Therapist's Guide to Learning and Attention Disorders

Therapist's Guide to Learning and Attention Disorders

Edited by

Aubrey H. Fine
California State Polytechnic University
Pomona, California

Ronald A. Kotkin
University of California, Irvine
Irvine, California

ACADEMIC PRESS
An imprint of Elsevier Science

Amsterdam Boston Heidelberg London New York Oxford
Paris San Diego San Francisco Singapore Sydney Tokyo

Academic Press
An imprint of Elsevier Science
525 B Street, Suite 1900, San Diego, California 92101-4495, USA
http://www.academicpress.com

Academic Press
84 Theobald's Road, London WC1X 8RR, UK
http://www.academicpress.com

Library of Congress Catalog Card Number: 2003106296

International Standard Book Number: 0-12-256430-8

PRINTED IN THE UNITED STATES OF AMERICA
03   04   05   06   07   7   6   5   4   3   2   1

Contents

v

110645

2 *Traditional and Innovative Assessment of Children with Attention Deficit Hyperactivity Disorder and Learning Disorders*   *43*

James M. Swanson, Dan Reschly, Aubrey H. Fine, Ronald A. Kotkin, Tim Wigal and Steve Simpson

3 *A Neurodevelopmental Approach to Differences in Learning*   *87*

Desmond P. Kelly and Melvin D. Levine

4 *Syndrome of Nonverbal Learning Disabilities: Effects on Learning*   *109*

Katherine D. Tsatsanis and Byron P. Rourke

5   *Educational Interventions for the Elementary Age Student in the Therapy Setting*   *147*

Joan Smith

6   *Educational Interventions for the Adolescent Student in the Therapy Setting*   *175*

Chris Zeigler Dendy, Aubrey H. Fine and Joan Smith

7   *Implementing School–Home Collaborative Treatment Plans: Best Practices in School–Home-Based Interventions*   *211*

Daniel Flynn, Ronald A. Kotkin, John Brady and Aubrey H. Fine

8 Parenting Children with Learning and Attention Disorders: Concerns and Directions for Therapeutic Intervention   *237*

**Aubrey H. Fine, Nadejda Karpova, Nicole Thorn,
Christine Holland and Ronald A. Kotkin**

9 Guidelines for Home Management for Disruptive Behavioral Challenges   *261*

Thomas W. Phelan and Aubrey H. Fine

Contributors

Numbers in parenthesis indicate the page numbers on which the author's contributions begin.

John Brady (215)
Chapman University
Orange, California

Micki Bryant (339)
Cal State Polytechnic University
Pomona, California

David Coffey (383)
UCLA
Westwood, California

Chris Zeigler Dendy (179)
Consultant, Author
Cedar Bluff, Alabama

Aubrey H. Fine (1, 43, 179, 215, 241, 265, 299, 339, 447)
Cal State Polytechnic University
Pomona, California

Steve Forness (447)
NPI, UCLA
Los Angeles, CA

Daniel Flynn (215)
UCI Child Development Center
Irvine, California

Mary Fowler (447)
Fair Haven, New Jersey

Christine Holland (241)
Cal State Polytechnic University
Pomona, California

Peter Jensen (447)
Center for the Advancement of Children's
  Mental Health
New York, New York

Nadejda Karpova (241)
Russian-US Young Leadership Fellows for
  Public Service
Novgorod, Russia

Mark Katz (447)
Learning Developmental Services
San Diego, California

Desmond P. Kelly (91)
Greenville Hospital System Children's
  Hospital
Greenville, South Carolina

Ronald A. Kotkin (1, 43, 215, 241, 299, 447)
University of California at Irvine
Irvine, California

Mark Lerner (447)
University of California at Irvine
Irvine, California

Melvin D. Levine (91)
University of North Carolina School
    of Medicine
Chapel Hill, North Carolina

Bruce McCandliss (468)
Weill Medical College of Cornell
    University
New York, NY

Thomas W. Phelan (265)
Child Management Inc.
Glen Ellyn, Illinois

Michael Posner (447)
Sackler Institute
New York, New York

Dan Reschly (43)
Vanderbilt University
Nashville, Tennessee

Byron P. Rourke (113)
University of Windsor
Windsor, Ontario

Joseph Sandford (425)
Braintrain
Richmond, Virginia

Steve Simpson (43)
University of California at Irvine
Irvine, California

Joan Smith (151, 179)
Learning Time Inc.
Seaside, California

James Swanson (43, 447)
University of California at Irvine
Irvine, California

Lynda Thompson (405)
ADD Centres LTD.
Toronto, Canada

Nicole Thorn (241)
City University of New York
New York, New York

Katherine D. Tsatsanis (113)
Harvard Medical School and Yale Child
    Study Center
Charleston, Massachusetts

Mark Turner (339)
Cal State Polytechnic University
Pomona, California

Tim Wigal (43)
University of California at Irvine
Irvine, California

Preface

Preparing a book with this magnitude is truly an arduous challenge and a tremendous opportunity. The primary aim of the book is to develop a practitioner's guide to document best practice approaches in treating children with ADHD and LD. Both editors (Ron and I) have first hand experience (as many of you) in regards to the mirage of challenges that many young people face on a daily basis. It is our intention to develop a manuscript that provides clinicians (both experienced and inexperienced) with practical insights into these learning/life challenges, and furnish you with practical solutions to make a difference.

Additionally, we hope that the insights of our contributors and ourselves will impart a greater sensitivity towards the needs of this population and their families. For over thirty years, both Ron and I have been involved in working with children and adolescents with learning and attention disorders. Being on the front line with families, has allowed us to witness the frustrations and challenges that many have experienced as well as the successes that they have also attained. Throughout the book, we have incorporated numerous case studies to make the materials more alive and practical. These life snapshots have been embedded in our minds and have helped us develop more realistic perceptions of what children and their families really need from clinicians.

We believe that families are in need of several things from practitioners. Families need clinicians who are at the cutting edge of diagnostic procedures as well as interventions that enhance behavior and learning. It is the intention of all contributors of this book, to provide up to date, cutting edge alternatives that clinicians can put right into practice. On the other hand, families need clinicians who are also sensitive to their challenges and can become their allies and safety nets. Like many other conditions, treating AD/HD and LD does not only pertain to those we directly serve, but rather the entire family.

In setting the tone for the book, we will provide you with this case example that we believe epitomizes life of many of the children under focus in this book. This snapshot may sound quite familiar. Andrew is now 16. He has been an enigma to his parents since he entered school. Although he is popular with his peers, the family began receiving negative feedback about their son when he was in the third grade. The family constantly was told that their son was "not living up to his expectations".

Over a course of a decade, the aftermath following the meetings was almost always identical. The parents would become discouraged with their son and arguments would begin. Often the father and the mother would shout derogatory statements at Andrew, calling him lazy, irresponsible and stupid. Usually, shortly after the outbursts, his parents would feel awful, and would apologize for their outbursts. Unfortunately, the emotional wounds and scars over the years made Andrew quite callous. He became a victim of failure, and misguided efforts.

In the case of Andrew, the years seemed to have a similar outcome. The school year was always a tough time, constantly filled with negatives and arguments about academic performance. Although he never failed any courses, his grades were always marginal. When given a psycho-educational evaluation, the outcomes did demonstrate that he had a mild learning disability. However, over the course of education he was only supported with generic accommodations and limited special education. Testing over the years revealed that he had a great deal of difficulty with auditory processing and his work production was very labored and slow. Findings also suggested that he had difficulty making inferences and applying higher order thinking. These deficits appeared to have an impact on his reading comprehension. Finally, Andrew's ability to stay on track, be organized and study was also remarkably labored (all areas of executive functioning).

Although Andrew seemed to work hard, he would become disillusioned when he constantly received poor grades. He would just shut down, even when others tried to encourage him.

Interestingly enough, the sense of incompetence and behavioral challenges were exhibited only in the academic year. Summers and the holidays were wonderful. His parents confessed that he did what he was told and was a pleasure to be around. What a difference from life "the other nine months".

This snapshot may be quite similar to those you have experienced. Perhaps the child's name isn't Andrew, but could be Matthew, Manuel, Angela, or Debbie. Andrew went for many years unidentified at school as a child with a learning disability along with ADHD. Unfortunately, this promoted a lot of misunderstandings both at home and at school. His parents became frustrated and angry because they believed that Andrew could do the work, but was just being lazy. Most of his teachers felt the same way and felt that Andrew wasn't accepting his share of the responsibility. They believed he was capable, if he would have just put his mind to it.

Serendipitously, the family eventually discovered that there probably was some legitimacy to Andrew's delays. He was misunderstood over the years, and the higher expectations were not very realistic. What the family and educators eventually discovered was that this wasn't a disability of effort, but rather of abilities. However, the time wasted waiting to identify and diagnose his challenges, had a strong impact on Andrew. By the time he became a young adolescent, he seemed to give up on himself. He chose to act as a class clown, primarily to gain respect and attention. He acted like this especially in classes that were very difficult for him.

Some clinicians, educators, and even parents under-estimate the magnitude of these disorders. They simply under-play the pervasiveness that both ADHD and LD have on the lives of children and their families. To compliment Andrew's case study, the following is a letter to the staff of the University of California at Irvine Child Development Center, a program specifically designed for children with ADHD and their families. The letter points to the significance of early intervention and treating the whole family.

For the 1996–2000 CDC Staff

All of you have enhanced our world and greatly improved the quality of our life. The process of bringing about family unity and the ability to work with instead of against our son seemed like a fairytale in 1996. But as we look back upon the last 4 years in 2000, gradually that fairytale has become much more of a reality than we could have anticipated. We are truly blessed.

We thank every one of the CDC staff for building our confidence as parents and the dignity of our son. We also thank you for the given tools so that we can continue to build. God only knows where we would be now if the center was nonexistent.

We admire your love and appreciation for the CDC students. Along with the support, care, encouragement and respect you give each child, you sustain a baffling amount of energy, patience and humor. The role you have played in each of our lives; whether separately or as a family, will never be forgotten.

Thankfulness and gratitude is extended to you all. Although your presence will be unseen in the future, your presence will always be felt in our hearts. We will truly miss you.

It is our intention and that of the other contributors, to clarify the magnitude of these challenges and to provide you with strategies that can provide solutions. The chapters within the book draw on the clinical and research backgrounds of some leading authorities in the field. The first four chapters provide you with a clear overview of the population. They incorporate current information on diagnostic methods as well as an in-depth discussion on Nonverbal learning disabilities as well as a phenomenological approach to identifying and supporting neurodevelopmental variations in children. The following final eleven chapters will discuss more clearly some alternatives and interventions in supporting these children over their school years and into higher education/careers. Contributors have written on a wide array of contemporary topics that will be useful in planning best practice solutions. In the final chapter we try and take a glimpse into what the future may have in store in identifying and treating this population.

In closing, we believe that this compilation should become a valuable resource for practicing clinicians. We anticipate that it will not only provide a blueprint for treatment, but that it will also be read to highlight some of the psycho/emotional challenges that children and their families face. There can be numerous metaphors and visualizations that can be applied to describe a child with the symptoms that we will focus upon. One excellent example could be illustrated through the magnificence of a rose. Like a rose, a child is a beautiful being. When you look at the pedals, and smell its poignant aroma, you are impressed with its innate beauty. This should be a similar phenomenon with children. Their grace and zest for life should also be miraculously appreciated. However, the beauty of the rose may be diminished when one accidentally grabs it by the stem, and gets pricked by one of its thorns. Unfortunately, this is the magnitude of an attention/earning disability. They both can literally be "the thorns" of a child's being. They can cause the child as well as the family tremendous pain and agony. Hopefully, the materials within this text will provide you with interventions that will aid you in cultivating the gardens within many families, so that they can celebrate and enjoy the beauty within their own children.

Aubrey H. Fine Ed.D.
Ronald A. Kotkin Ph.D.
November 2002

Acknowledgements

This book could not have been written without the support of all the contributing authors. Their insights into the field of LD and ADHD have made the development of this volume a remarkable experience. We would also like to thank Nikki Levy and Barbara Makinster from Academic Press who were very supportive throughout this project. The authors would also like to thank Robert Marvos for has wonderful illustrations which are presented in Chapter 1.

Finally, we would like to thank the many individuals who took the time to act as internal chapter reviewers. Their comments and feedback were important contributions to the formation of the final text. We acknowledge each of these individuals. Words cannot express our appreciation.

Frank Crinella, Ph.D., Ruth Deich, Ph.D., Cheryl Eastman, Christine Holland, Desmond Kelly, M.D. Loretta Kotkin M.A., Jeff Mio Ph.D., Rob Rutherford, Ph.D, Dale Salwak, Ph.D., James Sturgess, Ph.D., Nicole Thorne, Tim Wigal Ph.D.

Dedication

This book is dedicated to several of my early mentors. Mr. Herb Isenberg of Montreal Canada, who encouraged me and gave me my first opportunities to work with children with learning disabilities and the late Dr. Barry Lehrer (of Cincinnati, Ohio) who taught me to believe that all children thirst knowledge, but get to the fountain in different ways. Both of these individuals helped me discover that the greatest gift we can give children is the ability to discover their strengths and to enhance their desire to learn and believe in themselves.

I would also like to dedicate the book to the many parents and children who over the years have helped me become more sensitive to the challenges they face. Vikki, Barbara, Larry, Jonathan, Gary, and Jeffrey, (and to the thousands of others who I have met over the years) thank-you for helping me become a more sensitive clinician who realizes that every child has the right to learn and be respected.

In addition, I would like to acknowledge Margaret Gomez and Clement Papazzian M.D., two individuals who have always demonstrated that children and their families need more from professionals than their knowledge. Families need to associate with professionals who will walk the extra mile for their clients.

Finally, this book is dedicated to my loving family (Nya, Sean, Corey) and my companion animals (P.J., Hart, Shrimp, Snowflake, Starlight, Tikvah and Spike) that without their support and encouragement, life wouldn't be as rich and fulfilling. To all of you, my life is blessed because of your presence.

Aubrey H. Fine
November, 2002

I am dedicating this book to the children and the families that have made my life richer by sharing their caring, determination, hard work, persistence and unconditional love for one another. This book is also dedicated to all of the incredibly talented and commited staff of the Child Development Center, and to two very special teachers, Dave Agler and Dan Flynn, who epitomize the focus of this book. Most importantly the book is dedicated to Loretta Kotkin who has taught me the meaning of love and what it means to be a friend.

Ronald A. Kotkin
November, 2002

Attention Deficit Hyperactivity Disorder and Learning Disabilities: An Overview for Practitioners

Ronald A. Kotkin and Aubrey H. Fine

Every practitioner whose practice includes children will be faced with the challenges of assisting families whose children have behavioral and learning problems. The most prevalent disorders of childhood are attention deficit hyperactivity disorder (ADHD) and learning disabilities (LD) (NIMH, 1998; Kotkin et al., 2001). These disorders often coexist (Kotkin et al., 2001; Brown, 2000). This chapter outlines complexities involved in making a differential diagnosis using the criteria established by the Diagnostic and Statistical Manual (APA, 1994); issues in meeting the educational criteria for categorical placement in special education; the pervasiveness and the serious impact of the challenges of these disorders on the children and their families; the biological evidence for its existence; and an overview of contemporary strategies for treating the disorders. Since most children at some point exhibit some of the problem behaviors or learning difficulties associated with the symptoms of these disorders, skills in providing intervention for children with ADHD and LD will assist practitioners in providing assistance to any child who may have behavior problems or difficulty learning.

ATTENTION DEFICIT HYPERACTIVITY DISORDER (ADHD) AND LEARNING DISABILITIES (LD): MYTH OR REALITY

The estimated prevalence of learning disabilities in the general population is approximately 5% (Kotkin et al., 2001). A recent review of the estimated prevalence rates of ADHD in school-aged community samples (rather than referred samples) indicates rates varying from 4 to 12%, with estimated prevalence based on combining these studies of 8–10% (American Academy of Pediatrics, 2000). Studies of children with ADHD suggest a prevalence of comorbid learning disabilities ranging from 10 to 92% (Biederman, Newcorn, & Sprich, 1991), but when appropriate diagnostic criteria for learning disabilities are applied, the prevalence of comorbid learning disabilities appears to be in the range of 10 to 25% (Richters et al., 1995). The range of estimates for the prevalence of children with ADHD and LD underscores the difficulty in making a differential diagnosis of the disorders. The disorder of ADHD is made based on a behavioral symptom count. Behavioral symptoms are common behaviors exhibited by most children at times. Because the behavioral symptoms are common behaviors that most children are likely to exhibit, many families may question whether it is a true disorder. A learning disability is defined by a discrepancy between a child's cognitive functioning and performance on a standardized test of academics. Because most children may have some degree of difficulty learning academics, parents may question whether their child has a learning disability. As a practitioner, this may be the first question a family asks. The Clinical Practice Guidelines of the American Academy of Pediatrics (American Academy of Pediatrics, 2001) emphasize the importance of first educating parents and caregivers regarding the nature of the disorder and its effect on learning, behavior, self-esteem, social skills, and family function. A brief explanation of the disorder and current research supporting the biological basis of the disorder may help parents understand the difficulties the child is experiencing in an otherwise hidden disorder. Unlike physical disorders, such as blindness, deafness, or cerebral palsy, ADHD and LD are not immediately obvious disorders. Many parents may feel that their child is lazy or not trying hard enough and may have little empathy for their child's difficulties. The first step in treatment is helping the parents understand the nature of the problem.

Chapter 3 presents a phenomenological approach to understanding learning disorders. It describes the range of problems that teachers, parents, and practitioners may observe in students with learning difficulties and the possible patterns of dysfunction underlying deficient academic performance. They point out that learning problems may be due to a wide range of phenomena, including neurodevelopmental dysfunctions, fears about doing poorly in school, lack of experience, or inadequate teaching. Providing parents with a description of the complexity of the disorder and a summary of the biological basis of the disorder may help parents empathize with their child's difficulties and establish realistic expectations for treatment.

Understanding the biological basis of the disorders also has implications for the treatments of choice and the focus of treatment. For example, the use of stimulant medication for ADHD makes sense in the context of a neurologically based neurochemical problem. Behavior management makes sense when treating the behavioral symptoms of ADHD. The combination of medication and behavior modification makes sense as medication may assist in improving the integrity of the neurological system so it can better respond to behavioral interventions that directly target the behavioral symptoms of ADHD. In the case of a neurologically based learning disability, it makes sense that no amount of behavior modification will motivate a student to learn to read through a modality that they are incapable of using. However, if we are able to teach compensatory skills through a multisensory approach to reading instruction, behavior modification can be used to motivate the student to try their best even though it may be tedious or difficult. Although ADHD and LD often cooccur, they are discussed separately in the next sections. Case studies are used to illustrate the nature of the disorders and the complexities faced by parents, teachers, practitioners, and, most importantly, the child.

ATTENTION DEFICIT HYPERACTIVITY DISORDER: A CASE STUDY—A SNAPSHOT OF JOHN AND HIS FAMILY

John is a 6-year-old boy who has been a challenge for his parents since birth. He is an only child, which further complicates the situation for his parents. They have little experience with other children and are not sure what developmentally appropriate behavior is. John was very active as a toddler, getting into everything. At first the parents thought, "This is how all boys are." When he entered preschool, the teachers expressed concern with his behavior toward peers and difficulty staying with group activities. The parents had multiple conferences in which they were asked what they were going to do to get John to "behave." John's parents were frustrated and embarrassed by his silly disruptive behavior. He was eventually asked to leave the preschool. The parents tried several other preschools with similar results.

At home, John was a constant challenge. He did not do things to cause problems on purpose but rather impulsively. For example, he jumped off a high wall and broke his arm because he wanted to fly like superman. He also let go of the shopping cart in a parking lot, smashing into a moving car. His parents tried to anticipate potential problems, but even John could not predict what he might do. His mother spent most of the time closely supervising John. She became very stressed and resentful of the constant drain on her energies. She stopped seeing her friends and retreated into the world of her own home. She dreaded going out in public for fear of what John might do.

Dad worked long hours to support the family and spent little time with John. When he came home, he wanted to unwind and spend time watching television. When John became noisy and demanded attention, dad called mom to intervene. His constant irritability with John and mother's lack of control of John put a stress on their relationship. Dad felt that mom should be able to parent John, since her only job was being a houseparent. Mom tried to explain how difficult things were at home with John, but dad did not understand. Both mom and dad yelled at John and occasionally spanked him. John began to say that he was "no good" and wanted to run away from home. He said that he did not want to "be alive anymore." This deeply concerned his mother.

When John entered kindergarten, the problems continued. He constantly bothered the other children, often taking things from them, trying to control their play and saying inappropriate, silly comments. The other children began to avoid him. Despite his failure in preschool and kindergarten, he seemed to learn by osmosis. He began to learn to read and recognize his numbers. He began to write, although he did not like sitting for any length of time and often hurried through his work, writing illegibly. The teacher requested a conference and suggested that John might have attention deficit hyperactivity disorder. Mom was shocked to hear that her child might have ADHD. She asked the teacher what she should do. The teacher suggested referring him for testing to see if he qualified for special education assistance. He was tested and found not to qualify for services since he did not have a discrepancy between his IQ score and performance on standardized tests of academics. He continued to learn despite his behavior. This left the teacher and parent at a loss as to what to do. The teacher suggested that the parent learn more effective parenting skills, as it was obvious that he learned his inappropriate behavior at home. Mom was devastated. John did not have a problem according to test scores, yet the home and school both had problems with him and she felt it was obviously her fault. When mom talked with dad about the recommendation of the teacher, he felt that there was nothing wrong. Their relationship continued to become strained and deteriorated. Mom finally threatened to divorce dad, since he did not support her and she was getting extremely frustrated at having to defend herself.

They finally decided to take John to an outside psychologist who specialized in children with ADHD for a second opinion. First, the psychologist took a thorough developmental history and had the parents fill out rating scales rating the symptoms of ADHD. Next, he obtained rating scales from the teacher and arranged for psychoeducational testing. To verify the symptoms of ADHD acknowledged by the parents and teachers, he completed a structured interview. Finally, he referred John for a physical examination to rule out a physiological explanation of the problem. After reviewing all the sources of information, the psychologist confirmed the diagnosis of ADHD. He explained to both parents the nature of the problem and the challenges it posed for John. He explained that this was a neurologically based problem that was not the result of poor parenting. The parents also told him about John's wish "not to be alive." The therapist completed a suicide assessment and told them that although he did not think that John would commit suicide, his impulsive behavior made him at risk for hurting himself. He suggested removing all potential sources of serious harm from his reach as a precaution. He also gave them literature to read and told them about the treatments of choice for ADHD, medication, and behavior modification. He once again gave them a referral to a behavioral pediatrician to discuss the possibility of medication. He also agreed to attend the next Individual Educational Program (IEP) meeting to review his findings.

At the IEP, it was brought out that the IEP team had not assessed a functional impairment in the classroom. Children with limited alertness or overfocus and a functional impairment in the classroom can qualify for special education services under the category of other health impaired (OHI). They had tested him cognitively and academically and concluded that he did not have a discrepancy between his cognitive ability and his academic performance and therefore did not have a learning disability. The psychologist pointed out that federal law states that the discrepancy to qualify for special education services under the category of OHI must be a functional impairment in the classroom rather than a discrepancy between cognitive ability and performance on a standardized test of academics. If he is producing half or less of the academic work other children are completing, this is a functional impairment. Because he is above average cognitively and at grade level, he should be able to produce work at a rate that is equal to other children in the classroom with similar cognitive and academic abilities. However, because of his symptoms of ADHD, he is unable to consistently produce the same level work as his peers. In addition, he has no friends because of his behavior and he is therefore further functionally impaired.

Mom and dad were relieved to hear that John's problems were not strictly a result of their parenting skills. Dad became more understanding and more supportive. The teacher and support staff developed accommodations in the classroom with the help of the outside psychologist and enrolled him in an outpatient social skills program. Mom and dad enrolled in a parent training class together and John started social skills. The parents also took John to see the pediatrician and decided to try medication. John still has problems in school, but there is support for him when he has difficulty in class. John is one of the lucky children who got help early. The long-term prognosis for John is still a question that will be answered over time. Without help, his parents may have divorced, and John's self-esteem may have further eroded. ADHD is a disorder that affects the family, teachers, peers, and, most importantly, the child.

A clear understanding of the disorder, how it is diagnosed, and treatment options can help to avoid many months of pain for the family and child. The following sections summarize these components.

WHAT IS ATTENTION DEFICIT HYPERACTIVITY DISORDER?

ADHD is a family of chronic neurobiological disorders that interfere with an individual's capacity to regulate activity level (hyperactivity), inhibit behavior (impulsivity), and attend to tasks (inattention) in developmentally appropriate ways (NIMH, 2000). The core symptoms of ADHD are difficulty sustaining attention to tasks, developmentally inappropriate levels of activity, distractibility, and impulsivity. Diagnostic criteria and identification of ADHD in children have evolved over time based on professional consensus and evolving research. In the early 1970s, it was initially called "hyperkinesis" and "hyperactivity," emphasizing symptoms of overactivity. Further research focused on inattention (Douglas, 1980) as a core symptom of children previously labeled hyperactive.

Psychiatrists, pediatricians, and other primary health providers use the Diagnostic and Statistical Manual (DSM) in diagnosing psychiatric conditions. DSM criteria are based on clinical experience and an expanding research foundation (American Academy of Pediatrics Practice Guidelines, 2000). Over time, the ADHD concept has seen substantial changes in nomenclature and criteria. In the 1980s, DSM-III (American Psychiatric Association, 1980) first identified the syndrome of attention deficit disorder (ADD), recognizing inattention as a core symptom. It could be diagnosed with or without hyperactivity, emphasizing the symptoms of inattention. Many researchers and practitioners questioned the validity of recognizing children as having inattention alone and the distinction was not made in DSMIIIR (American Psychiatric Association, 1987). In 1987, the DSM-IIIR changed the name to attention deficit hyperactivity disorder, and a distinction between attention deficit disorder with and without hyperactivity was not made. Based on further clinical experience and research, the current DSMIV continues to use the term ADHD with three subtypes. ADHD may be diagnosed as a predominantly inattentive type, a predominantly hyperactive and impulsive type, or a combined type. Currently, DSMIV diagnostic criteria for ADHD (American Psychiatric Association, 1994) require the demonstration of at least six symptoms of either inattention or hyperactivity–impulsivity that were present before age 7 years, have persisted for at least 6 months, and manifested in two or more settings.

CURRENT EXPLANATIONS OF ADHD: MODELS FOR CONSIDERATION

Biological Bias

Although the exact cause of ADHD is undetermined, most researchers endorse a biological predisposition to the disorder (Barkley, 1990). In a retrospective 10-year (1986–1996) review of the literature, Dennis Cantwell (1996) concluded that rather than one etiological factor, there is most likely an interplay of both psychosocial and biological factors that may lead to the common pathway of the syndrome ADD.

Most of the current literature agrees that abnormalities in the prefrontal, frontal, and/or frontostriatal pathways may be indicative of a neural substrate of ADHD (Shue & Douglas, 1992). These brain areas are involved in the control of motor activity and attention. A positron emission tomography (PET) study by Zametkin et al. (1990) showed that compared with normal adults, adults with ADHD had lower cerebral glucose metabolism in the premotor cortex and in the superior prefrontal cortex. All adults in the study continued to manifest the syndrome from childhood into adulthood. Hynd et al. (1990) produced magnetic resonance imaging (MRI) findings suggesting that children with ADD had normal plana temporal, but abnormal frontal lobes. A number of investigators (Pennington & Ozonoff, 1996; Denkla, 1996; Barkley, 1997; Sergeant et al., 1999) have shown that key regions of the frontal lobes are underactive, which results in inefficiencies in attentional networks that control the flow of information in the human nervous system. There is also emerging evidence documenting reliable EEG differences between ADHD and non-ADHD children (Hughes & John, 1999). Children with ADHD have elevated frontal theta activity and diminished beta activity.

However, there appears to be more widespread differences in data identical in the brains of individuals with ADHD compared to others. Studies have shown several reliable differences in other brain structures in a study utilizing matched controls. Reports have indicated that children with ADHD have a reduced total brain mass, reduced caudate, cerebellum, and corpus callosum as compared to controls. Zametkin et al. (1990) used single photon emission-computed tomography (SPECT) to reveal focal cerebral hypofusion of striatum and hyperfusion in sensory and sensorimotor areas. It is important to note that no studies of brain differences as a function of stimulant exposure have ever been reported.

Problems with dopamine regulation may underlie the dysfunction in attentional processes found in ADHD. Animal studies (Shaywitz et al., 1978) suggest that animals with damaged DA-producing brain areas are hyperactive and poor learners. Some direct evidence from studies of cerebral spinal fluid in ADHD and normal children indicates decreased brain dopamine in ADHD children (Raskin et al., 1984). Pharmacolgical agents such as stimulants directly affect dopamine, further implicating dopaminergic dysfunction as a key problem. Stimulants increase the availability of catecholamines (dopamine and norepinephrine). Stimulants increase intrasynaptic dopamine and norepinephrine by inhibiting presynaptic reuptake and by releasing storage vesicles of dopamine into the synapse. The dopamine results might be explained on the basis of individuals having a "familial" and "persistent" subtype of ADHD (Cantwell, 1996).

Hereditary factors appear to play a large role in the occurrence of symptoms of ADHD in children. In fact, ADHD is one of the most recognized genetic-based disorders in all of psychiatry. Studies indicate that between 20 and 32% of parents and siblings of ADHD children also have the disorder (Biederman et al., 1986; Deutsch et al., 1982; Safer, 1973). Several studies of twins have shown a greater concordance between monozygotic as compared to dizygotic twins, thereby supporting an hereditary mechanism for ADHD (Cunningham & Barkley, 1978; Goodman & Stevenson, 1989; Heffron et al., 1984; Lopez, 1965). Barkley (1990) suggests that the genetic factor transmitted results in an underactivity of the prefrontal striatal–limbic regions. Although more research is called for in this area, dopamine depletion is common in all cases. At the genetic level, molecular genetic studies have implicated two candidate genes: the dopamine D4 receptor (DAD4) and the dopamine transporter (Cook et al., 1995). Studies of the DRD4 gene have demonstrated an increased frequency of the "seven-repeat allele" in subjects (Lahoste et al., 1996) and increased symptomalogy for those with the "seven-repeat allele" compared to those without it (Swanson et al., 1998). The next section discusses theories of executive functioning believed to be located primarily in frontal lobe functions (Barkley, 1990).

Executive Functioning: An Explanation for ADHD

A developmental delay in the executive functions of the frontal lobe of the brain has been proposed as an explanation for ADHD. Executive functions are functions of the brain that activate, regulate, and integrate a variety of other mental functions. In many ways, executive functions can be inferred as the internal ability of the brain to manage learning activities and behavior (Zeigler Dendy, 2000). These functions play a central role in our ability to think and problem solve. Barkley (1997) suggests that executive functions refer to those self-directed actions of the individual that are being used to self-regulate. These actions assist an individual in accomplishing self-control as well as maximizing future outcomes. Some believe that executive functioning is the hallmark of human intelligence and take an active role in our ability to perform complex

TABLE 1   Executive Functioning

- Butterfield and Belmont (1977) suggest that effective application of executive functioning allows an individual to control processes to reasonably respond to a change in an informational processing task
- Jacob Bronowski (1996) pointed out that language is the strongest element in a humans ability to delay responding so the individual can make a more informed decision
- Bronowski identified four functions in executive functioning. He attributed the prefrontal lobe as controlling those functions. Each of these functions are interactive. (A) Prolongation is demonstrative of the importance of human language and its ability to internalize language to refer both forward and backwards in time to construct reasonable behavioral solutions. (B) An internalized system that allows a human to separate emotion from a behavioral response. This form of inhibition is crucial in a human's abilities not to overreact quickly. (C) Internalization is the capacity to delay a response and construct solutions that may be the most appropriate to act with. (D) Reconstitution involves analysis, synthesis, selection, and monitoring
- Fuster's (1995) theory of prefrontal lobe functions concludes that the prefrontal cortex encodes the temporal aspects of behavior and provides the inhibition that an individual may need to delay the execution of behaviors in a correct temporal sequence.

---

symbolic activities, such as reading and writing (Lyon, 1996). In essence, executive functions are the processes used internally to make it easier for people to engage with new as well as old information. To assist in general understanding of the evolution of the concept of executive functioning, Table 1 summarizes some of the major contributions.

Russell Barkley (1998) has proposed a theory of prefrontal lobe functions or the executive system to explain the symptoms of ADHD. According to Barkley, inhibitory problems are what define the problem of children with ADHD, not attention deficits. Children with ADHD, the combined type, are delayed in the development of executive function. However, according to Barkley, this does not apply to ADHD, the inattentive type, who have a problem with processing information. Executive functions give a child self-control and self-regulation. Barkley identifies four executive functions: (1) nonverbal working memory, (2) verbal working memory, (3) covert self-directed affect/motivation/arousal, and (4) reconstitution. A prerequisite to the development of executive function is the ability to inhibit responses. Children with ADHD have difficulty inhibiting their response to immediate stimulus in their environment and function in the here and now. They seek immediate gratification and often do not learn from their experiences.

The psychological sense of time is an outcome of the executive system. Barkley points out that children with ADHD have a problem sensing time. He states that ADHD is the "consummate disorder of time management." Merely giving children more time to complete tasks does not solve the problem of task completion. Children with ADHD do not use the extra time efficiently. They need prompts such as timers or clocks that visually display the passing of time to help them manage time through an external prompt.

In his research on ADHD, Brown has made some additions to the understanding of executive functioning and ADHD. Brown (2001) suggests that executive functioning helps an individual connect, prioritize, and integrate various cognitive functions on a moment-to-moment basis. He suggests that numerous processes are incorporated for an individual to successfully guide thoughts to actual outcomes. He uses the metaphor of a conductor of an orchestra to illustrate how these functions take charge of the intricate mechanisms used in applied learning. Within his model of executive functions, Brown identified six variables that he sees as being critical.

The first variable focuses on the child's ability to organize, prioritize, and begin the actual work process. Other variables under this dimension are paying attention, as well as getting to finish the project under focus. Brown seems to acknowledge the crucialness of the individual's ability to modulate and monitor emotional strains such as frustration tolerance.

The dimension of memory is incorporated into Brown's conceptualization of executive functioning. It addresses the individual's ability to use working memory to stay organized as well as recall previously learned information. A critical aspect in this dimension is the individual's ability to monitor and self-regulate performance. Memory is also utilized to support the individual while he holds facts in his mind while manipulating new information. Self-talk is usually applied to direct behaviors.

Another key dimension to Brown's formula is the individual's ability to analyze information and break it apart. The individual is also capable of organizing the previously learned information into a new entity. A critical aspect in this dimension is the individual's ability to monitor and self-regulate performance.

To help crystallize an explanation of executive functioning, we have developed a simple illustration that may be useful for clients (Fig. 1). We use two river rafts heading down a river. Many of the dimensions noted earlier by Barkley (1998) and Brown (2001) are incorporated within this drawing. Figure 1 highlights a group that is clear and capable of

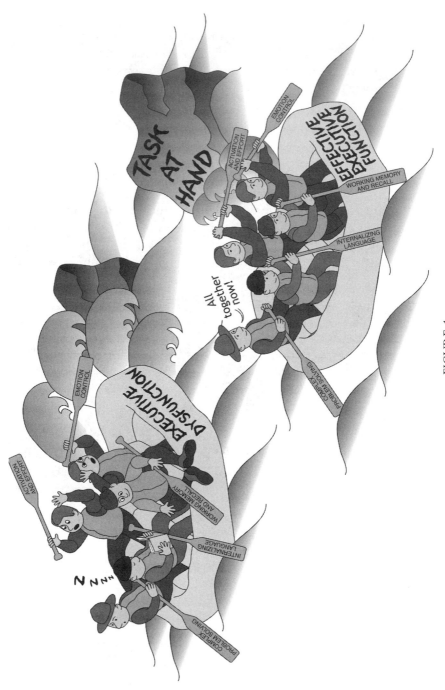

FIGURE 1

navigating through the rapids. However, there is a group that is not staying focused. They are likely to capsize or get themselves into a lot of trouble. We believe that this simple illustration will be valuable to the client in not only conceptualizing executive functioning, but how the various traits work in unison to support an individual.

ADHD: PSYCHIATRIC DIAGNOSIS AND EDUCATIONAL CRITERIA FOR SERVICES

The diagnosis of ADHD seems all too easy when we consider the core symptoms of hyperactivity, impulsivity, and inattention. Most children exhibit these core symptoms at one time or another. Very young children are likely to exhibit the majority of the behavioral symptoms in a preschool or home setting. Some children may not exhibit any of the symptoms in a one-on-one situation such as in a therapist's or physician's office, but show extreme symptoms in a classroom or family function. They may show symptoms during some activities at school and not during others. This variability in performance may result in conflicting diagnosis and a resultant mistrust of professionals. When diagnosis is based on observations in only one setting or with only one assessment tool, other disorders may be labeled ADHD erroneously or the diagnosis of ADHD may be missed completely. Comorbidity further complicates the process of a differential diagnosis of ADHD. Oppositional and defiant disorder and conduct disorder coexist with ADHD in 35% of cases (American Academy of Pediatrics, 2000). ADHD and mood disorders/depression coexist in 18% of children (American Academy of Pediatrics, 2000). ADHD and anxiety have been estimated to coexist in 25% of cases (American Academy of Pediatrics, 2000). Diagnosis of ADHD must include a multifaceted assessment to rule out other explanations for inattention or to identify coexisting disorders. The fact that many of these disorders may coexist with ADHD makes differential diagnosis even more complex. Pliszka and colleagues (1999) have written an excellent guide to the assessment and treatment of comorbid conditions. The authors recommend this book as a reference for practitioners. In Chapter 2, the complexities of making a differential diagnosis are discussed. They provide guidelines for making a differential diagnosis and case studies demonstrating best practices. Any diagnosis of ADHD must include a developmental history, physical examination, psychosocial assessment of environmental stressors, behavioral rating scales from parents or guardians and teachers, a structured interview to confirm the existence and severity of symptoms, and a psychoeducational evaluation (American Academy of Pediatrics, 2000). Practitioners should develop referrals to qualified professionals specializing in ADHD who can provide specialized assessments necessary to make a differential diagnosis. Many disorders may account for a child being inattentive. Children who are anxious or depressed may appear inattentive. Children whose home life is chaotic may appear inattentive. Medical problems may result in a child being hyperactive, impulsive, or inattentive. The treatment of choice for these disorders or medical conditions may differ from that of children with ADHD. A misdiagnosis of ADHD could lead to a course of treatment that does not address the core problem and to many months of unproductive therapy. Treating only one disorder when several may coexist may also lead to ineffective treatment. A multifaceted assessment increases the probability that a comprehensive diagnosis and treatment plan can be made that takes into account all of the child's needs.

Criteria for determining whether a child qualifies for special education services also present challenges for the practitioner. Children with ADHD and LD manifest their problems in the school setting. They are often failing academically, are disruptive to the class, have few friends, and, as a result, have low self-esteem (Barkley et al., 1990; Pehlam & Bender, 1982). Practitioners need to understand the educational criteria used to qualify children with ADHD for special education services and how to assist in providing the necessary clinical information to help their client's access-needed services. Prior to 1990, children with ADHD did not qualify for special education services based on their diagnosis of ADHD. Many school districts often stretched the educational criteria for existing special education categories in order to provide some level of service to children whose primary problem was attention deficit disorder, but often the core symptoms of ADHD were still not addressed (Swanson, 1990). The federal educational code, Individuals with Disabilities Education Act (IDEA, 1998), has changed to include children with ADHD for special education services under the category of OHI. In IDEA, the term disability is used rather than disorder. ADHD was included as a part of the OHI category based on part B of the IDEA and section 504 of the Rehabilitation Act of 1973 if ADHD produced "limited alertness" that seriously impaired school performance.

Limited alertness has since been defined to include heightened alertness to environmental stimuli, resulting in limited alertness in the educational setting (amendments to IDEA, 1998). If it is determined that the severity of the impairment is not sufficient to qualify for the OHI category under educational laws, then "504" accommodations to address a student's symptoms of ADHD can be developed in the regular classroom under civil rights laws. Children who are identified as having limited alertness or overfocus that results in a functional impairment in the classroom can qualify for special education services. A diagnosis of ADHD meets the criteria of demonstrating limited alertness. A functional impairment can be documented by comparing a child's actual work production to that of their non-ADHD peers. If their work production is significantly below that of their peers, they have a functional impairment. They are unable to produce work at the level that would be expected given the fact that they have average or above average IQ and average or above average performance on a standardized test of academics. This is a functional impairment because the impairment is in the setting where you would expect attention to be a problem. Many school districts are reluctant to use the federal guidelines in assessing a child for special education under OHI and use a traditional discrepancy model. Children whose primary disorder is ADHD without comorbid LD often do not have a discrepancy between their cognitive ability and their performance on a standardized test of academic performance. Children with ADHD are often able to complete academic tasks in a one-on-one situation with few distractions. As in the aforementioned case study of John, practitioners need to be aware of the educational law and assist parents in accurately documenting the need for service. A discussion of the federal laws and effective practices for serving children with ADHD in the general education setting is detailed in Chapter 7.

In a National Research Council Report on minority students in special and gifted education, as part of an Executive Summary for the White House Panel on Excellence in Special Education (Donovan & Cross, 2002), several recommendations were made in rethinking the current approach to special education. These recommendations recognize that in the current system of special education eligibility, children with ADHD and LD must fail significantly before receiving intervention. It suggests that teacher training must prepare general education teachers to provide a hierarchy of increasingly more intensive learning and behavioral interventions for students who fail to meet the minimal standards for successful educational performance as soon as a need is identified. This information will provide documentation of the need for more specialized interventions for those students who fail to respond to these more intensive interventions. Currently, teacher training does not include training in intensive learning and behavioral interventions. In an attempt to prepare teachers to intervene early, the council recommended that teachers be required to receive intensive supervised experience in the implementation of these strategies beyond exposure to inservice training and coursework. This should also include competency in behavior management in classroom and noninstructional school settings, instruction in functional analysis and routine behavioral assessment of students, competency in understanding and implementing reasonable norms and expectations for students, and core competencies in instructional delivery of academic content. The need for change is discussed in Chapter 2.

EXPLAINING ADHD TO PARENTS AND TEENS: VISUAL REPRESENTATIONS OF ADHD

We have developed several graphics that could be used with parents and teens to explain ADHD. The analogy of a baseball team was selected as a unique example to highlight the symptoms of the inattentive subtype as well as the hyperactive–impulsive subtype (Fig. 2 and 3). The symptoms are actually the 18 listed in the DSMIV. When using the illustrations, the practitioner could explain that any person could have any number of these symptoms. They become more synergistic when they are coupled with other symptoms. For example, the practitioner could show the family the inattentive subtype fielding team and explain that having any one of these symptoms could impact a team's performance. Nevertheless, a team (or a child or teen) that may have 6 or more symptoms undoubtedly will have a terrible time fielding the game.

The same is true with a child or an adult. Exhibiting six or more of these symptoms could place enormous hardships on a child. The clinician may find utilizing these illustrations very helpful in highlighting the interaction of the symptoms and discussing them with families.

However, there have been many other clinicians who have also developed visual illustrations to promote better understanding. For example, Mel Levine's cockpit is a convenient illustration to convey to a parent what ADHD represents. The meters on each of the panels clarify the intensity of each symptom. However, Zeigler Dendy (2000) suggests that many of the characteristics of ADHD are not apparently evident. She compared these phenomena to the tip of an iceberg (Fig. 4). She suggests that only the tip of the concerns is visible to others. The graphic infers that many of the symptoms are hidden beneath the surface. The tip of

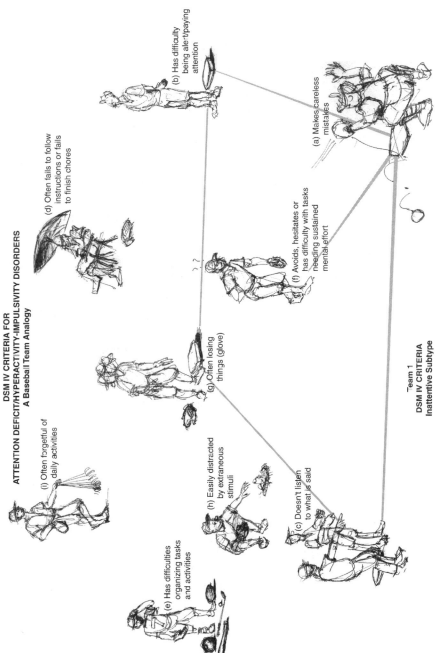

DSM IV CRITERIA FOR
ATTENTION DEFICIT/HYPERACTIVITY-IMPULSIVITY DISORDERS
A Baseball Team Analogy

(b) Has difficulty being alert/paying attention

(a) Makes careless mistakes

(d) Often fails to follow instructions or fails to finish chores

(f) Avoids, hesitates or has difficulty with tasks needing sustained mental effort

(g) Often losing things (glove)

Team 1
DSM IV CRITERIA
Inattentive Subtype

(i) Often forgetful of daily activities

(h) Easily distracted by extraneous stimuli

(c) Doesn't listen to what is said

(e) Has difficulties organizing tasks and activities

FIGURE 2

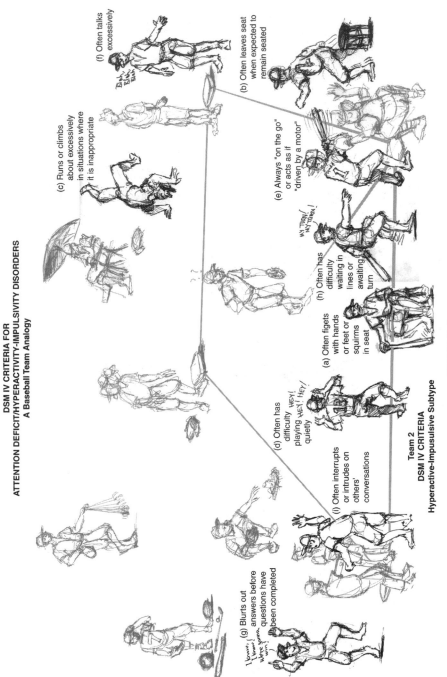

FIGURE 3

THE ADD/ADHD ICEBERG
Only 1/8 of an iceberg is visible!!
Most of it is hidden beneath the surface!!

THE TIP OF THE ICEBERG:
The <u>Obvious</u> ADD/ADHD Behaviors

IMPULSIVITY
Lacks self-control   Difficulty awaiting turn
Blurts out   Interrupts
Tells untruths   Intrudes
Talks back   Loses temper

HYPERACTIVITY
Restless   Talks a lot
Fidgets   Can't sit still
Runs or climbs a lot   Always on the go

INATTENTION
Disorganized   Doesn't follow through
Doesn't pay attention   Is forgetful
Doesn't seem to listen   Distractible
Makes careless mistakes   Loses things
Doesn't do school work

"HIDDEN BENEATH THE SURFACE"
The <u>Not So Obvious</u> Behaviors!!

NEUROTRANSMITTER DEFICITS IMPACT BEHAVIOR
Inefficient levels of neurotransmitters, *norepinephrine, dopamine, & serotonin,* result in reduced brain activity on thinking tasks.

COEXISTING CONDITIONS
<u>2/3 have at least one other condition</u>
Anxiety (37%)   Depression (28%)
Bipolar (12%)   Substance Abuse (5%)
Tourette Disorder (11%)
Obsessive Compulsive Disorder –
Oppositional Defiant Disorder (59%)
Conduct Disorder (43%)

WEAK EXECUTIVE FUNCTIONING
Working Memory and Recall
Activation, Alertness, and Effort
Internalizing language
Controlling emotions
Complex Problem Solving

SERIOUS LEARNING PROBLEMS (90%)
<u>Specific Learning Disability (25-30%)</u>
Poor working memory   Can't memorize easily
Forgets teacher and parent requests
Slow math calculation   Slow retrieval of information
Poor written expression   Difficulty writing essays
Poor listening and reading comprehension
Difficulty describing the world in words
Difficulty rapidly putting words together
Disorganization   Slow cognitive processing
Poor fine motor coordination   Poor handwriting
Inattention   Impulsive learning style

SLEEP DISTURBANCE (50%)
Doesn't get restful sleep
Can't fall asleep
Can't wake up
Late for school
Sleeps in class
Sleep deprived   Irritable
Morning battles with parents

TWO TO FOUR YEAR DEVELOPMENTAL DELAY
Less mature
Less responsible
14 yr. old acts like 10

IMPAIRED SENSE OF TIME
Doesn't judge passage of time accurately
Loses track of time   Often late
Doesn't have skills to plan ahead
Forgets long-term projects or is late
Difficulty estimating time required for tasks
Difficulty planning for future
Impatient   Hates waiting
Time creeps   Homework takes forever
Avoids doing homework

NOT LEARNING EASILY FROM REWARDS AND PUNISHMENT
Repeats misbehavior
May be difficult to discipline
Less likely to follow rules
Difficulty managing his own behavior
Doesn't study past behavior
Doesn't learn from past behavior
Acts without sense of hindsight
Must have immediate rewards
Long-term rewards don't work
Doesn't examine his own behavior
Difficulty changing his behavior

LOW FRUSTRATION TOLERANCE
Difficulty Controlling Emotions
Short fuse   Emotionally reactive
Loses temper easily
May give up more easily
Doesn't stick with things
Speaks or acts before thinking
Concerned with own feelings
Difficulty seeing other's perspective
May be self-centered
May be selfish

****
ADD/ADHD is often more complex than most people realize!
Like icebergs, many problems related to ADD/ADHD are not visible. ADD/ADHD may be mild, moderate, or severe, is likely to coexist with other conditions, and may be a disability for some students.

FIGURE 4

Reprinted with permission from Zeigler Dendy (2000).

the iceberg illustrates the three obvious benchmark features of ADHD (hyperactivity, impulsivity, and inattention). Nevertheless, Zeigler Dendy (2000) brings attention to the many features that may cooccur with the syndrome and may not be as apparent (e.g., many children with ADHD may have low frustration tolerance as well as coexisting conditions).

We suggest that when practitioners explain ADHD to parents that they incorporate all of these illustrations. It may make the discussion easier to understand.

HOW SERIOUS IS THE DISORDER?

ADHD is an externalizing disorder; it is one of the most prevalent disorders of childhood (Wells et al., 2000). Children with ADHD comprise one-third to one-half of all referrals to child mental health facilities (Popper, 1998). It is classified as an externalizing disorder because of the impact it has on others in the child's environment. For example, a child with ADHD who is impulsive and disruptive affects the harmony in a classroom. Students in the child's classroom may avoid being associated with the child with ADHD because the child is disruptive and often in trouble. Children with ADHD often have poor social skills and their peers actively reject them (Asarnov, 1988; Erhardt & Hinshaw, 1994). Many children with ADHD have no friends. They have no awareness of why others avoid them and are frustrated by the reactions of others. If this persists over time, they may develop an unhealthy self-esteem and become depressed. Often the non–ADHD sibling becomes resentful of the attention given to their brother or sister. They are embarrassed by the impulsive, disruptive, and socially inept behavior of their sibling. Parents often experience an enormous amount of stress and some resort to punitive strategies to control their child's behavior (Anderson et al., 1994; Danforth et al., 1991). They may avoid socializing with others or going out in public because they fear that their child will embarrass them in front of others. Parents often experience a great deal of strife over parenting the child with ADHD. This may put a tremendous stress on the marital relationship (Befera & Barkley, 1984; Barkley et al., 1990b). Children with ADHD are at risk for child abuse because of the extreme emotions they elicit in frustrated parents (Barkley, 1998). Children with ADHD are more likely to be retained in school and are also more likely to drop out of school, failing to complete high school (Barkley et al., 1990a; Hinshaw, 1992). They are more likely to get into car accidents as adolescents and adults (Weiss & Hechtman, 1993). Children with ADHD have more contact with the juvenile court system and later the criminal courts as adults (Ollendick et al., 1992; Parker & Asher, 1987). If not treated at an early age, they are more likely than their non-ADHD peers to develop further psychiatric problems. Girls are more likely to have premarital sex and become pregnant at an early age (Weiss & Hechtman, 1993). This is a serious disorder that needs early intervention to avoid the potentially catastrophic results from lack of therapeutic intervention.

EFFECTIVE PRACTICES FOR SERVING CHILDREN WITH ADHD

NIMH and the Department of Education funded a multimodal treatment study of children with ADHD (MTA) (MTA Cooperative Group, 1999) to gather up-to-date information concerning the long-term safety and comparative effectiveness of current treatments. Six different university medical centers and hospitals were brought together to evaluate the leading treatments for ADHD. These treatments included various forms of behavior modification and medications. The study included approximately 600 elementary school children (ages 7–9) assigned randomly to one of four treatment modes: (1) medication alone, (2) psychosocial/behavioral treatment alone, (3) a combination of both, or (4) routine community care. Medication consisted of a double-blind placebo-controlled evaluation of low to high doses of methylphenidate (Ritalin). If the child had a favorable response to Ritalin, he was put on maintenance with monthly visits for medication evaluation/adjustments. If he did not have a favorable response to Ritalin, he was put on an open trial of other medications used in clinical practice (amphetamine, pemoline, imipramine, buproprion, etc.).

The psychosocial/behavioral treatment consisted of parent training, a summer treatment program, and the University of California at Irvine (UCI) paraprofessional program (Wells et al., 2000). Parent training consisted of 8 individual and 27 group sessions covering behavior training and strategies for collaborating with teachers through a school/home daily report card. The summer treatment program took place over an 8-week period, 5 days a week, for 9 hours a day and consisted of direct behavior contingency management with a point system and a daily report card to parents for home reinforcement. In addition, a daily social and sports skill program was implemented emphasizing team membership, cooperation, and a buddy system. The UCI paraprofessional program (IPP) provided an extension from the summer treatment program to the next year's teacher through assignment of a classroom paraprofessional from the summer treatment program to help the teacher initiate the behavioral intervention in the classroom setting over a 12-week period. In addition, a therapist consultant from the summer program provided behavioral consultation to the teacher and reviewed the subject's progress.

Previous long-term studies comparing the two major forms of treatment have been for a 4-month period. This study extended treatment for 14 months (MTA Cooperative Group, 1999) and will track children involved in the study into adolescents. Initial results show that for most ADHD symptoms, children in the combined treatment and medication management groups showed significantly greater improvement than those given intensive behavioral treatment alone and community care. Combined and medication management treatments did not differ significantly on any direct comparisons, but in several instances (oppositional/aggressive symptoms, internalizing symptoms, teacher-rated social skills, parent–child relations, and reading achievement), combined treatment proved superior to intensive behavioral treatment and/or community care whereas medication management did not.

The MTA study identified medication and behavior modification as the primary treatments of choice currently used for children with ADHD. Skill in the use of behavior modification or applied behavior analysis is essential in treating children with ADHD. Children with ADHD are often able to perform as well as their non-ADHD peers if they are given more frequent feedback and more potent reinforcers (Pfiffner & Barkley, 1998). Practitioners must be able to complete a functional analysis of the child's problems in the context of the environments in which s/he must function. Because this is considered an externalizing disorder, the environment must be structured so as to give the child clear and consistent cues as to the appropriate behavior and contingent reinforcement for successful performance of the skill. In order to successfully program for the child to learn and maintain the newly acquired skills, others in his environment must be enlisted to help with treatment. This is a very different type of therapy than individual psychotherapy and requires the therapist to take on the role of consultant across many settings, including the home, school, and community. Parents must be taught behavior modification skills to structure their home routine to provide consistent support and opportunities for their child to practice new and more effective ways of interacting with others. Teachers must be taught practical behavior modification strategies that can be implemented in the classroom for children with ADHD. Additionally, whenever possible, all significant other contributors to the child's well-being, including camp counselors, child care workers, Sunday school teachers, and coaches, must be given simple and practical strategies for supporting the child with ADHD. Results point out that traditional outpatient group sessions focusing on social skills that do not also focus on strategies for including significant others in prompting and reinforcing children's efforts in the "real world" will not likely extend the use of these skills past the 1 hour of social skills a week (Mather & Rutherford, 1996). The children will do well in the social skills group but fail to change their behavior in the stressful and frustrating situations they find themselves in during the remaining nontherapeutic hours.

ADHD often leads to multiple life problems for the child and family. Practitioners who provide therapy for families of children with ADHD should develop a network of collateral therapists, psychiatrists, pediatricians, and educational specialists that are outside of the scope of their practice. The MTA study demonstrated the effectiveness of medication in treating children with ADHD, especially when monitored carefully. A close working relationship with a psychiatrist or pediatrician prescribing medication can help optimize the effects of both medication and behavioral intervention. Collecting objective behavioral data and systematically sharing it with the psychiatrist or pediatrician may help determine the effectiveness of medication or assist in making needed modifications to the medication regime.

One or both parents may have ADHD themselves and need help in seeking treatment for their ADHD symptoms before they can successfully help their child with ADHD. Parents may need to see a marriage and family counselor to address marital issues that are compounded by their child's problems. Without addressing the marital problems, there may be little progress in providing the consistency and support necessary to help their child with ADHD. The child with ADHD may have comorbid learning disabilities and need the assistance of a learning specialist. If his/her learning problems are not addressed, the attentional and behavioral problems may escalate. Children who have ADHD and are depressed may need additional individual therapy to address their depression.

Practitioners working with parents of children with ADHD can offer a parent training course to teach parents behavior modification skills to address home problems and strategies for supporting teachers and other caregivers. Parents must learn how to structure activities to increase the probability that their child will be successful. Once parents gain the confidence and experience in helping their child at home, they can extend their knowledge of what works with their child to others, such as teachers, camp counselors, and day care workers. Children with ADHD need specific instruction and practice in social skills. Social skills groups that provide the opportunity to assess the child's understanding of skills (skill knowledge), ability to know when to use the skill (social knowledge), and ability to perform the skill (skill performance) should be conducted in conjunction with parent training. Children practice their social skills in the group session and their parents learn to extend that practice to home and community. Parent training and social skills are discussed in a later chapter.

Teachers need to learn behavior modification for the general education classroom to support the child with ADHD in addressing symptoms of ADHD in the classroom. Difficulty completing tasks, following directions and rules, staying seated, raising their hand and waiting to be called on, getting along with peers and adults, and transitioning to the next activity by cleaning up and getting out required materials are skills that need to be taught and reinforced for children with ADHD. In addition, homework and completing long-term projects are skills that require systematic planning and feedback if the child with ADHD is to be successful in school.

The problem lies in how to provide the necessary training for teachers to feel confident and competent in intervening with children with ADHD in their classroom. A 1-day in-service course on strategies for working with ADHD is insufficient to train teachers in the necessary competencies of behavior modification. Innovative delivery systems need to be developed and implemented to allow teachers to gain the skills on the job. Strategies for parents and teachers to collaborate in supporting each other's efforts are presented in Chapter 7.

LEARNING DISABILITIES: A CASE STUDY—A SNAPSHOT OF ONE YOUNG MAN

Of the many students who we could identify with a learning disability, a young man named Terry came to mind. As you will quickly discover, Terry is an intelligent young man who is affected daily by his learning challenges. We became acquainted with him while he was in the seventh grade in a middle school.

Terry's parents gave us a comprehensive history of his academic and social challenges. His mother began describing Terry by stating "How can one explain this kind-hearted and sensitive young man? He is a student who can compose a six–page story, enjoy an eight-cassette audio book, and get an A or B on an exam that is read to him. He gets high marks on oral presentations at school because he has a remarkable memory and he does not read his note cards. He talks intelligently and expressively on his topic. However, he is also a student that cannot read a menu, the Sunday comics, or the written instructions on his Nintendo games." She went on to describe his graphomotor abilities and that his writing is unintelligible. Mom reported that Terry acted differently from others. He had a hard time understanding his peers and often became the victim of their blunt comments. For recreation, Terry loves to do stand-up comedy routines at family get-togethers. Recently, with the help of his father, they began producing a weekly live comedy radio show.

Developmentally, the family did not report any signs of abnormalities. His mother's pregnancy was normal as well as her delivery. She reported that Terry was an easy baby to take care of. He crawled, walked, and talked at developmentally appropriate times. In fact, his mother reported that he was a very articulate child.

His early educational experiences were uneventful. Preschool went quite well. The teachers did not seem concerned about his behavior and his academic readiness skills. However, socially, he did need some help interacting with peers. For example, he would often watch a game to see what the classmates were doing before he tried to join in. At 4 years of age he talked about Pluto, the planet, not Mickey Mouse's dog. His social interests appeared to be remarkably different from his peers.

When he entered kindergarten, the parents noted that they began to notice some definite differences. His kindergarten class was very structured and Terry appeared to be overwhelmed. He would often retreat under a table and curl up. When the school psychologist initially observed him, he did not seem to get an accurate perception of the challenges facing the child. He felt the family could wait until summer to test him and perhaps (he suggested) some of the developmental concerns would disappear.

Psychoeducational testing in the summer revealed intelligence in the gifted range with strengths in verbal abilities. However, fatigue, lack of vigilance, and distractibility during testing also seemed to indicate possible deficits in attention. It was at that time that Terry was seen by a child psychiatrist who diagnosed him with ADHD. The psychiatrist prescribed Dexedrine. His parents were somewhat impressed with the impact of medication for the first 18 months. Nevertheless, they became increasingly concerned about the side effects. Terry began to lose a great deal of weight and appeared depressed and withdrawn. Additionally, there did not seem to be any evident benefit to his academic challenges, although there was a subtle improvement in his motor control in his writing. It was not until the second grade that the parents became more alarmed about the prospect of a learning disability. Their son was not reading! Unfortunately, the school did not seem as alarmed. The teachers were pleased with his progress and encouraged the family to take a wait-and-see approach regarding his reading and writing. By the end of second grade he was reevaluated and referred to special education.

His third-grade teacher, a family friend, honestly told the parents that Terry was getting significantly behind his classmates in reading. Further visual perceptual motor testing was conducted and revealed there was some delay in visual processing, but not enough to account for the severity in Terry's reading delay. The parents became very concerned and called a meeting with his school. The principal insisted that the school had done everything possible. They confessed that Terry's lack of progress was an enigma to them.

As a consequence of the limited support from the school, the parents began securing outside services and supports for their son. They enrolled him in a program with an educational therapist as well as had a neuropsyhologist reevaluate him when he was 10. Data from the neuropsychological evaluation in Table 2 revealed similar findings, including superior intelligence and significant deficits in phonological processing.

It was when Terry was about 10 that his mother began spending most of her free time searching for answers. She would attend workshops, lectures, and conferences trying to learn about ways to help her son learn and read. The family became more acquainted with alternative remedial

TABLE 2   Neuropsychological Evaluation

WISC III	Test of memory and learning (TOMAL)
Verbal IQ = 134	Composite index scores
Performance IQ = 110	Verbal memory index = 126
Verbal comprehension index = 140	Nonverbal memory index = 103
Perceptual organization index = 122	Composite memory index = 115
Freedom from distractibility index = 101	Delayed recall = 103
	Attention/concentration index = 75
	Sequential recall index = 92
	Free recall index = 103
	Associative recall index = 151
	Learning index = 117

strategies and began enrolling Terry in outside clinics. The parents were very impressed with a learning disability specialist. She felt that Terry had a significant auditory processing problem and she recommended homework for reading. The parents took their son twice a week to her clinic for reading remediation and complemented those services with vision therapy and perceptual motor (patterning) therapy. Although they noticed small gains, they realized that the few hours a week of outside support were not enough.

Terry needed the same type of instruction during his school day. His special education teacher did not have this training (in phonemic awareness), and the parents prepared themselves to become advocates for their son.

In our interview with the family, the parents stressed that they had to attend many incredibly unpleasant meetings with school officials. They noted that the experiences were devastating. They felt that the meetings were extremely unproductive. A majority of the IEP goals were insignificant. The parents became more and more incensed as the years went by when the school refused to discuss specific reading methods and strategies that they would attempt. Over the years, the family left many meetings signing a dissent to the current IEP, hiring an advocate, and paying for other services.

As a family, they have had their share of upsets and tears over what to do. Even though he was identified for special education before first grade, the parents have witnessed valuable time slip by. Today, Terry is in high school, still having tremendous challenges with reading. He has made some improvements with his social cognition and is fitting in better with his peers. His parents became so discouraged with the public school system that they elected to put him in a private school specializing in learning disorders. He now seems to feel that there is hope and the school is committed to his progress.

We selected this case study not only to highlight the challenges of a student with a potential learning disorder, but also to stress the impact of the misunderstood disorder on the family.

WHO REALLY ARE CHILDREN WITH LEARNING DISABILITIES?

Kavale and Reese (1992) and McLesky (1992) prepared two revealing papers that identified some of the common characteristics of children with learning disabilities. In essence, both reports noted that there are more boys identified with learning disabilities than girls. The ratio is about one to four. It appears that the highest referral grades are third and fourth grade. Most students, who are identified early, continue to receive some sort of special education throughout their high school years. In most cases, the discrepancy model appears to be used to diagnose the challenges. There appears to be more children who are referred for learning disabilities in the language arts areas and less in mathematics. Many students with learning disabilities also appear to have the comorbidity of ADHD. In fact, some statistics highlight that over 20% can be identified. Many of the students have organizational and time management challenges similar to those of children with ADHD.

LEARNING DISABILITIES: AN OVERVIEW OF WORKING MODELS

Although the ramifications of this disorder are tremendous, the explanation of the pervasiveness and heterogeneity of this condition is equally as intricate. The educational challenge most identified to receive special educational services represents a group of children considered learning disabled. In fact, according to the U.S. Department of Education, nearly 50% of referrals for special education are from this population (which represents about 5% of the school age population). Unfortunately, as a condition, many people consider learning disabilities as a mild challenge. Martin (1996) strongly highlights that the idea that learning disabilities are a mild challenge may be misleading. For example, a considerable percentage of students identified with learning disabilities drop out of high school before they graduate (26.7%). A small minority of these students enroll in postsecondary education alternatives.

We have taken the liberty of gleaning the research that has led to a clearer understanding of learning disabilities. Table 3 identifies some of the historical trends that have impacted the current definition of the concept of learning disabilities. Table 4 highlights some of the research on the biological basis of the condition.

Lyon (2001) reported that the prevalence of learning disability identification has increased dramatically since the early 1980s. However, the major problem has been the lack of an agreed upon definition of LD with a comprehensive and reliable method for identification. Fletcher et al. (1996) pointed out that the identification of children with learning

TABLE 3   Learning Disabilities: A History of Theoretical Orientations—A Mixture of Points of Views

---

The evolution special education
- Jean Itard work with the Wild Boy of Aveyron
- Jean Ayres developed a sensory integration theory
- Helmer Myklebust research identifying the relationship between brain function and learning behavior
- Katrina deHirsh developed a theory that described receptive and expressive difficulties in linguistic processing
- Sam Kirk and William Cruickshank were both instrumental in suggesting the term specific learning disability. Kirk was responsible for one of the first working definitions of learning disabilities

Medical community—understanding disease or brain injury and its relationship to reading disabilities
- Schmidt (1676) first described the loss of a reading ability. This outcome was eventually named alexia in 1877 by Kussmaul. The term was modified by Berlin in 1887 to dyslexia (which represented partial reading loss)
- Samuel Orton believed that the fundamental difficulty lay in translating between what was heard and what was actually read (written words). He proposed the term strephosymbolia (twisted symbols) to replace the concept of congenital blindness
- Norman Geschwind (1985) proposed that dyslexia may be caused by the brain's manifestation of a broader spectrum of immune disorders

Minimal brain dysfunction
It was the observations of a British pediatrician in the early 1900s who linked defects in motor control to assumed infectious diseases or mild head injuries. Early in the 1920s, a number of reports illustrated that children recovering from encephalitis exhibited various behavior deficits. The term MBD had its greatest impact from Alfred Strauss. Strauss suggested that children with brain injuries, without any degree of mental retardation, could display deficits in perception, thinking, and emotional behavior

---

disabilities "represents a complex set of empirical and sociopolitical issues that are presently difficult to unravel" (p. 27).

As a disorder, LD should not be viewed as one generalized condition, but rather a grouping of delays in a variety of areas, including listening, speaking, writing, reading, reading comprehension, mathematics, and mathematical reasoning. *The standard definition under the Individuals with Disabilities Education Act suggests that a specific learning disability means a disorder in one or more basic psychological processes involved in understanding or in using language, spoken or written, that may manifest itself in an imperfect ability to listen, speak, read, write, spell, or to do mathematical calculations. The term excludes such conditions as perceptual disabilities, or environmental, cultural, or economic disadvantage (U.S. Office of Special Education, 1977, p. 6).* In the Diag-

TABLE 4   Biological Basis of LD

- Hinshelwood (1900) proposed that some brain damage must underlie reading disabilities, as children with severe reading disability often display behaviors associated with individuals with subtle brain damage.
- Greschwind and Levitsky (1968) documented in 100 normal brains that the region of the planum temporale was larger on the left side in 65% of brains while it was larger on the right side in only 11% of brains. The planum temporale was believed to be essential for linguistic comprehension and therefore rapid whole word comprehension in reading
- Galaburda and Kemper (1979) noted asymmetry of the planum temporale and focal cellular abnormalities widely distributed in the frontal and central language cortex in the left hemisphere of the brain. Symmetry of the planum temporale was not sufficient cause for reading disabilities to manifest but that reading disabilities may be potentiated by the presence of both symmetry of the planum temporale and focal brain abnormalities in the language cortex
- Heir, LeMay, Rosengerger, & Perlo (1978) used computed tomography (CT) to show that children with a severe reading disability had reversed asymmetry of the posterior cortex of the brain, which increased the risk of severe reading disability significantly
- Hynd, Semrud-Clikeman, Lorys, Novey, and Eliopulos (1990) used magnetic resonance imaging (MRI) to examine the asymmetries in nondisabled children, reading disabled children, and in children with ADHD. Both children with reading disability and ADHD had symmetry of the frontal lobes, and children with a reading disability had a smaller bilateral insular cortex. They reported a very significant incidence of symmetry or reversed asymmetry of the planum temporale among children with a reading disability. Brains of children with a reading disability are morphologically different from those of normal reading children
- Adults with a reported history of reading disability showed increased asymmetry of the right planum temporale due to a shift of tissue from the temporal to the parietal bank on the right side of the brain
- Four conclusions based on structural imaging studies: (1) the trajectory of brain development, especially in those areas subserving language and reading abilities, is often at variance from that expected in the brains of those without reading disabilities; (2) differences in brain morphology most likely first manifest during the middle trimester of pregnancy; (3) variations in brain structure are correlated with reading ability/disability and verbal intelligence; and (4) subtle differences in the development of the brain in persons with reading disability are potentially under the influence of genetic factors
- Genetic markers for reading disability have been found on the short arm of chromosome 6 (Cardon et al., 1994) and on chromosome 15 (Grigorenko et al., 1997)
- Functional magnetic imaging and positron emission tomography have been used to demonstrate differences in the functioning of the brain in normal and reading disabled individuals (Hynd, 2000)

nostic and Statistical Manual of Mental Disorders, 4th edition (DSMIV) (American Psychiatric Association, 1994), similar problems are referred to as disorders. *Learning disorders include reading disorder, mathematics disorder, disorder of written expression, and learning disorder not otherwise specified. A learning disorder is diagnosed when an individual's achievement on individually administered, standardized tests in reading, mathematics, or written language is substantially below that expected for age, schooling, and level of intelligence. In addition, the identified problem must significantly interfere with academic achievement or activities of daily living that require reading, mathematics, or writing skills. Substantially is defined as a discrepancy or two standard deviations between achievement and IQ that is not the result of an associated disorder in cognitive processing, a comorbid mental disorder, lack of opportunity, poor teaching, a general medical condition, or individual ethnic or cultural background* (American Psychiatric Association, 1994, p. 46).

COMMENTARY AND CONCERNS ABOUT THE PRACTICALITY OF THE LD OPERATIONAL DEFINITION

There have been many who have made comments on the definition and its value. We will review some of the salient comments and conclude this section of the chapter by reviewing Levine's phenomenological model, which differs conceptually from all the previous models presently being discussed.

Barbara Keogh (1987) revealed that one of the major challenges in remediating learning disabilities is our inability to define the syndrome accurately. The problem is largely due to the spectrum of characteristics associated with the disorder. The number of extraneous factors (education level, socioeconomic status, quality of education, etc.) also introduces more hurdles for professionals in the field of LD to jump.

Other researchers over the decades have argued about some of the aspects within the federal definition. For example, Hammill (1993a,b) noted that one problem with the federal definition pertained to differences in what has been considered the psychological processes noted in the definition. No exhaustive list of specific processes has been established and the federal government has refused to identify the criteria for judging if the deficits exist.

There has also been a tremendous argument in what constitutes a significant discrepancy in the formula. Probably the greatest weakness is the size of the discrepancy needed to qualify as being a serious problem. State guidelines vary in range from one to two standard deviations. Another problem is in the method used to determine a discrepancy. Professionals commonly use two methods to determine a significant discrepancy: the simple-difference method and the predicted-achievement method. Using the simple-difference method, scores on a standardized achievement test are subtracted from a measure of ability (such as the full-scale IQ). In the predicted-achievement method, IQ scores are replaced with estimated achievement scores predicted by the IQ scores. Predictions are made based on correlations between the ability-achievement measures. There is considerable controversy over the validity of the discrepancy approach (Kotkin et al., 2000). The choice of method carries a bias that favors individuals with low or high IQ (Swanson et al., 2000). Swanson et al. (2000) have pointed out that both methods have different statistical assumptions. Depending on which method is used, the number of cases identified may be very different.

Nevertheless, some researchers have noted exceptions to the discrepancy model. For instance, MacMillian and colleagues (1998) reported that many schools, although required, often do not even document a discrepancy between intelligence and achievement. In their study of 150 children evaluated in southern California in five school districts, 61 were identified as having learning disabilities. However, only 29 met the discrepancy criteria. The results highlighted that of the children who received the services, over 50% really did not meet the criteria of learning disabilities.

Torgeson (1991) pointed out that the currently accepted federal definition does not indicate that learning disabilities are a heterogeneous group of disorders that persist into adulthood. He prepared an excellent document in 1993 that argued for specific variations in a working model of learning disabilities. He suggested that a clear specification of academic or behavioral challenges must be addressed rather than using generic terms as a starting point. He pointed out that in a perfect world, a comprehensive definition should incorporate an information-processing model, which could be used to assess and describe the underlying failures. This information would articulate the processing deficits and possibly lead to a better understanding of the nature of the disorder. For example, a phonological theory of reading disabilities articulates clearly that children have a great deal of difficulty acquiring fluent word identification skills. The final two dimensions of his argument crystallize the importance of getting a clear understanding of the etiological concerns. With the advances in technology, Torgesen (1993) argued that we must begin to identify, as much as possible, more clearly the origin of brain abnormalities and also address the etiology of the central nervous system (CNS) dysfunction.

Fletcher et al. (1996) noted that a discrepancy model may be a necessary ingredient, but is not sufficient in explaining LD. We must accept the fact that there is a great deal of heterogeneity within this population. There appears to be some specific subtypes of impairments, but the reliability of capturing the essence within the subtypes is somewhat challenging and unreliable. Generally speaking, there is common acceptance of both language-based disabilities (which are associated primarily with problems in reading and spelling) and a nonverbal type (which is more associated with challenges in mathematics). Denckla (1991) suggested that no more than 10% of the learning disabled population falls into the category of nonverbal.

A PHENOMENOLOGICAL MODEL TO UNDERSTANDING LEARNING DISORDERS

Perhaps one of the most contemporary approaches to understanding childhood learning disabilities has been espoused by Mel Levine at the University of North Carolina. According to Kelly and Levine (authors of Chapter 3), "the field of learning disorders is in need of a conceptual model that will accommodate and respond to the extreme heterogeneity of the students that classroom teachers educate each day." Levine (2001) pointed out that children who struggle with learning deficits comprise a very large heterogeneous group of individuals. Levine argued that the use of labels, such as learning disabilities "or attempts to fit children with learning disorders into a few syndromes," represents an oversimplification of poor performance in the classroom (see Chapter 3).

Levine (2001) described a phenomenological approach to understanding learning disorders. This model "favors informed observation and description over labeling and attempts to take into account the great heterogeneity of children with disappointing school performance" (p. 2). In essence, the model takes a strong stand on identifying the affinities and strengths that a child exhibits that may help the child learn more efficiently. When a child has difficulties, Levine (2001) believes that it is more valuable to determine what subskills are weak and not doing their part to help the child learn and to determine what neurodevelopmental functions are actually needed to help support those skills that are deficient.

The neurodevelopmental model proposed by Levine suggests that diagnostic impressions of students would be clearer if clinicians applied well-informed descriptions, or profiles, of a student's areas of weakness, strength, affinity, and preferred styles of learning. According to Levine (2001) there may be different reasons why a child may display particular observable outcomes. He suggests that some children may have these gaps due to one or more neurodevelopmental dysfunctions, which are the actual gaps or variations in the way the child's brain is developing. There are many reasons why these variations occur neurobiologically, including chemical/metabolic abnormalities and uneven brain growth. Table 4 highlights some of the neurobiological evidence underlying reading disabilities. However, not all observable phenomena for academic deficits occur due to neurodevelopmental dysfunctions. Some may be due to the ways a child may cope with their learning obstacles, a lack of experience, or inadequate prior teaching.

Levine's model suggests that academic learning (or, for that matter, academic nonlearning) can be explored utilizing a neurodevelopmental model that incorporates eight neurodevelopmental constructs. Chapter 3 provides a thorough explanation of the model. However, we will identify the constructs at this point. They are attention controls, language, sequential ordering, high order cognition, memory, social cognition, spatial ordering, and neuromotor functions.

In essence, the goal of Levine's phenomenological approach "is to have clinicians, parents, teachers, and the students themselves understand why a student is struggling in school and to enable the development of a comprehensive descriptive profile of neurodevelopmental strengths, weaknesses, and affinities that leads to a focused and effective plan of management" (see Chapter 3). This way of addressing learning challenges appears to be optimistic, as it attempts to unearth the reasons for the challenges rather than identifying and labeling of the youngsters. The proposed phenomenological approach can be utilized as an alternative to a syndrome orientation to learning disorders (see Chapter 3).

EXPLAINING ADHD AND/OR A LEARNING DISABILITY TO A CHILD

Ultimately as we explain to children what is ADHD or LD, we need to provide them with useable information that they will absorb rather than ignore or fear. This information needs to be explained with sensitivity and humanism! The productive clarification should leave children realizing that there is hope in their lives and that they can learn to have an impact on their future. As clinicians, we need to be open and clear with our clients, but we should leave them with hope. Talon (2002), in an interview with Mel Levine, quoted him as stating, "Many kids are told that they will never amount to anything because of their learning difficulties. Parents, teachers and children need to understand that their future is as bright as any other child" (p. 23). It is cruel to rub a child's nose into his failures. Many children have become victims to their failures and it is hoped that with a clearer understanding they will engage in the first step in their healing process.

Levine (2002) calls the process "demystification" when one explains to children what they are dealing with. In our explanations, we should be trying to demystify and dispel fantasies as well as nightmares about what actually a child's learning challenge consists of. Rather than merely labeling a child as having LD or ADHD, the child needs to have a better understanding of how he is wired and the processes that work well or not as well. For example, a child may have strength in building things and in spatial memory, but falters in his ability to use rote sequential memory and attention. Simply telling a child he has ADHD may not be of any benefit. We need to help the child recognize that if we can get a better profile of how he learns, then we can better support his instruction. We must provide this explanation in a clear manner. It also should be conveyed with respect and optimism.

The hard part of explaining LD or ADHD is the fact that we are labeling a child with something that may be foreign. We owe it to the children to put their challenges into reasonable constructs that are easy for them to understand. In our discussion, a child needs to realize that no one is perfect and that every person has strengths and weaknesses. The key components in our discussion must be the highlighting of both strengths and weaknesses. In this manner, a child can begin to appreciate that s/he does have both. Children need to realize that everyone has positives and negatives in their profile. All people are wired to function better on various tasks and at different periods in their lives. With a clear and positive demystification, children may begin to have a better understanding of how they can learn better. Fine (2000) tells his clients constantly "that they all thirst knowledge, but get to the fountain in different ways." It is hoped that the information given helps children learn to appreciate their individual learning styles and gives them some direction of how they can make a better impact.

Once this is explained, we must put this profile into a perspective. We should try to be concrete and identify and clarify three or four symptoms that he needs to work on. By being clear about what a child needs to work on, we should be directly reducing the child's misconception of the pervasiveness of the symptoms. We actually do this by compartmentalizing the concerns and letting the child realize that he has work to do, but the future does not have to be that cloudy. In fact there are so many issues that haunt children in their youth that are totally avoidable as adults. We need to demystify these challenges so that hope can be felt.

Deciding what to say to a child about the fact that they have ADHD or LD can be a difficult task for parents and practitioners. The challenges faced by young children and adolescents differ. We have chosen to share a set of guidelines that focus on the challenges associated with the disorders and approaches that may serve to help the child meet those challenges. We feel that a focus on teaching children adaptive strategies is more productive than the overgeneralization about limitations that may occur. The following 12 guidelines may help anticipate potential problems and provide guidance in addressing them.

GUIDELINES FOR HELPING CHILDREN WITH ADHD AND LD UNDERSTAND AND MEET THEIR CHALLENGES

1. **Encourage children to always ask for help when something is difficult.** If something is hard to do, do not give up. Often children show their frustration by saying "I'm dumb," "this is too hard," and I can't do this." Teachers can reframe these statements into positive adaptive statements that can assist the child in getting help such as "I need help with this problem," can you show me how to do this," or "could you explain this in a different way so I can understand better?" The first set of statements does not provide an opportunity to get help and attributes the problem to a lack of ability that is inherent in the child. The second set of statements attributes the problem to the need for further help or presentation in a different way so the child can understand. Prompting the child to use adaptive statements and reinforcing them when they do will change the way in which the child perceives the difficulty he may be having at the moment.

2. **Be careful not to explain the disorder or disability in a way that suggests they are incapable of something, have no responsibility for their behavior, or it somehow excuses them.** For

example, some children announce that they have ADHD and have forgotten to take their medication. Therefore, they believe they have a license to act "crazy." They proceed to act on that belief. We let them know that they are still responsible for their behavior and that they will still receive consequences for their choices. The child needs to learn that others will judge them by the choices they make. While it may be difficult to control their behavior, they are still responsible for their outcomes.

3. **Remember to point out individuals as models who have overcome their challenges or excelled.** The challenges as well as the advantages of their uniqueness need to be emphasized. Many successful people have ADHD or LD, such as Einstein, Churchill, and Edison.

4. **Answer your child's questions at the appropriate developmental level.** Be prepared with an answer and use developmentally appropriate materials (to help you explain the answer to their potential questions).

5. **Be willing to share your own experiences if you also have struggled with similar challenges.** Sharing your challenges and how you have dealt with them successfully will prevent your child from feeling alone.

6. **Involve your child in support groups or create the opportunity for your child to meet other children who are struggling with similar challenges.** Setting up play dates with other children or enrolling them in a social skills group may help them realize that they are not alone.

7. **Be sensitive to your child's emotional state.** They may not be able to identify why they feel angry, frustrated, or sad when they are in a challenging situation. Children need empathy and understanding during these trying moments. For example, simply stating "I see that you are frustrated, and if you need help, I can help you" may serve to reduce their frustration.

8. **Anticipate some of the negative experiences that children may have and help them learn how to respond.** For example, children may often tease them. Helping your child know what to say and what to do may help prepare them when dealing with these difficult situations.

9. **Help your child understand that labels such as ADHD are for the purpose of allocating resources.** Children must be children first! The child is an individual that has challenges that can be helped by professionals who have expertise in providing specialized strategies and services.

10. **Help them to know how, when, and whom they can go to if they need help.** Contact professionals in your child's school, sports team, camp, and so on who can help them. Knowing how, when, and who to go to will reduce the child's stress and provide a support system.

11. **Be aware of situations that are a challenge for your child and try never to become frustrated, angry, or disappointed.** Prepare yourself to prompt, reinforce, and support your child when they are attempting to meet a challenge.

12. **Establish realistic expectations and make those the challenge.** Do not decrease your expectations, adjust them. Setting realistic goals and celebrating progress will encourage your child to value effort and feel successful.

CONCLUSION

Although many do not consider ADHD and LD serious disorders, their victims do. Although clinicians often underestimate the magnitude of the challenges, living with them can be frustrating. So many stories come to mind to express this occurrence. One example is in Neil Diamond's "Brooklyn Road." In this song, Diamond vocalizes the essence of defeat children experience as they are misunderstood. He tells the story of a child who is afraid of showing his mother his report card. Perhaps the fear is due to embarrassment, of knowing that he is not doing well. Perhaps the anger is due to feeling frustrated that he cannot do as well as others. This anger and a sense of disgrace are magnified even further when his mother is told at a teacher conference, "Got a good head if he'd apply it, but you know yourself it's always somewhere else."

Typically, the boy is misunderstood! Like most educators (who are not as aware of this subtle condition), he considers the boy lazy and not working up to his potential. As a result of being told he is incompetent, the child tries to escape the realities of his own life. Diamond continues his ballad by telling us that the boy builds a castle in his mind (filled with kings and dragons) and tries to ride off with them into "their never never land." He does this as he stands by his window daydreaming (really avoiding the hardships in his life) and looking out on those Brooklyn roads. In the boy's point of view, he dreams of escaping the realities of his own life. This ballad highlights one of our targeted missions. The outcomes could be avoided or perhaps not be as significant if the children were better understood, supported, and treated therapeutically.

REFERENCES

American Academy of Pediatrics (2001). Clinical practice guideline: Treatment of the school-aged child with attention-deficit/hyperactivity disorder, *Pediatrics*, 108:4, 1033–1044.

American Academy of P ediatrics (2000), Committee on quality improvement and subcommittee on attention-deficit/hyperactivity disorder. Diagnosis and evaluation of the child with attention-deficit/hperactivity disorder, *Pediatrics*, 105, 1158–1170.

American Psychiatric Association (1980). *Diagnostic and statistical manual of mental disorders* (3rd ed.). Washington, DC: author.

American Psychiatric Association (1987). *Diagnostic and statistical manual of mental disorders* (3rd ed.). Washington, DC: author.

American Psychiatric Association (1994). *Diagnostic and statistical manual of mental disorders* (4th ed.). Washington, DC: author.

Anderson, C. A., Hinshaw, S. P., & Simmel, C. (1994). Mother-child interactions in ADHD and comparison boys: Relationships with overt and covert externalizing behavior. *Journal of Abnormal Child Psychology*, 22, 247–265.

Asarnow, J. R. (1998). Peer status and social competence in child psychiatric in patients: A comparison of children with depressive, externalizing, and concurrent depressive and externalizing disorders. *Journal of Abnormal Child Psychology*, 16, 151–162.

Barkley, R. A. (1997). *ADHD and the nature of self-control*. New York: Guiford Press.

Barkley, R. A. (1997). Behavioral inhibition, sustained attention, and executive functions: Constructing a unifying theory of ADHD. *Psychological Bulletin*, 121, 65–04.

Barkley, R. A. (1990). *Attention deficit hyperactivity disorder; a handbook for diagnosis and treatment*. New York: Guilford Press.

Barkley, R. A. (1998). *Attention deficit hyperactivity disorder; a handbook for diagnosis and treatment* (3rd ed.). New York: Guilford Press.

Barkley, R. A., Depaul, & McMurray (1990a). Attention deficit disorder with and without hyperactivity: Clinical response to three dose levels of methylphenidate. *Pediatrics*, 87, 519–531.

Barkley, R. A., Fisher, M., Edelbrock, C. S., & Smallish, L. (1990b). The adolescent outcome of hyperactive children diagnoses by research criteria. 1. An 8-year prospective follow-up study. *Journal of the American Academy of Child and Adolescent Psychiatry*, 29, 546–557.

Befra, M., & Barkley, R. A. (1984). Hyperactive and normal girls and boys: Mother-child interactions, parent psychiatric status, and child psychopathology. *Journal of Child Psychology and Psychiatry*, 26, 439–452.

Biederman, J., Newcorn, J., & Sprich, S. (1991). Comorbidity of attention deficit hyperactivity disorder with conduct, depressive, anxiety, and other disorders. *American Journal of Psychiatry*, 32, 233–256.

Bronskowski, J., & Burke, J. (1996). Theories, models and measurements of executive functioning: An information processing perspective. In G. R. Lyon & N. A. Krasnegor (Eds.), *Attention, memory, and executive function* (pp. 235–262). Baltimore: Paul H. Brookes.

Brown, T. (2000). *Attention deficit disorders and co-morbidities in children, adolescents, and adults*. Washington, DC: American Psychiatric Press.

Butterfield, E., & Belmont, J. (1977). Assessing and improving the executive cognitive functions of mentally retarded people. In I. Bialer & M. Sternlicht (Eds.), *Psychological issues in mental retardation* (pp. 277–318). New York: Psychological Dimensions.

Cantwell, D. (1996). Attention deficit disorder: A review of the past 10 years. *Journal of Child and Adolescent Psychiatry*, 35(8), 978–987.

Cardon, L. R., Smith, S. D., Fulder, D. W., Kimberling, W. J., Pennington, B. F., & DeFries, J. C. (1994). Quantitative trait locus for reading disability on chromosome 6. *Science*, 266, 276–279.

Cook, E. H., Stein, M. A., Krasowski, M. D., et al. (1995). Association of attention-deficit disorder and the dopamine transporter gene. *American Journal of Human Genetics*, 56, 993–998.

Danforth, J. S., Barkley, R. A., & Stokes, T. F. (1991). Observations of parent-child interactions with hyperactive children: Research and clinical implications. *Clinical Psychology Review*, 11, 703–727.

Denckla, M. (1994). Measurement of executive functioning. In G. R. Lyon (Ed.), *Frames of reference for assessment of learning disabilities: New views on measurement issues* (pp. 117–142). Baltimore: Paul H. Brookes.

Denckla, M. B. (1996). A theory and model of executive function: A neuropsychological perspective. In G. R. Lyon & N. A. Krasnegor (Eds.), *Attention, memory, and executive function* (pp. 263–277). Baltimore: Paul H. Brookes.

Donovan, M. S., & Cross, C. T. (Eds.) (2002). *Minority students in special and gifted education*. Washington, DC: National Academy Press.

Douglas, V. I. (1980). Higher mental processes in hyperactive children: Implications for training. In R. M. Knights & D. J. Baker (Eds.), *Treatment of hyperactive and learning disordered children* (pp. 65–91). Baltimore, MD: University Park Press.

Erhart, D., & Hinshaw, S. P. (1994). Initial sociometric impressions of attention-deficit hyperactivity disorder and comparison boys: Predictions form social behaviors and from nonbehavioral variables. *Journal of Consulting and Clinical Psychology*, 62, 833–842.

Feagans, L., & McKinney, J. D. (1981). Pattern of exceptionality across domains in learning disabled children. *Journal of Applied Developmental Psychology*, 1(4), 313–328.

Fletcher, J., Francis, D., Rourke, B., Shaywitz, S., & Shavitz, B. (1996). Classification of learning disability: Relationships with other childhood disorders. In G. R. Lyon & N. A. Krasnegor (Eds.), *Attention, memory, and executive function* (pp. 27–55). Baltimore: Paul H. Brookes.

Fuster, J. M. (1995). Memory and planning: Two temporal perspectives of frontal lobe function. In H. H. Jasper, S. Riggio, & P. S. Goldman-Rakic (Eds.), *Epilepsy and the functional anatomy of the frontal lobe* (pp. 9–18). New York: Raven Press.

Galaburda, A., & Kemper, T. L. (1979). Cytoarchitectonic abnormalities in developmental dyslexia: A case study. *Annals of Neurology*, 6, 94–100.

Geschwind, N. (1985a). Biological foundations of reading. In F. H. Duffy & N. Geschwind (Eds.), *Dyslexia: A neuroscientific approach to clinical evaluation*, Boston: Little, Brown.

Geschwind, N. (1985b). Mechanism of change after brain lesions. *Annals of the New York Academy of Sciences*, 457, 1–11.

Geschwind, N., & Levitsky, W. (1968). Human brain: Left-right asymmetries in temporal speech region. *Science*, 161, 186–187.

Grigorenko, E. L., Wood, F. B., & Meyer, M. S. (1997). Susceptibility loci for distinct components of developmental dyslexia on chromosome 6 and 15. *American Journal of Human Genetics*, 60, 27–39.

Hammill, D. D. (1993a). A brief look at the learning disabilities movement in the United States. *Journal of Learning Disabilities*, 26, 295–310.

Hammill, D. D. (1993b). A timely definition of learning disabilities. *Family and Community Health*, 16(3), 1–8.

Hier, D., LeMay, M., Rosenberger, P., & Perlo, V. (1978). Developmental dyslexia: Evidence for a subgroup with a reversal of cerebral asymmetry. *Archives of Neurology*, 35, 90–92.

Hinshaw, S. P. (1992). Academic underachievement, attention deficits, and aggression: Comorbidity and implications for intervention. *Journal of Consulting and Clinical Psychology*, 60, 893–903.

Hinshelwood, J. (1900). Congenital word-blindness. *Lancet*, 1, 1506–1508.

Hughes, J. R., & John, E. R. (1999). Conventional and qualitative electrocephalography in psychiatry. *Journal of Clinical Neruopsychiatry and Clinical Neurosciences*, 11, 190–208.

Hynd, G. W. (2001). Neurobiological basis of learning disabilities. In D. Hallahan & B. Keogh (Eds.), *Research and global perspectives in Learning disabilities*. New Jersey: Lawerence Erlbaum.

Hynd, G. W., Semrud-Clikeman, M., Lorys, A. R., Novey, E. S., & Elioplus, D. (1990). Brain morphology in developmental dyslexia and attention deficit hyperactivity disorder with hyperactivity. *Archive of Neurology*, 919–926.

Kavale, K. A., & Reese, J. H. (1992). The character of learning disabilities: An Iowa profile. *Learning Disability*, 15, 74–93.

Keogh, B. K. (1987). Learning disabilities: Diversity in search of order. In M. Wang, M. Reynolds, & H. Walberg (Eds.), *The handbook of special education: Research and practice*. Oxford: Pergamon Press.

Kotkin, R. A., Forness, S. R., & Kavale, K. A. (2001). In D. Hallahan & B. Keogh (Eds.), *Research and global perspectives in learning disabilities*. New Jersey: Lawerence Erlbaum.

Levine, M. (2001). *Educational care: A system for understanding and helping children with learning problems at home and in school* (2nd ed.). Cambridge, MA: Educators Publishing Service, Inc.

Levine, M. (2002). *A mind at a time*. New York: Simon and Shuster.

Lyon, G. R., & Krasnegor, N. (1996). *Attention, memory, and executive function*. Baltimore: Paul H. Brookes.

MacMillian, D. L., Gresham, F. M., & Bocian (1998). Discrepancy between definition of learning disabilities and school practices: An empirical investigation. *Journal of Learning Disabilities*, 31, 314–326.

Martin, E. (1996). Learning disabilities and public policy. In G. R. Lyon, D. Gray, J. Kavanagh, & N. Krunegor (Eds.), *Better understanding of learning disabilities* (pp. 325–343). Baltimore: Paul H. Brookes.

Mathur, S. R., & Rutherford, R. B. (1996). Is social skills training effective for students with emotional or behavioral disorders? *Behavioral Disorders*, 22(1), 21–28.

MTA Cooperative Group (1999). A 14-month randomized clinical trial of treatment strategies for attention-deficit/hyperactivity disorder. *Archives of General Psychiatry*, 56, 1073–1086.

NIH Consensus Statement (1998). *Diagnosis and treatment of attention deficit hyperactivity disorder (ADHD)* (Vol. 16, No. 2, pp. 1–37).

NIMH (2000). *Attention deficit hyperactivity disorder (ADD) Questions and answers*, http://www.nimh.nih.gov.

Ollendick, T. H., Weist, M. D., Borden, M. C., & Green, R. W. (1992). Sociometric status and academic, behavioral and psychological adjustment: A five year longitudinal study. *Journal of Consulting and Clinical Psychology*, 60, 80–87.

Parker, J. G., & Asher, S. R. (1987). Peer relations and later personal adjustment: Are low-accepted children at risk? *Psychological Bulletin*, 102, 357–389.

Pennington, B. F., & Ozonoff, S. (1996). Executive functions and developmental psychopathology. *Journal of Child Psychology and Psychiatry*, 37, 51–87.

Pfiffner, L., & Barkley, R. A. (1998). Educational placement and classroom management. In R. A. Barkley (Ed.), *Attention deficit hyperactivity disorder: A handbook for diagnosis and treatment* (2nd ed. pp. 458–490). New York: Guilford Press.

Pliszka, S., Carlson, C., & Swanson, J. M. (1999). *ADHD with comorbid disorders: Clinical assessment and management*. New York: Guilford Press.

Popper, C. W. (1998). Disorders usually first evident in infancy, childhood, or adolescence. In J. A. Talbott, R. E. Hales, & S. C. Yudofsky (Eds.), *Textbook of psychiatry* (pp. 649–735).

Richters, J. E., Arnold, L. D., Jensen, P. S., Abikoff, H., Conners, C. K., Greenhill, L. L., Hechtman, L., Hinshaw, S. P., Pelham, W. E., & Swanson, J. M. (1995). NIMH collaborative multisite multimodal treatment study of children with ADHD. I Background and rationale. *Journal of American Academy of Child Adolescent Psychiatry*, 34, 987–1000.

Sergeant, J. A., Oosterlaan, J. N., & van der Meere, J. (1999). Information processing and energetic factors in attention-deficit/hyperactivity disorder. In H. Quay & Hogan (Eds.), *Handbook of disruptive behavior disorders*. New York: Plenum Press.

Shue, K. L., & Douglas, V. I. (1992). Attention deficit hyperactivity disorder and the frontal lobe syndrome. *Brain and Cognition*, 20, 104–124.

Swanson, J. M. (1990). *School-based assessment and interventions for ADD students*. Ivine, CA: K.C Publishing.

Swanson, J. M., Hanley, T., Simpson, S., Davies, M., Shulte, A., Wells, K., Hinshaw, S., Abikoff, H., Hechtman, L., Pelham, B., Hoza, B., Severe, J., Forness, S., Gresham, F., & Arnold, E. L. (2000). Evaluation of learning disorders in children with a psychiatric disorder: An example from the multimodality treatment study of ADHD (MTA). In *Learning disabilities: Implications for psychiatric treatment*. Washington, DC: American Psychiatric Press.

Talan, J. (2002). Stop Labeling our kids. *ADDtitude*, September/October, pp. 20–22.

Torgeson, J. K. (1991). Subtypes as prototypes: Extended studies of rationally defined extreme groups. In L. V. Feagans, E. J. Short, & L. J. Meltzer (Eds.), *Subtypes of learning disabilities: Theoretical perspectives and research* (pp. 229–246). Hillsale, NJ: Earlbaum.

U.S. Department of Education (1998). *Twentieth annual report to Congress on the implementation of the individuals with disabilities education Act*. Washington, DC: U.S. Office of Special Education Programs.

Wells, K., Pelham, B., Kotkin, R. A., Hoza, B., Abikoff, H., Arnold, L. E., Abramowitz, A., Cantwell, D. P., Conner, C. K., Del Carmen, R., Elliot, G., Greenhill, L. L., Hechtman, L. T., Hinshaw, S. P., Jensen, P. S., March, J. S., Schiller, E., Sevevre, J., & Swanson, J. M. (2000). Psychosocial treatment strategies in the MTA study: Rationale methods, and critical issues in design and implementation. *Journal of Abnormal Psychology*.

Westman, J. (1990). *The handbook of learning disabilities: A multisystem approach*. Needham Heights, MA.: Allyn and Bacon.

Weiss, G., & Hechtman, L. T. (1993). *Hyperactive children grown up: ADHD in children, adolescents, and adults*. New York: Guilford.

Zametkin, A. J., Nordahl, T. E., Gross, M., King, A. C., Semple, W. E., Rumsey, J., Hamburger, S., & Cohen, R. M. (1990). Cerebral glucose metabolism in adults with hyperactivity of childhood onset. *New England Journal of Medicine*, 323, 1361–1366.

Zeigler Dendy, C. (2000). *Teaching teens with ADD and AD/HD*. Bethesda, MD: Woodbine House.

Zeigler Dendy, C. (2002). *Five components executive function*. *Attention*, February, pp. 26–31.

Traditional and Innovative Assessment of Children with Attention Deficit Hyperactivity Disorder and Learning Disorders

James M. Swanson, Dan Reschly, Aubrey H. Fine, Ronald A. Kotkin, Tim Wigal and Steve Simpson

INTRODUCTION

Attention deficit hyperactivity disorder (ADHD) and specific learning disability (SLD) are two of the most commonly applied labels for children with school problems. Both are based on official definitions for categories of disorder (ADHD) or disability (SLD), and both have multiple domains or subtypes (i.e., the inattentive, hyperactive–impulsive, and combined subtypes of ADHD; reading, spelling, and math subtypes of SLD). Precise criteria based on etiology are lacking for either ADHD or SLD, but at any point in time detailed guidelines are presented in an "official" way (in manuals, laws, and regulations) to meet the practical needs of clinicians and educators. In ADHD there is close congruence between the construct definition and classification criteria, a circumstance that does not exist with LD. This chapter reviews the current definitions and what we consider to be the current state-of-the art methods for assessments for ADHD and LD. Also, we present a variety of innovative, nontraditional assessments directed by new hypotheses, theories, and discoveries that may shape the revisions of the official definitions and in the future may become accepted methods for assessments for ADHD and LD.

This chapter enhances the discussion presented previously in Chapter 1, which provided an overview of both ADHD and SLD, as well as their histories. The authors of Chapter 1 highlighted some of the difficulties in defining the syndromes as well as the heterogeneity of these populations. All of these variables may lead to challenges in diagnosing and assessing the symptoms accurately. Furthermore, this chapter is followed by two outstanding chapters providing a more in-depth view into nonverbal learning disabilities (NLD) and a neurodevelopmental approach to identifying learning challenges in children. Chapter 4 provides valuable suggestions for an accurate diagnosis of NLD. Chapter 3 also provides a detailed explanation of a phenomenological approach for assessing children with learning/attention challenges utilizing a neurodevelopmental approach. Clinicians will be able to combine what they read in this chapter and use the information in the Chapters 3 and 4 to obtain a more comprehensive perception of assessment options.

OFFICIAL DEFINITIONS

ADHD

Currently, the most widely accepted definition of ADHD is listed in the *American Psychiatric Association's Diagnostic and Statistical Manual, Edition IV* (DSM-IV, 1994). This definition evolved from the definitions of hyperkinetic reaction to childhood listed in DSM-II (1968), attention deficit disorder (ADD) in DSM-III (1980), and attention deficit hyperactivity disorder in DSM-III-R (1987). Another definition is provided in the *International Classification of Diseases, Revision 10* (ICD-10, 1993), which uses the label hyperkinetic disorder (HKD) that has evolved from the ICD-9 (1978) definition of HKD and is often used outside of the United States. In the early 1990s, after decades of differences, the specific symptoms specified in these most recent revisions of these manuals (ICD-10 and DSM-IV) converged so that now they both list the same set of 18 core symptoms (see Table 1). The definitions in both manuals also require early onset (by age 7 years), impairment in multiple settings (typically at home and school), and long duration (to ensure chronic not episodic presence). However, DSM-IV and ICD-10 criteria still differ in a number of ways, which are discussed in a section on innovative assessments.

TABLE 1   DSM-IV/ICD-10 Symptoms: The SNAP Rating Scale with Items Defined as Psychopathology

1. Often fails to give close attention to detail or makes careless mistakes in schoolwork or tasks
2. Often has difficulty sustaining attention in tasks or play activities
3. Often does not seem to listen when spoken to directly
4. Often does not follow through on instructions and fails to finish school work, chores, or duties
5. Often has difficulty organizing tasks and activities
6. Often avoids, dislikes, or reluctantly engages in tasks requiring sustained mental effort
7. Often loses things necessary for activities (e.g., toys, school assignments, pencils, or books)
8. Often is distracted by extraneous stimuli
9. Often is forgetful in daily activities
10. Often fidgets with hands or feet or squirms in seat
11. Often leaves seat in classroom or in other situations in which remaining seated is expected
12. Often runs or climbs excessively in situations in which it is inappropriate
13. Often has difficulty playing or engaging in leisure activities quietly
14. Often is "on the go" or often acts as if "driven by a motor"
15. Often talks excessively
16. Often blurts out answers before questions have been completed
17. Often has difficulty awaiting turn
18. Often interrupts or intrudes on others (e.g.,butts into conversations or games)

A definition of ADHD is also provided in educational laws and regulations. Under the Education for the Handicapped Act (EHA, 1978), neither ADHD nor any of its predecessors were recognized as a handicapping condition. However, during the process of revising the EHA and reauthorizing it as the Individuals with Disabilities Education Act (IDEA, 1990), a partial recognition of ADHD was proposed by the U.S. Department of Education (Davila et al., 1991; "Memorandum to Chief State School Officers: Clarification of Policy to Address the Needs of Children with Attention Deficit Hyperactivity Disorders within General and/or Special Education"). This memorandum was based on broad input generated by a notice of inquiry on ADHD (Federal Register, 1990) and provided guidance on how children with ADHD could be determined eligible for services under two laws (i.e., Part B of the IDEA and Section 504 of the Rehabilitation Act of 1973). As specified in this memorandum, if ADHD produced "limited alertness" that seriously impaired school performance, then qualification under the other health impaired (OHI) disability category was allowed. In amendments to the IDEA (1997), "limited alertness" was defined to include a heightened alertness to environmental stimuli resulting in limited alertness to relevant stimuli in the educational setting. If the severity of impairment due to ADHD is not sufficient to qualify for the OHI disability category, then accommodations for ADHD in the regular classroom were recommended under a civil rights law, the Rehabilitation Act of 1973 (Section 504), which prohibits discrimination on the basis of disability.

SLD

Diagnostic constructs are composed of conceptual definitions and classification criteria. Consistency is important in the definition and classification criteria in order for the diagnostic construct to have coherence, meaning, and consistent application. If gaps emerge in the construct, conceptual definition and classification criteria, one or both nearly always change over a period of time. An example of this phenomenon is the change in conception of mental retardation (MR) that occurred in about 1960 (Grossman, 1973; Heber, 1959, 1961), which continues today (Luchasson et al., 1992, 2002).

Conceptual Definition

Conceptual definitions of diagnostic constructs specify what the diagnosis means, what it is, and its key features. The most commonly used conceptual definition of SLD was formulated by a panel in 1968 (U.S. Department of Education, 1968). This definition of SLD was incorporated into regulations governing the Federal Education of the Handicapped Act (1975) and continues in the current version of that law (Individuals with Disabilities Education Act, 1997, 1999). The special education rules adopted by most state departments of education adopted this definition or a slight variation thereof (Mercer et al., 1996). Other authoritative guides to the diagnosis of disorders of children and adolescents use similar SLD definitions (American Psychiatric Association, 1997). The definition stresses SLD as a disorder in underlying psychological processes related to learning.

The term "specific learning disability" means a disorder in one or more of the basic psychological processes involved in understanding or in using language, spoken or written, which may manifest itself in an imperfect ability to listen, think, speak, read, write, spell, or to do mathematical calculations. The term includes conditions such as perceptual handicaps, brain injury, minimal brain dysfunction, dyslexia, and developmental aphasia.

The term does not include children who have learning disabilities that are primarily the result of visual, hearing, or motor handicaps, or mental retardation, or emotional disturbance, or of environmental, cultural, or economic disadvantage (USOE, 1968, p. 34).

Definitions of LD are also provided in psychiatric manuals. The current definition provided in DSM-IV evolved from the definitions in DSM-III-R (academic skills disorders) and DSM-III (specific developmental disorders). DSM-IV definitions of LD incorporate the ability–achievement discrepancy: reading disorder, mathematics disorder, and disorder of written expression are diagnosed when achievement is ". . . substantially below that expected for age, schooling, and level of intelligence." The current definition of LD in the ICD-10 manual also uses an ability–achievement discrepancy that makes diagnosis dependent on achievement ". . . below the level expected on the basis of the child's chronological age and general intelligence."

There are three critical components of the SLD conceptual definition: (a) disorders in psychological processes that are (b) manifested in problems with achievement (c) not due to other causes such as sensory deficits or mental retardation. Each of these components has significant implications for classification criteria.

Classification Criteria

Classification criteria must be established for diagnostic constructs to define cases, to determine who does and does not qualify for the diagnosis. Classification criteria for SLD have *not* been stable since 1968, and significant variation exists today across different states and educational and clinical agencies. The reasons for this variation will become apparent from the review of research on traditional LD classification practices in a subsequent section.

Subsequent to the passage of mandatory national special education legislation in 1975 [Education of the Handicapped Act (EHA), 1975, 1977], development of SLD classification criteria was essential. In congressional hearings, different experts described widely varying anticipated prevalence rates if SLD was included in the law that varied about 2% to as high as 32%. Fearing massive fiscal consequences, Congress required the Department of Education to develop a special set of regulations regarding SLD, which, if not developed in a timely manner, would be replaced by what in essence would be a 2% cap on SLD prevalence. There was, however, no agreement in the profession on SLD classification criteria due in large part to the recently exposed failure of processing deficit models (see later section).

The solution in the mid-1970s, a compromise with which no one was particularly satisfied, established what were titled, Additional Procedures for Evaluating Children with Specific Learning Disabilities in federal regulations (34 C.F.R. 300.540 through 543). Unlike any of the other 10 disabilities officially defined in EHA, SLD was the only category with a special set of regulations about classification criteria. The special SLD regulations established the following requirements: (a) the multidisciplinary team had to include the child's regular education teacher and someone authorized by the state to conduct diagnostic evaluations, (b) severe discrepancy criterion to determine if an SLD exists, (c) classroom observations, and (d) a written report. The additional SLD regulations reflected congressional concerns that this category of disability was not supported by a consensus about classification criteria, which, along with the huge variations in estimated prevalence, created great uncertainty just at the time when the federal role in mandating appropriate education services for students with disabilities was just beginning.

The critical feature of the special SLD regulations was the requirement of a "... a severe discrepancy between achievement and intellectual ability in one or more of the following areas, oral expression, listening comprehension, written expression, basic reading skill, reading comprehension, mathematics calculation, or mathematics reasoning." (34 C.F.R. 300.541). The severe discrepancy requirement was far from universally supported by the professional community; however, it solved a pressing problem, meeting the congressional mandate to establish a method to control SLD prevalence. In addition to the severe discrepancy requirement, the poor academic performance could not be due to a visual, hearing, or motor impairment, mental retardation, emotional disturbance, or environmental, cultural, or economic disadvantage.

These regulations established classification criteria that were partly consistent with the SLD conceptual definition. SLD was unexpected low achievement with expectations based on the child's performance on a measure of general intellectual ability. Unexpected low achievement could occur in one of seven areas and that low achievement could not be due to other plausible explanations, such as MR or sensory deficits. Conspicuous by its absence was any mention of underlying processing disorders as a cause of SLD or among the required classification criteria.

Virtually all states now require the existence of a severe discrepancy between intellectual ability and achievement in the state education agency rules governing eligibility for special education programs; however, several states do not provide guidance regarding the determination or magnitude of this discrepancy (Mercer et al., 1996; Reschly et al., 2003). For example, although 95% ($N = 47$) of states require the establishment of a severe discrepancy in order for a student to gain eligibility for special education in the category of SLD, only two-thirds of the states actually define the magnitude of the severe discrepancy. Moreover, 21 states provide no guidance on how the discrepancy is to be determined, leaving enormous discretion to multidisciplinary teams.

Approximately half of all states specify both a discrepancy determination method and the magnitude of the discrepancy. The two most common discrepancy determination methods are the standard score deviation and regression method. These methods have slightly different effects. The standard score deviation method involves applying a simple criterion to determine how large the discrepancy has to be in order to be severe, e.g., one standard deviation or 15 points, 1.5 SDs or 23 points. The other common method when a method is specified by a state is a regression function that takes into account errors of measurement, the correlation of the two tests, and regression to the mean. The practical effects of the two methods are to advantage and disadvantage students in different parts of the distribution regarding SLD eligibility. The regression method makes it more likely that students with IQs below 100 and less likely that students with IQs greater than 100 will be eligible for SLD, whereas the standard score deviation method has the opposite effects. Some states have severe discrepancy requirements that are virtually uninterruptible and impossible to apply to individual cases. All states allow multidisciplinary teams the discretion to classify students as SLD even though they do not meet the severe discrepancy standards if the team believes the student "really" has a SLD and should be eligible for special education.

The discussion in the preceding paragraph should leave the suspicion that SLD diagnosis has a large subjective element. In fact, research since the mid-1970s clearly supports this suspicion. Students with the SLD diagnosis differ dramatically from each other within and between states.

Characteristics of Children with SLD

A recent volume composed of major chapters and response papers from a federally funded "summit" on learning disabilities provides an excellent summary of the characteristics of children and adults with SLD (Bradley et al., 2002). First, persons with SLD are highly diverse in terms of levels of ability, achievement, social skills, and behavioral difficulties (Gottlieb et al., 1994; MacMillan et al., 1998). The one common feature is low achievement. Second, many children in school programs for SLD do not meet state-adopted IQ achievement discrepancy criteria (MacMillan et al., 1998). Rather, they are placed in special education as SLD because the school staffing team decides academic assistance is needed and uses the override provisions that exist in all states. Third, the vast majority have reading problems as the sole basis for the placement or with or without other academic deficits, such as mathematics or written language. Fourth, approximately one-half to two-thirds of students with SLD have behavioral patterns that interfere with efficient school learning, complicating instruction in general or special education.

Other key characteristics of children and adults with SLD include a preponderance of males in a ratio of two males to one female, despite reports that there are equal numbers of male and females with very low reading achievement (Shaywitz et al., 1990). Most children with SLD are in part-time special education programs, although patterns vary significantly across the states (USDE, 2001). Finally, most students with SLD have special education programs that emphasize reading instruction.

TRADITIONAL ASSESSMENT METHODS

ADHD

Evaluating Presence by Domain and Source

DSM-IV uses a categorical classification system that separates "mental" disorders into types based on defining features that are organized hierarchically. ADHD and LD fit into this organization as "disorders usually first diagnosed in infancy, childhood, or adolescence," which imposes a broad and overarching early age-of-onset criterion for 10 categories each with multiple disorders having some common qualifying features: mental retardation, learning disorders (where RD is placed), motor skills disorders, communication disorders, pervasive developmental disorders, attention-deficit and disruptive behavior disorders (where ADHD is placed), feeding and eating disorders, tic disorders, elimination disorders, and other disorders. DSM-IV criteria for ADHD and LD are summarized in Table 2.

TABLE 2   DSM-IV Criteria for ADHD and LD

ADHD (DSM-IV, pp. 78–85)
  a. Age-inappropriate levels of inattention and/or impulsivity/hyperactivity
     (at least six of nine symptoms present in one or both domains)
  b. Onset by the age of 7 years
  c. Impairment in two or more settings
  d. Interference with appropriate functioning
  e. Not better accounted for by other psychiatric disorders

LD (DSM-IV, pp. 48–50)
  a. A discrepancy between ability and achievement
  b. Significant impairment in activities that require reading (or written expression)
  c. Difficulties not solely due to a sensory deficit

The DSM-IV approach emphasizes phenomenology not etiology and reliability not validity of diagnoses. In a categorical system, diagnosis (classification) is based on the presence of abnormal patterns of behavior assumed to be qualitatively different than the pattern of normal behavior in the population, with clear boundaries between normal and abnormal classes that are mutually exclusive and with high within-class homogeneity. Of course, for ADHD and LD, these conditions may not hold so the use of the categorical system of DSM-IV and the qualitative psychiatric diagnoses that it generates may not be optimal. In the section on innovative assessments, an alternative approach is discussed based on dimensional descriptions of ADHD and LD that are based on the quantification of attributes distributed continuously across the range of defining behaviors without clear boundaries to define separate categories of psychopathology and normality. However, in traditional assessments of ADHD and LD, the DSM-IV approach currently is the state-of-the-art approach, so it will be described here.

The multimodality treatment study of ADHD (MTA) provides an example of traditional assessment of ADHD in a research setting (Hinshaw et al., 1997). To follow the DSM-IV guidelines, the MTA assessment used the diagnostic interview schedule for children (DISC). This structured interview with the parent is based on specific questions designed to estimate the age of onset, severity, and impairment associated with each symptom of the disorders of childhood listed in DSM-IV. The result for ADHD is a count of the number of symptoms endorsed, which can be compared to the cutoff values stated in DSM-IV (i.e., the presence of at least six of the nine symptoms in either or both of the two symptom domains: inattention and hyperactivity–impulsivity).

The length of the DISC interview depends on how many "modules" are included and how many are excluded by the negative answers to probe questions that allow the remainder of the module to be skipped. In the MTA assessment the typical length was one hour or more, which makes the use of the DISC impractical. Also, the DISC is "structured" so no deviation from the questions is allowed. As a result it could be administered by a nonclinician or by computer. However, this impersonal nature of the interview led to a review by a clinician in the MTA assessment, who could overrule the DISC diagnosis based on information from an informal, nonstructured clinical interview and from information from other assessment instruments (to be described later). Based on this review, in the MTA the clinician made the final determination whether the diagnosis of ADHD was warranted.

The full MTA assessment battery included over 50 instruments, and its size, time to administer, and redundancies make it impractical for use in clinical practice. Fortunately, the MTA data reduction procedures identified six key instruments (see Swanson et al., 2000), which provides an empirical basis for a streamlined state-of-the-art assessment organized in the "source by domain" conceptual framework. The two primary instruments in this streamlined assessment battery are rating scales that have parallel forms for two sources (parents and teachers): the Swanson, Logan, and Pelham (SNAP) rating scale and the social skills rating system (SSRS).

The SNAP questionnaire, introduced in the early 1980s by Swanson et al. (1983), was the first rating scale that used the exact DSM-III symptoms of ADD (and later the DSM-III-R and DSM-IV symptoms of ADHD) as items to be rated (see Table 3). The SNAP was renamed the disruptive behavior disorder (DBD) rating scale by Pelham et al. (1992), but this may be an inaccurate name, as ADHD in DSM-IV is no longer considered to be a "disruptive" behavior disorder. DSM-defined symptom lists were also used as items for the ADHD rating scale (Dupaul et al., 1998) and for the Vanderbilt rating scale (Wolraich et al., 1998) so these rating scales are almost identical to the SNAP (and to each other). All of these rating scales assign a score to each DSM-IV symptom of ADHD based on a four-point impairment scale (e.g., for the SNAP, the assignment is not at all, 0; just a little, 1; pretty much, 2; and very much, 3). The average rating per item (instead of the total score) can be

TABLE 3   The SNAP Rating Scale[a]

	For each item, check the column that best describes this child			
	Not at all	Just a little	Quite a bit	Very much
1. Often fails to give close attention to details or makes careless mistakes in schoolwork or tasks	—	—	—	—
2. Often has difficulty sustaining attention in tasks or play activities	—	—	—	—
3. Often does not seem to listen when spoken to directly	—	—	—	—
4. Often does not follow through on instructions and fails to finish schoolwork, chores, or duties	—	—	—	—
5. Often has difficulty organizing tasks and activities	—	—	—	—
6. Often avoids, dislikes, or reluctantly engages in tasks requiring sustained mental effort	—	—	—	—
7. Often loses things necessary for activities (e.g., toys, school assignments, pencils, or books)	—	—	—	—
8. Often is distracted by extraneous stimuli	—	—	—	—
9. Often is forgetful in daily activities	—	—	—	—
10. Often has difficulty maintaining alertness, orienting to requests, or executing directions	—	—	—	—
11. Often fidgets with hands or feet or squirms in seat	—	—	—	—
12. Often leaves seat in classroom or in other situations in which remaining seated is expected	—	—	—	—
13. Often runs about or climbs excessively in situations in which it is inappropriate	—	—	—	—
14. Often has difficulty playing or engaging in leisure activities quietly	—	—	—	—
15. Often is "on the go" or often acts as if "driven by a motor"	—	—	—	—
16. Often talks excessively	—	—	—	—
17. Often blurts out answers before questions have been completed	—	—	—	—
18. Often has difficulty awaiting turn	—	—	—	—
19. Often interrupts or intrudes on others (e.g., butts into conversations/games)	—	—	—	—
20. Often has difficulty sitting still, being quiet, or inhibiting impulses in the classroom or at home	—	—	—	—
21. Often loses temper	—	—	—	—
22. Often argues with adults	—	—	—	—
23. Often actively defies or refuses adult requests or rules	—	—	—	—
24. Often deliberately does things that annoy other people	—	—	—	—
25. Often blames others for his or her mistakes or misbehavior	—	—	—	—

(Continues)

TABLE 3   (*continued*)

	Not at all	Just a little	Quite a bit	Very much
	For each item, check the column that best describes this child			
26. Often touchy or easily annoyed by others	___	___	___	___
27. Often is angry and resentful	___	___	___	___
28. Often is spiteful or vindictive	___	___	___	___
29. Often is quarrelsome	___	___	___	___
30. Often is negative, defiant, disobedient, or hostile toward authority figures	___	___	___	___

ADHD-In	ADHD-H/Im	ODD
#1 ___	#11 ___	#21 ___
#2 ___	#12 ___	#22 ___
#3 ___	#13 ___	#23 ___
#4 ___	#14 ___	#24 ___
#5 ___	#15 ___	#25 ___
#6 ___	#16 ___	#26 ___
#7 ___	#17 ___	#27 ___
#8 ___	#18 ___	#28 ___
#9 ___	#19 ___	(#29) ___
(#10) ___	(#20) ___	(#30) ___
Total = ___	= ___	= ___
Average = ___	= ___	= ___
95th Percentile T 2.56	2.00	1.70
95th Percentile P 1.56	1.33	1.23

a The four-point response is scored 0–3 (not at all, 0; just a little, 1; quite a bit, 2; and very much, 3). Subscale scores on the SNAP-IV are calculated by summing the scores on the items in the specific subset (e.g., inattention) and dividing by the number of items in the subset (e.g., 9). The score for any subset is expressed as the average rating per item. ADHD items are grouped by the DSM-IV symptom domains of inattention (items #1–#9) and hyperactivity/impulsivity (items #11–#19), with a summary item for each domain (#10 and #20). The ODD domain (items #21–#28) is supplemented by an item from DSM-III-R (#29) that was not included in the DSM-IV and a summary item for the ODD domain (#30). The inclusion of items in parentheses (#10, #20, #29, and #30) is optional, but their inclusion makes scoring easier, as division of subset totals is by 10.

used to compare relative standing on scales based on a different number of items (i.e., the 9-item subscales for inattention or hyperactivity–impulsivity symptom domains of ADHD, the 18-item total ADHD scale, or the 26-item SNAP scale based on ADHD and ODD items). Data reduction procedures of the MTA identified 6 subscales from the SNAP (for both the parent and teacher sources, the inattention, hyperactivity–impulsivity, and ODD subscales) as "marker variables" in the source × domain framework.

The social skills rating system (SSRS) by Gresham and Elliott (1989) does not provide a direct assessment of the symptoms of ADHD, but does provide a broad assessment of children's social behaviors based on parent and teacher ratings on a three-point scale (never occurs, 0; sometimes occurs, 1; and very often occurs, 2). The SSRS covers three domains of positive social skills—cooperation (e.g., volunteering to help with household tasks or using free time appropriately at school), assertion (e.g., initiating conversations with others or inviting others to join in games or activities at home or school), and self-control (e.g., compromising in conflict situations and responding appropriately to teasing at home or school)—as well as three domains of problem behaviors that interfere or compete with either the acquisition or the performance of social skills, externalizing problems (e.g., fights with others, threatens or bullies, temper tantrums), internalizing problems (e.g., appears lonely, acts sad or depressed, shows anxiety with other children), and hyperactivity problems (e.g., easily distracted, fidgets, and acts impulsively). The data reduction procedures of the MTA identified total social skills as marker variables in the source x domain framework.

In addition to the measures of externalizing behaviors (ADHD and ODD), the MTA data reduction identified two measures of internalizing behaviors: scores based on parent and teacher impression of internalizing behavior on the SSRS, from the problem behavior subscales, and a summary anxiety score derived from an interviewer rating problems listed on the multidimensional anxiety scales for children (MASC; March et al., 1997). The MASC acquires information directly from the child, who is asked about anxiety-driven physical symptoms (tense/restless and somatic/autonomic), social anxiety symptoms (humiliation/rejection and public performance fears), harm avoidance symptoms (anxious coping and perfectionism), and separation anxiety symptoms. It uses a four-point rating scale to document how often the child considers each item to be true (never, 1; rarely, 2; sometimes, 3; and often, 4).

Combining Information across Sources

Clinicians can combine information across sources by using an "AND" rule (ADHD symptoms are counted if they are reported by the parent AND the teacher) or by using an "OR" rule (ADHD symptoms are counted if they are reported by the parent OR the teacher). DSM-IV criteria for ADHD call for some impairment due to the symptoms to be present across settings, but does not require each symptom to be present in two settings. Also, the correlation between parent and teacher ratings on the SNAP (as for most such scales) is low ($r \sim .3$ to $.4$) so disagreement is not uncommon. In fact, in the MTA assessment, in complex cases where parents and teachers did not agree, the "OR" rule was adopted for up to two symptoms so that many clear cases would not be excluded from the study. In the assessment of the MTA sample, the correlation between parent and teacher ratings on the SSRS was also low (about .2), which is in line with the norms from this instrument for total social skills ($r = .36$) and internalizing problem behaviors ($r = .27$). Low parent–teacher correlations (even for the best instruments) mean that for comparisons of the parent and teacher ratings, less than half of the cases will exceed the 95th percentile cutoffs for *both* sources.

A discrepancy does not necessarily mean that either source is invalid or erroneous, as situational specificity (a true difference in manifestation of symptoms at home and school), situational tolerance (different standards for behavior at home and school), and situational requirements (different task demands at home and school) could all exist and produce discrepancies. However artifactual discrepancies could be produced by common biases in parent and teacher ratings, such as "halo" effects (the presence of a salient behavior may impact ratings of other behaviors) and measurement errors (subjective ratings vary on retest and typically show regression to the mean). We discuss how a clinician could evaluate parent–teacher discrepancies in the sections on innovative assessments.

In the MTA assessment of non-ADHD symptoms, discrepancies were also apparent. Interviews with the parent (on the DISC) and the child (on the MASC) produced discrepant reports of anxiety, with the DISC suggesting higher levels for parent-reported child anxiety than the MASC for child-reported levels of anxiety. March et al. (2000) have discussed the rationale for considering DISC-defined anxiety as a manifestation of negative effect rather than anxiety.

Research on LD Diagnoses

Success of SLD

The rate of growth in the use of the SLD category has been incredible since the mid-1970s as shown in Table 4. The 260% increase rate from 1976 to 1977 when the U.S. Office of Special Education first gathered data on the prevalence of students with disabilities receiving special education services in public schools to the 1998–1999 school year overshadows the increase of any other disability by a large margin. Although SLD is only 1 of 13 disabilities recognized currently in the IDEA, it accounts for slightly over half of all students with disabilities receiving special education in public schools. The rapid increase in students with disabilities has been accompanied by, and is in part related to, the 40% decline in MR over the same time period (USDE, 2001).

LD Diagnostic Models

Three diagnostic models have dominated SLD diagnosis since the mid-1970s. The research supporting each is dubious. None are closely related to interventions and the diagnoses based in each have questionable reliability and stability.

Processing Deficits

The classification criteria for SLD as it was emerging as an official diagnostic category in the 1960s emphasized information processing factors such as input (auditory or visual), manipulation of information (integration of information across modalities, perceptual processes), and response modalities (verbal, nonverbal, motoric) (e.g., Kirk & Kirk,

TABLE 4   Prevalence of MR and SLD in U.S. Public Schools (U.S. Department of Education, 2001)

	1976–1977	1998–1999	Change	% change
LD	797,213	2,861,333	2,064,120	260
MR	969,547	613,207	−356,340	−36

1971). Other formulations emphasized visual perceptual skills visual–motor integration and auditory perception (Mann, 1979). These formulations were applied most often to children and adolescents with serious reading problems who then might have been diagnosed as dyslexic or SLD in reading.

Clinical practice in this early era focused on comprehensive evaluations of children and adolescents with learning problems, typically in school settings, most often in the area of reading. Measures of general intellectual functioning and educational achievement were almost always administered as well as screening for sensory deficits and other factors that might provide an explanation for the low educational performance. In addition to these assessments, and, at that time, crucial to the diagnosis, were measures of the underlying processes that were presumed to cause the learning problem or "block" normal acquisition of skills. Some of the more commonly used processing measures were the Illinois Test of Psycholinguistic Abilities (Kirk et al., 1968).

Rapid demise of the processing focus in SLD diagnosis occurred in the early to mid-1970s due to research studies of children and adolescents with SLD. This demise occurred at a crucial time, corresponding closely with the congressional mandate to establish SLD classification criteria. First, the processing measures typically had poor technical characteristics in the crucial areas of reliability, validity, and norms (Mann, 1979). Children found to have a processing deficit with one measure of a particular process often performed normally on other measures of the same process, leading to poor diagnostic reliability, a potentially fatal problem. Furthermore, it was assumed that improved functioning on processes through direct teaching routines would remove the block to efficient learning and rapid gains in academic achievement would result. A scathing critique of this basic assumption about remediating processes and improved academic achievement appeared in the early 1970's. Hammill & Larsens' (1974) review of the literature suggested that the improved functioning on the processes was difficult to achieve, did not transfer beyond training materials, and, most important, did not produce improved acquisition of academic skills. In short, focusing on improving children's functioning on underlying processes had little benefit and was costly in terms of time and effort. Those conclusions continue with little change in recent authoritative reviews of the relevant literature (Kavale & Forness, 1999). If not processing deficits as specified in the conceptual definition, then what should be used as criteria for SLD?

Severe Discrepancy–Ability and Achievement

To develop classification criteria in the critical mid–1970s, one approach was to require a severe discrepancy between achievement and ability (see prior discussion). This was not a model but, rather a practical solution to very real problems: differentiating SLD from other kinds of low achievement and providing some method to control the potential population of students with SLD. Application of the ability–achievement discrepancy varied significantly across states and within states, depending on the specific test used and the methods adopted to estimate discrepancy (i.e., the "simple difference" of the "predicted achievement" method—see Reynolds, 1992).

In the MTA data reduction methods, scores from the psychometric tests of ability (the WISC) and achievement (the WIAT) were used in a traditional assessment of SLD. Despite concerns about the use of discrepancy scores (see Fletcher et al., 1998), IQ–achievement discrepancies were calculated (see Swanson et al., 2000). In DSM-IV guidelines, a significant discrepancy is described as achievement substantially below expectations for age, schooling, and level of intelligence, where "substantially below" is defined as a discrepancy of ". . . more than 2 standard deviations between achievement and IQ." Thus, to conform to DSM-IV guidelines, the "simple difference" method was used to calculate the difference between the WISC measures of ability and the WIAT measures of achievement.

ICD-10 also specifies the use of a discrepancy score, but recommends a cutoff for an ability–achievement discrepancy ". . . that is at least 2 standard errors of prediction below the level expected on the basis of the child's chronological age and general intelligence." To meet this ICD-10 guideline, the "predicted achievement" method was used to calculate the difference between the achievement levels predicted from the WISC IQ score given by tables in the WIAT manual and the actual achievement scores on the WIAT.

The psychometric assessment of the MTA revealed that this large sample of ADHD children manifested the expected distribution of ability (IQ) scores in terms of mean (about 100), SD (about 15) and shape (approximately normal). The distribution of achievement scores was similar in terms of shape (approximately normal), but the mean was about five points lower than the mean for the estimate of IQ. Here we present the IQ and achievement distributions for this traditional assessment of ability and achievement (see Figs. 1 and 2) and ability–achievement discrepancies (see Figs. 3 and 4).

Combining Domains of LD

Based on the MTA assessment battery, qualification for the SLD label depends on which method is used to calculate discrepancy (i.e., simple difference (see Figure 3) or predicted achievement (see Figure 4)), the statistical significance level adopted (e.g., 05 or .01, (as specified in Figure 3 and 4)), and whether a discrepancy in any of the domains of achievement or on some combination of multiple domains is required. In one evaluation of the MTA sample (Swanson et al., 2000), one combination of these factors was used to define comorbid SLD by the predicted achievement method (see Figure 4) if the discrepancy was statistically significant at $p < .05$ for any of the three domains (reading, spelling, or math). Under these conditions, about 35% of the MTA sample qualified for the SLD label.

It is clear that discrepancy alone is not acceptable to define SLD. In fact, federal guidelines (e.g., "Assistance to the States for Education of Children with Disabilities"; CFR, Title 34, Part 200) specify that a qualified team, consisting of professionals from the school (including the teachers who know the child), as well as the parents of the child, should conduct the assessment, and if a disability (e.g., SLD or OHI) is verified, then this team must develop an individualized educational plan (IEP) tailored to meet the specific needs of the child. Thus, a comprehensive assessment and review of each child are necessary to determine if a disability exists. In the MTA assessment, because the focus of the study was not on SLD, a rigorous state-of-the-art assessment in this area was not performed. In the MTA follow-up phase, records of school assessments that did follow the IDEA guidelines and obtain a full, rigorous assessment of LD will be obtained.

Neuropsychological Profiles and Matching Strengths

One of the most prominent theories of SLD focuses on neuropsychological profiles as a means to diagnose SLD and the use of profile strengths in designing educational programs (Hynd et al., 1986; Swanson et al. 2000). Psychometric profiles using ability, achievement, visual motor, and other tests are interpreted in terms of presumed underlying neurological functions. Students with achievement problems accompanied by a

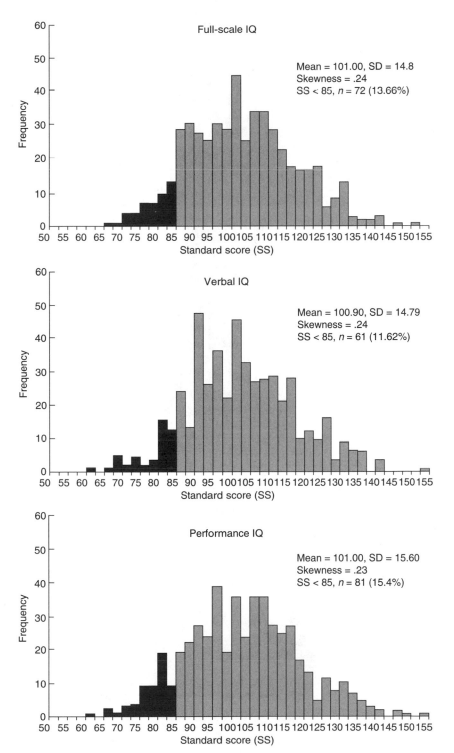

FIGURE 1 Distributions of WISC-III IQ scores and WIAT-S scores for the MTA sample.

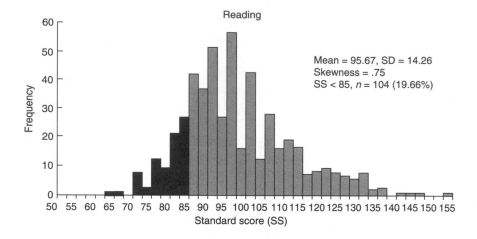

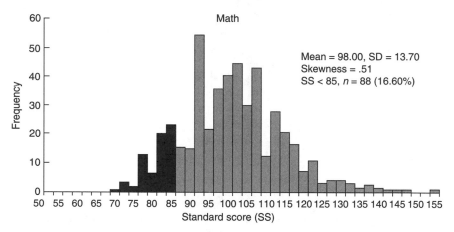

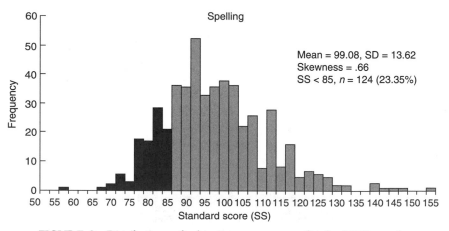

FIGURE 2   Distributions of achievement test scores for the MTA sample.

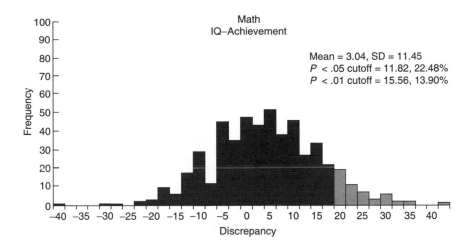

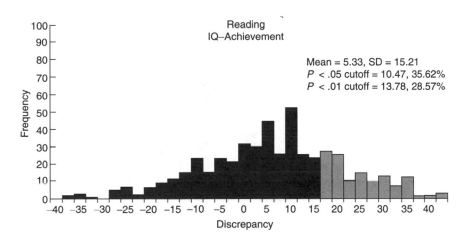

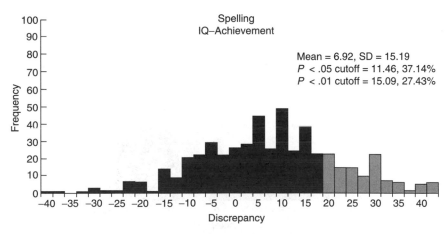

FIGURE 3 Distributions of the predicted achievement discrepancies of the MTA sample.

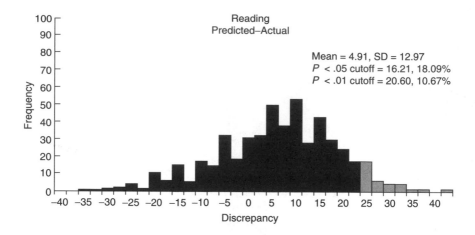

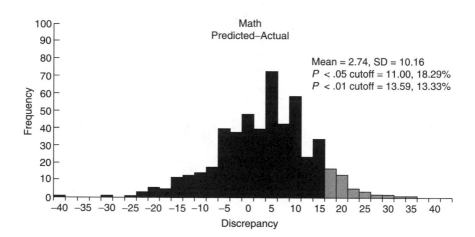

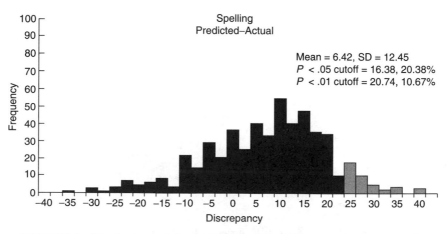

FIGURE 4   Distributions of simple difference discrepancies in the MTA sample.

variety of kinds of profiles are asserted to display different kinds of SLD. For example, a cardinal feature of nonverbal SLD is poor performance in certain domains such as social comprehension that is accompanied by, among other things, higher verbal than nonverbal performance on a test battery. The profile analyses are used to diagnose SLD, i.e., profile differences based on subtest scatter are interpreted as signs of learning disorders, a subtle assumption that normality is defined as a flat profile (i.e., normal learners have few differences across a variety of tasks and activities).

The second use of the profile information is to recommend teaching methodology based on presumed learning strengths and avoiding learning processes that are deficient. For example, the recommendation for a child with a particular profile indicating left hemisphere strengths (similar to sequential or successive information processing and auditory–vocal channel) likely would be a phonic method of teaching reading. Neurologizing of these psychometric profiles sometimes is rather extreme as in Reynolds' suggestion for avoiding "dead tissue" (Reynolds, 1992).

Serious problems with both uses of the profiles exist. First, and most fundamental, scatter or differences among subtests within and between measures of psychological constructs related to learning are normal, not a sign of abnormal performance. High degrees of scatter are found in all normal samples of students. If scatter is a sign of neurological disorder, then nearly all children must be disordered!

Second, many of the neuropsychological interpretations reflect ignorance of the actual complexity of neurological functioning. The relationship between performance on a complex behavioral task in underlying brain functioning rarely involves simple, discrete areas of the brain; rather both hemispheres and multiple areas of the brain typically are involved in complex behavioral tasks. Moreover, there typically is no confirmation of the neuropsychological interpretations regarding brain–behavior relationships, despite significant advances in methods for studying brains. Without such confirmation, the neuropsychological interpretations are speculative at best and are not confirmed or even, in many instances, confirmable by objective evidence of actual brain function (Heinrichs, 1990).

If the treatment recommendations from these neuropsychologists who diagnose SLD based on psychometric profiles worked, the criticisms cited could be mitigated. In fact, there is virtually no support for these treatment recommendations and considerable evidence that they do not work. The neuropsychological treatment recommendations assume that matching estimated neuropsychological strengths to specific teaching methods will produce improved learning for students with SLD. The matching of processing strengths assumes the existence of aptitude by treatment interactions, a largely discredited, but enormously popular theory (Cronbach, 1957, 1975; Kavale & Forness, 1999). Matching presumed strengths seems like it should work. It is enormously popular. It is not supported empirically.

INNOVATIVE ASSESSMENTS

ADHD

Evaluating Parent–Teacher Discrepancies

The MTA provides rich information from a large sample of ADHD children to consider new assessment methods and strategies. One innovative strategy addressed the discrepancies between the two primary sources. We (see Swanson et al., 1999) proposed that the clinician focuses on the parent–teacher discrepancies between SNAP ratings of the specific ADHD symptoms (i.e., whether just one or both sources rated an item more than "just a little"). This strategy was based on the clinician using a standard dialogue with the two primary "sources" to pose the same question: "The rating scales that you completed don't allow you to tell everything about this child, but they do give us a good starting place for a discussion of the symptoms of ADHD. I reviewed the forms you and the (teacher or parent) completed about (the child's) behavior, and I summarized the areas where you agreed and disagreed. To help me understand the overall situation, let's focus on an area of discrepancy." A sample dialogue with the parent might be the following: "When you completed the forms about Linda's behavior at home, you identified significant problems in the areas of inattention and hyperactivity/impulsivity (show the rating forms as reminders). Linda's teacher completed the same forms about her behavior at school and noted less serious problems in both areas. Have you discussed this discrepancy with her teacher?" A sample dialogue with the teacher might be the following: "When you completed the forms about Linda's behavior at school, you identified some mild problems with inattention and hyperactivity/impulsivity (refer to the rating forms as a reminder). Linda's parents completed the same forms and identified more serious problems in both areas at home. Have you discussed this discrepancy with her parents?" The discussion focusing on discrepancies, which may be based on true differences or artifacts, allows the clinician to become the "third source" to break the "tie" when the parent and teacher disagree about the presence of ADHD symptoms.

Defining a Refined Phenotype

One refined phenotype of ADHD, suggested for studies of biological factors of ADHD, is based on cases with the full syndrome ADHD-combined type; concurrent treatment of another disorder (depression or anxiety) and without very restrictive school placement due to aggression. This refined phenotype has been used in studies of the biological bases of ADHD, such as the molecular genetic studies of the DRD4 gene (LaHoste et al., 1996; Swanson et al., 1998e), and it is similar to the phenotype of ADHD defined by the MTA.

The MTA data set is made available to other investigators who propose innovative ways to use it. One proposal came from Taylor and his colleagues from the institute of psychiatry in London, UK, who set out to rediagnose the MTA cases based on ICD-10 definitions of HKD. Even though ICD-10 lists the same 18 symptoms as DSM-IV, DSM IV and ICD-10 differ in decision rules to define these disorders. For example, ICD-10 guidelines (1) impose cutoff values for hyperactivity (at least 3) and impulsivity (at least 1), as well as inattentiveness (at least 6), to ensure pervasiveness across the symptom domains and to exclude all but the combined subtype of ADHD, (2) exclude cases with comorbid emotional disorders (anxiety and depression), and (3) require that the symptom severity (i.e., symptom count) cutoff be met in both the home and the school setting, which excludes some cases that are subthreshhold in one setting and thus are considered to have home-specific or school-specific forms of the disorder. When these ICD-10 guidelines were applied to the 579 MTA cases, only 145 passed all three and met the more conservative criteria for HKD. This process will avoid false-positive diagnoses, but will increase false negatives (misses) and may be preferred by some who are critical of the more liberal criteria for ADHD.

Assessment of Response to Treatment

Assessment does not stop with diagnosis, assessment and screening methods. In the MTA the full assessment incorporated on the evaluation of response to treatment. For example, during the 14-month treatment phase of the MTA, monthly medication reviews were scheduled to monitor effectiveness and side effects of the MTA medication algorithm. An innovative part of this assessment was a short (5 to 10 minute) monthly telephone call to the child's teacher to supplement the information derived from the parent and child at the office visit. At each of these monthly visits, a common set of questions were asked of both sources (parents and teachers) to obtain standard information about change from the prior month (general, improved, worsened) in the area of core symptoms of ADHD (hyperactivity, impulsivity, and inattention) and in the area of associated features (fighting, following school rules, etc.). Based on the answers for both sources, the clinician rated seven categories of status (see Table 5) to indicate a clinical global impression (CGI) of severity of impairment. This innovative algorithm provided the information for a course of action: (1) continue medication as prescribed, (2) change the dose and/or time of administration of the current medication prescribed, (3) change the medication prescribed, or (4) stop the current medication.

Another way that the MTA assessment utilized treatment response was to define "success" by low ratings of symptoms (i.e., equal to .05 or less than 1.0 (just a little) in the 0 to 3 snap scale, which logically represents normal or non-pathological behavior). At the end of treatment, a quali-

TABLE 5   Sample Questions Based on the MTA Teacher Phone Interview

---

How would you describe overall progress at this time?

Please describe specific problems that have improved or that have gotten worse.

Has the child occasionally or frequently missed doses of medication, to your knowledge.

What is this child's current level of restlessness or fidgetiness?

What is this child's current level of impulsivity, such as calling out or interrupting?

How would you describe this child's ability to focus over the last month.

Are there times of the day that are a special problem or a behavior difference from morning to afternoon?

Has there been any change in academic production in classwork or homework in the past month?

How are social relations with peers and teachers? Have there been fights, disciplinary action, or suspensions from school since our last discussion?

---

tative outcome measure was defined by a 1.0 cutoff on the average/item on the SNAP ratings summed across sources (parent and teacher) and domains (inattentive, hyperactive–impulsive, and ODD). This revealed that that the percentage of cases normalized was 35% for treatment with the intensive behavior (Bch) modification treatment, 56% by the medication management (Med/Mgt) treatment, and 68% by the combined (Comb) treatment (see Swanson et al., 2001). The fact that some cases were normalized by nonpharmacological (Beh) treatment is significant and may lead some to question whether these cases were false-positive diagnoses at entry to the study. Also, the statistically significant increase (12% = 68% − 56%) in normalization by the multimodal (Comb) treatment over the medication only (MedMgt) treatment suggests that multimodality treatment is superior to pharmacological treatment (in contrast to the initial report based on the evaluation of the quantitative measures from the SNAP).

Dimensional versus Categorical Evaluation of ADHD Symptoms

The SNAP (and almost all other standard rating scales of ADHD symptoms) define items categorically to represent psychopathology by asking about the presence of weaknesses (i.e., inattention, overactivity, and impulsiveness). Thus, when ratings are obtained in a schoolwide population that distribution of the summary score on the SNAP is highly skewed (see Fig. 5). This creates serious problems for the use of cutoff values from norms, especially if the cutoffs assume a normal distribution and are based on standard scores with a mean = 0 and SD = 1 (z scores) or with a mean = 50 and SD = 50 (T scores). To correct this psychometric flaw, the SNAP was revised for an innovative assessment of the dimension of ADHD as it relates to normal behavior rather than psychopathology. Each SNAP item (defined by the presence of "psychopathology" in Table 2) was reworded to develop the strengths and weaknesses of ADHD symptoms and normal behaviors (SWAN) ratings scale (Table 6).

This scale can capture the full range of behavior in the population and generates a distribution of summary scores that is approximately normal distribution in a sample of nonselected preschool and school-aged children. The SNAP (and all other rating scales positive scores representing "psychopathology") may have a fatal psychometric flaw due to possible artificial categorical definition of behavior that may be dimensional in nature.

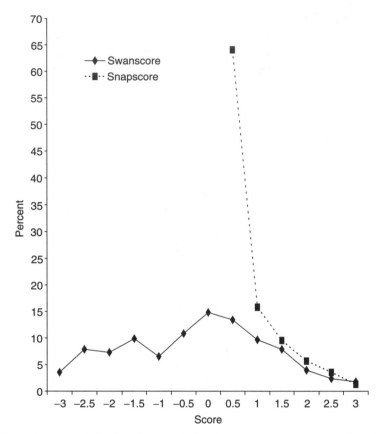

FIGURE 5   Norms (school–wide ratings) for the SNAP (ADHD as psychopathology, n = 847) and the SWAN (ADHD as a dimension encompassing normal behavior, n = 506).

Neuropsychological Assessment of ADHD

Many investigators have tried to identify a cognitive deficit that is unique to ADHD. For example, Douglas (1972) started the modern view of attention deficit as the primary feature of ADHD instead of overactivity, but later concluded that "... the basic infromation processing capacities of ADDH children are intact" and hypothesized that "... the cognitive deficits of ADDH children can be traced to a faulty self-regulation" (Douglas, 1988). Sergeant (1981) adopted the stages of information processing (encoding, comparison, response selection, and response execution) as a framework for evaluating attentional deficits, but concluded that

TABLE 6   DSM-IV/ICD-10 Items Reworded to Reflect Dimensions of Attention and Action: The SWAN Rating Scale with Items Defined by Dimensions Encompassing Normal Behavior

	Compared to other children, how does this child do the following						
	Far below average	Slightly Below	Slightly below average	Far Average	above average	Above	above average
1. Gives close attention to detail and avoids careless mistakes	—	—	—	—	—	—	—
2. Sustains attention on tasks or play activities	—	—	—	—	—	—	—
3. Listens when spoken to directly	—	—	—	—	—	—	—
4. Follows through on instructions and finishes school work or chores	—	—	—	—	—	—	—
5. Organizes tasks and activities	—	—	—	—	—	—	—
6. Engages in tasks that require sustained mental effort	—	—	—	—	—	—	—
7. Keeps track of things necessary for activities	—	—	—	—	—	—	—
8. Ignores extraneous stimuli	—	—	—	—	—	—	—
9. Remembers daily activities	—	—	—	—	—	—	—
10. Sits still (controls movement of hands or feet or controls squirming)	—	—	—	—	—	—	—
11. Stays seated (when required by class rules or social conventions)	—	—	—	—	—	—	—
12. Modulates motor activity (inhibits inappropriate running or climbing)	—	—	—	—	—	—	—
13 Plays quietly (keeps noise level reasonable)	—	—	—	—	—	—	—
14 Settles down and rests (controls constant activity)	—	—	—	—	—	—	—
15 Modulates verbal activity (controls excess talking)	—	—	—	—	—	—	—
16 Reflects on questions (controls blurting out answers)	—	—	—	—	—	—	—
17 Awaits turn (stands in line and takes turns)	—	—	—	—	—	—	—
18 Enters into conversations and games without interrupting or intruding	—	—	—	—	—	—	—

". . . there is no evidence to indicate clearly a failure of one of more of these stages" and hypothesized that the deficiencies of ADHD children are due to an inability ". . . to control their behavior, rather than a structural deficit of attention" (Sergeant, 1988). Barkley (1994) developed a "new complete theory of ADHD" based on the hypothesis that a core deficit in behavioral inhibition caused ADHD and concluded that there was ". . . no attention defcit in ADHD" and recommended that the term "attention deficit" be dropped and replaced with "behavioral inhibition deficit." Pennington and Ozonoff (1996) reviewed the literature and concluded that the tasks that most consistently showed these deficits were the Stroop color-word naming task, the matching familar figures test requiring detailed comparison of objects, Tower of Hanoi test of planning, and the trails B test of search in the face of distraction.

The emergence of the new field of cognitive neuroscience (see Gazzaniga et al., 1998) led to new concepts of attention linked to specific brain circuitry. Posner and Raichle (1994) developed a neuroanatomical network theory of attention that is based on the concepts of alerting (supressing background neural noise by inhibiting ongoing or irrevevant activity or mental effort to establish a state of vigilance), orienting (mobilizing specific neural resources by facilitation of one specialized process and inhibiting others), and executive control (coordinating multiple specialized neural processes by detecting targets, starting and stopping mental operations, and ordering multiple responses to direct behavior toward a goal), each with a well-defined neural circuitry (right frontal, bilateral parietal, and anterior cingulate).

Swanson et al. (1998b) used this theory as a framework for evaluating attentional deficits in ADHD and concluded that deficits were most prominent on tasks that relied on anterior brain regions (alerting and executive control) and were least prominent on tasks that relied on posterior brain regions (orienting). This framework can be used for a level of analysis (behavioral, cognitive, and neural) of ADHD that may provide some new insights about the cognitive component of this disorder (Morton & Frith, 1995). Using Posner and Raichle's (1994) neuroanatomical network theory, each symptom was classified based on its relationship to alerting, orieinting, and executive control (see Table 7). The nine symptoms of inattention (description at the behavioral level) logically split into three groups of three when aligned with the concepts of attention (description at the cognitive level) and the underlying networks (description at the neural level). The three symptoms of impulsivity are behavioral manifestations of deficits in self-regulation, which align with the executive control network. The link to attentional networks is less clear for the six symptoms of hyperactivity, which fall into two groups based on deficits in fine motor and gross motor control, so networks related to the cerebellum were suggested in Fig. 3.

The application of multiple levels (see Morton & Frith, 1995) of analysis (e.g., behavioral, cognitive, and neural) may provide some new insights

TABLE 7   Symptom Domains

Symptom domain	Cognitive process	Neural network
Inattentive—Alerting	Sustained attention	Alerting
Difficulty sustaining attention	Vigilance level/ decrement	Cortical: right frontal
Fails to finish	Persistence	Midbrain: locus coruleus
Avoids sustained effort	Performance	Other
Inattentive—Orienting	Selective attention	Orienting
Distracted by stimuli	Visual cueing	Cortical: parietal
Does not seem to listen	Auditory cueing	Thalamic: pulvinar
Fails to give close attention	Visual search	Other
Inattentive—Memory	Memory/planning	Executive control
Has difficulty organizing tasks	Planning	Cortical: prefrontal
Loses things	Memory for objects	Striatal: basal ganglia
Is forgetful	Memory for time	Other
Impulsivity	Cognitive regulation	Executive control
Blurts out answers	Conflict resolution	Cortical: anterior cingulate
Interrupts or intrudes	Behavioral inhibition	Striatal: nucleus acumbens
Can't wait	Delay aversion	Other?
Hyperactivity—Fine motor	Motor/vocal control	Fine motor control
Fidgets	Fine motor control	Cortical: left frontal
Can't play quietly	Nonverbal control	Striatal: cerebellar vermis
Talks excessively	Verbal	Other?
Hyperactivity—Gross motor	Activation level	Gross motor control
Leaves seat	Gross motor control	Cortical: right frontal
Runs about and climbs	Novelty seeking	Striatal: caudate
Always on the go	Arousal level	Other?

about the dopamine theory of ADHD (Wender, 1971; Levy, 2001). To organize our levels of analysis approach, we have used the neuroanatomical network theory of Posner and Raichle (1994), to classify each symptom (see column 1, Table 6) based on the relationship to cognitive processes (see column 2, Table 6) and a proposed neuroanatomy of each network (see column 3, Table 6).

Using the Community Parent Education Program (COPE) in a Screening/Treatment Delivery Program

One of the primary concerns in the assessment of ADHD school-aged children is the possibility of false-positive diagnoses. In fact, Baron and Swanson (1998) point out (as have many others) that the use of instruments for screening a school-wide sample, even if the false-positive and false-negative rates are at "acceptable" levels of about .15, will identify many more non-ADHD (false positive) than ADHD (true positive) cases as having ADHD. This is due to the large difference in the base rate (3 to 5% for ADHD cases vs 95 to 97% for non-ADHD cases).

One contributing factor to false-positive diagnosis is the limited information obtained from the standard assessments with questionnaires and interviews. This is particularly crucial in the assessment of preschool children.

In an innovative collaborative program between Children's Hospital of Orange County (CHOC) and UCI, the community parent education program (COPE) developed by Cunningham et al. (1995) to provide service to "at-risk" families was adopted for a screening program combined with a service delivery program. COPE has been demonstrated to be effective in teaching parenting strategies to parents and child care providers across a variety of settings (Cunningham et al., 1993, 1994). Its use as a screening tool to assess the need for clinical services in a preschool population is somewhat unique. The collection of data over a 10-week period across multiple settings is expected to reduce the number of false-positive diagnoses substantially, as well as providing clinical insight into treatment interventions.

SLD

Changes in SLD Diagnostic Construct

The SLD diagnostic construct is undergoing change as this chapter is being prepared. The conceptual definition has not been changed, but key classification criteria are changing significantly. The reasons for these changes become apparent from a review of the highly influential dyslexia studies funded by the National Institute of Child Health and Human Development (NICHD).

NICHD Dyslexia Studies

Determining an ability–achievement discrepancy is crucial in most states as part of the SLD classification criteria. The IQ–achievement discrepancy has severe psychometric deficiencies, especially the stability of the discrepancies over short periods of time, rendering unreliable SLD diagnoses. Moreover, the discrepancy has highly questionable validity, as IQ–achievement discrepant and nondiscrepant poor readers do not differ in the instructional interventions needed or in responsiveness to that instruction (Fletcher et al., 1998).

Criticisms regarding the reliability and validity of the IQ–achievement SLD classification criterion have appeared periodically since the 1970s without much reaction from the field or change in practices. A well-documented effect called "wait to fail" was highlighted by the NICHD investigators. This refers to the fact that young children, regardless of the severity of reading problems, rarely meet the IQ-achievement criteria. Typically, children do not meet the IQ–achievement criterion until age 8 or 9 can be identified accurately in kindergarten by low achievement. Delaying treatment allows reading problems to worsen, as well as causing enormous frustration for children, teachers, and parents. Fletcher et al. (1998) summarized this case with "Classifications of children as discrepant versus low-achievement lacks discriminative validity. . . . However, because children can be validly identified on the basis of a low-achievement definition, it simply is not necessary to use an IQ test to identify children as learning disabled. . . . For treatment, the use of the discrepancy model forces identification to an older age when interventions are demonstrably less effective" (pp. 200–201).

The major SLD organizations have recommended abandoning the IQ–achievement classification criterion, making changes highly likely. The current federal administration is also strongly committed to eliminating the discrepancy criterion in the reauthorization of the IDEA currently before congress. The question now is what replaces the discrepancy criterion in SLD classification practices.

Problem Solving and Response to Intervention

The most likely replacement to current SLD classification criteria is a combination of problem-solving approaches and response to intervention rather than the current heavy reliance on standardized tests of intelligence and achievement. The overall framework is problem solving involving a multistep set of procedures for defining problems behaviorally, measuring their severity, analyzing conditions, developing interventions, monitoring progress and enhancing interventions based on progress data, and evaluating outcomes (Bergan & Kratochwill, 1990; Deno, 1985; Reschly et al., 1999).

Measurement within the problem-solving framework for the identification of disabilities focuses on behavioral assessment methods involving direct measures of behaviors in natural contexts such as classrooms, playgrounds, and homes. Curriculum-based measures (CBM) are the principal means of assessing academic problems (Howell & Nolet, 2000; Shinn, 1989, 1998; Shapiro, 1996; Shapiro & Kratochwill, 2000). The goal is to apply powerful instructional design and behavior change principles to learning and behavior problems in general education as part of special education eligibility determination (Kavale & Forness, 1999). Responsiveness to these high-quality, carefully implemented and assessed interventions then becomes a major part of SLD eligibility criteria.

Decisions about SLD eligibility are formulated by multidisciplinary teams just as they are in the traditional system; however, data considered by the team and eligibility criteria are significantly different. Basic data involve direct CBM and behavioral assessment results comparing the child's current skills to expectations based on peers using local or national norms. Large deficits compared to peers justify the development of problem-solving interventions in general education. The responsiveness to these interventions constitutes an essential criterion on which SLD eligibility is determined. Eligibility then is based on large deficits in relevant domains compared to peers, an insufficient response to high-quality interventions, and a need for specially designed instruction and related services in order to receive an appropriate education.

Several school districts have adopted problem-solving approaches to special education eligibility determination in SLD and other high-incidence disabilities (ED and mild MR). These systems typically do not use IQ testing as part of eligibility determination for any disability category. Descriptions of these systems are available in several sources, including Ikeda et al. (1996), Reschly et al. (1999), and Tilly et al. (1999). Evaluations of these systems generally find that the same students are found eligible by traditional and alternative systems, but that the students in the alternative systems usually receive assistance earlier (avoiding the wait to fail effect) and their special education programs are more likely to incorporate powerful instructional design and behavior change principles (Fuchs & Fuchs, 1986, 1989; Kavale & Forness, 1999).

SUMMARY

Advances in the field of brain research, brain imaging, and cognitive neuroscience offer the potential for a better understanding of the underlying cause of ADHD and LD. Current research refining our knowledge of the biological basis of the disorders may lead to more refined treatment. This is an exciting era in the field of LD and ADHD that witnesses the blending of several disciplines in the understanding and treatment of ADHD and LD.

The MTA experience provides several lessons that may have clinical relevance regarding ADHD. First, the MTA study identified key instruments (see Table 1) for acquiring information from parent and teacher "sources," as well as reasons for discrepancies across these sources. Based on the MTA experience, we recommend a telephone call to the child's teacher, specifically to inquire about any discrepancy in the "source by domain" summary, as an efficient way to make a meaning connection between developmental or educational (school-based) assessments and health-related (medical practice-based) services for children with ADHD (see Swanson et al., 2000b). Based on the MTA experience, we recommend frequent telephone contact with the teacher specifically to inquire about the peak effects and dissipation of effects of medication that are expected to occur during the school hours as a way to improve the assessment of effectiveness and side effects that may have time-course effects that require different or dual assessments at home and at school.

Innovative approaches to the diagnosis of ADHD are evolving from the field of cognitive neuroscience. The neuroantomical network theory of attention (Posner & Raiche, 1994) has led to a framework for evaluating attentional deficits in ADHD that may provide some insights about the cognitive component of this disorder (Morton & Frith, 1995).

In the area of learning disabilities, new and innovative approaches to assessment are currently being proposed that also rely on response to treatment. Changes in SLD classification are underway because of persistent problems in the traditional system, particularly the dubious reliability and validity of the IQ–achievement method of determining eligibility and the pernicious wait-to-fail effect. Alternative methods emphasizing problem solving are being implemented in several places in the United States, a movement that is likely to expand with the reauthorization of the IDEA in 2003. Further evaluations of the problem-solving methods and response to treatment criteria are needed to ensure that these approaches identify students with the greatest needs and that they support the development of effective interventions.

REFERENCES

Abikoff, H., Courtney, M., Pelham, W. E., Jr., & Koplewicz, H. S. (1993). Teachers' ratings of disruptive behaviors: The influence of halo effects. *Journal of Abnormal Child Psychology*, 21(5), 519–533.

Achenbach, T. M., Verhulst, F. C., Baron, G. D., & Akkerhuis, G. W. (1987). Epidemiological comparisons of American and Dutch children. I. Behavioral/emotional problems and competencies reported by parents for ages 4 to 16. *Journal of the American Academy of Child and Adolescent Psychiatry,* 26(3), 317–325.

American Psychiatric Association (1994). *Diagnostic and statistical manual of mental disorders* (4th ed.). Washington, DC: American Psychiatric Association.

Arnold, L. E., Abikoff, H. B., Cantwell, D. P., Conners, C. K., Elliott, G., Greenhill, L. L., Hechtman, L., Hinshaw, S. P., Hoza, B., Jensen, P. S., Kraemer, H. C., March, J. S., Newcorn, J. H., Pelham, W. E., Richters, J. E., Schiller, E., Severe, J. B., Swanson, J. M., Vereen, D., & Wells, K. C. (1997). National Institute of Mental Health Collaborative Multimodal Treatment Study of Children with ADHD (the MTA): Design challenges and choices. *Archives of General Psychiatry* 54(9), 865–870.

Baren, M., & Swanson, J. M. (1996). How not to diagnose ADHD. *Contemporary Pediatrics*, 13, 53–64.

Barkley, R. A. (1994). Impaired delayed response: A unified theory of attention deficit hyperactivity disorder. In D. K. Routh (Ed.), Disruptive Behavior Disorders: Essay in honor of Herbert Quay (pp. 11–57). New York: Plenum.

Barkley, R. A., DuPaul, G. J., & McMurray, M. B. (1991). Attention deficit disorder with and without hyperactivity: Clinical response to three dose levels of methylphenidate. *Pediatrics*, 87(4), 519–531.

Barr, C., Wigg, K., Malone, M., Schachar, R., Tannock, R., Roberts, W., & Kennedy, J. (1999). Linkage study of catechol-o-methyltransferase and attention deficit-hyperactivity disorder. *American Journal of Medical Genetics (Neuropsychiatric Genetics)*, 88, 710–713.

Barr, C. L., Feng, Y., Wigg, K., Bloom, S., Roberts, W., Malone, M., Schachar, R., Tannock, R., & Kennedy, J. L. (2000). Identification of DNA variants in the SNAP-25 gene and linkage study of these polymorphisms and attention deficit hyperactivity disorder. *Molecular Psychiatry*, 5, 405–409.

Barr, C. L., Wigg, K. G., Schachar, R., Tannock, R., Roberst, W., Malone, M., & Kennedy, J. L. (2003). 5'-untranslated region of the dopamine D4 receptor gene and attention-deficit hyperactivity disorder. *American Journal of Medical Genetics*.

Bergan, J. R., & Kratochwill, T. R. (1990). *Behavioral consultation and therapy*. New York: Plenum.

Bradley, R., Danielson, L., & Hallahan, D. P. (2002). Specific learning disabilities: Building consensus for identification and classification. In R. Bradley, L. Danielson, & D. P.

Hallahan (Eds.), *Identification of learning disabilities: Research to practice* (pp. 791–804). Mahwah, NJ: Lawrence Erlbaum.

Cantwell, D. P. (1990). Empiricism and child psychiatry. The 1990 C. Charles Burlingame, M.D. Award Lecture. The Institute for Living, Hatrford, CT.

Collier, D., Curran, S., & Asherson, P. (2000). Mission: Not impossible? Candidate gene studies in child psychiatric disorders. *Molecular Psychiatry*, 5, 457–460.

Cook, E. H., Stein, M. A., Krasowski, M. D., Cox, N. J., Olkon, D. M., Keiffer, J. E., & Leventhal, B. L. (1995). Association of attention-deficit disorder and the dopamine transporter gene. *American Journal Human Genetics*, 56, 993–998.

Cronbach, L. J. (1957). The two disciplines of scientific psychology. *American Psychologist*, 12, 671–684.

Cronbach, L. J. (1975). Beyond the two disciplines of scientific psychology. *American Psychologist*, 30, 116–127.

Crowe, R. R. (1993). Candidate genes in psychiatry: An epidemiological perspective. *American Journal of Medical Genetics*, 48(2), 74–77.

Cunningham, C. E., Bremmer, R. B., & Boyle, M. (1995). Large group community-based parenting programs for families of preschoolers at risk for disruptive behaviour disorders: Utilization, cost effectiveness and outcome. *Journal of Child Psychology and Psychiatry*, 36, 1141–1159.

Cunningham, C. E., Davis, J. R., Bremmer, R., Dunn, K., & Rzasa, T. (1993). Coping modeling problem solving versus mastery modeling: Effects on adherence, in-session process, and skill acquisition in a residential PT program, *Journal of Consulting and Clinical Psychology*, 61, 871–877.

Curran, S., Newman, S., Taylor, E., & Asherson, P. (2000). Hypescheme: An operational criteria checklist and minimal data set for molecular genetic studies of attention deficit and hyperactivity disorders. *American Journal of Medical Genetics* (*Neuropsychiatric Genetics*), 96, 244–250.

Davila, R. R., Williams, M. L., & MacDonald, J. T. (1991). Classification of policy to address the needs of children with attention deficit hyperactivity disorders within general and/or special education. (memorandum from the US Department of Education: Office of Special Education and Rehabilitative Services).

Deno, S. L. (1985). Curriculum-based measurement: The emerging alternative. *Exceptional Children*, 52, 219–232.

Deutsch, C. K., Matthysse, S., Swanson, J. M., & Farkas, L. G. (1990). Genetic latent structure analysis of dysmorphology in attention deficit disorder. *Journal of the American Academy of Child and Adolescent Psychiatry*, 29, 189–194.

Deutsch, C. K., Swanson, J. M., Bruell, J. H., Cantwell, D. P., Weinberg, F., & Baren, M. (1982). Over representation of adoptees in children with attention deficit disorder. *Behavior Genetics* 12, 231–238.

Diagnosis and Treatment of Attention Deficit Hyperactivity Disorder (1998). National Institute of Health Consensus Development Conference, Nov. 16–18. *Diagnostic and Statistical Manual, Version IV*. (1994) Washington DC: American Psychiatric Association.

Douglas, V. I. (1972). Stop, look, and listen: The problem of sustained attention, and impulse control in hyperactivity and normal children. *Canadian Journal of Behavioral Science*, 4, 259–282.

Douglas, V. I. (1988). Cognitive deficits in children with attention deficit disorders with hyperactivity. In L. Bloomingdale, & J. Sergeant (Eds.), *Attention Deficit Disorder: Criteria, Cognition, and Intervention* (pp. 65–82). New York: Pergamon Press.

DuPaul, G. J., Power, T. J., Anastopulos, A. D., & Reid, R. (1998). *ADHD Rating Scale-IV: Checklists, norms, and clinical interpretation.* New York: Guilford Press.

Education of All Handicapped ChildrenAct of 1975, 20 U.S.C. §1400 *et seq.* (statute); 34 CFR 300 (regulations published in 1977).

Faraone, S., Doyle, A., Mick, E., & Biederman, J. (2001). Meta-analysis of the association between the dopamine D4 gene 7-repeat allele and attention deficit hyperactivity disorder. Submitted for publication.

Fletcher, J. M., Francis, D. J., Shaywitz, S. E., Lyon, G. R., Foorman, B. R., Stuebing, K., & Shaywitz, B. A. (1998). Intelligent testing and the discrepancy model for children with learning disabilities. *Learning Disabilities Research and Practice,* 13, 186–203.

Fuchs, D., & Fuchs, L. S. (1989). Developing, implementing, and validating a prereferral intervention system. *School Psychology Review,* 18, 260–283.

Fuchs, L. S., & Fuchs, D. (1986). Effects of systematic formative evaluation: A meta-analysis. *Exceptional Children,* 53, 199–208.

Gazzaniga, M. S., Ivry, R. B., Mangun, G. R. (1998). *Cognitive Neuroscience: The Biology of the Mind.* New York: W. W. Norton.

Gottleib, J., Alter, M. Gottlieb, B., & Wishner, J. (1994). Special education in urban America: It's not justifiable for many. *Journal of Special Education,* 27, 453–465.

Greenhill, L. (1998). Safety and efficacy of treatments-short and long term: Stimulant medications. NIH Consensus Development Conference on Diagnosis and Treatment of Attention Deficit Hyperactivity Disorder (ADHD).

Greenhill, L. L., Abikoff, H. B., Arnold, L. E., Cantwell, D. P., Conners, C. K., Elliott, G., Hechtman, L., Hinshaw, S. P., Hoza, B., Jensen, P. S., March, J. S., Newcorn, J., Pelham, W. E., Severe, J. B., Swanson, J. M., Vitiello, B., & Wells, K. (1996). Medication treatment strategies in the MTA study: Relevance to clinicians and researchers. *Journal of the American Academy of Child and Adolescent Psychiatry,* 35(10), 1304–1313.

Greenhill, L. L., & Osman, B. B. (Eds.) (1991). *Ritalin: Theory and patient management.* New York: Mary Ann Liebert.

Gresham, F. M., & Elliot, S. N. (1989). *Social skills rating system-parent, teacher, and child forms.* Circle Pines, MN: American Guidance Systems.

Gresham, F. M., MacMillan, D. L., Bocian, K. M., Ward, S. L., & Forness, S. R. (1998). Comorbidity of hyperactivity-impulsivity-inattention and conduct problems: Risk factors in social, affective, and academic domains. *Journal of Abnormal Child Psychology,* 26(5), 393–406.

Grossman, H. (Ed.) (1973). *Manual on terminology and classification in mental retardation.* Washington, DC: American Association on Mental Deficiency.

Grossman, H. J. (Ed.) (1983). *Classification in mental retardation.* Washington, DC: American Association on Mental Deficiency.

Hammill, D., & Larsen, S. (1974). The effectiveness of psycholinguistic training. *Exceptional Children,* 41, 5–14.

Heber, R. (1959). A manual on terminology and classification in mental retardation. *American Journal of Mental Deficiency Monograph Supplement,* 64(2).

Heber, R. (1961). Modification of the "Manual on terminology and classification in mental retardation." *American Journal of Mental Deficiency,* 65(4), 499–500.

Heinrichs, W. R. (1990). Current and emergent applications of neuropsychological assessment: Problems of validity and utility. *Professional Psychology: Research and Practice,* 21, 121–126.

Hinshaw, S. P., March, J. S., Abikoff, H., Arnold, L. E., Cantwell, D. P., Conners, C. K., Elliott, G. R., Greenhill, L. L., Halperin, J., Hechtman, L. T., Hoza, B., Jensen, P. S., Newcorn, J. H., McBurnett, K., Pelham, W. E., Richters, J. E., Severe, J. B., Schiller, E., Swanson, J. M., Vereen, D., & Wells, K. (1997). Comprehensive assessment of childhood attention-deficit hyperactivity disorder in the context of a multisite, multimodal clinical trial. *Journal of Attention Disorders*, 1, 217–234.

Howell, K., & Nolet, V. (2000). *Curriculum-based evaluation: Teaching and decision making* (3rd ed.). Atlanta, GA: Wadsworth.

Hynd, G. W., Obrzut, J. E., Hayes, F., & Becker, M. G. (1986). Neuropsychology of childhood learning disabilities. In D. Wedding, A. M. Horton, & J. Webster (Eds.), *The neuropsychology handbook: Behavioral and clinical perspectives* (pp. 456–485). New York: Springer.

Ikeda, M. J., Tilly, W. D., III., Stumme, J., Volmer, L., & Allison, R. (1996). Agency-wide implementation of problem solving consultation: Foundations, current implementation, and future directions. *School Psychology Quarterly*, 11, 228–243.

Individuals with Disabilities Education Act (1997, 1999). 20 U. S. C. Chapter 33, Sections 1400–1485. (Statute), 34 C.F.R. 300 (Regulations) International Classification of Diseases, Edition 10. World Health Orgnaization, Geneva, 1993.

Jensen, P., Mrazek, D., Knapp, et al. (1997). Evolution and revolution in child psychiatry: ADHD as a disorder of adaptation. *Journal of the American Academy of Child and Adolescent Psychiatry*, 36, 1672–1681.

Kavale, K. A., & Forness, S. R. (1999). Effectiveness of special education. In C. R. Reynolds & T. B. Gutkin (Eds.), *The handbook of school psychology* (3rd ed., pp. 984–1024). New York: Wiley.

Kent, J. D., Blader, J. C., Koplewicz, H. S., Abikoff, H., & Foley, C. A. (1995). Effects of late-afternoon methylphenidate administration on behavior and sleep in attention-deficit hyperactivity disorder. *Pediatrics*, 96(2 Pt 1), 320–325.

Kephart, N. (1960). *The slow learner in the classroom*. Columbus, OH: Merrill.

Kirk, S. A., & Kirk, W. (1971). *Psycholinguistic learning disabilities: Diagnosis and remediation*. Champaign, IL: University of Illinois Press.

Kirk, S. A., McCarthy, J., & Kirk, W. (1968). *Illinois Test of Psycholinguistic Abilities*. Champaign, IL: University of Illinois Press.

Levy, F., Swanson, J. M. (2001). Timing, space, and ADHD: The dopamine theory revisited. *Australian and New Zealand Journal of Psychiatry*, 35, 504–511.

Lou, H. C. (1996). Etiology and pathogenesis of attention-deficit hyperactivity disorder (ADHD): Significance of prematurity and perinatal hypoxis-haemodynamic encephalopathy. *Acta Paediatr* 85, 1266–1271.

Luckasson, R., Brothwick-Duffy, S., Buntinx, W. H. E., Coulter, D. L., Craig, E. M., Reeve, A., Schalock, R. L., Snell, M. E., Spitalnik, D. M., Spreat, S., & Tasse, M. J. (2002). *Mental retardation: Definition, classification, and systems of support* (10th ed.). Washington, DC: American Association on Mental Retardation.

Luckasson, R., Coulter, D. L., Polloway, E. A., Reiss, S., Schalock, R. L., Snell, M. E., Spitalnik, D. M., & Stark, J. A. (1992). *Mental retardation: Definition, classification, and systems of support* (9th ed.) Washington, DC: American Association on Mental Retardation.

MacMillan, D. L., Gresham, F. L., & Bocian, K. M. (1998). Discrepancy between definitions of learning disabilities and school practices: An empirical investigation. *Journal of Learning Disabilities*, 31, 314–326.

Mann, L. (1979). *On the trail of process.* New York: Grune & Stratton.

March, J. S., Parker, J. D., Sullivan, K., Stallings, P., & Conners, C. K. (1997). The multidimensional anxiety scale for children (MASC): Factor structure, reliability, and validity. *Journal of the American Academy of Child and Adolescent Psychiatry,* 36(4), 554–565.

March, J. S., Swanson, J. M., Arnold, L. E., Hoza, B., Conners, C. K., Hinshaw, S. P., Hechtman, L., Kraemer, H. C., Greenhill, L. L., Abikoff, H. B., Elliot, L. G., Jensen, P. S., Newcorn, J. H., Vitiello, B., Severe, J., Wells, K. C., Pelham, W. E. (2000). Anxiety as a predictor and outcome variable in the multimodal treatment study of children with ADHD (MTA). *Journal of Abvormal Child Psychology,* 28(6), 527–541.

Mercer, C. D., Jordan, L., Allsopp, D. H., & Mercer, A. R. (1996). Learning disabilities definitions and criteria used by state education departments. *Learning Disability Quarterly,* 19, 217–232.

Milich, R., & Loney, J. (1980). The role of hyperactive and aggressive symptomatology in predicting adolescent outcome among hyperactive children. *Annual Progress in Child Psychiatry and Child Development,* 336–356.

Morton, J., & Frith, U. (1995). Causal modeling: A structural approach to developmental psychopathology. In D. Cicchetti, & D. Cohen, (Eds.), *Manual of developmental Psychopathology* (Vol 1, pp. 357–390).

Moyzis, R., Swanson, J., Ding, Y., Grady, D., Chi, H.-C., Spence, A., Flodman, P., Schuck, S., & Kidd, K. (2001). Sequence variation in exon 3 of the DRD4 gene: Implications for ADHD. *International Society for Research in Child Psychopathology.*

MTA Cooperative Group (1999a). 14-month randomized clinical trial of treatment strategies for attention deficit hyperactivity disorder. *Archives of General Psychiatry.* Vol 56, 1073–1086.

MTA Cooperative Group (1999b). Moderators and mediators of treatment response for children with attention-deficit/hyperactivity disorder. *Archives of General Psychiatry,* 56, 1088–1096.

National Institute of Health Consensus Conference on Attention Deficit Hyperactivity Disorder (1999). Washington, DC.

Pani, L. (2000). Is there an evolutionary mismatch between the normal physiology of the human dopaminergic system and current environmental conditions in industrialized countries? *Molecular Psychiatry,* 5, 467–475.

Pelham, W. E., Gnagy, E. M., Greenslade, K. E., and Milich, R. (1992). Teacher ratings of DSM-III-R symptoms for the disruptive behavior disorders. *Journal of the American Academy of Child and Adolescent Psychiatry,* 31(2), 210–218.

Pelham, W. E., Jr., Swanson, J. M., Furman, M. B., & Schwindt, H. (1995). Pemoline effects on children with ADHD: a time-response by dose-response analysis on classroom measures. *Journal of the American Academy of Child and Adolescent Psychiatry,* 34(11), 1504–1513.

Pelham, W. E., Lang, A. R., Atkeson, B., Murphy, D. A., Gnagy, E. M., Greiner, A. R., Vodde-Hamilton, M., & Greenslade, K. E. (1997). Effects of deviant child behavior on parental distress and alcohol consumption in laboratory interactions. *Journal of Abnormal Child Psychology,* 25(5), 413–424.

Pennington, B. F., & Ozonoff, S. (1996). Executive functions and developmental psychopathology. *Journal of Child Psychology and Psychiatry,* 37, 51–57.

Posner, M. I., & Raichle, M. E. (1994). *Images of mind.* Scientific American Books.

Reschly, D. J., & Gresham, F. M. (1989). Current neuropsychological diagnosis of learning problems: A leap of faith. In C. R. Reynolds & E. Fletcher-Janzen (Eds.), *Handbook of clinical child neuropsychology* (pp. 503–519). New York: Plenum Press.

Reschly, D. J., Hosp, J. L., & Schmied, C. (2003). *State learning disabilities conceptual definitions and classification criteria: Storm before reform.* Nashville, TN: National Research Center on Learning Disabilities, Department of Special Education, Peabody College.

Reschly, D. J., Tilly, W. D., III, & Grimes, J. P. (Eds.) (1999). *Special education in transition: Functional assessment and noncategorical programming.* Longmont, CO: Sopris West.

Reynolds, C. R. (1992). Two key concepts in the diagnosis of learning disabilities and the habilitation of learning. *Learning Disability Quarterly,* 15, 2–12.

Richters, J. E., Arnold, L. E., Jensen, P. S., Abikoff, H., Conners, C. K., Greenhill, L. L., Hechtman, L., Hinshaw, S. P., Pelham, W. E., & Swanson, J. M. (1995). NIMH collaborative multisite multimodal treatment study of children with ADHD. I. Background and rationale. *Journal of the American Academy of Child and Adolescent Psychiatry* 34(8), 987–1000.

Safer, D. J., Zito, J. M., & Fine, E. M. (1996). Increased methylphenidate usage for attention deficit disorder in the 1990s. *Pediatrics,* 98, 1084–1088.

Schachar, R. J., Tannock, R., Cunningham, C., & Corkum, P. V. (1997). Behavioral, situational, and temporal effects of treatment of ADHD with methylphenidate. *Journal of the American Academy of Child and Adolescent Psychiatry,* 36(6), 754–763.

Sergeant, J. A. (1981). *Attentional Studies in Hyperactivity.* Groningen, the Netherlands: Veenstra.

Sergeant, J. A. (1988). From DSM III attentional deficit disorders to functional defects. In L. Bloomingdale and J. Sergeant (Eds.) *Attention Deficit Disorders: Criteria, Cognition, and Intervention* (pp. 183–198). New York: Pergamon Press.

Shapiro, E. S. (Ed.) (1996). *Academic skills problems: Direct assessment and intervention* (2nd ed.). New York: Guilford Press.

Shapiro, E. S., & Kratochwill, T. R. (Eds.) (2000). *Behavioral assessment in schools: Theory, research, and clinical applications* (2nd ed.). New York: Guilford Press.

Shaywitz, S. E., Shaywitz, B. A., Fletcher, J. M., & Escobar, M. D. (1990). Prevalence of reading disability in boys and girls: Results of the Connecticut longitudinal study. *Journal of the American Medical Associatioin,* 264, 998–1002.

Shinn, M. R. (Ed.) (1989). *Curriculum-based measurement: Assessing special children.* New York: Guilford Press.

Shinn, M. R. (Ed.) (1998). *Advanced applications of curriculum-based measurement.* New York: Guilford Press.

Stein, M. A., Blondis, T. A., Schnitzler, E. R., O'Brien, T., Fishkin, J., Blackwell, B., Szumowski, E., & Roizen, N. J. (1996). Methylphenidate dosing: Twice daily versus three times daily. *Pediatrics,* 98(4 Pt 1), 748–756.

Stevens, J., Quittner, A. L., & Abikoff, H. (1998). Factors influencing elementary school teachers' ratings of ADHD and ODD behaviors. *Journal of Clinical Child Psychology,* 27(4), 406–414.

Stevenson, J. (1992). Evidence for a genetic etiology in hyperactivity in children. *Behavior Genetics,* 22, 337–344.

Swanson, J., Castellanos, F. X., Murias, M., LaHoste, G., & Kennedy, J. (1998a). Cognitive neuroscience of attention deficit hyperactivity disorder and hyperkinetic disorder. *Current Opinion in Neurobiology,* 8(2), 263–71.

Swanson, J., Flodman, P., Kennedy, J., Spence, A., Moyzis, R., Schuck, S., Musrias, M., Moriarity, J., Barr, C., Smith, M., & Posner, M. (2000a). Dopamine genes and ADHD. *Neuroscience and Biobehavioral Reviews*, 24, 21–25.

Swanson, J., Grenhill, L., Pelham, W., Wilens, T., Wolraich, M., Abikoff, H., Atkins, M., August, G., Biederman, J., Bukstein, O., Conners, K., Efron, L., Fiedelkorn, K., Fried, J., Hoffman, M., Lambrecht, L., Lerner, M., Leventhal, B., McBurnett, K., Morse, E., Palumbo, D., Pfiffner, L., Stein, M., Wigal, S., & Winans, E. (2000b). *Journal of Clinical Research*, 3, 59–76.

Swanson, J. M., Hawley, T., Simpson, S., Davies, M., Shulte, A., Wells, K., Hinshaw, S., Abikoff, H., Hechtman, L., Pelham, W., Hoza, B., Severe, J., Molina, B., Odbert, B., Forness, S., Gresham, F., Arnold, L. E., Wigal, T., Wasdell, M., Greenhill, L. (2000). Evaluation of learning disorders in ADHD (MTA). In L. L. Greenhill (Ed.). *Learning Disabilities: Implications for Psychiatric Treatment*, 19(5), 97–125.

Swanson, J. M., Lerner, M., March, J., Gresham, F. (1999). Assessment and intervention for ADHD in the schools. Lessons from the MTA study. *Pediatric Clinics of North America*, 46(5), 993–1009. Philadelphia: W. B. Saunders.

Swanson, J., McStephen, M., Hay, D., Levy, F., & Schuck, S. (2001). The potential of the SWAN Rating Scale in genetic analyses of ADHD. *International Society for Research in Child Psychopathology*.

Swanson, J., Posner, M., Cantwell, D., Wigal, S., Crinella, F., Filipek, P., Emerson, J., Tucker, D., & Nalgioclu, O. (1998b). Attention-deficit/hyperactivity disorder: Symptom domains, cognitive processes and neural networks. In R. Parasuraman (Ed.), *The attentive brain* (pp. 445–460). Boston; MIT Press.

Swanson, J., Schuck, S., Mann, M., Carlson, C., Hartman, C., Sergeant, J., Clarke-Stewart, A., Wasdell, M., McCleary, R., & Beck, R. (2000c). Over-identification of extreme behavior in the evaluation and diagnosis of ADHD/HKD, ADHD.

Swanson, J. M. (1992). *School-based assessments and interventions for ADD students*. Irvine, CA: K. C. Publishing.

Swanson, J. M., Castellanos, X. F., Murias, M., & Kennedy, J. (1998c). Cognitive neuroscience of attention deficit hyperactivity disorder and hyperkinetic disorder. *Current Opinion in Neurobiology*, 8, 263–271.

Swanson, J. M., Gupta, S., Guinta, D., Flynn, D., Agler, D., Lerner, M., Willimas, L., Shoulson, I., & Wigal, S. (1999). Acute tolerance to Methylphenidate in the treatment of attention deficit hyperactivity disorder in children. *Clinical Pharmacology and Therapeutics*.

Swanson, J. M., Kinsbourne, M., Roberts, W., & Zucker, K. (1978). A time-response analysis of the effect of stimulant medication on the learning ability of children referred for hyperactivity. *Pediatrics* 61, 21–29.

Swanson, J. M., McBurnett, K., Christian, D. L., & Wigal, T. (1995). Stimulant medications and the treatment of children with ADHD. In T. H. Ollendick, & R. J. Prinz (Eds.), *Advances in clinical child psychology*. New York: Plenum Press.

Swanson, J. M., Oosterlaan, J., Murias, M., Sachuck, S., Flodman, P., Spence, M. A., Wasdell, M., Ding, Y., Chi, H. C., Smith, M., Mann, M., Carlson, C., Kennedy, J., Sergeant, J., Leung, P., Zhang, Y. P., Sadeh, A., Chen, C., Whalen, C. K., Babb, K., Moyzis, R., & Posner, M. I. (2000d). Attention deficit/hyperactivity disorder children with a 7-repeat allele of the dopamine receptor D4 gene have extreme behavior but normal performance on critical neuropsychological tests of attention. *Proceedings National Academy of Science USA*, 97, 4754–4759.

Swanson, J. M., Posner, M., Potkin, S., Bonforte, S., Youpa, D., Fiore, C., Cantwell, D. P., & Crinella, F. M. (1991). Activating tasks for the study of visual-spatial attention in ADHD children: A cognitive anatomic approach. *Journal of Child Neurology*, 6, S119–S127.

Swanson, J. M., Sandman, C. A., Deutsch, C., & Baren, M. (1983). Methylphenidate hydrochloride given with or before breakfast. I. Behavioral, cognitive, and electrophysiologic effects. *Pediatrics*, 72(1), 49–55.

Swanson, J. M., Sergeant, J. A., Taylor, E., Sonuga-Barke, E. J. S., Jensen, P. S., & Cantwell, D. P. (1998d). Attention-deficit hyperactivity disorder and hyperkinetic disorder. *Lancet*, 351, 429–433.

Swanson, J. M., Sunohara, G. A., Kennedy, J. L., Regino, R., Fineberg, E., Wigal, T., Lerner, M., Williams, L., LaHoste, G. J., & Wigal, S. (1998e). Association of the dopamine receptor D4 (DRD4) gene with a refined phenotype of attention deficit hyperactivity disorder (ADHD): A family-based approach. *Molecular Psychiatry*, 3, 38–41.

Swanson, J. M., Wigal, S., Greenhill, L. L., Browne, R., Waslik, B., Lerner, M., Williams, L., Flynn, D., Agler, D., Crowley, K., Fineberg, E., Baren, M., & Cantwell, D. P. (1998f). Analog classroom assessment of Adderall in children with ADHD. *Journal of the American Academy of Child and Adolescent Psychiatry*, 37(5), 519–526.

Terwilliger, J. D., & Weiss, H. H. H. (2000). Gene mapping in the 20th and 21st centuries: Statistical methods, data analysis, and experimental design. *Human Biology*, 72, 63–132.

The ADHD Molecular Genetics Network (2000). *American Journal of Medical Genetics (Neuropsychiatric Genetics)*, 96, 251–257.

The ICD-10 classification of mental and behavioral disorders: Clinical descriptions and diagnostic guidelines (1992). Geneva: World Health Organization.

Tilly, W. D., III., Reschly, D. J., & Grimes, J. P. (1999). Disability determination in problem solving systems: Conceptual foundations and critical components. In D. J. Reschly, W. D. Tilly III, & J. P. Grimes (Eds.), *Special education in transition: Functional assessment and noncategorical programming* (pp. 285–321). Longmont, CO: Sopris West.

United States Department of Education (1968). *First annual report of the National Advisory Committee on Handicapped Children*. Washington, DC: U.S. Department of Health, Education, and Welfare.

United States Department of Education (2001). *To Assure the Free Appropriate Public Education of All Children with Disabilities: Twenty-Second Annual Report to Congress on the Implementation of the Education of the Individuals with Disabilities Education Act*. Washington, DC: Office of Special Education Programs, Author.

Volkow, N., Wang, G.-J., Fowler, J., Gatley, J., Logan, J., Ding, Y.-S., Hitzemann. R., & Pappas, N. (1998). Dopamine transporter occupancies in the human brain induced by therapeutic doses of oral methylpehnidate. *American Journal of Psychiatry*, 155, 1325–1331.

Weiss, K. (1993). *Genetic variation and human disease: Principles and evoluntionary approaches.* Cambridge: Cambridge University Press.

Well, K., Conners, C. K., Del Carmen, R., Elliott, G., Greenhill, L. L., Hechtman, L. T., Hinshaw, S. P., Jensen, P. S., March, J. S., Schiller, E., Severe, J., & Swanson, J. M. (1999). Psychosocial treatment strategies in the MTA study: Rationale, methods, and critical issues in design and implementation. *Journal of Clinical Child Psychology*.

Wender, P. H. (1971). *Minimal brain dysfunction in children.* New York: Wiley-Interscience.

WIAT Manual (1992). *Wechsler individual achievement test.* San Antonio: Harcourt Brace.

Wilcutt, E. G., Pennington, B. F., & DeFries, J. C. (2000). Twin study of the etiology of comorbidity between reading disability and attention-deficit/hyperactivity disorder. *American Journal of Medical Genetics (Neuropsychiatric Genetics)*, 96, 293–301.

Wilson, M. (2000). Coloboma mouse mutant as an animal model of hyperkinesis and attention deficit hyperactivity disorder. *Neuroscience and Biobehavioral Reviews*, 24, 51–57.

Wolraich, M. L., Feurer, I. D., Hannah, J. N., Baumgaertel, A., & Pinnock, T. Y. (1998). Obtaining systematic teacher reports of disruptive behavior disorders utilizing DSM-IV. *Journal of Abnormal Child Psychology*, 26(2), 141–52.

## CHAPTER 3

A Neurodevelopmental Approach to Differences in Learning

Desmond P. Kelly and Melvin D. Levine

THE NEED FOR A NEW MODEL

The learning disorders of school-aged children are remarkably complex. There are numerous possible patterns of dysfunction underlying deficient academic performance. Furthermore, children and adolescents with learning disorders vary widely in their associated strengths, affinities (positive orientations toward particular topics or subjects), and levels of motivation and resiliency (Levine & Swartz, 1995a). These patterns of strengths, dysfunctions, and affinities are not captured on traditional measures of aptitude and achievement. As a result, clinicians, educators, and parents often misunderstand the nature of learning disorders and the potential for effective management. Consequently, the field of learning disorders is in need of a conceptual model that will accommodate and respond to the extreme heterogeneity of the students that classroom teachers educate each day (Levine et al., 1993). The use of labels, such as learning disabilities, or attempts to fit children with learning disorders into a few syndromes represent an oversimplification of poor performance in the classroom. We propose that students will benefit from the use of well-informed descriptions, or profiles, of a student's areas of weakness, strength, affinity, and preferred styles of learning.

This chapter explores a phenomenological approach to recognizing and managing students with learning disorders. Observable phenomena are particular problems with learning and performing that are clearly visible as one watches a child over time or during some form of testing, such as trouble remembering new material while studying for tests (Levine & Reed, 1999). There are many different reasons why a child might exhibit a particular observable phenomenon. In some instances the phenomenon may be a manifestation of one or more neurodevelopmental dysfunctions that are gaps, delays, or variations in the way a particular child's brain is developing. Some observable phenomena may represent acquired behaviors, such as aggression in children who are trying to hide inner fears about doing poorly in school, whereas others are delayed skills that may themselves result from neurodevelopmental dysfunctions, a lack of experience, or inadequate prior teaching.

The proposed phenomenological approach is an alternative to a syndrome orientation to learning disorders (Levine & Swartz, 1995b). The goal is to have clinicians, parents, teachers, and the students themselves understand why a student is struggling in school and to enable the development of a comprehensive descriptive profile of neurodevelopmental strengths, weaknesses, and affinities that leads to a focused and effective plan of management.

A NEURODEVELOPMENTAL APPROACH

A neurodevelopmental approach to differences in learning requires that clinicians become adept at identifying the neurodevelopmental functions that are needed for the mastery of academic subskills. These neurodevelopmental functions represent a range of highly specific and basic cognitive developmental abilities or basic brain processes that may be needed for learning and productivity in school (Levine, 2002). An individual's neurodevelopmental function is likely to contribute to learning across a range of performance areas. For example, the ability to retain sequences of data in short-term memory is a neurodevelopmental function that plays a role in following directions, acquiring procedural knowledge in mathematics, and remembering a person's telephone number. Thus, short-term memory is a function that participates in a range of tasks. A neurodevelopmental dysfunction is a weakness in a particular neurodevelopmental function that may stand in the way of school performance. The differences in neurodevelopmental strengths and weaknesses that exist between individuals are termed neurodevelopmental variations. A neurodevelopmental profile is the spreadsheet of neurodevelopmental strengths and weaknesses that we all carry with us. Such profiles are not fixed, they can change over time.

Neurodevelopmental functions are especially critical to academic success as they collaborate to enable a student to master and apply subskills with increasing sophistication and automatization. The latter are the critical subcomponents of academic skills (Levine, 2002). For example, the neurodevelopmental status of a student's phonological abilities and awareness is closely tied to their word decoding skills: a critical subskill of overall competency in reading (Olson et al., 1994; Vellutino et al., 1994). Neurodevelopmental functions are not only confined to playing a role in subskill attainment, they are also critical for the comprehension, retention, and application of knowledge.

NEURODEVELOPMENTAL CONSTRUCTS

Neurodevelopmental functions can be grouped into eight capacities or "neurodevelopmental constructs" (Levine & Reed, 1999). They help organize thinking and communication about learning differences by focusing on the roles and the interactions of neurodevelopmental functions with regard to specific behaviors. They also allow for flexibility in the ways that differences in learning are evaluated, while at the same time, pinpointing areas of learning breakdown and creating very specific plans for helping students succeed. The constructs are not isolated areas of function, and the functions within constructs overlap and transact extensively (Levine, 2002). The neurodevelopmental constructs and their constituent functions are as given.

Attention

Attention is much more than just "paying attention" (Lyon & Krasnegor, 1995). It includes such aspects as the ability to concentrate, to focus on one thing rather than the other, to finish tasks one begins, and to control what one says and does. Attention can be conceptualized as a network of controls over conscious functioning. The attention controls can be grouped into three interactive systems.

1. *Mental energy controls* are related to initiating and maintaining the energy level needed for optimal learning and behavior. Components of mental energy are alertness (attaining an effective level of focused listening and watching), mental effort (initiating and maintaining the flow of energy needed for cognitive work output), sleep–arousal balance (sleeping well at night and being sufficiently alert during the day), and performance consistency (maintaining a steady, reliable, and predictable flow of the mental energy needed for dependable functioning).

2. *Processing controls* regulate information intake and utilization. The processing control system is composed of five basic controls: saliency determination (discriminating between important and unimportant information; also known as selective attention), depth and detail of processing (focusing with sufficient intensity to capture specific details of information), cognitive activation (linking incoming information with prior knowledge and experience), focal maintenance (sustaining and monitoring concentration for the appropriate period of time; also known as attention span or sustained attention), and satisfaction level (focusing sufficiently on activities or topics of moderate or low levels of interest).

3. *Production controls* regulate academic and behavioral output. They allow the mind to operate slowly and deliberately. Five production controls can be described: previewing (anticipating likely outcomes of actions, events, and problems), facilitation and inhibition (selecting the best option before acting or starting a task—problems in this area manifest as impulsivity), pacing (doing tasks at the most appropriate speed), self-monitoring (watching one's own output and making necessary modifications), and reinforceability (using previous experience to guide current behavior and output).

Memory

Memory is a major contributor to the learning process (Mayes, 1995). Even if students are able to understand, organize, and interpret the most complex information, an inability to store and then later recall that information will impede their performance dramatically. Memory involves a number of components, processes, and steps. It can be divided broadly into three systems.

1. *Short-term memory* is the ability to briefly register new information that is used, stored, or forgotten. Components of short-term memory are saliency determination (determining quickly whether new information is relevant), recoding (transforming information to fit into short-term memory by condensing or shortening it), and depth and detail of processing (capturing important, newly introduced information at the level or depth needed for retention).

2. *Active working memory* has been called the "workspace of thinking." Active working memory allows one to mentally suspend information while using or manipulating it (Swanson & Bentinger, 1994). There are several different forms of active working memory, including idea maintenance (keeping prior information in mind while continuing to take in new information), task component maintenance (holding onto different parts of a task while undertaking it), proximal and distal planning (balancing immediate objectives with long-term goals), and short-term to long-term memory linkage (holding incoming information in short-term memory while activating prior knowledge or skills stored in long-term memory).

3. *Long-term memory* allows for the permanent storing of information, including knowledge, skills, and experiences. The two primary processes of long-term memory are storage (consolidation) and access. The *consolidation* of information in long-term memory is accomplished by at least four highly specific formats: paired association storage (linking and storing two related data bits), procedure storage (storing new skills and processes), rule, pattern, and schema storage (filing recurring sets of information as they fit with rules, common patterns, or systems of organization), and category storage (classifying information in meaningful groupings). Long-term memory *access* refers to the recovery of information, including knowledge, skills, and experiences. The three academically relevant access routes are association (remembering one-half of a pair after seeing or hearing the other half), pattern recognition and method transfer (detecting a familiar pattern and transferring the methods that have worked with that pattern in the past), and recall (recovering information or skills with only minimal cueing).

Language

Being able to understand and articulate language is central to the ability to succeed as students and learners. Language functions involve elaborate interactions between various parts of the brain and include many separate abilities: pronouncing words, being aware of different sounds, comprehending written symbols, understanding syntax, and telling stories.

Language functions can be divided broadly into *receptive* and *expressive* domains, and within each domain there is a developmental progression of increasingly complex and sophisticated abilities.

1. *Receptive language* encompasses the processing and understanding of incoming oral and written information. Components or dimensions of receptive language include phonological processing (receiving, distinguishing, and manipulating the sounds in words), morphological sense (interpreting parts of words that convey some meaning), semantic understanding (knowing the meanings of words), sentence comprehension (understanding sentences and sentence structures), and discourse processing (interpreting language beyond the boundaries of a sentence).

2. *Expressive language* is the production and communication of ideas orally and in writing. There is a similar hierarchy of dimensions within expressive language: articulation and fluency (using mouth muscles effectively and generating smooth and intelligible speech), semantic use (properly utilizing word meanings), word retrieval (finding the right words quickly and easily), sentence formulation (expressing thoughts in complete sentences when speaking and writing), discourse production (communicating information in a cohesive chain of sentences), and verbal elaboration (extending and developing ideas through language production).

Temporal-Sequential Ordering

Whether it involves reciting the alphabet, following the steps toward solution of a math problem accurately, or getting to the right class on time, the ability to understand time and sequence is a key component of learning. The elements of sequential ordering include *sequential awareness*, the ability to be alert to the presence of, and identify, an incoming sequence or array. *Sequential perception* is the ability to process the order of the parts of incoming information. Such sequential details may be processed visually, auditorially, or kinesthetically. The appreciation of serial order most often demands that such order be preserved in *sequential memory*, which retains the order of steps, events, or other sequences. *Sequential output* is the creation of products in which the content is arranged in the optimal order. Both motor and nonmotor procedures and products depend on such organization. *Time management* is, of course, heavily dependent on sequential ordering abilities, and *higher sequential thinking* utilizes serial order to enhance concept development and problem solving. Many sophisticated cognitive activities are organized sequentially, such as the discernment and analysis of cause-and-effect relationships.

Spatial Ordering

Closely related to the functions of time and sequence, spatial ordering is the ability, for instance, to distinguish between a circle and a square or to use images to remember related information. On a more complex level, spatial ordering helps musicians to be able to "see" a piano keyboard and enables architects to "imagine" the shape of a particular room. *Spatial awareness* relates to being alert to the presence of, and identifying, an incoming configuration or array. *Spatial perception* includes the interpretation of relationships within and between spatial patterns. Spatial patterns such as shapes and symbols are stored as image representations in *spatial memory*. *Spatial output* is the creation of products that have spatial characteristics. Examples of spatial output in the classroom setting include a student arranging numbers in a column or spacing words consistently and arranging them on the line when writing. *Material management* (organizing the various resources and supplies needed for a task) is highly dependent on intact spatial-ordering abilities. Reasoning and conceptualizing without language through the use of mental imagery is an example of *higher spatial thinking*.

Neuromotor Functions

Whether students are trying to write their first words, catch a football, or punch away at a computer keyboard, their brains' ability to coordinate their motor or muscle functions is key to many areas of learning. There are three broad domains of motor function.

1. *Gross motor function* is the ability to use the body's large muscles in a coordinated, effective manner. Effective gross motor function requires the integration of components that include outer spatial processing (interpreting and using spatial information when implementing motor activities), body position sense (keeping track of one's body while balancing or moving), gross motor production (mobilizing the right muscles in the best order to achieve a motor goal), gross motor memory (remembering how to engage in specific motor procedures or skills), and gross motor problem solving and logic (responding to the challenges of gross motor activities with appropriate plans).

2. *Fine motor function* is expressed as manual dexterity. The elements of fine motor function are eye–hand coordination (using visual information efficiently when working with one's hands), fine motor procedural memory (remembering how to do things with one's hands), and fine motor problem solving and logic (knowing how to meet the challenges of manipulating objects).

3. *Graphomotor function* is the motor aspect of handwriting. Efficient graphomotor function requires the integration of key elements: Previsualization (picturing a letter or number before creating it), graphomotor memory (recalling letter and number forms rapidly and accurately), graphomotor production (implementing the act of handwriting; coordinating the motor actions needed for each aspect of the handwriting task), and graphomotor feedback (knowing where the writing utensil is during letter formation).

Social Cognition

One of the most often overlooked components of learning is the ability to succeed in social relationships with peers, parents, and teachers (Levine, 2001). Students (and adults) may be strong in other construct areas and yet have academic difficulties because of an inability to make friends, work in groups, or cope effectively with peer pressure. Important areas of social ability are as follow

1. *Verbal pragmatics* or the use and understanding of language within social contexts. Verbal pragmatic strategies include communication and interpretation of feelings (conveying and discerning true or intended feelings through language), code switching (being able to speak somewhat differently depending on the context and people involved), topic

selection and maintenance (knowing what to talk about, when, with whom, and for how long), humor regulation (making use of tasteful humor at appropriate times and responding to others' jokes), and conversational technique (engaging in the give-and-take of verbal interaction).

2. *Social behaviors* foster optimal relationships with others. These behaviors include self-marketing (building and displaying an image that is appealing to others), social information processing (figuring out the true meaning or agenda in a social encounter), collaboration (working and playing in a cooperative manner with others), initiation technique (knowing how to begin a relationship or enter into a social activity), social control regulation (maintaining the optimal level of personal choice and will when relating to others), timing and staging relationships (knowing how to pace a relationship, i.e., when it is okay to do what), social conceptualization (understanding the meaning of different kinds of relationships), and conflict resolution (resolving interpersonal disagreement without aggression).

3. *Political acumen* is the ability to nurture positive relationships with important people, particularly adults. The student who is able to establish a positive relationship with his or her teacher is much more likely to be successful in that class.

Higher Order Cognition

Higher order cognition involves the ability to understand and implement the steps necessary to solve problems, attack new areas of learning, and think creatively. It is the pathway to complex thinking. Higher cognition is composed of a number of interrelated processes (Levine & Reed, 1999).

1. *Concept formation.* Concepts are groupings of facts, attributes, steps in a process, or ideas that commonly go together. Conceptualization can be verbal (forming concepts using language), nonverbal (forming concepts without using language), or process (forming concepts that explain a mechanism or how something works).

2. *Critical thinking.* The critical evaluation of products, ideas, and opinions.

3. *Creativity/brainstorming* is the capacity to elaborate, to discover unusual similarities or analogies, to link ideas or objects that are not ordinarily associated with each other, and in so doing to fuse new and

meaningful relationships. Creativity is often an important component of giftedness.

4. *Problem solving* is the application of a systematic stepwise approach to complex questions or challenges. Effective problem solving requires an individual to slow down and think through a challenge in a deliberative and systematic fashion.

5. *Rule use.* The discovery of rules that predict and account for phenomena is a vital developmental acquisition during school years.

6. *Reasoning and logical thinking* facilitate the generation of sensible and thoughtful answers to complex issues.

7. *Mental representation* is the ability to portray new ideas in one's mind so they are meaningful and lasting.

NEURODEVELOPMENTAL FUNCTIONS AS RELATED TO ACADEMIC SKILLS

An academic subskill is a capability that develops when and if teaching activates particular required neurodevelopmental functions and those functions are able to respond effectively (Levine, 2002). Various academic skills (such as writing) are composed of specific subskills (such as letter formation and spelling for writing), which, in turn, are composed of the needed neurodevelopmental functions. The same neurodevelopmental functions needed to acquire a subskill are likely to become strengthened through the use of that subskill. When a subskill is not attained or is mastered incompletely, the functions underlying it may subsequently fail to develop to the extent they would in other children.

For example, strong semantic abilities, or knowledge of word meanings, facilitates the attainment of certain reading subskills, while reading, in turn, greatly strengthens a student's capacity to appreciate word meanings. Similarly, a lack of academic success can inhibit the growth of a neurodevelopmental function. If a child does not read very much because of a memory dysfunction, some gaps in language ability may become apparent during adolescence.

There are no important academic subskills and skills that draw upon only a single neurodevelopmental function. In fact, there is a constant demand for dynamic collaboration among multiple neurodevelopmental functions. These relationships among functions, and between functions and content, demand synchronization and a reasonable sharing of mental effort. Thus, to contribute effectively to the mastery and subsequent application of an academic subskill, a neurodevelopmental function must be able to operate at a rate synchronized with that of other participating functions and it must perform without exhausting more than its share of a student's effort resources (Levine & Reed, 1999). When inordinate effort is drained to fuel a particular neurodevelopmental function, the other participating neurodevelopmental functions are likely to be deprived of their needed attentional resource and energy allocation, resulting often in a generalized delay in acquiring or using the desired skill. Any academic pursuit can undergo expectations analysis, a process whereby a specific task, a specific subskill, or even a subject area at a particular grade level can be parsed into the neurodevelopmental functions that must be intact and interactive to engender success. For example, one observable phenomenon that may result from a dysfunction between phonological abilities and active working memory is a student's inability to maintain in memory the multiple sounds within a word while trying to read that word aloud. An informed observer would discover that by the time the child articulates the last of three sounds, she has forgotten the first one and so cannot reblend the sounds to form a whole word. This neurodevelopmental dysfunction at the junction between the functions of phonology and active working memory may undermine the acquisition of the subskill of decoding for reading that, in turn, will deter the attainment of overall skill in reading (Velluntino et al., 1994). The following examples illustrate observable phenomena and breakdown points in writing (Levine & Swartz, 1995b).

Example 1

A 12-year-old boy has many good ideas and well-developed language abilities. In class discussions he reveals a slight articulation problem, but expresses himself very well. However, he is reluctant to submit written assignments. When he does so, his ideas on paper are not at all sophisticated, and the language content is equally simple—more like that of a 7 year old. His writing is slow and labored. Legibility is poor. He employs a right-handed and tight grip, holding the pencil near the tip and applying much pressure to the page. He is good at spelling and understands rules of punctuation, but he commits numerous spelling and punctuation errors when he writes. He is succeeding in mathematics, and he reads well.

This child may well be experiencing significant graphomotor dysfunction. His tight pencil grip and labored output are likely the results of difficulty with graphomotor production, a problem affecting a student's ability to assign and coordinate muscle groups in the hand during letter formation. Many of these children also manifest speech problems. Frequently, as in this case, the great motor effort required for writing undermines other functions (such as omitted or misspelled words). Students like this often feel self-conscious about writing and may be unwilling to submit their written products.

Example 2

An 11-year-old boy has had a long history of attentional difficulty. He has shown evidence of distractibility, impulsivity, mental fatigue, and weak self-monitoring. Writing has always been a serious problem. Although he is a very bright and competent boy in other areas of education, his written output is unsophisticated and laden with careless mistakes in spelling and mechanics. The boy claims that he hates to write, and that is what makes him hate school in general. He recently said, "Whenever I try to write, my whole mind goes dumb on me." His parents report that getting him to do homework requires relentless coercion and causes serious disruptions in their home life.

Many children with attention deficits have serious problems with writing. When they try to write, they may experience overwhelming mental fatigue. Additionally, they have trouble coordinating and synchronizing the multiple developmental functions needed for writing. Their difficulties with planning, filtering out distractions, and self-monitoring represent additional writing barriers. In particular, these students have trouble managing the junctions between the functions. It is hard for them to orchestrate the interactions among memory, language, ideation, and motor function. For example, the flow of ideas may be too rapid for their fingers to keep pace. In children with attention deficits, it is also important to look for additional neurodevelopmental dysfunctions such as problems with retrieval memory or language complicating the underlying attentional dysfunction.

In the examples just cited, each student exhibits some observable phenomena that suggest the presence of one or more neurodevelopmental dysfunctions impeding writing (Hooper et al., 1994). In such cases it is important to verify the presence of the neurodevelopmental dysfunctions while also trying to uncover other relevant areas of weakness as well as associated strengths. This justifies a collaborative and multifaceted approach to assessment.

ASSESSMENT OF STUDENTS WHO ARE STRUGGLING IN SCHOOL

When a student is having difficulty, it is important to begin the diagnostic process by posing the following questions, "Where is the breakdown occurring?" and "Which of the neurodevelopmental functions required to learn and apply this subskill are weak or unable to assume their share or play their vital roles?" Thus, a child may harbor a neurodevelopmental dysfunction in a particular function and/or a dysfunction may exist at the junctions between functions. In either case, the breakdown prevents the student from succeeding.

The valid assessment of a child's profile of neurodevelopmental strengths and dysfunctions is a critical step in devising an effective plan for her or his management at home and in school. The following general principles can guide the assessment process.

a. Clinicians and teachers need to be cognizant of the common observable phenomena that thwart the acquisition of particular subskills at specific grade levels. They also need to be receptive to the possibility of encountering some unusual or even unique phenomena in individuals.

b. Any assessment process should stress the search for strengths and content affinities, i.e., strong intellectual orientations toward certain subject matter.

c. Multiple forms and sources of assessment information should be gathered. Evidence should derive from direct observations by teachers and parents, interviews with the child, and careful analyses of work samples, as well as formal testing procedures. The choice of tests is not nearly as important as the kinds of observations and inferences that occur during the testing.

d. The assessment process should consist of the search for recurring themes. That is, it is important to seek patterns that are evident in the observations and/or tests of more than one individual and across time. For example, a particular form of memory dysfunction may be suspected on samples of spelling, math work, comments by the parents, and some direct tests of memory function. For a particular finding to be considered valid it should be verified. Any single observation or any one source of data should be considered incomplete and unready for interpretation until and unless it is compatible with other forms of evidence.

Depending on the complexity of individual cases, different forms of assessment are likely to be appropriate. Four levels of assessment intensity can be defined: (1) informed observation and discussion by parents and teachers, (2) evaluation by a professional (e.g., psychologist, educational diagnostician, or developmental pediatrician), (3) evaluation by a multi-disciplinary team within the school, and (4) evaluation by an independent evaluation team in the community (Kelly, 2002).

Not every neurodevelopmental function or academic skill can be *tested*, but every phenomenon can be *assessed*. Assessment is a broad-based process in which data are gathered and analyzed. These data could include test scores, but should also include other information. Assessment should include qualitative observation (e.g., in the classroom and/or during testing), work sample analysis, and review of history. Also, we should not forget to ask the student where s/he thinks the breakdown is occurring. Assessments should combine flexible and standardized testing procedures. Flexible procedures allow the clinician to better elicit the best possible performance and search for effective management strategies, embodying principles of dynamic assessment and single case study methodology. Standardized procedures permit reliable comparisons of task performance and skill level with same-age peers. Standard scores can be useful as measurements of phenomena and can enable clinical judgments about a student's performance level in specific areas. One can think of qualitative data as belonging to one of two categories: *process* and *product*. Process observations involve how the student arrived at the response or completed the task. For instance, how quickly and/or efficiently did the student work? Did the student plan, use strategies, and self-monitor? Did certain tasks or types of problems seem to make the student anxious? What kind of work did the student appear to enjoy? Product observations are targeted toward the features of the student's response or output. Examples of product observations include accuracy of response, types and patterns of errors, and organization of work.

Both academic skills and neurodevelopmental functions should be assessed in relation to one another. In a sense, academic skills are on the surface—these skills are salient and readily observable. The mystery, however, is what factors underlie weak (or strong) academic skills. For example, weak *reading comprehension* (academic skill) could result from any number or combination of weak functions, including *receptive language, active working memory, sequencing, attention,* or *higher order cognition.* Either or questions ("is it '*x*' *or* is it '*y*'?") should not constrain assessment. Students commonly harbor more than one area of dysfunction or risk (i.e., it could well be '*x*' and '*y*'), and one should consider the relative contributions of multiple factors. Effects are usually transactional. An example of such a two-way street is that neurodevelopmental dysfunctions can lead to mental health problems, and mental health problems can lead to impaired neurodevelopmental functions.

Clinicians should pay close attention to the timing of a student's difficulties when forming hypotheses about his/her possible weaknesses. For example, a child with weak active working memory may show few if any problems with learning in the first years of school when there are few demands on multitasking. As he enters the third or fourth grade, however, he may begin to struggle with multistep math word problems or with simultaneously managing all of the skills needed for writing lengthier passages (Swanson & Bentinger, 1994). A child with insufficient phonological skills may be an adequate reader at the first-grade level but begin to have problems with decoding and reading comprehension in the late second and early third grades. As the topics of the reading texts become less familiar and fewer illustrations are included, her previous reliance on contextual and picture cues for decoding becomes less effective and her comprehension weakens. A student with poor higher order language skills may begin to struggle in high school as more abstract concepts are introduced in a rapid-fire, straight lecture setting. He may have difficulty with analytic reasoning and complex problem solving. In earlier grades, he may have been more successful because language was delivered in a slower, more concrete fashion, supported by many visuals and examples.

The report of an assessment should consist of an accurate description of a child, one that extends well beyond the invocation of labels and the reporting of test scores. If the latter are a necessity to qualify for services or facilitate reimbursement, they should be regarded as necessary evils and not as the end point of evaluation! A descriptive report should include an account of neurodevelopmental strengths and dysfunctions, relevant observable phenomena, current skills and subskills, and content affinities. Description can lead logically to prescription. An accurate profile of strengths and weaknesses is replete with implications for helping a child overcome the effects of his or her learning disorder. A profile of strengths and weaknesses should be generated and communicated in a meaningful way. Management planning is much more effective when working from a profile than from a label. Ultimately, the uncovering of strengths and affinities is as important as the exposure of relevant weaknesses or dysfunctions.

MANAGEMENT BY PROFILE

The successful management of a child with a learning disorder requires a multifaceted, coordinated approach. The parents, teachers, and clinicians must share goals and make use of strategies that are truly complementary. In working together, all must recognize the need to manage an entire profile of strengths, weaknesses, and affinities rather than just an attention deficit or language problem in isolation. That means that management has to be highly individualized, custom fitted to students' unique needs. The following are the components of effective management.

Demystification

It is often futile to try to motivate a student to work on a problem he does not understand. Therefore, the education of a student about the nature of the learning disorder, as well as associated strengths, is a critical component of management. A clinician or teacher should explain the profile to the child using accessible language, multiple examples, and, when appropriate, vivid analogies. The demystification should be upbeat and nonaccusatory. It should not sound like a sermon or an admonition. Demystification should aim to destigmatize, i.e., assure the child that "no one is perfect," and to overcome defensiveness and denial. Description of a child's assets should include concrete examples of strengths (as observed during the assessment). Weaknesses should be enumerated in nontechnical language and there should be introduction of optimism regarding future opportunities for success.

Bypass Strategies

In order to help a child keep pace with the flow of expectations, certain strategies may need to be devised to enable him or her to circumvent any breakdown points that are impeding subskill learning or application. Such bypass strategies include modifications in the rate, volume, or complexity of information being conveyed to the student, such as stopping frequently to review and summarize material, allowing additional time on tests, or decreasing the amount of reading. Other strategies could include allowing shorter written assignments or assigning fewer math problems for homework or simplifying the difficulty level of tasks such as by assigning essay questions that require discussing only one concept at a time. There can also be accommodations in what that student is being asked to produce, such as by letting a child print instead of using cursive writing or enrolling the student in an extra art class rather than requiring a foreign language. Technology and instruments such as calculators and word processing can be used to bypass weaknesses. Procedures or rules can be modified to accommodate the student's needs, such as changing class schedules, permitting breaks or allowing doodling or use of objects (e.g., bean bag) to redirect energy, or allowing an oral report instead of a written report. Accommodations in grading policies and feedback modes could include alternatives to tests, such as portfolio assessment, or utilizing recognition memory items for tests, such as multiple choice or true/false instead of recall items. In the case of a student with graphomotor dysfunction (such as in the first example described earlier), it would be helpful to allow more time for writing, permit the student to write shorter reports, arrange for some reports to be given orally rather than on paper, and encourage the use of a word processor. While none of these accommodations actually cures the graphomotor dysfunction, they represent important bypass techniques that can prevent the student from being discouraged and ceasing to be productive in school.

Intervention at the Breakdown Points

A wide range of techniques can be applied to enhance deficient subskills. These include the following.

1. Exercises to automatize (render fast and effortless) slow and labored writing, such as vigorous practice with letter formation or the recall of spelling.

2. Scaffolding of tasks utilizing instructional techniques to bridge gaps between what students can do on their own and what they can do with support. Examples of scaffolds include checklists, diagrams, outlines, verbal prompts, and guided questions. Scaffolds are used until the function is strengthened or the skill is improved and then scaffolds are "dismantled" gradually, moving the student toward independent performance.

3. Design of activities that end at the breakdown point. Teachers can design many tasks and learning activities that target weak functions or skills. Often, this involves analyzing a skill carefully, identifying its components, and basing a new task on a problematic area. For example, a

student may have difficulty with written expression because he has trouble organizing thoughts. A breakdown-specific task for such a student would be to give him a list of ideas or terms and ask him to sequence them into an outline; the task would not necessarily involve going on to write a paper using the outline.

4. Utilization of a stepwise approach. Some students, such as those with weak temporal–sequential ordering or production controls of attention, often feel overwhelmed when confronting a task or project because they try to do it all at once. They may lack a stepwise approach that enables them to break tasks down into manageable, incremental "chunks." One way to promote "step wisdom" is to require students to devise work plans for complex or long-term assignments. In addition, students can be required to give progress reports as they work through their timeline. Ideally, students will then develop their own capacity for working and learning in a stepwise fashion.

5. Modeling a task for a child. With the student watching, the teacher solves the first problem on the page, providing a model the student can refer to while completing other, similar problems on the page.

6. Providing strategies. Students can be challenged to come up with strategies for approaching tasks and improving neurodevelopmental functions. Usually, the first step is for the teacher to offer examples or model strategic approaches that students can then implement independently. Ultimately, students need to progress to inventing strategies on their own.

7. Using strong neurodevelopmental functions to help support weaker ones. Teachers, in addition to modifying specific tasks or activities to focus on students' strengths, should encourage students to continuously practice using their strengths on their own. An instance of the latter would be the use of graphic designs to help a child with strong spatial abilities use these to overcome the effects of possible problems with linear and sequential data formats and multiple step procedures.

8. Use of advance organizers. Often these strategies, such as letting students know what pieces of information to listen for in a lecture or learning video, act as early warning systems. Advance organizers are often beneficial to all class members and can be particularly helpful in guiding reading or listening to a presentation.

Other helpful techniques include talking through a task or self-coaching. One way to promote self-coaching is to ask students to pretend they are teaching the skill to someone else. This activity might be followed by having students develop their own self-coaching script.

Self-evaluation and self-regulation are good habits for all students to form, especially students with weak production controls of attention. To promote these habits, teachers can ask students to estimate how they fared on a report or test and provide them with very specific checklists that can be used to guide the monitoring of work such as writing assignments.

The Strengthening of Strengths and Affinities

Any management plan should include provision for the growth and development of a child's areas of competency. Ultimately, the strength of a child's strengths is likely to have the greatest implications for success and gratification during adult life (Levine, 2002). Strengthening affinities is a process of helping children discover and deepen their natural interest in particular topics or subject areas (such as cars, horses, or nature). This is also important for a sense of gratification, especially if students become an expert on a topic of interest. Taking advantage of a student's special interests or content orientation—her "affinities"—can motivate as well as help her work through or around a learning impasse. For example, reading about something that excites you can help enhance reading skills. The same can be said for writing, remembering information, and concentrating. Opportunities must be sought at home and in school for children to apply, exhibit, and practice what they are good at and that for which they display a true inclination.

Other Forms of Intervention and Service

A range of additional options for management exists, although their availability varies from community to community. These include targeted tutoring outside of school, specific forms of developmental therapy, such as language or occupational therapy, psychological counseling, and structured group activities, including social skills training. In some cases, children may be helped by taking medication (Kelly, 2002). Psychopharmacological management may be necessary to strengthen attention. Every effort should be made to shield a child with a learning disorder from public embarrassment, particularly in front of peers. Teachers, in particular, must avoid the temptation to be openly critical or to put children in a position where their shortcomings are displayed publicly. Students with writing difficulties should not have other children correcting their papers, and their written products (when messy) should not be displayed. Recurring humiliation in school is likely to result in serious emotional and motivational complications that are far more dangerous than any leaning disorder itself.

IMPLICATIONS FOR PRACTITIONERS

This chapter portrayed and exemplified a phenomenological approach to learning disorders during childhood. We have explored its implications and some of its applications. In particular, we have emphasized the vital importance of specificity. Thus, rather than feeling comfortable with the notion that a child has "dysgraphia," we explore and describe the neurodevelopmental functions that are not operating and interacting optimally to produce the needed subskills for writing. We then base our understandings and our interventions upon such rich description. If we adopt this approach, we lose the undeniable convenience of the labels as we gain in our likelihood of customizing management to the needs of individuals.

It should be evident that there are trade-offs when one adheres to a phenomenological approach to children's learning disorders. Categories, labels, and gold standard test scores are certainly tidier than phenomena. They make it easier to derive uniform practices and policies for children in groups. However, this chapter portrayed an approach that is more individualized and less convenient for research, but, in all likelihood, more applicable to the realities of human diversity. Strengthening strengths and accommodating a student's content interests are rarely traveled instructional paths. We must not only recognize these strategies as practical, but apply them widely in an effort to help students achieve their potential.

REFERENCES

Hooper, S. R., Montgomery, J., Swartz, C., Reed, M. S., Sandler, A. D., Levine, M. D., Watson, T. E., & Wasileski, T. (1994). Measurement of written language expression. In G. R. Lyon (Ed.), *Frames of reference for the assessment of learning disabilities: New views on measurement issues* (pp. 375–417). Baltimore: Paul H. Brookes.

Kelly, D. P. (2003). Patterns of development and function in the school-aged child. In R. Behrman, R. Kliegman, & H. Jenson (Eds.), *Nelson textbook of pediatrics* (17th ed.). Philadelphia: Saunders.

Levine, M., Oberklaid, F., & Meltzer, L. (1981). Developmental output failure: A study of low productivity in school-aged children. *Pediatrics*, 67, 18–25.

Levine, M. D. (2001). *Jarvis clutch: Social spy.* Cambridge, MA: Educators Publishing Service, Inc.

Levine, M. D. (2002). *Educational care: A system for understanding and helping children with learning problems at home and in school* (2nd ed.). Cambridge, MA: Educators Publishing Service, Inc.

Levine, M. D., Hooper, S., Montgomery, J., Reed, M., Sandler, A., Swartz, C., & Watson, T. (1993). Learning disabilities: An interactive developmental paradigm. In G. R. Lyon, D. B. Gray, J. I. Kavanough, & N. A. Krasnegor (Eds.), *Better understanding learning disabilities: New views from research and their implications for education and public policies* (pp. 229–250). Baltimore: Paul H. Brookes.

Levine, M. D., & Reed, M. (1999). *Developmental variation and learning disorders* (2nd ed.). Cambridge, MA: Educators Publishing Service, Inc.

Levine, M. D., & Swartz, C. W. (1995a). The unsuccessful adolescent. In R. Lillie (Ed.), *Secondary education and beyond: Providing opportunities for students with learning disabilities* (pp. 3–12). Pittsburgh: Learning Disabilities Association.

Levine M. D., & Swartz, C. (1995). The disabling of labeling: A phenomenological approach to understanding and helping children who have learning disorders. In A. Thomas (Ed.), *Plain talk about K.I.D.S, a summit on learning disorders: Transforming crisis into success.* Cambridge: Educators Publishing Service Inc.

Lyon, G. R., & Krasnegor (1995). *Attention, memory and executive function.* Baltimore: Paul H. Brookes.

Mayes, A. R. (1995). The assessment of memory disorders. In A. D. Baddeley, B. A. Wilson, & F. N. Watts (Eds.), *Handbook of memory disorders.* New York: Wiley.

Olson, R., Forsberg, H., Wise, B., & Rack, J. (1994). Measurement of word recognition, orthographic, and phonological skills. G. R. Lyon (Ed.), *Frames of reference for the assessment of learning disabilities: New views on measurement issues* (pp. 243–277). Baltimore: Paul H. Brookes.

Swanson, H. L., & Bentinger, L. W. (1994). Working memory as a source of individual differences in children's writing. In E. C. Butterfield (Ed.), *Children's writing: Toward a process theory of the development of skilled writing* (pp. 31–56). Greenwich, CT: JAI Press.

Velluntino, R. R., Scanlon, D. M., & Tanzman, M. S. (1994). Components of reading ability: Issues and problems in operationalizing word identification phonological coding, and orthographic coding. In G. R. Lyon (Ed.), *Frames of reference for the assessment of learning disabilities: New views on measurement issues* (pp. 279–329). Baltimore: Paul H. Brookes.

## CHAPTER 4

Syndrome of Nonverbal Learning Disabilities: Effects on Learning

Katherine D. Tsatsanis and Byron P. Rourke

INTRODUCTION

This chapter brings attention to an oft-unrecognized type of learning disability: the syndrome of nonverbal learning disabilities (NLD). Our goal is to provide a clear description of the characteristics and dynamics of NLD derived from our clinical experience with this disorder and empirical investigations. The NLD syndrome is so named because the clinical presentation is thought to arise from deficits that are primarily nonverbal in nature. These primary deficiencies, which include visual, tactile, and motor functioning, also impact apprehension and use of nonverbal aspects of communication, such as facial expressions, gestures, and general body language. The term learning disability (LD) is applicable to the syndrome in two ways. First, the NLD syndrome was isolated in the context of research attempts aimed at the identification of reliable and valid subtypes of LD. In this series, two particular groups of children were examined: those with relatively deficient reading and spelling performances and those who showed markedly impaired arithmetic performance. Second, the term learning disability captures the fundamental challenge for children with NLD. In short, these children are capable of learning virtually anything but need to learn almost everything. Children with NLD are often very pleasant and eager to please, and can appear quite capable under certain conditions. However, they must cope with core learning vulnerabilities that include dealing with new learning, especially in complex or novel situations; an overreliance on previously learned rote information, such that overlearned procedures are used without regard for unique aspects of a new learning task; and a preference for processing information through one modality, namely auditory–verbal, in the context of a limited capacity for intermodal integration. We find that with practice and preparation, and given conditions that are sensitive to the individual's strengths and weaknesses, persons with NLD can develop a level of competence in many areas of their functioning.

BACKGROUND

The historical context for our research endeavors lies in Johnson and Myklebust's (1967) early work on LD. The authors advanced a notion (unfavorable at the time) that subtypes of LD were distinguishable and, more than this, that the identification of distinct patterns of strength and weakness in children's performance would inform learning approaches and intervention strategies. We agreed with this observation, and research at the University of Windsor laboratory has since focused on this effort. We have engaged in concentrated investigation of two subtypes of LD— basic phonological processing disorder (BPPD) as well as NLD (see Rourke 1975, 1978, 1982, 1987, 1988a, 1989, 1993; Rourke & Finlayson, 1978; Rourke & Fisk, 1992; Rourke & Fuerst, 1992; Rourke & Strang, 1978, 1983; Strang & Rourke, 1983, 1985a,b).

Children with BPPD exhibit many relatively deficient psycholinguistic skills in combination with very well-developed abilities in visual–spatial organizational, tactile–perceptual, psychomotor, and nonverbal problem-solving skills. These children also display poor reading and spelling skills and significantly better, although still impaired, mechanical arithmetic competence. Their outstanding problem is in the area of phonological awareness and processing.

The opposite pattern of results was obtained in the group of children with NLD. We have found that NLD represents a distinct and discrete diagnostic entity; almost two decades of systematic research led to

Rourke's (1989) comprehensive description of the syndrome and model. There are three facets to the syndrome that are especially relevant for discussion: (1) a characteristic neuropsychological profile, (2) a particular pattern of academic strengths and weaknesses, and (3) vulnerabilities in psychosocial functioning (i.e., social emotional/adaptability deficits). In addition, the model offers a unique perspective: a developmental framework is applied to both behavior and brain to explain NLD, resulting in a dynamic approach to understanding the disorder.

Others have described similar groups of children. Mykelbust (1975) first coined the term nonverbal learning disabilities; later investigators have described children with "minimal brain dysfunction," "developmental learning disability of the right hemisphere," "social and emotional learning disability," and "developmental right-hemisphere syndrome" (Denkla, 1983; Gross-Tsur et al., 1995; Tranel et al., 1987; Voeller, 1986; Weintraub & Mesulam, 1983). The clinical accounts of these children share some features, namely an association between a lack of ability to make sense of and navigate the social environment and deficits in visual–spatial and mathematical skills.

Although these basic features are noted consistently, clinicians and researchers have approached this type of learning disability from varied perspectives and/or disciplines, reflected in a varied nomenclature. Thus, a child might be described to have a right hemisphere learning disability if seen by a neurologist and a semantic pragmatic disorder if seen by a speech and language therapist. In addition, we have observed that the literature is comprised largely of clinical studies of groups of individuals with apparently similar learning difficulties selected out of a larger clinical population. Although the similarities are noteworthy, an understanding of why these particular difficulties should fall together is minimally explicated. The usual account involves right hemisphere dysfunction. In our empirical and theoretical work, we attempt to be more exhaustive.

CHARACTERISTICS OF THE NONVERBAL LEARNING DISABILITIES (NLD) SYNDROME

The principal clinical manifestations of the NLD syndrome are listed. These features have been identified through a process of intensive clinical examination and are manifested in a profile of relative strengths and weaknesses. A more detailed description of the clinical presentation of children with NLD, in conjunction with relevant research findings, follows. We then report on a tentative classification system based on our recent efforts and identify a useful battery of neuropsychological measures.

Children with NLD typically exhibit the following neuropsychological assets:

- simple repetitive motor skills, such as finger tapping and static steadiness, that tend to normalize with increasing age
- strong rote verbal capacities, including extremely well-developed rote verbal memory skills
- little difficulty with the phonologic and syntactic aspects of language
- a well-developed vocabulary and varied store of rote verbal (factual) material as well as verbal associations
- an ability to benefit from repetitive acts and particularly repetitious input through the auditory modality
- an ability to deploy selective and sustained attention for straightforward, repetitive verbal material
- simple visual discrimination, especially for material that can be verbalized, that usually approaches normal levels with age
- much verbosity as well as intact receptive language skills
- well-developed auditory perception, segmentation and sound blending skills
- proficiencies in reading (word recognition) and spelling
- handwriting may reach age-appropriate levels with much practice
- a propensity for making use of language to problem solve and gather information

The following neuropsychological deficits are identified in children with NLD:

- problems in dealing with complex tactile input; tactile–perceptual deficits are bilateral, but are usually more marked on the left side of the body
- bilateral psychomotor coordination deficiencies, often more marked on the left side of the body; complex psychomotor skills, especially when required within a novel framework, tend to worsen relative to age-based norms
- marked deficiencies in visual–spatial–organizational abilities

- notable difficulty in adapting to novel and otherwise complex situations
- marked deficits in nonverbal problem solving, concept formation, and hypothesis testing, as well as the capacity to benefit from positive and negative informational feedback in novel or otherwise complex situations
- significant difficulties in dealing with cause–effect relationships and marked deficiencies in the appreciation of incongruities (e.g., as reflected in some aspects of humor)
- a distorted sense of time, reflected in poor estimation of elapsed time during common activities and poor estimation of time of day
- difficulty with comprehension of more complex verbal material, including written text, usually because the material is novel, abstract, inferential, or requires an appreciation of relevant versus irrelevant detail
- outstanding relative deficiencies in mechanical arithmetic as compared to advanced reading/decoding (word recognition) and spelling; misspellings that occur are almost exclusively of the phonetically accurate variety
- language is relied on as the principal means for social relating, information gathering, and relief from anxiety but may be of a repetitive, straightforward, rote nature and not contextually appropriate
- deficits in social perception, social judgment, and social interaction skills; of note, there is a marked tendency toward social withdrawal and even social isolation as age increases and the older child or adolescent with NLD is very much at risk for the development of psychosocial disturbance, especially "internalized" forms of psychopathology such as anxiety and depression

As is characteristic of most disorders, there are varying degrees of expression of the NLD syndrome and there are children who exhibit many but not all of the neuropsychological assets and deficits outlined earlier. The vital aspect of expression is the pattern of performance; we are interested in the respective gap between the child's strengths and weaknesses and in manifestations over time. As such, the level of intellectual functioning is not a reason for diagnostic exclusion. A child may perform in the range of mental retardation or in the superior range of intelligence and exhibit the NLD syndrome, which will be evident in his or her neuropsychological profile and adaptive behaviors.

We also expect to find some modifications in manifestation depending on course. A child may manifest most but not all NLD features as a result of related early events; for example, chronic ear infections may lead to auditory perceptual deficiencies, although the child shows many other critical aspects of NLD. Children who are affected with NLD since the earliest stages of development and those who onset at older ages (e.g., acquired through head injury) may show differences in their performance. Relevant aspects of the child's history should be taken into account when formulating a diagnosis. The other point to be made is that we generally expect to see an increasing discrepancy between assets and deficits over time. One account for this finding is that children with NLD will tend to overrely on their strengths, with learning restricted primarily to one modality, and show a concomitant decline in areas of weakness.

DETAILS OF NLD CHARACTERISTICS

Auditory–Verbal Assets

The neuropsychological strengths of children with NLD include rote verbal learning, word knowledge, word associations, and auditory perception. In general, children with NLD are inclined to experience less difficulty with the dimensions of language that are structured or easily routinized. Formal language skills, such as syntax and grammar, are well developed and these children display an excellent vocabulary. Verbal output is typically high; children with NLD tend to say a lot and say it well. They exhibit good auditory perception and typically advanced phonemic encoding and decoding, sound blending, and segmentation skills. In some cases, the phonological aspects of language may be attended to more than the semantic features of discourse. Children with NLD give the appearance of being facile with language content; they are verbose, use advanced words, and show well-developed reading skills. In addition, because these children exhibit strong verbal memory skills, often they are able to recall facts and details and repeat verbatim segments of prose or lines from cartoons and movies with little difficulty. As such, children with NLD can give the impression of being very bright and more capable than may be the case, at times masking their level of need.

These children are observed to use their words as a means to regulate behavior and problem solve; they may need to talk to themselves as they work but also sometimes cue their behavior with rote phrases (said quietly or aloud, depending on the child's working memory capabilities). Results of comparisons using the California Verbal Learning Test (CVLT; Delis et al., 1987, 1994) indicate a preference for a sequential versus semantic style of learning new information (Fisher & DeLuca, 1997). Children with NLD may learn best by speaking (talking things through) and using a step-by-step approach; in other words, by breaking tasks down into their component parts and drawing on verbal mediation strategies to help process information.

An overreliance on language for mediating behaviors and feelings is also common; disparate events are related by making the connection in words and experiences too may be recoded into words. Whereas language is structured to deal well with factual knowledge and categorical information, it is less effective for conveying and apprehending direct experience.

The content of language is often associative and may not be well organized. During anxiety-provoking situations, these children may be especially tangential and long-winded in conversation. A conversation that begins with a simple question about where one lives could end with a discussion of skunks (i.e., Canada—Quebec—speaking French—Pepe Lepu—skunks). Children with NLD display their humor, often expressed in the form of word play. Incongruities in nonverbal and verbal expression (as in sarcasm, irony, or other forms of humor) are more problematic. Further deficits in nonverbal (pragmatic) and higher order language skills are addressed.

Primary Deficits

The primary neuropsychological deficits in NLD include complex motor, tactile, perceptual, and visual–spatial–organizational skills. Harnadek and Rourke (1994) confirmed these areas of deficit to be most discriminative in a comparison of children with NLD, reading/spelling disabilities, and normal controls. In addition to exhibiting relative weaknesses on complex psychomotor tasks, children with NLD are often described to be clumsy and ill-coordinated, to have trouble in gym class, and to have difficulty with team sports, such as soccer and baseball. Complex psychomotor deficits are also seen to affect the performance of constructional activities and handwriting; handwriting is initially quite poor but does improve with practice over time for many children with NLD. We have also found that these children can become proficient at other kinds of more solitary sports activities, such as running and swimming, as well as sports that can be practiced routinely such as racket sports (e.g., tennis). We know of individuals who have excelled in these areas, in turn fostering greater self-esteem and gaining recognition among peers.

Early social experiences as well as self-care competencies (such as tying shoelaces, dressing) are impacted by fine motor and tactile deficiencies. These deficits are seen to have wider implications for the child's experience of himself or herself and the world. Much of early learning activity is gained through motivated exploration; the infant and toddler learn about their world through motor exploration and physical manipulation. Children's early play also is physical in nature rather than verbal; children engage through constructive play and physical games, and later more organized activities, such as sports. However, children with NLD prefer to hear about the world rather than to see or touch it and are less likely to engage with their peers through this kind of activity. Play can be considered the predominant childhood arena for practicing social skills, developing relationships, exercising new capacities, and permitting a mode of self-expression (Piaget, 1951). For children with NLD, there is a disproportionate reliance upon language (compared to play-based activity) as the principal means of social relating, information gathering, and relief from anxiety.

Motor and tactile deficits may affect development in critical ways that are easily overlooked. The impact of visual–spatial–organizational deficits also can be wide-ranging. Simple visual discrimination is generally not an issue for children with NLD—they are able to complete basic visual matching tasks and show good memory for pictures or visual material that can be verbalized readily. The strongest deficiency is in the area of visual spatial performance involving, for example, pattern construction, puzzle arrangement, or recall of a spatial array. In terms of day-to-day behavior, children with NLD typically do not show an interest in, or propensity for, building blocks or legos.

In school, these children have difficulty working with materials that are visually overwhelming, such as charts, graphs, maps, number lines, or homework sheets. On math assignments, errors may result from poorly aligned columns, failure to pay attention to the mathematical sign, and/or lack of appreciation of numerical position. In addition, copying from the board can be problematic; this activity requires graphomotor skill (generally an area of weakness for the child with NLD) and demands that the child translate visual information from a distal vertical plane (the board) to a proximal horizontal plane (the desk). Copying information from the board can be a time-consuming activity, with little information retained and potentially much information lost in the translation.

Children with NLD often exhibit directional confusion and experience trouble navigating space. This is particularly evident in middle school when they must change classrooms and negotiate hallways. Working on the identification of salient visual cues or a set of verbal directions may be helpful. During social exchanges, children with NLD are observed to have trouble maintaining appropriate interpersonal distance and recognizing how much space is appropriate. We also expect that visual imagery, mental representation, and estimation (including awareness of time) are impacted and these are areas that would benefit from further exploration.

Novelty, Problem Solving, and Concept Formation

The outstanding core deficit in NLD is adaptation to novelty. The capacity to cope with novelty is important for learning and adapting spontaneously to changing demands, whether in social discourse or day-to-day activity. Children with NLD have a fundamental difficulty adapting to novel situations and often rely on rote schemata, rigidly adhering to the use of overlearned strategies. Parents describe their child as repeatedly asking what will happen next and becoming upset with novel circumstances or changes in routine. The familiar is comfortable and organizing whereas uncertain or ambiguous situations are especially anxiety provoking for children with NLD. Their need to know what to expect is related to their desire to know how to respond. As such, children with NLD tend to form scripts, which represent an internalized concept of how things should happen in order to inform their behavior. These scripts are quite useful until they are violated and then it becomes a major challenge to make the adjustment and assimilate the new information. Direct instruction includes learning new scripts, flexible problem solving, learning how to adapt new information, but also being prepared in advance.

This need was captured delightfully by one child who was presented with a problem-solving task. He was given the information he needed to apply in order to solve the problem, but was required to arrive at the solution himself. When he appreciated the demands of the task, he was unable to suppress a grin and his relief, and commented, "But the answer is there, you gave me everything I need to know—that's like cheating." Of course, he still needed to perform the steps to arrive at his answer, but his relief was palpable because he was presented with the information he needed in advance, in static form, and the steps were clear for him to work toward the solution.

The child who avoids novelty is unlikely to explore his or her environment, yet motivated exploration and manipulation of the environment furnishes the child with the necessary information to begin forming mental schemata. This early activity is thought to yield the development of higher order mental processes, such as an understanding of cause-and-effect relationships, hypothesis testing, nonverbal concept formation, and reasoning abilities. We have observed children with NLD to use overlearned descriptive systems or to apply previously learned strategies to new situations in a rigid fashion. Although these children are capable of learning the rules well, the challenge is one of knowing what strategy to apply in which situation. In older children and adolescents with NLD, this difficulty is manifest in elevated numbers of errors on novel problem-solving measures, such as the Wisconsin Card Sorting Task or Category Test (Fisher et al., 1997).

Academic Strengths and Weaknesses

The profile of academic functioning in NLD was generated on the basis of Wide Range Achievement Test (WRAT; Jastak & Jastak, 1965; Wilkinson, 1993) scores; children with NLD showed advanced reading/decoding and spelling skills in the context of marked difficulties in arithmetic. We have observed that a phonetic approach is typically used when reading and words that are phonetically predictable are read and spelled more easily. In addition, over time, reading/decoding skills are superior to those required in reading/understanding. This finding is thought to reflect in part the difficulties inherent in reading for meaning (e.g., abstracting relevant vs irrelevant details). Reading comprehension measures that involve simple regurgitation of text (e.g., main points) are completed successfully. However, shortcomings in reading comprehension are observed when the child with NLD is required to paraphrase what he or she has read, to apply the information read, or to draw out implications of the material read.

Mechanical arithmetic skills are an area of relative deficiency and have been observed to rarely exceed the grade 5 or 6 level. Some children with NLD may excel at committing arithmetic facts or mathematical theorems to memory and reciting this information when asked to do so, thus relying on their verbal memory strength. The challenge lies in their capacity to reason through a problem, to know how to apply math facts or rules, or to problem solve adaptively. In advanced grades, geometry and physics are also problematic subjects. Written expression is an area of vulnerability with regard to organization and production of ideas.

Psychosocial/Adaptive

Vulnerabilities in psychosocial functioning are another aspect of the developmental picture for children with NLD. These children are socially interested and are eager to please and to be liked. However, they encounter difficulty navigating the social world, particularly when interacting with peers and in the context of group situations. They are often more comfortable in the company of adults who are more predictable in their behaviors and willing to scaffold or support the child's unconventional behaviors.

We have observed that children with NLD tend to exhibit an excessive reliance on language as a means for social relating in the context of deficits in social perception and social judgment. They show a preference for a single modality, namely auditory–verbal, when processing information. Difficulties ensue when they attend to what the person says but not how it is said (i.e., the underlying meaning), affecting appreciation also of the nonliteral aspects of language (e.g., ambiguities, idioms, inferences, sarcasm). Information that is conveyed through nonverbal aspects of communication, such as facial expression, tone, and gestures, is not integrated as readily. This is especially true when individuals with NLD must sustain a natural to-and-fro conversation, analyzing and integrating the elements necessary for this exchange in real time.

Another important aspect of social and adaptive behavior involves being able to determine what is most relevant in a given situation. This use of context requires a capacity to determine those aspects of the situation that are most salient. Children with NLD may have trouble in this arena; for example, perceiving how a particular stored memory involving a strategy or procedure may apply to a particular situation.

We have found that over time, children with NLD are at risk for anxiety and depression. A series of studies have shown that there are clear relationships between patterns of academic achievement and psychosocial outcome (Rourke & Fuerst, 1991; Tsatsanis et al., 1997; Pelletier et al., 2001). At least one-third of children with NLD do not show significant emotional disturbance, another one-third show mild concerns, and the remaining one-third are at risk for severe psychopathology (Pelletier et al., 2001). Among the affected groups, internalized forms of psychopathology tend to predominate.

Course and Outcome

Children with NLD encounter early challenges and it is unfortunate that their behaviors are often poorly understood at this time. In preschool and kindergarten, children with NLD may be diagnosed with ADHD or even early reading difficulties. This is in part because the learning environment largely invites interaction with the world that is tactile, motor, and visual and thus does not as readily engage children with NLD who show a proclivity for talking. Indeed, parents often report that their children talk at a young age, even before acquiring motor skills such as walking. Because these children show an early preference for learning about their environment through language and eschew physical exploration, their exposure to a large range of experiences and novel stimuli is more limited. Concerns about reading difficulties arise in the primary grades when a visual or whole word versus phonetic approach is applied to reading learning.

The gap between areas of strength and weakness, such as rote overlearned types of knowledge or learning and visual spatial or novel problem-solving skills, typically increases over time. Similarly, increasing discrepancies between reading/decoding and arithmetic skills are observed. However, graphomotor skills are generally poor in the primary school years but improve with age and practice. In addition, activity levels change over time; apparent hyperactivity in the young child tends to turn to normoactivity in the school age child and then to hypoactivity in the adolescent with NLD. Preadolescents and adolescents with NLD are also at risk for depression as well as anxiety.

It remains to be seen whether and to what extent these conditions may be explained by neurobiological or family genetic factors. More commonly, an association is posited between increasingly negative experiences in adolescence and feelings of depression. Rates of peer isolation and victimization are high for the school-aged child with NLD (Little, 2001). It may not be surprising, then, that varying degrees of depression are found as age and social pressures increase. The middle school years are often especially challenging as there is a shift in the social and academic environment; schools tend to be larger and require more transitions and learning is increasingly abstract and less rote in nature.

Adults with NLD are expected to do reasonably well in academic courses and jobs that involve rote verbal skills and patterns of responding that are highly predictable and straightforward. Programs and work environments that require on-the-spot flexible thinking and problem solving or place an emphasis on speeded visual motor coordination or spatial analysis are less suited to persons with NLD. We are familiar with adults with NLD who have gone on to college and those who have encountered job success in an academic setting or, for example, employment settings such as a travel agency.

CLASSIFICATION SYSTEM

At present, there is no formal provision for NLD in the DSM-IV; rather, for the purposes of obtaining services the needs of these children may be partially captured by diagnostic labels, such as mathematics disorder, disorder of written expression, pervasive developmental disorder, or other health impaired. Diagnosis is often considered to be one of the goals of assessment and it certainly carries important information. However, what is needed for programming is a consideration of the whole child—information related to his or her cognitive and academic profile, as well as behavioral and emotional functioning, that is understood both within a developmental framework and the environmental context.

Knowledge gained toward identifying children with NLD is intended to inform their programming needs. For example, we have encountered children with NLD who are placed in inappropriate classroom environments because their behavior is misjudged to be a problem rather than to be a manifestation of a significant developmental disability. The reverse scenario is also encountered; the cognitive strengths and verbal abilities of children with NLD mask the degree of information processing difficulties they are experiencing. We are working toward classification to aid the process of identification and in response to parents of children with NLD who have been frustrated in their attempts to gain appropriate recognition of and support for their children's needs.

The principal or primary dimensions of NLD have been confirmed through a series of studies (Casey et al., 1991; Harnadek & Rourke, 1994; Pelletier et al., 2001). In the most recent paper, the rules for classification of NLD and BPPD were refined to improve their utility and increase ease of use. These criteria were based on data obtained from subjects who were initially classified as definite or probable NLD.

Numbers in parentheses represent the percentages of children who met these criteria.

REVISED RULES FOR CLASSIFYING
CHILDREN WITH NLD (AGES 9–15 YEARS)

1. Less than two errors on simple tactile perception and suppression versus finger agnosia, finger dysgraphesthesia, and astereognosis composite greater than one standard deviation below the mean (90.9%).
2. WRAT/WRAT-R standard score for reading is at least eight points greater than arithmetic (85.7%).
3. Two of WISC/WISC-R vocabulary, similarities, and information are the highest of the verbal scale subtests (77.9%).
4. Two of WISC/WISC-R block design, object assembly, and coding subtests are the lowest of the performance scale (76.6%).
5. Target test performance is at least one standard deviation below the mean (63.6%).
6. Grip strength within one standard deviation of the mean or above vs grooved pegboard test greater than one standard deviation below the mean (63.6%).
7. Tactual performance test right, left, and both hand times become progressively worse vis-à-vis the norms (59.7%).
8. WISC/WISC-R VIQ > PIQ by at least 10 points (27.3%).

It should be noted clearly that not all of these are mutually exclusive. For experimental purposes, we propose the following criteria: first five features, definite NLD; seven or eight of these features, definite NLD; five or six of these features, probable NLD; three or four of these features, questionable NLD; and one or two of these features, low probability of NLD.

These criteria are neither mutually exclusive nor are they intended to replace the need for a thorough evaluation. These classification rules have been developed as a means to support diagnosis and to highlight some important caveats in this process. First, although a Verbal IQ–Performance IQ discrepancy may serve as a red flag, it is not a necessary criterion for a diagnosis of NLD. Some children with NLD may not show a significant VIQ–PIQ split. In part, this reflects the fact that the Verbal and Performance dimensions of the Wechsler scales are not pure (e.g., a child with a solid base of verbal knowledge may perform poorly on the arithmetic subtest due to poor numerical skills, and both elements factor into overall verbal IQ). In addition, many children with learning difficulties have received multiple evaluations. Subtests within the performance scale of the WISC are especially sensitive to practice effects and certainly the novel element of these subtests (especially taxing for children with NLD) is reduced with each subsequent testing. Service provision also may impact performance when a child has received practice with some of the skills that are being measured. As is always true, test scores need to be interpreted within the broader context in order to achieve a more complete understanding of the child.

ASSESSMENT BATTERY

Much of the research on NLD has involved children between 9 and 15 years, and we are most confident identifying this disorder when children are 8 or 9 years of age. At this stage in their development, we are able to sample a fuller range of abilities, and psychological tests as well as school demands do not emphasize rote learning alone but also draw upon problem-solving skills. A recommended battery of tests is presented in Table 1, which represents those measures used originally for delineation of the NLD subtype. For more information on these measures, the reader is referred to Rourke (1989).

We have also found several other tests to be useful in the clinic setting, which warrant further research. The *Test of Visual Perceptual Skills Revised* (Gardner, 1996) provides multiple subtests measuring varied aspects of visual perception and discrimination. We have found the Form Constancy and Visual Closure subtests to be of particular interest for children with NLD. It is important to note that the items in this test battery are forced choice; this response approach may enhance performance for some children, especially those who are higher functioning. Other measures that may be useful include the Judgment of Line Orientation (Benton, 1994), Mental Rotation task (Vandenberg & Kuse, 1978), and Progressive Planning subtest of the NEPSY (Korkman et al., 1997). The Fluid Reasoning composite from the Woodcock Johnson III (Woodcock et al., 2001), particularly a comparison of the analysis, synthesis, and concept formation subtests, can also be informative with regard to appreciating the child's capacity to derive and apply newly formed rules.

TABLE 1

Domain	Relative strength	Relative weakness
Motor and psychomotor	Grip strength Static steadiness	Grooved pegboard test Maze
Tactile perceptual	Simple tactile perception	Finger agnosia Tactile form recognition Fingertip number writing
Visual–spatial organizational	Simple visual perception/ discrimination Trail-making test, part A	Wechsler object assembly Wechsler block design Trail-making test, part B
Visual attention/ memory		Target test Rey-Osterrieth Complex figure test
Auditory perceptual	Speech sounds perception test Auditory closure test	
Auditory–verbal	Digit span (forward)	Sentence memory
Attention memory	Seashore rhythm	
Language	PPVT Wechsler similarities Wechsler vocabulary	
Problem solving		Tactual performance test Category test
Academic achievement	WRAT reading WRAT spelling	WRAT arithmetic
Adaptive/social emotional		Vineland PIC

DYNAMICS OF NLD

A hierarchical and causal account has been formulated for NLD. From this perspective, the clinical dimensions of the NLD syndrome are best understood within the context of the dynamic interplay between several neuropsychological assets and deficits. These are couched within a model that suggests a role for the left and right cerebral hemispheres in the acquisition, integration, and application of descriptive systems. The precise dynamics of NLD have been discussed in detail elsewhere (Rourke, 1989) and are presented briefly here. The hypothesized asset–deficit streams are illustrated in Fig. 1. We will confine our discussion to the deficit stream.

PRIMARY NEUROPSYCHOLOGICAL ASSETS	PRIMARY NEUROPSYCHOLOGICAL DEFICITS
Auditory Perception Simple Motor Rote Material	Tactile Perception Visual Perception Complex Psychomotor Novel Material

SECONDARY NEUROPSYCHOLOGICAL ASSETS	SECONDARY NEUROPSYCHOLOGICAL DEFICITS
Auditory Attention Verbal Attention	Tactile Attention Visual Attention Exploratory Behavior

TERTIARY NEUROPSYCHOLOGICAL ASSETS	TERTIARY NEUROPSYCHOLOGICAL DEFICITS
Auditory Memory Verbal Memory	Tactile Memory Visual Memory Concept Formation Problem Solving

VERBAL NEUROPSYCHOLOGICAL ASSETS	VERBAL NEUROPSYCHOLOGICAL DEFICITS
Phonology Verbal Reception Verbal Repetition Verbal Storage Verbal Associations Verbal Output	Oral–motor Praxis Prosody Phonology>Semantics Content Pragmatics Function

ACADEMIC ASSETS	ACADEMIC DEFICITS
Graphomotor (Late) Word Decoding Spelling Verbatim Memory	Graphomotor (Early) Reading Comprehension Mechanical Arithmetic Mathematics Science
SOCIOEMOTIONAL/ADAPTIVE ASSETS	**SOCIOEMOTIONAL/ADAPTIVE DEFICITS**
???	Adaptation to Novelty Social Competence Emotional Stability Activity Level

FIGURE 1   Content and Dynamics of the NLD Syndrome.

The primary neuropsychological deficits experienced by the child with NLD involve tactile and visual perception, complex psychomotor skills, and the capacity to deal adaptively with novel material. Such deficits are expected to eventuate in disordered tactile and visual attention and reduced exploratory behavior; in turn, problems in memory for material delivered through the tactile and visual modalities, as well as deficits in concept–formation and problem solving, would be expected to follow. This set of deficits is considered to eventuate in the particular linguistic deficiencies outlined in Fig. 1 (for a more extensive explanation of these linguistic deficits, see Rourke & Tsatsanis, 1996). In addition, this set of neuropsychological deficits is expected to lead, in a necessary way, to a particular configuration of problems in psychosocial/adaptive behavior both within and without the academic situation (Rourke, 1988a, 1989, 1995; Rourke & Fuerst, 1992).

The notion that a particular pattern of neuropsychological assets and deficits (resulting in a particular subtype of learning disability) can lead to both a particular pattern of academic assets and deficits and a partic- ular pattern of psychosocial disturbance is well illustrated by the NLD syndrome. In a series of investigations (Casey et al., 1991; Harnadek & Rourke, 1994; Rourke & Fuerst, 1991), we have been able to demon- strate the concurrent and predictive validity of these formulations relat- ing to the academic and psychosocial consequences of NLD. Also, it has been possible to demonstrate that particular patterns of academic assets and deficits are reliably related to particular patterns of psychosocial dys- function across the age span of interest (Fuerst & Rourke, 1993; Pelletier et al., 2001; Tsatsanis et al., 1997).

In addition to describing the content and dynamics of the NLD syn- drome, a model to explain the dynamics of the syndrome has been proposed (Rourke, 1987, 1988b, 1989, 1995). The model involves an inte- gration of Piagetian developmental theory and a concept of brain devel- opment that extends the theoretical tenets of Goldberg and Costa (1981). An approach is advanced in which the manifestation of this syndrome is viewed in terms of the complex and complementary interaction of cog- nitive, brain maturational, and experiential factors.

Developmental Perspective

The NLD model is distinctive in its attempt to understand the manifes- tation of this disorder within a developmental framework. The primary deficits experienced by the child with NLD are also those that are integral to early learning. Piaget (1954; Piaget & Inhelder, 1969) emphasized sensorimotor functioning as one of the early developmental features upon which formal operational thought is founded (Casey & Rourke, 1992; Strang & Rourke, 1985a). Observations of young children's behavior show that the external world is known principally through touch, vision, and movement. Early learning also takes place in the context of goal-directed behavior, which is manifested outwardly in action or active experimentation (Piaget, 1954). Motivated exploration and manipulation of the environment furnish the child with the necessary information to begin forming mental schemata. This early activity is thought to yield the development of higher order mental processes, such as an understanding of cause-and-effect relationships, hypothesis testing, nonverbal concept formation, and reasoning abilities.

From this perspective, development is characterized as an emerging and continuing process of organization, integration, and consolidation of one's experiences that are engendered by newly emerging capacities. At the earliest stages, the interaction between self and environment is organized through the body (sensory processes) and action (Piaget, 1954).

Within this formulation, it follows then that the adequacy of the child's sensorimotor experience is related in a direct way to his or her cognitive development (Piaget, 1954). The primary deficits of NLD—tactile perception, psychomotor coordination, and visual perception—are precisely those domains identified as essential to early learning. Furthermore, children with NLD have considerable difficulty adapting to novel stimuli and are unlikely to explore their environment or seek out stimulation. It may be argued that, for the child with NLD, there is little organized interaction between him or her and the external world, and a fundamental inability to make sense of the complex and novel stimuli.

For children with NLD, some areas of language development are quite adequate whereas other areas are more impaired. On the one hand, language is transmitted to the child in ready-made and compulsory form (Piaget & Inhelder, 1969). Young children receive structured auditory input and highly directed speech in their "conversations" with caregivers. In addition, some language skills (e.g., verbal output, syntax and grammar, word knowledge, and word decoding) are readily routinized behaviors that are governed by explicit rules. On the other hand, the meanings of words may be manifold and may have a literal or nonliteral sense. Children learn these distinctions by hearing how words are associated with particular actions and behaviors in a social context and then assigning meanings to those words. Eventually, context is not needed to understand what the word represents (Boone & Plante, 1993). In this process, the importance of experience is underscored. Inasmuch as words may operate as symbols or representations of experiences, it is also the case that the association between words and their referents (external as well as internal events) occurs through experience.

The role of contextual information is also relevant to this discussion. In language and in social situations, the number of contextual cues available is very rich. We make use of prosody, gestures, affect, body movements, situation, knowledge of the speaker, or relation to that person both to convey and to understand the message. Language development involves greater sophistication or refinement in the use of context (Milosky, 1992). This would also appear to be true of reading/understanding at higher levels. Accordingly, the process of understanding language relies on increasing flexibility in the use of context, the capacity to adapt to novel contexts, and the ability to draw upon a knowledge base (incorporating past and salient features of the present experience) that pertains to different aspects of context.

From this description, it is easy to understand why children with NLD may have difficulty making use of contextual information. One of the primary deficits experienced by these children is an inability to deal with novelty. Children with NLD are likely to experience difficulty in adapting spontaneously to changing demands in social discourse; instead they usually rely on routinized or programmatic exchanges.

A similar distinction may be drawn between areas of mathematics that are learned in a formulaic manner and those that are acquired through reasoning. Number facts are taught explicitly and achieved largely through a process of rote memorization, a relative strength for children with NLD. However, in addition to the formal mathematics instruction that takes place, children must also develop an appreciation for number concepts. That is, they must develop an idea of what is meant by "number," "more and less," "greater than and less than," "fraction," "conservation of quantity," and so on. An understanding of these mathematical constructs is built upon principles that derive from physical experience. The concepts are revealed in the children's ability to think about and mentally represent the relations between objects and their experiences of them (Piaget & Inhelder, 1969). Higher level mathematics further draws upon spatial visualization and representation, a relative area of deficit for children with NLD.

A pervasive difficulty in making sense of and adapting to external events is also expected to affect the ability to interact socially. In Piagetian terms, schemata are developed and applied to the social experience (Piaget, 1954). This process is dependent on a capacity to draw out the common, more general, features of interpersonal events. More basic problems in intermodal integration, reasoning, and concept–formation are also thought to contribute to deficits in social judgment and interaction (Rourke, 1993; Strang & Rourke, 1983). Specifically, limitations in the capacities of persons with NLD for intermodal integration are expected to give rise to the following adaptive difficulties: (a) problems in the assessment of another's emotional state, which depends on the analysis and synthesis (integration) of information gleaned from facial expressions, tone of voice, posture, psychomotor patterns, and the like; (b) impaired assessment of social cause-and-effect relationships, which arises because of a failure to integrate data from a number of sources, as is often necessary to generate reasonable hypotheses regarding the chain of events in social intercourse; (c) failure to appreciate humor because of the complex intermodal judgments required for assessing the juxtaposition of the incongruous; and (d) misinterpretation of the behavior of others, such as attributing unreasonable or oversimplified causes for their behavior, and making such attributions in situations that would lead to embarrassment for that person.

Social competence also requires adaptability to novel interpersonal situations and a constantly shifting pattern of exchange. A basic deficit identified in persons with NLD is coping with novelty, which is exacerbated by poor problem-solving and hypothesis-testing skills. This constellation of difficulties conspires to render a smooth adaptation to the constantly changing milieux of social interactions all but impossible for the child or adult with NLD. Although some social rules may be learned, a formulaic descriptive system is not likely to eventuate in the spontaneous give and take of a social exchange. Despite an initial desire to interact with others, the totality of these problems may create an unrewarding social experience for the child with NLD. With increasing age and social pressures, they may be ostracized or ridiculed. These experiences are expected to lead to an increased likelihood of social withdrawal, isolation, and depression on the part of the person with NLD. As noted, evidence suggests that depression and suicide attempts are greater than average in individuals who exhibit this syndrome (Bigler, 1989; Fletcher, 1989; Rourke et al., 1989).

Neurodevelopmental Perspective

Three principal axes of neurodevelopment are considered for their role in the integrative action of the brain. From this perspective, the role of neural pathways (i.e., axonal or "white matter" connections) in flexibly processing information and responding to changes in functional demands is seen as crucial. Events that lead to damage or perturbations in the development of these pathways are hypothesized to be the cause of the phenotypical manifestations of NLD. A brief account of this aspect of the model is presented later. For a full description of the syndrome and the "white matter" model designed to account for it, the interested reader is referred to Rourke (1989, 1995) and to Tsatsanis and Rourke (1995).

The development of axonal connections (white matter pathways) and the process of myelination are far from complete in the brain of the very young child (Dietrich & Bradley, 1988; Kolb & Fantie, 1989; Rourke et al., 1983). In addition, the excess production and eventual elimination of neurons, dendrites, and synapses are important events in postnatal development (Huttenlocher, 1984, 1994). A description of these events also underscores the notion that brain development involves a dynamic interplay between two main processes: differentiation and integration. The brain evolves to greater complexity through the integrative action of neuronal growth and differentiation and associated organization of these component parts to yield more refined neural systems (Majovski, 1989). Similarly, the mark of higher order processing is the activation of specialized subsystems as well as the capacity to integrate them toward an identified goal.

In the current white matter model, functions that involve inter- rather than intramodal processing are expected to be more likely affected by white matter perturbations. It follows that white matter disturbances will have a more profound effect on neural systems that are characterized by a high degree of interregional connectivity. In their capacity to deal with novel and complex information, it is expected that both right hemisphere and frontal systems display greater interregional connectivity (e.g., Damasio, 1990; Tulving et al., 1994). Moreover, the integrity of these systems is expected to bear upon the child's ability to adapt to increasing environmental demands.

The finding of an anterior–posterior gradient of development in the formation of these connections has been interpreted to suggest a mechanism of integration by frontal systems of elemental sensorimotor units to form higher level abstractions and systems of abstraction (Thatcher,

1994). Another dimension of interest would appear to be the long fibers projecting from subcortical and limbic system structures to cortical areas, particularly frontal regions.

Evidence suggests that reciprocal connections between these regions influence information processing at higher levels. Such roles include the assignment of affective meaning to external events, formation of novelty encoding networks, and synchronization and desynchronization of cortical activity (Barth & MacDonald, 1996; Damasio & Anderson, 1993; Mega et al., 1997; Steriade et al., 1993; Tulving et al., 1994). Developmentally, a perturbation in these pathways would be expected to result in diminished subcortical-limbic influences on refinement and organization of the cortex, thereby affecting regulation and coordination of higher order mental activity.

The pattern of development displayed by children with NLD has also been interpreted by Rourke (1982, 1987, 1989), on the basis of formulations of the Goldberg and Costa (1981) model, to involve right hemisphere dysfunction. Through an analysis of differences in the neuroanatomical organization of the right and left hemispheres, Goldberg and Costa (1981) identified distinct roles for the cerebral hemispheres in the acquisition, integration, and application of descriptive systems. Their examination suggested that the right hemisphere has a crucial role in the initial stages of the acquisition of descriptive systems, whereas the left hemisphere is superior at deploying these codes in a routinized manner once they have been assembled. Hence, it is hypothesized that systems within the right hemisphere are highly efficient at processing novel information for which the individual has no preexisting code. In contrast, left hemispheral systems are thought to be superior at processing that takes advantage of these fully formed codes, i.e., the storage and application of multiple overlearned descriptive systems. The specific pattern of neuropsychological assets and deficits displayed by children with NLD is expected to develop under conditions that compromise the functioning or accessibility to right hemispheral systems in particular.

The NLD syndrome is manifest most clearly on a "developmental" basis and persists into adulthood (Rourke & Fisk, 1992). However, it is also seen in the clinical presentation of persons suffering from a wide variety of types of neurological and neuroendocrine disease, disorder, and dysfunction (Rourke, 1995; Rourke et al., 2002). These include significant tissue destruction within the right cerebral hemisphere (Rourke et al., 1983) and some types of hydrocephalus (Fletcher et al., 1995), callosal agenesis (Smith & Rourke, 1995), congenital hypothyroidism (Rovet,

1995), and other pathological processes that have as one of their results significant perturbations of neuronal white matter (long myelinated fibers). Some other examples include persons with Williams syndrome (Anderson & Rourke, 1995; MacDonald & Roy, 1988; Udwin & Yule, 1991) and Asperger syndrome (Klin et al., 1995). It is because of this that we refer to the NLD phenotype as the "final common pathway" for a variety of neurological disorders. It is also why we maintain that significant right hemisphere damage or dysfunction is sufficient to cause the NLD syndrome, but it is not necessary (Rourke, 1995).

INTERVENTION

Children with NLD display many important strengths and our broad approach to treatment is to utilize those strengths to remediate areas of weakness. However, a key first step is that these children be recognized and evaluated appropriately. Well-developed rote verbal skills, good vocabulary, and verbosity sometimes give the impression that the child with NLD is more capable than is actually the case. The result is that these children do not receive the kind of attention that they need. Their problems are overlooked, and they become increasingly overwhelmed and socially isolated. Parents often report that "meltdowns" present at home before they manifest at school.

Remediation and habilitation for the child with NLD are critical and are assisted by a good understanding of the child and shared vision by all who work with him or her. Children need to receive educational programs that are appropriate for their special learning needs. In addition, parents and families will benefit from support to guide their expectations and parenting approach so that they fit the child's most salient developmental needs. Although the behavioral manifestations are similar among children with NLD, it is expected that outcome is impacted by the degree of neuropsychological impairment. In addition, early intervention is integral to later development, particularly toward building adaptive coping strategies.

It is critical that the work be conducted with all of the child's caregivers to help them with insight and direction regarding the child's most salient development needs. It should be clear to everyone involved that children and adolescents with NLD and, for that matter, most adults with NLD require fairly continuous monitoring of their adaptive behavior. The principal challenge for parents and other caregivers is the necessity to meet these continuing needs. Often, the interventions required are rather minimal, but the absence of such can have a rather far-reaching negative impact on the person with NLD. Each of the principles of intervention described here can be incorporated by all caregivers into their interactions with a child with NLD. We have found that well-motivated caregivers who have an intuitive or learned appreciation of their child's adaptive strengths and weaknesses most often create a milieu at home or elsewhere in which the child prospers and in which adaptive deficits are minimized.

An approach to treatment is outlined here. For further information regarding principles of intervention and their applications for the child and adolescent with NLD, the interested reader may wish to consult the following: Cermak and Murray (1992), Foss (1991), Rourke (1985, 1989, 1991), Rourke et al. (1983, 1986), Rourke and Del Dotto (1994), Rourke et al. (1986), Rourke and Fuerst (1991), Rourke and Tsatsanis (1995) and Thompson (1997).

1. Observe the child's behavior closely, especially in novel or complex situations. One approach to dealing with a child's behavior is to view it first as a form of communication. The child's behavior is information—an indication of what they might be feeling or thinking, or how they might be challenged. It is particularly informative when working with children with NLD to focus on what the child *does* versus what the child *says*. This should also help the parent, therapist, and/or teacher develop a better appreciation of the child's potentially outstanding adaptive deficits. One of the most frequent criticisms of remedial intervention programs with this particular type of child is that remedial authorities are unaware of the extent and significance of the child's deficits. Through direct observation under these conditions, it should become apparent that the child is very much in need of a systematic, well-orchestrated program of intervention.

2. Adopt a realistic attitude. Once it has been established that the child's behavior is nonadaptive, particularly in new or otherwise complex situations, adults working with this child must be realistic in assessing the import and impact of the child's neuropsychological assets (e.g., "automatic" language skills, rote memory) and deficits (e.g., visual–spatial–organizational skills). In the classroom, for instance, it should be readily apparent that the child's well-developed word recognition and spelling abilities are not sufficient for him or her to benefit from many approaches to formal and informal instruction, especially for those subjects requiring

visual–spatial–organizational and/or nonverbal problem-solving skills. This being the case, there are really only two educational alternatives: to adopt special procedures for the presentation of material of the latter variety or to avoid such material altogether. [For further information relevant to these matters, see Brandys and Rourke (1991) and Rourke and Tsatsanis (1996).] Some suggestions for "special procedures" follow.

3. Teach the child in a systematic, "step-by-step" fashion. Whenever possible, a parts-to-whole verbal teaching approach should be used. As a rule of thumb, the therapist or teacher should take note that if it is possible to talk about an idea, concept, or procedure in a straightforward fashion, then the child should be able to grasp at least some aspects of the material. However, if it is not possible to put into words an adequate description of the material to be learned (e.g., as in explaining time concepts), it will probably be quite difficult for the child with NLD to benefit from the instruction.

It should also be kept in mind that the child will learn best when each of the verbal "steps" is presented in the correct sequence because of his or her difficulties with problem-solving skills and associated organizational challenges with novel (even linguistically novel) material. A secondary benefit of this teaching approach is that the child is provided with a set of verbal rules that can be written out and then reapplied whenever it is appropriate to do so. This is particularly important for the teaching of mechanical arithmetic operations and procedures.

The principal impediment to engaging in this rather slow and painstaking approach to teaching the child with NLD is the faulty impression that the child is much more adept and adaptable than is actually the case. This increases the probability that the adult working with this child will start the program at a level that is too sophisticated for the child and will proceed at too fast a pace for the child's information-processing capacities. The child with NLD tends to respond quite appreciatively and appropriately to an approach that is slow, repetitive, and highly redundant.

4. Encourage the child to describe in detail important events that are transpiring in his or her life. This principle applies not only to teaching sessions with the child, but also to any situation in which the child does not seem to appreciate fully the significance of his or her behavior or the behavior of others. For example, when there is an incident on the playground in which the child has encountered interpersonal difficulty, the teacher or therapist should ask the child to explain in detail the events that transpired and his or her perceptions of the cause of the incident and its effects. The caregiver should encourage the child to focus on the rel-

evant aspects of the situation and point out the irrelevancies therein. Through discussion, the child should be helped to become aware of discrepancies between his or her perceptions (regarding the situation in question) and the perceptions of others. In teaching situations, one useful technique is to encourage the child to "reteach" the teacher or therapist (or, in some situations, to teach other children) the procedure or concept that he or she has been taught. This will help increase the probability that the child has understood the necessary information, that it has been analyzed and integrated, and that it will be applied in future situations.

5. Teach the child appropriate strategies for dealing with particularly troublesome situations that occur on a frequent, everyday basis. In many cases, children with NLD do not generate appropriate problem-solving strategies independently because they are unaware of the actual requirements of the situation. At other times, these children may be unable to generate appropriate strategies because this particular type of endeavor requires basic neuropsychological competencies that they have not developed. For both of these reasons, they need to be taught appropriate strategies for handling the requirements of troublesome situations that are occurring frequently. The teacher or therapist will find that the step-by-step requirements for teaching this type of child are quite similar to those that would be employed effectively for much younger children. Once again, it should be emphasized that the most frequent error made by adult caregivers in such situations is to overestimate the capacities of children with NLD to learn and to apply adaptive problem-solving solutions and techniques for coping.

6. Encourage the generalization of learned strategies and concepts. Although the vast majority of children see how one particular strategy or procedure may apply to a number of different situations and/or how certain concepts may apply to a wide range of topics, the child with NLD usually exhibits difficulties with this form of generalization. For example, it is common to find that although the child with NLD has been trained assiduously in visual attention and visual-tracking skills in the laboratory or therapeutic setting, he or she fails to employ the skills effectively in everyday life (e.g., when it would be propitious to examine some aspects of a person's physical characteristics in order to enhance recognition of that person in the future). The child with NLD not only needs to be taught specific skills in a step-by-step fashion, but also that transitional or generalization skills need to be addressed in an identical manner.

Related to these difficulties is a very persistent and pervasive deficit in the judgment of cause-and-effect relationships. The relationships between events (e.g., thoughts and behaviors, settings and behaviors) need to be brought quite explicitly to the child's attention because children with NLD do not make the same sort of inferences regarding cause and effect that are arrived at spontaneously and without difficulty by children not so afflicted.

Another point to bear in mind is that virtually all generalizations need to be taught to children with NLD. There is little reason to infer that the learning of one generalization by the child with NLD will, necessarily, enhance the acquiring of another generalization.

7. Teach the child to refine and use appropriately his or her verbal (expressive) skills. As has been pointed out previously, it is quite probable that children with NLD will come to use verbal (expressive) skills much more frequently and for many different reasons than do most children. For example, children with NLD may repeatedly ask questions as a primary way of gathering information about a new or otherwise complex situation. This may be quite inappropriate for many situations (e.g., those of a social nature), in which nonverbal behaviors are much more important for feedback and direction.

The content of the child's verbal responses may also be problematic. A common observation is that the child with NLD may begin to make a reply by directly addressing the question asked, but then may gradually drift off into a completely different topic. At the very least, the tangential nature of such utterances has the effect of alienating the listener. Specific training should be undertaken that is directed at the "what to say," "how to say," and "when to say" aspects of language as these questions apply to the child's problem areas. However, as with other aspects of remediation mentioned earlier, there is the problem of generalization of learning in this sort of training exercise. The child with NLD tends not to be flexible and adaptive in the application of learned habits, even when these are in his or her areas of "strength" (i.e., verbal skills). The interested reader may wish to consult Rourke and Tsatsanis (1996) for further explanations of these dimensions.

For these and other reasons, it is usually necessary to spend considerable time and effort to train the child to stop, look, listen, and weigh alternatives, even in what may appear to the casual observer to be mundane, straightforward situations. Failure to anticipate the consequences of their actions often leads children with NLD to rush into situations where they are very likely to suffer physical and/or psychological harm. Their usual tendency is to avoid such situations after repeated failure and pain. The caregiver's role is to help the child deal effectively with such situations, rather than to encourage the child's understandable tendency to avoid them altogether.

8. Teach the child to make better use of his or her visual–perceptual–organizational skills. It should be borne in mind that children tend to "lead with their strong suit" in situations that are in any way problematic for them. For example, if a child exhibits an outstanding area of disability (e.g., visual–spatial skills) in combination with relatively intact abilities (e.g., verbal receptive and expressive skills), he or she tends to use the better-developed (verbal) skills whenever it is possible to do so, even though this approach is not the most appropriate. This encourages a situation in which the poorly developed skills (e.g., visual–spatial skills) are not challenged or "exercised"; hence, their optimal level of development may not be realized. The tendency to "play the strong suit" also encourages the child with NLD to develop a very wide variety of ways to use language-related skills but in ways that are clearly maladaptive.

To increase the likelihood that the child's visual modality and associated perceptive and analytic abilities will be developed and used optimally, a younger child with NLD could be taught to name visual details in pictures as a way of encouraging him or her to pay attention to these details. In conjunction with this exercise, the child could be asked to talk about the relationship between various details in a picture (e.g., intersecting lines) as a way of drawing attention to the complexity, importance, and significance of visual features of stimulus presentation.

When the child is older, remedial suggestions and exercises should be more "functional" or practical in nature, but at the same time should address directly the child's outstanding areas of difficulty. For example, most social situations require the child to decipher or decode the nonverbal behaviors of others in order to interpret them properly. It is clear that the child with NLD is quite deficient in abilities that are crucial for the development of nonverbal social–analytic skills. Therefore, a caregiver or therapist might create "artificial" social situations that require the child to rely only on his or her visual receptive and other nonverbal skills for interpretation. This could be done with pictures, films, or even contrived "real-life" situations for which there is no verbal feedback available. After an exercise of this type, the caregiver should discuss the child's perception of the social situation and of his or her most appropriate role in the situation. At the same time, the caregiver might provide the child with strategies for deciphering the most salient nonverbal dimensions inherent in these contrived social situations.

9. Teach the child to interpret visual information when there is "competing" auditory information. Training the child to focus on visual stimuli when auditory stimuli are available is usually more complex than the suggested remedial interventions already mentioned. This recommendation is particularly important in attempting to teach the child to deal more effectively with novel social situations. In these situations, it is important not only to interpret others' nonverbal behavior correctly, but also to interpret what is being said in conjunction with these nonverbal cues. In most cases, this type of training should be undertaken only when there has been adequate work and progress in the previously mentioned areas.

10. Teach appropriate nonverbal behavior. Many children with NLD do not appear to have adequately developed nonverbal behavior. For example, such children often present with a somewhat "vacant look" or other inappropriate facial expressions. This is especially true of those individuals who are found to exhibit marked neuropsychological deficits. A child with NLD may smile in situations in which such behavior is quite inappropriate (e.g., when he or she is experiencing failure with a task). It is important to attempt to teach more appropriate nonverbal behavior, keeping in mind the concepts introduced in association with the refinements of the child's verbal expressive skills. In this connection, teaching the child "what to do" and "how and when to do it" should be the focus of concern. For example, some children may not know how or when to convey their feelings in a nonverbal manner. The use of informative pictures, imitative "drills," work with a mirror, and other techniques and concrete aids can prove to be invaluable in this type of training. This sort of intervention may also serve to make the child more aware of the significance of the nonverbal behavior of others.

11. Facilitate structured peer interactions. It is not always possible to promote social training in unstructured social situations because these are largely beyond the reach of the remedial therapist or teacher. For instance, when the child is on the playground, it is not often possible to regulate his or her play in any way (at least to the extent that it promotes positive social growth for the socially impaired youngster). However, intramural activities of one sort or another, clubs, and formal community groups can provide a forum for social training if these are exploited in a proper manner. Unfortunately, many children with NLD tend to be somewhat socially withdrawn. That being the case, they may not be encouraged to join their peers in social activities of any kind because their parents and other caregivers may see a need to protect the children from such encounters.

This raises the thorny issue of "overprotection." Although sensitive caregivers are often accused of this, it is clear that they may be the only ones who have an appreciation for a child's vulnerability and lack of appropriate skill development. Balancing the need for protection with the need for expanded horizons and encounters with physical and social reality is never easy. Understanding that this is a difficult realm within which to exercise prudence (i.e., to dare wisely) is the first—and very necessary—step to engaging in the complex series of judgments and activities that constitute effective intervention for children with NLD.

12. Promote, encourage, and monitor "systematic" explorative activities. One of the most potentially harmful tacks that a well-meaning therapist can take with a child with NLD is to leave the child to his or her own devices in activities that lack sufficient (or any) structure (e.g., ambient play situations with other children). However, it is also quite worthwhile to design specific activities through which the child is encouraged to explore his or her environment. For example, exploratory activity may be encouraged within the structure of a gross motor program. In this setting, the child could be provided with the opportunity to explore various types of apparatus and the exercises that would suit each apparatus. In this situation, it is important that such children do not feel that they are competing with their peers. In addition, following the lesson, the child with NLD should be required to give the instructor some verbal feedback and perhaps accompanying demonstrations regarding the activities that have transpired.

13. Teach the child how to use age-appropriate aids to reach a specific goal. One potential "aid" for an older child with NLD is a hand calculator, which can be used to provide the child with a way of checking the accuracy of his or her mechanical arithmetic work. After the child has completed a question independently, he or she can be allowed to redo the same question with a hand calculator. This gives the child a means for checking the accuracy of the answer, provided that he or she uses the calculator correctly. If it is found that the solution is incorrect, the child should then be encouraged to rework the question with pen and paper. At the high-school level, hand calculators should probably be used whenever possible so that the adolescent or young adult will develop at least a functional grasp of common mathematical operations and their applications in everyday life situations.

Another aid that can be used, especially for the younger child with NLD, is a digital watch. Many children with NLD have difficulty in reading the hands of a traditional clock face, which imposes further limitations on their already impoverished appreciation of time concepts. A digital watch is read more easily and can serve as a concrete tool for the teaching of elementary time concepts.

In all of this, there is no substitute for creative approaches to the provision of therapeutic "aids." This is especially the case for exploitation of the vast potential of computers as prosthetic/therapeutic devices. Programs that allow for appropriate and helpful corrective feedback for difficult academic subjects; those that take the child in a step-by-step fashion through any number of quasi-social and problem-solving situations; and those that present material in a systematic, sequenced fashion that draws the child's attention to the process of problem-solving development—all of these and many more dimensions of the creative use of computer software—are potentially of considerable benefit for the child and adolescent with NLD.

14. Help the child gain insight into situations that are easy for him or her and those that are potentially troublesome. It is important for older children and adolescents with NLD to acquire a reasonably realistic view of their capabilities. This is certainly more easily said than done. In this regard, a therapist's expectations always need to be in concert with a child's abilities because gains in this area may prove to be marginal at best. For instance, a child's practical insight may be limited to "I am good at spelling and have problems with math." However, if the child is provided with consistent and appropriate feedback from concerned and informed adults regarding his or her performances in various kinds of situations, fairly sophisticated insights may develop. This is especially important with respect to perceiving the need to use prelearned strategies in appropriate situations. Furthermore, it is important for children with NLD to learn that they do have some cognitive strengths and that these strengths can be used to advantage in specific situations.

15. Be cognizant of the therapist's/remedial specialist's role in preparing the child with NLD for adult life. Special educators, in particular, should assume a major role in preparing the child with NLD for adult life. Unlike most educational programs, in which the primary goal is to help the child master a particular curriculum, the program required by children with NLD is one that focuses primarily on the development of social/life skills. A child's mastery of the standard academic curriculum is insignificant if he or she is not prepared to meet the social and other adaptive demands of independent living. Indeed, we have found through longitudinal follow-up that some children with NLD as adults have developed rather seriously debilitating forms of psychopathology. Thus, it is

clear that remedial/habilitational interventions with such children should always be consonant with their short- and long-term remedial needs and with their remedial capacities.

A FINAL NOTE

The person with NLD can learn practically anything. For example, with intensive practice and close monitoring of progress, very complicated psychomotor skills, such as racquet sports, martial arts, and the like, can be learned to rather high levels of attainment. Once mastered to a reasonable level, such activities usually provide a considerable source of self-esteem for the person with NLD. The same applies to learning social skills that will help them "get through" many, if not most, social situations without tremendous difficulties. Although we have emphasized the difficulties involved in interventions for persons with NLD (primarily because so many actual and potential caregivers tend to overestimate their capacities), this emphasis should be seen against a backdrop of tremendous potential for learning—under the proper circumstances and within a context that acknowledges the actual neuropsychological assets and deficits of the individual.

REFERENCES

Anderson, P., & Rourke, B. P. (1995). Williams syndrome. In B. P. Rourke (Ed.), *Syndrome of nonverbal learning disabilities: Neurodevelopmental manifestations* (pp. 138–170). New York: Guilford Press.

Barth, D. S., & MacDonald, K. D. (1996). Thalamic modulation of high-frequency oscillating potentials in auditory cortex. *Nature, 383,* 78–81.

Benton, A. (1994). *Judgment of line orientation.* Los Angeles: Western Psychological Services.

Bigler, E. D. (1989). On the neuropsychology of suicide. *Journal of Learning Disabilities, 22,* 180–185.

Boone, D. R., & Plante, E. (1993). *Human communication and its disorders* (2nd ed.). Englewood Cliffs, NJ: Prentice-Hall.

Casey, J. E., & Rourke, B. P. (1992). Disorders of somatosensory perception in children. In I. Rapin & S. J. Segalowitz (Eds.), *Handbook of neuropsychology* (Vol. 6, pp. 477–494). Amsterdam: Elsevier.

Casey, J. E., Rourke, B. P., & Picard, E. M. (1991). Syndrome of nonverbal learning disabilities: Age differences in neuropsychological, academic, and socioemotional functioning. *Development and Psychopathology, 3,* 329–345.

Cermak, S. A., & Murray, E. (1992). Nonverbal learning disabilities in the adult framed in the model of human occupation. In N. Katz (Ed.), *Cognitive rehabilitation models for intervention in occupational therapy* (pp. 258–291). Boston: Andover Medical.

Damasio, A. R. (1990). Synchronous activation in multiple cortical regions: A mechanism for recall. *Seminars in neuroscience*, 2, 287–296.

Damasio, A. R., & Anderson, S. W. (1993). The frontal lobes. In K. M. Heilman & E. Valenstein (Eds.), *Clinical Neuropsychology* (3rd ed., pp. 409–460). New York: Oxford Univ. Press.

Delis, D. C., Kramer, J. H., Kaplan, E., & Ober, B. A. (1987). *California verbal learning test: Adult version manual*. San Antonio, TX: The Psychological Corporation.

Delis, D. C., Kramer, J. H., Kaplan, E., & Ober, B. A. (1994). *CVLT-C: California verbal learning test—Children's version*. San Antonio, TX: The Psychological Corporation.

Denckla, M. B. (1983). The neuropsychology of social-emotional learning disabilities. *Archives of Neurology*, 40, 461–462.

Dietrich, R. B., & Bradley, W. G. (1988). Normal and abnormal white matter maturation. *Seminars in Ultrasound, CT, and MR*, 9, 192–200.

Fisher, N. J., & DeLuca, J. W. (1997). Verbal learning strategies of adolescents and adults with the syndrome of nonverbal learning disabilities. *Child Neuropsychology*, 3, 192–198.

Fisher, N. J., DeLuca, J. W., & Rourke, B. P. (1997). Wisconsin card sorting test and Halstead category test performances of children and adolescents who exhibit the syndrome of nonverbal learning disabilities. *Child Neuropsychology*, 3, 61–70.

Fletcher, J. M. (1989). Nonverbal learning disabilities and suicide: Classification leads to prevention. *Journal of Learning Disabilties*, 22, 176–179.

Fletcher, J. M., Brookshire, B. L., Bohan, T. P., Brandt, M., & Davidson, K. (1995). Early hydrocephalus. In B. P. Rourke (Ed.), *Syndrome of nonverbal learning disabilities: Neurodevelopmental manifestations* (pp. 206–238). New York: Guilford Press.

Foss, J. M. (1991). Nonverbal learning disabilities and remedial interventions. *Annals of Dyslexia*, 41, 128–140.

Fuerst, D. R., & Rourke, B. P. (1993). Psychosocial functioning of children: Relations between personality subtypes and academic achievement. *Journal of Abnormal Child Psychology*, 21, 597–607.

Gardner, M. F. (1996). *Test of Visual Perceptual Skills Revised*. Wood Dale, IL: Stoelting Co.

Goldberg, E., & Costa, L. D. (1981). Hemisphere differences in the acquisition and use of descriptive systems. *Brain and Language*, 14, 144–173.

Gross-Tsur, V., Shalev, R. S., Manor, O., & Amir, N. (1995). Developmental right-hemisphere syndrome: Clinical spectrum of the nonverbal learning disability. *Journal of Learning Disabilities*, 28, 80–86.

Harnadek, M. C. S., & Rourke, B. P. (1994). Principal identifying features of the syndrome of nonverbal learning disabilities in children. *Journal of Learning Disabilities*, 27, 144–154.

Huttenlocher, P. R. (1984). Synapse elimination and plasticity in developing human cerebral cortex. *American Journal of Mental Deficiency*, 88, 488–496.

Huttenlocher, P. R. (1994). Synaptogenesis in human cerebral cortex. In G. Dawson & K. W. Fischer (Eds.), *Human behavior and the developing brain* (pp. 137–152). New York: Guilford Press.

Jastak, J. F., & Jastak, S. R. (1965). *The wide range achievement test*. Wilmington, DE: Guidance Associates.

Johnson, D. J., & Myklebust, H. R. (1967). *Learning disabilities*. New York: Grune & Stratton.

Klin, A., Volkmar, F., Sparrow, S. S., Cicchetti, D. V., & Rourke, B. P. (1995). Validity and neuropsychological characterization of Asperger syndrome: Convergence with nonverbal learning disabilities syndrome. *Journal of Child Psychology and Psychiatry*, 36, 1127–1140.

Kolb, B., & Fantie, B. (1989). Development of the child's brain and behavior. In C. Reynolds & E. Fletcher-Janzen (Eds.), *Handbook of clinical child neuropsychology*. New York: Plenum Press.

Little, L. (2001). Peer victimization of children with Asperger spectrum disorders. *Journal of the American Academy of Child and Adolescent Psychiatry*, 40, 995–996.

MacDonald, G. W., & Roy, D. L. (1988). Williams syndrome: A neuropsychological profile. *Journal of Clinical and Experimental Neuropsychology*, 10, 125–131.

Majovski, L. V. (1989). Higher cortical functions in children: A developmental perspective. In C. Reynolds & E. Fletcher-Janzen (Eds.), *Handbook of clinical child neuropsychology*. New York: Plenum Press.

Mega, M. S., Cummings, J. L., Salloway, S., & Malloy, P. (1997). The limbic system: An anatomic, phylogenetic, and clinical perspective. *The Journal of Neuropsychiatry and Clinical Neurosciences*, 9, 315–330.

Milosky, L. M. (1992). Children listening: The role of word knowledge in language comprehension. In R. S. Chapman (Ed.), *Processes in language acquisition disorders*. St. Louis, MO: Mosby Year Book.

Myklebust, H. R. (1975). Nonverbal learning disabilities: Assessment and intervention. In H. R. Myklebust (Ed.), *Progress in learning disabilities* (Vol. 3, pp. 85–121). New York: Grune & Stratton.

Pelletier, P. M., Ahmad, S., & Rourke, B. P. (2001). Nonverbal learning disabilities and basic phonological processing disorder: Rules of classification and a comparison of psychosocial subtypes. *Child Neuropsychology*, 7(2), 84–98.

Piaget, J. P. (1954). *The construction of reality in the child*. New York: Basic Books.

Piaget, J. P., & Inhelder, B. (1969). *The psychology of the child*. London: Routledge & Kegan Paul.

Rourke, B. P. (1975). Brain-behavior relationships in children with learning disabilities. *American Psychologist*, 30, 911–920.

Rourke, B. P. (1978). Reading, spelling, arithmetic disabilities: A neuropsychologic perspective. In H. R. Myklebust (Ed.), *Progress in learning disabilities* (Vol. 4, pp. 97–120). New York: Grune & Stratton.

Rourke, B. P. (1982). Central processing deficiencies in children: Toward a developmental neuropsychological model. *Journal of Clinical Neuropsychology*, 4, 1–18.

Rourke, B. P. (1987). Syndrome of nonverbal learning disabilities: The final common pathway of white-matter disease/dysfunction? *The Clinical Neuropsychologist*, 1, 209–234.

Rourke, B. P. (1988a). Socio-emotional disturbances of learning-disabled children. *Journal of Consulting and Clinical Psychology*, 56, 801–810.

Rourke, B. P. (1988b). The syndrome of nonverbal learning disabilities: Developmental manifestations in neurological disease, disorder, and dysfunction. *The Clinical Neuropsychologist*, 2, 293–330.

Rourke, B. P. (1989). *Nonverbal learning disabilities: The syndrome and the model*. New York: Guilford Press.

Rourke, B. P. (1993). Arithmetic disabilities, specific and otherwise: A neuropsychological perspective. *Journal of Learning Disabilities*, 26, 214–226.

Rourke, B. P. (Ed.) (1995). *Syndrome of nonverbal learning disabilities: Neurodevelopmental manifestations*. New York: Guilford Press.

Rourke, B. P., Ahmad, S. A., Collins, D. W., Hayman-Abello, B. A., Hayman-Abello, S. E., & Warriner, E. M. (2002). Child clinical/pediatric neuropsychology: Some recent advances. *Annual Review of Psychology*, 53, 309–339.

Rourke, B. P., Bakker, D. J., Fisk, J. L., & Strang, J. D. (1983). *Child neuropsychology: An introduction to theory, research, and clinical practice*. New York: Guilford Press.

Rourke, B. P., & Del Dotto, J. E. (1994). *Learning disabilities: A neuropsychological perspective*. Thousand Oaks, CA: Sage.

Rourke, B. P., & Finlayson, M. A. J. (1978). Neuropsychological significance of variations in patterns of academic performance: Verbal and visual-spatial abilities. *Journal of Abnormal Child Psychology*, 6, 121–133.

Rourke, B. P., & Fisk, J. L. (1992). Adult presentations of learning disabilities. In R. F. White (Ed.), *Clinical syndromes in adult neuropsychology: The practitioner's handbook* (pp. 451–473) Amsterdam: Elsevier.

Rourke, B. P., & Fuerst, D. R. (1991). *Learning disabilities and psychosocial functioning*. New York: Guilford Press.

Rourke, B. P., & Fuerst, D. R. (1992). Psychosocial dimensions of learning disability subtypes: Neuropsychological studies in the Windsor Laboratory. *School Psychology Review*, 21, 360–373.

Rourke, B. P., & Strang, J. D. (1978). Neuropsychological significance of variations in patterns of academic performance: Motor, psychomotor, and tactile-perceptual abilities. *Journal of Pediatric Psychology*, 3, 62–66.

Rourke, B. P., & Strang, J. D. (1983). Subtypes of reading and arithmetical disabilities: A neuropsychological analysis. In M. Rutter (Ed.), *Developmental neuropsychiatry* (pp. 473–488). New York: Guilford Press.

Rourke, B. P., & Tsatsanis, K. D. (1995). Memory disturbances of children with learning disabilities: A neuropsychological analysis of two academic achievement subtypes. In A. D. Baddeley, B. A. Wilson, & F. N. Watts (Eds.), *Handbook of memory disorders* (pp. 501–531). London: Wiley & Sons.

Rourke, B. P., & Tsatsanis, K. D. (1996). Syndrome of nonverbal learning disabilities: Psycholinguistic assets and deficits. *Topics in Language Disorders*, 16, 30–44.

Rourke, B. P., Young, G. C., & Leenaars, A. (1989). A childhood learning disability that predisposes those afflicted to adolescent and adult depression and suicide risk. *Journal of Learning Disabilities*, 21, 169–175.

Rovet, J. F. (1995). Congenital hypothyroidism. In B. P. Rourke (Ed.), *Syndrome of nonverbal learning disabilities: Neurodevelopmental manifestations* (pp. 255–281). New York: Guilford Press.

Smith, L. A., & Rourke, B. P. (1995). Callosal agenesis. In B. P. Rourke (Ed.), *Syndrome of nonverbal learning disabilities: Neurodevelopmental manifestations* (pp. 45–92). New York: Guilford Press.

Steriade, M., McCormick, D. A., & Sejnowski, T. J. (1993). Thalamocortical oscillations in the sleeping and aroused brain. *Science*, 262, 679–685.

Strang, J. D., & Rourke, B. P. (1983). Concept-formation/non-verbal reasoning abilities of children who exhibit specific academic problems with arithmetic. *Journal of Clinical Child Psychology*, 12, 33–39.

Strang, J. D., & Rourke, B. P. (1985a). Adaptive behavior of children who exhibit specific arithmetic disabilities and associated neuropsychological abilities and deficits. In B. P. Rourke (Ed.), *Neuropsychology of learning disabilities: Essentials of subtype analysis* (pp. 302–328). New York: Guilford Press.

Strang, J. D., & Rourke, B. P. (1985b). Arithmetic disability subtypes: The neuropsychological significance of specific arithmetic impairment in childhood. In B. P. Rourke (Ed.), *Neuropsychology of learning disabilities: Essentials of subtype analysis* (pp. 167–183). New York: Guilford Press.

Thatcher, R. W. (1994). Cyclic cortical reorganization: Origins of human cognitive development. In G. Dawson & K. W. Fischer (Eds.), *Human behavior and the developing brain* (pp. 232–266). New York: Guilford Press.

Thompson, S. (1997). *The source for nonverbal learning disorders.* East Moline, IL: LinguiSystems.

Tranel, D., Hall, L. E., Olson, S., & Tranel, N. N. (1987). Evidence for a right hemisphere developmental learning disability. *Developmental Neuropsychology, 3,* 113–120.

Tsatsanis, K. D., Fuerst, D. R., & Rourke, B. P. (1997). Psychosocial dimensions of learning disabilities: External validation and relationship with age and academic functioning. *Journal of Learning Disabilities, 30,* 490–502.

Tsatsanis, K. D., & Rourke, B. P. (1995). Conclusions and future directions. In B. P. Rourke (Ed.), *Syndrome of nonverbal learning disabilities: Neurodevelopmental manifestations* (pp. 476–496). New York: Guilford Press.

Tulving, E., Markowitsch, H. J., Kapur, S., Habib, R., & Houle, S. (1994). Novelty encoding networks in the human brain: Positron emission tomography data. *NeuroReport, 5,* 2525–2528.

Udwin, O., & Yule, W. (1991). A cognitive and behavioral phenotype in Williams syndrome. *Journal of Clinical and Experimental Neuropsychology, 13,* 232–244.

Vandenberg, S. G., & Kuse, A. R. (1978). Mental Rotations, a group test of three-dimensional spatial visualization. *Perceptual and Motor Skills, 47,* 599–604.

Voeller, K. K. S. (1986). Right-hemisphere deficit syndrome in children. *American Journal of Psychiatry, 143,* 1004–1009.

Weintraub, S., & Mesulam, M.-M. (1983). Developmental learning disabilities of the right hemisphere: Emotional, interpersonal, and cognitive components. *Archives of Neurology, 40,* 463–469.

Wilkinson, G. S. (1993). *WRAT3 administration manual.* Delaware: Wide Range.

Woodcock, R. W., McGrew, K. S., & Mather, N. (2001). *Woodcock-Johnson III.* Itasca, IL: Riverside Publishing Company.

## CHAPTER 5

Educational Interventions for the Elementary Age Student in the Therapy Setting

Joan Smith

Gina, a 7 year old with blonde curls surrounding her angelic face, was perched on her knees on a hassock in my office. She had her rear in the air and was peering intently at the underside of the cushion. She looked strikingly like a petticoat clad ostrich with its head buried in a hole. She had completed one item of a digit span test and wandered off before the second item could appear.

Gina was in first grade this year and had not yet developed a reading or spelling system. Her teachers had to work with her individually because she could not stay on task if left unattended. They suggested she needed medication to stay on task. Her parents were concerned that she might have an attention problem and had requested the testing.

Her mother shared: *"We are so worried about Gina. Her teachers think she needs to be medicated so she will pay attention but we really don't like that idea. We don't want her drugged. She is such a happy child and interested in every- thing around her. We thought she would do very well when she went to school even though she always seemed a bit flighty. Her teachers say that unless they sit right with her she does not stay on task and can't finish anything. Even when it is something she likes to do, she is easily distracted."*

Her father added: *"Gina loves to work with me outside. She is a big help. Her teachers say she likes to help around the classroom, too. We are worried about her because this year she is in a combination kindergarten first grade classroom and she is the only first grader. There are two teachers and one of them works with her alone quite a lot. Next year going to second grade will be a big change."*

It would be simple to observe Gina briefly and conclude that she did indeed have an attention problem and possibly a dyslexic learning problem since she was not learning to read despite normal intelligence and considerable instruction. In fact, Gina experienced a complex series of attribute inefficiencies, which created her attention and learning issues.

Although Gina appeared to be impulsive because she wandered off in the midst of a task, she actually experienced a dual attention issue of in-attention and delay in response time. It is likely that the delay in her response time, coupled with a very bright inquisitive nature, caused much of her inattention and subsequent impulsivity. It took Gina at least twice the time it would take another child of her age to process incoming information.

When children experience a delay in response time they can easily appear to be impulsive because they do not mediate stimuli. A simple example of this would be that Roy walks into the kitchen and sees a newly frosted cake on the counter. He loves chocolate cake and immediately cuts a piece. He knows that the family is going to a picnic today but does not make the connection that the cake was prepared as his family's contribution at the picnic. The stimulus—response occurs without thinking through the behavior. This type of behavior places children in difficult circumstances very often because they cannot explain *why* they acted as they did. The response is triggered by the stimulus. The delay in processing prevents them from thinking about what or how to respond. Their behavior appears impulsive. A rapid response time allows children to think through a behavior before or as they are initiating it. The thinking or mediating process creates thoughtful, rule-governed behavior.

Because Gina is not developing a reading system, it was important to look at her memory skills for recall of symbols. Memory assessments showed that Gina held up to three numerals or letters on short-term visual presentation and two items in auditory memory. This is a severely restricted memory attribute for a 7 year old. In order to establish a reading system she will need to be recalling four to five units for short term or inputting memory. Even as Gina's attention focus issues are addressed she will continue to have learning issues until her visual and auditory memory attributes are strengthened.

The lesson to be gained from Gina's profile is that it is important to look at a wide range of attributes in establishing a comprehensive therapeutic intervention for children. Attributes that respond to interventions include the following.

1. Attention. A variety of behaviors or characteristics are included under this heading. The most obvious in the classroom setting is *impulsivity*. This is easy to see because the level of movement, energy, activity, and reactivity is usually exaggerated and inconsistent to the setting. It is usually characterized by difficulty in staying on task or complying with instructions. Interruptive comments, combative responses, or inappropriate verbalizations often draw attention to the child. It is often labeled as *hyperactive*. These children will be very distracted in a stimulating or complex environment, and their behavior responsiveness will escalate with the level of stimulation. This is often best described as *exaggerated reactiveness to stimuli*. A second type of attention issues is seen in children who are characterized as *daydreamers*. These children have difficulty in focusing attention on a task and appear to be distracted by either internal or external thoughts or activities. The *far-away* look in the eye or the pencil poised, as if suspended, over the paper often characterizes this type of inattention. Time on task is a difficulty in this type of *inattention*. They are unable to work for any length of time and sustain the attention to low-stimulus materials or tasks. A third type of attention issue is one that is often masked by impulsive-appearing behaviors and an inability to maintain task focus. It is recognized by the primary characteristic that is a *delay in response time*. This was described in Gina's case. Basically it causes a delay in receiving, evaluating, and formulating an appropriate response to a stimulus. It is characterized by inappropriate responses, a lag in response to stimuli, or frequent changes of the subject. It is very difficult to observe and is measured through a computer-tracking task such as the test of variables of attention (Greenberg, 1996).

2. Memory. The input mode for memory may be visual, auditory, kinesthetic, tactile, taste, smell, or any individual or combination of the sensory modes. Two different types of memory are related to learning issues: (a) short-term memory and (b) long-term memory. Short-term memory is used primarily for inputting information. It is recognized as an electrical trace through the brain and usually is recalled for seconds to hours. Long-term memory is identified as cellular in nature and is

recorded for extended use. Long-term memory is established by repetition, building upon existing information or by novel, unusual experiences. It is very important to evaluate memory skills and build on any inefficiencies for effective and efficient productivity.

3. Language. Reception and expression of language are important skills, which must be considered for a thorough evaluation of learning issues. Although blatant misarticulation in speech is easy to recognize, language difficulties are readily missed. Low levels of communication are often assumed to relate to behavior, shyness, embarrassment, or low intellectual prowess. Language skills often are related to auditory processing inefficiencies and may overlap with auditory memory deficits. Language issues are often observed in student's written work where their internal language appears in writing.

4. Motor skills. Motoric skills are critical for writing, seat sitting, balance, inhibiting early reflexes, and coordination. Students are often described as *clumsy* or *disoriented*. These are good indicators that there are motor coordination issues that may be interfering with learning (Shea, 1993). It is often difficult to discriminate between writing issues which are motor in nature versus related to a slow response time or to visual memory confusion.

5. Executive function skills. The ability to identify a strategy for performing effectively on a task, implementing it, and evaluating its effectiveness is a critical learning skill (Lyon, 1996). Students in third grade and above are assumed to be developing executive function strategies when they are asked to perform on tasks such as writing a paper, studying for a test, taking notes, or preparing a project. The assumption that children under the age of 12 can implement executive function skills without explicit teaching and practice reflects a serious error among our educational systems. Executive function skills correlate with frontal lobe development and should be recognized as control processes (such as withdrawing from one thing to focus on others) (Lyon, 1996).

INTERVENTIONS FOR THE THERAPIST

Attention Skill Development

Interventions for inattention are varied. In the therapy setting interventions may include direct focus training through sustained on-task intervention activities, biofeedback intervention, dietary identification and modification, nutritional supplements, and/or medically prescribed interventions. In addition to these direct interventions, it is consistently appropriate to work with parents, child, and siblings regarding expectations and changes. It is often difficult for a child to make changes, and even small changes need to be recognized and reinforced within the family and school settings.

Interventions that can be used in the therapy setting require the therapist to establish a task or activity for the child. For instance, a good sustained concentration task may be to ask the child to stack several blocks on a piece of paper. The task is to move the paper from one end of a table to the other (5 to 6 feet). Obviously, a few blocks can be moved with good stability, but a stack of six or more blocks must be moved with great care slowly. Develop a chart with the number of blocks across the top and the times beginning with 15-second increments along the side. Chart the times with the child for one block, two blocks, etc.

This task will become frustrating to the child who is accustomed to speeding through a task when the numbers of blocks increase and he must slow the movement of the paper. Work with the child on strategies to accomplish the task and reduce the frustration. Some of the strategies include taking a deep breath before beginning, moving the paper very slowly, and pretending that the paper is very heavy and it has to be pulled very slowly. As the child is accomplishing the task, provide verbal suggestion phrases about being focused: *"You are very focused and concentrating quite nicely. You can feel what it is like to really focus your attention. I see that you have good attention to this task."*

Young children who have serious attention issues often respond to the *check* system. The child learns that when they hear the word *check* they are to assume a specific position and are rewarded for it (Lovaas, 1975). The five-point system that is effective is (1) feet on the floor, (2) seat on the chair, (3) eyes on the speaker, (4) ears on the speaker, and (5) hands on the table. You can *play* the *check* game by telling the children to do anything they want to do until they hear the word *check* and then they need to assume the position. We usually are doing table-top activities with the child and when we want to bring them back to listening we will use *check*. When they come back to attention immediately, they are rewarded with points toward playing a game with the therapist. Although children often work well for prizes, it is our goal to teach them to enjoy interaction with the therapist (or parent or teacher) and would prefer using these for reinforcement. As we are working with a child, he will often assume the *check* posture when it has not been prompted and sit quietly, waiting to be recognized with a point. At that stage children are demonstrating recognition of the desired compliant behavior and are using it to accomplish their own goals.

Older students often benefit from practicing their attention focus during planned interruption tasks. A *planned interruption* might be that the therapist asks the student to read out loud from a story while the therapist attempts to divert their attention. The student is not going to let the therapist disrupt them. We like to set the timer for 1 minute and instruct the student to read from his book and not let us take their power of concentration away. The therapist must gauge the interruptive effort based on the student's ability to stay on task. For instance, the therapist with one student may rattle papers, cough, make "oh" noises, or get up and walk around behind them. With a student who has stronger attention skills, the therapist may talk, tell jokes, touch their book, or other more invasive types of attention disruption. Our students are often laughing as they are reading but they do not stop their reading until the time is up.

This attention training activity may be extended for the student by having him work in a stimulating environment such as a library or hall. The student's focus on task may be charted and he can be given feedback regarding the length of time the attention was sustained. The student and therapist can then begin to plan strategies to extend the time on task with good focused attention.

Therapists may want to trade roles with the child on these activities and model what the behavior should be. The therapist may show how he was focusing on work and continue with it even though the child was moving around the room and being distracting. The therapist will want to verbalize how they are doing it so that the child understands what it takes to be focused. Verbalizing of inner thoughts such as *"I am going to continuing looking at the book and thinking about my topic because I am reading about hound dogs and I need to know where they originated and what their main job was and I can stay focused and do that"* will assist the child in learning how to use his inner voice as an aide in maintaining attention focus.

A coding sheet makes an excellent attention focus exercise medium. A partial page example follows. The student is asked to fill in the numerals that match the symbols at the top of the grid.

The therapist needs to prepare or decide on the *interrupter signal*. This can be a tape that is recorded with a *beep* or other sound that is a signal to

□	–	✓	–	→	☒
1	2	3	4	5	6
→	☒	□	–	✓	☒
–	□	→	✓	–	☒

the student to stop working, record a tally at the top of the sheet, and *immediately* return to task. If a tape is not used, the therapist may provide a verbal signal as the interrupter.

The student begins the coding exercise transferring the information to the boxes on the work page. Whenever the *interrupter signal* is heard, the student marks a tally at the top of the page and returns to work. This exercise teaches the student to return to task quickly from an interruption. This is an important skill in a classroom setting because teachers frequently interrupt the class to give additional instruction, correct one student, or respond to a student. All of the students are drawn off task in these circumstances, but the student with attention issues often remains off task because she is unaccustomed to returning to task immediately. This exercise will retrain this habit and aid the student in becoming focused for sustained periods of work.

Memory Skill Development

The first step toward establishing improved memory skills is identification by assessment. It is important to know the level of memory competence related to input and output of information. The memory strands used most commonly in school include visual > verbal (see and say what was seen, as in reading), visual > motor (see and write, as in copying from the board or book), auditory > verbal (hear and repeat), and auditory >

motor (hear and write, as in taking a spelling test or notes). A variety of simple diagnostic instruments may be used for identifying these skills. The *receptive-expressive observation* (REO) (Smith, 1978, 1999) measures these four channels directly for ages 5 and up through seven digit recall and provides standardized scores for interpretation. A computerized assessment that is competency based, *competency assessment battery* (CAB) (Smith, 1993, 2002), provides memory information in a different format. It separates out visual and auditory memory skills looking at the ability to match to a stimulus item, recall and choose an item from similar items, and recall and select the elements to recreate an item. These are each critical levels of memory, which build from the matching level.

Once memory digit span is identified, programming should be implemented to assure that the student has adequate recall to input information appropriately. Expectations for children below age 6 would be for digit recall and accurate sequencing of up to four digits from visual input and up to five from auditory input. For most students, verbalizing the information will be easier than writing it, and the digit recall is usually one element greater for verbalization than writing. Children age 8 and above should recall at a five digit level. This information is based on standardization studies for test development (Smith, 1978, 1999).

School requirements for digit recall actually exceed the average levels that children achieve. Students subsequently have to develop skills for chaining or grouping multiple digit recall strands in order to remember long words for reading or spelling. Generally, for application of memory, students work at an automatic level at one element below their digit span. If they are at a four digit span in testing, their automatic level will be three digits. While this is not an efficient process, it is a survival skill that successful students utilize until their memory skills increase to a six to seven element level. An example of the challenge that a student may experience is observed with Mary. Mary, a first grader, can recall four letters. When she has to copy a sentence (*The postman delivers mail to our homes*) she has to divide it into many segments. Her visual chunking to write it may look like this as she segments the words: *The/ pos/ tm/ an/ del/ iv/ ers/ mai/ l/ to/ our/ hom/ es.* Because her memory will drop one element, she will be chunking the information at a three digit level. It will require her to track and write with from 11 to 14 fixations in order to record the sentence that another student with a six or seven element memory may write from memory with fewer observations (Smith, 1991, 1996).

Memory skills are easily taught and transitioned when specific steps are observed. First, the therapist will identify the apparent memory inefficiency and whether an input–output pathway is involved. Memory is primarily an *input* issue. If a student experiences difficulty with see–write (visual input–motor output) activities, it does not necessarily mean see–say (visual input–vocal output) tasks will be a problem. It depends on where the memory strand breaks down. The question to answer is *"Does this inefficiency relate to input or output issues?"* If the challenge in this example is in the motor output of writing, then the student may be perfectly comfortable in the see–say task because visual input is working well and it is not a memory issue, it is a motor attribute problem.

Once the memory issue is identified, there are two steps to improving learning skills. The first is to *increase* memory. The second is to teach *how to use* the new memory as a skill and a strategy. Individuals who have not had adequate memory skills at the appropriate developmental levels miss the experiences that help them learn to use memory as a strategy for executive function skills (Smith, 1998).

Increasing Memory

Visual memory skills may be increased with a variety of exercises. The input in the exercises is always visual (seeing) information. Exercises should start at the level of the child or adult.

Beginning Level

Young children or adults with brain interference that has created memory issues begin with pictures, colors, or shapes. They learn to observe the information, have it removed, and then recall it in sequence. The visual input should be rehearsed with using output modes of verbal or written (writing or manipulating of symbol cards). Both modes should be practiced because they each have a different brain pathway (*i.e.*, *visual input —occipital > verbal—temporal > vocalized output—frontal* for visual input > vocal output). The exercise of *observe > remove stimulus > respond* is used throughout the training program.

Primary Level

Children or adults who recognize letter or numeral symbols and have a digit span recall of three or more items practice with the same processing sequence but with letters, numbers, or words. Visual stimuli may be presented on a card, paper, or computer. The stimulus is then removed and the student is asked to verbalize or write (or assemble from letter/-numeral cards) the item that he recalls. Simple drill exercises are useful *only* when they are coupled with a discussion about *how the student is recalling the information.* It is critical to call the student's attention to how he is doing something. He needs to be aware of the strategy that he is using to gain information.

Adults can often provide insights that would be difficult for a child to articulate. For example, a 36-year-old adult with a mild head trauma was working on increasing his auditory memory skills. When he heard a series of numerals and was asked to recall them he had great difficulty. He was observed to squint his eyes, while looking up, and obviously exerting considerable mental energy for the task as he repeated the numbers back slowly and with great effort. After watching him go through this extreme frustration on several items, I could stand it no longer and asked, "How are you doing this?" He explained that he had been told to make mental images of what he heard by a prior therapist. He was attempting to create a mental image of the numbers as he said them to himself and then to read them back to me! I asked him if it might not be easier just to say them outloud and skip the middle step for this task. He was delighted to eliminate his imaging of the symbols and just repeat the information back and jumped quickly in recall from four digits to seven.

We discussed the practical application of his listening memory and when it would be appropriate to use the strategy of visualization, such as when given directions to a new location, listening to a story, or following a lecture. In contrast, if he was recalling a telephone number someone just gave him, there was no point in attempting to visualize it when he could either write it down (motor output) or dial the number. The same type of discussion should occur with younger students.

Memory practice should be done with *planned interference.* Because we do not have many experiences in which we are working in a quiet, totally focused setting, we must be able to use our memory skills in a traditional active environment (classroom, business place, home with family around.)

Interference may include sensory stimulation or manipulation of time. Typical sensory stimulation include the following.

1. Auditory. Require the student to listen to information after hearing or seeing the stimulus. The information may be a joke, an instruction, a phone number, or anything distracting from the stimulus.

2. Visual. Provide the students with visual information in the form of a puzzle, word, picture to study, maze, or other distracter.
3. Motor. Ask the student to perform a sequence of movements, such as walk to the door and tap twice and then return to your chair and tap the seat three times before sitting down.
4. Verbal. Require the student to verbalize information such as his telephone number, address, or information from a category (male names, colors, mammals, etc.)

Time interference usually involves establishing a set time to wait between stimulus and response. The interference may be 5 to 60 seconds. Longer times may be used for working with isolated series of information. An adult might be given a code to recall and to provide it at the end of the session.

Detailed exercises for developing specific input channels and extended memory training exercises are provided in "You Don't Have To Be Dyslexic" (Smith, 1991, 1996). An effective computerized program for increasing memory is produced by Advanced Brain Technologies and is called the *Brain Builder* (Doman, 1997, 2000). It provides excellent attention focus exercises called an intensity activity and three types of memory exercises for both auditory and visual input inefficiency. It should be used with a therapist initially in order to establish appropriate strategy patterns and provide reinforcement for increasing memory.

Although memory appears to be absolutely an automatic skill to people with strong skills, it is very difficult for many children and adults. Memory skill does not relate to intellectual prowess. Some of the brightest children and adults have very specific memory difficulties. They spend considerable time and energy compensating for their inefficiencies. Many are unaware that they have specific inefficiencies in a memory attribute. Others are very aware of frustrations and avoid doing tasks that require a specific skill.

Children often interrupt whoever is speaking or appear to be oblivious that someone is talking when they want to talk. It is appropriate to use the insights gained from working with an articulate adult in order to understand this behavior in our elementary age students.

Brad came for an assessment and therapy at age 42. He wanted to go to college and become a writer. He had attempted to take classes numerous times over the past years but found that he never finished a class. During the memory portion of his assessment it was apparent that he had inefficiencies in his auditory memory. This challenge was very apparent in a conversation with Brad. He frequently interrupted the speaker to insert a thought or comment. When we discussed this behavior, he stated, *"If I don't tell you what I am thinking while you are talking, I will forget it."* He believed that he had to say what he was thinking immediately upon experiencing the thought. He felt he would forget what he wanted to say if he waited for a pause from the speaker.

This articulate gentleman with a very sophisticated vocabulary had considerable frustration with his memory for listening. He had incredible skills in his visual memory but had decided that the visualizations he was experiencing when he was a youngster distracted him from listening. In second grade he *turned off* his visualization ability. He had spent the next 35 years attempting to learn and work with his inefficient auditory system as his primary input mode.

The first exercises with Brad were in beginning to extend his auditory memory beyond the five digit recall he experienced. Simple listen and repeat exercises were used to stimulate his memory function. A sample lesson dialogue would include:

> Therapist: *Brad, I am going to say a series of numbers. Please repeat them back when I have finished. You will know when I am at the end of the sequence because I will drop my voice. You can listen for that clue. 2, 5, 1, 7, 9*
>
> Brad: *2, 5, 1, 7 . . . I can't remember the last one. Was it a nine?*
>
> Therapist: *What do you hear in your inner voice?*
>
> Brad: *I thought I heard a nine. Then I questioned myself and wasn't sure about it. I didn't want to make a mistake and be wrong.*
>
> Therapist: *Perhaps you will do some experimenting with this process. Let yourself relax and give yourself permission to play with different strategies for remembering. Some will probably give you more confidence than others. Remember to use your inner voice to focus on what you are repeating and bracket out any distracting doubts. It will increase your memory immediately.*

Both children and adults become very concerned about being correct. When they experience early memory inefficiencies they tend to think they are going to be wrong. Instead of staying focused on the item or subject they are attempting to remember, they flood their inner language with past fears and haunts: *"I'll never remember this. See, I can't remember like everyone else."* And the most often reported: *"I am so stupid."*

When Brad was ready to increase to the next level we used a doubling technique to assist him in recalling the sequence. He was using his strategy of repeating the item immediately in his inner voice before saying it.

> Therapist: *Brad, it seems that five digits sequences are very comfortable for you and you are ready to experiment with longer sequences. You may want to continue to use*

*your strategy of repeating the information, hearing it in your inner voice, and then
writing it on your paper. Listen, 8, 4, 5, 2, 1, 1, write it.*

Brad: *I think I got it. I wrote 8-4-5-2-1-1.*

Therapist: *How did you recall the sequence?*

Brad: *I repeated it in my head. It seemed like I could hear your voice saying it
to me. It feels good to know I can do this.*

When a student is ready to increase the number of digits in memory,
it is effective to ease him into the longer sequence by doubling the final
items (8-4-1-9-9, recency model), doubling the initial items (8-8-4-1-9,
primacy model), and doubling the internal items (8-4-1-1-9 or 8-4-4-1-
9). Each of these exercises is done with interference, and a comfort level
with this number of items and model is established before moving to a
next step. We must anticipate that younger children will require more
practice and patience than older students. The most important skill is to
understand when to move on and when a student requires additional
rehearsal. An appropriate rule for gauging when to move a student to the
next level is when he can achieve 10 items at a specific digit level with
80% accuracy *and* with interference.

Using Memory Skills

Children who have missed the developmental stage associated with specific memory targets will need to be taught how to use their new
memory competence for processing information. It cannot be assumed
that this transition will occur automatically. Habit patterns and compensating techniques have been in place for the individual for many years
and must be actively replaced with new patterns and strategies.

It would seem that if a child were unable to remember information
and then developed their memory to be sufficient to perform that they
would use it. A good lesson in the need for doing specific transitioning
of a skill was provided by Luci. Luci was a fourth grader who had experienced a serious dyslexic learning style associated with a lag in visual
memory. When she began therapy in third grade she could only recall a
sequence of two symbols with her visual memory. By midfourth grade
she was at a six symbol level in her memory.

During math class Luci was required to copy down the problems from
the book and then work them. Every day she labored over copying the
problems, one symbol at a time, and then had to take the work home to
do for homework. Her one symbol recall for copying was logical for her

two symbol level of memory. When she was able to recall six symbols, I called her teacher to, hopefully, hear that she was no longer having trouble with copying her problems. When I asked how her math was progressing the teacher responded, *"There doesn't appear to be any change. Why, are you working on it?"*

This was, obviously, not what I was hoping to hear. I mumbled something about *"moving in that direction next"* and asked the teacher to let me know when she saw any changes emerging. That afternoon when Luci came in, I gave her a math problem and asked her to copy it and work the problem. She immediately repeated her old habit of copying the problem, one numeral at a time. When she had finished, I asked her to try and *experiment* with me. I had her look at the problem, which involved four single digits (24 + 36), and then visualize it on her paper. She looked for a few seconds and then immediately transferred it to her paper without a second glance at the problem.

When she had finished I suggested that we extend our experiment to her class the next day. I asked if she would use this new strategy of imaging the problem to copy her math problems. She was always enthusiastic for experiments and agreed easily.

At three o'clock the next afternoon I had a phone call from Luci's teacher. She said, *"Luci copied down all the problems in a few moments and completed her paper before class was over. What did you do?"* I confessed to the teacher that *"I made a mistake."* Then, I continued to explain, *"I assumed that she would make the transition using her new memory skills and I was wrong. I had to show her how to use this as a strategy now that she had the memory skill."*

The strategies that must be taught include using inner language skills of visualization and reverbalization. Visualization or imaging skills are a difficult concept to explain to young children. Although they are experiencing imagery in many ways, they are often *unaware* of it. Two effective training techniques may help in establishing this skill.

1. Place three lines on a white board. Ask the student to look at the board while you trace a letter with your finger above each line: <u>c</u> <u>a</u> <u>t</u>. Make the letters slowly and clearly with your finger and say the letter (or sound of the letter) as you trace it. Then return to the first line and ask the student to come up and trace over and say the letter she is imagining on the first line. Continue until she has traced over all the letters. Now work with the image by taking the last letter and moving the image and the line to another part of the board. Ask what letter you just moved.

If she can track the letters and can tell you what the letters are that remain on the first two lines, she is holding the image. Reinforce that she is *imaging* the symbols and *visualizing* the word. Remember to put the letters back together before finishing the exercise.

2. Another imaging exercise asks the student to listen to a description and enjoy the picture it creates. You might say, *"I am going to tell you about a picture I am seeing and I want you to enjoy seeing it also. I see a large tree in the middle of my picture. It is a fat oak tree with sturdy branches and lots of leaves. It must be summer because the leaves are shiny like it is in full bloom. As I study the tree I realize that I can see a bird in a nest on the left side of the tree about half way on the outer edges of a branch. The bird is bright blue and seems to be sitting on a nest made of twigs and leaves. Can you see my picture so far?"* If the student appears to be following the picture, you may want to involve them in building on the imagery by having them add more details to the picture.

These are both very different imaging exercises but they are effective in establishing the concept of imagery. It is important to talk with the student about how an *image* looks. When we use examples such as *seeing a movie, taking a picture,* or similar references, we create the impression that the image is clear, solid, and detailed. In fact, an image is often wispy, transparent, and without detail. The details are added by talking about them and creating the picture. When we add a detail, such as the color of the bird in the prior example, we become aware of it. Students often claim that they cannot visualize because they assume that their wispy, vague images are inadequate forms of visualization. By helping them understand that this is typical of imagery, it will heighten their understanding of this important brain function and increase its usage.

The inner voice is understood more easily because we are more accustomed to *thinking with our voices*. Several steps in an exercise sequence assist in developing inner voice awareness for students, such as the following.

1. Ask the student to count out loud as you clap 15–20 times and tell you how many claps he heard.
2. Ask the student to count by whispering as you clap 15–20 times and tell you how many claps he heard.
3. Ask the student to listen and count *in his brain* as you clap 15–20 times and tell you how many claps he heard.

Once the student is able to do the third step, he is using his inner voice. Ask the students if they were aware of themselves counting with their inner voice. If they need more experience, have them say the letters of the alphabet in sequence to themselves as you tap. Ask them what letter they are on when you stop tapping (6 times, 12 times, etc.).

Students who have had delays in memory development will need to learn *when* to use their memory, visualization, and inner voice skills. They need instruction to visualize spelling words, image a story they are hearing, image a story they are reading, and image following directions. They will not use the skills automatically because they have missed the developmental experiences when this would occur. They did not have the memory skills to support the implementation and compensated by using other strategies, avoided the task, or failed in their attempts.

If they have not learned to use inner voice skills, they will have difficulty in listening. They will have challenges in integrating what they are hearing with what they are seeing. Without integration it is very difficult to take notes, write down assignments, develop a report or composition, and perform the many different tasks assumed to be automatic in a school setting. When we are using our memory skills we will have the resources to support the development of executive function skills.

Language Skill Development

Language is one of our earliest developing skills. Along with motor skill, language awareness is stimulated from birth. Children begin language development with the imitation and vocalization of sounds (ba, ma, da). They rapidly refine their vocalizations to feature individual words (wawa—water, mama, dada, me, up) and then begin to link words in noun verb sets (me go, cookie now, me want, go bye bye). Once the linking of words occurs a rapid change begins, which features talking in phrases and sentences.

There is a difference between language skills and articulation skills. A child may have language but experience articulation, phonology, errors (*Duh bown dog hath duh bawa*—The brown dog has the ball). Although articulation may make the child difficult to understand, the actual sentence structure, syntax, may be appropriate. If the distinction is difficult to determine, a referral for speech and language assessment through the public school or private vendor is beneficial. Specific speech and language assessments will provide the necessary observation, testing, and interventions.

As a therapist working with children with inefficiency in their language attribute it is important to provide several services.

1. Identification of the issue and referral to an appropriate resource for speech and language therapy.
2. Establish expectations regarding communication during therapy.
3. Provide support for communication during therapy.

A professional speech and language specialist will be able to identify the issues surrounding articulation and language expression and reception. The report from the assessment should provide assistance in understanding any modifications or unique expectations that should be included in therapeutic work with the child. Specific issues that may influence communication with the child include memory and response time attribute inefficiencies. When therapy requires dialogue or interaction through word communication, children with either of these issues will experience difficulty. They may appear to be uncooperative or unmotivated. In fact, they have shut down because they are unable to process incoming information—receptive language—at a level that allows appropriate response. They subsequently become confused, lose track of the topic, and experience negative feedback. They will claim to be *bored* by the activity. By definition, *bored*, in this context, usually means. *"I can't follow what you are saying, I can't relate it to anything I know about,* and/or *I am lost and need to feel like I am okay so I will divert you from this topic."* It is very easy to become insulted when told what we are teaching is boring. The appropriate response is to question what is happening, *"Are you saying it is difficult to follow this subject? Are you saying you don't want to talk about (or do) this? Are you feeling lost? Would you feel like you were participating if we changed to another topic?"*

Children may not have the language skills to express themselves adequately. The use of cue cards is often helpful with them. Simple yes, I don't know, and no cue cards may be helpful in these situations. The child merely has to indicate the answer card while they are being asked a series of questions. Sally, a child who had shut down and refused to go to school, emerged with this questioning technique. She was identified as having auditory processing issues and did not talk about feelings readily. She seemed to have difficulty in formulating her thoughts. In limiting the choices for responses she was able to focus on the issue and we could target the solution. Her dialogue illustrated this technique in the following sequence:

> Therapist—*Hi, Sally. Did you go to school today?* (no response) *I hear you stayed in school all day.* (no response) *Did you enjoy playing with your friends?* (no eye contact, shrugs shoulders.) *Sally, I have three cards here. This one says yes, this*

one says I don't know, because sometimes we really don't know or can't think of a response, and this one says no. Now, just to experiment with using these, show me the one that says yes. (Points to card and quickly looks away.) *Good job, Sally. You got a point! Every time you point to a card as an answer, you get a point. When you have 15 points, we will play a game that you can choose for 5 minutes. Are you ready?* (Points to yes and watches to see if she is given a point.) *Okay!*

Sally—*What you ask?*

Therapist—*Well, most of these are too easy for you, like the first one. Did you go to school today?*

Sally—Points to yes.

Therapist—*Yes, you get another point. Let me see, oh, I know, did you play with your friends today?*

Sally—Points to no, eyes downcast.

Therapist—*Another point, wow, you have four points already! Okay, next question, is having friends important to you?*

Sally—Points to no, then looks up and points to yes.

Therapist—*Another point for you, now we have five! Okay, next one. Do you want to have friends at school?*

Sally—Points to I don't know.

Therapist—*Nice job, another point for you. I am looking forward to our game.* (Sally smiles.)

At this point we are carrying on two parallel conversations. One in the present about the points and another about what was happening at school today. As this interaction continued, Sally revealed that the other girls were teasing her because she "talked funny." She was afraid to talk in front of them, shut down her language expression, and did not want to go to school. Once she had revealed the issue she abandoned the cards and began to talk about her feelings and distress. We talked about a plan to handle her needs and she became very cooperative. It appeared that having an ally who understood her was a new experience and she had so much to share.

Some children limit their language or shut down because they are overwhelmed by sound sensitivity. These children appear to have hyperacuity. They will often complain about the loud lights, the clock ticking, or other environmental sounds of which few are aware. Classroom or family activities are distressful for them and they often act out or shut down. When we talk in a normal voice volume, they feel like we are yelling at them. These children respond very well to a quiet therapeutic environment and a very soft, quiet voice with a low volume. They will immediately engage in eye contact and communicate because they have found someone who understands what they need. This is a frequent issue with children who were born with fetal alcohol syndrome or who experienced maternal drug use in utero. They appear to have other neurologically based issues, including clumsiness, tactile defensiveness, or sensory confusion.

It is often difficult to *hear* language problems unless we are alerted to their existence. Children learn very early to mask their speech by using short phrases for responses or slang phrases. Sara, a sixth-grade girl, consistently tells me to *hang on* whenever she cannot think of an answer or needs time to correct herself. She kind of *blurts it out* as though I am doing something wrong or moving inappropriately fast. It is her way of saying, *"I am not getting this and need more time to figure it out."* She will benefit from addressing her communication skills. Several of the following exercises that are effective for her also benefit other students with language inefficiencies.

Echo Technique

This technique begins with the selection between the student and the therapist of an interesting story, novel, or article. The therapist instructs the student that they are going to listen to the story and repeat what they hear. The therapist reads the story to the student in short phrases. The length of the phrase must be adjusted to the auditory memory level of the student. It will become apparent quickly if the phrases are too long because the student will be unable to echo them back. Most students with learning issues can begin with three-word phrases.

As the student becomes adept at repeating the information, the therapist can increase the length of the phrases until they are repeating 7- to 10-word sentences. This provides the student with practice in speaking in appropriate phrases and with fluency. The therapist models vocal expression by adding emphasis to important words and varying the voice volume and tone.

This is a simple technique to teach parents to practice between sessions and can be used with the student's school materials, as well as recreational books. It has the added benefit of enhancing comprehension for listening and reading development (Smith, 1998).

Sentence Strips

With minimal preparation ahead, the therapist can create sentences on the computer with a 20 point type font. Each sentence is then cut into phrases and words and clipped together. The task for the student will be to take the sentence and put it back together so that it makes sense. Most sentences can be reassembled in at least two ways and the student is encouraged to find more than one solution. For instance: *The cat was very tired after climbing the tree. Was the cat very tired after climbing the tree? After climbing the tree, the cat was very tired.* The activity of exploring other ways of putting the words together is an important learning experience. It provides an opportunity to dialogue about how words work together, syntax, and develop a familiarity of appropriate language.

Written Language

Students who have developed good skills in concealing their language inefficiencies by minimizing their expression are identified easily when they express themselves in writing. Writing samples can be elicited by providing pictures or story stems. When the student is provided with a topic or stimulus to use in writing the first challenge in writing is avoided—*trying to decide what to write about.* The picture or story stem provides the stimulus but it is helpful to the student to talk about it before beginning. If the student needs words spelled they can be recorded and the student will feel more confident in approaching the task. The intent of the exercise is not to evaluate spelling or punctuation but instead to look at the syntax.

There are a variety of good materials for the therapist to use to stimulate writing efforts. One program that is available on computer disk or workbook format is provided by Critical Thinking Press and is called *Editor in Chief* (Baker, 2002). This program is effective in exploring language development and in improving written language.

Motor Skill Development

Clumsy, uncoordinated, or last one chosen for teams—all of these describe the child with motor skill issues. These refer to large motor skills and are identified easily in observing a child's gait, posture, and movement through space. Serious issues with large motor coordination tend to be referred to the physical or occupational therapist for evaluation and therapy. Mild coordination issues may become part of the therapy program in conjunction with other learning issues.

Large Motor Coordination Training

Specific exercises for improving large motor coordination should begin with cross-lateral movements. Two exercises that are very useful come from different sources: *Edu-K for Kids*, Dr. Paul Dennison (1990), and *Infinity Walk*, Dr. Deborah Sunbeck (2002). Both of these authors and therapists encourage doing movements that require left arm–right leg and right arm–left leg alternating movements. Dennison has multiple training books and most of them train students to march in place and touch a hand to the opposite knee as they are marching. Left hand to right knee and then right hand to left knee. This activity stimulates both sides of the brain with good activity going across the corpus callosum, which hosts the transfer of messages from one side of the brain to the other. It also stimulates the motor area of the brain. Younger children who have difficulty doing this *cross crawl* movement often benefit from having a sticker put on the top of their right hand and the same sticker on their left knee. The job is to match up the two stickers by putting the right hand on the sticker on the left knee, thus creating the pattern for the movement.

Infinity Walk exercises ask the student to walk a figure eight (infinity sign) path while performing other integrated movements, such as swinging arms in opposition to the legs, tapping the fingers in a pattern, and performing cognitive exercises. This series of exercises appears to engage multiple brain territories as well as left/right brain integration. Students frequently report that they can feel their brain *heat up* when they are doing this activity. It appears to stimulate blood circulation in the brain. This series of exercises is especially powerful when children are upset about something that has happened. If they can walk the pattern as they are telling about the problem it appears to engage their cognitive reasoning very effectively and they engage in rationale thinking and problem solving.

Children who have difficulty with a cross crawl movement may need to begin their exercises with angels in the snow described by Belgau in *A Perceptual Motor and Visual Perception Handbook of Developmental Activities* (1970) and Roach and Kephart in the *Purdue Perceptual Motor Survey* (1966). This activity is reminiscent of children playing in the snow. It is named after the observation that when one lies in the snow and slides his arms over his head and opens his legs in and out the image of an angel remains when he leaves. This movement is used in therapy to develop the child's ability to move parts of the body separately, smoothly, and in synchrony or opposition to other parts of the body. The activity starts with the child lying on his back on the floor or mat with legs closed and arms touching the side of the body. A typical exercise is to ask the child to move his arms over his head, sliding them on the floor until they are up by his ear on each side. Then return to the starting position. Oppositional movements might include moving the right arm and left leg or left arm and right leg. Lateral movements would include moving the limbs on one side while keeping the other side still. When observing these exercises, the therapist is looking for the ability to work one limb without initiating movement from the opposite limb, move left and right side, simultaneously, and move upper limbs while lower limbs remain still. Physical prowess in large motor skills benefits when these skills are in place.

Fine Motor Skills

Handwriting, drawing, and finger dexterity issues are all apparent when the attribute of fine motor coordination is inefficient. The symptom of poor handwriting should be explored to understand the etiology. The inefficient attribute may be fine motor control, visual memory confusion, or slow response timing. No matter what the attribute is that is creating the issue, it is likely that the child will be resistive to engaging in writing behaviors. By identifying the underlying issue, a therapeutic approach can be designed that will reduce the stress the child is experiencing and assist them to reengage in developing writing skills.

Serious fine motor issues are usually assisted by the occupational therapist. There are a series of evaluations that will assist in identifying the extent of the motor issues and programming required for resolution. More basic issues may be addressed during the therapeutic intervention with other academic activities.

Simple patterns of movement will improve the coordination for handwriting. Patterns might include a series of cursive letters such as m, u, i, or l's. The pattern hooks the letters together, creating a smooth repetitive movement. These are initiated most appropriately on a white board (chalk board) and then transferred to paper and pencil when the pattern skill is in place. The therapist can guide the child's hand in developing the pattern more readily at the board.

The child who is experiencing frustration because she cannot visually image the letter to the paper has a different type of attribute inefficiency.

She will need to learn to image the letter by studying it, tracing it, and then imaging it in another location on the paper (or board). It is often necessary to start with simple shapes before working with complex letter or numeral patterns. These activities will need to be repeated and rehearsed on a daily basis to establish the necessary image memory and motor pattern recall for written comfort.

Executive Function Skills

The fourth-grade teacher knows that Jane's mother will be waiting outside the classroom door for the children to exit at the end of the school day. She will come in and check the chalkboard for the homework assignments and go to Jane's desk. She will need to mow through papers, books, and objects that Jane has collected to find the books she needs. Jane will be pulling on her mother and telling her *"Come on, it's time to go."* It is apparent that Jane has not developed her executive function skills yet. She does not write down her assignments and does not leave the classroom with the materials she will need to do her homework. She does not organize her materials in her desk. She survives in fourth grade with her mother's constant support. Her teacher feels that Jane should be doing this herself and that she is never going to learn if her mother keeps doing it for her.

Somewhere in the middle ground between the teacher's judgement versus the mother's action is the child who has not matured in her frontal lobe development with the executive function skills she needs. This maturation is likely to occur during the next 4 years, between ages 10 and 14. The reality in our education system today is that children are being asked to perform independent executive function skills for which they do not have the necessary maturation. When the skills are not emerging naturally, then they need to be taught.

The teacher's recommendation to *require that Jane do it herself* is nonproductive. If Jane understood how to organize her work on her own the problem would not exist. Failing her for her lack of understanding and capability to perform independently further complicates the problem by diminishing Jane's self-esteem. The mother organizing for Jane is productive for the mother, but possibly not for Jane. At least, with the mother's approach, Jane is getting her homework done and is not flunking her classes. The mother does not have to call classmates and return to school to try to get the materials.

Executive function skills are best taught through a system analysis. In other words, the skills need to analyzed and broken down into the basic steps. Jane, her mother, and therapist would sit down and discuss the goal—getting home with her homework assignment and materials. Jane would be asked to help everyone understand where the hurdles are for her in performing this task.

Some children will say that they do not have *time* to copy down the information. Others will report that they *forget* to copy down the information. A few will say they do not *want* to copy it down and do not want to do homework. These are all valid feelings and observations and need to be acknowledged with listening.

Next, the mother will be asked to share her feelings about how things are working. Jane will benefit from hearing her mother's frustration and her desire that Jane become capable and will be able to do this herself. The mother can be asked how she is modeling this expectation for Jane. It is likely that she thinks that by doing it for Jane, she is showing her how to do it. At this point the mother often recognizes that she is not actively modeling it for Jane.

The therapeutic technique of identifying strategies by enlisting the participation of both Jane and the mother is very effective. The therapist can model with questioning and recording the information: *What has to happen first? What happens next* and so on. It is important for Jane to begin to verbalize the sequence and an understanding of the task.

It is important to get Jane's agreement to engage in the process she has just identified. The first step may be as simple as putting her books on top of her desk. As this becomes consistent behavior for Jane, the second step may be activated—copying the assignment from the board before the mother arrives. Finally, the third step in the planning strategy would be leaving the classroom with the assignment and her books.

As Jane takes each of the steps toward independence, it is crucial that she be reinforced with recognition of her independent behavior. Teacher, mother, and therapist may all be part of the cheerleading team recognizing and verbalizing Jane's progress. At this point Jane has participated in the process of developing an executive function skill—the questions that the therapist may encourage Jane to use to establish this process include:

1. What do I want to accomplish?
2. What is my plan–strategy to make this work?
3. Am I using my plan?

4. Is my plan being effective?
5. Should I change my plan to make it work more effectively?
6. What other activity do I do where this strategy (plan) would work?

When children have not developed executive function skills it is important to begin teaching them the process needed to accomplish the goal. There are a variety of expectations in our schools that assume the existence of skills in planning and organizing. Common examples are a state project, Indian tribe paper, mission building project, science fair project, studying for spelling words, studying for a test, writing an essay, and so on. In many classrooms it is assumed that the children have the skills necessary to perform these tasks. In most homes it is the parents who are structuring, teaching, and organizing these projects. The fact that the child comes to school with the completed work reinforces the schools assumption that these are appropriate and realistic assignments.

If a child is expected to perform with executive function skills it will be necessary to teach the steps and process to the child because he may not have the luxury of waiting for maturation to complete the cycle. The six steps for analysis of the task are effective guidelines for the therapist in initiating this process.

One mother who was home schooling her 11-year-old son, Mike, decided to begin to teach him about strategies. He had difficulty in completing his work and tended to spend most of the time distracting himself from doing his work. She began by having him locate the dictionary definition of *strategy*. They decided that *having a plan for achieving a goal* was a good working definition but they added their own description: *"A good strategy is like a good tool. Using it helps us get the job done well."*

She then asked her son five questions as follows.

1. What is your goal? (She adjusted the questions to his response that he wanted to complete his work more quickly and ccurately and have more time to do other things.)
2. Why do you want to get your work done fast?
3. Why do you want to get 100%?
4. How can you get your work done fast?
5. How can you get 100%?

She wrote Mike's answers to these questions on a dry-erase board. She reported that she helped him brainstorm a little, but left his answers unedited. After establishing the goal and *why* it was important she asked him *how* he would achieve his goal. He identified a number of things that would help him stay on task but mostly he thought of the things he should not do, such as drumming his pencil on the table.

Between them they discussed some of the strategies that would help. She introduced some alternatives, and he chose those that he thought would work for him. Then Mike agreed to use these diligently during his math lesson all week. She had charted him unobtrusively the prior week and had identified that during his math session he was off task 34 times. She noted that even though she is his mother and works with him everyday, she was shocked to note how often he was off task. She commented, "No wonder we are both exhausted at the end of our school day!"

The next day Michael wrote his strategies on the board and verbalized how he would use each one. Then he began his math lesson. She continued to chart and found that he was off task one time as compared to 15 times the prior Monday. At the end of the week he had six tallies for being off task. She reported, *"Mike was amazing. I expected improvements but not the drastic modification that became apparent within the first 10 minutes. He sat at his desk working quietly, staying completely on task for 20 minutes. It was if his loose energies had merged and he was impelled toward a magnet. He knew* what *he was doing and* why *and he knew exactly* how *to do it. I felt as if, finally, he was able to tap into his inner resources. All of his goodness and potential had found a channel through which to emerge and there he was—calm, focused and triumphant!"*

Learning attributes must be taught when they do not emerge naturally at the appropriate developmental level or when the demands of the environment require that they are in place prior to development. The benefits for teaching these skills are observed with the emergence of a competent, effective learner who experiences success in school and self-esteem.

REFERENCES

Amen, D. G. (1998). *Change your brain, change your life.* New York: Random House, Inc.

Baker, M. (2002). *Editor in chief.* Seaside, CA: Critical Thinking Books and Software.

Belgau, F. (1970). *Handbook of developmental activities.* Port Angeles, WA: Balametrics, Inc.

Dennison, P. (1990). *Edu-K for kids.* Ventura, CA: Edu-Kinesthetics, Inc.

Doman, A. (2000). *Brain builder.* Denver, CO: Advanced Brain Technologies.

Greenberg, L. M., & Kindschi, C. L. (1996). T.O.V.A. test of variables of attention. St. Paul, MN.

Klob, B., & Whishaw, I. Q. (1985). *Fundamentals of human neuropsychology*. New York: Freeman.

Lovaas, O. I. (1975). Attention training in the school: Compliance techniques. Lecture presented at the annual Behavior Modification Techniques Conference. University of California, Los Angles.

Lyon, G. R., & Krasnegor, N. (1996). *Attention, memory and executive function*. Baltimore: Paul Brookes.

Lyon, G. R., & Rumsey, J. M. (1996). *Neuroimaging*. Baltimore: Paul Brookes.

Roach, E. G., & Kephart, N. (1966). *Purdue perceptual motor survey*. San Antonio, TX: The Psychological Corporation.

Shea, C. H., Shebilske, W. L., & Worchel, S. (1993). *Motor learning and control*. Englewood Cliffs, NJ: Prentice Hall.

Smith, J. M. (1996). *You don't have to be dyslexic*. Carmel, CA: Learning Time Publications.

Smith, J. M. (1998). *Learning victories*. Carmel, CA: Learning Time.

Smith, J. M. (1999). *The receptive-expressive observation*. Carmel, CA: Learning Time Publications.

Smith, J. M. (2002). *The competency assessment battery*. Carmel, CA: Learning Time Publications.

Sunbeck, D. (2002). *The complete infinity walk*. New York: The Leonardo Foundation Press.

Zimmerman, M. (1996). *The ADD nutrition solution*. New York: Henry Holt and Company.

## CHAPTER 6

Educational Interventions for the Adolescent Student in the Therapy Setting

Chris A. Zeigler Dendy, Aubrey H. Fine and Joan Smith

Chris is an 11th grader in a public high school. He was diagnosed as having attention deficit/hyperactive disorder (ADHD) when he was in third grade. Like many students with ADHD, Chris is a very bright student. He does well on most of his tests. Nevertheless, his final grades on most of his classes are very poor. His major pitfalls are organization and prioritization (executive function skills.). He does not seem to be capable of finishing what he starts. He gets overwhelmed with small details and very often copes by avoiding or not completing assignments. As noted earlier, all of these behaviors are impacted by his weaker executive functioning.

However, Danielle is a 10th grader in a private high school. Early in elementary school she was identified as having an auditory processing disorder as well as significant reading comprehension challenges. Although the parents were cautioned that she would have benefited from special education, the parents declined. They believed that with proper outside support she would adapt. Unfortunately, that optimal outcome did not occur. Education has continued to be demanding for Danielle. Attending school and completing all her assignments have become relentless. Danielle GPA is about a 1.4. In most instances, like Chris, Danielle copes by avoiding and denying. There is no question that she wants to do better, but she appears lost in knowing how. In her case, just trying harder will not do. She has a legitimate barrier and she needs to learn more efficient study strategies. To further complicate matters, Danielle's support team members (parents and teachers) are not utilizing optimal strategies to enhance her progress.

These two case examples represent some of the real hardships that teens with ADHD/learning disorder (LD) face on a daily basis. Although the names may be different, the outcomes for many teens with ADHD/LD, who have not learned compensatory strategies, are about the same. They struggle to keep pace with their classmates and are often misunderstood by their teachers and parents. Some of the teens are considered lazy and are treated harshly. Often, uninformed parents and teachers believe that these students should be capable of overcoming their deficits and do not realistically evaluate the magnitude of ADHD or LD in this era of time. To make matters worse, these challenges in learning are compounded, with normal teenage hardships (peer challenges and other social constraints).

This chapter focuses on strategies (both interventions and accommodations) to aid a student in becoming a more competent student. Interventions are those strategies that are applied to enhance or strengthen skills, while in most case accommodations are used to avoid putting pressure on the weak skill. Efforts will be made to provide the reader with practical solutions to educational challenges. We realize that clinicians are not tutors, but as members of the front-line support team, they can provide valuable insight and suggestions to ameliorate the difficulties. The following provides the reader with a basic overview of the major components within the chapter.

1. Introduction.
2. Educational philosophy guiding educational interventions.
3. Characteristics of the adolescent learner with specific learning disabilities (SLD) or ADHD.
4. Attributes and symptoms that impact learning.
5. Educational interventions, including attention training, strategies for executive functioning, and strategies for common educational problems.

INTRODUCTION

Traditionally, therapists leave educational matters in the hands of school officials. After all, is not educating students really the teacher's job? Practical knowledge regarding learning disabilities and ADHD varies widely among mainstream educators. For example, some educators lack information regarding effective accommodations for LD or ADHD. Sadly, some teachers still do not believe that ADHD even exists. Furthermore, they may not be aware of some of the more subtle aspects of LD and ADHD, e.g., the impact of executive functions on academic performance. In addition, new information (watch for 2002 revisions to IDEA) from major changes in law such as the requirements for functional behavior assessments and positive behavioral intervention plans in the 1997 revisions to IDEA take significant time before filtering down from the federal level to each individual school. Unfortunately, some educators are not acquainted with this broad source of information, and parents turn to therapists to find solutions.

Unfortunately, some educators are not aware of the latest research about learning issues that are unique to this population. For example, many teachers view the behaviors that are characteristic of ADHD, such as forgetfulness and disorganization, as simply a matter of choice or laziness. Thus they fail to recognize that these problems are often linked to deficits in *executive functions*. Consequently, many teachers and parents punish students for these behaviors that are actually DSM-IV characteristics of the condition. Yet punishment only teaches students what not to do, it does not teach them the proper skill or behavior they should use (Jordan, 2000). Sometimes we must educate teachers to this truth. Just as teenagers with a math deficit must be taught the information and skills they lack, a child with SLD, ADHD, and/or an executive function deficit must also be taught (1) specific academic skills, (2) compensatory skills, or (3) be given accommodations.

The bottom line is that the therapist cannot assume that their client's academic needs are being met by the school system. So how do we go about ensuring academic success for our clients? Ideally, when a student is struggling at school, a therapist will accompany parents to meetings with school officials to determine their level of awareness and make suggestions for correcting problem situations. If the school is not well informed, then a key element of the therapist's job is to educate them and request accommodations needed to help the student succeed academically. Because parents are often intimidated and outnumbered at school meetings, the therapist also serves a key role as an effective advocate on behalf of the teenager and family. This chapter focuses on suggestions that a clinician can provide teens in various academic areas. We realize that therapy is not tutoring, but feel that clinicians can give great input and support.

EDUCATIONAL PHILOSOPHY GUIDING ACADEMIC INTERVENTIONS

Before discussing specific intervention strategies, it is important to briefly discuss the educational philosophy that should guide these academic interventions. Because these students are 2 to 4 years developmentally behind their peers, adults must provide *developmentally appropriate supervision* (Zeigler Dendy, 2000). In other words, parents must provide greater support and supervision as would be expected for a younger age group. It is important for therapists to give parents permission to be involved at this more intensive level of supervision rather than admonishing them for being too involved.

Parents and treatment professionals must teach these students missing skills by beginning at the student's current level of performance. In other words, parents and treatment professionals must *shape* the desired behavior by taking small steps and moving the student toward mastery of a new skill. Dr. Russell Barkley reminds us that behavioral intervention strategies are not particularly effective at changing behavior long term. This brings to mind the insightful quote from Michael Gordon, "Students with ADHD know what to do, but they don't always do what they know." However, there are some things we can do to maximize the effectiveness of our interventions. First of all, one of the most important tips is to make the learning process as concrete and visual as possible. These students are more likely to remember facts and concepts that they can see, touch, manipulate, or talk about. If the student is eligible for special accommodations pursuant to IDEA or Section 504, several suggestions are listed in this section that could be incorporated in the IEP or 504 plan.

It may be a good idea for the therapist to accompany the parent to the IEP or Section 504 planning meeting. In fact, the therapist and parent should consider developing a draft IEP complete with learning issues and possible accommodations before the meeting. Some of the most helpful accommodations are (1) extended time on assignments and tests, (2) having a copy of the class notes, (3) use of a calculator or grid for math facts, (4) using a child's affinities in areas where they can enhance a strength, (5) scaffold where appropriate to provide temporary solutions for students to function effectively, and (6) shortening homework assignments. Of course, the student must be experiencing some difficulty to be eligible for these accommodations. For example, a student with slow processing speed would be eligible for shortened assignments and extended time on tests if needed. Furthermore, this chapter highlights various strategies to implement a viable IEP or a 504 plan, including utilizing the ISS form developed by Flynn and Kotkin (2000).

The therapist mayh also consider modifying some of these same teaching strategies for use by students and parents. Unfortunately, because of the need for daily supervision, parents are frequently called upon to be teachers too, especially when their teenager is struggling in school. The suggestions in the following paragraphs could be especially helpful to parents as they help their teen achieve academic success. Of course there may be situations where parent involvement in school work may cause serious family conflicts. In that case, the therapist may have to assist in developing alternative strategies, such as hiring an academic coach or possibly a local college student who might be willing to help monitor school work.

Sometimes assistive technology can be beneficial to the students by helping them with organizational, memory, and hand-writing problems, e.g., laptop computers, books on tape, or pocket personal computers. Local libraries have information on applying for the books on tape program. If needed, assistive technology needs should be written into the student's IEP or Section 504 plan.

Clinicians should encourage parents to add a LD/ADHD mentor to the support team. Over the years we have had great success encouraging parents to get mentors to help the students stay on top of their work. Although we are utilizing the term mentors, coaches is the more acceptable term. However, we have found that college students and other paraprofessionals can be trained to be aware of how to best support a teen with LD/ADHD. Therefore, for families who do not have certain resources, they can still get someone who can aid them in monitoring and supporting their child. Coaches can help teens by creating practical strategies so that the adolescents can be more effective in their daily lives. Whitworth et al. (1998) pointed out that in coactive coaching the relationship is focused entirely on getting the results that the client determines. The client has a great say in setting the agenda and goals. Hallowell and Ratey (1994) suggested that the coaches "keep the players focused on the task at hand and offer encouragement along the way". Our major difference with this definition is that a mentor will not only help the teen focus on the goal at hand, but will also model and teach strategies that will aid the learner in becoming a more efficient and reliable student.

CHARACTERISTICS OF THE ADOLESCENT LEARNER WITH SLD OR ADHD

Traditional and nontraditional learning problems and related mental health issues often impact the student's academic performance and are common among this population. Although most researchers (Barkley, 1998) conservatively report that 3–5% have an attention deficit, more recent research by the Mayo Clinic (7.5%) and Dr. Mark Wolraich (12.4%) place it significantly higher. According to researchers at the CDC (2002), 50% of all students have learning disabilities. In one study, Mayes and Calhoun (2000) reported that the majority of students with learning disabilities (SLD) also have ADHD (82%). Although Barkley (1998) reported data showing that only 25% of students with ADHD also have learning disabilities, Mays and Calhoun (2000) placed rates much higher, at 70%. These researchers speculate that this discrepancy might be explained by the failure of earlier researchers to evaluate for learning disabilities in written expression, which is very common among students with ADHD.

Currently, students with learning disabilities or ADHD may be diagnosed with one of these seven specific learning disabilities, as established in IDEA, the federal education law: (1) oral expression, (2) listening comprehension, (3) written expression, (4) basic reading skills, (5) reading comprehension, (6) mathematics calculation, and (7) mathematical reasoning. Unfortunately, it is not uncommon for the diagnosis of these learning problems to be overlooked. In some cases the learning issues may cause serious problems yet not be severe enough to meet strict special education eligibility criteria.

To further complicate matters, other serious conditions may also cooccur with SLD or ADHD. According to the recent landmark National Institute of Mental Health study (1999) on ADHD, **two-thirds of children with ADHD have at least one other coexisting problem**, such as depression or anxiety. Obviously, these coexisting conditions have a significant impact on learning and must also be identified and treated.

Of the seven specific learning disabilities, here are the most common academic skills that cause students with ADHD to struggle: (1) written expression (65%), (2) math, especially math computation (12–30%), (3) reading (8–39%), and (4) spelling (12–27%). In addition, teachers and parents often report that there are two major reasons why these students do poorly in school: disorganization and forgetfulness often result in the student's failure to remember, complete, and turn in (1) homework and (2) long-term projects.

Surprisingly enough, the student's intelligence and academic skills may be well above average, yet he or she may still be failing classes. This fact has baffled parents, teachers, and treatment professionals for years, especially when an intellectually gifted student teeters on the brink of school failure. Recently researchers may have solved part of this challenging puzzle; deficits in *executive function* often interfere with a student's ability to succeed in school. For example, completion of homework and special projects requires memory and organizational skills, which are critical elements of executive function. As would be expected, the very symptoms of ADHD, forgetfulness and disorganization, wreak havoc on the student's academic performance. This may explain why bright students with ADHD can struggle so terribly in school. Specific strategies for addressing executive function deficits are provided in a subsequent section later in the chapter.

Specific Symptoms of Teens with ADHD: A Quick Review

Adolescent behavioral challenges are complicated by a heightened sensitivity to peers and social pressures. The symptom of *impulsivity* continues to drain the child. It may take the form of showing off, making inappropriate or untimely remarks, interrupting learning situations, and/or entertaining peers. It appears to be a choice that the student is making, although it is more an inability to inhibit the choice than to initiate one. Typically restlessness replaces hyperactivity in adolescence. In many ways we believe that it is one of the reasons why doctors often say that a teen outgrows hyperactivity. We believe it just gets displaced. The excessive motor movement may be channeled into skateboarding or other sports activities which are acceptable. It will likely still be apparent in the classroom with continual shifting in the seat, a need to move around, or fidgety behaviors such as drumming a pencil or tapping a foot.

Although *daydreaming* behavior may continue into adolescence, it is often misconstrued as more lethargic or apathetic behavior. A student may be characterized as having low motivation, not trying, or uninterested. In fact, this is the continuing issue of *inattention*.

The slow response time does not disappear as students enter adolescence. It continues to create havoc for the student. Response speed issues may appear to have an impulsive component with characteristic types of behavior goofs, such as *acting without thinking*. The impulsive nature will have become chronic for the student and will be difficult to distinguish from classical impulsivity. The different components of attention should be measured through a good continuous response task.

Memory

Visual and auditory memory skills may continue to be a challenge for the adolescent. Visual memory issues will be apparent as correlated with a difficulty in spelling and inaccuracy in word attack. The student will be observed to make frequent word-calling errors such as saying "*family*" for familiar or "*from*" for form. Auditory memory issues will be apparent in inefficient reading comprehension, following of assignments or instruction, and peer interactions. It is likely that both short term and long-term memory function may be involved. Students may have compensated for short term recall but will not be able to mask the longer retention issues.

Motor Skills

By the adolescent years, students have either developed keyboarding skills to compensate for fine motor issues or developed intensive avoidance issues related to writing. If they have found it difficult to write during the initial 6 to 7 years of school, they often will refuse to participate on assignments requiring written performance. Their handwriting will appear *frozen* at mid-second grade with awkward printed-letter formations.

Large or gross motor skills may continue to be a challenge for some students. They may avoid physical education activities or refuse to dress out. The avoidance behavior should be evaluated carefully to identify the underlying etiology and recognition.

Self-esteem and Impact School Failure

The adolescent as a student has experienced years of struggling to learn. He has probably developed many avoidance behaviors, inappropriate habits, or learned to compensate in order to avoid being cited for his lack of learning strengths. While it will be essential to teach him to develop appropriate learning attributes, it is also important to address the student's image of *self*. Learning to distinguish between Sally the math student and Sally the person is important for the adolescent's sense of perspective. Failure in school unfortunately makes it difficult to motivate a teen to continue trying. It is hard to encourage students to take risks or make a commitment when their reservoirs of academic successes are limited. As noted in Bear et al. (1991) numerous research studies on self-esteem and children with ADHD and LD indicate that many of these youngsters become victims to academic failure and are likely to have an unhealthy self-esteem. Overall, a majority of research paints a pessimistic picture. Nevertheless, we must help the teens evaluate the efficacy of their efforts by getting them to realize that there will be a payoff at the end of the road. We have to help them begin to appreciate their assets and recognize that everyone has individual differences. Fine (2000) makes a point to explain to teens that all youth thirst knowledge but get to the fountain in a different way. This metaphor enables teens to recognize that they are not as different as they imagine themselves to be. It is our ultimate role as clinicians to help our clients develop strategies that enable them to quench their thirst of knowledge and to avoid frustration.

It is crucial to therefore have in place appropriate accommodations, where the teen can meet some degree of success. If this does not occur, the teens will continue to falter and will see no reason to put forth the needed efforts. Although this will be difficult, as clinicians we also will need to teach our teens how to judge their successes more realistically. Unfortunately, they still may not be getting the grades they feel they deserve (with all the extra efforts put forth) but their progress is the most important thing. With all members of the team working together, we should make a conscientious effort to help motivate a student externally and alter his sense of pessimism to optimism. The reader is encouraged to review several of the practical suggestion on motivation, which are presented in Chapter 10.

The impact of school failure takes a huge toll on the self-esteem of children with SLD and ADHD. Researchers such as Barkley (1998) tell us there are several possible negative outcomes associated with school failure: (1) damaged self-esteem; (2) higher rates of class failure, suspension, and expulsions; (3) lower academic achievement; (4) increased risk of dropping out of high school; (5) increased risk of substance abuse; (6) increased risk of involvement with juvenile justice system; (7) and decreased likelihood of graduating from college. Continual negative school experiences often bombard these students. Sometimes they finally shut down emotionally, give up, and possibly even drop out of school. Due to repeated bouts of constant failure, many of these students begin to believe they are not competent. They give up or begin to put their efforts into other areas where they display degrees of success. In class, some may also cause behavior problems by being oppositional, preferring to look defiant rather than dumb in front of their peers. Consequently, it is incumbent upon the therapist to be alert in checking for coexisting conditions, especially if the teen is being treated but is still struggling academically. For example, a student's misbehavior may actually be masking undiagnosed learning problems or depression.

EDUCATIONAL INTERVENTIONS FOR THE THERAPIST

A Neurodevelopmental Developmental Model: A Brief Comment on a Phenomenological Approach

As noted in Chapter 3, the neurodevelopmental model places a strong emphasis on identifying the strengths that all children possess. As was explained in the previous chapter, the model is based on clinical, educational, and research experience and favors informed observation and description over labeling. The true utility of the model is in its ability to place strong emphasis on identifying and taking advantage of a child's innate strengths. According to Levine (2001), a neurodevelopmental variation refers to differences in the neurodevelopmental strengths and weaknesses that exist in all children.

Levine (2001) believes there can be many different reasons why a child may exhibit a particular educational delay. The crucial dimension in a successful evaluation is the clinician's ability to unearth the elements in the child's neurodevelopmental profile that represents a functional strength. We also need to determine what innate weaknesses in the profile may deter from academic performance. A thorough assessment should reveal recurring themes in specific functional areas. Once this information is determined accurately and a learning profile is established, a set of strategies can be put into place to help support the child. Interventions can be developed accurately at breakdown points so that the youngsters can learn commensurate strategies. Furthermore, the teens may also benefit from legitimate accommodations in the classroom or the home that systematically bypass their challenges. These accommodations, along with appropriate interventions, will support the students' learning and will protect them from continued public humiliation and frustration (Levine, 2002). The readers are strongly encouraged to read Levine's *A Mind at a Time* or *Educational Care* to get a clearer perspective of the model. We believe that this phenomenological model has tremendous merit and applicability. It can demystify to youth the source of their challenges and give them hope that their challenges can be remediated. As clinicians, our role will be to help teens (taking advantage of their strengths and affinities) overcome the impact of their neurodevelopmental dysfunction and to help them learn new ways of learning so they will be successful.

Attention Skill Development

By adolescence the complexity of attention deficit issues has compounded significantly. In addition to being off task, the student's behavior has been shaped by peer reaction. The *class clown* has become an entire entertainment component; the *happy wanderer* who was unable to remain in the desk is now unable to stay in the classroom and is often found wandering the halls, visiting or checking out lockers; the *daydreamer* has retreated deeper and appears to *care less* about studying; and the *impulsive* student is either enjoyed or detested by the teachers.

A complex range of emotions is experienced by the adolescent with attention issues. In addition to the complexity of attempting to survive in a teenage environment, he possesses a brain that constantly gives unnecessary or irrelevant feedback. It is these issues that tend to bring him to the attention of a therapist for intervention.

The initial task for the therapist is to identify the components of the apparent behavior that are associated to attention. In this task the importance of the student's history is immense. It is likely that the student will have a history of impulsivity, inattention, or delay in response time throughout early childhood and elementary school. The early behaviors provide the unencumbered observations that are needed to determine where to begin in addressing attention issues.

Students are often unaware that their behavior is unique or different. They know that their teachers, parents, and others disapprove or complain about them but they do not understand what provokes the complaints. They know that adults want to make them take medications to change their behavior, but they are not sure of why and how these medications would work.

For example, Marty was 13 years old and preparing to go to high school the next year when he was referred for therapy. He had been taking Ritalin for 4 years and was upset about having to continue going to the school office for his *pills* when he went to high school. He wanted not to **have to** take the medication and was willing to work on changing his behavior to achieve this.

The file observations on Marty's therapy provide good insights into a student with classic symptoms of ADHD. *"Marty was observed during the intake interview and testing. During the spelling test, he was apparently unable to remain still in his chair. The chair teetered on the edge of falling backwards. Prior to writing each word he would shift his weight and lurch forward toward the table. It was difficult to video tape him during the initial task because he kept appearing in and out of the camera frame. He was talking at the same time and explaining loudly why he did not understand why everyone talked about his behavior."*

Several interventions were used to assist Marty in changing his behavior to help him manage his ADHD. He learned relaxation techniques, breathing exercises, developed an awareness of the stimuli in his environment, which attracted his attention, and learned to time his attention to a task. The technique of learning relaxation and breathing techniques for adolescents and adults is very effective. It provides them with a way of gaining control of their bodies and energy levels. They need to learn to recognize that they can receive messages from their inner voice and can learn to guide their own behavior through their inner voice. The therapist can use one of a variety of relaxation tapes or dialogues to initiate the process. The selected sequence should include strong suggestions using breathing. The use of deep breathing as a control gives the client the *time* to analyze choices or behaviors and review with his inner voice. A colored sticky dot placed in strategic places can be used as a reminder signal to take a deep breath, relax, and function with control. With students, the dot(s) may be on a pencil, binder, desk, or other object that is commonly used. Adults often will put dots on their cell phone, pager, car mirror, schedule, palm pilot, or computer.

STRATEGIES IMPACTING EXECUTIVE FUNCTIONING

Although the impact of executive function deficits on school success is profound, this fact is often unrecognized by many parents and teachers. Practically speaking, these deficits may cause problems for students with either SLD or ADHD in several important areas: getting started and finishing work, remembering homework, memorizing facts, writing essays or reports, working math problems, being on time, controlling emotions, completing homework and long-term projects, and planning for the future.

Although scientists have not yet agreed on the exact elements of executive function, two ADHD researchers, Dr. Russell Barkley (1998) and Dr. Thomas Brown (2000), have provided helpful information. Dr. Barkley describes executive function as those "actions we perform to ourselves and direct at ourselves so as to accomplish self-control, goal-directed behavior, and the maximization of future outcomes." Through use of a metaphor, Dr. Brown gives us a helpful visual image by comparing executive function to the conductor's role in an orchestra. The conductor organizes various instruments to begin playing singularly or in combination, integrates the music by bringing in and fading certain actions, and controls the pace and intensity of the music.

Components of Executive Function

The components inherent to executive functioning have been discussed in various chapters throughout the book. We do not want to belabor the definition, but feel it is imperative that we identify some of the elements. Based on material from Barkley and Brown, here are five general components of executive function that impact school performance.

1. **Working memory and recall** (holding facts in mind while manipulating information; accessing facts stored in long-term memory).
2. **Activation, arousal, and effort** (getting started; paying attention; finishing work).
3. **Controlling emotions** (ability to tolerate frustration; thinking before acting or speaking).

4. **Internalizing language** (using "self-talk" to control one's behavior and direct future actions).
5. **Taking an issue apart, analyzing the pieces, and reconstituting and organizing it into new ideas** (complex problem solving).

Table 1 provides a more in-depth look at just one element of executive function—deficits in working memory and recall—and its impact on school work and life at home.

COMMON ACADEMIC PROBLEMS LINKED TO ADHD AND EXECUTIVE FUNCTION DEFICITS

Problems with executive function are often manifest in a variety of ways. Here are several of the most common ones with which families struggle and often result in school failure. Suggested intervention strategies from *Teaching Teens with ADD and ADHD* (2000) and *Teenagers with ADD* (1995) are also provided.

Two other resources that readers may find helpful include Sandra Rief's *How to Reach and Teach All Students in the Inclusive Classroom* and *How to Reach and Teach ADD/ADHD Children*, plus Dr. Don Deschler's *Teaching Adolescents with Learning Disabilities.*

Not Completing Homework Assignments or Having Assignments That Take too Long to Complete

Students with ADHD are notorious for getting zeros for not completing and turning in homework. They often forget their assignments and books necessary for competing homework. Sometimes the problem may be that the student is disorganized and forgetful. Other teens may have homework assignments that are too long. According to Goldstein and Zentall (1999), most teachers underestimate how long it takes students with special needs to complete homework assignments. The NEA and PTA developed a joint policy statement that suggests that the total of all homework assignments should not take more than 10 minutes per grade, in others words a 9th grader should spend not more than roughly 90 minutes total on homework for all his subjects.

TABLE 1   Impact of Poor Working Memory and Recall on Home and School Performance or on Behavior and Academic Performance[a]

---

1. Affects the **here and now**
    Limited working memory capacity
    Weak short-term memory (holding information in mind for roughly 20 seconds; capacity is roughly the equivalent of seven numbers)
    Forgetfulness—cannot keep several things in mind
  As a result, students
    Have difficulty remembering and following instructions from parents and teachers
    Have difficulty memorizing math facts, spelling words, and dates
    Have difficulty performing mental computation, such as math in one's head
    Forget one part of a problem while working on another segment
    Have difficulty paraphrasing or summarizing
2. Affects their sense of **past events:**
    Difficulty recalling the past
  As a result, students
    Do not learn easily from past behavior (limited hindsight)
    Repeat misbehavior
3. Affects their **sense of time**
    Difficulty holding events in mind
    Difficulty using their sense of time to prepare for upcoming events and the future
  As a result, students
    Have difficulty judging the passage of time accurately
    Do not estimate accurately how much time it will take to finish a task; consequently, they may not allow enough time to complete work
4. Affects their sense of **self-awareness**
    Diminished sense of self-awareness
  As a result, students
    Do not examine or change their own behavior easily
5. Affects their **sense of the future**
    Students live in the present—focus on the here and now
    Less likely to talk about time or plan for the future
  As a result, students
    Have difficulty projecting lessons learned in the past, forward into the future (limited foresight)
    Have difficulty planning ahead to complete a task in a timely manner
    Have difficulty preparing for the future

---

[a] Reprinted by permission from Zeigler Dendy (2000).

190 Chris A. Zeigler Dendy et al.

Strategies

- Sometimes teachers will ask another student to remind the teenager to write down his assignments. Dr. Clare Jones, a teacher and educational consultant, suggests that teachers appoint *"row captains"* to check to see that all students have written down their assignments and to pick up homework from each student.
- Some teachers post homework assignments on the school or their own person web page. Some schools have homework hotlines.
- Students may get phone numbers from a knowledgeable student in each class in which the teenager often forgets his assignments. Then the teen may call during the evening to find out his assignments.
- If a student is in danger of failing, some teachers are willing to *send home homework assignments in writing for the whole week.* Then once the student is passing again, a simpler strategy may be implemented.
- Ask a friend, parent, or teacher aide to meet the student at his locker to get the necessary homework materials together. Ultimately, this process of *"modeling"* and *"shaping"* behavior at the critical *"point of performance"* will help the student master skills or, at a minimum, teach him to compensate for deficits.
- *Consider utilizing a weekly report* in the event a student is failing. However, keep in mind that one of the key symptoms of ADHD is forgetfulness. So do not ask the student to get a weekly report signed in all his classes if he is failing only one, as otherwise he is being set up to fail.
- Goldstein and Zentall suggest a great strategy to *determine whether homework assignments are too long.* The teacher is asked to write on the student's paper how long they anticipate the homework should take to complete. In return, the parents and teenager write down how long it actually took to complete the assignment. If there is a discrepancy where the student is spending more time than should be expected, then this information provides a good argument for reducing the length of the assignments.

Teachers and educators with whom we have worked identified five areas as primary reasons for school failure among students with ADD/ADHD. These issues, as well as intervention strategies to help eliminate academic agony, are discussed in Table 2.

TABLE 2   Five Common Reasons for School Failure: Eliminating Academic Agony[a]

Problems	General strategies
1. Not doing homework/getting zeros	
Due to disorganization, forgetfulness, executive function deficits	**Use an assignment notebook**
	1. Have the student write down assignments
	2. Have a classmate double check assignments
	3. Teacher double checks assignment and initials it.
Forgets assignments	Give assignments at the beginning of class rather than during the rush at the end of class
	Provide a variety of ways for student to get assignments
	1. Provide a couple of classmates' phone numbers so the student can phone them at home for the assignment
	2. Fax or e-mail a copy of assignments to parents, perhaps daily or weekly
	3. Ask a student or teacher's aide to write down assignments to send home
	4. Give assignments and test dates in writing (every week or month)
	5. Record homework assignments on a classroom answering machine or teacher voice mail
	6. Have a "homework hotline," a school-operated phone line that students can call to get homework assignments
	7. Post homework assignments on the school or teacher web page
	8. Post homework assignments on an outside window so students can return to check it after school hours
	9. Make homework assignments available at the local library
	Tell parents the homework pattern
	Algebra: homework 4 nights weekly; test every 2 weeks or at the end of a chapter
Forgets books	Have student borrow a book from a classmate
	Allow student to keep an extra book (or set) at home
	Be flexible: allow work to be turned in late

(Continues)

TABLE 2 (*continued*)

Problems	General strategies
	Develop a plan to turn it in on time
	Use a weekly report to reinforce completion of work
Forgets to turn in assignments	Enlist other students' help
	Ask "row captains" to check that assignments are written down and to collect homework
	Pair all students. Ask them to spend the last 5 minutes checking to see that assignments are written down and homework turned in
No medication when doing work medication is still effective	**Start homework during the time when**
Too much homework	Determine whether too much homework is being assigned. If appropriate, reduce the amount of homework
2. Failing tests	
Does not do homework or study	Ensure homework completion using strategies listed earlier
	Provide a study review sheet of key facts
	Modify testing format
	1. Use word banks
	2. Avoid essay exams
	Allow the student to earn extra credit
Does not have time to finish tests	Give extended time on tests
	Give tests in an area without distractions or interruptions
3. Forgetting key assignments, tests, and long-term projects	The teacher or row captain reminds the student of due dates
	Send a notice home to parents regarding special projects or tests
	Break projects into three or four segments
	Grade each segment separately
	Teach time management
	Complete a weekly/monthly schedule
	1. Divide task into required steps
	2. Schedule each step
	3. Work backward to complete the timeline
4. Not taking notes/difficulty copying from the board	Teach the student to take notes
	Teach students to make up their own shorthand
	Designate a note taker for the whole class

(*Continues*)

TABLE 2   (*continued*)

Problems	General strategies
	1. Make photocopies of a student's notes and leave them in a designated spot for any student who needs them
	2. Have the note taker use noncarbon replica paper and tear off the bottom copy to give to the student with ADD/ADHD
	Give guided lecture notes
	Outline the key points, leaving spaces for students to write additional notes
	Allow the student to tape record the class lecture (this strategy may be ineffective for students who are unwilling to listen to the same material twice)
	Minimize copying from the board
	When copying is necessary, allow the student to copy from the book or a handout
5. Difficulties making the transition from elementary to middle to high school	Encourage parents to notify a new school about ADD/ADHD
	1. Notify in May June or check with the guidance counselor at the new school to find out when student schedules are developed
	2. Provide input on the Fall schedule
	Develop an IEP for special education students before they transition to the next school.
	Schedule a student support team meeting (SST)[b]
	Assign an upper class mentor to help with the transition.
	Give parents an update on grades after 2–3 weeks in the new school.

[a] Reprinted by permission from Zeigler Dendy (2000).

[b] Although not mandated by federal law, many states have developed teams of educators that meet to discuss ways of helping students who are struggling. These teams may have different names in different states, such as student support team or child study team (CST). The SST is not the same thing as an IEP team. IEP teams are mandated by federal law to screen students for special education eligibility. The SST team is available to help any student regardless of whether she is eligible for special education services. Team members may include veteran teachers and ideally also a guidance counselor, school psychologist, or social worker.

Monitoring Homework Completion

Parents are often faced with conflicting feelings about how much to be involved in their teenager's homework completion. Some teachers may feel that parents are too involved in their child's school work. Obviously, teens should do as much as possible of their work independently. If, however, a student with ADHD is failing classes, parents should become more involved and provide more supervision, despite what teachers are saying. Remember because of the 2- to 4-year ADHD developmental delay, these students will need more supervision and support than their peers. It is important to give parents permission to be involved—to provide *developmentally appropriate supervision*. Of course, the level of supervision required will vary from student to student.

The one caution here is that if this approach causes damaging conflicts between the teen and one of his parents, some changes must be made. For example, the other parent may take the lead on homework or a tutor or neighbor may take over this task. Keep in mind also that a parent who also has ADHD and problems with organization may not be able to provide the required level of supervision, despite their best intentions.

Since encouraging students to do their work independently is so important, some parents elect to tell their teens that as long as they are passing all their classes with at least a grade of C, the parents will not intervene. However, if they are failing, then homework will be monitored more closely. This way there is an incentive to do his work and pass his classes so parents will stop monitoring his work so closely.

Strategies

- Set a homework routine. Involve the teen in developing this routine. Give student's some choices about the time to start their homework and which subjects they start on first. What time and where will he study? In setting the routine, help the student recognize that she needs to take a preplanned break. Breaks are important because they help rejuvenate and give you energy. When breaks are taken, we must teach the teen to learn to stay with the prescribed amount of time.
- Students often benefit from doing some preset up prior to working. Students are encouraged to set up their study area prior to studying. They can place all their materials on a table. Be certain there is note paper, pencil, paper, computer, or whatever is

going to be needed to study. They can review their assignments and select the necessary materials from texts or notes. Then they take a break until it is study and anticipating the activities that they will do. It will take them less time. Often students just go ahead and complete their studying once it is set up rather than waiting for a later time!

- Consider setting a timer or ask him to set his watch to remind him when to start. Providing a 10-minute warning may be helpful to assist with the transition to doing his homework. Shifting from one activity to another is always difficult for these teens so the warning allows them some time to get ready mentally to work.

- Help the student learn to prioritize the work that s/he has to complete. Each afternoon, the teen should review the work and identify how long each subject should take. A routine should be established where the homework is done from hardest to the simplest. This will make it easier at the end of the day when the less complicated assignments will be attempted.

- By helping the students learn to prioritize what they do, they can begin to make plans about their school work. The students will have to learn that they must learn to be in charge and must assume responsibility for their choices. In doing so, many will have to learn how to delay gratification and to prioritize what they are doing. Readers are encouraged to get their clients to review the book *Take Control of Your Time and Life* by Alan Lakein. Basically, Lakein provides simple strategies to learn time management, including learning how to label tasks as A's, B's, or C's. A's actually represent items on a list that are the most important and urgent, whereas C's do not require immediate attention.

- The student may need a break at 20- to 30-minute intervals.

- Since problems getting started are linked to their ADHD, parents may consider checking in initially simply to make certain they have started working. Sometimes just the sight of the parent at the door is enough to prompt the teen that they need to begin work. They may check in near the end to review the finished homework product.

- For some students and some subjects, medication will be critical for homework completion. So analyze the time periods that the medication coverage lasts and make certain that is lasts through the homework period. Parents should check with their doctor to see if a short-acting (3–4 hours) dose of medication is required in the early evening.

- Use a computer as often as possible for doing homework.
- Have the student learn to use various self-monitoring strategies that can help them learn to evaluate their actual output.
- Some parents ask students to study even on those evenings that no homework is assigned. This practice should be discouraged.

    Because school is such an aversive situation for most students with ADHD, they need social, recreational, and family interactions that build self-esteem and give them some joy each day.

PREPARING TO STUDY: GUIDELINES FOR PARENTS

Middle school and high school students often find that they improve in their studies when they set the stage for learning. Students often feel that they want to have the television or music on when they are studying. Obviously, they are limiting their effectiveness if they are attempting to split their attention between two tasks that require language processing. Instead, students are encouraged to use the new CDs that provide anchor sound but do not distract from language processing necessary for studying. Excellent CDs are available through Advanced Brain Technologies—Sound for Health Series and Samonas International— SONAS Classic Edition. Listening to specially selected music will provide a base for background sound and stimulate the brain appropriately for learning.

Some educators note that some physical exercises can be used to help the brain to get ready to study. Use of the infinity walk exercises suggested by Deborah Sunbeck may provide important preparatory brain organization for learning. Some families may find it helpful to suggest that students follow the figure eight pattern and perform exercises at several levels of complexity prior to studying. Early research suggests that these procedures provide good brain stimulation, activates right and left cortex areas, and stimulates the corpus callosum to activate learning. Additional activities are suggested in the "brain gym" work by the Dennisons. Their suggestions to drink water while working and many other exercises have been noted as very appropriate in activating learning in the student.

Suggestions for Helping Students Who Have Difficulty with Planning and Have an Impaired Sense of Time

Students with ADHD are often described as "living in the here and now." Unfortunately, that means that they do not plan ahead very well. Dr. Barkley (1998) linked this problem to their impaired sense of time, more specifically, they do not judge the passage of time accurately. One of the more common reasons for school failure is a forgotten long-term project that students do not remember at all or at least not until the night before it is due. Parents and teachers are also reminded that accommodations are often needed because after all, forgetfulness is a characteristic of the disorder. Typically, failure to complete these projects is not simply intentional defiance.

Strategies

- Parents may take the opportunity at a school open house to ask each teacher whether they assign a semester long-term project.
- Some parents have asked to include the following statement in the IEP or 504 plan: "Parents will be notified of any long-term projects." Teachers may email or send a note home as a reminder.
- Some teachers divide these assignments into two or three segments and give separate grades. These due dates are more likely to come to the parents' attention earlier so that failure is less likely.
- Parents may ask the teacher to modify the timeline when assignments may be due. This may help some students who may benefit from a little more time. This strategy should also be considered for in class assignments as well.
- Try using graphic organizers to summarize project requirements, to check completed steps, and to teach organizational skills through modeling.
- Starting with the due date, teach the students to schedule backward to estimate how long it will take to complete the project. This form of previewing helps the students determine what is necessary to complete.
- The student may need a watch alarm that vibrates to help them be on time for family activities or appointments.

Disorganization

Parents are well aware of the terrible disorganization that these young-sters exhibit. It is not unusual for them to lose clothes, shoes, jewelry, games, tools, books, homework, reports, and backpacks. In addition, dis-astrously messy desks, backpacks, lockers, and rooms are the rule rather than the exception.

Strategies

- Parents must work hard to teach and model good organizational skills for these teenagers. Teaching this skill will not be easy and will take considerable time and practice. It will require setting aside *"maintenance time"* to teach this skill, e.g., checking the notebook and backpack weekly to see if assignments have been submitted, especially for those classes the student is in danger of failing.
- Keep any assignments or reports until after the semester is over and grades have been released. This back-up insurance is critical, as sometimes the teacher indicates that an assignment is missing when in fact the student did the work but never turned it into the teacher.

Slow Processing Speed and Recall of Information

Many students with ADHD *read and write more slowly* than their peers. Furthermore, when combined with *poor fine coordination*, these students often take longer to complete assignments and will often produce less written work during the same period of time as their classmates. Under these circumstances, adults should not be surprised that homework avoid-ance is a major issue for many of these students.

Strategies

- Frequently, the overall goal is to reduce the amount of written work required. If appropriate, ask that homework assignments be shortened. This may be very helpful for students who work slowly. If a child has graphomotor difficulties, we may ask if the student could word process rather than write or, for that matter, print instead of use cursive writing.

- On some assignments, write the answers only and not the questions. Photocopy questions and fill in the blanks. For in-class presentations, a student may be allowed to present an oral report (with great detail) rather than always having to do a written report.
- Encourage use of a computer, which enables these students to complete work more easily, in a timely manner, and preserves a written copy in the event earlier work is lost. Furthermore, according to Dr. Mel Levine (1994), use of a computer requires less memory than writing cursive and printing also requires less memory than writing cursive. This may explain why so many of these students prefer to print even when they are in middle or high school.
- Ask for extended time on tests, if appropriate. Many students (Zeigler Dendy, 1999) often say that extra time on tests is the most helpful classroom accommodation they receive.
- If a lot of reading is required, for example, in literature, students may get classic novels on an audiocassette tape through Books on Tape. It is easier to stay focused on the story if they can read the text while listening to the story on tape. Furthermore, some teachers may be willing to decrease the amount of reading or give the students an abstract of the materials presented.
- A variety of assistive devices are available that can provide student support in reading. Computer programs are available that scan the text a student must read and then "read" it back verbally to the student. These programs usually light up the word as it is verbalized and can be set at a pacing the student can follow. Additional programs are available that allow the student to dictate to the computer. These resources are important advances that benefit the learning disabled and/or dyslexic individual.

Writing Essays and Reports

Students with ADHD/LD often have a *limited working memory* capacity and difficulty *quickly recalling information* stored in long-term memory. As a result, they frequently have difficulty getting their ideas written down on paper for essays or reports or doing complex manipulations to solve math problems. In addition, some of these students may also have *slow processing speed*, thus they read or write more slowly than their peers. All three of these skills are important elements of executive function. Obviously, they are critical for writing essays and working math problems. With these challenges, it should come as no surprise that it takes longer for these students to complete assignments; consequently, many of these students will produce less written work. Without help, their essays may be very brief, consisting of the bare minimum of sentences.

- The Mayes and Calhoun study identified *written expression* as the most common learning problem among students with ADHD (65%). Consequently, writing essays, drafting book reports, or answering questions on tests or homework is often very challenging for these students. Specifically, these students have trouble holding thoughts in short-term memory long enough to get their ideas down on paper; using their working memory to remember what they want to write next; remembering the original question; and organizing the information in a logical manner utilizing the working memory system. For these students, having a graphic organizer for essay writing provides *written* guidelines for the student to follow.
- Write ideas on "post-it" notes for brainstorming essay ideas. Then the student can focus on producing ideas without any worries about remembering them. Next, move the ideas on "post-it" notes around and group them by broad topics and ideas for each paragraph.
- Ask for two grades on written assignments: one for content and the other for grammar compliance. This gives the student credit for the skills he has demonstrated plus increases the likelihood that he will pass the class.
- *Modeling* is an especially effective way to assist students in learning to write essays. Some teachers will actually write an essay on an overhead while soliciting assistance from the class. Initially, if the student is really struggling and assignments are too long, the parent may alternate writing paragraphs with the student. The parents gradually phase out their support as the student's writing skills become stronger.
- Referring to an encyclopedia for an easily understood overview of a topic can be very helpful when writing a report. Using *Encarta*, an encyclopedia software program, can be beneficial.

Completing Math Problems

Since learning is relatively easy for most of us, sometimes we forget just how complex seemingly simple tasks such as memorizing multiplication tables or working a math problem really are. For example, when a student works on a math problem, he must fluidly move back and forth between analytical skills and several levels of memory (working, short-term, and long-term memory). With word problems, he must hold several numbers and questions in mind while he decides how to work a problem. Next he must delve into long-term memory to find the correct math rule or formula to use for the problem. Then he must hold important facts in mind while he applies the rules and shifts information back and forth between working and short-term memory to solve the problem and determine the answer.

Frequently, these students are not able to automatize math facts easily. Parents often complain that earlier attempts by their children to memorize multiplication tables often resulted in disaster. Many of these students learned the multiplication tables one day only to have forgotten them by the next morning. Later during the teen years, parents and teachers also often observe that these students cannot quickly retrieve their math facts and rules from long-term memory without assistance from calculators or math grids. Typically this slows them down, resulting in completion of fewer math problems and, more importantly, energy wasted on routine computation rather than focusing on the mastery of critical new math concepts.

Strategies

- *Use paired learning.* In this strategy, the teacher explains the problem, students make up their own examples, and then swap problems and discuss their answers. (After barely passing high school and college algebra, one student with ADHD made an A in calculus plus had a 100 average on tests when the professor used this strategy. At the same time, he also tutored a friend.) Parents can also use this same strategy at home with a teenager.
- *Find a peer tutor or allow the teenager to tutor a younger student.* Frequently, the person providing the tutoring learns more than the recipient of the tutoring.

Listening Comprehension and Note Taking

A limited working memory capacity also contributes to problems with listening comprehension and note taking. Consequently, these students may have difficulty following directions, particularly if they are too long or complicated. When they are taking notes in class, they may not be able to identify key points in a teacher's lecture. *Poor fine motor skills* may also interfere with the student's ability to write easily and fluidly without great concentration.

Strategies

- Teachers and parents should *give brief, clear instructions*, perhaps even numbering them and writing them down on the board or "post-it notes."
- *Teaching a modified note-taking system* may also be helpful, e.g., T = the, rd = read, > = more than, w/o = without, p = page, ? = question.
- The teacher may *ask another student to take notes* for the teenager. Sometimes they may use noncarbon replica paper, which the note taker simply pulls apart the bottom sheet and gives it to the student, or they may photocopy a student's notes and make them available to any student who needs them.
- Laptop computers may be very helpful for note taking and class work. Some schools provide *AlphaSmart*, which is a less expensive laptop computer with an adequate but somewhat limited capacity.

READING COMPREHENSION: GENERAL EDUCATIONAL IMPLICATIONS

Before we give some specific suggestions for reading, we thought it would be helpful to give a basic overview of potential problems. In general, there are three different issues with reading comprehension in adolescent students. The issue may be poor word recognition skills, which causes laborious reading, errors in word identification, and reduced energy for understanding what is being read (comprehension). Reading comprehension challenges with teens who have ADHD may also be influenced by their inability to concentrate and stay with the content.

The third possibility is that the student has a tremendous challenge comprehending, whether he is listening or reading information. This deficit appears to be rooted as a language problem. We believe that to best help support a teen in the area of reading, a therapist will need to identify clearly what aspect of language impedes on the reading performance. This can be done easily by reviewing assessment information (which would identify word recognition issues), talking to the student, and asking questions regarding "What happens when you attempt to read?"

Good information can be gained from asking the student to identify the differences between reading a textbook and reading magazines, comics, or other pleasure text. The student with language challenges will have trouble in gaining information from any reading. She will have difficulty in getting information from lectures or discussion. The student who is distracted while reading will find that some material holds his attention. The student with word recognition issues will experience stress in all areas of reading, but may be strong in discussion and verbal reception.

General techniques that are applicable to the therapist's setting include neurological impress reading developed by R. G. Heckelman. Heckelman found that when he had students impress read 10 minutes a day for a total of 5 hours (30 days), they gained 1 to 2 years of progress in their reading ability. The technique requires the therapist to place a finger above the word in a reading selection and the student to place a finger below the word. Then they read together through the selection. The therapist may say the word before the student if the student is having difficulty identifying it. The therapist establishes a methodical, slow pace and uses considerable expression in reading. The importance of the technique is for the student to see the word, hear it, and say it.

The EDU-therapeutics echo tap technique, which was discussed previously in an earlier chapter, is especially useful for improving comprehension with students who are distracted in reading or who have language challenges. The approach provides auditory–vocal exercise, which stimulates the listening efforts and improves the retention of information. Both of these techniques are helpful for students with attention issues or learning disabilities. They experience success, which inspires confidence; rehearsal in reading, which improves the reading brain pathway; and gain information, which improves comprehension. The tasks are usually comfortable for the student to use. Neurological impress reading can be done independently once the student has mastered word recognition. It serves to focus attention by tracking with the finger on the print, thus improving concentration.

Working Memory and Reading Comprehension

Students with *working memory* problems are very likely to have poor reading comprehension skills. Their limited working memory capacity interferes with their ability to remember key information they are trying to retain as they read. Sometimes they cannot remember what they have just read and have to reread material. Understandably, students also complain of having great difficulty when asked to summarize or paraphrase information they have read, heard, or seen.

Students who learn to paraphrase improve their reading comprehension skills greatly. Please remember that it is not enough simply to tell a teen how to do these skills. An adult will need to practice them with the teen until it is obvious they have mastered the skill.

Strategies

- Discuss the importance of the structure of their textbook, for example, the importance of **bold** and *italics*, heading and subheadings. Ask the student to point out several examples as he turns through a book. Remind him that the first sentence in the paragraph usually conveys the key idea of the whole paragraph. Make certain he knows how to find the subject and verb for the first sentence and highlight them. Copy a practice paragraph and show him how to do this. Then let him highlight the noun and verb and then summarize the main idea of the paragraph.
- *RAP* is a self-management strategy used to help with paraphrasing and remembering what has been read. This strategy comes from Dr. Don Deschler's book, *Teaching Adolescents with Learning Disabilities* (1996): *r*ead a paragraph, *a*sk yourself what the paragraph was about, and *p*ut the main ideas and two details in your own words. Dr. Deschler and colleagues at the University of Kansas have developed a detailed curriculum known as the strategic instruction model (SIM) to methodically teach this skill to adolescents.
  - Deschler (1966) has also developed a four-step process that he calls PASS. This approach may be very helpful, especially when

using textbooks. **P**review by reading the heading and one or two of the sentences. This may help the student predict what will be coming up. **A**sk content-focused questions such as who, what, why, and where. This helps students become more interactive with the materials and helps them learn to monitor what is being presented. **S**ummarize to yourself what was the essence of the paragraph or section that was read. Again the most important aspect of this section is to interact and think about what you are reading. **S**ynthesize what you have read and assess how it fits in with the other materials already reviewed.

- Students may *take notes* as they read. Another option is to pencil information lightly in the margins or *write the information* on "post-it notes."
- They may also *highlight key points* in their reading if the school allows them to write in the book. If this is the strategy you choose to implement, erasable highlighters are also available.
- To help students remember what they have read, some teachers suggest the **SQ3R method** (**s**urvey, **q**uestion, **r**ead, **r**ecite, and **r**eview). In other words (1) *survey* the chapter title, first paragraph, section headings, pictures and captions, the summary paragraph, and questions at the end of the chapter; (2) *make up your own questions* about the chapter; (3) *read* the chapter; (4) at the end of a section, look away from the book and *recite* or summarize what you have read; and (5) finally *review*—look back over the chapter to see how the parts are related.
- Developing *a graphic organizer* for the student to complete after reading class material may be helpful. For example, in literature, you may include the setting (time and place), main characters, conflicts, events, climax, and solution of conflicts. Basically, list these topics and leave blank lines to the right of the terms for students to fill in the answers. By providing this visual prompt, the student does not have to rely on his faulty memory to recall what information he should be searching for during his reading. Another approach espoused by Idol (1987) is known as a story map. Within this strategy the teen reads a story and then develops a map of all the main idea and events. The map is a tremendous visual tool for visualizing and remembering important story events.
- Creating a *diorama, pop-up book, or scrapbook* for history or literature that includes drawings of the major leaders/characters, maps of

countries involved, pictures of the key battles, or a drawing of the final outcome should also be beneficial.

Students with ADHD often seem to be superficial processors of information so any activities that create a greater opportunity to talk about, write, draw, perform in a play, or cut out pictures related to the topic will enhance the student's memory regarding the material. Information in the next section should also be helpful.

Memorizing Facts or Information

Some students have a terrible time memorizing information such as multiplication tables, math formulas, science or history facts, or a foreign language. Students who struggle with memorization may be processing the information superficially. Consequently, they have difficulty remembering information they read.

Understanding working memory capacity is very important. To help us visualize working memory capacity, Dr. Claire Wurtzel, Banks Street College of Education, refers to this capacity as *"cognitive counter space."* When the student has memory problems, then the "counter" quickly becomes cluttered with information such as brainstorming ideas, major issues to be included in the essay, rules for writing an essay, grammar rules, and, for many, anxiety about performance. Because these students have significant memory problems, it is important to remove any unnecessary information from the "counter space." For example, clear the space occupied by rules for writing an essay by giving them a graphic organizer as a visual prompt. This helps free up additional working memory to focus more energy on writing, organizing, and editing the essay content.

Strategies

These three general strategies will help students improve their ability to memorize information.

- *Link words or concepts with pictures or a story.* For example, some teachers have students develop a book report by drawing or cutting out pictures of the main characters, the author, events in the story, and creating a four to five page report. If the teacher assigns a book report, the parent may suggest this strategy or a more creative one such as filming his report on video.

- *Elaborate on or discuss information.* Getting a student to talk about the information and possibly linking it to his own personal experiences will also help his memory. For example, when studying adverse weather conditions, such as tornadoes or thunderstorms, students may be asked to tell about the worst weather conditions they have ever experienced.
- Carefully *organize information in a visual format.* Many teachers are now using graphic organizers, which lay out information in a logical sequential order, thus enhancing the student's memory. As discussed earlier, an organizer may contain guidelines for writing an actual essay. For example, to write an essay a student must start out with a thesis paragraph, which contains three things: a definition of the essay topic, its importance, and three key traits. Consequently, having these guidelines means the student does not have to use up his limited working memory to remember the rules for writing an essay.

In addition, here are some specific memory strategies.

1. *Use mnemonics* (memory tricks), such as acronyms or acrostics, e.g., HOMES to remember names of the Great Lakes or My Very Educated Mother Just Gave Us Nine Pizzas for remembering the order of the planets. These techniques provide a simple code that makes it easier to remember information. Two of the most popular mnemonics are the reduction mnemonics where you try and reduce a large body of information to a shorter form. The previous example highlighted this form (HOME). However, rhyming mnemonics are where rhymes are developed to help one remember key information.

2. Use *visual posting* of key information on strips of poster board taped on the board or wall. The parent/teacher refers to these poster strips as she discusses the key facts. Then she asks a question and the student answers while looking at the answer. Parents might write key facts for a test on butcher paper and tape it on the wall at the foot of the student's bed so that it is last thing the student sees before he falls asleep. (Information is often consolidated into memory at night while we sleep.) Later, while taking a test, the student can often visualize the answers in his mind.

3. One other approach that has been used widely to support memory is to use places in your mind to remember specific things. By placing an associative object into a certain location and then by going back into your mind to find that specific location, the object or the fact should come back to you quite easily. For example, you can visualize a room and all

the items in it. You then can proceed and place certain important facts that are to be remembered in or on top of the various places. Many people have found this approach to be very helpful.

Test-Taking Anxiety

Students with ADHD have so many learning issues to cope with that taking tests is often an anxiety-producing situation. As you know, they must struggle with limited working memory capacity, slow processing, difficulty retrieving information quickly, and poor fine motor skills. So a few tips may be helpful for test taking situations. Additional tips are also available in *Thinking Smarter* by Carla Crutsinger (1992).

Strategies

- Always spend more time on the part of the test that earns the most points.
- "Brain dumping" may help. As soon as the student receives his paper for the test, he may write down any key facts that he is afraid he may forget.
- For multiple choice, read questions carefully, mark an "x" beside any choices that you know are wrong, and if there is no penalty, always guess.
- For fill in the blank/sentence completion, suggest that they write down something, even if students do not know the answers to test questions. They may earn partial credit.
- For discussion questions, look for key words—list, outline, describe, discuss, compare, and be certain to address those issues.
- For true/false, *all, always, never, none,* and *only* are words often used in false statements. *Often, rarely,* and *generally* are words usually used to indicate true statements.
- With matching questions, determine if the two columns are equal in length. Ask if you can use an answer more than once.
- Sometimes an answer in an earlier question may trigger information that answers a later question. If you get stuck, glance back over the test to see if anything reminds you of the answer.
- Do not go back and change answers. Your first choice is usually correct.

- Most importantly, teach your client how to relax. Guided imagery or a simple hypnotic approach may be helpful to practice so when needed the teen can put it into place. Additionally, we need to let our clients know about the need for rest, eating a hearty breakfast, and drinking water.

CONCLUSION

Clearly school is often very difficult for students with LD/ADHD. In some ways, the learning challenges are even more significant than in the elementary years because so many people do not appreciate their magnitude. Additionally, when coexisting conditions occur with the presence of deficits in executive functioning, the accompanying problems are often overwhelming to the student and family. Unfortunately, some parents and teachers have had little awareness or sympathy for the challenges presented by these combined deficits. As clinicians, teachers, and parents it is hoped that we can appreciate that these disorders are often very complex conditions! Consequently, with guidance and support, these students will benefit from individually prescribed accommodations and methods.

In forthcoming chapters, other authors will discuss best practice approaches in home/school consultation, which may complement what parents can do to get what their child needs in school. Furthermore, there is also a chapter that focuses on what clinicians need to be aware of in aiding their teen in transitioning from high school into postsecondary options.

The greatest gift that we can give these students is an awareness that they are capable and can learn. They may need to learn more efficient, consistent, and comprehensive strategies to support themselves. "Succeeding in school is one of the most *therapeutic* outcomes that can happen to a teen!" *(Zeigler Dendy, 2002). So it behooves clinicians to do whatever it takes to help the child succeed in school and in their daily life.*

REFERENCE

Barkley, R. (1998). *Attention-deficit hyperactivity disorder* (2nd ed.). New York: Guilford Press.

Bear, G., Clever, A., & Proctor, W. (1991). Self-perception of nonhandicapped children and children with learning disabilities in an integrated setting. *Journal of Special Education*, 24, 409–426.

Brown, T. (2000). *Attention deficit disorders and comorbidities in children, adolescents, and adults.* Washington, DC: American Psychiatric Press.

Centers for Disease Control and Prevention (CDC) (2002). CDC study confirms ADHD: Learning disability link. *Mental Health Weekly*, 12(21), 6–7.

Crutsinger, C. (1992). *Thinking smarter: Skills for academic success.* Carrolton, TX: Brainworks, Inc.

Dennison, P. (1990). *Edu-K for kids.* Ventura, CA: Edu-Kinesthetics, Inc.

Deshler, D., Ellis, E., & Lenz, B. (1996). *Teaching adolescents with learning disabilities: Strategies and methods.* Denver, CO: Love Publishing.

Doman, A. (1999). Sound for health series: Advanced brain technologies. Denver, CO. Advanced Brain Technologies.

Fine (2000). *Fathers and sons.* Dubuque, IA: Kendall Hunt.

Flynn, D., & Kotkin, R. (2000). Intervention Strategies for Success (ISS). Unpublished rating scale, Irvine, CA: Flynn & Kotkin Associates.

Hallowell, E., & Ratey, J. (1994). *Driven to distraction.* New York: Pantheon.

Idol, L. (1987). Group story mapping: A comprehensive strategy for both skilled and unskilled readers. *Journal of Learning Disabilities*, 20, 196–205.

Jensen, P. (1999). Moderators and mediators of treatment response for children with AD/HD: The multimodal treatment study (MTA) study of children with AD/HD. *Archives of General Psychiatry*, 56, 1088–1096.

Jordan, D. (2000). *Honorable intentions: A parent's guide to educational planning for children with emotional or behavioral disorders* (2nd ed.). Pacer Center.

Levine, M. (1994). *Educational care.* Cambridge, MA: Educators Publishing Service.

Levine, M. (2001). *Educational Care.* Cambridge, MA: Educators Publishing Service.

Levine, M. (2002). *A mind at a time.* New York: Simon and Shuster.

Mayes, S., & Calhoun, S. (2000). Prevalence and degree of attention and learning problems in ADHD and LAD. *ADHD Reports*, V. 8, N. 2, April.

Rief, S. (1996). *How to reach and teach all students in the inclusive classroom.* West Nyack, NY: Center for Applied Research in Education.

Whitworth, L., Kimsey-House, H., & Sandahl, P. (1998). *Co-active coaching: New skills for coaching people toward success in work and life.* Palo Alto, CA: Davies-Black.

Zeigler Dendy, C. A. (2002). Five components of executive function and how they impact school performance. *Attention Magazine*, February, pp. 26–31.

Zeigler Dendy, C. A. (2000). *Teaching teens with ADD and ADHD.* Bethesda, MD: Woodbine House.

Zeigler Dendy, C. A. (1995). *Teenagers with ADD.* Bethesda, MD: Woodbine House.

Zeigler Dendy, C. A. (1999). *Teen to teen: The ADD experience (video), (www.chrisdendy.com).*

Zentall, S., & Goldstein, J. (1999). *Seven Steps to Homework Success.* Plantation, FL: Specialty Press.

## CHAPTER 7

Implementing School–Home Collaborative Treatment Plans: Best Practices in School–Home-Based Interventions

Daniel Flynn, Ron Kotkin, John Brady and Aubrey H. Fine

Children spend 6 hours a day at school, and it is in these school settings where the core symptoms of attention deficit hyperactivity disorder (ADHD) and learning disabilities (LD) have the most profound and potentially negative effect upon the child, creating a challenge for teachers, support staff, and the children themselves. Practitioners can play an essential role as case managers in helping parents and teachers collaborate to provide an effective program to support children with ADHD and LD in the school setting.

Research on children's learning shows that the connection and relationship between home and school can significantly affect the child's academic and behavioral functioning (Christenson et al., 1992). This approach is variously labeled conjoint behavioral consultation (Sheridan et al., 1996) or ecobehavioral consultation (Gutkin and Curtis, 1999) as it takes into consideration the child's school and home environments that can affect behavior or achievement. Conjoint behavioral consultation with both parents and teachers has been found to be successful (Sheridan et al., 2001) in changing behavior in home and school environments in that it coordinates a unified, consistent approach to the child by both the parent and the teacher.

A practitioner is in a unique position to facilitate collaboration between home and school. This type of school–home collaboration can include coordination of many collateral therapies that may impact the child's performance. This chapter reviews four areas that relate to school–home collaboration: (1) general guidelines in the development of a school and/or home behavior management program, (2) implementing a school–home behavioral report card system, (3) identifying and sharing information to accommodate a child with ADHD and/or LD, and (4) facilitating access to special education services in the public sector.

GENERAL GUIDELINES IN DEVELOPING A SCHOOL–HOME BEHAVIOR MANAGEMENT PROGRAM

Identifying the Problems

Consultation with the teachers and parents in developing a behavior management plan has a number of critical factors that contribute to its success. Initially, the practitioner must help define the problems that jointly affect school and home in as clear concise and objective manner as possible. Clarity in definition helps in working toward a solution and in determining when the problem is solved. Prior to the process of face-to-face interviewing, it is helpful to have both parents and teachers fill out a behavior problems worksheet (Appendix 2) to get a preliminary idea of the scope of their problems. Often the parent and teacher will have only a partially shared perspective of the problem. The practitioner next interviews the parents, teachers, and student (when appropriate) as the final step in identifying the problems.

Prioritizing the Problems

The next stage of behavioral case management is prioritizing the identified behavioral problems. Often there are too many specific concerns or problems to practically address at one time. The practitioner needs to develop consensus upon one or two behaviors that will be the initial focus of intervention. Utilizing the behavior problem worksheet and interviews, practitioners can identify behavior problems shared by both parents and teachers, and communicating this consensus facilitates a sense of collaboration. At this stage the parents or the teachers may need reassurance that all of the problem behaviors will ultimately be addressed. In choosing the initial behavior, it is helpful to choose a behavior that has a high probability of responding quickly and favorably to intervention. Favorable behavior change creates a positive attitude and optimism about the use of behavioral management strategies and facilitates commitment to future interventions.

Operationally Defining the Problem Behaviors and Collecting Baseline Data

Once the target behaviors are agreed upon between teachers and parents, these behaviors need to be operationally defined as clearly as possible. The behaviors should be defined so that two independent observers could record the occurrence of the behavior accurately. Once the behaviors have been operationally defined, it is important to establish a preintervention level (frequency and/or duration) of the problem behavior—this is referred to as the baseline. Both the parent and the teacher need to collect baseline data until the present level of the behavior is established. To facilitate determining the baseline of the behavior, a simple set of instructions and a data collection sheet on which parents and teacher note the frequency or duration of the target behavior (Appendix 3) or a standardized tool such as the SKAMP (Appendix 4) (Swanson, 1992; Swanson et al., 1999) can be utilized. Recording baseline data allows the parents, teachers, and practitioner to track the child's response to intervention once intervention is initiated.

Developing and Implementing an Intervention Plan

The next step is developing the intervention plan. Interventions can focus on decreasing a particular behavior, substituting a replacement behavior, or a combination of these two strategies. Most teachers and parents initially focus on reducing the frequency of a problem behavior not realizing that a replacement behavior is often necessary to maintain a child's progress. For instance, one can reduce "yelling out in a classroom" (attention seeking) by punishing the behavior. However, the child still needs to be taught how to get attention in acceptable ways. A replacement behavior serves this purpose. When considering what replacement behavior to train, it is essential to determine the function of the negative behavior. Was the child trying to gain attention or trying to avoid or escape work that is too hard? In the first case you may want to teach the child more acceptable ways of getting attention (raising his hand), whereas in the second case you may also want to teach and encourage the child to ask for help when the work is too difficult.

After selection of the problem behaviors, several considerations exist before choosing an intervention. First, is the intervention research based? Interventions that are research based and validated in professional literature provide teachers and parents sound evidence that an intervention has been shown to be effective and may facilitate treatment compliance. In addition to the interventions detailed later in this chapter, a number of compilations of researched-based academic and attention interventions are easy to set up and monitor (Rathvon, 1999; Sprick & Howard, 1999).

The ease of use and acceptability of an intervention must also be considered. Because most practitioners are usually limited to weekly 50-minute sessions with the family and phone calls to the teacher, the interventions have to be simple enough to explain in a short period of time or to write down as a short set of instructions. Behavioral interventions that are simple facilitate implementation in the home and classroom by the parents and teachers. Simplifying can be accomplished by focusing on interventions that the parents and teachers were successful using in the past. The intervention must also be comfortable and acceptable to parent and teacher because they are less likely to implement an intervention program they find unacceptable (Axelrod et al., 1990). Due to either cognitive dissonance or a desire to please the practitioner, both parents and teachers tend to agree with the practitioner's wishes even when they have doubts as to the effectiveness of the plan. Probing may be required to understand if they see programs as feasible and potentially effective so that the practitioner can address obstacles to implementation seen by either party.

In addressing the obstacles, parents and teachers often indicate they have tried a procedure, independently or in isolation, and it did not work. Practitioners can point out that these procedures may be made more effective when all parties work together, focusing on the systematic application of the procedures and daily monitoring of success. It is very helpful at this point for the clinician to offer several alternatives from which the teacher and parent choose.

Do not assume that teachers or parents are skilled in the aspects of any particular intervention. Practitioners must be prepared to provide any materials and/or training (directions, report forms, check sheets, etc.) necessary for the implementation of any suggested intervention. Because this is usually done with the parents in an office and with the teacher over the phone, it is important to write out the behavior plan (Appendix 5) that can be given to the parents and mailed (or emailed) to the teacher. This literally keeps everyone "on the same page" in relation to the steps of the intervention and enhances overall treatment integrity. The intervention strategies for success (ISS) form reviewed later in this chapter provide a prioritized list of interventions that teachers and parents can use to identify and prioritize what can be done in the classroom for a specific child.

Treatment Integrity and Compliance

Once the intervention has been agreed to and initially implemented, the next concern is that of treatment integrity—following through and implementing the program as it was designed. Regular communication with the parents and teachers is needed to keep the intervention on track. Therapists rely heavily on parent and teacher verbal reports (through office visits, phone calls, email, notes, and receiving the weekly report of behavior). However, if an intervention appears to be off track or there are conflicting reports then determining treatment integrity is most effective through direct observation. Once the treatment integrity has been confirmed, an intervention needs time to facilitate results. Both parents and teachers desire quick results but such results are rare and not longstanding. Keeping parents and teachers motivated until the behavior is changed is crucial.

Motivating parents and teachers to start and follow through with interventions is most critical at the beginning of the intervention or when it is not working well and needs to be modified. Motivation to stay with the plan can be enhanced by warning participants about plan pitfalls prior to the initiation of the intervention. Often letting both parents and teachers know that a target behavior may not change immediately, the possibility of regression, and/or that the plan can be revised if it is not working supports a realistic and motivated attitude. Let them know that behavioral change is a process that the practitioner will be engaged in until the problem is solved. If the first solution does not work, modification and adjustment will continue until a solution is achieved as a team. The best motivation for parents and teachers to keep up the intervention is seeing the behavior change over time. Weekly follow-up phone calls to support teacher and parent efforts are helpful in maintaining motivation and providing input for making necessary adjustments to the program. Reviewing the objective recording of behavior change is critical in communicating the effects of treatment.

Data Collection

Data collection is critical. Effective data collection on the target behavior will give an objective measure of success. Relying only on the parent's or the teacher's anecdotal comments of the effectiveness of the intervention can be misleading. These subjective memories can be affected positively or negatively by many factors and are often not accurate. A simple but accurate data collection procedure is always needed. Parents and teachers are more likely to collect the information needed to determine the success of the intervention when the data collection procedure is simple and easy. The same behavior report form (Appendix 3) or the SKAMP (Appendix 4) that was used for the initial collection of data can be used for this purpose.

IMPLEMENTING A SCHOOL–HOME REPORT CARD SYSTEM

The previous section outlined general guidelines for the development of a school–home behavior management program. A specific strategy for coordinating a school–home intervention is the use of a school–home report card, and the challenge is how a home program can reinforce appropriate behavior at school. The answer to this question lies again in effective and proactive communication between these two environments. The typical communication between school and home happens infrequently. Typically there are between two and eight reporting periods per year. Schools have long used a weekly and sometimes daily behavioral written report as a reaction to inappropriate behaviors in the form of a daily or weekly communication to the home. The weekly or daily written communication is often not an intervention but merely intended to inform parents regarding their child's inappropriate behavior. A more proactive and very prescriptive use of a daily behavioral report card (DBRC) has been found to be a simple, inexpensive, efficient, and adaptable tool for coordinating a school–home behavioral intervention (Chafoulcas ct al., 2002; Wright, 2000). Historically, DBRCs have been found to be feasible and effective in promoting positive studcnt behavior (Dougherty & Dougherty, 1977; Pelham, 1993).

Steps in Developing an Effective Daily Behavioral Report Card

Developing a Collaborative Parent/Teacher Team

Step one in developing a sound and effective DBRC is the development of a sound and effective home program. All effective home programs have behaviors that are objective and identifiable to both the child and the parents. In preparing for a home program to be integrated with input from the teacher, it is important for the child to view and perceive the parent and the teacher as collaborative authority figures. The parents and teacher must work closely together and present a unified front to the child. This avoids a potential for the child to split the parents and teachers, resulting in the child undermining the effectiveness of the report card system. When the teacher's input is used as a component of the home program, data must be viewed as valid and reliable by the parents (as implementers of the home program). Any questions or disagreements between the parents and the teacher regarding the report card should take place in private. While it is natural for a parent to question components of the report card, it would be inappropriate for a parent to minimize the teacher's input if a child reports that the teacher is unfair or irrational. This is the reason why it is critical in the development of a home program to seek input from the teacher and demonstrate to the child that the information will be utilized as reported, regardless of what the child attributes to the situation.

Identifying Core Information/Target Behaviors

After developing the home program, the practitioners in collaboration with the parents should identify the core information necessary from the teacher(s) that will be utilized within the home program. The practitioners in collaboration with parents need to determine how many behaviors the teacher can track and how often the teacher is able to give feedback to the student on the DBRC. In an elementary school setting, identification of three target behaviors is usually viewed as feasible. Some possible target areas are on-task behavior, initiating an assigned task, keeping hands to self, having materials, and completing classroom assignments. Each of these behaviors needs to be described fully and objectively to assure that the student, teacher, and parents are clear on what is expected. In middle and high school settings, the use of a DBRC is more complex because of the number of teachers that must collaborate in completing the DBRC. In addition, middle and high school students may be more resistant to using a DBRC because of the stigma that may be attached to having a DBRC. This can be overcome with a more covert DBRC, such as a small label put in the student's notebook.

Scale and Data

Following the identification of the target behaviors, the form of input from the school should be determined. In the typical school contract, broad areas such as "grade" and "behavior" are used in which the teacher writes daily notes home. Providing this type of information is usually daunting to the teacher who has to use their precious time to write something into the empty cell/box on the form. A simpler DBRC offers the advantage of merely circling a yes or no or the appropriate rating on a likert scale. Using a likert scale allows more flexibility in recognizing improvement as opposed to an all-or-none rating. For this reason, it has been found that the use of a likert scale is more effective and teacher friendly. In his *Classroom Behavior Report Card Resource Book*, Wright (2000) offers many examples of single-sheet DBRCs. As discussed earlier, simplicity facilitates compliance. A 1 to 3 scale with a "4" as a bonus to recognize exemplary behavior is simple and easy enough for most teachers, although any scale that both the parents and the teacher can agree to will work. The 1–3 scale forces categorization and therefore more objectivity. A rating of "3" could be the desirable and appropriate behavior within the category stated. A rating of "2" can be defined as "needing improvement." A rating of "1" can be defined as unacceptable and inappropriate behavior. The "4" rating is reserved for exemplary behavior where extra effort on the part of the student was clearly noted.

Sometimes ascribing of a numerical value may not be necessary. In some cases, circling a symbol may be more age appropriate for younger children, such as a thumbs-up, thumbs-medium, and thumbs-down, or happy/unhappy faces. The primary grade teacher at the UCI-Child Development Center states that the unhappy face scale has a negative effect. The child who is rated with the unhappy face then feels labeled as "unhappy" for the day and the ability to recover behaviorally at home is potentially undermined (Agler, 2002, personal communication). With the younger children, Agler (2002) prefers a color rating using the thermometer where red is "red hot—good, yellow is warm—needs to improve, and blue is cold—needs a lot of improvement." With older latency aged children (grades 4–6), happy faces combined with numeric ratings can be appropriate, in such cases the "1" rating could be an unhappy face symbol, a "2" rating a neutral face symbol, and the "3" a happy face symbol. Whether numbers or symbol, it is important to determine and clearly communicate the meaning of these symbols for the student, teacher, and parents alike.

Frequency of Data Collection

Different educational settings will dictate the frequency that data can be recorded on the DBRC. In a setting where there are support staff or aides available, target behaviors may be rated two or three times during the school day. More frequent data collection may be needed with younger children in that they may not be able to wait for feedback until the end of the day. Also, multiple ratings during a day may benefit a younger or more needy student in that a difficult morning may be rated while still allowing the student to recover and get better ratings later in the same day.

Back-up Reinforcers

The most critical component of the school–home report card is the consistent use of effective back-up reinforcers. A back-up reinforcer is the consequence given at home based on performance reported to the home through the DBRC. If the child brings the report card home and the parent forgets to provide reinforcement, the system will fail. If the child is not interested in the daily back-up reinforcer, the system will also fail. It is extremely important that the practitioner assists the parent in identifying a wide range of potential reinforcers that can be used on a daily basis. A menu of back-up reinforcement choices that the child can choose from increases the probability that the child will not become bored or disinterested in the back-up reinforcers. Parents should be encouraged to share with the teacher the back-up reinforcers they are using so the teacher can use them as a prompt. This also reassures the teacher that the parents are doing their part.

Consistent Application and Collaborative Adjustment

Once the DBRC home program is developed, it needs to be documented. A simple contract letter allows all parties to demonstrate consensus. Appendix 6 is an example of a DBRC definition and contract letter for elementary school with three target behaviors rated once a day by the teacher. This DBRC was printed onto a sticker, which was placed into the school-provided planner/agenda. The contract letter simply states steps 2–5 and defines the responsibilities of the child, the parents, and the teacher and can be developed in collaboration with the practitioner and the parents. Consistent application of the DBRC intervention is critical if behavioral change is to be achieved. The practitioner needs to utilize either reports or direct observation of DBRC data to determine treatment integrity. It would be prudent to have the parents provide copies of the child's DBRCs as data. The DBRC can be utilized as a data collection device superseding the more general behavioral reports or standardized scales because the DBRC serves as a child-specific scale.

If parents or teachers are demonstrating difficulty in complying with the DBRC program, it would be necessary to identify the obstacles to compliance and then either overcome the obstacles or modify the intervention to better meet the collaborative situation. If all parties are complying with the treatment plan and the target behaviors are not being modified following an appropriate length of time, then collaborative adjustment and the implementation of additional behavioral interventions may be necessary.

Ancillary Use of Daily Behavioral Report Cards for Pharmacological Interventions

As discussed earlier, collaboration among parent, teacher, and clinician is critical during the development, implementation, and adjustment of any intervention. As with any intervention, motivation to persevere is best facilitated through successful behavioral change. Sometimes true change may not come about through consultation and behavioral interventions. In these situations, pharmacological interventions may be explored through the addition of a psychiatrist or physician to the existing team of psychologist, teacher, and parent. Where pharmacological intervention is being considered, the DBRC can contribute to the pharmacotherapy as well (Pelham, 1993). DBRCs can offer baseline data for the psychiatrist to review. Regardless which DBRC scale is chosen initially, data points provide a prepharmacological intervention baseline. If the psychiatrist or physician chooses a chemical intervention, the existing DBRC will allow for objective determination of medication efficacy specifically to the target behaviors already identified. Whether utilized for behavioral or medical intervention efficacy, the DBRC will only provide useful data if the implementation is consistent over both home and school settings.

IDENTIFYING AND SHARING INFORMATION TO ACCOMMODATE CHILDREN WITH ATTENTION DEFICIT HYPERACTIVITY DISORDER AND LEARNING DISABILITIES

Diagnostic criteria change and are refined over time—the current version of the *Diagnostic and Statistical Manual* (American Psychiatric Association, 1994) is in its fourth revision. Special education laws and legislation change over time (i.e., the inclusion of ADHD as a qualifying condition under the other health impairment category in 1991) and between states (the presence or absence of the behaviorally disordered qualifying condition in different states). In this dynamic situation that straddles educational and mental health settings, one mind-set best serves the individual student with ADHD or LD: programming for an individual student's needs.

Starting with a clear understanding of a child's academic and behavioral needs rather than whether a child qualifies for categorical placement in special education creates a proactive program of intervention. Whether the child qualifies for special education or not, a prescription for addressing the identified problem is developed. Discrepancy models focusing only on weaknesses and discrepancies may miss critical information, such as the strategies that have been successful for the individual student in previous settings and that are necessary for the student to continue to grow and succeed.

The Intervention Strategies for Success (ISS) and Behavioral Intervention Responsibility Plan (BIRP) form (Appendix 7) grew out of extensive experience transitioning children following completion of an intensive clinical day treatment intervention and has proven effective in communicating the necessary programming (program components) to continue the academic and/or behavioral gains made in the program.

The key element is focusing on the individual needs of the child. Identifying a child as having ADHD does not effectively communicate much about the individual. When looking at diagnostic criteria, there are 252 six-item combinations of the nine criteria for DSM-IV's ADHD impulsive subtype and an additional 252 six-item combinations of inattentive subtype. This yields 63,504 possible combinations for mixed subtype children with ADHD. While many of the symptoms may be interdependent and the number less than suggested by the possible combinations, the point is still made that there are dramatic variations in children with the ADHD diagnosis.

Components of Programming Success Using the Intervention Strategies for Success (ISS) and Behavioral Intervention Responsibility Plan (BIRP)

Matching the needs of a child with ADHD or LD has five main components in the process of programming for success: (1) identifying successful strategies, (2) prioritizing the strategies that are essential to success, (3) identifying the resources that are available or that need to be available, (4) matching the student to the environment where the highest degree of necessary resources are available to the student, and (5) developing consensus between all team members.

Identifying Successful Strategies

There is a multitude of strategies a teacher has available to use in his/her classroom. There are many very specific and specialized behavioral interventions that are effective and continue to be documented in research and practice. The challenge comes when looking at an individual child and identifying what strategies that individual needs.

In the clinical setting, strategies are systematically tried and successes measured. The effectiveness of a strategy is determined by systematically implementing a strategy at increasing levels of intensity until the student is successful and then removing the intervention for a brief time to establish if a functional relationship exists between the intervention and the student's success. When a child's success decreases with removal of the intervention and increases with reinstitution, it is shown to have a functional relationship. The intervention is identified as being critical to the child's success. A list (or scaled checklist as is the case with the ISS form) is generated of the necessary strategies for that individual child's success.

The ISS form is more than just a list of interventions/accommodations. There are 91 specific strategies that it currently addresses. These are divided into six broad categories: namely 23 behavioral interventions, 8 strategies for environmental or physical arrangement of the room, 9 organizational strategies, 15 strategies for lesson preparation, 25 strategies relating to assignments or worksheets, and 11 test-taking strategies. With 91 strategies, the tailoring of programs to address academic interventions is not limited to solely addressing fluency, skill development, and productivity, but also includes behavioral management.

Prioritizing Strategies

Obviously, many children would benefit from many if not all of the strategies taught to teachers during their training. However, the reality is that very few teachers use all that they learned in their teacher training program on a day-to-day basis, nor should they—not all kids need all the special strategies available to teachers. Thus the need for step two of focusing on the child—prioritization of the strategies. Looking specifically at the ISS, each and every strategy on the form could be deemed helpful to any student. The ISS rating scale was developed to assist in prioritizing individual strategies that should be in place in the classroom to increase the academic and social success of the child with ADHD or LD. The rating is based on the degree of importance of each item to the child's predicted success. The form uses a 0–4 rating scale. An intervention is rated as "0—not recommended" when the intervention strategy does not increase desired behaviors. This strategy may provoke an undesirable student response or may be counter to previously identified "critical" interventions. An intervention is rated as "1—not critical" when the intervention strategy has demonstrated neither a positive nor a negative impact on desired behavior. An intervention is rated as "2—helpful" when the intervention strategy is helpful in combination with other strategies. The individual strategy does not increase desired behavior in isolation of other strategies. As mentioned earlier, almost every listed intervention could be considered "helpful" to most students (that is due to the fact that all these strategies are supportive by definition).

An intervention is rated as "3—highly recommended" when the intervention strategy has been demonstrated to increase desired behavior. Desired behavior decreases shortly after the intervention has been withdrawn. An example would be item number 514 on the ISS form, "develop school-based reinforcement for homework completion." A child receiving a rating of "3—highly recommended" for this item will be successful when the daily reinforcement is present. When the daily reinforcement is withdrawn, his homework compliance will decrease. While all students can benefit from daily reinforcement, the specific child in question has been identified as needing this intervention in order to be successful.

An intervention is rated as "4—critical" when the intervention strategy has demonstrated a direct correlation in increasing desired behavior. Consistency of this intervention is critical to student success. The commitment of the school site should be to deliver the intervention daily and consistently throughout the student's placement in that setting.

Identifying Available Resources

Following prioritization of the intervention list, the next step in focusing on the student should be identifying available resources. When a child's needs exceed the offerings of his/her current classroom placement, the teacher usually brings the issues to their school resources. These may include a special education teacher, a school psychologist, or other identified individuals. If the student study team feels that the child should be assessed for special education, then a referral is made. The typical special education assessment and placement process includes testing. Following testing, usually done by the special education teacher and psychologist, the "IEP" meeting is conducted to inform the parents of the results of the testing and to discuss placement options. If the testing indicates qualification (according to the federal guidelines), then the placement is discussed. If the testing results do not indicate a qualification, then there is no need for placement discussion (or the disagreement is stated and the process is moved the next level). This next level could include mediation and/or fair hearing.

It is essential in the IEP assessment process to talk with the current teacher and assess the current level of functioning. Obviously, if the child is encountering problems, the teacher's comments will reflect these concerns. If the child is doing well, the teacher may simply summarize the successes. When a child is being assessed, regardless of their special education qualification, diagnosis, or their current placement, it is essential to discuss what strategies or interventions are facilitating any successes. Often an IEP qualification/placement meeting will be held without the successful interventions being discussed. Even as the goals and objectives are being written, the methods and strategies to achieve these goals are not discussed. Administrators and school psychologists often assert that the method with which a teacher reaches the goals should be left up to the professional discretion of the teacher working with the student, successful strategies a previous teacher may have discovered for a specific child are seldom documented. This is corrected with the use of the ISS form.

MATCHING THE STUDENT TO THE ENVIRONMENT WHERE NECESSARY RESOURCES ARE AVAILABLE

Matching the Student to the Environment

Using the ISS as a platform for discussion (whether in the student study team, an IEP meeting, or just in an informal transition meeting) facilitates communication between school staff and parents by clearly articulating the program needs of the child. It fosters a less confrontational discussion. In discussion with parents, a discussion focusing on interventions that are successful and critical to their child's success rather than a discussion of whether their child qualifies for special education services is quite easy to accept. When each intervention is discussed, it is easier to address why it is necessary. When the whole of the ISS is discussed, a profile of critical and highly recommended interventions emerges. This profile actually defines the needs of the child (or more specifically for the child's success in the school setting).

This type of discussion is also very appropriate between teachers from year to year. What teacher would not want to know what has been successful in previous years? Whether qualified for special education or not, the knowledge of successful strategies is significant to a new school year. The situation where a teacher or setting may meet some but not all of the critically rated items does not necessarily cause problems. If many but not all critically rated interventions are present in one setting, the discussion now becomes how to supplement the needed interventions. The second part of the ISS is the behavioral intervention responsibility plan. The BIRP identifies individuals who have the ability to implement the strategies as identified on the ISS that are not possible by the teacher alone.

Examples of the ISS-BIRP in Action

Often student intervention teams, student study teams (SST), or individual education program teams identify the present level of functioning, long- and short-term objectives, and when those objectives should be met. While there is consensus on the objectives, there is no discussion of the strategies to accomplish the goals or the skills necessary to implement the strategies. While the goals may be appropriate, the teacher may not have the skills or the time to implement the strategies necessary to meet the goals. Because the SST or IEP team often does not include a discussion of specific strategies needed to accomplish short- and long-term goals, it is difficult to assess the potential for success of the plan. For example, a child is in a school setting and the previous teacher has discovered and documented with the ISS that this student has a critical need to have his homework assignment that he writes in his homework planner checked by staff in order assure that it is accurate. The next setting does not have time in the teacher's schedule to check his homework daily. While completing homework assignments successfully may be a goal on the student's IEP or accommodation plan, the teacher may not have the time or resources to implement a simple accommodation to assure that the child meets his homework goal.

The BIRP may identify an aide or other school staff to check and verify that the assignments are written accurately into the planner. The advantage of using the ISS-BIRP is that it is quick and simple in communicating what strategies are needed to meet identified academic and behavioral goals and who has the expertise to implement them.

The best way to illustrate how the ISS-BIRP can be used to facilitate success is to demonstrate how it has been used in planning and programming for some very divergent students. Both of the students in these case studies were originally seen with the primary concern of ADHD. The two students were not qualified for special education prior to the transition meeting used in the case study.

Case Study 1

Student 1 was a fifth-grade student with a high IQ. Although qualified for gifted education, the child was unable to access these classrooms due to behavior issues. Student 1 would become easily frustrated, especially when bored. When frustrated he would become aggressive and volatile. His level of frustration would frequently escalate to the point of throwing furniture and becoming a physical threat to himself and others. During the treatment phase, his parents were put through parent training and taught how to utilize home-based reinforcement for the child's appropriate behavior at school. The child also responded to a positive reinforcement model with a high frequency of verbal and nonverbal redirections prior to escalation. The student was also taught how to participate in a guided problem-solving model when he began to feel frustrated. Although some interventions were usually successful, the incidents of unsafe behavior were still possible if the other interventions were not successful.

Student 1's needs included the development of a positive intervention plan (following the Hughes bill in California that requires a written functional behavior analysis and plan prior to any hands-on or physical intervention). Additionally, it was determined that the staff needed some formal training in the management of assaultive behavior. The home–school link was also identified as critical. It was determined that the student needed a daily home/school behavioral report card that would allow the parents to positively reinforce appropriate behavior at school. The staff at the school site needed to be aware of the problem-solving model that proved successful in the previous setting and a mechanism by which the student could access this trained staff member. Finally, the student needed an educational environment that had the academic stimulation that addressed his cognitive level. This would prevent him from becoming bored and frustrated and hopefully decrease the incidents of escalation and aggressive behavior. In the placement meeting (which in effect was also an IEP placement meeting), one member of the new school team jokingly said, "What this child needs is a gifted-special day class." While stating a true oxymoron, the teacher was correct. This statement pointed out the problem with identifying placements rather than placement plans.

Rather than enter into a discussion on the existence or lack of a gifted–SDC in that particular district, the topic was changed to how can we create an environment that meets this child's needs? Utilizing the BIRP, the child was placed into the gifted classroom. In order to facilitate special education resources, the child was qualified for special education services under the other health impairment category using his diagnosis of ADHD. This qualification thus facilitated the written behavioral intervention plan to be completed by a behavioral intervention case manager in order to meet the requirements of the Hughes bill. In the intervention plan, the classroom teacher, the aid, the playground staff, and the principal were all trained in that district's approved management of assaultive behavior course. In effect, a gifted–SDC classroom was created.

Case Study 2

Student 2 was also in the fifth grade and had a high IQ. Although qualified for gifted education, the child was unable to access these classrooms due to behavior issues. Student 2 was very different from Student 1 in the previous example. Student 2 would become very anxious and experienced a high degree of separation anxiety. Initially having only a diagnosis of "ADHD," this student also benefited from the clinical day treatment center. The clarity of rules and directions necessary for the program's token economy also decreased any ambiguity—such ambiguities were antecedents for his anxiety attacks. Student 2 expressed his anxiety in a flight response and had a history of leaving school grounds for home when in his previous school. When the student encountered anxiety at the clinical day treatment program, the opportunity to process his feelings with the school psychologist would frequently allay the panic response. Knowing that the psychologist could call his parents was all that this student needed to know, although the process of actually calling was not necessary in the treatment center. The parents also benefited from parent training and were able to facilitate home reinforcement for school behavior.

Student 2 also needed an academic environment that attended to his higher cognitive functioning. He needed a high degree of clearly defined rules and expectations. This was especially true when it came to the consequences of leaving school grounds during the school day. Identifying and fully sharing with the school psychologist in the receiving school the strategies to allay the anxieties and to proactively create a therapeutic alliance between the student and this counselor was critical. Developing a home program to positively reinforce the appropriate school behavior and contingency planning in the event that the anxiety was triggered was done with both the home and the school. Finally, the student was actively involved in the planning and transition meetings, visited the campus, and met all involved faculty prior to transition.

In communicating the ISS for Student 2, the issue of qualification for special education services was not necessary. The BIRP identified placement in the gifted cluster of classes. These gifted teachers had no problem committing to the daily report card with which to communicate daily behavior to the parents for reinforcement. The key with this child was the development of a counselor/psychologist to address crisis management and issues of anxiety should they occur. Student 2's needs were met without qualifying for special education and or writing a 504 accommodation plan.

Considerations in Using the ISS–BIRP

The ISS–BIRP is a useful tool that highlights a collaborative process for identifying or developing a successful educational environment for a child. It is designed to facilitate collaboration between home and school in identifying or developing an effective program for a student. It adds the "how" to the "what," "when," and "where" that is often not the focus of discussion in SST, IEP, or teacher meetings. The ISS–BIRP is a seemingly simple and effective tool to communicate student's needs but it is not without some caveats and warnings.

The ISS is best completed by a practitioner in collaboration with teachers or support staff who are familiar with and have had demonstrated success with the child. The practitioner should guide the teacher offering data to complete the ISS and not filter and second guess the receiving environment. It is contradictory to the spirit and purpose of the ISS to limit the number of items receiving a rating of "4" to that which the teacher feels is possible in the next environment. If a child's profile does not match the next environment, that is exactly the information the ISS is trying to reach. In such a situation the BIRP may indicate that additional resources are necessary in the child's programming. Additionally, raters should not exaggerate the ratings in an effort to necessitate a more intense environment. A word of wisdom is "be careful what you ask for, because you might just get it." As in the case of Students 1 and 2, a special day class would not be appropriate.

The practitioner should assure the teacher that the goal of the process is not to make value judgements about the teacher, the school, or the programs, but to determine the appropriateness of the match between a program and the child's needs. It should be used to develop creative solutions by brainstorming resources that can be accessed to assist in meeting the child's needs.

Using the ISS–BIRP to Reduce Conflicts between Parent and School

Practitioners may often be consulted when there is an existing conflict between the parents and the school regarding the appropriateness of a placement. The steps outlined in the above mentioned case studies were used to foster collaboration and reduce conflict by using the ISS–BIRP to better match a child's behavioral and academic needs. Independently interviewing parents and teachers to first gain consensus on the "critical" accommodations that need to be in place to increase the probability of the child's academic and/or behavioral success facilitates communication. Both parties have an objective and clear picture of what a successful setting would look like. What would they see the teacher and/or support staff doing that matches the ISS–BIRP profile? The district has an objective criterion through use of the ISS–BIRP profile and the parents can use the profile to judge appropriateness. Focusing on the child's needs and the means to achieve them foster a sense of trust.

FACILITATING ACCESS TO SPECIAL EDUCATION SERVICES

Practitioners assume the role as direct service providers, rendering diagnostic impressions and direct interventions to those served. Practitioners are also involved in supporting the family as a consequence of having a member with ADHD/LD. The challenges created by the child's ADHD or LD can cause a ripple effect within the whole family system and have a direct effect on the functioning of the family. This suggests that outcomes that pertain specifically to the child at some level may have an effect on the stability within the home and have a strong impact on the functioning of both the child and the nuclear family.

Jaska (2002) points out that parents of children with mild disabilities may not choose their roles as advocates, but are thrust into that role when they discover their child may have special needs. To be a truly effective advocate, parents must have a good understanding of their child. Parents also must become cognizant of the practical applications of disability law and how it applies to their child. Too often, many parents are not aware of their child's entitlements. These parents find themselves lost in the bureaucracy of education and habitually failing to secure what the child needs. Lack of awareness and assertiveness puts these parents at a great disadvantage. Practitioners, in accepting them as clients, assume the role of helping these parents become educated consumers. In seeking the assistance of a trained and licensed therapist/psychologist, they are soliciting the professional's training and insight into these problems. Just as the parents are thrust into the role of advocate, so too is the practitioner when they offer their services as consultants and case managers to the clients. Practitioners must also become educators, exposing parents to their role as advocates for their child. Through example, the practitioner's positive consultation and collaboration with local school officials will model the avoidance of adversarial situations and thereby avoid negative and conflict-laden outcomes. Practitioners must encourage in word and deed that advocacy can be implemented in a collaborative manner. Parents that communicate in a respectful, assertive, and considerate manner are possibly more likely to get the services that their child needs. The crucial components to being a change agent are not only the parents' ambitions, but also their conscientiousness and their ability to be informed consumers/advocates.

In defense of educators, there are many school officials who will walk the extra mile for their students and will make tremendous efforts to accommodate individual differences. However, the realities of public education sidetrack institutions from meeting the global psycho/social needs of their students and providing the minority (of which ADHD and LD children are members) with the most appropriate education.

Practitioners must develop an atmosphere of trust and cooperation with local school officials if they are to truly serve their clients. This degree of cooperation will encourage school personnel to act more collaboratively with the clinician and those he serves. Nevertheless, when necessary, practitioners must act more forcefully to help families get the services that are needed. It is therefore essential in the role of practitioner to have a current and fundamental working knowledge of the local laws that pertain to education and federal and state special education laws and legislation (including the most current authorization of the Individuals with Disabilities Education Act—P.L.105–17), as well as any legislation and laws addressing the disabled population as a whole (Civil Rights Section 504 of the Vocational Rehabilitation Act revised in 1973—P.L. 93–112).

The Individual with Disabilities Education Act (IDEA) addresses many minimum requirements to implement a free and appropriate education for children and youth with disabilities. This law also covers early intervention services. Although subtle differences exist between the various states, the law entitles parents with certain provisions. If the parent believes that the child is in need of special education, they have the right to request an evaluation of their child. Furthermore, if the district feels that a child may need to be evaluated, the parent has the right to be notified and must give consent. It is important for families to realize that they have the right to also obtain an independent evaluation outside the school system. Parents can request that the school district pay for this consultation if they believe that the evaluation conducted by the district was not appropriate.

When a child is found by the school district as not qualifying for special education and it is evident that they need special accommodations, parents can request a 504 hearing based on the fact that ADHD is the disability impacting the ability to access public education. According to Section 504, the child with a disability may receive accommodations and modifications that support his/her access to education. It is incumbent upon the parents (with the support of various practitioners) to document the disabling features and the accommodations that would be necessary to help support the child. It is now the role of the practitioner and the parents to understand the accommodations as stated in the written 504 accommodation plan and to ensure that these accommodations are implemented in the school setting. It is also necessary for the practitioner to inform and support the parents in the appropriate course of action and process that may be necessary if the written accommodations are not implemented.

Practitioners may find it helpful to recommend to parents that they read up on both of the laws and become more aware of their rights. Wrightslaw (http://www.wrightslaw.com), which is based in Deltaville, Virginia, and the National Information Center for Children and Youth with Disabilities (NICYD) in Washington, DC, are two excellent resources to gain information on both laws. In fact, Ferguson and Ripley (1991, with NICYD) developed a parent's guide on how parents can communicate their concerns about their child to school districts through letter writing. They state that letters provide families with an excellent tool to record their concerns, suggestions, and ideas to school officials. Letters can be a first step for parents to clarify their apprehensions to their school districts and request what they believe would be helpful.

With the permission of NICYD, Appendix 8 includes core letters that could be used as a guide for families. The core letters address six areas where parent documentation is critical in the process of accessing special education in the public setting. These six areas are (1) requesting initial evaluation for special education services (to initially determine qualification for special education services), (2) requesting a meeting to review the IEP (if an existing IEP's goals and objectives are in question or progress is not being noted), (3) requesting a change of placement (in the event that the child's needs change or that the needs are not being addressed appropriately), (4) requesting records, (5) requesting an independent education evaluation at public expense, and (6) requesting a due process hearing (the formal name for the conflict resolution process where an independent hearing officer hears both sides of a disagreement between parents and school personnel with the goal of providing an appropriate education for the child). These core letters are valuable but the source document stands on its own as an educational tool for both practitioners and parents regarding communication strategies within the legal/educational environment. The NICYD provides this publication via the internet (http://nichcy.org/pubs/parent/pa9txt.htm) and thereby provides the practitioner the ability to educate the parents by directing them to the source document. Practitioners should not only know the laws, but the tools by which to navigate the legal system within which the education system is bound. Practitioners should access these tools and educate their parent–clients to access them as well.

CONCLUSION

Challenges for children with ADHD and/or LD cross the home and school environment. This chapter is designed to foster collaboration between home and school through practical and effective practitioner-facilitated interventions. First, practitioners must help parents and teachers strengthen their home and school behavior management programs. General guidelines are provided to assist parents and teachers in selecting target behaviors, collecting baseline information, developing an intervention, and monitoring the effectiveness of intervention.

The steps in setting up, implementing, and monitoring a school–home daily behavior report card are presented as a method of collaboration between home and school. A sample DBRC is provided in Appendix 6. Using a DBRC, parents can play a critical role in motivating their child to give their best effort in the classroom. Teaming with parents allows teachers to provide more frequent and more potent back-up reinforcers than can be provided by the teacher alone.

When the style of the teacher and the strategies implemented in the classroom match a student's needs, the student is often less symptomatic. A process for communicating the needs of a student using the ISS-BIRP is presented as a nonconfrontational approach to collaboration between home and school for the purpose of obtaining a good match. This process describes the components of a setting that best matches the individual student's needs. The ISS-BIRP is developed through consensus between the practitioner and the school and shared and documented to the parents. This serves as an objective profile that can be referred to in determining if a given classroom or combination of support services matches a student's needs. The process of qualifying for special education is deemphasized, instead emphasizing the process of identifying resources and expertise necessary for the student's success. The need to access services is identified on the student's ISS profile. Through this process a BIRP is developed regardless of whether the student qualifies for special education services. The question of qualification for special education under IDEA or the development of a 504 accommodation plan is based on the extent of the student's needs. The importance of being versed in current federal laws and civil rights codes is discussed to assist practitioners in helping parents access needed services.

While teachers and parents have a common goal of helping students reach their potential, often the process for accomplishing this goal is not clear. Practitioners who focus on assisting parents and teachers to clearly articulate the needs of the students they serve and collaborate in matching these needs with services create a foundation for success.

REFERENCES

American Psychiatric Association (1980). *Diagnostic and statistical manual of mental disorders* (3rd ed.). Washington, DC: author.
American Psychiatric Association (1987). *Diagnostic and statistical manual of mental disorders* (3rd ed. revised). Washington, DC: author.

American Psychiatric Association (1994). *Diagnostic and statistical manual of mental disorders* (4th ed.). Washington, DC: author.

Axelrod, S., Moyer, L., & Berry, R. (1990). Why teachers do not use behavior modification procedures. *Journal of Educational and Psychological Consultation*, 1, 309–320.

Chafouleas, S., Riley-Tillman, T., & McDougal, J. (2002). Good, bad, or in-between: How does the daily behavior report card rate? *Psychology in the Schools*, 39, 157–169.

Christenson, S., & Christenson, C. (1998). *Family, school, and community influences on children's learning: A literature review (Report No. 1). Live and learn project.* Minneapolis, MN: University of Minnesota Extension Service.

Christenson, S. L., Rounds, T., & Gorney, D. (1992). Family factors and student achievement: An avenue to increase students' success. *School Psychology Quarterly*, 1(3), 178–206.

Dougherty, E., & Dougherty A. (1977). The daily report card: A simplified and flexible package for classroom behavior management. In L. A. Hersov & M. Berger (Eds.), *Aggression and antisocial behavior in childhood and adolescence* (pp. 73–79). London: Pergamon Press.

Ferguson, S., & Ripley, S. (1991). *A parent's guide: Special education and related services: Communication through letter writing.* Washington, DC: The National Information Center for Children and Youth with Disabilities.

Gutkin, T. B., & Curtis, M. J. (1999). School–based consultation: Theory, techniques, and research. In T. B. Gutkin & C. R. Reynolds (Eds.), *The Handbook of School Psychology* (3rd ed., pp. 598–637). New York: Wiley.

IDEA Amendments of 1997 (1997). Pub. L. No. 105–17.

Jaska, P. (2002). Be your child's Strongest Advocate. *ADDitude, p. 4–6.*

Pelham, W. (1993). Pharmacotherapy for children with attention deficit hyperactivity disorder. *School Psychology Review*, 22, 199 227.

Rathvon, N. (1999). *Effective school interventions.* New York: Guilford Press.

Sheridan, S. M., Kratochwill, T. R., & Bergan, J. R. (1996). *Conjoint behavioral consultation.* New York: Plenum Press.

Sheridan, S., Eagle, J., Cowan, R., & Mickelson, W. (2001). The effects of conjoint behavioral consultation results of a 4-year investigation. *Journal of School Psychology*, 39(5), 361–385.

Sprick, R., & Howard, L. (1999). *Teacher's encyclopedia of behavior management.* New York: Guildford Press.

Swanson, J. (1992). *School-based assessments and interventions for ADD students.* Irvine, CA: KC Publishing.

Swanson, J. M., Agler, D., Fineberg, E., Wigal, S., Flynn, D., Fineberg, K., Quintana, Y., & Talebi, H. (1999). UCI Laboratory School Protocol for PK/PD Studies. In L. Greenhill & B. Osman (Eds.), *Ritalin: Theory and practice* (2nd ed., pp. 405–430). Mary Ann Liebert, Publishers.

Wright, J. (2000). Classroom behavior report card resource book. Retrieved 25 Oct 02 from http://www.jimwrightonline.com/pdfdocs/tbrcExcerpt.pdf

Parenting Children with Learning and Attention Disorders: Concerns and Directions for Therapeutic Intervention

Aubrey H. Fine, Nadejda Karpova, Nicole Thorn, Christine Holland and Ronald Kotkin

Recently I was given a letter by a parent expressing her feelings about having a son with attention deficit hyperactivity disorder (ADHD). Cindy (not her real name) is a single mom who has a son in high school. Over the years she has experienced some rough episodes in parenting her son. She writes:

> As a young mom, I was presented with a beautiful infant who I prayed was healthy. I gloated over my son. To me he was the most adorable child. As a new mom, I relished the opportunity of having a child! This was going to be my chance to make a difference. We want our children to grow up and become happy, fulfilled, spiritually grounded, financially successful human beings. We have so much hope and aspirations. Unfortunately, my story has more downs than ups. It has been hard to sit and present my thoughts. I often avoided putting my thoughts into words. Perhaps because the experience was going to be too painful. Well, here it goes . . . let me tell you what it has been about for me. I won't bore you with all the details, but I will get right to the point. Here are some of my reflections.
>
> As an infant, Alan (not his real name) had trouble getting to sleep. Bedtime and naps could turn into great ordeals. He generally needed rocking and singing prior to his nap. He chattered and was very vocal at an early age. I initially thought the

behavior was cute but as he aged he never stopped! At an early age he became very mobile. When he began to walk it was at a high speed. People began to comment (to my face and behind my back) that he was very busy. In fact, even my father used to refer to him as hyper (which terribly hurt my feelings).

Social challenges and traumas came early in our lives together. He had so many tantrums, from leaving a friend's home, to fighting when he didn't get his way in stores and restaurants. It was horrible to deal with. Perhaps even more appalling was (and it still is) to hear others state that all this child needs is discipline. I had been made to feel incompetent and there were many who insinuated that it was obviously due to my indulgence and lack of skill. I found myself retreating and not even socializing with friends for months just to avoid their negative, painful comments and looks.

Shortly after entering the toddler years, invitation to parties and get-togethers were very sparse. I learned to accept these realities. Over the years, I cannot tell you how many parties I had to carry my son out of. In some ways it was a relief not to get invitations in that I didn't have to deal with his behavior. However, I was heartbroken my son couldn't enjoy this type of interaction. He was being excluded, and he still was so young and innocent.

The word school brings a horrible, sour taste to my mouth. In fact, it began right when Alan entered preschool. The day would start off with an extremely crabby and difficult child to wake up (which still is the case at age 14). I found myself praying every morning that he would have a good day. I would always dread picking him up from school and listening to all the things he had done. In retrospect, I wish the teachers would have appreciated how hard it was becoming for me! By the end of our 2 years of preschool, I found my son sitting in the "director's office" everyday waiting for me to pick him up. They were tired of working with him. I later found out from another parent that he spent an hour (most days) by himself in the chair next to the director. They were not sure of the root of his problems, but they had a hunch that he may have ADHD. However, the doctors I brought him to wouldn't address this issue until he started kindergarten.

In the first week of kindergarten, we went to see a neurologist. The doctor stated that my son was probably the most hyperactive, bright child he had seen in 20 years. He cautioned me that the road would be a difficult one and if I could survive raising him to the age of 20, I would deserve a medal. From that day on, the merry go round of raising a child with ADHD began. We had our challenges finding a medicine that was effective. Ritalin worked for a while. However, during the second grade, we needed to adjust his medication, as the dose of Ritalin was not effective in holding him. All the while I did research on ADHD, attended CHADD meetings. . . . struggling with parenting and life. We also started counseling for my son.

The second grade was a challenging year for Alan and me. I became more frustrated with the trial and error of medication, the constant challenges at school, and the personal lack of reward of raising a child who was oppositional and argumentative. I truly felt it was "me and him" against the world. We were both so alone. My husband even stated my inability to parent was the reason for Alan's problems. This lack of sensitivity and support was detrimental to our marriage.

During Alan's third-grade year we took a parenting class where we learned more sophisticated applied behavior modification techniques. The suggested formula utilized medication, along with behavior modification and counseling, and was the first real successes we had. We worked extremely hard to create a process of communication with the teachers and principal at the school building, and we recorded the various behaviors throughout the day during school. We monitored the data closely and developed a school/home reward system.

Once we established a formula for success, I continued applying this pattern for a few years. I organized constant meetings with his teachers, which seemed to decrease the negative outcome. The energy necessary to get this accomplished was consuming; however, as his major advocate, all I could think of was making things better for my only son.

All of the above took its toll on our marriage and when he was in fourth grade we were divorced. I am thankful that he had the supporting relationship with his counselor prior to the divorce, as this was critical during this sad time. However, my son and I now live in an environment that is much healthier, less negative, and our quality of life is dramatically better.

I often wondered where was the "joy of parenting," as I rarely felt any. The work was constant; however, I knew that the formula started in third grade was the key. But the personal pain was tremendous. It not only affected my home life, but also my relationships with friends. I constantly felt the need to protect my son from social events so that there was relief from the critical eye of the world.

People were often cruel. For example, there was even a teacher who asked why my son was even allowed in school. He was in a Catholic school with teachers with limited abilities to accommodate children with special needs. My hope was that the smaller school and universe would help particularly in junior high. Alan graduated from junior high last week, and looking back, I think all the effort really made a difference. He scored very well on the placement test for high school (which I was thrilled for him).

Sports were another dimension with similar outcomes over the years. Coaches did not want him on their teams. They never really said this to my face, but how they treated Alan, and the attitude they presented to me, easily inferred it. Out of convenience, I found that I needed to put extra energy into relationships with teachers and coaches. Over the years I learned to become the best room mom, or always the team mom.

Alan's overall ability to make friends, and have friends, has always been bad. His overall stubborn and argumentative personality can be difficult for everyone. At this time of his life, he has very few good friends.

As we have aged together, I can now look back and see my son's good qualities. He is thoughtful, in touch with his feelings, and, with support from counseling over the years, has learned more about communication. He continues to be stubborn and defensive at times. Nevertheless, when he thinks about his behavior, he quickly apologizes. He does have compassion for others and can be very caring. He is now more like a "typical teenager." The energy I have expelled over the years will still be needed to help him become successful. I am very tired . . . it isn't fun, but I won't give up on him!

Over the years, I have recognized that my own self-worth has been greatly damaged due to my son's needs. Although I know I have worked extremely hard and have been successful in providing him with the sound tools he needs to be successful,

I continue to feel frustrated. It is painful to live with a child who gives back very little and takes so much.

My overall comment to any parents of a child with ADHD is to be the foundation for your children. Support them with the formula I referred to earlier. Try not to get angry. Laugh and look at every gain. Love your child. But realize it will take a lot of thankless work to help your child grow into the healthy adult that you dreamed of when you first held him in your arms.

This letter reflects the uncertainty and frustration that a parent experienced over the years in bringing up her child. The emotional tolls she identifies (feeling alone, hopeless) are reflective of what many other parents express while bringing up their children. It is as if they are living on a roller coaster, and unfortunately (as she says) there are more downs than ups.

This chapter identifies the various challenges that parents experience as they rear their sons and daughters. We review the literature, incorporate some of the major findings, and follow up with some suggestions that clinicians should incorporate while working with families. Chapter 9 highlights specific home management guidelines.

RESEARCH TO PRACTICE: WHAT DOES THE LITERATURE SAY?

During the past three decades, much research has focused on the problems and characteristics families of children with learning disabilities (LD) and ADHD. From these studies, it seems that the challenges faced by parents of sons and daughters with mild disabilities may be considered somewhat different from those of families who have children with severe disabilities.

Ross (1964) pointed out that the family with a child with a mild handicap has more difficult problems arising from parent–child relationships. These challenges arise from such variables as the invisibility of the disability, the lack of awareness of the disability, and the difficulties in parenting the child. Unfortunately, the realities that many of these families face are the episodes of disruptiveness and tension within their families. Family genograms have been found to be valuable tools as they clearly illustrate where disputes actually arise within families. In some cases, the entire family may be impacted, whereas in others there may be conflict between specific members of the family and the child. With the support of the genogram the clinician can illustrate visually the challenges that a

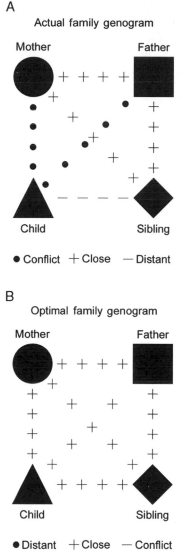

FIGURE 1   (A) An actual family genogram. (B) An optional family genogram.

family faces, and perhaps where the dynamic difficulties are. Figure 1 illustrates a possible family scenario, highlighting actual family functioning versus the desired change.

The nature of the handicap determines how the family and society respond to it. For example, Faerstein's research (1986) showed that "invisible" handicaps of the children caused their mother's isolation within the community and made their adjustment and coping more difficult. It is commonly thought that if the child's behavior is not acceptable and he/she does not do well at school, the parents are often blamed initially. This can result in a transient stress disorder; it can also have a permanent debilitating effect on the entire family (Schulz, 1987). As noted in Cindy's letter, many outsiders did not understand why Alan behaved the way he did. To these outsiders, Alan was acting like a brat and all he needed was firm discipline and consistency.

Current research such as that by Anastopoulous (1992) suggests that parents of children with the combined form of ADHD (rather than those diagnosed with the predominant inattentive form) expressed more dissatisfaction in their parenting roles. Specifically, mothers noted that a child's inattention and oppositional conduct problems contributed uniquely to role distress (dissatisfaction related to parenting or parenting performance). For fathers, parenting role distress was associated uniquely with child oppositional or aggressive behaviors, but not with ADHD symptom severity. Anastopoulous et al. (1993) concluded by suggesting that role distress may be most related to a disruption of family relations and may be amenable to intervention.

Perhaps a great challenge in parenting children with LD and ADHD is the revelation that there is a legitimate reason for the behaviors being displayed. For example, Faerstein (1986) reported that the average age of diagnosis for children with LD was 5.9 years (with a range from 2 to 12). This suggests that there is an enormous delay for some parents between their suspecting that something was wrong with their children and their obtaining a professional diagnosis. There is a similar phenomenon with the diagnosis of ADHD. Moghadam (1988) stressed that there was a 2- or 3-year lapse from the time the parents suspected that something was "not quite right with their child" until the diagnosis was made. It is only logical to appreciate the impact of this delay on how parents cope with their children.

The cause of the disorder (or the search for the cause) may also have a great impact on the family. Parents often search aimlessly in trying to get a better understanding of the problem. They may not find professionals who are well trained in this area, and an accurate diagnosis may not be secured for a while. This will only make situations harder on the child and the family. For instance, in Alan's case the family did not secure a clear diagnosis until he was in kindergarten. If a diagnosis and a plan had been put into place earlier, some of the initial trauma could have been avoided.

The literature suggests that if a source to the problem is not found, parents begin to blame themselves. The outcome of Faerstein's (1986) and Chodoff et al. (1964) research points out that many parents internalize the disabilities. However, Podolski and Nigg (2001) discovered that parents who cope by the use of more positive framing (thinking about problems as challenges rather than obstacles) were associated with higher role satisfaction for both mothers and fathers. A reoccurring finding in the literature suggests that the strongest predictor of both a child's progress and maternal efficiency was the mother's perception of whether she could be effective with her child. This leads us to believe that one of the strongest ingredients that we can give to the parents we serve is hope. We have to help them recognize the legitimacy of the behavior they are seeing and that with proper care and support their child can make gains.

THEORETICAL MODELS FOR UNDERSTANDING PARENTAL RESPONSES

As clinicians, we may want to illustrate for parents and others the phases that so many go through while rearing their child. Over the years, many have attempted to use a stage theory to explain the emotions of new parents who have a child with a disability. Kubler-Ross's (1969) theory of the stages of grief is often used as a method of explaining how one deals with a child with a disability. When a child is born who does not fulfill the parents' hopes, or when a child is diagnosed at a later age with a disability, a parent's dream of having a "normal child" dies. This profound loss is a normal initial reaction, but it can become detrimental for the parent as well as the family. The loss of the dream, and the stages of mourning that a parent may face, is the subject of the next few paragraphs.

Duncan (1977) is credited with adapting Kubler-Ross's theory and applying it to parents with children with disabilities. Duncan (1977) suggested that the birth of a child with any disability (or discovering the child's disability later, as it is with LD) is similar to the loss of a loved one. The model incorporates the five stages: denial, bargaining, anger, depression, and acceptance.

Denial

Denial and shock are the parents' initial response. This defense mechanism operates on an unconscious level and is aimed at warding off anxiety. According to Duncan's theory, parents deny the frightening reality that their child has a challenge. They are often confused, disorganized, and helpless. Cindy, for example, experienced a lot of confusion and frustration while coping with her son. She felt rejected. She was also hurt that many people did not accept her son. There was also some denial that there was anything significantly wrong with her son. He simply needed more time to mature. Cindy's reaction is typical. She was trying to make sense of a terrible situation. She did this by trying to disguise the behaviors to justify their existence. Seligman (1979) pointed out that some parents disguise their child's condition rather than deny or accept it. With this disguise, a causal factor is put forth as the reason for the child's problems such as being lazy or uncooperative.

Bargaining

The second stage is the bargaining stage and is characterized by "positive thinking," e.g., "If I work hard on helping my child, he will recover." Some parents seek help from organizations for the disabled, some turn to religion, and some wait or pray for a miracle. Parent organizations such as Learning Disability Association (LDA) or Children and Adults with ADD (CHADD) provide strong support. They help parents meet others who are in a similar situation.

Anger

As some parents begin to realize that their child cannot improve quickly, they become angry. It is apparent that these parents will become discouraged over time. They come to believe that their attempt to find a solution and to help their child does not dramatically improve the situation. Living with a frustrating child (and getting no support from a community and family members), compounded with professionals who have different opinions, can trigger the anger stage. It is at this time that many professionals get to see their parents.

Depression

The stage of depression usually begins with guilt evoked by parents' condemnatory attitude toward themselves. Negative feelings about a "normal" child can challenge the parents to accept the child for who she or he is. This outcome was clearly highlighted in the letter prepared by Cindy. She was having a hard time accepting Alan for who was, and she felt guilty. Seligman (1995) describes a long-term effect of chronic demoralization that lingers throughout the parenting cycle. He calls this process "chronic sorrow." This is not a temporary stage, but rather a feeling that may accompany parents of children with exceptionalities throughout life. This does not imply that such parents are always sad or depressed, but rather that they may experience demoralized feelings at crucial life milestones (e.g., when a child's formal K–12 schooling has concluded and the parents do not see any possibilities to further the child's education).

Acceptance

Gradually, most parents begin to "awake" from depression and move toward acceptance. However, numerous variables impact the outcome of the grieving stages. For example, anger can become a rehearsed response to having to deal with the behaviors of a child. It is at this stage that parents begin to respond rationally to their child's realities. In most cases, parents begin to take a more active stance in their child's life. Seligman (1995) described the characteristics of parents' behavior that can be observed at this stage. The parents are willing to attend parent–teacher conferences, can discuss their child's disability with relative ease, can abandon overprotective and rejecting behavioral patterns toward their child, can collaborate with the teacher and make plans, will pursue personal interests unrelated to their child, can discipline the child appropriately without feeling guilty, and evidence a balance between encouraging independence and showing love.

This is the stage that parents need to arrive at. With professional support we can help parents see the light at the end of the tunnel. They need to see value in their efforts and the call for their continued involvement.

Acceptance waxes and wanes during parent's lives, as does depression. It is crucial to highlight that the process may become cyclical. At various stages in a child's life, a parent may regress to an earlier stage. For example, a child may do well in elementary school after being identified with a learning disability. However, once entering middle school, some of the initial problems dealt with may reoccur and begin to frustrate the parents who regress to the depression stage.

Although Duncan's theory is well accepted by the professional community, other points of view exist. Moses (1982) describes the grieving process in parents of children with disabilities as *gradual grieving* that may have "feeling states," such as denial, anxiety, fear, depression, guilt, and anger. However, Moses argues that these states do not have to follow any specific pattern. He views grieving as "not a step-by-step process that evolves through discrete stages." Each person can experience different feeling states at different times, depending on his own unique manner and order. Within his theory, he did not incorporate the final stage as acceptance. He believed that "the concept of acceptance is totally unfounded" and may never really occur. It is important to recognize that not all family members experience the same stages of mourning at the same time. When one parent is bargaining and the other is still denying, then the process of adjustment may slow down.

Each possible phase (rather than stage) seems to have a specific rational purpose. For example, anxiety may serve to mobilize the parents to make changes in their lives (perhaps in their attitudes, priorities, values, beliefs, and/or day-to-day routines). Fear is a warning that alerts the person to the seriousness of the internal changes that are demanded. Guilt may be necessary when parents are trying to explain why the tragedy has happened to them. Moses (1986) suggests that the experience of deep pain can be used to reorder the rightness of the world. Guilt is the feeling state that facilitates this struggle to order. Finally, the anger expressed by some parents may serve as a medium through which they redefine their concepts of fairness and justice in the world.

It is apparent that these stages may have a conceptual place in understanding the dilemmas of treating the affected families. To some degree, parents of children with LD and ADHD have experienced most of the stages. For some parents, the identification of learning disabilities may bring false hope. The nature of the disability may cause stronger denial in the parents, as well as more active attempts in seeking ways to treat their children. Feelings of anger may be more intensive because, although the child seems "normal" and has a high IQ, it seems incomprehensible that a disorder does exist and the child is merely lazy or the teachers "cannot teach."

The stage theory has not been supported by extensive theoretical data. Rather, these models are the result of clinical judgements based on interviews. Moreover, there has not been much research on parents of children with LD and ADHD that clearly describes the way parents attempt to cope. Additionally, there is no research that demonstrates abnormalities in the personalities of parents with children with disabilities. In general, most families with exceptional children function well. Many of the difficulties that the parents experience with family life may occur in a family without a child with LD or ADHD.

AN ECOLOGICAL MODEL TO DISABILITIES: ITS IMPACT ON OUR UNDERSTANDING AND PRACTICE

The ecosystem model developed by Bronfenbrenner (1979) seems applicable in describing the support mechanisms that people use for overcoming the stresses of having a child with a disability. The model consists of a series of nested contexts called microsystem, mesosystem, exosystem, and macrosystem. It has been used to describe many significant challenges confronting families, including divorce and child abuse (Belsky, 1980a). Gorcy et al. (2000) point out that the model views a person's life as a social unit embedded within various formal and informal social units.

It is apparent that the quality of life for families with children with LD and ADHD depends on available support mechanisms. Quality of life is defined as an overall well-being that encompasses physical, material, social, and emotional welfare (Felce & Perry, 1993). It is believed that the perceived quality of life for families depends, in part, on how the family attempts to cope with their child's disability. When one feels supported and perceives fewer challenges, it is possible that the individual will cope more effectively as a family.

This model is similar to the way that naturalists would describe the layers of an ecosystem. Figure 2 illustrates the model under focus. Each of the layers is connected, with the central, innermost layer being the microsystem. It includes everything within the child's home and can either support or contaminate the growth of that child. A child with a support system at home may adapt more effectively to his or her disability.

The impact of the disability seems to depend on factors such as family resources, relationships within the family, and the social support system

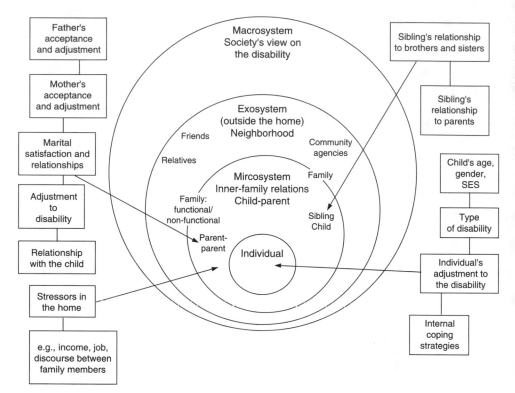

FIGURE 2   Bronfenbrenner's ecological model.

within both the family and the community. The exosystem consists of support systems found outside the home. Financial, medical, and emotional supports found in formal and informal neighborhood opportunities can make the life of a family more livable or more of an ordeal. The formal options can be found at school, clinics, religious institutions, and community social service agencies. Informally, contributions from family members and close friends can lift a person's sense of well -being. The outer layer, the macrosystem, incorporates the larger culture of the world in which we all live. It may represent the culture's biases and reactions to LD and ADHD; unfortunately, this may be where the stigma of the disability is developed. There is a positive relationship between the resources secured and an individual's ability to function and adapt more effectively.

Within the exosystem, members included in the system (friends, relatives, self-help organizations) provide support to parents of children with

ERRATUM

Therapist's Guide to Learning and Attention Disorders

PAGE 53, CHAPTER 2

Please note the disk for scoring the SNAP-IV-C is not included in the book, although Appendix 5 does contain complete instructions for hand scoring or computer scoring the SNAP-IV-C.

PAGE 71, CHAPTER 2, TABLE 6

The SWAN rating scale headings listed are incorrect. Please refer to the correct headings on Page 501 in Appendix 6.

PAGE 175, CHAPTER 6

The copyright line for this chapter should be:

Copyright © 2003 by Elsevier, Inc.
Table 1, Table 2, Appendix 3, and Figure 4 copyright © Chris A. Zeigler Dendy.

Therapist's Guide to Learning and Attention Disorders
Edited by Aubrey H. Fine and Ronald A. Kotkin
ISBN: 0-12-256430-8

exceptionalities. Families with an abundance of these social resources definitely cope better with the problems of rearing such a child. Podolski and Nigg (2001) point out that mothers who demonstrated a high level of stress lacked social support, family cohesion, family opportunities, and financial independence. Cunningham and colleagues (1988) enhanced this position when their research revealed that parents of children with ADHD had fewer extended family contacts, and those with contacts were less helpful and supporting. It is evident that this research agrees with the importance of having and utilizing resources.

It is within the mesosystem that all the provided services and the family interact to hopefully provide quality assistance to the child and his/her family. Parents feel more support when all unite in their attempt to help the families.

In our modern society, families that do not produce "perfect" children are considered "different." This difference usually creates a stigma for parents. Within a macrosystem that is accepting of disabilities, families may find social agencies and a society that will be supportive.

Bronfenbrenner urges mental health professionals to view the psychological health of any individual as a direct result of the forces operating within the systems that he or she lives within. The model permits simultaneous consideration of numerous factors within the microsystem, the mesosystem, the exosystem, and the macrosystem that can help an individual adapt to his/her obstacles.

Ecological transition is a term used by Bronfenbrenner to highlight the shifting in roles or settings in an individual's life. It can be applied to every person, including parents of exceptional children. After identifying a child with special needs, the parents change their roles, even if they already have had children. This usually occurs because of the additional burden of care and stress that the parents experience rearing their child.

OTHER FACTORS WITHIN THE MICROSYSTEM

Divorce and dysfunction in families can contribute to the stress of raising a child with ADHD/LD. Based on the limited research done in this area, Seligman and Darling (1997) concluded that there are several reasons for this. One is that the preference of the disability can aggravate an already existing marital dysfunction. Many families will cope successfully with external support; however, others will be unable to cope with the marital discord and they will turn to divorce, leading to single parenthood (Seligman & Darling, 1997). For example, families with children with significant behavioral challenges would appear to be more likely to have developed dysfunctions if the parents are having a hard time communicating with one another.

Coleman (2001) identifies various types of families that clinicians should be aware of. The four most common are the following.

a. *The chaotic family, which* represents a family where much dysfunction exists. These families may be highly disorganized and friction may exist between numerous members. There also may be numerous psychosocial stressors that the family is dealing with. These stressors may include issues such as income, health, domestic difficulties, and changes in employment/career. It appears that these families may struggle with or without having a child with a disability.

b. The second type of family identified is called the *discouraged family*. These families often appear to feel hopeless. They are discouraged about the life events they are confronting and they are extremely overwhelmed. We may often encounter this type of family, especially early on in identification.

c. Coleman (2001) discusses the third type of family as one who *appears stuck on how to solve family challenges or has set very unrealistic goals within the family or for their child*. This type of family often finds itself disillusioned. This appears to be a common outcome with parents who do not understand their child's disability or have difficulty respecting its magnitude.

d. Finally, the last type of family that Coleman (2001) highlights are those who *appear angry, resentful, and aggressive*. These families may also be frustrated, but their coping mechanisms are often counterproductive.

Parents of children with LD or ADHD often merely need to be heard. Because some of these parents might know about the disability when the child first starts school, the educators and therapists can be incredibly important in aiding parents to be more informed. They can get the parents on the right track in getting the support for their child.

Another source of support for the child are the members of his/her family. When one member family member does not accept the child, it is more difficult for other members to develop coping skills. It is especially true when one parent does not accept the child. In this case, the other parent must bear the burden of care. The siblings in this case are more likely to reject their brother or sister or to develop ambiguous feelings about him/her. Perhaps this outcome occurs because the siblings see this behavior sanctioned by their parent. Sometimes siblings of children with ADHD can feel neglected because parents focus attention on the special child more often than on children without the disability. So siblings (especially older ones) should understand the problem and avoid causing additional problems within the family.

HELPFUL TIPS AND SUGGESTIONS FOR THERAPEUTICALLY SUPPORTING PARENTS

There are many suggestions that a clinician can provide to parents as they begin to establish a relationship. The next chapter discusses in more detail home management strategies. However, we now provide some basic ideas in no particular order.

1. Most important, give the parents confidence that they are not alone. Help them realize that the best thing they can do for their son or daughter is to understand the condition they are dealing with and to learn how to best manage it.

2. Give the parents their due. One of the greatest tragedies that parents face is feeling inadequate. Having a clinician who respects their integrity aids in the therapeutic process. These parents need to be heard. Although as clinicians we may have a lot of information to share, parents may need time to just talk, without having any solutions. They just need a healthy, reflective listener.

3. Help your parents to be honest about the challenge. Over the course of therapy, it is imperative that we help the parent to open up and talk about the child's challenge. That challenge should not be kept as a family secret. Rather, by helping the parents and other family members understand the condition, everyone can talk more openly about it. Once this occurs, we must make sure that our client (the child with ADHD/LD) does not feel uncomfortable with the family being open about his/her concerns.

4. Provide parents with practical solutions that are easily implemented. Help them to understand that their role may be demanding. Nevertheless, it takes as much effort to get children to learn and behave positively as it does when you intervene when they are misbehaving. Parents must learn that being proactive and making changes before challenges arise is the best and truly the only option.

5. Help parents find the resources they need. Too often, parents find themselves searching for resources that may be obvious to you. Possibly develop a list of useful locally available services for their child (e.g., tutors, physicians).

6. Provide parents with guidelines on how to advocate for their child with the schools and other agencies. Some parents are not aware of their legal rights under the IDEA act or Section 504 of the rehabilitation act. Show them methods that will make it easier for them to get what they need (some of these strategies were discussed in Chapter 7).

7. Be available for the parents. Although therapy appointments are valuable, parents may need to contact you to ask questions. Although guidelines may be needed for excessive consultations, parents need to know that they can count on clinicians beyond the traditional therapy sessions.

8. Help parents keep the child's disability in a perspective. They need to be able to see the positives in their child and realize that beyond the disability there is a child that needs nurturing and love (just like any other child).

9. Help parents put their lives in a perspective. Let them see that there will be light at the end of the tunnel, even though for some families the outcome will be positive and for others the story may not have such a positive ending. Parents must be encouraged to realize that they can only do the best they can.

10. Being unrealistic with goals will only lead to sorrow. Parents may benefit from clinicians who act as a reality check for them. Sometimes the clinician's perceptions may initially appear too candid and unfair, but parents do need professionals to help guide them. Sometimes that means sharing information that may be somewhat unpleasant. However, when providing this information, therapists should be aware of how the parent hears what is said. Compassion may make sad news easier to accept.

11. Although explaining a disability to a parent may be easy for a clinician to do, the explanation needs to be as personal as possible. As a clinician, recognize that your explanation will be with a family for the rest of their lifetime. They may recall your exact words for years to come. Although you cannot avoid the truth, sharing it with clarity, simplicity, and sensitivity may make it easier for parents to digest.

12. Parents might also need help with the child's sibling. How can we help in making them allies rather than enemies? Having a brother or sister with LD or ADHD can become an incredible drain for siblings. Recognizing that one does not live in a vacuum, it is apparent that many homes

that have children with ADHD (and possibly with LD) lead stressful and possibly negative lifestyles. Barkley (1995) pointed out that siblings tend to get exasperated by living with disruptive behavior. They can become overwhelmed with the arguing and usually find themselves in unhealthy family relationships as a consequence. Barkley (1995) also suggests that some siblings eventually begin to resent all of the responsibilities that they are expected to fulfill in comparison to their sibling. At times, the siblings are forced to grow up emotionally faster because of all the attention that is placed on their brother or sister. Finally, the research of Barkley and others indicate that jealousy can be heightened as a result of greater time spent rearing the child with ADHD. In fact, some siblings eventually even feel guilty that they are jealous of the attention because they realize the impact that their sibling has on the family. Nevertheless, their feelings must be recognized, and we should encourage parents to be aware of this challenge. It is important to highlight that the strongest single factor affecting the normal sibling's acceptance seems to be how the parents, especially the mother, react to the child (Seligman, 1983; Fine, 1988). Parents may need to demonstrate and model compassion and understanding so that the sibling will follow their lead.

Fine (1988) points out that normal siblings may be burdened with excessively high parental aspirations to compensate for parental frustrations due to having a child with a disability. Therapists need to help parents become more cognizant of some of the pressures placed on their nondisabled child. They must be cautioned not to ignore the behaviors of the sibling, but rather to give them optimal attention and time. That may mean taking outings and perhaps not bringing the other sibling along (the divide and conquer strategies discussed in Chapter 9).

Although having a sibling with a disability can be a hardship, there has been some research that highlights a few benefits. For example, the normal sibling may develop empathy and understanding for people with disabilities and, for that matter, all people. Powell and Ogle (1985) showed that siblings may become more mature and responsible as a consequence of being in a family with a disabled child.

Although the previously cited benefits have psychosocial value, the sibling does deserve the opportunity to grow up and have as normal a life as possible. It is sad to hear about families in which brothers and sisters alienate themselves from their siblings. They recall all the volatility and they want to avoid it. In serious situations, some are in need of psychotherapy. For example, Cleveland and Miller (1977) and Vine (1982) reported that normal siblings may feel the need for counseling in later life and may feel jealous, guilty, frightened, or embarrassed about their disabled siblings.

The important ingredient for clinicians to take from this tip is that they need to make sure they talk to parents about the siblings and how they are coping. Clinicians need to serve the family as a unit as they all learn to cope with the ramifications of learning/attentional challenges.

13. Books and publications may play a significant role in the coping process. Clinicians may find it helpful to provide various readings for parents to help them to better understand the conditions of their children and to provide support, encouragement, and a sense of universality. In recommending certain publications, the clinician should be cautious. The literature offered to parents may offend them or differ from their philosophy of how to bring up children. Therapists should establish a list of literature that would be useful for understanding the etiology of the condition. This basic information can be complemented with resources on various methodologies and strategies to aid the child. Parents may also enjoy reading about other families and how they coped with having a child with LD or ADHD. These readings will show parents that they are not alone and that the future can have positive outcomes for their child and themselves. The readings usually leave the parents uplifted and feeling a sense of hopefulness.

14. Encourage your parents to enroll in a parent education/training class. Children with ADHD need consistent structure and reinforcement to maintain their efforts in situations where inattention, hyperactivity, and impulsivity would be a problem. Parents often approach their child's problems from a crisis management perspective. If their child has a problem at school or home, they seek advice from a professional on how to best handle the latest crisis. However, intervening with a crisis situation is often complex and difficult to manage. Parents are given specific suggestions on how to handle the latest crisis until the next crisis arises. However, some parents do not have the skill to solve problems proactively. Parent training classes that teach parents the range of choices they have in parenting their child using sound behavior management strategies may provide them with the skill and confidence to address problems as they arise. Parents of children with ADHD need to become paraprofessional behavioral psychologists if they are to help their child throughout life. ADHD is a chronic problem that does not go away. Therefore, some degree of structure will be needed to support the child's effort to adapt to the fact that they have ADHD.

A parenting class offers parents the opportunity to learn about the mechanics incorporated in behavioral strategies as well as how they can be applied. Through a group process they learn that they are not alone. These parents learn quickly that they are not "bad" parents, but guardians who need to learn a more sophisticated level of parenting to support their child. All children can benefit from good behavior management strategies. For the child with ADHD, however, it is critical. Parents can practice applying the principles of behavior management to the problems of their child and other children in the group. They can learn a wide range of interventions from problem solving the range of problems identified in the group. Parent training classes should be designed to systematically teach parents how to complete a functional analysis and design a behavioral intervention. There are a number of excellent manualized parent training programs that practitioners can use to train parents in behavior modification, including those developed by Barkley (1997a), Cunningham et al. (1997), and Forehand and McMahon (1981). Both programs lend themselves to easy application with families of children with ADHD. Barkley's and Forehand and McMahon's programs provide parents with a systematic overview of behavior management. The program of Cunningham et al. (1997) utilizes a systems approach that facilitates parents' problem-solving skills in addressing common ineffective parenting strategies. The program encourages the participant to evaluate the efficacy of a parent's solution to common behavioral problems through viewing vignettes. No matter what class a parents attends, he/she becomes better prepared to benefit from individual behavior therapy.

15. Finally, helping parents become more aware of self-help organizations may provide them with an alternative support network. These support organizations can be a valuable adjunct to traditional therapy. Fine (1988) suggested that parent organizations develop as a response to parents' needs to share information, to identify themselves as a group, to be heard by others who have similar problems, to be socially involved, and to find better opportunities for their children.

The two major support groups are LDA and CHADD. Within most states there are numerous local chapters that parents can get involved with. Table 1 identifies several organizations that may be helpful to families.

Support groups provide opportunities for increased communication and a forum for solving difficult problems. They also provide increased information and suggestions to help parents in raising children and an

TABLE 1   Self-Help Organizations for Parents of Children with ADHD and LD

CHADD—National Headquarters
499 Northwest 70th Ave.
Suite 109
Plantation, FL 33317

ADDA
P.O. Box 972
Mentor, OH 44061

Learning Disability Association
4156 Library Road
Pittsburgh, PA 15234

National Center for Learning Disabilities, Inc.
381 Park Ave. S. Suite 1420
New York, NY 10016
Orton Dyslexia Society
Chester Bldg., Suite 382
Baltimore, MD 21286

For books on tape, parents can contact the following two agencies:
    National Library Services for the Blind and Physically Handicapped
    1291 Taylor Street NW
    Washington, DC 20542

    Recording for the Blind, Inc.
    20 Roszel Road
    Princeton, NJ 08540

---

opportunity to share their experiences and information with other families (Millier & Hudson, 1994).

Support groups are also an effective way for parents to gain access to information about the child's condition. They can provide continuing education about ADHD of both parents and professionals. They are also helpful in helping parents locate quality professionals who provide comprehensive assessments and other services needed by the family within a particular community. Most of these organizations have local, regional, and national conferences.

Probably the greatest benefit of nationally based support groups is their role in advocacy. Over the years, support groups have formed alliances to demand equity in educational opportunities for children with ADHD and LD. With the support of these organizations, parents feel some relief that they are not on their own in fighting for the legitimate needs of their sons and daughters.

Support groups also provide a positive outlet for parents. They can become healthy forums for them to vent their concerns about rearing their child. The two most popular types of support groups are the internet and face to face. Face to face is the traditional type in which the parents meet weekly or monthly at an arranged location, usually a community center or a parent's house. This group provides a valuable personal connection but such groups may not be available to all parents (because of time, lack of childcare, or distance).

If these problems occur, the internet support group is an alternative. Many on-line sites contain live chat areas or message boards. Questions can be answered easily and stories can be submitted as well. Usually these internet sites are sponsored by national organizations (LDA and CHADD) or by other interested parties, including other parents. The sites are easy to find. Most people today know how to use internet search engines, such as ask.com, yahoo.com, or google.com, and type in specific information such as "support groups and ADHD or LD." It can be uplifting for parents to read stories from other parents and to realize that they are not alone. An advantage of these sites is that they are available at all hours of the day so if a crisis does arise at any hour of the day there may be access for some support. All a parent needs to do is sign onto the support group page and get involved.

SUMMARY

Throughout the chapter, we have highlighted some of the current research that articulates concisely the challenges that parents face in living with a child or children with attention/learning challenges. It is imperative that clinicians become more sensitive to these challenges so that clinically we can do a better job supporting the entire family.

Years ago, the lead author published an article about how having a child with an attention/learning challenge could affect the entire family. In writing the article, the author compared the emotions felt with those experienced while confronting a hurricane.

In many ways, there are similar feelings experienced by both groups. Parents who have children with learning and behavioral challenges fear that their personal hurricane will never cease. The physical damage to the family may differ dramatically from the actual natural disaster, but the emotional strains placed on the family are similar. Too often families are left feeling alone and incompetent. They develop a sense of detachment and resentment because they do not see an end to the storm. It is hoped that this tragedy can be avoided with the support of insightful and sensitive mental health care providers.

To conclude this chapter, we would like to leave you with words from a parent. Years ago, the lead author received a letter from one of his parents articulating the importance of not giving up and of trying to confront the challenge within their home. His words express eloquently and succinctly our major message in the chapter. He concludes his letter by stating:

> *Our advice to other parents is simple. Never give up! Be your child's constant ally and devoted advocate. Seek out the right professional people to help your entire family along the journey. It is never too late to set your child on a course of rebuilding self-esteem to ensure success in school and in life. As parents, we must all believe in ourselves and continue to support our children. Too often we may feel overwhelmed, not only by the challenges of our own children, but additionally by the insensitive feedback from others as well by our inability to make the change for our children. I tell you now, and please never forget this: The battle may be hard to fight, but never, never give up!*

It is important for clinicians to understand how parents' feel and to give them hope. Life may be hard for some of our clients, but that does not mean that they should give up. Unfortunately, life's adventures don't always turn out favorably as in many fairy tales, but with a sense of dignity and direction, parents can acknowledge that they are doing the best that they can. As Ben Stein once declared, "It is inevitable that some defeat will enter even the most victorious life. The human spirit is never finished when it is defeated . . . it is only finished when it surrenders."

ACKNOWLEDGMENTS

Miss Karpova's contributions for this chapter were supported in part by a grant from the Russian–US Young Leadership Fellows for Public Service (YLF) Program, a program of the Bureau of Educational and Cultural Affairs (ECA) of the United States Department of State, funded by the FREEDOM Support Act (FSA), and administered by the International Research & Exchanges Board (IREX).

REFERENCES

Anastopoulos, A. D., Guevremont, D. C., Shelton, T. L., & DuPaul, G. J. (1992). Parenting stress among families of children with attention deficit hyperactivity disorder. *Journal of Abnormal Child Psychology*, 20, 503–519.

Bailey, J., Barton, B., & Vignola, A. (1999). Coping with children with ADHD: Coping styles of mothers with children with ADHD or challenging behaviors. *Early Child Development and Care*, 148, 35–50.

Baker, D. B., & McCal, K. (1995). Parenting stress in parents of children with attention deficit/hyperactivity disorder and parents of children with learning disabilities. *Journal of Child and Family Studies*, 4, 1.

Barkley, R. (1995). *Taking charge of ADHD*. New York: Guilford Press.

Cunningham, C. E., Bemness, B. B., & Siegel, L. S. (1988). Family functioning, time allocation, and parental depression in the families of normal and ADHD children. *Journal of Clinical Child Psychology*, 17, 169–177.

Barkley, R. A. (1997). *Defiant children* (2nd ed.): *A clinician's guide to assessment and parent training*. New York: Guilford Press.

Coleman, W. L. (2001). *Family-focused behavioral pediatrics*. Philadelphia: Lippincott, Williams and Wilkins.

Cunningham, C. E., Bremmer, R. B., & Secord-Gilbert, M. (1997). COPE (Community Parent Education Program): A school based family systems oriented workshop for parents of children with disruptive behavior disorders (leader's manual). Hamilton, Ontario: COPE Works.

Dyson, L. L. (1996). The experiences of families of children with learning disabilities: Parental stress, family functioning, and sibling self-concept. *Journal of Learning Disabilities*, 29(3).

Edwards, G., Barkley, R., Laneri, M., Fletcher, K., & Metevia, L. (2001). Parent-adolescent conflict in teenagers with ADHD and ODD. *Journal of Abnormal Psychology*, 29(6).

Faerstein, L. M. (1986). Coping and defense mechanisms of mothers of learning disabled children. *Journal of Learning Disabilities*, 19(1).

Fine, A. (1988). Parents: Their perceptions and input. The importance of collaboration. In A. Fine & N. Fine (Eds.), *Therapeutic recreation for exceptional children*. Springfield: Charles C. Thomas.

Forehand, R. L., & McMahon, R. J. (1981). *Helping the noncompliant child: A clinicians guide to parent training*. New York: Guilford Press.

Grossman, F. K. (1972). Brothers and sisters of retarded children. *Psychology Today*, 5.

Moghadam, H. (1988). *Attention deficit disorder: Hyperactivity revisited*.

Moses, K. (1987). *The impact of childhood disability: The parent's struggle*. Ways Magazine.

Podolski, C., & Nigg, J. T. (2001). Parent stress and coping in relation to child ADHD severity and associated child disruptive behavior problems. *Journal of Clinical Child Psychology*, 30, 503–513.

Schulz, J. B. (1987). *Parents and professionals in special education*. Boston: Allyn and Bacon.

Seligman, M. (1979). *Strategies for helping parents of exceptional children*.

Seligman, M. (1983). *The family with the handicapped child*. New York: Grune and Stratton.

Wagonner, K., & Wilgosh, L. (1990). Concerns of families of children with learning disabilities. *Journal of Learning Disabilities*, 23(2).

## CHAPTER 9

Guidelines for Home Management for Disruptive Behavioral Challenges

Thomas W. Phelan and Aubrey H. Fine

In the previous chapter, attention was given to highlighting the challenges that parents face in rearing their child with attention deficit hyperactivity disorder (ADHD) and learning disabilities (LD). One of the major reasons why parents seek out professional support for their family (after a diagnosis) is to gain a better understanding of how to manage their child's behavior.

Children with LD and ADHD have problems with complex verbal signals, sustained motivation, impulsive responding, and emotional over-arousal (Barkley, 1995; Ingersoll & Goldstein, 1993). Furthermore, many of these children have weak self-control and poorly integrated executive functions. Both of these variables strongly impact the way a child reacts and behaves. To complicate matters, some of their parents suffer from the same traits due to genetic similarities as well as extreme frustration. If a successful home management program for disruptive and other problematic behavior is going to be implemented, these parents are the ones who are going to have to carry out the task. Although research has shown that parent training can work (MTA, 1999) with an ADHD/LD population, the job will not be easy. Consequently, it is essential that the clinician come up with a course of parent instruction that meets four criteria: (1) the advice is easy to learn, (2) the suggestions are simple to do (communication required is clear and brief), (3) the program provides reinforcement that is immediate and strong to both parent and child, and (4) the plan minimizes emotional arousal (and thus cognitive regression) in both parent and child.

UNDERSTANDING PARENTING STYLES: HELPING PARENTS RECOGNIZE THE STYLE OF PARENTING THEY APPLY

Before parents learn about strategies that they can apply within their homes, it is helpful for them to evaluate the way they parent their own children. Some parents will quickly confess that they are inconsistent and do not follow through with consequences. Others may find that they rescue and baby their children. They may also parent the child with ADHD/LD differently than their other children, being either too strict or too lenient.

Numerous terms have been used to classify parents' styles of discipline, ranging from inconsistent and very relaxed (laissez-fare) to irrational and very stern (autocratic). Jim Fay (1994), in his book entitled *Helicopters, Drill Sergeants and Consultants*, talks about three types of parenting styles. One style is the "helicopter" parent. These are parents who hover over their children and protect them from life. Parents who apply this philosophy frequently try to rescue their kids. A helicopter may eventually get the child to complete what is expected, but the cost may be exorbitant. This type of parent nurtures dependence by doubting the child's capabilities and by sending a message to the child that he is not capable of solving his own problems.

There are times when we see this overprotective parenting style in families with children with ADHD/LD. Some parents feel sorry for their children and will do whatever they can to get their child to be successful. As a parent, doing what is essential is certainly appropriate, but feeling sorry for children and hovering over them will only lead to children feeling helpless. Boone and Hartman (1972) have identified a condition of which they term the "benevolent overreaction syndrome." This syndrome focuses on parents who are so overwhelmed by their child's challenges that they find themselves overprotecting and overreacting to try and compensate. However, parents who nurture their children excessively also pamper them, and overindulged children are often not treated as accountable for their own actions. When these children lack self-control, the parent rescues them.

Fay calls the second parenting style "drill sergeant." This is the parent who is very dogmatic and rigid with his or her child. The drill sergeant does not want to hear any excuses. Children who have parents like this often feel dominated and oppressed. Although parental control is often necessary, overcontrolled children feel overpowered by their parents and do not appreciate what their parents can do to help them. The controlling parent also damages the relationship with his child because the youngster grows up believing her destiny is predetermined. As a consequence, children with over controlling parents may act out because they do not believe they have any control.

It is not so bad if parents act like drill sergeants periodically. This approach becomes problematic though when it makes up one's entire parenting style. Parents who are drill sergeants do not try to talk and listen to their children; they just demand. These parents may eventually receive respect from their "subordinates," but it is often out of fear.

Children need parents who are more than drill sergeants or helicopters. Certainly families have many tasks that must get done, and kids need parents who let them know the bottom line and help them learn from their actions. They need parents who are consistent and firm, but they also need parents who believe in them, listen to them, and really understand them. Fay describes this firm but understanding type of parent as his third style of parenting, which he calls the "consultant." The consultant parent holds children accountable for their actions, provides them with warmth and support, and teaches them to fend for themselves.

APPROACHES THAT HELP CHILDREN FEND FOR THEMSELVES

Let's look at one program that fosters the consultant parenting style, *1-2-3 Magic: Effective Discipline for Children 2-12* (Phelan, 1995). This program was developed in the 14 years prior to 1984, when it first appeared as a seminar and a book. The book is about to appear in its third edition, and video and audio formats also exist. The program was based on first-hand experience raising a child with ADHD, as well as an outpatient psychological practice that involved numerous pediatrician referrals. We'll

TABLE 1   Helpful Clinical Habits

1. Sympathy and empathy
2. Down-to-earth language
3. Sense of humor
4. Use of personal experience
5. Adjustment of expectations

describe how the "1-2-3" works, and as we do that, we will explain how it helps meet the four criteria described earlier for a successful parent training program.

To help parents to start using positive home management strategies and to help them continue to use them, several habits are useful when it comes to the clinician's style (Table 1). First, the clinician needs to be sympathetic and empathic (the distinction between these two adjectives is not relevant). There's nothing wrong, for example, with saying, "That's an awful thing to have happen to you!" Second, the therapists' language should be down to earth and simple; "street" (nonprofane) language is better than verbal emissions that sound as though they came from a professional journal.

Third, a good sense of humor is invaluable. The ability to laugh, from time to time, with or at anyone—child, parent, or yourself—helps client–clinician bonding and also helps open parents' minds to new ways of thinking. Fourth, therapists who use their own personal experiences—when they are relevant—are more credible to clients. A clinician may or may not have children with ADHD or LD, but she often does have kids. Thus she will have experienced most of the basic challenges of parenting. Clients like to know from time to time that their therapist has been in the same boat that they are in.

Finally, any mental health professional working with families where LD and ADHD are involved should be ready to adjust expectations rapidly. When a therapist feels that he is getting angry with a client, it is often the case that he is expecting something that is impossible, and his expectations need to be revised, usually downward. Along these lines, clinicians will usually find that parents of preteens are usually more motivated and easier to work with than parents of adolescents. Parents of younger children are more enthusiastic, more anxious, and less burned out. Consequently, they are more likely to do what you ask.

PARENTAL ATTITUDE ADJUSTMENTS

Before any adults with children with ADHD and LD can really be effective in changing their own parenting behavior, they must be led through a few simple cognitive adjustments. Cognitive therapy (Beck, 1995), which involves reducing emotional upset by changing the way people think, has been shown to work. However, the phrases "cognitive therapy" or "psychoeducational intervention" are a little too obtuse for most parents, so it is often better to describe this part of the treatment as straight thinking, getting back to reality or simply as an attitude adjustment.

In therapy, there are basically two parts to this process: (a) understanding the youngster with ADHD/LD and (b) understanding the parenting job.

Understanding the Youngster with ADHD/LD

When parents have one or more children with specific challenges, it is critical that parents understand the nature of these challenges so they can have realistic expectations of what their children are capable of doing. This basic knowledge helps moms and dads avoid some of the distorted and unrealistic thoughts that can lead to severe emotional upset as well as to poor parenting. Parents need to understand the (1) nature of their child's deficits, (2) the fact that these problems do not constitute willful disobedience, and (3) the origin of their youngster's difficulties. Parental understanding is especially necessary when the disorders, as is the case with learning disabilities and attention deficit, are not visible to the naked eye (Table 2).

The Nature of Deficits

Chapters 1, 3, and 4 took a more in-depth look at some of the deficits that children with LD and ADHD experience. However, each child's

TABLE 2   Understanding the ADHD/LD Youngster

---

1. The nature of the deficit
2. Not willful disobedience
3. The cause of the problem

---

particular version of these problems needs to be understood. Many parents, for example, can tell you that their child has a learning disability. but when you ask exactly what the learning disability is, the parents cannot describe it. Parents need to know specifically what their child's problems (what are the constructs that impede the behavior—memory, language, attention, etc.) are and also how these problems manifest themselves in everyday life. If a bright child has an inordinate amount of trouble with word recognition, for example, he is not going to spend his weekend reading books, even though mom and dad may want him to turn the TV off for a while. A child who has trouble reading nonverbal social cues is not going to get a lot of calls for sleepovers. A child who cannot hold a pencil well enough to put together a coherent sentence is going to find many ways to avoid a writing assignment. The behaviors may be symptoms of dyslexia, nonverbal learning disability, and dysgraphia, but these terms are useless unless their particular daily manifestations are clear to parents.

The same is true with ADHD. The terms inattentiveness, impulsivity, and hyperactivity may be easier to understand than some of the language used to describe learning disabilities, but parents still need to be aware of the specific behavioral manifestations of these traits in their own offspring. Their 8-year-old son with AD/HD, for example, may be more likely than other children to not listen to parental instructions for how to behave at Aunt Sally's, more likely to blurt things out and interrupt at the dinner table, and more likely to act like a total maniac at his own birthday party.

Not Willful Disobedience

Many people grumble about the negative effects of having labels for children's problems. What these people miss is the fact that a label (dyslexia), plus a grasp of the behavioral manifestations of dyslexia in a particular child (this child hates to read books), is extremely helpful for parents and teachers. Labels with meaningful descriptive meat attached to them help adults understand that certain youngsters are not just being ornery when they produce disruptive or otherwise problematic behavior.

Another useful way of helping parents to not attribute willful negativism to their child's activities is what we call the "thirty percent rule." For example, children with ADHD are often described as "immature"— as behaving, in other words, like they were younger than their true chronological age. This is, in fact, the case, and in attempting to quantify this immaturity some writers such as Barkley (1998) have come up with a figure of around 30%. For instance, a 9-year-old child with ADHD may be expected to behave more like the average 6 year old.

The thirty percent rule helps parents and teachers form more realistic expectations for children with ADHD and to make more informed decisions about them. At the age of 16, for example, a child with ADHD may want his driver's license. Nevertheless, if we use the thirty percent rule as a formula for decision making, at the age of 16 this child may actually not have the emotional maturity that comes with driving (s/he may be functioning like a 12 year old). Let us look at another illustration. Mrs. Simpson is Linda's seventh-grade science teacher. This teacher does not feel she should help Linda remember to complete her assignment sheet anymore because she believes seventh graders should be totally responsible for such a task, but Linda has been diagnosed with ADHD. If you apply the thirty percent rule, would this teacher help a third grader with the same task? She probably would.

The Origin of Difficulties

Before embarking on a course of professional evaluation and counseling for a child, most parents probably labor under the belief that their child's problems are either largely or totally the result of their parenting. While poor parenting, such as that involving physical or sexual abuse, can definitely cause behavioral dysfunctions, parents need to understand that ADHD and learning disabilities are largely or entirely genetic. The behavioral problems that result, therefore, are not learned or produced by dysfunctional families. On the contrary, ADHD and LD (in kids and parents) often cause family dysfunction. In counseling this notion needs to be reinforced again and again: While parents can and do hurt their children by bad parenting, these same parents need to appreciate the fact that they did not produce their child's ADHD or LD to begin with.

Parents, therefore, must learn to alter their thinking about their roles as moms and dads. They must begin to think "I'm not a horrible person who has scarred my child for life," and "My kid is not a brat, but rather has a particular psychological problem that she cannot control at will." This more realistic thinking helps produce a reduction in negative emotional arousal, and less emotional upset helps considerably with the implementation of any home behavioral management program.

TABLE 3   Understanding the Parenting Job

1. The warm/demanding parenting model
2. The "countertransference" problem
3. The little adult assumption
4. Parent–child similarities

Understanding the Parenting Job

After coming to an understanding of their child and her deficits, the next step is for parents to come to grips with their particular parenting job in relation to this child. This step involves understanding (1) the warm/demanding parenting model, (2) the "countertransference" problem, (3) the little adult assumption, and (4) the possible similarities between the child's disorders and the parents' own weaknesses (Table 3).

The Warm/Demanding Parenting Model

Some parents are naturally so warm, comforting, and supportive that they have trouble setting limits (like the helicopter parents). Others parents, it seems, are irritable nags who can never see anything good about anyone else. Unfortunately, parents of children with LD, especially parents with children who have ADHD, tend toward irritability and nagging. Parents need to be reminded that their job has *two* critical parts: warmth and support on the one hand and reasonable expectations, reprimands, and encouragement on the other (Baumrind, 1971).

The "Countertransference" Problem

All mental health professionals have had clients who are irritating and difficult to like. When these people present themselves in the office, the would-be therapist is put in a difficult position trying to be a supportive provider of care to an obnoxious individual. Parents of children with ADHD and LD are usually in the same position; they may love their children but often they may not like them. A therapist's explaining this difficult parental role and showing empathy for the dilemma are very helpful. Most parents have very disturbing internal reactions to being angry at or not liking their own children (e.g., "I must be a rotten father"), and these reactions can compromise greatly their behavior management efforts. Learning to accept frequent dislike and anger toward your own children is very important: These children can be extremely irritating!

The Little Adult Assumption

Before attempting to implement a home management program, parents also need to understand the pitfalls involved in what we call the "little adult assumption" (Phelan, 1995). This is the idea that children are just smaller than we are, but they are basically reasonable and unselfish. Little adults, it is thought, will always respond to words and reason. Pouring more information into the child's brain through explanations and discussion, it is therefore hoped, can cure behavioral problems.

Parents of nonproblem children are certainly subject to this type of wishful thinking, but so are most parents of children with LD and ADHD. The presence of the little adult assumption in adult brains is why most parents talk far too much in discipline situations. Unfortunately, all this talking usually produces more irritation and less cooperation in the children who are on the receiving end of it.

Parent—Child Similarities

Once parents have had their child through an evaluation and have bonded some with the professional involved, they may be ready to hear some bad (or perhaps good) news: Because ADHD and LD are often genetic (Ingersoll & Goldstein, 1993), mom and dad may have had for their entire lives deficits or weaknesses that are similar to their child's. They too may have trouble paying attention during conversations, get too excited over little things, be disorganized, hate paperwork, and be unable to sit for long periods of time. Before parents can start implementing a behavioral management program, they should be aware of how their own strengths and weaknesses are going to affect this process. For many adults this is a humbling but enlightening experience.

UNDERSTANDING LIMIT SETTING AND BEHAVIORAL BOUNDARIES

In teaching a child responsible behavior and self-control, it is often necessary to institute behavioral boundaries. Sometimes boundaries within the home will be established through verbal discussions where limits are clarified. For some children, of course, limits have to be clearer and put into place more firmly. The limits that parents set for children with AD/HD and LD should be dependent on the child's maturity (age appropriate) and willingness to conform. Applied boundaries will also change over the years during different developmental periods (e.g., toddler years vs teenage years).

Boundaries help clarify parental expectations for children's behavior. Unfortunately, some parents are indecisive with their discipline and their children frequently test the limits. Consequently, these parents then either relent or act inconsistently. This inconsistency causes children to become more argumentative and to challenge the parents' authority.

Behavioral expectations and boundaries support the convictions of a parent. Children need to know that their parents are serious about their discipline. Boundaries are like fences, and parents may find themselves adjusting their boundaries (lowering or heightening the fences) depending on their child's needs. Sometimes children need boundaries that keep their behavior in line, almost like bumper lanes at a bowling alley. You would not throw gutter balls if the bumpers help your ball carom into the middle. In a sense, as a child becomes more capable and self-controlled, parents can remove the bumpers and allow the youngster to bowl more independently. Boundaries should be considered as disciplinary tools that will be replaced when they are no longer necessary.

The boundaries that parents place within their homes are instituted without negotiation. They represent the guidelines that parents believe they need to support their teaching. Boundaries clearly articulate the degree of limits that a parent will enforce. In their book, *Raising a Son*, Ellum and Ellum (1990) discussed various types of behavioral boundaries. We were particularly impressed with their explanation and will therefore discuss a few of the positions they describe.

When helping parents think about the boundaries they institute, they will quickly see that some children just need friendly reminders to adhere to household limits. When these children do not follow the guidelines, only minor consequences are necessary. This type of boundary is classified by the Ellums as a "picket fence." Picket fences are not very strong; they act as a deterrent merely by identifying where the boundaries are. However, some children need firmer borders because they have difficulty setting their own limits. These kids may benefit from "rubber walls," which help them bounce in the correct direction (similar to what we earlier called "bumper lanes"). For example, a nightly curfew, which a child has to conform to, keeps him in line. If he chooses to come in late, he will lose this privilege temporarily. Rubber walls help give the child more guidance so that he can "bounce off of" and thus learn from the experience.

The Ellum's final two boundary types are more restrictive and are applied when children need extra firmness to teach them appropriate expectations. When children require very strong limits in order to give them a wake-up call, metal fences and the "brick wall" boundary (the most restrictive) may need to be enforced. The brick wall represents a set of boundaries that are quite tough and restrictive. These brick walls might be in place on a temporary basis until a child gains control of his behavior. The "tough love" approach for parenting is an example of this type. However, brick walls can also be utilized with young children who are acting out and need rigidity to help them settle in.

MANAGING BEHAVIOR IN PRETEENS

Once the evaluation has been done, the presence of ADHD and/or LD has been determined, and the aforementioned education/cognitive therapy has been initiated, it is time to actually try to change the child's behavior! With parents of the preteen population, the first thing we explain to parents in the *1-2-3 Magic* program is that there are basically two kinds of behavior problems: (1) the youngsters are doing something obnoxious that you want them to stop and (2) the youngsters are not doing something good that you want them to start.

To help parents remember the distinction, we often refer to these two categories as "stop" behavior and "start" behavior. Stop behavior includes the minor but aggravating things children do during the day, such as arguing, teasing, fighting, screaming, tantruming, and whining. Each of these items is not so bad alone, but a steady diet of them is. Start behavior includes getting up and out in the morning, eating dinner, doing homework, being nice to people, and picking up after yourself.

The reason for distinguishing between these two types of problems is twofold. First of all, the motivational requirements for cooperation from a child are different for each. Terminating a stop behavior such as whining, for example, takes potentially only 1 second. The same is true with ceasing a tantrum, an argument, or a fight; little time is required to accomplish the objective. With start behavior, however, a lot of time may be required. Homework may take 45 minutes. Getting up and out in the morning can take 25 minutes, going to bed 15 minutes. Obviously, to get these jobs done, constructive motivation must be maintained for some time in the child, and often in the parent as well.

The second reason for the distinction between stop and start behavior follows from the first: There are different tactics for managing each—different tactics, in other words, for helping to stimulate (stop behavior) or to stimulate and maintain (start behavior) the necessary motivation in children. For stop behavior, we teach parents the principles of counting, or the "1-2-3," and for start behavior we suggest several different tactics that can be used individually or in combination. Sometimes, but not always, stop and start behavior are different sides of the same coin so the problem can be approached from one or both perspectives. For example, teasing your sister is the opposite of being nice to her and throwing your coat on the floor is the opposite of picking up after yourself.

Counting for Minor Obnoxious Behavior

Perhaps the most useful, as well as the most simple, aspect of the *1-2-3 magic* program is the use of a procedure known as "counting" to manage minor unpleasant behavior such as arguing, yelling, fighting, whining, and tantrums. The counting method has preserved the sanity of many parents of children with ADHD and LD and, according to those same parents, it has also saved quite a few marriages as well. Counting is simple, but not always easy. We will describe the simple part first and then the not so easy part.

When a child is doing something he should not be doing, the parent (or teacher) holds up one finger and says *calmly*, "That is 1." This statement constitutes the child's first warning that it is time to shape up. Nothing else is said. If the child behaves, the adult does nothing, or the adult may smile or otherwise reinforce the positive change in behavior. If the child continues the obnoxious behavior, however, the second count, "That is 2," can be given within as few as 5 seconds from the time of the first. If cooperation follows the second warning, praise or no adult response may again follow.

If the child's misbehavior continues further at this point, the parent will say "That is 3." This means that a consequence will follow. The consequence may be a time out or "rest period" (approximately 1 minute per year of the child's life) or what we call a "time-out alternative": partial loss of allowance, earlier bedtime, loss of computer or TV access for an hour or two, brief chore, etc. Following the third count, the consequence is either administered or simply noted, and no other discussion takes place.

When this counting procedure is done correctly, what usually happens is that children quickly learn to terminate their obnoxious behavior after the first or second warnings. Some children learn this procedure and shape up immediately, whereas others may take a few weeks to come around. Once the counting is working, parents feel more effective as well as more affectionate. There is more time for fun and family members enjoy one another more.

If we stopped the discussion right here, there would be many skeptics among our audience. Some people would think, "That is too simple, anyone could have come up with that," "the child I am working with is a wild man!" or "we have already tried counting and it did not work." In response to the first two thoughts, remember that our goal is, in fact, a simple method that will work with these children.

In response to the third objection, "We have tried that," the following observation is offered: When counting (as described earlier) does not work, 90% of the time the problem is this: The adults are (1) getting too excited and (2) talking too much. This is the heart of the disciplinary matter. Parental frustration or parental tantrums, accompanied by incessant talk and endless chatter, are simply futile exercises in emotional ventilation. Too much parental talk and too much parental emotion have nothing to do with effective behavior management. In fact, these misplaced efforts are especially confusing and irritating to children with ADHD and LD.

Why is this the case? An example will help. You recall from our earlier discussion that children with ADHD/LD have trouble with complex verbal signals, sustained motivation, impulsive responding, and emotional overarousal. Imagine that a child with ADHD and LD asks his mother for a small bag of potato chips right before dinner.

1. Child: "I want some potato chips."
2. Mother: "Not right now."
3. Child: "Why not?"
4. Mother: "Cause we're eating dinner in 10 minutes."
5. Child: "Aw, come on. I never get anything."
6. Mother: "You never get anything? Do you have clothes on? Am I making dinner for you? Now don't start bugging me when I'm busy. Go finish your homework."
7. Child: "You go finish my homework!"

8. Mother: "Don't talk to me like that, young man. We're eating in 10 minutes!"
9. Child: "I don't want any of your stupid dinner!" Throws magazine across kitchen.
10. "Listen here, young man!"

Statements 1–4 represent a fairly reasonable interchange. The child asks a question and the parent gives an answer. The trouble starts with statement 5. The impatient youngster presses his parent with a straightforward piece of martyr-like badgering. Unfortunately, Mom's response (statement 6) is a complex verbal signal that clearly arises from the little adult assumption in her brain: If I can just give the child the right information, the problem will be solved. Unfortunately, however, Mom's elaborate communication here is now attempting to deal with three problems: the child's apparent view of himself as deprived, his badgering about the potato chips, and his homework.

For this child with ADHD and LD, therefore, statement 6 is confusing. The first part of it (arguments against the deprived child concept) is irrelevant; the second part ("don't bug me") is the real problem, but the message is buried in a verbal garbage heap; and the third part of statement 6 (homework) represents a weak attempt at distraction. In addition to being confused, the child is now aggravated by (1) not getting his way and (2) having to listen to a parental lecture. As a result his motivation to cooperate and leave his mother alone has evaporated, and his irritation erupts in his smart aleck retort in statement 7. Although badgering your parent is a stop behavior that can take only 1 second to terminate, by this point in the conversation the child's motivation to cooperate has disappeared.

To make matters worse, Mom is also getting frustrated. In her brain, emotional and cognitive regression are setting in so instead of coming up with an effective or more creative approach, she resorts to a comment (statement 8) that involves an instruction about disrespect as well as another futile attempt at the little adult assumption, "We're eating in 10 minutes!" This comment serves to irritate her son further, and his traits of impulsivity and emotional overarousal kick in. The magazine is thrown across the kitchen. Where this battle will end, no one knows.

The Efficiency of Counting

Now let us take a look at the same scene, but we will have our parent trained and equipped to use the 1-2-3, or counting method. Mom's focus on doing very little talking and remaining as calm as possible will help her son when it comes to his troubles with complex verbal signals, motivation, impulsive responding, and emotional overarousal.

1. Child: "I want some potato chips."
2. Mother: "Not right now."
3. Child: "Why not?"
4. Mother: "Cause we're eating dinner in 10 minutes."
5. Child: "Aw, come on. I never get anything."
6. Mother: "That's 1." Parent holds up one finger.
7. Child: "Please, just this once."
8. Mother: "That's 2." Parent holds up two fingers.
9. Child: "Oh, brother." Leaves room.

Statements 1–4 are again the same reasonable interchange. The child asks a question and the parent gives an answer. At statement 5 the child pushes further with "Aw, come on. I never get anything." This time, however, Mom responds with a short, clear signal, which has a simple verbal part, "That's 1," and an equally simple visual part, holding up one finger. The count notifies the child that what he is doing is out of line. The child still does not like this parental response, but it is perfectly clear and the dual-mode presentation (verbal and visual) reinforces the seriousness of the message. Children with learning disabilities and ADHD often grasp concepts better with dual-mode presentations.

With the counting procedure, it is understood between parent and child that the youngster will get two chances, the first two warnings, to stop minor, undesirable behavior. If the undesirable behavior continues, however, so that the child hits a third count ("That's 3"), a mild and usually brief consequence will follow. The consequence can be a time out (1 minute per year of the child's life) or a "time-out alternative," e.g., 50 cents off allowance, no electronic entertainment for 2 hours, bedtime 15 minutes earlier, or a brief chore.

When children (with a mental age of at least 2) have been exposed to counting for only a few trials, they quickly learn that "That's 1" from a parent or teacher means the following:

1. I am doing something I should not be doing.
2. I had better figure out what it is.
3. I had better stop or there will be a consequence.

This clear communication keeps the focus on the misbehavior and puts the responsibility for change where it belongs—on the child.

Compare this sequence to one in which the parent's responses are based on the little adult assumption: "You never get anything? Do you have clothes on? Am I making dinner for you? Now don't start bugging me when I'm busy. Go finish your homework." These little adult-based responses take the focus off the child's actual and current misbehavior (badgering mother) and transfer the child's attention to the discussion/ argument, most of which is now off track. Noncounting responses also put the burden for change on the parent, who now has the difficult task of giving a frustrated child several compelling reasons for shaping up. It is as if the parents is waiting for the child to have an "Aha!" experience, suddenly exclaim, "Gee, I never looked at it like that before!" and then leave the kitchen quietly and happily.

Inefficient attempts at problem resolution also take time, and parents of children with ADHD/LD do not have time to waste time when it comes to conflict with their children. The reason for this is the fact that the longer any frustration in these kids lasts, the more their emotional overarousal kicks in and the greater the likelihood that angry impulsive behavior by the child (e.g., throwing a magazine across the kitchen) will escalate the hostilities. All this, of course, happens in only a few heart-beats, but it is a well-established fact that a full-blown attack of rage can occur in less than 10 seconds. This biological reality often makes for an unfortunate combination. Impulsive and emotionally excited children are overly provocative, and impulsive and emotionally excited parents are overly punitive. These vicious cycles can take on a life of their own.

Counting (or other brief signals), however, has the following advantages. First of all, counting keeps the focus on the misbehavior, not on a complex verbal message or on a conversation. Second, the message is singular, simple, and easy to understand for a child. Third, when counting is done calmly and early on in a conflict situation, the procedure elicits cooperation from the child before his anger, emotional overarousal, and desire for revenge overwhelm his desire to cooperate (Fig. 1).

Although the child is frustrated, the continuation of a ridiculous conversation does not force his frustration to boil over. The child with ADHD and LD will often forget about minor inconveniences quite rapidly if parents keep quiet. It is not uncommon for parents to ask the clinician how to apply these strategies in a public setting, during sibling rivalry, or when the offense is more serious. Our response is simple but guarded. The strategies are the same, but need to be designed for different situations. Attention needs to be given to how to help the child control her behavior. For example, in public settings it is harder to be unemotional

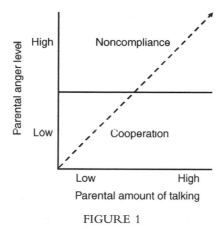

FIGURE 1

and just institute consequences. Parents must also be prepared to leave the situation if necessary, but they should also let the child know that there will be a chance in the following days to try again.

Testing and Manipulation

Parents of children with LD and ADHD who master the art of counting obnoxious behavior soon find that their silence speaks louder than their words. They are by no means out of the behavioral woods, however. It is one thing to suggest to parents that they count minor offenses, but it is quite another thing to prepare parents for their children's responses to this new type of disciplinary frustration. Children are unlikely to thank moms or dads for their parents' efforts to raise them to be responsible adults.

The next item for discussion, therefore, is what we call "testing and manipulation" (Phelan, 1995). Generally speaking, testing and manipulation are children's efforts to get their way by undermining parental resistance. In the course of a typical parenting day, for example, moms and dads have to ask their children to do things the youngsters do not want to do or to stop doing things the children do want to do. At other times parents must deny children's requests to get or do something. In each of these instances, kids can either cooperate or they can test and manipulate.

If children "decide" to test and manipulate, they usually apply one of these following six choices listed in Table 4. With the exception of butter-up strategies, all testing tactics attempt to create unpleasant feelings in

TABLE 4   The Six Kinds of Testing and Manipulation

1. Badgering
2. Temper
3. Threat
4. Martyrdom
5. Butter Up
6. Physical Tactics

parents, such as weariness (badgering), anxiety (temper and threat), guilt (martyrdom), or just plain fear (physical tactics). After the parent is uncomfortable, the child is essentially offering a deal to the targeted adult: Give me what I want and this obnoxious behavior will stop. If the parent does give the child what she wants, the testing will, in fact, stop. The child, however, will have won the battle. She will also have received reinforcement for using testing again in the future.

In training parents to manage testing and manipulation, the first job, therefore, is for adults to learn how to recognize testing. This process includes memorizing the list of the six types and then identifying their own children's favorite tactics. Some parents say, for example, "My kid's a whiner," or "My daughter has a tantrum whenever she doesn't get her way!" Once testing is recognized, moms and dads are then reminded that they have three jobs. First, parents should not give in to testing once they have set down, and if necessary explained, a certain rule or limit. Second, parents need to remember the rules about not getting too excited and not talking too much. Parents who become too aroused will allow the kids to use testing as an effective means of revenge.

Third and finally, how should parents respond to testing? Two options are possible: (1) no response at all to passive forms of testing by a child (which may include buttering up or whining) or (2) counting. In our previous example, mom counted her son's testing when he pushed her about getting the potato chips:

1. Child: "I want some potato chips." (Reasonable request)
2. Mother: "Not right now." (Legitimate denial of request)
3. Child: "Why not?" (Reasonable question)
4. Mother: "Cause we're eating dinner in 10 minutes." (Legitimate explanation)
5. Child: "Aw, come on. I never get anything." (Testing: badgering and martyrdom)

6. Mother: "That's 1." Parent holds up one finger. (First warning)
7. Child: "Please, just this once." (Testing: badgering and butter up)
8. Mother: "That's 2." Parent holds up two fingers. (Second warning)
9. Child: "Oh, brother." Leaves room. (Conflict is over)

Initially, children's testing often throws parents for a loss. The adults feel they are doing the right thing in setting a limit, but then "the kids just push and push, or she throws a terrible tantrum." Parents then think, "What am I doing wrong?" The elegant solution to this problem is to simply redefine (or reframe) testing and manipulation as simply another kind of obnoxious (stop) behavior that should be managed by counting.

The Teeter-Totter Approach

We have found that visual illustrations can be valuable tools to explain to parents the interaction between their behavior and their child's. The graphic of a teeter-totter (Fig. 2) can be applied easily to illustrate how parents' behavior may be triggered by their child's misbehavior. For example, when a child misbehaves, in effect, s/he pushes down on the teeter-totter. The natural outcome of pushing down on the teeter-totter is that the other side will rise (in this case, the rise may be seen in the parent's overreaction). As clinicians, we can help parents realize that the outcome of their reaction to their child (parent possibly reacting

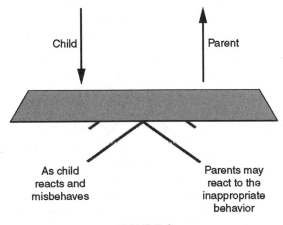

FIGURE 2

TABLE 5   Managing Testing and Manipulation

1. Do not give in
2. Stay cool (do not reinforce revenge)
3. Ignore or count

harshly) may be influenced directly by their frustration to the child's misbehavior. If the parent is more conscious of this outcome, she may try to not become reactive, but rather put into place more consistent and reliable behavioral strategies. When appropriate strategies are applied and one responds effectively, the teeter-totter outcome can be avoided (Table 5).

Encouraging Positive Behavior

The chief distinction between stop and start behavior is the length of time that a child's motivation must be sustained in order to comply with a parental objective. Counting is useful for stop behavior because counting can trigger the 1 or 2 seconds worth of compliance that it takes for a child to cease and desist when arguing, screaming, whining, or tantruming.

Several seconds worth of motivation, however, are not sufficient to encourage and sustain start behavior. Homework, going to bed, getting off to school, picking up after oneself, and completing chores require more time to complete. The time necessary to complete these daily activities may range from approximately 10 to 40 minutes, or perhaps even longer. This fact hits children with ADHD and LD right where they live. As most of us know, these children have an awful time sticking with tasks that are not especially interesting. Playing Game Boy for 40 minutes is no problem at all, but staying on track and completing mundane homework for 40 minutes—or completing boring chores—is almost impossible.

The parent's job with start behavior, therefore, involves three elements: structuring the task, sustaining motivation, and rewarding compliance (Table 6). To illustrating this start behavior scenario, let us look at a typical example: getting a child to go to bed. Keep in mind that even parents of children with ADHD and LD can fall into the little adult trap. Imagine at 9 o'clock one night Dad gives an instruction to his son, who is watching TV in the family room: "Time to get ready for bed." Then Dad lets

TABLE 6   Managing Start Behavior

1. Structure
2. Help sustain motivation
3. Reward cooperation

the matter drop. Fifteen minutes later he reenters the family room, finds his son still watching TV, and then screams at him, "I said it's time for bed! What's the matter with you!"

In analyzing the interaction, the father in this example made two mistakes in his thinking. First, he expected his child, like a little adult, to want to comply with his parent's request. Second, dad forgot that children with ADHD and LD are even less likely than their peers to follow through on any start behavior.

The solution to these start behavior challenges is not as complicated as parents may believe. The first requirement is for parents to recognize that a start behavior issue is involved. It must be understood that getting compliance from a child will not be as simple as it is with counting. More effort will not only be required of the child, but more effort will also be required from the parent. The adult can not simply give an instruction and then walk off into the land of wishful thinking. Instead, it is necessary to think of ways to structure the situation, sustain the child's motivation, and reward positive behavior.

The parent will also have to learn that if you want a child to follow through with a request, you must mean what you say and also monitor the child's performance. Children often know when a parent will not monitor their behavior, and they will wait until they see the parent really means it (in this case, when the parent begins to display anger).

Here is how a positive outcome might work with our bedtime example. The child is told that every night bedtime will be 9:00 and that at 8:30 she will be told it is time to get ready for bed. This notification means that she must do everything required for bed (brush teeth, put on pajamas, make any requests, etc.) and then she is to report to her parent. If everything is, in fact, completed properly, the rest of the time until 9:00 is time for a story or time to just sit on the bed and talk. Then at 9:00 it is light out.

This structure gives the child a clear idea of what she is supposed to be doing once the notice has been given at 8:30. The notice, which could be as simple as an alarm on a watch, activates the child to follow through. The hope of a reward (story or talk) helps the child sustain her focus and motivation. Smart parents, however, knowing that children are not little adults and that children with ADHD and LD forget easily what they are supposed to be doing, will also provide encouraging and reinforcing comments as needed after their first announcement about bedtime. Within the already established structure, these verbal rewards ("You're really moving along there!") help sustain motivation.

The procedures for most start behavior should be as routine as possible each day: same time, same place, and same way. Children with ADHD and LD do not handle change (and certainly not chaos!) especially well. Therefore the more routine we make things, the better off the child will be. For example, homework is done at 4:00. We use a kitchen timer and chart the expected behaviors after they are completed. Chores other than homework are done at particular times and are also charted. Failure to complete a chore on time means that the child pays a consequence for noncompliance. There is no arguing, no nagging, no lecturing, and no spanking.

When counting stop behavior emphasis is placed on the threat of a mild punishment (time out or time-out alternative), but with start behavior the emphasis should be on positive rewards. Consistent reliance on punishment to encourage good behavior simply does not work that well, probably because the fear of punishment does not sustain motivation as well as the hope of reward. Verbal rewards from parents are also very useful in sustaining the children's motivation, and artificial rewards (sometimes referred to as bribery) are also helpful when the task the child is being asked to do is extremely difficult or distasteful to the youngster (homework).

GUIDELINES FOR APPLYING STRATEGIES WITH TEENS

As the children get older and they head into adolescence, other behavior management strategies will become useful and even necessary. Counting obnoxious behavior can be continued into the teen years, especially if the children were used to the procedure as preteens. However, counting should be used less and less, as adolescents who are physically almost as big as their parents sometimes start to feel that this type of discipline is disrespectful. The basic rules having to do with minimizing both talking and emotion during conflicts continue to be just as important as they

TABLE 7   Possible MBAs

1. Teen's use of phone
2. Messy room
3. Appearance
4. Musical preferences

were with smaller children. This section borrows some advice from the second edition of *Surviving Your Adolescents* (Phelan, 1998).

MBAs: Picking Your Battles

In many ways the art of parenting teenagers revolves around the issue of knowing when to talk and when to keep quiet. Teens do not take kindly to what they see as unnecessary parental intervention into their affairs. Before opening their mouths, therefore, parents need to ask themselves two questions: (1) Is what I am about to say really necessary? and (2) Will what I am about to say inspire hostility and provoke a needless argument?

In this regard it is helpful to point out to mothers and fathers that their teens already have their "MBAs." An MBA is a *minor-but-aggravating* problem that may cause parental outrage but which at the same time is not a sign of serious psychological disturbance. In other words, many of the irritating things adolescents do are simply signs of adolescence, not indications of a need for further psychiatric care (Table 7).

A good example of an MBA is the teenager's use of the phone. Teenagers, including those with ADHD and LD, love to engage in long, drawn out, and apparently useless conversations on the phone. These conversations reflect the teens' obsession with peers and their growing social skills. This endless chatter, however, often irritates parents because the adults focus not on growing social skills, but rather on growing phone bills. Another example of an MBA is the adolescent's messy room. Parents, especially mothers, find their stomachs churn at the very sight of their child's bedroom. Yet a messy room is a legitimate MBA. There is no research that indicates that teens who have messy rooms grow up to be professional criminals, homeless persons, or have a higher divorce rate. We have to help parents learn to pick their battles. Certain things are not worth fighting for. Energies need to be put into areas that truly need attention and change.

Others MBAs *might* include the youngster's musical tastes, choice of friends, sleeping habits, avoidance of family gatherings, clothes, and grammar. Parents need to be reassured, however, that it is not the place of any professional to define their MBAs for them. Parents must define these pseudo problems for themselves.

Labeling certain issues as MBAs may help clinicians direct parents as to when they should keep quiet. Consequently, parents will find that they upset their teens much less frequently with such acts as nagging, lecturing, and arguing. Many parents find that accepting MBAs as truly minor issues not only helps keep peace in the house, but it also helps people to enjoy one another more.

THE FOUR DOS AND FOUR DON'TS OF RELATIONSHIP BUILDING

Parents of teens with ADHD and LD often focus a good deal on how to manage the problems their child presents. What will we do about homework, about medication, about his/her lack of friends, about his/her losing his job, or about his/her terrible irritability in the morning? These concerns are certainly legitimate and do require careful thought, but focusing solely on problems overlooks an extremely important matter. Although helping a teenager overcome some of their disabling characteristics is critical, it is also crucial for parents to recognize that they also need to concern themselves with strengthening their family's bond. We must encourage parents to consider this: "How do you simply get along, day by day, with a teenager who appears to have come from another planet?"

Just getting along in a friendly way with an adolescent is very important for several reasons. First of all, some research (Millstein & Irwin, 1998) has shown that teens who have reasonably open and amiable relationships with their parents are less likely to get hurt by driving, drugs and alcohol, or sexual experience. Second, life is more pleasant and the self-esteem of everyone in the family is increased when people get along with each other (Phelan, 1995; Fine, 2000). Finally, it is obviously easier to solve problems when you are negotiating with someone you like rather than talking with a hostile stranger.

Our advice for getting along comes in the form of four dos and four don'ts. Although some of these eight suggestions do not involve rocket science and they may appear quite obvious, it is surprising how often

TABLE 8   The Four Don'ts

1. Arguing
2. Nagging
3. Lecturing
4. Spur-of-the-moment problem discussions

these recommendations are either ignored or not implemented. In many ways it is easier for parents to enjoy and interact with preschoolers because these little ones are cute and engaging. With teens, however, parents tend to worry on the one hand, but lose their ability to interact on the other. Because parents find teens less enjoyable and more intimidating, getting along becomes more difficult. The following are a few simple suggestions that can be beneficial.

What Not to Do with Teens

On the to-be-avoided list regarding parent–child interactions are arguing, nagging, lecturing, and spontaneous problem discussions. Parents often blunder impulsively into these activities due to immediate and intense frustration with their older children. When irritated parents engage in these four verbal mistakes, however, they in turn infuriate their kids. Repeat this mutual aggravation process dozens and hundreds of times, and relationships within the family deteriorate. Getting along becomes more difficult and negotiating problems becomes impossible (Table 8).

Arguing

Teens love to argue, and adolescents with ADHD/LD are no exception. Although arguing can be a form of entertainment for some people, most arguments range from unpleasant to destructive. Although it may be easy to fall into an argument, getting out of one is much harder. Although arguing rarely solves anything, it can easily become addictive.

Nagging

Nagging may be defined as a series of repetitive and often hostile comments directed from person A to person B, where person B does not share person A's enthusiasm for the project. We tell parents that nagging is based on a psychotic parental delusion: the repetition delusion. If giving the advice 74 times did not do the trick, surely the 75th time will be the charm! Why some parents nag so much also brings up an interesting question: Why would a parent, who is basically a reasonable and practical person, continue to employ a tactic that has been repeatedly proven not to work? Nagging can quickly make a parent's very presence obnoxious to a teen, and the youngster will go out of her way to avoid the older, unpleasant adult.

Lecturing

The third destroyer of good relationships is lecturing, or what we sometimes call "insight transplants." A parent, wanting to be helpful, recalls one of life's important lessons. Dad might remember, for example, that while in high school he studied for at least 2 hours every night at the same time and in the same place with no phone interruptions or TV. Appreciating the wisdom of this approach, Dad then tries to communicate this notion to his offspring who is currently getting three Ds and three Fs as a sophomore. Dad is surprised when his 30-minute explanation is met with indifference and then hostility.

Dad should not have been surprised. Although the ideas concerned adults offer are usually rational and potentially helpful, teenagers find parental lectures humiliating.

Spur-of-the-Moment Problem Discussions

Finally, a sure-fire way to irritate an adolescent and make her never want to see her parent again is to bring up problems on the spur of the moment. For example, while the teen is watching TV on a Tuesday evening in March, her mother begins to stew about her latest bad report card. As Mom's irritation builds she can no longer resist asking the obvious question, "Do you have your homework done?" The comment prompts a tantrum from her daughter, who then storms out of the room—not to do schoolwork, however. Bringing up a sore subject when another person is not ready for it is a sure way to provoke anger.

What should parents do about arguing, nagging, lecturing, and spontaneous problem discussions? Several pieces of advice have proven helpful. As a clinician, one should advise parents as follows.

1. If the problem you want to discuss is really an MBA, keep your mouth shut.

2. If the problem is important, make an appointment with the teen to talk it over (more about negotiation later).
3. If any discussion becomes an argument, briefly say what must be said, terminate the "dialogue," and then leave.

WHAT TO DO ABOUT GETTING ALONG

Eliminating arguing, nagging, lecturing, and spur-of-the-moment problem discussions can go a long way toward improving the quality of the time spent between a parent and a teenager, but adding the positive must complement eliminating the negative. The following four positive strategies are used for improving relationships: active listening, talking about yourself, shared fun, and praise (Table 9).

Active Listening

Teens often catch their parents off guard with unexpected statements. Fielding emotional outbursts and responding constructively are difficult when an adolescent blurts out "My history teacher is an idiot!," "I like Camels better than Nows," or "This family is so boring." Parents are tempted to react with comments such as, "So what are you, a star student?" "That's just great, smoking is really a brilliant maneuver!" or "You're not so exciting yourself." These responses cut off all hope of meaningful conversation.

Communication involves learning to be honest and understanding what others need. For parents to become more encouraging with their children, they have to be able to talk with them. Unfortunately, there are many levels of listening. Some parents believe they are receptive to their children, but they are in fact selective listeners. These parents may listen

TABLE 9   What to Do

---

1. Active listening
2. Talking about yourself
3. Shared fun
4. Praise

---

in spurts. They do more hearing of content than really hearing the emotions, which generate the words. Often this type of listening can be judgmental.

Empathetic listening, however, reflects a nonjudgmental attitude. The listener sincerely tries to understand the words as well as the feelings being expressed. It is this level of communication that can enhance family relationships because the speaker feels more connected and heard. We have to help parents realize that communication is the key to healthy relationships. Moms and dads must learn to listen for the moment and not get distracted.

Some parents may find this type of communication a little awkward. Their approach may be to quickly resolve challenges that they have with their children. They do not see the need to allow the kids to express themselves. If parents want to build an effective relationship, however, they may want to consider improving their communication with their teen. Being an effective communicator will help them be a better parent and also a more effective individual.

Barriers to effective listening include constantly interrupting (interpreting what is being said) and being judgmental. Parents sometimes find themselves sympathizing, analyzing, and agreeing or disagreeing before the speaker is even finished. During discussions, some parents become aggressive and act as an interrogator. However, some may become passive and find themselves daydreaming. Both of these approaches are destructive to the communication process.

Unable to let their teens occasionally manage for themselves, some parents find it easier to communicate by ordering, directing, or commanding. Directions are given with force. For example, "Go right back there and tell her you are sorry!" Constant use of this tactic will discourage communication with a teen.

The opposite of this style, but just as deadly, is the parent who preaches and moralizes. These parents use cliches such as "you should have" or "you ought to" in their interaction with their child. Most adolescents become quickly impatient with this type of conversation and simply stop listening.

Shaming, ridiculing, and name calling are other options that some parents apply. These tactics create major relationship barriers by demonstrating basic disapproval. Such comments are given with the intent of correcting the behavior through shame. With some children, this negative approach may actually bring about a change, but it does so at great cost to the parent–child relationship. With other kids, these approaches prevent any change because the child just begins to shut out the parent, with-drawing emotionally and avoiding any interaction.

As many parents are aware, active listening is an attempt to (1) under-stand what your child is trying to say, even if you do not agree with it (the listening part) and (2) check the accuracy of your understanding and let the child know you understand by periodically feeding back to the youngster what you think it is they are trying to express (the active part). Although it takes patience and some skill, listening well and often is one of the best ways there is to both get along with and understand a teenager. We have developed a small handout that you may want to share with your parents as a guideline for instituting reflective listening. It can be found in Appendix 9.

Talking about Yourself

Most parents of teens with ADHD/LD are familiar with this dinner table dialogue. The parent attempts to start things off:

"How was your day?"
"Fine."
"What did you do?"
"Nothing."

This is the verbal equivalent of a dead-end street. The problem here is that the solicitous parent's attempt to start the conversation is—to a teenager—both too obvious and too condescending. In addition, many teens, especially those who have experienced problems, such as attention deficit or learning disabilities, translate the parent's question. Instead of hearing "How was your day?" the adolescent hears, "Did you mess up anything today that I need to know about?" Naturally, the child does not want to engage in this self-esteem-reducing contest so his answers are vague and noncommittal.

A parent has to decide here if she wants to really just talk or if she really does want to conduct a day-end minidiagnostic on the child. If the goal is the latter, it is better to simply keep quiet and eat in peace. If the goal is the former, there are better ways to start conversations. One is to simply express an opinion about an interesting or controversial issue. "I think the President was absolutely wrong when he sent troops to Aphro-disia," for example, might pique the interest of an otherwise reserved and moody teen. Anxious parents must wait for a response, however, and not solicit communication directly. "Johnny, what do you think about what the President did?" is an all-too-obvious frontal attack on the communication problem. Teens, once again becoming translator/interpreters, will hear, "Please talk to me!" and will clam up.

Another way to engage an adolescent is for a parent to simply rattle on about some of his own interesting experiences, whether recent or distant. Many kids enjoy hearing their parents talk about what mom or dad did when they were teenagers, especially if the tales include some of the parents' more "newsworthy" exploits. The one caution is that these parental anecdotes must be provided for entertainment value only, not as ways of conveying a hidden moral or lesson.

Shared Fun

It may be that the best way to improve a relationship with anyone is to simply have fun on a regular basis. People who frequently have fun together will like each other. Having fun with children does not have to be elaborate or expensive. A ride in the car, a sporting event on TV, or shared internet interests can qualify. All that is necessary is that two people be in the same place at the same time enjoying the same thing. One on one is best and no problem discussions are allowed. A good suggestion for parents who feel they can not find a common interest with their teen is a movie followed by food. A parent who pairs himself regularly with his teen's fun is wisely using a modern-day example of good old-fashioned classical conditioning.

Praise

It is a well-known but unfortunate fact that parents of teenagers praise their children much less often than parents of preschoolers. Because preschoolers are cute and engaging, parental verbal approval flows naturally. Because teens are often irritating and funny looking, praise is much less forthcoming. Praise, however, is a simple thing to do if parents of adolescents remember to do it. A daily quota system is often a handy idea ("I will compliment my 15 year old three times today"). It is also usually true that teens respond better to praise that is less sugary and more business-like.

The Divide and Conquer Routine

When it comes to family bonding, the divide and conquer routine is—perhaps paradoxically—one of the most beneficial and easily applied strategies that we have for families that are affected by ADHD and LD. When they got married, most moms and dads (especially moms) had a definite idea of what they wanted their family of the future to be like. What they imagined were pleasant scenes in which everyone was together. The children would be playing and enjoying one another. Mom and Dad would not only be getting a kick out of the kids' activities, but they would also be taking pleasure from one another's reactions. The feeling would be one of warmth, joy, and family togetherness.

It would be nice if that scene could be duplicated in all families with children with ADD and LD, but unfortunately it can not. On the contrary, in some of these families these little bits of interpersonal heaven are extremely rare, and the brief pieces that do occur are often marred initially by anticipatory anxiety and then shattered by angry explosions. The fact of the matter is the opposite of the famous "The more the merrier." When ADD and LD are involved, the more people who get together in one place at one time, the greater are the chances for noise, aggravation, and conflict.

So in families with ADHD/LD, the dream of a congenial, peaceful, and enjoyable family life may have to be given up to a large extent. It is hard and it is sad to be honest about this unwanted limitation. Nevertheless, by trying to plan accordingly, many pitfalls can be avoided. If a mother says to a father, for example, "Wouldn't it be fun if we took the kids to Disney World?," the correct answer might really be "No, it would not be fun. The children would fight on the plane, in the rental car and in the hotel room. When we'd try to decide what to do, no one would be able to agree. Sit-down meals would be a chore and our son with ADHD would want to buy everything he saw. The whole experience would make him overly excited and his tantrums would become even more frequent than they are now, with audiences wherever we went."

The dream of family togetherness dies hard. After some fairly miserable vacations, for instance, many parents try to remember only the fun parts, which may have been relatively few. These adults may then use this selective memory to predict what the next vacation is going to be like. Making matters worse, magazines, radio, and TV constantly urge families to do things together in order to prevent mental illness, drug abuse, low self–esteem, and crime. In the family that eats together all kinds of good things will happen, it is claimed.

When it comes to spending time with your children, whole-family get-togethers also have a sort of pseudo–efficiency about them. The thought is this: "If we all get together to eat or go out to a show, we can accomplish the goals of bonding and togetherness quickly and easily." It is impossible to estimate how much harm has been done in the innocent, hopeful, and naive pursuit of this difficult dream.

The bright side is that positive interactions between family members are possible, but usually not when the whole family is together. With the divide and conquer routine we take advantage of a useful and proven fact about children with ADHD and LD: these children are much more manageable in one-on-one situations. So what we recommend is that the family group be divided up as much as possible. It is a bit sad, but this routine is a tremendous help when it comes to encouraging positive and enjoyable interpersonal interactions.

Illustrations of the divide and conquer routine are easy to come by. Imagine that a family of four goes to a fast food restaurant. If they have no ADHD or LD children, they can go sit at the same table and probably enjoy themselves reasonably well. However, let us imagine that they have one child with and one child without ADHD. After getting their food, they split up. One parent takes one child to one table, while the other parent takes the other child to another table, preferably out of sight of the first one. Both parents and children enjoy their meals.

Here is another example. Imagine that a couple with an ADHD son and an ADHD/LD daughter, in a moment of insane perversity, determine to take the children to Disney World. The divide and conquer method can still be used to ease the burden. On the ride to the airport, one child sits in the front and one in the back. On the plane, mom and daughter sit in seats 23 E and F, while dad and son sit in seats 17 A and B. Halfway through the flight the kids switch places. In the motel room, both kids use sleeping bags. One child sleeps on the floor on one side of the king–size bed and the other child sleeps on the floor on the other side of the bed.

While at the park, mom takes one youngster for the morning and dad takes the other. The family meets for lunch, but sits at adjacent tables. Then parents and kids switch partners for the afternoon. If the parents are up for it, they can have the entire family together for short periods. Nevertheless, they will need to be careful and not overdraw on their investment. Children need to learn to get along, but by placing boundaries into the expectations, the outcomes can be more fruitful. The ultimate goal of being a parent is to have a family one enjoys being with. Applying these strategies will promote more cohesion within the home and less friction and disappointment.

CLOSING REMARKS

This chapter provided an overview of best practice strategies for families to implement within their homes. It provided clinicians with ideas that can be taught and applied easily in any home. Clinicians must be aware of methods that can make a major difference in the lives of the families they serve. By doing so they increase their therapeutic efficacy. We highlighted at the outset of this chapter four major therapeutic guidelines that we believe increase the likelihood of actual generalization and application. They are as follows.

1. The strategies must be easy to learn.
2. The strategies must be simple to follow.
3. The outcomes should provide reinforcement that is immediate and strong.
4. The process and the outcomes should minimize emotional arousal.

Strategies that meet these criteria will allow our clients to enjoy their ADHD/LD children and to improve the quality of their lives.

REFERENCES

Barkley, R. A. (1995). *Taking charge of ADHD*. New York: Guilford.

Barkley, R. A. (1995). *Your defiant child*. New York: Guilford.

Barkley, R. A. (1998). *Attention-deficit hyperactivity disorder: A handbook for diagnosis and treatment* (2nd ed.). New York: Guilford Press.

Baumrind, D. (1971). Current patterns of parental authority. *Developmental Psychology, Monograph*, 4 (No. 1, Pt. 2).

Beck, J. (1995). *Cognitive therapy: Basics and beyond*. New York: Guilford.

Boone, D. R., & Hartman, B. H. (1972). The benevolent over-reaction. *Clinical Pediatrics*, 11, 268–271.

Ellum, D., & Ellum, J. (1990). *Raising a son: Parents and the making of a healthy man*. Hillsboro, OR: Beyond Words Publishing.

Fine, A. (2000). *Fathers and sons*: Dubuque, IA: Kendall Hunt.

Fay, J. (1994). *Helicopters, drill sergeants, and consultants.* Golden, CO: The Love and Logic Press.

Ingersoll, B., & Goldstein, S. (1993). *Attention Deficit Disorder and Learning Disabilities.* New York: Doubleday.

Millstein, S. G., & Irwin, C. E. (1988). Accident-related behaviors in adolescents: A biosocial view. *Alcohol, Drugs and Driving,* 4, 21–29.

MTA Cooperative Group (1999). Fourteen month randomized clinical trial of treatment strategies for attention–deficit hyperactivity disorder. *Archives of General Psychiatry,* 56, 1073–1086.

Phelan, T. (1995). *1-2-3 magic: Effective discipline for children 2-12* (2nd ed.). Glen Ellyn, IL: Child Management, Inc.

Phelan, T. (1998). *Surviving your adolescents: How to manage and let go of your 13–18 year olds* (2nd ed.). Glen Ellyn, IL: Child Management, Inc.

## CHAPTER 10

Social Skills and Children with Attention Deficit Hyperactivity Disorder and/or Learning Disabilities Realities and Direction for Treatment

Aubrey H. Fine and Ronald Kotkin

INTRODUCTION

Eric is a 16-year-old high school student who was diagnosed as having attention deficit hyperactivity disorder (ADHD), with the comorbidity of a learning disability (LD). One of Eric's greatest life challenges is his inefficient and awkward approach in relating with peers. Although he is kindhearted, he lacks social graces and relates poorly with others. He communicates inappropriately, asking constant irrelevant questions. He spends much of his time alone or on the sidelines of most social clusters. Recently, while discussing social rejection, he said how horrible it felt to be "invisible" to others. "It is like you are not even there, and nobody really cares."

Josh is a fourth grader who was diagnosed with ADHD when he was 6 years of age. Emotionally, Josh is very sensitive and often gets his feelings hurt, especially when things do not go his way. Because of his hyperactivity, many of his peers do not like to be around him. He is bullied frequently, especially because his classmates know how to get him to react.

Josh gets excited when he is invited to parties or to the homes of others, but the invitations are very few. He talks about his loneliness and feeling different. He tells his parents that he wishes he were normal and that people would be kinder to him.

Growing up with ADHD and/or a learning disability goes beyond the classroom or the home and impacts the social lives of many children tremendously. The social wounds of being ostracized, ignored, picked on, or being laughed at are all elements that can make a child feel inferior. Factors that contribute directly and indirectly to the social success or, for that matter, the social failures of most children may also include the way the child looks, the way he presents him/herself to others, and perhaps even the way the child feels about him/herself.

This chapter provides practitioners with a snapshot of the literature and then follows with best practice alternatives for assessing and teaching social skills. The following areas are discussed.

1. Assessing social skills deficits
2. Objectives of social skills training
3. Problems in the generalization of social skills: An overview
4. Strategies for facilitating generalization of social skills in individual therapy, group therapy, and natural settings
5. Special topics, e.g., bullying and teasing and self-esteem and social competence

SOCIAL SKILL DEFICITS AND ADHD/LD: A SNAPSHOT OF THE LITERATURE

It is widely accepted that children with ADHD and learning disabilities have considerable problems with peer interactions. In fact, some believe that social problems may be considered the hallmark of ADHD, with serious interpersonal difficulties and peer rejection being two unfortunate outcomes (Bagwell et al., 2001).

Within the literature, numerous studies suggest that peer rejection may lead to associated feelings of loneliness, unhealthy self-esteem, poor school work, and possibly even school dropout. In fact, peer ratings of dislike, taken as early as the third grade, were shown to be better predictors of emotional maladjustment some 11 years later than other traditional adjustment indices, including, IQ, grades, academic achievement, and ratings by teachers (Fine, 1993).

Fine (1993) identified some of the specific behaviors that seem to cause children with ADHD and learning disabilities to receive negative peer feedback. Some of these children do not recognize or respect social boundaries and at times can act intrusively. Their interactions with peers may appear to be annoying to others and may cause their peers some irritation. Pelham and Bender (1982) noted that children with ADHD are often rejected by peers even after very brief interactions. Their findings appear to be in direct agreement with those of Fine (1993). Furthermore, a benchmark feature that is often reported by children and adults is the boisterousness of some children with ADHD and their lack of awareness of the impact their behaviors have on others. Some of the children also demonstrate intractable traits of stubbornness and inflexibility. All of these characteristics in excess can have an impact on any social situation. A behavior that probably has the most adverse impact on the social well-being of children with ADHD is aggression (Fine, 2000).

Levine (2001) suggested that children with social skill deficits can be divided into two groups: those who are aggressive and disruptive and those who are shy and withdrawn. Levine (2001) discussed social cognition as a key variable in social skills. He suggested that "social cognition is an array of functions necessary for successful interpersonal relationships" (p. 10). These skills can aid a child in fitting into social situations and sidestepping rejection from peers. These cognitive skills can be divided into verbal and nonverbal skills. Verbal skills may include the selection of a right topic to talk about, the use of appropriate modes of speaking depending on the social situation, and so on. However, nonverbal skills include problem resolution skills, turn taking, and an internal ability to conceptualize social cues and feedback (Levine, 2001).

It is important to point out that those who are aggressive and disruptive often may not even realize that their behavior and actions are offensive to others. However, those who are withdrawn may show little social initiative and sadly may often spend time in isolation. Levine (2001) suggested that children who are impulsive seem to have difficulty with predicting their social responses. In addition, their weaker sense of internal monitoring makes it hard for them to effectively self-regulate if they are offending or losing the respect of their peers.

Some children with language-related learning disabilities may have social challenges due to their verbal pragmatics. These children may not recognize the impact of the words they select and the tone of their voice utilized.

Over the years Dodge (1986) developed a theory to explain social skill deficits in this population. He explained that the deficits begin because of perception, understanding, or interpreting environmental cues. Many children with ADHD or learning disabilities show deficits in encoding and perceiving social cues in the environment. A deficit in encoding appears to be evident in children with nonverbal learning disabilities (Tur-Kaspa and Bryan, 1994). Furthermore, there also is a deficit in the child's limited behavioral repertoire to generate possible behavioral solutions to behavioral problems. Many children with ADHD have a social perform-ance deficit. They know how to behave appropriately, but they seem to be unable to consistently apply their skills in everyday interactions. It is our strong belief that their stimulus-bound behavior has the greatest impact on the outcome. This may be further evidence in the deficit of executive functioning where children fail to inhibit their responses before considering their behavioral choices. Performance deficits often explain the behavior of impulsive children with ADHD; however, children with the predominantly inattentive type of ADHD may demonstrate perform-ance deficits in a different fashion, including often being disengaged and reclusive, thus limiting social interactions (Zumpfe & Landau, 2002).

Bullying is one of the main concerns for children with ADHD and LD. Because of their social deficits, they are more susceptible to bully-ing—by being either the perpetrator or the victim (Salmon et al., 2000). Throughout the remaining aspects of this chapter, we will highlight strate-gies that may be useful in offsetting these difficulties.

To simplify the review of literature and to demonstrate the consisten-cies in the findings, Tables 1 and 2 have been prepared. This synthesis should be helpful in understanding some of the clinical applications dis-cussed in the latter portion of the chapter.

STRATEGIES TO ENHANCE SOCIAL SKILLS

When one discusses social competence in children, the process requires an evaluative judgment of a child's behavior within a specific context. It is the behavior, and not the child, that is judged. However, social skills are specific strategies used to successfully perform social tasks in order to be judged as being socially competent. In the case of the children under focus, it is apparent that both of these variables appear to be affected.

Hall et al. (1999) suggested that nonverbal behavior may be misinter-preted by children. Many of these children appeared to receive or send nonverbal emotional information that differs from that of their main-stream friends. The awkwardness that some of the children display while

TABLE 1   A Snapshot of Research as It Pertains to Social Skills and LD[a]

Baum et al. (1988) studied the prevalence of social dysfunction among students with learning disabilities in the public schools of Iowa. Their results found that 38% of students with learning disabilities were in need of social skills training.

Bryan (1998) reported that students with learning disabilities demonstrated less effective communicative competence. They were found to be less tactful in most situations as well as being less persuasive in arguing their point of view.

Bryan (1974) in her pioneer study provided evidence that youngsters with learning disabilities (when compared with their mainstream contemporaries) were less well accepted and often socially rejected.

Bryan (1974) suggested that many children with LD are rejected by their peers.

Carlson (1987) noted that children with LD have been found less skilled than their NLD contemporaries in the quantity of strategies chosen for hypothetical social situations.

Conte and Andrews (1993) concluded that the absence of limiting conditions in definitions of learning disabilities makes it difficult to exclude any particular skills or type of knowledge from falling within the bounds of the definition.

Flicek (1992) reported that the combination and quality of ADHD along with LD was associated with the greatest risk of social status problems.

Kavale and Forness (1966) suggested that 75% of children with learning disabilities manifest social skill deficits. The perceptions on how one does in school may have great bearing on the rejection that the student's face.

Kavanaugh and Truss (1988) recommended that the definition of learning disabilities should be changed to include social skill disorders as one of the challenges.

Kistner and Gatlin (1989) pointed out that close to 60% of children with learning disabilities experience social problems and that many are rejected and ignored by their peers.

Levine (2002) discussed social language as a potential obstacle for optimal social development. He noted that children with language challenges have trouble regulating their tone of voice, may have weak greeting skills, poor verbalization of feelings, may have trouble alternating their speech with various groups (code-switching), the prosody of the speech, and their overall ability to convey what exactly they mean may also be hampered. Some of these children may also have a lot of difficulties perceiving what others are actually trying to convey.

Levine (2001) identified several other common skill deficits that some children may also display. These children may struggle with the use of humor and have difficulty asking for things, as well as knowing what to talk about and when.

Margalit (1994) reported that children with LD are more likely to experience loneliness and engage in more solitary activities.

Martlew and Hodson (1991) acknowledged that children with mild learning disabilities were teased/bullied more and made fewer friends than mainstream children.

Pearl and Bay (1999) identified that many children with LD "are less accepted, more rejected, or more neglected than their nondisabled classmates." Although academic concerns appear to be a priority, children with learning challenges face disproportionate levels of rejection than their mainstream friends.

(Continues)

TABLE 1   (*continued*)

Pearl and Bay (1999) in their review of the psychosocial correlates of learning disabilities found numerous studies highlighting the fact that many of these children have deficits in interpreting social displays, especially understanding nonverbal emotional expressions. Furthermore, youngsters with learning disabilities had definite deficits in social insight, which included their ability to evaluate realistically their social status.

Schachter et al. (1991) examined the prevalence of emotional problems among children with learning disabilities. The children displayed a broad spectrum of behavioral problems.

Strain (1981) suggested that children with LD do not generally employ reinforcing behaviors (e.g., verbal compliments) and, as a result, are rarely sought out for social interactions by others.

Swanson and Malone (1992) found that social skill difficulties may not be due to social inefficiency, but rather to the inability to learn more positive social behaviors. It is important to emphasize that children with NVLD may have a hard time distinguishing what a person is trying to say when there is a contradiction between verbal and nonverbal messages.

Vaughn et al. (1993) reported that there is extensive research documenting that children with learning disabilities have tremendous difficulty forming and maintaining relationships.

Wiener (1987) reviewed 25 studies that compared the peer status of children with learning disabilities and students without learning challenges. The findings suggested overwhelmingly that children and adolescents with learning disabilities were lower in peer status than their mainstream peers. Academic failure may have much to do with peer status and how one is accepted.

[a] It appears from the literature review that many of the studies highlight that young people with LD appear to have some break down in one or more of the stages in perceiving and initiating social scenarios.

relating to others may be caused by their inability to interpret the actions of others accurately. These behavioral inadequacies may be more related to the ability to understand the emotions and feelings of others. For example, Richard has a hard time reading facial expressions. He has a hard time telling if students are trying to tease him or if they are being truthful.

Many commercial programs are designed to teach social skills. Instead of reviewing selective programs, we have chosen to provide a guide in selecting and using programs to teach social skills effectively. The basic questions that must be addressed in reviewing social skills programs include

TABLE 2   Social Skills and ADHD: A Snapshot into the Literature

Bagwell (2001) reported that children with ADHD were, as a group, more rejected by their peers in their teenage years than those teens without ADHD.

DeWolfe et al. (2000) suggested that for some school-age children with ADHD, negative social situations will ultimately result in social rejection by their peers. Furthermore, these disruptive and intrusive behaviors may eventually receive tremendous negative sanctions from parents and teachers, as well as their own peers.

Dodge and Coie (1987) identified that early aggressive reactions are a viable predictor to later social impairments.

Fine (1993) reported that although children with ADHD seem to know the correct answer to social dilemmas in real-life situations, there appears to be significant difficulty generating solutions to their own difficulties.

Fine (1993) identified that children with ADHD have difficulty adapting their behavior to situational demands. They do not seem as cognizant to the social cues.

Flicek (1992) pointed out that beyond aggression, the traits of off-task behaviors, disruptiveness, defiance, and the inability to exhibit self-control were other features that seem to dramatically impact social acceptance.

Levine (2001) identified several traits that children who are impulsive and hyperactive may display. The following lists some of the issues presented: Problematic conflict resolution skills, poor social predicting, failure to self-monitor social behavior accurately, and aggressiveness.

Martlew and Hodson (1991) suggested that children with MLD or ADHD tend to be bullied/teased more by peers and are subjected to increase amounts of teasing as they get older.

O'Moore and Hilley (1989), in their study of Dublin schools, found that children with ADHD or MLD were bullied twice as much as nonremedial children.

Salmon et al. (2000) found that the most common disorder associated with bullying was conduct disorder, with ADHD being the most common comorbid disorder.

Stormont (2001) pointed out that children with ADHD often misread subtle social cues that can easily lead to teasing/bullying or being ostracized by peers.

Stormont (2001) suggested that children with ADHD are less popular among their peers and that aggression toward peers is strongly associated with peer rejection.

Stormont (2001) suggested that children with ADHD have a bias toward aggressive solutions and are less desirable to work with.

Stormont (2001) found that teachers are often negative when interacting with children with ADHD and may influence how the teacher interacts with the entire class.

Stormont (2001) pointed out that one of the most pervasive problems for children with ADHD is aggression. It appears that children with ADHD start more fights and arguments as compared to non-ADHD children.

Wolfe et al. (2000) pointed out that preschool children with ADHD were rated by their parents as being more aggressive, noncompliant, demanding, and less adaptive and socially competent than their peers.

(1) how are social skill deficits assessed, (2) how is treatment matched to deficits, and (3) how to encourage generalization of the new skills.

ASSESSING SOCIAL SKILLS DEFICITS

Gresham (1983) suggested that there are three types of measures to consider in planning social skill interventions. The first type concerns social validity. Socially valid treatment goals are ones that schools, courts, mental health agencies, parents, and teachers have in mind when referring children for evaluation and intervention. The effectiveness of the intervention is evaluated based on the perception of positive change in the child's social competence. Others see the change and recognize the child's progress. According to Gresham (1998), social validity is a sound measure because it predicts long-term outcomes that are important to society. Thus, measures in this category could include peer acceptance, friendship status, parent and teacher judgments, and some type of archival data (e.g., school attendance, disciplinary referrals, and school suspensions).

The second type of assessment is observations of the child's behavior in the natural environment. Did the child's behavior change in the predicted direction? The child may have made a change in the behavior, which is measured objectively, and others did not recognize the change or see the change as important. Objective observations of the child's behavior in the natural or clinic setting indicate that behavior did or did not change. It does not tell us whether the change was perceived as important. Objective measures of change, such as direct observational recording, may help significant others (parents, teachers, peers, etc.) recognize that change has actually occurred. This may be an initial step in helping others to recognize the social validity of the behavior.

The third type of measurement is the least socially valid measure. This is a measure of how the child does in role-play tests, problem-solving measures, and measures of cognition. It is a measure of component skills and does not necessarily consider whether the child will be able to use the skills in the natural setting. These measures may assist in assessing the prerequisite skill development necessary for socially valid behavior changes to occur. Gresham (1998) pointed out that a child may have to exhibit behavior for a long time and in a variety of situations before others recognize the change. It is often more difficult to change adult and peer perceptions than to change behavior. For example, a child who has developed a reputation for aggression and disruptive behavior may need many months of appropriate behavior before others recognize and accept that he has changed.

SOCIAL SKILLS TRAINING

There are four main objectives of social skills training (Gresham, 1998): (a) promoting skill acquisition, (b) enhancing skill performance, (c) reducing or removing competing behaviors, and (d) facilitating generalization and maintenance. A deficit in any of these areas may contribute to a lack of social competence. A social skill acquisition deficit refers to either the absence of knowledge of how to execute particular social skills or the failure to discriminate when certain social behaviors are appropriate. For example, a child might not recognize that he may only ask one question during a 30-minute academic period. He could ask 20 questions but not see the frustration in the teacher's face. A social performance deficit refers to the presence of social skills in a behavioral repertoire, but failure to perform these behaviors at an acceptable level in specific situations. In the aforementioned example, the child has learned the social skill of asking questions in an assertive style; however, he has not learned when and how often it is appropriate to ask questions. This may also be due to competing maladaptive behaviors in the child's repertoire that have been shaped by a history of reinforcement. The child may use inappropriate social behavior instead of the socially skilled behavior because the competing behavior is more efficient in meeting the immediate needs than the socially skilled behavior. For example, a child may choose to grab a ball from a peer rather than ask for the ball assertively because grabbing the ball is more efficient and achieves the goal more often than assertion. This example illustrates the third goal of social skills training: reducing or removing competing behaviors.

Often, social skills programs take on a "one size fits all" approach to training (Gresham, 1998). This is highly inefficient and does not recognize the individual needs of the child. Implementing a social skills program should always start with a functional analysis of the nature of the child's current social skill deficits. The assessment should first determine the type of social skill deficit the child has. Does the child lack the knowledge to execute particular social skills or fail to discriminate when certain social behaviors are appropriate? Is there a performance deficit? Is the social skill within his repertoire, but he fails to perform those behaviors at acceptable levels in specific situations? Is the social skill deficit one of fluency? That is, has there been a lack of sufficient exposure to appropriate modeling of behavior or has he been given insufficient rehearsal, practice, or reinforcement of skill performance? Through a thorough assessment of the child's performance in the natural setting, strategies should be developed to address the identified skill deficit.

GENERALIZATION OF SOCIAL SKILLS TRAINING

Most social skills training programs are conducted as small group outpatient sessions that are held once a week for a period of several weeks. The most effective social skill strategies appear to be some combination of modeling, coaching, and reinforcement procedures. Several reviews (Gresham, 1998; Dupaul & Eckart, 1994; Mathur & Rutherford, 1996) of social skills programs have identified the basic weakness in the effectiveness of most social skills programs: *failure to generalize beyond the therapeutic setting.* The reviewers pointed out that the failure of social skills to generalize to the natural setting is not surprising given the lack of programming to facilitate generalization. Most programs take "a train and hope" approach, i.e., they train social skills in the context of a clinical setting and hope the child uses the skills in the natural settings such as home, school, and community. This approach has been found to be minimally effective in facilitating generalization.

Most social skills training programs have neither recognized nor incorporated the behavioral technology to facilitate generalization described originally by Stokes and Baer as early as 1977. The classification of strategies to program for generalization was outlined by Stokes and Baer (1977) and further refined by Stokes and Osnes (1986). They identified 12 tactics that they grouped under three basic principles. These principles and tactics are listed in Table 3 and will be reviewed as a guide in planning for generalization to occur outside the clinical setting.

EXAMPLES OF SOCIAL SKILLS TRAINING IN CLINICAL AND NATURAL SETTINGS

The University of California at Irvine, Child Development Center (CDC) offers a specialized multicomponent treatment program (Swanson, 1992;

TABLE 3   Generalization Strategies

Principle 1: Exploitation of current functional contingencies
- In selecting a target behavior to change, one could choose behaviors that are highly likely to be reinforced in the natural setting each time they are exhibited. Also known as trapping (Stokes & Baer, 1977).
- Another approach is to program opportunities for the child to come into contact with environmental settings, which may naturally prompt and reinforce appropriate social skills.

Principle 2: Social skills can also be viewed from a competing behaviors framework
- Some social skills either are not learned or performed because of the presence of stronger, competing, or interfering problem behaviors.
- Interfering problem behaviors include behaviors that are internalizing or overcontrolled (e.g., anxiety, fear, social withdraw) and those that are externalizing or under controlled (e.g., aggression, disruption, impulsivity). One must help the child by perhaps scheduling consequences that maintain inappropriate behaviors so that more appropriate behaviors can be developed. For example, one might recruit the cooperation of peers in the child's classroom to ignore disruptive behavior and reinforce the child for appropriate behavior.
- Temporarily interrupting the contingency of peer attention by extinguishing disruptive behavior and reinforcing appropriate behavior strengthens the appropriate behavior.

Principle 3: Emphasizes training diversity
- When the goals and procedures of training are more widespread so are the outcomes widespread.
- The more similar the training setting is to the natural environment the more likely the stimuli from training setting will elicit the trained response.
- If there are peers from the child's classroom in the social skills training group, they will help increase the likelihood the child will respond with learned responses in the natural environment with the peers present.
- The more similarities to the natural setting that can be presented in the clinical setting the greater the probability of these stimuli prompting appropriate social behavior.
- Another strategy in training diversity is to allow a variety of conditions of training so that the child will not readily discriminate performance to a particular set of circumstances.

Principle 4: The use of functional mediators
- A mediating stimulus is usually one that can be carried easily by the child to a diversity of conditions to facilitate generalization.
- One strategy is to incorporate salient physical stimuli; physical items common and obvious in natural and relevant generalization environments are incorporated into the training. For example, a simple report card targeting specific social skills taught in the weekly clinical sessions could be used in the school setting to prompt the use of these skills in school. The report card itself serves as a cue to use appropriate social skills.
- A strategy that incorporates many of the generalization strategies reviewed earlier is incidental learning. Incidental learning takes advantage of the naturally occurring behavioral incidents or events to teach social behavior.

Kotkin, 1995, 1998) that has incorporated suggestions from a technology for facilitating generalization (Stokes & Baer, 1977; Stokes & Osnes, 1986) and applied it to its social skills program. The center has conducted social skills outpatient training sessions as well as implemented comprehensive training within the natural setting of the school and home. This section shares practical suggestions from the CDC and other selected programs for establishing and incorporating social skills training through individual sessions, group sessions, and in the natural setting. Special emphasis will be placed on highlighting strategies that have been programmed to facilitate generalization. Three tables are incorporated at the end of the following three distinct sections (Tables 5–7) to demonstrate the increasing strategies for facilitating generalization in the various treatment options (individual therapy, group therapy, and the natural setting).

Individual Therapy

Therapists may choose to focus on social skills training through individual sessions. If this is done, it is then important to find significant others in the child's life to prompt and reinforce the use of appropriate social skills in natural environments, including the home, school, and community. Social skills by their very nature require interaction with others. Individual social skills training lacks the opportunity for practice with peers, siblings, parents, and others. However, an advantage of individual training sessions is the opportunity to work closely with the child in ensuring that the social skill concepts are grasped. Strategies can be tailored to ensure that the child knows when to use them and that they are within the child's repertoire.

An excellent example of an intensive individualized training program is one implemented in a Visalia unified school district at a middle school. This is an excellent approach that a therapist could apply easily in individual therapy sessions. Here, the participants were students who had been identified as hostile and aggressive. They were avoided by their peers and seen as poor students in the classroom. Their demeanor frightened most of their peers. These students were targeted for intervention through a daily resource specialist program (RSP). In keeping with Gresham's (1998) stance that interventions need to be individualized, the RSP teacher evaluated students individually and determined their specific areas of need. The general approach for each student was that the RSP teacher first identified socially valid goals or intervention. The goals were to increase the student's positive interactions with peers and therefore increase friendships. Second, the RSP teacher decided to teach the students individually how to be good students. What did students who were perceived as good students do and how could this be taught through social skills training? The specific behaviors that were targeted were behaviors that were likely to be reinforced naturally by individuals in the child's environment, or said to be trapped. The first skill they decided to teach was a more natural smile. Students in the program went through school with scowls on their faces. They looked threatening. They were unaware of how they appeared to others. The RSP teacher used videotapes of their attempts to smile as a way of first assessing and then softening their appearance. They practiced smiling in a more inviting way. They observed themselves via videotape until they were able to produce a more inviting smile. In addition, the teachers helped the students assess the reciprocal interactions they were having with their peers. The children chose specific individuals with whom they wanted to become friends and collected baseline data on their interactions with these students. They noted what the target student liked, how often the student returned their greeting, and what their interests were. With this information, they designed a behavioral program to increase positive interactions with the target student. The social skills they developed and the method of analysis became trapped in that the targeted peer began to interact more positively and frequently with the student in the program.

Next the RSP teacher helped the students identify what successful students did naturally to create a positive image of themselves with teachers in the classroom. For example, they taught them to have an interested look, to ask questions about topics they already knew the answer to, thank teachers for their help, and to ask if they could help them after class. As a result of changing their behavior in class, they were better accepted by teachers and suddenly perceived as excellent students. They were reinforced for their excellent progress in academics and given positive feedback. This also served to "trap" the behavior in the natural setting by increasing the natural positive interactions with teachers.

These approaches were done through intensive individual sessions. However, they focused on socially valid behaviors, behaviors that were the cause for referrals. They also selected behaviors that were likely to be maintained in the natural setting. This is an example of how an individual session can be used to teach a social skill that is generalized beyond the individual session. The trainers also assessed social validity by obtaining feedback from teachers and peers on whether the changes in the students' behavior were recognized.

Many unique and dynamic strategies can be applied in individual therapy, such as those mentioned previously. Clinicians should first do a functional analysis to identify a repertoire of social skills that a child possesses as well as deficits the child needs to work on. Fine (1991) developed the **Get Along Gang program**, which was designed to promote social skills for children with ADHD and LD. The program identified various social skills that needed attention and implemented a comprehensive training program to address these needs. The participants met weekly to work on their established goals. To assist with the generalization, parents were required to attend a weekly parent session explaining how both they and the teachers could help transfer the skills into the natural environment. To enhance the direction of the treatment, emphasis was placed on selecting the behaviors that needed to be improved. The program included the development of a taxonomy of various social skills to give specific direction to the treatment. The protocol of behaviors was reviewed not only by the clinician and the parents, it also had input from the child's educator and the child. Table 4 is an example of the taxonomy developed within the get along gang program. Nevertheless, numerous other social skill inventories could be applied for this purpose, such as the social skill rating system by Gresham and Elliott (1989; American Guidance Service). All of these documents allow the clinician more guidance in the direction they need to take, as well as a more concrete approach for evaluation.

There are many books and sources that a clinician can use to guide a child through social skills development. For example, Mel Levine has prepared a valuable resource for middle school-age children entitled *Jarvis Clutch Social Spy*. There are many tools that are provided in this book that serve to facilitate generalization. The book incorporates several chapters that contain concrete descriptions explaining the various social skills youths need to develop to make friends and sustain healthy reputations. Each chapter highlights a major area that a young person may need to work on to develop more appropriate social behaviors. The chapters stress Levine's neurodevelopmental model as it applies to social abilities and social cognition. Levine, with the help of Jarvis (a fictitious middle school student), has prepared a valuable book, rich with wonderful examples and suggestions on such topics as (a) seeming right (topics include the way you look and dress, your interests), (b) talking right (dealing with language function's impact on socialization), and (c) acting right (learning

TABLE 4 Taxonomy of Social Skills: Evaluate the Child on Each of These Variables

- Communication skills
  - Introducing oneself
  - Beginning a conversation
  - Sustaining a conversation
  - Utilizing proper nonverbal behaviors
  - Ending a conversation
  - Speaks in an appropriate tone
  - Learning to evaluate how you sound to others (e.g., friendly or unfriendly)
  - Matching your language style to the group you are speaking to
- Friendship skills
  - Giving compliments
  - Accepting compliments
  - Sharing
  - Inviting others to play
  - Coping with not always getting one's way
  - Listening
  - Saying nice things to others
  - Asking others if you can play
  - Asking for favors and doing a favor
  - Demonstrating kindness
  - Monitoring activity level
  - Playing fairly
  - Being assertive
  - Helping others
  - Controlling talking
  - Dealing with teasing
  - Taking turns
  - Follows rules of a game
  - Recognizing how your behavior impacts others
  - Being patient
  - Joins activities
  - Being a good sport
  - Dealing with teasing
  - Dealing with embarrassment
  - Coping with losing
  - Monitoring how you are doing with others
  - Being able to call a friend on the phone
  - Demonstrates compassion and concern for others
  - Conflict management skills (avoiding fights and using positive solutions)
  - Avoiding arguments
  - Apologizing
  - Handling criticism
  - Dealing with losing or not getting your way
  - Negotiating and problem solving
  - Learning how to interact with more than one person (do not dominate)
- Skills for dealing with your feelings
  - Identifying various feelings
  - Recognizing the feelings of others (both verbally and nonverbally)
  - Demonstrating an awareness of how other's feel
  - Regulating one's anger
  - Dealing with fears and novel situations
  - Controlling temper in conflict situations

how to act appropriately in various social settings and conditions). The book is easy to follow and could be applied by both therapists and parents to help support the child.

Fine et al. (1996) pointed out that there are numerous table games that can be used in individual therapy to help children deal with aggressive and competitive urges in a more socially acceptable manner. Many clinicians have noted that some games can promote social learning as well as be a method to help children cooperate, learn to respect governing rules, and control anger while in competition. *The Center for Applied Psychology—Childswork/Childsplay* has published many therapeutic games that can be applied easily. The center may be a good initial resource to review products that have specific benefits. They have also published several products that are geared specifically to enhancing social skills of this population. The use of table games in individual therapy can facilitate generalization to the natural setting because of their portable nature. Parents, teachers, and peers can engage in these table games in the natural setting as well.

Over the years, we have also experimented and developed a few specific techniques taught in individual sessions that have been found to be useful in aiding our clients to learn useful social skills and generalize their use to the natural environment. Here are two examples.

1. ***Knowing your temperature.*** Helping children to learn to gauge their anger is a very useful technique. Children are introduced to how a thermometer helps estimate the actual temperature. The concept can be adapted to help children learn to determine their emotional temperature. After an initial introduction, the clinician should get the child to visualize certain scenarios and discuss which ones escalate the temperature. The desired outcome from these initial lessons is to get clients to visualize the mercury rising whenever they find themselves getting frustrated. Once this concept is understood and is engrained, the clinician should follow with instruction on methods that can be applied to cool down. Through exposure to a variety of therapeutic techniques, a child can begin to develop strategies that help him/her cool off. The clinician may find it useful to have small thermometers in the office to serve as examples or to keep various drawings, such as the one illustrated in Fig. 1. The small thermometers can be taken by the children as a portable reminder of the strategies to cool their temperature.

2. ***A toolbox.*** Similar to the thermometer, the toolbox can serve as a prompt for the child to use the strategies learned in a natural setting. The

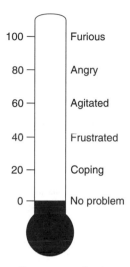

FIGURE 1   Knowing your "temperature" using a good sport thermometer.

TABLE 5   Individual Therapy: Summary of Strategies to Facilitate Generalization

---

Select socially valid social skills behavior
Target behaviors that have a high probability of being trapped in the natural setting
Assess the students current social skill deficits
Teach portable strategies

---

toolbox is a visual cue that allows the child to access strategies learned in the individual sessions. The client can make his own portable toolbox out of a decorated shoebox. Within the box, the child places cut-out tools, which have specific techniques that were learned to solve social problems in the individual sessions. For example, on specific tools, the child may write stop and think, take a deep breath, ignore, use your words, etc. The intention of the toolbox is to highlight strategies that the child has learned and to encourage outside generalization (Table 5).

Group Therapy

Group sessions provide children with the opportunity to practice social skills in a group setting. Strategies can be implemented to facilitate generalization within the social skills training session and in the natural setting. Social skills group therapy gives counselors or therapists the opportunity to assess social skills through the direct observation of interactions during selected social activities and role plays. In the CDC outpatient social skills program, several strategies have been used to facilitate generalization beyond the group social skills training session. First, parents attend a parallel group session to learn strategies for programming generalization in the home and school. The focus of the parent group is to learn, through observation and group discussion, what their child is learning in the children's social skills group session. They learn the language used to prompt specific social skills, the specific definitions and situational role plays used to practice social skills, and the level of competence their child has in using the social skill. They plan strategies for facilitating generalization through prompting, role plays, and reinforcement.

Second, each of the social skills taught has specific language prompts that are paired with the class of behavior being taught. For example, the use of assertion is taught through puppet characters whose names represent different styles of interaction. "Cool Craig" is the assertive character, "Mean Max" is the aggressive character, and "Whimpy Wally" is the passive character. Children learn the nuances of each style. They practice, through role plays, a wide range of relevant situations provided by parents in which assertion could be used. They then practice the skill through specially selected games under a heightened emotional situation approximating the natural setting. Using the language from the social skills group in the home setting becomes an efficient prompt for choosing an assertive response in the home. For example, a parent might prompt a child with the term "Cool Craig" just prior to a situation in which they typically are aggressive. They might say, "Remember to be a Cool Craig. Now ask your brother if you can borrow his skateboard." The term "Cool Craig" prompts a class of behavior, assertion, not solely a splinter skill such as eye contact. If the child chooses to be a "Cool Craig," parents are taught to immediately reinforce the behavior of making a good choice. There are a multitude of situations in which children can practice and be reinforced for being assertive in the natural setting. In addition to reinforcing children for assertive behavior, it is important to decrease the effectiveness of alternate competing strategies the child might choose. For example, if being a "Mean Max" or "Whimpy Wally" is more efficient than a "Cool Craig" in getting their needs met, then they will choose to be a "Mean Max" or "Whimpy Wally." Strategies such as time out, the loss of privileges, or point losses in their token economy need to be implemented to decrease the effectiveness of alternate maladaptive approaches.

Third, the strategy of teaching appropriate social skills can be shaped in the natural setting. For example, children often are at a loss for how to initiate a response, or they lack the sophistication to respond diplo matically when questioning an adult or peer. A child may have the cognitive skills to assess accurately whether the information presented to him/her is accurate, but may not have the diplomacy to bring errors to the teacher's attention in a diplomatic way. The child may choose to interrupt the teacher in midsentence and state "that's wrong, wrong, wrong." The child may not see the need, or have the appropriate social awareness, to question the teacher in a more appropriate manner. Questioning inaccuracies is a skill that should not be eliminated. However, rudeness will result in others avoiding the child. In this situation, the child can learn appropriate pivotal sentences to help question the accuracy of the teacher's statements without creating resentment. Pivotal sentences are those such as "I've heard that, . . ." "could it be possible that, . . ." "is it possible that . . . ?" These pivotal sentences can be written on a sheet of paper and taped to the child's desk to prompt him to start his questions appropriately. If he starts to respond in a rude manner, the teacher can point to the sheet of paper as a prompt. If the child chooses to redo the question starting with the pivotal sentence, he or she will be allowed to continue. If the child is rude, the teacher will administer a time out and the child will not be allowed to continue. In this situation there are competing behaviors. Blurting out a challenge to the teacher has worked for the student. By decreasing the effectiveness of the rude response and reinforcing the use of appropriate pivotal sentences, the teacher can encourage the child to learn to get needs met in a more appropriate manner. This system can be taught and practiced in a group social skills setting and then transferred to the natural setting of the classroom.

Another portable strategy taught to parents is the use of visual prompts to facilitate generalization from the social skills group setting to the natural setting. For example, children in the group are taught to ignore minor provocations. They can choose to ignore someone who is teasing them. They should not ignore their parents, teachers, or other adults, but they may ignore a peer who is trying to upset them. Many children with ADHD have great difficulty ignoring peers and escalate their responses, drawing negative consequences to themselves in the home, school, and community. In our social skills groups we teach a sophisticated definition of ignoring and practice ignoring through role plays and selected games. We teach children to use a hand sign to tell us when they are ignoring. They curl a pinky and hide it from the person they are ignoring. They are taught to look at the teacher until the teacher acknowledges their sign with a wink and then to put it away. They are reinforced for choosing to ignore minor irritating behavior directed at them. The sign is used to let the counselor or parent know that they are actively choosing to ignore since it may not be apparent what the child is ignoring. The counselor or parent can ask the child privately what is being ignored if it is not clear. The hand signal can also be used to prompt a child in the natural setting to choose to ignore a behavior. A teacher or parent can use the sign to communicate nonverbally that ignoring might be an appropriate choice. If the child chooses to ignore, it can be reinforced immediately.

Visual prompts are an excellent method to foster generalization of skills taught in a social skills group to the natural setting. One simple strategy used in our group settings is a simple red and green signal. A red circle on one side of a poster board means you must first raise your hand and wait to be called on before speaking. A green circle on the reverse side of the poster board means it is okay to speak out without being called on. The visual cue is placed where children in the group can see it readily. Changing the visual cue helps students learn not to interrupt counselors and teachers leading a group. The visual sign is more effective because it remains visible as a reminder even after the teacher has stated the rule. It also prompts counselors and teachers to be consistent in their consequences for rule violations or compliance. Another portable visual cue that is used to accomplish the same goal is a simple hand gesture that means to "wait until I acknowledge you before entering the conversation."

Another strategy that can be used to bridge the gap between the counseling setting and the natural setting is a group contingency focusing on anyone in the group using social skills in the natural setting. One example of a group contingency used at the CDC is called "big deals." "Big deals" are a form of a token system in which parents, teachers, and significant others operantly reinforce a child for using a learned social skill by immediately giving him/her points that are turned in during the social skills counseling session. The number of points is written on a piece of paper outlining the skill demonstrated, and the paper is signed by the parent. This is called a "big deal home challenge." The "big deals" are brought to the social skills group and counselors make a big deal over the points the children earn. They first ask if anyone has "big deals" from home. They have various cheers that children can choose from to recognize their accomplishment. The child calls on others to guess what he has earned.

The child then gets to put the points up on a "big deal" chart that is a group contingency. When the chart is full, the group earns a "big deal" fiesta. The "big deals" are both an individual reinforcement and a social reinforcer. "Big deals" are an efficient cost-effective way for parents to increase the use of appropriate learned social skills in the home setting. This illustrates why it is important for parents to be a part of the social skills training process. They know through observation what social skills are being taught and to what level their child is capable of using the skill. Parents also contribute valuable information about the actual situations where the child has difficulty with role playing. A variation of the "big deal" fiesta for the children in the group is a parent–child "big deal" fiesta. The children can give their parents "big deals" for exhibiting the appropriate social skills. This prompts parents to model the behavior they want their child to exhibit. Modeling is a powerful form of learning. It is also a reminder to parents to recognize the use of appropriate social skills by their child.

Another portable social skills group contingency is the good sport pizza. All of the individual social skills are taught through playing group games in addition to role plays and group discussion. They are taught to be good sports. Children are taught that there are nine specific skills that are part of being a good sport in a group game. Before going out to play a game, they review the rules of the specific game they are about to play. Then each child is assigned one of the specific skills to assess during the game. The children assess how the group did on that skill during the game, not how an individual did. They next play the game and then come back to the group session to debrief the leader on how the group did on good sportsmanship. The children report on the skill they were assigned. For example, "Did the group stay with the game all of the time, some of the time, or none of the time?" Thumbs up means all of the time, thumbs to the side means most of the time, and thumbs down means none of the time. Each of the children is asked to evaluate the group's performance on their assigned skill. Next the group votes on how the group did in overall good sportsmanship using a 1–5 scale on a group good sport thermometer. A vote of 1 means that they were not good sports most of the game. A score of 5 means they were good sports all of the time. For each 5 that they earn, they get a pepperoni on the good sport pizza. A picture of a pizza with "x's" is placed prominently in the social skills room. If the group earns a 5, then an x on the pizza is covered with a round sticker. When the group covers all the "x's" with stickers, social skills turns into a pizza party for the group. Parents, during a group or individual

FIGURE 2   Example of big deals.

sporting event, can use this process easily. A small portable good sport thermometer can be created for use during a group sporting activity. Children can be asked to set a personal good sport goal. Meeting their goal successfully can be reinforced immediately following the activity. During the game, parents may periodically get and give feedback on how the child is doing using a thumbs up, thumbs sideways, or thumbs down. This can serve as immediate feedback during the activity. At the end of the game, the child will be asked to self-evaluate using the concept of the good sport thermometer learned in the social skills group sessions.

In addition to the visual cues discussed earlier, pictures depicting the skills can be posted in conspicuous places to prompt the use of the skill. Each time the child sees the poster, he/she is reminded of the skills learned in the social skills session (Fig. 2).

Once a child has been taught a repertoire of social skills, a problem-solving strategy can be taught in the social skills groups to help generalize the use of these skills to the natural setting. Children learn a four-step procedure for problem solving. First, they give the counselor or parent a visual prompt that they want to try problem solving. The prompt is a "T" using a hand gesture. This signifies that they want to step aside and solve the problem privately that is angering, frustrating, or puzzling them. They

TABLE 6   Group Therapy: Summary of Strategies to Facilitate Generalization

---

Technology for facilitating generalization

 Select socially valid social skills behavior
 Target behaviors that have a high probability of being trapped in the natural setting
 Assess the student's current social skill deficits
 Teach portable strategies
 Practice with a different peers and adults
 Practice in a heightened emotional game situation approximating games that are
  played in the natural setting
 Include significant others (parents) in planning generalization
 Practice the use of visual and auditory cues in a simulated social situation
 Decrease the effectiveness of maladaptive competing behaviors

---

step aside with the counselor or parent and state the problem and three possible solutions. Then they select the one most likely to solve the problem, go back into the setting and try it, and pat themselves on the back if it works or try another solution if it does not. This approach facilitates incidental learning in the natural setting. Children give the "T sign," which interrupts an impulsive response. They stop, think, and then act. If significant others are aware of the problem-solving procedure and respond immediately by stepping aside to allow the child to problem solve, the child gets an opportunity to practice across a variety of situations and settings, and with a variety of individuals.

Finally, Fine developed a curriculum entitled the ***Magic within You*** (Fine & Salwak, 1989) that applied magic, drama, communication skills training, art therapy, and social skills training (Fig. 3). The intention behind the program was to help the child learn that s/he had the power to make changes in his/her life. Although the children participated because they wanted to learn magic, they were exposed to much more, including traditional social problem-solving strategies. The youngsters were also taught stagemanship, which eventually also enhanced their ability to express themselves more clearly (Fig. 4). Readers are encouraged to review several good books on magic such as Windley (1976), Wilson (1988), Fitzkee (1988), as well as Fine and Salwalk (1989) and Fine (2000) for further information.

Therapy in the Natural Setting

At the CDC, the staff has developed practical strategies for teaching social skills in the natural setting, the general education classroom (Kotkin, 1995,

FIGURE 3   The Magic Within You.

1998; Swanson, 1992), and a school/clinic setting (Swanson, 1992). The Irvine Paraprofessional Program (IPP) is designed to provide direct intervention in the public school setting to students with ADHD and behavioral consultation to the classroom teacher. A specially trained instructional aide (behavioral specialist) provides direct intervention. The school psychologist or outside consultant provides behavioral consultation to the teacher. Intervention takes place over a 12-week period. Students having extreme behavior problems are referred to the student study team (SST) for intervention. An assessment is done to determine whether the severity of the problem is beyond what the teacher can handle alone. If

FIGURE 4   The Magic Within You: Cognitive Problem Solving Steps.

the team agrees that there is a need for additional resources, a behavioral specialist is assigned to the classroom for a 12-week period. A schedule of bimonthly consultation meetings is programmed over a 12-week period to evaluate the effectiveness of intervention and to strengthen the teacher's behavior management program. The role of the behavioral specialist is to implement a systematic token system in the classroom and on the playground in order to shape the student's behavior in the natural setting. The behavioral specialist also assists in managing the classroom and serves as an instructional assistant to the entire class. Target behaviors are identified in collaboration with the teacher and support staff. Socially valid behaviors are prioritized and targeted for intervention through the token system. The behavioral specialist monitors and provides direct feedback to the student on a predetermined schedule of reinforcement that is faded over the 12-week period. Students receive daily reinforcement based on their performance in the token system. The time intervals for feedback are increased based on a predetermined criterion of success in the token system. Feedback in the token system starts at 15-minute intervals with a goal of fading to feedback only three times a day; in other words, to a level that the teacher can monitor without assistance. Once a consistent level of performance is reached, the intervention is turned over to the teacher. The behavioral specialist monitors progress in the token system through graphing of the target behaviors. This information is used in bimonthly meetings with the school psychologist or consultant and teacher. Data are reviewed, and adjustments to the token system are made as necessary. In addition, the school psychologist or consultant reviews the teacher's current behavior management strategies in an effort to strengthen them. Suggestions are made and information provided on how existing strategies can be modified to better support the target child's gains. The goal is to work collaboratively with the teacher to make practical modifications to the teacher's classroom behavior management system that can assist in maintaining the student's gains.

A significant component of this program is a group social skills session taught by the behavioral specialist. Twice a week, the behavioral specialist leads a social skills group that meets outside of the classroom with selected peers. The function of social skills group is similar to the outpatient social skills program described earlier with the exception that it takes place in the setting where the social skill problems occur. This is part of the token economy. The behavioral specialist serves as a cue to use the social skills taught in the school setting because s/he is in the student's classroom. Other peers also serve as a prompt to use the newly learned skills. Situations role played in the social skills sessions are drawn from actual situations identified in the school setting. The teacher also learns the language and prompts used in the social skills session as strategies for facilitating generalization. Teaching social skills in the context of the natural setting incorporates many of the strategies for generalization suggested by Stokes and Baer (1977) and Stokes and Osnes (1989).

The IPP was developed as an extension of the CDC school/clinic program. It differs in that children with severe ADHD and comorbid conditions such as learning disabilities go to the clinic/school program rather than their home schools. Many of the components are identical to the outpatient program. It differs, however, in the fact that the staff is blended with clinical and educational staff focusing on educational and clinical goals all day long.

Parents first complete a 6-week parenting class to learn basic behavior management strategies. Extending social skills to the home setting is

TABLE 7   Therapy in the Natural Setting: Summary of Strategies to
Facilitate Generalization

- Select socially valid social skills behavior
- Target behaviors that have a high probability of being trapped in the natural setting
- Assess the student's current social skill deficits
- Teach portable strategies
- Practice with a different peers and adults
- Practice in a heightened emotional game situation approximating games that are played in the natural setting
- Include significant others (parents) in planning generalization
- Practice the use of visual and auditory cues in a simulated social situation
- Decrease the effectiveness of maladaptive competing behaviors
- Use multiple stimuli conditions for training
- Use multiple examples of responses to the targeted behavior in training
- Allow a variety in the conditions of training so that the student will not readily discriminate performance to a particular set of circumstances
- Incorporate common salient physical items common and obvious in natural environments into training
- Incorporate important persons from generalization settings in the training setting
- Use self-mediated physical stimuli that can be transported by the student as part of training
- Self-mediated verbal and/or covert discrimination stimuli are produced by the student across relevant settings

---

accomplished by the use of multiple family groups to which parents are assigned following the completion of the parent training sessions. Parents meet 1 day a week every other week in a multiple family group at the school to observe and plan strategies for generalizing social skills to other settings. All the parents from their child's classroom meet during the school day to plan and practice using what they learned about in the parenting class. They practice the skills they will use in the home and community in simulated and in vivo activities. For example, parents plan play dates with the children's peers from the school. They practice their plan at the school and then try it as a scheduled play date at their home. They incorporate strategies for prompting their child to use appropriate social skills and they reinforce them. Parents receive feedback and supervision from the clinical staff on their skill in implementing their plan. Over the course of a year, parents refine their skill at planning activities for generalization of what their child learns at the CDC.

BULLYING AND TEASING: STRATEGIES TO APPLY IN INDIVIDUAL THERAPY

The National Safety Organization reported that 15% of school age children are involved in bully–victim problems. Most children are bullied because they act differently than their peers. This makes children with LD and ADHD prime victims. At times, the children who are picked on are children who have difficulty defending themselves (either physically or mentally) from others. These children are loners, too small, underachievers, overweight, possibly younger, lack social savoir-faire, or behave somewhat differently. They just have difficulties fitting in and they are left feeling less competent and humiliated.

Unfortunately, our experience with most bullying suggests that it occurs outside the purview of adults. Bullies are cautious and usually intimidate their victims only when they will not get caught. In most cases, it seems that children bully others because it makes them feel powerful and it gains them attention. Often bullies pick on the same victim repeatedly. Sometimes bullies justify their behavior by believing irrationally that the victim provoked the altercation (e.g., "he looked at me the wrong way").

Researchers studying bullying have found that most bullies have their friends join in while they victimize their target. Interestingly, in the elementary years (grades 1 and 2), male bullies appear to be the most popular in the class. However, by the fourth grade, it is the less popular children who usually become the bullies. This may suggest that some children with both these disorders may also become perpetrators.

In most cases, children usually do not like to tell others that they are being bullied. They have been humiliated in front of others and they would rather not confront the challenge. Often times the victim feels hopeless. He/she believes that very little can be done to alter the predicaments. The child believes that very few people (including their parents) will understand how they feel.

What Clinicians Can Do to Help Their Clients

Helping the bullied child is not easy. However, there are some guidelines and suggestions that perhaps could help.

1. Help your client become more assertive when others are attacking him. Teach him/her strategies that will help him/her become more

confident and assertive. Help the child learn some conflict management strategies. Two popular commercially available programs are the Peacemaker Program and Bully Proofing. Learning how to problem solve and apply the strategies will ultimately be helpful. Role play the use of eye contact and proper body posture when one is confronted. Demonstrate in therapy how to speak firmly with the bully. Sometimes just learning how not to be afraid and trying to talk it out can be a viable option.

2. Explain to children why people tend to bully others. Often times some children just enjoy watching others overreact and fall apart. When the child does not react, the bullies may not find it reinforcing to bother him. Help the child recognize that the bully wants him to react. That is the way the bully gains power. Help the child to realize that sometimes the best approach to being bullied is just to walk away. Help the youngster realize that sometimes refusing to fight or get involved is a healthy solution. While the child is in therapy, develop a reporting system that s/he can apply at home to practice the new learned skills. Have the child record his progress (or lack of it) for use as a forum for further therapeutic discussions.

3. We have always found the analogy of "fishing" to be a useful example when explaining the bullying process. Many children who bully try to hook a child into reacting. We must persuade the child that instead of taking the bait, s/he should try to avoid getting caught. We need to help the child realize that ignoring, avoiding a reaction, or merely staying away and avoiding interactions contribute to a positive solution. Furthermore, helping the child realize that at times just learning to agree with a bully (even if it is not true) may actually get the bully to leave him alone (because they are not reacting!). Once the child comprehends that bullies want (and desire) confrontation, it is imperative that we help the child develop a plan of action to put into place. Discuss with the child when, where, and for how long s/he will try the new strategies. Give children realistic guidelines on how to evaluate the outcomes of their efforts. Additionally, make sure that a safety net is also in place just in case a given strategy does not work. Encourage the children to be honest with you. Let them know that whatever outcome occurs, they are always able to discuss it with you.

4. Encourage some families to enroll their child in a self-defense class. For example, karate helps teach a child how to defend himself/herself when s/he is being assaulted. It helps a child learn how to protect himself/herself rather than to begin a fight. Enrolling a child into a

self-defense program will also enhance a child's confidence. While in the class, the child will be exposed to a whole group of other youngsters who may also model positive approaches for handling conflict.

5. Help your client learn ways to deflect comments and not internalize the commentary.

6. Help the child recognize when s/he can get help from a nearby adult. Let the child know that it is not a weakness to get someone to intervene.

SELF-ESTEEM AND SOCIAL COMPETENCE

"Winners are those people who will do the extra things that losers won't do." This quotation from Jack Canfield (lead author from the *Chicken Soup* series) identifies that winners recognize that they have to work harder than others to achieve at a higher level. This strong belief system represents the values of certain people who do not give up. They do not take for granted their inherited assets and they continue to strive to be their best.

Conclusions from numerous research studies on self-esteem and children with ADHD and LD indicate that many of these youngsters experience academic failure and are likely to have low self-esteem (Bear et al., 1991). Overall, the majority of studies paint a pessimistic picture. Nevertheless, the research as it relates to the child's social sense of self is not as conclusive. Pearl and Bay (1999) have noted some studies that failed to demonstrate conclusively that the children felt maladjusted as a consequence of their disability. It is apparent that the social supports made available to children, and how others relate to these children, are factors that affect the child's sense of self.

As clinicians it is crucial that we support the whole child. We need to make ourselves available and to attempt to modify negative traits that impact the child adversely. Self-concept and self-esteem are closely linked. McGuire and Padawer-Singer (1976) identified six of the situational determinants of one's self-concept. They include the following.

1. Situational demands (e.g., the self-perceptions that are evoked by questions about oneself in a job interview differ from those evoked by a conversation with a new acquaintance).
2. Stimulus intensity (e.g., gross characteristics, such as hair color, are more likely to be a part of self-concept than more subtle characteristics, such as eye brow shape).

3. Availability (e.g., people are more likely to think of themselves in terms of recent activities than earlier ones).
4. Momentary needs (e.g., currently unfilled desires are likely to be incorporated into the immediate self-concept).
5. Enduring values (e.g., a long-term religious affiliation is likely to be a part of one's self-concept).
6. Past reinforcement history (e.g., what has determined rewards and punishments in the past).

The California State Task Force to Promote Self-esteem and Personal Social Responsibility adopted a couple of working definitions. One definition identified self-esteem as a *social vaccine that may be used to innoculate individuals from life's misfortunes*. Perhaps the key term in this definition is that of a social vaccine. When one is vaccinated, it is assumed that he/she will be protected from something. In this case, it is believed that healthy self-esteem will promote more individuality and assist an individual in promoting and living a healthier lifestyle. It likely will enhance an individual's quality of life and allow him/her to live more fruitfully. The other definition identified self-esteem "as appreciating my own worth and importance and having the character to be accountable for myself and to act responsibly toward others."

David Brooks (1990), a nationally recognized authority on self-esteem, suggests that self-esteem is built by a step-by-step progression of successes' and that successes are the result of action. He refers to the four A's as key ingredients for healthier self-esteem. Brooks believes that one must have the right **attitude** to succeed. Without the attitude, the process is not ready to begin. From there, the individual must take the steps for proper **action**, which will lead to **achievements**. This suggests that there must be a plan to **attain** success. Finally, for there to be growth, the individual must acknowledge those **achievements**.

In many ways this simplified perception of how to maintain a healthy self-esteem makes sense. A proper attitude may spur an individual to act more forcefully in accomplishing something. This ultimately leads to some recognition (either internal or external) and then to self-acknowledgment.

THE SOURCE OF SELF-ESTEEM

Healthy self-esteem is a commodity that is in wide demand. It is discussed frequently and desired greatly, but it is difficult to change. Many youngsters genuinely misunderstand the source of self-esteem. They seem to be confused about where it comes from. This is understandable because our society gives them a mixed message about it.

One analogy of understanding self-esteem is to distinguish between valid and invalid perceptions. Valid self-esteem comes from the inside out. It develops and stems from a solid, clear place within us and it is a variable we can control. Although situations in our life change, our self-esteem and our healthy way of coping are the same in all situations.

The difficulty, of course, is that children confuse valid self-esteem with invalid self-esteem. Children may interpret anything that makes them "feel good" as a valid source of self-esteem. That is understandable because valid and invalid self-esteem can feel similar in some ways. At first, meeting a difficult challenge leaves us "feeling good," but so might other alternatives that are somewhat antisocial, such as abusing drugs or joining gangs.

One of our primary tasks as clinicians is to help our children recognize the difference between valid and invalid self-esteem. If children can do that, then they will be better able to make the kind of choices that will provide them with valid self-esteem: The "feeling good" that comes from a strong, clear place within us will endure. As children grow in their ability to recognize sources of valid self-esteem, they will also learn to approach with caution those situations that let us feel good but which come from something outside ourselves and will not endure.

UNHEALTHY SELF-ESTEEM: WHERE DOES IT LEAD?

Children who have unhealthy self-esteem appear to have many common harmful characteristics. Glenn and Nelsen (1987) have identified many characteristics that they believe are damaging outcomes of unhealthy self-esteem. We have taken the liberty and utilized some of their perceptions as a stepping stone for discussion.

Many of these children seem to have unhealthy self-assessment skills. They do not seem to evaluate social situations and their personal impact on the outcome. Many children with unhealthy self-esteem also use inadequate judgment skills and do not take advantage of what they learned in the past.

Many children with unhealthy self-esteem struggle in believing in themselves and are not willing to except responsibility for their actions that they influence. Some children blame others for consequences and do not seem to recognize their impact on the result. Finally, children who have an unhealthy self-esteem have weaker perceptions of their value and significance to others. They do not appreciate their capabilities. They often act against themselves and put themselves down. They feel incompetent, and in many ways they do not recognize and appreciate their significance and uniqueness.

BELIEFS THAT HELP CHILDREN LIVE MORE EFFECTIVELY AND HEALTHY

As clinicians, we realize that it is quite difficult to challenge our youngsters to help them learn to believe in their own attributes. Over the years, many of the children have suffered inequities that have caused them to feel different. They feel like failures and are perceived by others to be failures. In authors' years of treating children with LD and ADHD, we have made it a practice to identify several belief systems believed necessary to have them focus upon. Some of these belief systems are from the work of Anderson (1981). Fine and Sachs (1998) elaborated upon these belief systems and made them more relevant to this specific population. We will continue to refine these beliefs and provide the reader with some concrete suggestions that apply to those that you serve. They are as follows:

Belief 1: It Is Okay to Make Mistakes—Do Not Confuse a Child's Mistakes with Sins

Making mistakes is something we all do. Children who accept this position recognize that they are worthwhile individuals despite their mistakes. These are individuals who recognize that it is inevitable to make errors and they can cope with this. Children must realize that failure is an event, not a person. It is realistic to assume that a child will fail many times in life. As Robert Kennedy stated so elegantly, "Only those who dare to fail can ever achieve greatly."

Belief 2: I am Responsible for My Day

Many children aspire to learn that they control their destiny. They must learn that they are responsible for how they feel and, for that matter, what they do.

Belief 3: I Can Handle Things
When They Go Wrong

Children need to relax and recognize that they cannot deliberately control all outcomes. They need to accept the position that things usually go well, and when they do not, they can handle it. Would not this be an excellent belief for all ages to follow? As clinicians, we need to be sensitive that this dimension can be very difficult for the youngsters to overcome, especially because they find themselves so often doing things that might be wrong. Children need to recognize that they can handle things when they are not working out. They have to implement a plan that will help them offset their deficits. They need to recognize that they might not be able to change the past, but they still have the power to influence the future.

Belief 4: It Is Important to Try

This belief is extremely important. Children must be ready for the challenges of daily living. Even though they might be confronted with difficult tasks, they must believe that it is better to try than avoid them. Outcomes worth having are deserving of the effort. Children must be challenged to accept this point of view.

Belief 5: I am Capable

One needs to genuinely develop a sense of self-respect. A child who recognizes a positive sense of self is a child who is willing to take chances. Children also need to realize that they should not compare their strengths with those of anyone else. We recognize that this is difficult, but self-comparison is probably more constructive, at least initially. For example, a child could compare his/her performance to previous outings. As time goes on, external comparisons can also be made. All a child needs to think is "I am capable and productive." Productivity between children may differ, but believing in capabilities will not. Children need to try to seek the positive in every situation instead of bemoaning what they lack.

Belief 6: I Can Change

Children need to know that they are capable of changing their behaviors. Every day is a new experience, and children need to realize that they can have an impact on their own destiny. For example, a child who has difficulty controlling his/her behavior or, for that matter, learning a specific academic skill must accept the challenge. Children have to realize that they can enhance their abilities with effort. Unfortunately, some children use negative thinking, which predetermines their behaviors. When children empower themselves to believe they have an impact, surprising outcomes may occur.

THE MAGIC INGREDIENTS FOR HEALTHY SELF-ESTEEM

A question asked frequently by many parents is "What can I do to help my child's self-esteem. Is there any magic?" Unfortunately, the answer is not as simple as the question. As can be seen throughout this section of this chapter, self-esteem is affected in many ways. If we were to select three broad dimensions that we believe impact a child's overall sense of competency, they would be (1) helping children to recognize that they belong, (2) helping them appreciate their competence, and (3) helping them recognize that they are worthwhile. Although easy to explain and write about, these are three very tough dimensions.

Belonging is of utmost importance. Children need to know that they fit in. When this occurs, they feel more comfortable because they realize they are accepted. One of the saddest experiences to watch on a playground is a child wandering around aimlessly trying to find a friend. What compounds this problem even more is that children need to be accepted by the group they want to belong to. If a child has a desire to be accepted by one group, but is only accepted by another, the child would walk away feeling empty. Acceptance and belonging to a specific group are important. Children see more value in life when they feel a part of something.

A sense of competence is the recognition that one is capable and has something to offer. When children discover their talents and are appreciative of them, they will grow even further. Their sense that they are worthwhile comes from the recognition they receive from others, and this indirectly applauds them for their accomplishments. Children also need to pat themselves on their backs for challenges that they feel they have mastered.

Children need to develop a belief system that affirms their convictions. Somewhere in their lives they will learn to take a stance and note that "I am a capable person who can change if I choose to."

TABLE 8   Guidelines for Parents to Enhance Self-esteem in Their Children

1. When you are accepting of who you are and like and respect yourself, it is assumed that you have healthy self-esteem. Parents need to be encouraging to their children. They have to help their children discover their inner talents and become more grounded. Children who are accepting of their skills are more willing to try to change. They do not walk around feeling discouraged because they have not lived up to their own and others expectations.

2. As much as possible, parents should set a goal to build a home *that is open and supporting*. A home that is open and supporting will mostly likely nurture risk taking rather than being full of anger and ridicule. Criticism and negative comments from others can be very incriminating and damaging. Continued rejection and unrealistic unpleasant expectations will eventually convince a child that others do not believe he is worthwhile.

3. Parents need to take their time and try to understand what motivates their children. With this insight, parents may be able to apply (or, for that matter, discontinue) approaches that will assist their child in becoming more emotionally energized.

4. Parents must attempt to energize children so they become empowered to reach for their dreams. Empowering children means helping them develop self-respect as well as dignity for their actions. These efforts will enable them to affirm their dreams. As parents, we must be cautious and not discourage our children. We should not tell them that their dreams are impossible to reach. Our children must be more willing to reach out and touch the stars.

   A guideline that all parents should try to institute within their home is a clear understanding of failure. A good lesson is to instruct our children that failure is an event not a person. Parents should help children respect the realities of life circumstances and recognize that any failure should not be personalized. It is merely an event that can be learned from. Children can take lessons of failure and turn them into challenges for the future or lessons to be learned from. What is important for parents to recognize is that it is realistic to assume that a child will fail at various episodes throughout life. Efforts have to be initiated to help children cope with this dimension of the game.

5. Things worth having are deserving of the effort. Parents have to help children appreciate that it takes some effort to attain achievement. Tenacity and hard work are two principles that have to be modeled and taught to our charges. Eventually, children who are more driven will take these principles more to heart. Ultimately, they will have to develop more realistic reliance in themselves. This eventually will help children discover that they have hidden talents that will blossom if the appropriate attention is given.

6. When children empower themselves to believe they have an impact, they will. Again, we return to this crucial premise. The old Zen proverb, "when the mind is ready the teacher comes," really makes extraordinary sense. Children have to be ready and willing to enable themselves in all aspects of their life. When this does occur, surprising outcomes may happen.

7. As parents, we have to teach children that if they always say they cannot, they probably in the end will be right. Negative thinking deteriorates performance. We must become more conscious of our child's attitude and help model more

(Continues)

TABLE 8   (*continued*)

---

appropriate alternatives. The major point is that as parents we should be aware of children's internal thinking and help as much as possible to alter its origins. **Cannot** usually stands for not wanting or preferring not to rather than not being able to.

8. *Parents, should help children focus on positive self-talk rather than negative, destructive self-talk.* Finally, to continue with what was noted in the previous thought, positive affirmations are one of the most powerful procedures we can utilize to change our thinking and our reactions. Children with a healthy self-esteem recognize the shattering effects of negative thinking. These children will try to apply positive procedures, which enhance their performance or, for that matter, the outcome.

STRATEGIES TO PROMOTE HEALTHY SELF-ESTEEM: GUIDELINES FOR PARENTS

Now that we have provided a clear overview of self-esteem, it is only logical that we provide a simple handout that can be used to identify some of the principles highlighted within this component. Table 8 identifies some of these strategies.

FINAL THOUGHTS

This chapter has provided insight into strategies that could be applied to enhance social skills and self-competence. It may be useful to develop a protocol of best practice approaches to implement with our clients. It is hoped that we can have some impact on their quality of life. We have chosen to provide a rubric rather than solely reviewing existing programs that may or may not fit your individual client's needs. Our bias in writing this chapter was to provide clinicians with an understanding of strategies that will enhance the effectiveness of social skills interventions by addressing the importance of planning for generalization. We believe that this component is missing from most clinical procedures and practices. It is because of this belief that we formatted this chapter as a blueprint for effective clinical practice.

REFERENCES

Anderson, J. (1981). *Thinking, changing, rearranging.* Eugene, OR: Timberline.

Bagwell, C., Molina, B., Pelham, W., & Hoza, B. (2001). Attention-deficit hyperactivity disorder and problems in peer relations: Predictions from childhood to adolescence. *Journal of the American Academy of Child and Adolescent Psychiatry*, 40(11), 1285–1292.

Baum, D., Duffelmyer, F., & Geelan, M. (1988). Resource teacher perceptions of the prevalence of social dysfunction among students with learning disabilities. *Journal of Learning Disabilities*, 21(6), 380–381.

Bear, G., Clever, A., & Proctor, W. (1991). Self-perception of non-handicapped children and children with learning disabilities in an integrated setting. *Journal of Special Education*, 24, 409–426.

Brooks, D. (1990). *The self-esteem repair and maintenance manual.* Newport Beach, CA: Kincaid House.

Bryan, T. (1974). Peer popularity of learning disabled children. *Journal of Learning Disability*, 7, 621–625.

Bryan, T. (1994). The social competence of students with learning disabilities over time: A response to Vaughn and Hogan. *Journal of Learning Disabilities*, 27(5), 304–311.

Bryan, T. (1998). Social competence of students with learning disabilities. In B. Wong (Ed.), *Learning about learning disabilities* (pp. 237–275). San Diego: Academic Press.

Bursuck, W. (1989). A comparison of students with learning disabilities to low achieving and higher achieving counterparts. *Journal of Learning Disabilities*, 22(3), 188–194.

Carlson, C. I. (1987). Social interaction goals and strategies of children with learning disabilities. *Journal of Learning Disabilities*, 20, 306–311.

Conte, R., & Andrews, J. (1993). Social skills in the context of learning disability definitions: A reply to Gresham and Elliot and directions for the future. *Journal of Learning Disabilities*, 26(3), 146–153.

Cummings, R. L., Vallance, D., & Brazil, K. (1992). Prevalence and patterns of psychosocial disorders in children and youth with learning disabilities: A service provider's perspective. *Exceptionality*, 2(3&4), 91–108.

Dodge, K. A. (1986). A social information-processing model of social competence in children. In M. Perlmutter (Ed.), *Cognitive perspective on children's social and behavioral development: The Minnesota Symposia on Child Psychology*, (Vol. 18, pp. 77–125). Hillsdale, NJ: Lawrence Erlbaum Associates.

Dodge, K.A. (1987). Social information processing factors in reactive and proactive aggression in children's peer groups. *Journal of Personality and Social Psychology*, 53(6), 1146–1158.

Dodge, K. A., & Coie, J. (1987). Social information processing factors in reactive and pro-active aggression in children's peer groups. *Journal of Personality and Social Psychology*, 53(6), 1146–1158.

DuPaul, G. J., & Eckert, T. L. (1994). The effects of social skills curricula: Now you see them, now you do not. *School Psychology Quarterly*, 9(2), 113–132.

Fine, A. (1991). The Get Along Guy Manual. Pomona, CA: Graphics Communication.

Fine, A. (1993). Friendship, Social Skills, and Getting Along: LDA CA State Conference, Pomona, CA: Oct. 21–24, 1993.

Fine, A. (2000). The magic within you: Enhancing personal competence. *The Brain Journey: 2000.* Monterey, CA: Technology, Medicine and Education for Attention Deficit Disorder.

Fine, A. H., & Sachs, M. (1997). *The total sports experience for kids.* South Bend: Diamond Communications.

Fine, A., & Salwak, D. (1989). *The magic within you.* Geni, 53, #2, 122–122.

Fine, A., Lee, J., Zapf, S., Kriwin, S., Henderson, K., & Gibbons, F. (1996). Broadening the impact of services and recreational therapies. In A. Fine, & N. Fine (Eds.), *Therapeutic recreation for exceptional children* (2nd ed., pp. 243–300). Springfield, IL: Charles C. Thomas.

Fitzkee, D. (1988). *Showmanship for magicians.* Pomeroy, CA: Lee Jacobs Productions.

Flicek, M. (1992). Social status of boys with both academic problems and attention-deficit hyperactivity disorder. *Journal of Abnormal Psychology,* 20(4), 353–365.

Glenn, S., & Nelsen, J. (1987). *Raising self-reliant children in a self-indulgent world.* Rocklin: Prima.

Gresham, F. M. (1983). Social validity in the assessment of children's social skills: Establishing standards for children's social competency. *Journal of Psychoeducational Assessment,* 1, 299–307.

Gresham, F. M. (1998). Social skills training: Should we raze, remodel, or rebuild? *Behavioral Disorders,* 24(1), 19–25.

Gresham, F. M., & Elliot, S. N. (1989). Social skills assessment technology for LD students. *Learning Disability Quarterly,* 12, 141–152.

Haagar, D., & Vaughn, S. (1995). Parent, teacher, peer, and self-reports of the social competence of students with learning disabilities. *Journal of Learning Disabilities,* 28(4), 205–216.

Hall, C., Peterson, A. D., Webster, R. E., Bolen, L. M., & Brown, M. B. (1999). Perception of nonverbal social cues by regular education ADHD, and ADHD/LD students. *Psychology in the Schools,* 36(6), 505 512.

Kavale, K. A., & Forness, S. R. (1996). Social skill deficits and learning disabilities: A meta-analysis. *Journal of Learning Disabilities,* 29(3), 226–247.

Kawanagh, J. F., & Truss, T. J., Jr. (1988). *Learning disabilities: Proceedings of the national conference.* Parkton, MD: York Press.

Kistner, J. A., & Gatlin, D. G. (1989). Sociometric differences between learning-disabled and nonhandicapped students: Effects of sec and race. *Journal of Educational Psychology,* 81, 118–120.

Kotkin, R. A. (1995). Irvine Paraprofessional Program: Using paraprofessionals in serving students with ADHD. *Intervention in School and Clinic,* 30(4), 235–240.

Kotkin, R. A. (1998). Irvine Paraprofessional Program (IPP): A promising practice for serving students with ADHD. *Journal of Learning Disabilities,* 31(6), 556–654.

Levine, M. (2001). *Educational care*: Cambridge, MA: Educators Publishing Service.

Levine, M. (2001). *Jarvis Clutch-Social Spy.* Cambridge, MA: Educators Publishing Service.

Levine, M. (2002). *All kinds of minds.* New York: Simon and Shuster.

Margalit, M. (1994). *Loneliness among children with special needs: Theory, research, coping and interaction.* New York: Springer-Verlag.

Martlew, M., & Hodson, J. (1991). Children with mild learning difficulties in an integrated and in a special education school: Comparisons of behavior, teasing and teacher's attitudes. *British Journal of Educational Psychology,* 61(3), 355–369.

Mathur, S. R., & Rutherford, R. B. (1996). Is social skills training effective for students with emotional or behavioral disorders? *Behavioral Disorders,* 22(1), 21–28.

McGuire, W. J., & Padawer-Singer, A. (1976). *Journal of Personality and Social Psychology,* 33(6), 743–754.

Moore, A., Hillery, B. (1989). Bullying in Dublin schools. *Irish Journal of Psychology, Vol.* 10(3), 426–441.

Pearl, P., & Bay, M. (1999). In J. Schwean, & S. Saklofske (Eds.), *Handbook of psychosocial characteristics of exceptional children* (pp. 443–469). New York: Kluwer Academic/Plenum Press.

Pellham, W. E., & Bender, M. E. (1982). Peer relationships in hyperactive children: Description and treatment. In K. D., Gadow, & I. Bialer (Eds.), *Advances in learning and behavioral disabilities* (pp. 365–436). Greenwich, CT: JAI Press.

Salmon, G., James, A., Cassidy, E., & Javaloyes, M. (2001). Bullying a review. *Clinical Child Psychology and Psychiatry*, 5(4), 563–579.

Schachter, B., Bless, M. B., & Bruck, M. (1991). The prevalence and correlates of behaviour problems in learning disabled children. *Canadian Journal of Psychiatry*, 36, 323–331.

Stokes, T. F., & Baer, D. (1977). An implicit technology of generalization. *Journal of Applied Behavior Analysis*, 10, 349–367.

Stokes, T. F., & Osnes, P. G. (1986). Programming the generalization of children's social Behavior. In P. S. Strain, M. J., Guralnick, & H. Walker (Eds.), *Children's behavior: Development, assessment and modification* (pp. 407–443). Orlando, Fl: Academic Press.

Stormont, M. (2001). Social outcomes of children with ADHD: Contributing factors and implications for practice. *Psychology in the Schools*, 38(6), 521–531.

Swanson, H. L., & Malone, S. (1992). Social skills and learning disabilities: A meta-analysis of the literature. *School Psychology Review*, 21, 427–443.

Strain, P. S. (Ed.) (1981). The Utilization of Classroom Peers as Behavior Charge Agents. New York: Plenum.

Swanson, J. M. (1992). *School-based assessments and interventions for ADD students.* Irvine, CA: K. C.

Tur-Kaspa, H., & Bryan, T. (1994a). Social attributions of students with learning disabilities. *Exceptionality*, 4, 229–244.

Tur-Kaspa, H., & Bryan, T. (1994b). Social information processing of students with learning disabilities. *Journal of Learning Disabilities Research and Practice*, 9, 12–23.

Vaughn, S., McIntosh, R., & Spencer-Rowe, J. (1991). Peer rejection is a stubborn thing: Increasing peer acceptance of rejected students with learning disabilities. *Learning Disabilities Research and Practice*, 6(2), 83–88.

Vaughn, S., & Sinaugub, J. (1998). Social competence of students with learning disabilities: Interventions and issues. In B. Wong (Ed.), *Learning about learning disabilities* (pp. 453–487). San Diego: Academic Press.

Vaughn, S., Zaragoza, N., Hogan, A., & Walker, J. (1993). A four-year longitudinal investigation of the social skills and behavior problems of students with learning disabilities. *Journal of Learning Disabilities*, 26(6), 404–412.

Wiener, J. (1987). Peer status of learning disabled children and adolescents: A review of the literature. *Learning Disabilities Research*, (2), 62–79.

Wilson, M. (1988). *Mark Wilson's complete course in magic.* Philadelphia: Courage Books.

Windley, C. (1976). *Teaching and learning with magic.* Washington DC: Acropolis.

Wolfe, N. A., Byrne, J. M., & Bawden, H. N. (2000). ADHD in preschool children: Parent-related psychosocial correlates. *Developmental Medicine and Child Neurology*, 42, 825–830.

Zumpfe, H. J., & Landau, S. (2002). Peer problems: Managing peer rejection. *Attention*, 8(5), 32–35.

## CHAPTER 11

Transitions into Higher Education

Micki Bryant, Mark Turner and Aubrey H. Fine

INTRODUCTION

In your work with children and adolescents with learning and attention disorders you have guided students and their families through various developmental stages. Efforts thus far have probably focused on helping the student adapt within structured school systems while providing solid foundations in behavioral, academic, and social–emotional arenas—establishing the "roots" that are essential to all youth.

It is also important to help your clients grow the "wings" that will be necessary for a successful transition into higher or vocational education, career selection, and the life tasks of adulthood. Such a daunting developmental task is especially challenging for those with cognitive differences and their effect on everyday life functioning. Your guidance now will be oriented toward helping them make critical decisions about their life path and the development of the skills necessary to find the "best fit" for themselves in this wider world. Higher education is a whole new world for most students, one that maintains elements of structure and rules, but one that also allows greater freedom of choice that requires internalized individual direction. Students who are not prepared for this often flounder or experience failure at this important juncture. Your ability to help students and families make important decisions about this next phase can be critical to your clients' ultimate success.

The impact that therapists can have on such clients may be illustrated by the experiences of two very different students. At a recent graduation ceremony, one of the writers encountered a young man that he had worked with when the student was 8–12 years of age (whom we will call Gilbert). The author had reconnected with this student when he attended our university, and he had the opportunity to have Gilbert in one of his classes. Going to college was a big deal for him! Things did not come easily for Gilbert, and it took great perseverance for him to reach this plateau. He benefited from his hard work, use of services such as tutoring, and excellent family support. His parents shared their excitement about their sons achievement, and the author felt a sense of pride and satisfaction that they included his efforts in Gilbert's quest for success.

In a situation with a less successful outcome, one of the writers worked with a young man since he was in the sixth grade (we will call him David). Diagnosed with Attention–Deficit/Hyper-Activity Disorder (ADHD) from an early age, David faced many challenges socially and academically. He was always getting himself into trouble, but over time, David made tremendous progress, especially during high school. Through the insights made in therapy as well as maturation, David appeared to learn and apply numerous compensatory strategies that helped support him. He received positive feedback from his teachers and family and he became more self-confident. In therapy, the author and David began discussing college selection in a methodical manner, looking at his interests and abilities, matching them with campuses that could support him. David selected a community college and appeared motivated to begin. His family believed that the need for therapy was less important at that juncture so sessions became bimonthly.

Despite his former progress, David encountered difficulties upon entering college. His family did not have realistic expectations for their son's transition, encouraging him to take a full load of classes as well as getting a part-time job. Clinically the therapist believed that the adjustment to the greater freedom in higher education could pose challenges for David. He had been used to having more supervision and now would need to be more independent to be successful. David also decided that he did not want to be identified with his college's disabled student services. All these poor choices left David with an ineffective support system from the college and his family.

Unfortunately, things did not go well—he failed several classes and was ultimately unsuccessful in his college transition. All of the previous efforts to help a child grow into a responsible adult seemed to come unraveled when he entered college. What could have been different for David? What were the needed ingredients for him to transition to college successfully and become a more effective adult?

This chapter provides a "road map" to help assess and prepare your clients for successfully navigating this transitional phase and for understanding the landscape of higher education. As therapists working with such students, you will need to make a thoughtful assessment of your client's abilities in cognitive and social–emotional areas, evaluate their support network, and help them prepare for this new world. Understanding the options available in various types of postsecondary settings is also important. Integrating your understanding of the student with information about the options will enable you to offer sound guidance upon which successful decisions can be made. Your influence may lead to more positive outcomes such as the graduation of "Gilbert" instead of less successful experiences like those of "David."

Within the chapter, suggestions and information are offered in the following areas to support your clients' success in planning and achieving their educational goals.

- Assessment of your clients' internal and external resources for identifying and meeting educational goals.
- Disability-related information about postsecondary environments.
- Perspectives on integrating this into a "success profile" for students with learning and attention disorders.
- Access to additional resources.

ROLE OF THE THERAPIST IN APPROPRIATE PATH SELECTION

The consensus among clinicians experienced with these populations is that the therapist needs to assume a more directive and structured role than might be used for other clients. Hallowell (1995) recommends a less neutral stance in favor of one that is encouraging and directive. Although he values some aspects of traditional therapy due to issues such as low self-esteem, he suggests that the therapist act as ". . . a guide through thoughts and associations, helping prioritize mental productions so as to pay attention to what is germane, while letting go of what is extraneous" (p. 151). Helping a client feel truly understood, especially a client who already feels different, is also seen as an important goal and a powerful therapeutic experience (Murphy, 1995; Hallowell, 1995).

Nadeau (1995) sees the role of the therapist as encompassing several aspects: (1) an educator who improves understanding of the diagnosis and the individual; (2) a supporter who empowers the person to "manage" the disability; (3) an interpreter who validates the client's experiences regarding the disability (especially when others do not); (4) a structurer who provides structure initially, while helping clients learn to self-structure; and (5) a rehabilitation counselor, who suggests practical modifications to daily routines across many environments.

Working with college students who have learning and attention disorders has reinforced our support of a therapeutic approach that provides both a deep-felt understanding of the client's world and greater direction and guidance. Within this framework, it is important to remember that the ultimate goal is one of personal empowerment (Murphy, 1995), which is especially critical for students transitioning to adulthood. Initially, however, the therapist may need to model methods by which the clients can come to a more complete understanding of the "true self," including areas of disability. This will be critical for helping clients make the path selection of "best fit" for them.

The following section suggests areas to assess when evaluating your client's readiness for transitioning into an appropriate environment for their needs. Recommendations for helping your clients to prepare for a successful transition will also be included.

FEARLESS ASSESSMENT OF CLIENT FUNCTIONING (AND WHAT TO DO ABOUT IT)

Therapists naturally want to see their clients improve and be able to succeed in meeting their goals. However, it is also important for clients and their therapists to be realistic in an assessment of the capabilities necessary for achieving their goals. We thus recommend a "fearless assessment" of a variety of areas of the student's functioning in order to help arrive at the best match of student and environment. With a clear picture in mind, therapist and client can then work together to capitalize on strengths and improve weaknesses in preparing for meeting their goals.

A thorough assessment involves all aspects of functioning, including such areas as cognitive and academic functioning, general academic preparation, interests and intrinsic motivation, executive/organizational abilities, and social–emotional skills and support resources. Experience with this population reminds us that it is often those general "life-functioning" skills we may take for granted that are the most important rather than academic skills alone. Students by no means have to be proficient in all of the areas reviewed here, although they should possess a good balance of strengths and weaknesses.

Throughout this review of important areas to assess, we will suggest some ideas of how clinicians might work with their clients to augment their readiness for the higher education setting. Appendix 10 includes a form to help you integrate your clinical impressions.

Cognitive and Academic Functioning

An updated comprehensive assessment of a client's cognitive and academic functioning is a key element in determining the best fit between a student and the postsecondary environment. Although college settings may accept existing documentation, you should critical evaluate the adequacy of this documentation. While some reports are excellent, many may lack the depth desired when determining specific strengths, weaknesses, and readiness for college settings. Because ADHD can be diagnosed without formal testing, some students may not have a comprehensive report. College campuses will prefer to see a recent assessment emphasizing the functional limitations for students with either learning or attention disorders. It is therefore in the best interests of your client to have a thorough assessment or reevaluation done within 1–2 years of attending a postsecondary setting. If the school district cannot provide one of sufficient depth, encourage your client's family to seek an outside evaluation, preferably from a specialist in the field.

The assessment will provide an overall IQ or intellectual functioning score and help you understand the way your client processes information of varying types. For example, you should have a clear idea of strengths

TABLE 1

Cognitive performance
  Verbal abilities
  Nonverbal or performance abilities (including visual–spatial and hands-on skills)
  Perceptual abilities (such as auditory and visual processing)
  Memory (short and long term)
  Attention
  Visual–motor skills
  Executive functioning abilities, especially for those with ADHD
Academic performance
  Reading (decoding and sight word recognition)
  Reading comprehension
  Written language (basic mechanics and broader quality of content)
  Mathematics (calculation and applied problem solving)

---

and weaknesses in the cognitive and academic areas shown in Table 1. Additionally, the assessment should address the cognitive style that works best for the way the student learns. For example, information might be best presented in a visual, auditory, or combined modality or the student might be a strong kinesthetic learner.

The assessment results can assist you in three important ways: (1) provide you with an in-depth profile of your clients' resources, (2) help you educate your client about their own strengths and weaknesses, and (3) guide both of you in making choices of best fit for specific majors, career goals, and specific campus settings.

Once you have an understanding of the student's profile, discussing these test results with your client is vitally important. This should be done with a minimum of technical terminology so that students have a clear understanding of their disability and how these challenges may impact them in college and throughout life. Knowledge of their own profile of strengths and weaknesses enables students to better understand their need for specific accommodations. Having the student share their perceptions and reactions to the test results is also important (Brinckerhoff et al., 2002). Unfortunately, the more typical experience in the higher education setting is that students who have been diagnosed from an early age still do not understand the nature of their disabilities by the time they reach college. This makes it difficult for the student to understand his or her own needs and to advocate for these with professors.

The profile of strengths and weaknesses derived from the assessment can help you evaluate your client's potential for higher education and also guide the student in making informed choices about specific majors and career goals. For example, students who have strong verbal abilities and writing skills may do well in areas such as English, social sciences, or journalism. Those with stronger nonverbal or visual–spatial abilities could do well in fields such as science, architecture, graphic design or engineering, and other technical fields. Other students may have a similar pattern of strengths, but lack sufficient overall resources or verbal abilities to do well in an academic environment with heavy demands for reading and writing. Vocational schools may therefore be a better choice. Adults with ADHD may possess strong academic skills, but have poor executive functioning abilities, which could indicate the need for a more supportive environment, such as community college. These are just a few examples of how assessment results can help guide important decisions for career goals and specific settings.

Academic Preparation

While an assessment will reveal general performance in academic areas, it is also important to assess the student's overall academic background and readiness for continued education. For instance, does the student possess good skills in fundamental academic areas of reading, writing, and math? If not, the client should seek additional tutoring or other supplemental instructional programs to improve these skills. Because most colleges have general education standards in areas such as English and math, students who are underprepared in these areas may face significant obstacles to passing these basic courses.

To gain a sense of the client's academic preparation, clinicians will most likely need to consult professionals involved in the student's educational life. Feedback from teachers, school counselors, and parents will be very useful. Grades, standardized achievement testing, and feedback from specific projects, school conferences, or Individualized Education Plan (IEP) meetings can also help assess general academic background.

In assessing academic preparation it is critical to consider the study skills and strategies that students possess. So many college students lack the basic knowledge of how to approach learning, particularly when a higher order of learning is required. You can encourage your client to learn basic study strategies, such as how to read chapters and take notes effectively, determine the essential elements being taught, and outline and write papers and projects. If workshops or classes on this topic are not available in high school, they may be found elsewhere, perhaps at tutoring centers. Some colleges also offer these programs in summer camps or other learning experiences prior to entering the first term. While most colleges have such programs on campus for all students, it would be best for students with learning and attention issues to obtain these skills as early as possible prior to matriculation.

It is also important to consider the type of courses that students are taking when they are receiving special education services. Students with learning disorders that affect English or math abilities, for example, may not be taking the courses designated as college entrance requirements (i.e., 4 full years of English, 2 years of algebra, and 1 of geometry). While altering their high school course requirements due to areas of disability may seem logical, when it comes time to apply for college, they may not qualify. Although some colleges do allow for circumstances of "special admittance," it is best to have all requirements in place prior to graduation. You may need to check with your client's parents and/or school to make sure that proper courses are being taken.

If your client seems to lack a good academic background, beginning at a community or vocational college may be a better option than initially attending a 4-year institution. This can offer the student a better chance to feel successful and improve on skills that may be lacking. Bear in mind that such decisions should include consideration of the specific disability and how the individual may be able to compensate. Students with dyslexia or other reading disorders will naturally have lower reading skills; however, if they can perform well with accommodations such as additional time, taped books, or electronic text, this should not be viewed as a significant obstacle to higher education.

In fact, we suggest that students who are most familiar with strategies for compensation, such as the use of assistive technology, will be better prepared than high school students who were not allowed to use such accommodations. Even if a school district does not allow such strategies for test taking and learning, you should encourage your client and their family to utilize adaptive strategies outside of the classroom. This will ease their transition greatly, as most postsecondary settings expect students to rely on these assistive resources and accommodation strategies within a mainstreamed environment. Some resources that provide additional information on this topic include "*Learning How to Learn—Getting Into and Surviving College When You Have a Learning Disability*" (Cobb, 2001), "*How The Special Needs Brain Learns*" (Sousa, 2001), and "*ADD and the College*

Student: A Guide for High School and College Students with Attention Deficit Disorder" (Quinn, 1994).

Interests/Motivation

An important area to assess in determining the best path for your client is, of course, what the client wants to do. Is there sufficient interest in and motivation for pursuing higher education or vocational goals? Without this basic drive, students will find it very difficult to persist in the face of the challenges posed by their learning disabilities. While it may be difficult for students who lack such ambitions to admit this to families who have high expectations, the therapist may be in a unique position to explore the truth of the situation.

Obtaining information about various careers or vocations prior to entering college may stimulate the person with learning issues to feel informed, confident, and enthusiastic regarding the possibilities that are available. A variety of ways to explore career options have been suggested (Brinckerhoff et al., 2002), including vocational classes, volunteer or work experiences, field trips to work sites, and meeting with adults in fields of interest. Student organizations, clubs, or hobbies can also be sources of inspiration, and interest inventories may help focus students' interests into specific areas. Brinckerhoff et al. (2002) also suggest that students work with the Department of Rehabilitation and opportunities under the School-to-Work Opportunities Act, which allow for more real-world explorations of career possibilities.

Throughout this exploration process, it will be important to link the student's profile of strengths and weaknesses with the fields of interest. If a student is weak in math, for instance, majors and careers that depend heavily on that subject will not be suitable. Students may not realize what a certain field requires and how their disability may impact that career choice. You can assist them to consider such factors as they explore various areas of interest in the manner described earlier. It is equally important to help the client discover his or her own values and whether they fit with career choices.

A therapist's role can be crucial in guiding clients with disabilities to effective path selections for education and careers. Gently confronting unrealistic expectations regarding your client's estimation of his/her own abilities can be a delicate but potent process. Addressing the hope of family members for their child's goals can also help relieve the tension of "unspoken" expectations. Discussing these issues in a realistic but supportive manner will help enormously with preparing to make the most of students' potential and find the "best fit" for fulfilling educational and career paths.

Executive Functioning

Executive functioning is an area often unexplored in therapeutic settings. However, because of its strong correlation with academic functioning, it is a particularly critical area to assess when determining your client's readiness for higher education. As noted in earlier chapters, executive functions (EF) are processes of the brain that activate, regulate, and integrate a variety of other mental functions. They play a central role in learning activities (Dendy, 2000), problem solving (Butterfield & Albertson, 1995), and self-regulation (Barkley, 1998). By allowing for higher order, symbolic reasoning, they serve as hallmarks of human intelligence (Lyon, 1996). While executive dysfunction is only sometimes noted in those with learning disabilities, it is considered by many to be a hallmark characteristic of ADHD (Barkley, 1997).

Because of the breadth of cognitive skills commonly subsumed under the label of EF, evaluating this area can be challenging and time-consuming for clinicians. For that reason, we tend to focus on those aspects of EF that consistently play a disproportionately large role in determining successful academic functioning. These components include effective planning, organization, time management, behavioral modulation, and attentional/memory controls, although we often find it useful to selectively include other constructs (e.g., affective lability) where indicated. Each of these core components is first described in some detail, emphasizing their importance to successful college functioning. We then propose an "academic audit" method to help clinicians assess their clients' EF skills.

Planning

Planning activities are future-oriented and include skills such as goal setting, resource investigation, and strategy formulation. They are vital to ensuring the success of any long-term educational endeavor. Navigating the curriculum of a higher education institution is a complex process requiring the tracking of an extensive array of curriculum information both during and across academic terms.

Lack of planning may be problematic even within the context of a given term or course. For example, a computer science student may find as he begins work on a programming project Saturday evening that he failed to anticipate the need for a key software program found only in the school lab that is closed on weekends. In this situation, the student will likely be graded on his weakness in planning rather than on his strength in programming.

Effective counseling and advising will encourage such students to develop a checklist of materials necessary for a given project to be completed at the time the assignment is given. A step-by-step outline can also be generated so that students do not skip an important aspect of the project. This allows the student to keep him or herself on track and allows plenty of time to gather or acquire the necessary components.

Failures in long-term planning can significantly disrupt the student's completion of specified course sequences in a timely manner. Many students fail to carefully and comprehensively investigate when required courses are offered and/or which courses are needed as pre- or corequisites. Either of these may lead to several problematic situations, including (a) an inability to take any required courses during a given term, (b) last-minute scrambling to add or change course enrollments, (c) delays in receiving accommodations for newly added courses, (d) having to combine more (or more difficult or time-consuming) courses during a given term than is appropriate for the student, or (e) being compelled to extend the length of their studies.

Such situations can be avoided by encouraging the student to work with an academic counselor early in their academic tenure at the school to map out their anticipated course schedule several terms in advance. Students may need to be reminded to check this plan before registering each term and to meet with their advisors regularly to make any necessary modifications to this plan.

Organizational Skills

Organizational skills, while similar to planning in several respects, can be distinguished by their greater emphasis on present rather than future demands. In a higher education setting, organizational skills can most simply be characterized as the efficient matching of available resources (e.g., study time, money, a home computer) to academic demands. An effective organization system thus requires two core elements. The first is a holistic, real-time tracking system for both resources and demands (e.g., a planner or personal digital assistant). The second is a mechanism to periodically evaluate the efficacy of the tracking system. In our experience, both are vitally important. Students may purchase planners, but fail to review or update them consistently. They therefore stop using them in a very short period of time, rendering a potentially helpful strategy useless.

For this reason, we believe that a review of the student's learning and memorization styles should be factored in before recommending a particular organizational system. Rather than imposing a standard organizational strategy on all students, it is useful to involve the student in selecting or even generating his or her own strategies. While some students have trouble maintaining structure, they are often good at judging what will and will not work for them.

Time Management

Time management encompasses several related but ultimately distinct skills, including accurate time estimation for tasks, the capacity to monitor the passage of time, and the ability to prioritize tasks according to both importance and time demand required. Inadequate time estimation in particular can be extremely damaging to students. It often leads to a false sense of time availability, subsequent overcommitment, and persistent tardiness and failure to meet deadlines.

For some students, merely keeping a journal of time commitments or auditing a month's worth of appointments can be sufficient to determine where their estimations run astray. For others, it becomes more beneficial to either build in guaranteed blocks between commitments or, where appropriate, to use a simple rule of thumb multiplier (e.g., take their initial estimate and add 50% for safety).

Difficulties in accurately monitoring the passage of time may take several forms. For students with LD or ADHD, they may overestimate the actual duration of activities such as reading with which they struggle, while similarly underestimating the amount of time during which they engaged in pleasant activities. This can lead to more frequent and lengthy breaks from studying than are warranted. For this reason, we often encourage students to set timers (often turned away from them to avoid "clock watching") to provide independent verification of time spent studying.

Time-monitoring problems may also take the form of periods of "zoning out" during which the student was unaware that they were not engaging in any activity whatsoever. In these circumstances, it is important to determine whether these occur as a result of waning attention, physical fatigue, difficulties with reading comprehension, or some other underlying problems. In some cases, it may be useful to have the student set predefined, short-term timers that will bring the student back "on line" or at the very least encourage them to transition into a different activity until their focus returns.

Finally, students often commit time to activities based less on their actual import than on their feelings about the activity in that moment. Procrastination, denial, and anxiety may serve to delay the scheduling of a particular task. Even worse, students may purposely prescribe an inadequate period of time to accomplish a task that they know will engender a great deal of discomfort. Time commitments, rather than being perceived as burdens, should be reframed by counselors as opportunities to advance the student's own goals.

Attentional and Behavioral Modulation

Difficulties with behavioral modulation are generally among the easiest areas of executive functioning to evaluate because their manifestation is often readily observable. Indeed for students with executive dysfunction, ineffectual modulation of behavior is often the principle presenting complaint. It is our belief that behavioral modulation is intimately related to attentional modulation in that they are distinct facets of a singular process of adaptive environmental response. We see attentional modulation as the internalized, neurological process that allows successful orientation to, and preparation to interact with, their environment. Behavioral modulation, however is the more externalized manifestation of the unfolding environmental response.

Modulation difficulties are quite common among students with executive dysfunction. They typically arise in response to discrete academic tasks, such as sitting down to read course material, completing end-of-chapter problems, writing a midterm report, or even focusing while attending lectures. Students may characterize this experience in terms or phrases that suggest they perceive their body or mind to have a will of their own (e.g., "My hands just wouldn't listen to my brain") or that attempts to begin tasks are counterproductive (e.g., "The more I try to get going, the harder it is to get anything done").

In situations where this affects the initiation of action or thought such "behavioral paralysis" is often due to modulation dysfunction in the student's arousal and attentional systems. Specifically, the initiation problems may be due to neurological overstimulation (potentially affective, cognitive, or sensory) that overwhelms the student's processing capacity. Conversely, it may be due to neurological understimulation that precludes the availability of adequate mental resources to activate, motivate, and guide the student. Such students tend to need guidance in breaking tasks down into more manageable parts (e.g., outlines, brainstorming, mind mapping, or free writing). Active coaching may also be important (e.g., encouraging students to separate the production stages from the editing stages when writing in an attempt to reduce the required cognitive load necessary for task completion).

When the modulation difficulties revolve around struggling to sustain attention or adaptive behavior, students tend to report far shorter periods of effective reading, writing, studying, or listening than their nondisabled peers. While the initial presentation may appear more behavioral, it is our experience that underlying these struggles are deficits in working memory, the arena for computation and information processing (Torgesen, 1996). When these students attempt to exceed their processing threshold over longer periods of time, they may report substantially reduced effectiveness, sleepiness, headaches, or even agitation that manifests itself in the behavioral realm. Given the volume and scope of typical postsecondary projects, this has the potential to be quite disruptive to the student's academic progress.

In such situations, we tend to recommend a schedule management system in which students build in regular breaks between classes, between study sessions, and between classes and study sessions. It is also important to consider avoiding scheduling several classes within the same academic term that tap the same executive weakness (e.g., courses that are extensively technical in detail or whose professors utilize exclusively auditory presentation styles). Further, it may also be important to explore whether certain times of day have a particularly pronounced impact on the student and to modify scheduling as course availability allows. Those who are stimulated excessively may need to modify their environments to reduce such stimulation, e.g., avoiding sitting near windows or near other people who may generate noise or movement. They may also find it useful to use equipment such as earplugs or noise-canceling headphones to further reduce stimulation. Those who are understimulated may find it useful to work in environments that provide some neurological stimulation, whether by using study groups or study halls instead of libraries or perhaps by using equipment such as white noise generators or low-level ambient music while working.

Modulation of focus and behavior may also be impaired in the area of switching tasks. Behaviorally, this may involve a level of switching that is inappropriately high (e.g., external or internal distractibility) or inappropriately low (e.g., mental and behavioral perseveration). Both tend to preclude or significantly retard task completion. These are particularly problematic in situations where a project requires independent action in the absence of structure or environmental feedback that would otherwise occur in a group or lab setting.

In response to high levels of switching, we tend to suggest that students limit the materials they bring to a study environment, limit the location of studying to places that do not offer tempting alternatives to their required activities, and set electronic timers to check periodically whether they are "on task." In response to low levels of switching, we tend to suggest that students impose strict time limits of tasks and that they make use of external mechanisms to monitor and enforce these tasks (e.g., scheduling tasks at locations that have restricted hours and using electronic timers to mark the conclusion of a study period).

Evaluating Executive Functioning

Given the extensive variations in scope and intensity of executive dysfunction typical of LD and ADHD populations, along with the extent to which executive functioning demands are pervasive throughout the postsecondary curriculum, clinicians working with such populations are strongly encouraged to spend time individualizing their assessment and recommendations for their clients.

We use the term "academic audit" to characterize the process we use to conduct such an assessment in the postsecondary disability setting. The academic audit is a two-step process designed to the extent and manner in which EF issues may play a role in a student's academic progress. The first step in this approach is a careful analysis of the student's strengths and weaknesses within the EF domain that are most relevant to their postsecondary functioning. Understanding the internal resources that the student brings to the postsecondary setting is of tremendous utility because it provides information about how the student approaches the task of learning. However, the absence of formal executive functioning measures in most assessment evaluations often necessitates the use of other assessment techniques. For example, many questionnaires designed to gauge ADHD symptomology include ratings of cognitive, affective, and behavioral difficulties that are consistent with executive dysfunction. We prefer those instruments that allow for both first- and third-person reports and that further allow an assessment of both contemporary and early childhood school periods to discern any significant changes in functioning.

Additional information can often be gleaned from a careful and comprehensive analysis of the student's behavior in the course of daily interactions. Specifically, we often note difficulties with speech (e.g., problems with word retrieval, tangentiality, poverty, or excessively detailed content), as well as difficulties with managing appointments (e.g., frequent tardiness, forgetting appointments, having to change appointments due to conflicting commitments) and with paperwork completion (e.g., attentional errors such as skipping over or misreading questions, forgetting personal information such as their own telephone number or zip code, and planning problems such as running out of space in a response field of a form). Finally, we often find that a process-oriented analysis of existing assessment data can provide numerous examples of executive dysfunction. Such examples may be found in examiner's behavioral observations (e.g., unusual response latencies, frequent requests for the administrator to repeat items, impulsive approaches to problem solving, and frequent break requests) or in an analysis of the student's responses to test items (e.g., uneven responses with subtest responses scored incorrectly due to misperceiving the test question or responses involving long-term memory that were provided beyond the ascribed time limit). Information derived from these nonstandard sources is often quite illuminating and nicely supplements the existing empirical data. For this reason, we encourage clinicians working with students to explore some of these approaches, including incorporating rating scales into their regular intake process, including an awareness of EF issues when evaluating client behavior, and reviewing previous assessment findings and behavior when such material is available.

The second step in the academic audit involves identifying any environmental variables specific to the student's chosen field of study that may be particularly relevant for those with executive dysfunction. Different fields of study often manifest significant variations in executive load within and across the traditional curriculum elements (e.g., lecture attendance, reading demands, written projects, field studies, and comprehensive examinations). A computer science curriculum, for example, tends to require a large number of projects, with short time lines and a high degree of independent work. Such a curriculum will be significantly more challenging for those students whose EF deficits lay in the areas of initiation, time estimation, and planning. Conversely, the principle demands of a liberal studies curriculum center around a consistently high reading load, punctuated by periodic, integrative written work and a great deal of critical discussion. A curriculum of this sort will be more problematic for students that struggle with working memory, perceiving the passage of time, and organization.

Whereas mainstream students take such differences in stride—modifying their approach to course demands with a fair amount of automaticity—students with executive dysfunction are often more sensitive to such differences and less able to shift to meet these demands. Therapists can help guide students in their identification of educational goals by integrating issues of EF into early discussions of potential career choices. One of the most significant issues that may arise during these discussions is the question of how to respond when information derived from evaluating the student's EF suggests a conflict between the academic expectations of the institution and the student's previously articulated interests and goals. Clearly the student's ability to meet the demands of the environment needs to be considered during the transition into postsecondary education. Equally important, however, is the need to ensure that the student is connected with and passionate about their proposed field of study. The process of exploring and balancing these issues for a given individual can provide rich material for therapeutic work and will certainly better prepare the student for the transition process.

The ideal end result of an academic audit is a clear sense as to what potential EF issues are likely to arise for a student in their intended academic path. This, in turn, should encourage the clinician and student to begin the process of identifying what environmental resources may be available to the student to mediate the affects of the underlying executive dysfunction (e.g., services, technology, or changes in student behavior). Both philosophically and pragmatically, specific, individualized recommendations serve to bridge the gap between the student's internal executive resources and the executive demands imposed by the academic environment. By optimizing the student's functioning in this manner, the student is better able to engage in successful, adaptive academic performance.

Social–Emotional Functioning

While cognitive, academic, and executive functioning abilities are vital to a student's success, it is equally important to consider a client's social–emotional skills, along with their general level of psychosocial development. As presented in earlier chapters, individuals with learning and attention disorders may also experience difficulties in social competence, communication skills, and even nonverbal learning disabilities (see Chapter 4) that inhibit the ability to read social cues. Many students also suffer from low self-esteem, a poor self-concept, and difficulties sustaining positive interpersonal relationships (see Chapter 10). Secondary and/or comorbid conditions such as anxiety and mood disorders are also often experienced by those who have struggled with the implications of differences in cognitive functioning. Research has also indicated that the psychosocial difficulties often first evident in childhood can persist throughout the life span (Weiss & Hechtman, 1993; Smith et al., 1997). Clinical experience in working with college students with learning and attention disorders has shown us that a student's social–emotional maturity is often a critical factor in their ultimate ability to achieve their goals. In fact, this may even be a more important factor than the degree to which they have worked through academic obstacles.

It is important to consider these areas of functioning in the context of the developmental stage of adolescents and young adults. According to Erickson's (1963) stages of development, adolescents are dealing with issues of identity formation (versus role confusion). They are coming to terms with who they are, especially in the context of their peer, social, and cultural reference groups. Individuation from family influences is also occurring. Developing a clear sense of one's strengths and weaknesses, values, and purpose is also part of this phase. While this is a difficult period for most people, those who feel "different" in any way may struggle even more in this search for self.

Early life experiences may have also adversely affected any one of the previous developmental stages, including basic trust vs mistrust (of the environment, but also of one's self), autonomy (vs shame and doubt), initiative (vs guilt), and industry (vs inferiority) (Erickson, 1963). For those cognitive processing difficulties, it may be harder for an individual to develop a basic trust in his or her own abilities or feel autonomous and unashamed of their differences. Lack of basic confidence can make it more difficult to take initiative and to experience a feeling of industry and productivity due to feelings of inferiority compared to others. While environmental influences and internal resources will mitigate some of these difficulties, all of these factors can lead to a reduced capacity to form a positive identity during adolescence.

It is also critical to keep in mind that the neurological deficits inherent in learning and attention disorders can alter the individual's perceptions and general subjective experience of the world. As described by Palombo (2001), there is a complex set of interactions among the child, the deficits, and the social and emotional milieu in which the child is raised. While the specific combination of these factors and subsequent compensations by the child leads to a variety of outcomes, the learning disorder will have a definite effect. These problems will persist into adulthood, even if they may change forms, precisely because of the underlying neurological deficits. Palombo (2001) continues to emphasize the importance of keeping this neurological perspective in mind when working with those with learning disorders: "Children with learning disorders are commonly misunderstood because caregivers and therapists fail to consider the children's thoughts and behaviors as neurologically driven rather than motivated by psychological factors" (p. 7). This is just as true when these children become adolescents and adults.

With this developmental perspective in mind, let us turn to some of the areas of social–emotional functioning that are most important to assess when considering your client's readiness for postsecondary environments.

Self-awareness and Self-acceptance

Upon entering a college or workplace setting, a higher level of adaptation to a diverse environment is expected. This entails understanding one's own abilities and needs, the demands of the setting, and how to successfully integrate the two. For the student with learning differences, this will demand an even greater degree of self-awareness and self-acceptance than for other students.

An important part of identity formation is the capacity to look within from an "observing" stance that is not burdened by harsh, critical judgment. Developing a balanced, realistic self-assessment can be especially painful for those with learning and attention difficulties. These students must integrate the concept of a "disability" into their self-image, which may result in low self-esteem, lack of self-confidence, and a general feeling of inadequacy.

Unfortunately, we see many students who are coming to terms with this for the first time in the college setting—usually when they have gotten themselves into academic trouble because they denied the possible implications of their difficulties to themselves and others. Many students have limited awareness of the effects of their disabilities on their cognitive and academic abilities, career interests, or organizational skills. Their emotional reactions to these difficulties may be buried even deeper, which in turn keeps them from seeking needed support. Students all too often have not had the guidance and support needed to develop a realistic awareness of their disability, which still enables them to feel good about themselves. If students could enter the postsecondary environment with greater awareness and acceptance of their disabilities, their potential for success would be increased markedly.

In our experience, a major obstacle to success for college students with learning disabilities is their avoidance of using accommodations and support services. Many students tell us that they want to feel and be seen as "normal," which may cause them to reject academic accommodations because other students do not use them. These students often fail to use services for fear of being noticed as "different," "weak," or "less than" by peers and professors. While these initial emotional reactions to having a disability are expected, the continuation of unexplored feelings may sabotage the very assistance that is needed.

Increased self-awareness and acceptance of the disability will provide an important emotional foundation for the student in postsecondary settings to utilize the following skills.

- Advocate for their needs in a mature, proactive manner.
- Accept assistance where needed to meet their goals.
- Emphasize their strengths while supporting their areas of weakness.
- Feel more at ease in a demanding and stressful environment.
- Interact more successfully with peers, groups, and in the classroom.
- Be open to major and career choices that best fit their abilities.

As a therapist, you can be a wonderful guide and "mirror" in helping students develop their disability-related self-awareness in a manner that allows for honesty, acceptance, and honor for their unique self. Focusing directly on the emotional attitude towards one's disabilities can be an especially powerful tool in helping individuals moving into a world where their greatest obstacle may well be their own negative attitudes toward themselves. Unless they can know and accept both their limitations and their strengths, these young adults may never actualize their true potential. Following are a few ideas of how to explore these issues with your client (Table 2).

TABLE 2   Therapeutic Tips for Addressing Disability Self-Awareness

---

Ask your client to describe feelings about having a disability. If it is difficult for them to verbalize this, they could also write about it, draw a picture, or make a collage

Explore ways their disabilities may/may not limit them; emphasize holistic integration of strengths and weaknesses

Practice or role play how they might describe their disabilities to others, but in a more autonomous and proactive manner. Include situations with staff, faculty, and peers

---

Dependence, Independence, and Interdependence

Postsecondary settings also call for a greater degree of independent functioning than previously required. Students will determine how they spend their time, including whether they attend classes or do their homework. This requires good organizational skills and other EF skills, in addition to the capacity to operate effectively when structure is not provided. Sometimes the emotional aspect of appropriate independent behavior is a critical component to success.

Identity formation entails achieving a balance between dependence and independence, resulting in mature interdependence. Adolescents and young adults are often struggling between rejecting dependence and developing greater independence (while most likely fearing both). This struggle may lead those with learning and attention disabilities to either reject assistance that they see as reflecting dependence on others or seek more support than is expected in these settings.

A more dependent student who has relied too much on strong parents, teachers, siblings, or peers will suddenly find that these support systems cannot be used effectively anymore. This makes it difficult to interact effectively with professors and administrators and to fulfill the basic obligations of producing homework and papers and studying for tests. Attempts to use the campus disability office as a substitute will not be effective in a mainstreamed environment. They may have trouble advocating for themselves in a setting that is trying to teach them that they must "own" their disabilities and their strengths and that they are ultimately responsible for their own success or failure.

Conversely, students who try to be too independent may not seek the support they legitimately need to perform equally with nondisabled peers. In their push to "do it on my own," such students often fail to even inform instructors that they have a disability that affects learning. These

TABLE 3   Therapeutic Tips for Addressing Dependency Issues

Overly dependent student

    Address any fears the client has about being more independent, responsible, or "grown up." For example, they may fear making mistakes if responsible, based on negative feedback or from interacting with more controlling role models

    Select one small area where the client would like to be more independent and plan steps to achieve that goal; generalize this model to other situations

    Help your client to think as well as act more independently. Encourage them to have opinions and express themselves without fear of judgment or abandonment

    Devise projects to do inside or outside of therapy that will enable the client to take an original idea and follow it through to completion. This can help develop initiative, productivity, creativity, planning, and "ownership" of ideas and actions

    Work with family members or teachers as needed to allow greater freedom for the client to act, take risks, make mistakes if necessary, and learn from that feedback

    Use the research, planning, and application phase of seeking college or work placements to practice increasing independence

Overly independent student

    Address any fears the client has about being dependent, irresponsible, or being "told what to do." For example, they may not trust others to come through or they may be invested in having greater control over the outcome and their own process

    Select one small area where the client wants to be less independent/responsible or increase their ability to depend on others and plan steps to achieve that goal. This process can then be generalized once the student experiences comfort and success in a new role

    You might encourage activities or even support groups where your client can increase their interaction with others in a group or cooperative project

    Work with teachers or family members to encourage greater use of accommodations or explore other ways to relieve the stress of relying exclusively on oneself

---

students may fail to use accommodations and develop strategies that are actually designed to help them achieve the very independence that they seek, such as reading services and assistive technology (Table 3).

As students approach greater balance in this area, they can better utilize their skills in the following areas.

- Accept responsibility for their own success or failure.
- Adhere to time lines and procedures required in the setting.
- Develop independent thinking and critical judgment.
- Seek needed accommodations and support services.
- Develop disability–related independence (e.g., use assistive technology).

Ego Strength and the Capacity to Cope

We have worked with many college students who have great difficulty in coping with common academic situations with professors, roommate issues, and personal relationships. Poor internal resources or "ego strength" often underlies these difficulties in coping, resulting in limited capacity for good judgment, insight into the behavior of self and others, and effective regulation of emotions—the more "intangible" aspects of successful coping skills. These same areas are often lacking in students with learning disorders due to the underlying neurological issues, including difficulty interpreting social cues that can inhibit the capacity to cope when relating to others. Low self-esteem, lack of motivation and initiative, or comorbid disorders such as anxiety or depression can also impair the capacity to cope with stress. Regardless of their genesis, deficits in these areas can impede a student's ability to successfully navigate the postsecondary setting and to function effectively in the world. These difficulties are often most apparent when students are confronted with the need to use their coping skills in solving everyday problems.

Research has indicated that students with learning disabilities often lack good problem-solving abilities (Williams, 1990) or may need to be taught these skills more directly than others. Helping students develop good problem-solving skills in coping with the more subtle aspects of academic and social situations can make a tremendous difference in their overall experience in college. As a clinician, you will most likely be working with issues of ego strength at a core level of the client's sense of self. It is also beneficial to work directly on improving coping and problem solving skills for the student transitioning to the more complex higher education environment.

For example, therapists may want to provide their clients with a structured problem-solving approach that can be used as a model for various situations. Several models exist for using problem-solving schemas (Williams, 1990). They generally include phases such as defining or identifying the problem; generating possible solutions; selecting a solution to implement; gathering feedback about the effectiveness of that solution; and selecting alternative solutions to try, as needed. Practicing the application of such a model on "real-world" problems can enhance your client's ability to generalize this to the complex environments that they will encounter as they mature.

While some of these skills can be taught, the therapist can also provide "corrective" modeling through feedback about a variety of everyday

TABLE 4   Therapeutic Tips for Promoting Problem-Solving Skills

---

Provide a structured problem-solving approach and practice using it with your client
Have your client take on perspectives of others who might be involved in the problem, not just their own
Use role play to increase their confidence in problem solving "in the moment" without becoming too upset to think and act effectively
Provide on-going, gentle feedback about how your client reacted in a given situation and explore alternatives
Use the exploration and planning process of preparing for college or the workplace as a model in problem solving

---

feelings and situations in a nonjudgmental way. Practice with "perspective taking" can help clients see problems from a broader, more flexible perspective. This helps strengthen the capacity to cope with stress in general and prevents feeling overwhelmed and paralyzed when confronted with problems in everyday life (Table 4).

As students develop these stronger abilities in these areas, they can function more effectively in the following ways.

- Interact proactively with professors, roommates, and groups.
- Cope better with stress when problems arise.
- Develop the capacity for logical, analytical thinking.
- Improve judgment and insight into others' behavior.

Social and Interpersonal Skills

For students with disabilities, social and interpersonal abilities may play as significant a role as their academic skills in determining success. Many researchers have attested to the social and interpersonal difficulties associated with both attention issues (Murphy, 1997; Hallowell & Ratey, 1994) and learning disabilities, especially those with nonverbal learning disorders (Chapter 3). Poor coping and problem-solving abilities can be compromised even further by poor social skills. Difficulties in this area can lead to miscommunication with faculty, office staff, peers, and within close relationships. Daily functioning includes a great deal of interaction on the social level, from participating in class to joining campus or work groups and making friends. The developmental task of forming intimate relationships can also be quite problematic for individuals with deficits in this area.

TABLE 5   Therapeutic Tips for Improving Social Skills

Encourage participation in interest groups during high school and college, where
students can improve social interaction skills while emphasizing an area of interest

Many students benefit from group therapy to facilitate social and interpersonal skills or
specific social skills training programs

Role playing of specific anticipated encounters can help improve skills and reduce
anxiety about social interactions. Situations such as interviewing for college,
describing their disability to a teacher, or joining a peer organization could be
utilized

Many college settings also offer support groups, either through their counseling services
or programs through their offices for students with disabilities

---

College students who feel socially inadequate or awkward may find it
difficult to interact with peers and professors alike. They may have trouble
making friends, joining academic support organizations, forming study
groups, or meeting with tutors to help with academic preparation. Many
students with difficulties in these areas will have trouble meeting with
professors and advocating for their needs. Due to the additional academic
burden they face compared to their nondisabled peers, these students
might also focus so much time and energy on their studies that they
neglect the important interpersonal developmental tasks of this stage. If
they have entered college already behind others in this regard, the higher
education setting may make them feel even more estranged from other
students.

For clients who experience difficulties in this area, Table 5 offers some
suggestions for improving your clients' interpersonal abilities. Students
who already possess excellent social skills will find that it is among their
greatest assets. In evaluating your client's readiness for educational
advancement, remember that deficits in this area do not preclude success
or personal fulfillment.

Comorbid Factors

You may already be aware that your client has psychological issues in
addition to a learning or attention disorder. Psychological disorders that
most commonly coexist with these disabilities include depression and
anxiety (including panic and generalized anxiety disorders and obsessive-
compulsive disorder). These and other disorders can either coexist or
mimic symptoms of ADHD, in particular. Bipolar disorder and personal-

ity disorders such as borderline, histrionic, antisocial, and intermittent explosive disorders may need to be ruled out or can also cooccur. Although incidence rates vary widely, it is estimated that comorbid conditions may be present in children with attention deficit disorders up to 46% of the time (Barkley, 1998). Studies of comorbid psychiatric conditions for learning disabilities are less prevalent, although some survey results show that 36 to 50% of adults with learning disabilities have either participated in therapy or felt the need for such services (Hooper & Olley, 1996). If you are unsure whether a comorbid disorder is present, you may wish to seek a consultation with an expert in these areas. A medication evaluation with a psychiatrist may also be indicated.

If a comorbid condition has been diagnosed, this may be a factor in determining your client's readiness for a postsecondary setting. Many students with comorbid conditions can be successful. However, that success may depend somewhat on factors such as the degree of severity of the cooccurring condition, effective management through medication or psychotherapy, and the degree to which that condition may fluctuate. While this may not preclude attending college, the impact on academic performance should be considered (e.g., a longer stay might be anticipated, given the variability of functioning). Students with comorbid disorders will most likely need additional support in college, much of which is available on campus (see college services). It is important to anticipate their needs and to arrange for services to be in place from the beginning.

Evaluating the Support Network

Although the postsecondary setting clearly requires greater independence, this does not imply that students should do without a network of support. In addition to accommodations and support services provided through an office for students with disabilities, there are many other sources of support that may be of benefit. In fact, additional support is often crucial for the student with the added burden of coping with learning and attention disorders, especially if comorbid factors are present.

Family Support

Although the role of the family will most likely diminish during college years, the family can still offer vital support. The family may be instrumental in offering full or partial financial support, which can reduce the student's need to work during college. Students may also be part of a family's health insurance plan. Such support can minimize the potential stress of financial burdens or health care crises.

The type and degree of personal support will vary depending on whether the student lives at home or on campus. Even if living apart, families may continue to offer interest in the student's progress and encouragement in the face of struggles and disappointments. If the student is at home, family members may continue to provide similar support available during high school (i.e., encouraging structure such as routine studying hours).

In either case, it will be the *quality* of family contact that is most important. In some families, the interpersonal dynamics create a less supportive environment. Family responsibilities or expectations of support *from* the student could create a drain on their time and energy. As the therapist, it will be important to evaluate how much support your client might receive or how much "burden" they may be expected to carry. You can assist your client to anticipate both financial and emotional aspects of family support by discussing this realistically in advance. Helping the family understand and prepare for the type of support needed is also useful. Given your therapeutic perspective of the nature of the family relationships, you may also need to advocate for either greater or lesser involvement according to the best interests of your client. Keeping issues of phase development and individuation needs in mind are also essential.

Friend/Relationship Support

An important source of support includes friends and/or significant relationships. For students with social skills deficits, even greater encouragement will be needed to assist them in seeking new relationships. In most cases, it can be especially important for students to have some contact with others who are facing similar challenges. Some campuses offer support groups for students with learning and/or attention disorders, either through the disabilities or counseling departments. Enhanced service programs tailored specifically for these students may be available (see the college services section later). Such programs can also provide a tremendous sense of community for students with disabilities and can lead to the discovery of understanding friends.

Student organizations are a good way to meet friends and may be particularly important for the student who initially wants to avoid disability-related groups in an attempt to feel more "normal." Campus orientations provide an overview of student activities from which to choose. You could go over these to help your client select ones most suited to their interests, needs, or areas requiring some development.

Therapeutic Support

Many students with learning and attention disorders would benefit greatly from continued support from their therapist. If distance precludes this, students could still check in via phone or email or meet in person when they return home during school breaks. Knowing there is someone familiar to turn to "just in case" is important. A source of support outside of the family can be especially beneficial during this phase of individuation if students begin to experience feelings that they are ashamed to share with their families (such as fears or a sense of failure). Continuation of such support may depend on the student's felt need for independence or financial considerations.

If it seems appropriate to discontinue the traditional therapeutic relationship, other professionals may be of help. For example, coaching has been found to be very helpful for some individuals with ADHD or executive functioning weaknesses. Coaching provides a structured, practical approach to functioning more effectively in academic and daily life, which can help enormously with achieving specific goals. These services are available privately through certified coaches specializing in ADHD. Many campuses also offer programs based on the coaching model through peer-mentoring programs. You can help your client research this as a potential service when deciding which campus to attend. For example, the learning disabilities services program at the University of North Carolina at Chapel Hill offers a well-developed coaching program (Parker & Byron, 1998).

Medication Intervention

Students diagnosed with ADHD or comorbid disorders such as depression or anxiety may have been utilizing medication successfully. If so, it would be wise to continue this important source of support, especially since the demands will only increase as the student adjusts to a new environment. Unfortunately, many students decide instead to go off of medication as part of their desire to be "independent" or because they believe they have outgrown the need for such assistance. For those with ADHD, it may be that their more hyperactive-impulsive symptoms have decreased as they have matured. However, it is important to consider whether symptoms of inattention still persist or whether the student has benefited in other ways, such as being more organized in speech, behavior, or written expression. While it may be difficult to encourage your client to either initiate or remain on medication, this may be one of the most crucial sources of support for them in an environment that will demand even more of their focus and potentially weak areas (i.e., sustained reading, initiative and follow through) than ever before.

College Services

Many colleges offer support services in a variety of areas. Services offered by disabilities offices will vary by campus. These are discussed more fully later, but such services typically include assistance with accommodations, intervention with faculty as needed, and some degree of academic or disability-related counseling. Specialized or subject area tutoring may be provided, but if not, tutoring is usually available somewhere on campus (typically in a program such as a learning resource center or specialized programs such as educational equity services). Some campuses offer specialized programs for students with learning and/or attention disorders designed to provide a broader range of support services and more individualized attention. For example, the University of Arizona's Strategic Alternative Learning Techniques (SALT) program offers an array of services to maximize student success. This fee-for-service program offers access to learning specialists, writing specialists, workshops, a computer resource lab, and tutoring services. SALT was highlighted as a model program in the August edition of the C.H.A.D.D. magazine *Attention!* (Katz, 2002). Similar, smaller scale programs offering enhanced services may be free for students due to subsidized funding. At Cal Poly Pomona University, for example, a grant-funded program emphasizes academic retention efforts through enriched support services. ARCHES (Achievement, Retention and Commitment to Higher Education Services) provides academic advisement, disability-related counseling, and peer mentoring and tutoring.

For more general psychological counseling, most 4-year campuses have a counseling center, which typically provides some brief therapy at no cost (e.g., they may offer 6–10 sessions per academic year). Crisis counseling is also available. Only some 2-year colleges will offer counseling services. Many counseling centers work closely with disability offices when serving disabled students, which can be a major source of support for students. It is important to note that even when campuses offer counseling services, a psychiatrist may not be available or medical doctors may not be certified to prescribe stimulant medications (considered to be controlled substances). Medication management may therefore have to be maintained off campus, preferably with the student's original prescribing physician.

Career counseling services allow students to work with a career counselor and take interest inventory assessments to help direct decisions regarding the choice of major and career goals. Because cognitive test results and the specific nature of the learning disorder provide crucial information in making these choices, it is recommended that career and disability centers work closely on behalf of the student. While most 4-year colleges have such centers, they are not available at all 2-year colleges.

You now have an overview of how to assess the internal and external resources that your client will bring to the higher education environment. This is the first part of the "road map" that you will need to assist your clients in the transition into higher education settings. The next section offers a glimpse into the "landscape" of disabilities in the higher education setting. Students with learning and attention disorders must learn the features of this landscape in order to operate effectively and be successful. As their therapist, we believe it is important for you to understand how higher education differs from the K–12 system that the student will be leaving, the types of disability services available in higher education, and alternatives to the traditional postsecondary setting.

DISABILITIES IN THE HIGHER EDUCATION SETTING

We believe strongly that higher education is a realistic and achievable goal for many students with learning disabilities. College enrollment figures are proving this, as persons with disabilities are seeking entrance to higher education in rapidly growing numbers. The percentage of incoming freshman reporting a disability in American 2- and 4-year universities has grown fivefold during the past 20 years, rising from only 2% in 1979 to 10% in 1999 (Henderson, 1999).

Yet there is also sobering evidence that many secondary students with disabilities arrive ill-prepared to begin this journey and tend to disproportionately struggle in the postsecondary realm. Vogel and Adelman (1990), for example, found that college students with LD had lower college GPAs throughout their academic tenure and took longer to complete their studies. Research on the academic performance of secondary level students with LD points to similar results (Zigmond & Thornton, 1986).

Students with learning disabilities often need specialized assistance to adequately prepare for the unique challenges they will face in this environment. An enormous number of these students arrive at colleges and universities without the necessary planning, information, attitudes, habits, and resources to meet these challenges and ensure their success. Principal among these challenges is learning to navigate a higher education disability service system that bears little semblance to the familiar K–12 system they have recently left behind.

As a guide for your clients into the world of higher education, it is important to know what kind of assistance is available to students with learning and attention disorders. The type of support offered depends on the nature of the setting and the laws and regulations that govern it. We therefore turn our attention to providing a working knowledge of the features, options, and demands of the disability service system that await the postsecondary student with LD.

Higher Education versus K–12 Disability Service Systems

Students and service providers accustomed to the K–12 disability environment often find the transition to the postsecondary setting challenging. Different rules, roles, and responsibilities apply that necessitate a shift in approach. These differences are summarized in Table 6.

Differences in Intent

The laws governing higher education disability services differ in several important ways from the K–12 realm. Within the K–12 disability service system, the principal statute is the Individuals with Disabilities Education Act (IDEA) of 1990, which governs the special education system. IDEA (and its subsequent amendments, 1997) mandates that elementary and secondary schools provide a "free and appropriate public education" for all students, with the specific intent of reducing or eliminating any academic deficiencies that are secondary to the student's disability. To achieve this goal, a school must identify all students suspected of possessing a

TABLE 6   Comparison of K–12 and Higher Education Disability Services

K–12 disability services	Postsecondary disability services
Educational statutes that focus on educational interventions	Civil rights statutes that focus on equal access
Philosophy of remediating weaknesses	Philosophy of accommodating weaknesses
Specific emphasis on curriculum access	Covers all institutional activities/ resources
Serves those within specific diagnostic categories	Serves those with functional limitations irrespective of diagnosis
Disability services may substantially modify or individualize the curriculum	Disability services may not fundamentally alter the essential features of curriculum
Institutional responsibility to identify students eligible for disability services	Student responsibility to self-identify as eligible for disability services
Institutional responsibility to document service eligibility and service prescriptions	Student responsibility to document service eligibility and service prescriptions
Institutional responsibility to coordinate service utilization and advocacy	Student responsibility to coordinate service utilization and advocacy

disability and subsequently develop a program of supplemental or alternative educational services. These services result in IEPs and Individualized Transition Plans (ITPs).

Conversely, the higher education community is governed by Section 504 of the Rehabilitation Act of 1973 and the more recent Americans with Disabilities Act (ADA) of 1990. A fundamental difference is that 504 and ADA are civil rights statutes rather than educational equity statutes. Their intent is to ensure equal participation by, as well as prohibit discrimination against, persons with disabilities rather than to ensure educational parity.

This difference in legal philosophy tends to result in a significant shift away from remediation and a corresponding shift toward accommodation of functional impairments. While the K–12 system's focus on remediation might result in skill building in phonics to improve spelling for the dyslexic student, the higher education setting would prescribe the use of a computerized spell checker during exams. Some students who are accustomed to disability service programs that target skill development may find the accommodative emphasis on environmental adaptation somewhat disappointing, interpreting it as an indication the institution does not want to encourage their academic progress. Others find the shift refreshing by allowing them to focus their time on areas of academic interest rather than on areas of weakness. In either case, students should consider the extent of their interest in, and need for, remediation services and identify whether the institutions they are considering offer them.

Differences in Scope

Both 504 and ADA are substantially broader in scope than IDEA. Section 504 impacts all programs, activities, facilities, and procedures of entities (not merely colleges and universities) receiving federal money. ADA broadens this further to include all entities that interact significantly with the public whether or not they receive federal money. While both obligate an individualized plan of support services, they also cover all aspects of campus life as well, such as access to classrooms and campus housing and extracurricular activities. This clearly extends beyond the classroom accommodations typical of an IEP in the K–12 system.

However, postsecondary entities vary widely in the extent to which the notion of universal access pervades the campus. Students considering postsecondary schools should explore what curricular (as well as extracurricular activities) are offered by the campus and confirm with the disability office whether accommodative services are available where desired.

Differences in Coverage

In a K–12 environment, IDEA identifies several discrete disability categories whose members are afforded coverage under the statute. Students with a diagnosis of a learning disability, for example, are specifically covered if they meet the designated criteria, whereas those with ADHD may (depending on the school district) be covered under the "other health-related" category of IDEA or may need to request a separate 504 service plan. In either case, the diagnosis itself serves as the eligibility criterion while the functional impact of the disability determines the particular educational services to be offered.

In a higher education environment, Section 504 and ADA do not use specific diagnostic categories to determine eligibility. Instead, these laws establish broad criteria by which a person may be evaluated to determine whether they are protected as a covered individual with a disability. Specifically, 504 and ADA stipulate that a disabled person "means any person who (1) has a physical or mental impairment that substantially limits one or more major life activities, (2) has a record of such impairment, or (3) is regarded as having such an impairment" (Americans with Disabilities Act, 1990).

What this means for students is that their functional impairments, rather than their diagnosis, will determine their eligibility for services as well as the nature and scope of services they will be offered. Students with identical diagnoses may end up with somewhat different services based on differences in functional impairments. Further, the same disability service (e.g., books on audio tape) may be offered to students with significantly different disabilities (LD vs low vision) but overlapping functional limitations (inadequate or inaccurate visual perception of printed materials). This highlights the importance of ensuring that the student provides documentation that indicates not merely the presence of a diagnosis, but also the measurable, functional repercussions of that diagnosis on the student in an academic environment.

Another difference that students should become familiar with is the right of higher education environments to impose entrance, maintenance, and graduation requirements for its participants. Higher education participation is neither mandated nor guaranteed in a manner similar to the K–12 system. Under 504 and ADA, higher education entities still maintain the right to establish limitations to participation in the curriculum as long as these limitations do not have the specific effect of discriminating against persons with disabilities. Thus when students request reasonable accommodations under 504 and ADA, they should understand that educational entities still retain the ability to make decisions about the curriculum even if they affect a particular student with a disability. For example, colleges and universities are not required to waive elements of the curriculum considered essential, need not provide accommodations that alter the curriculum fundamentally, and are not required to provide accommodations that would disrupt the academic environment. Moreover, each higher education institution reserves the right to determine the specific accommodations that students may receive for their functional limitations. Students should be encouraged to explore the accommodations that would be prescribed for them prior to final acceptance of college admittance.

Differences in Student Responsibilities

In the K–12 environment, it is the responsibility of the school to conduct a diagnostic evaluation, determine service eligibility, design the IEP and

ITP goals, implement any academic interventions, and ensure that the student participates in the programmatic activities. While parents are sometimes involved in IEP meetings and may even be encouraged to provide input on programmatic decisions, it is our experience that students typically are uninvolved in this process. The result is that they arrive at colleges and universities ill-prepared for the extent of responsibility and involvement imposed upon them by higher education disability service programs.

Self-identification

This shift in the burden of responsibility from school personnel to the college student begins upon entrance to the university. For example, it is the responsibility of the student to self-identify to the disability service program. If they elect to 'go it alone' once they reach the higher education level or if they are unaware of the presence of a disability office, they will generally fall through the cracks as colleges and universities are not required to conduct outreach activities for students with disabilities.

Students are therefore strongly encouraged to become familiar with what disability services are available at the postsecondary institutions they are considering and to begin the process of registering for disability services as soon as they are accepted to the university.

Documentation

In most 4-year schools, it is the student's responsibility to provide accurate and complete documentation of a learning disability. Students are often surprised to find that colleges and universities are not required to conduct such evaluations. While 2-year schools more typically elect to provide basic diagnostic assessments, students who transition straight from high school into 4-year schools or who suspect a learning disability only later in their academic career may be required to seek out an assessment in the private sector. This often involves great cost, as few insurance programs provide coverage for psychoeducational evaluations. It is also sometimes challenging to find clinicians in the community with the expertise to conduct specialized disability assessments.

Students who possess documentation of a learning disability are still responsible for ensuring that their documentation (which may have been adequate for the K–12 system) will meet the standards imposed by the higher education entity. This arises most commonly when secondary schools elect not to conduct a full evaluation during the recertification process or when a secondary assessment does not include a cognitive evaluation due to either legal mandates or philosophical positions at the school district. The student may then be responsible for either updating or supplementing the documentation to the standards of the school.

Because issues around documentation requirements and procedures are often quite time-consuming to address, it is vitally important that the secondary school, the family of the student, and the student themselves work together to ensure that appropriate and current documentation be made available for the student. Parents should ensure that a recent reevaluation was conducted and that the documentation is complete, including clear, specific information on diagnosis, functional impairments, and service history.

Service Utilization

Students with learning disabilities are often surprised to find that they are now responsible for many of the logistical procedures regarding their accommodations as well. Whereas in the past they were sought out by service providers and guided actively through the use of disability services, they must now initiate specific requests for service such as modifying examinations for a particular class as well as following through on any necessary intermediate steps (e.g., scheduling the accommodation, securing professor signatures, and ensuring they bring any requisite equipment or supplies). While students can reasonably expect programs to disseminate information about such procedures and deadlines, they are unlikely to find more proactive measures in place (e.g., phone call reminders) or the same degree of flexibility in shifting/waiving of academic procedures to which they may be accustomed.

In response to this increase in responsibility, students should attend any orientation services offered by the disability office. They should also ensure they have the contact information of the coordinator for any disability service for which they are eligible. Finally, they should inquire about whether some of the information they may need in order to utilize the resources of the campus (and the disability office in particular) is available electronically on the internet. Students should also determine whether request forms can be submitted electronically on the internet or by fax in situations where the student is unable to provide information to the office during standard office hours.

Self-advocacy

Students with disabilities in higher education are also given more responsibility for self-advocacy. Whereas the student's instructors in the K–12 environment were often involved in the IEP process and thus familiar with the student's issues and needs, faculty and staff in higher education schools are typically provided only the information necessary to ensure their participation in the accommodation process (e.g., providing a copy of the exam to the disability office). Whether due to a desire to assist students with disabilities, concerns about accommodations, or mere curiosity, faculty do approach students with disabilities with questions regarding the student and/or their service plan. The most common queries center around the nature of the student's disability, the manner in which their disability affects their academics, why their accommodations are needed, what if any modifications the professor may need to provide, etc. However, in our experience, few secondary students are provided with detailed information about the nature of their disability or the educational rationale for the services they receive. Even fewer of these students have received any instruction in how to explain their disability to others in an appropriate manner—either in terms of communicating the educational impact of their disability or with respect to justifying the need for disability-related assistance. This is frequently exacerbated by a general intimidation incoming students feel toward a postsecondary faculty with the result that students do not receive the type of individualized assistance they often need.

Students must resolve to become better self-advocates in order to improve the assistance they receive as well as in preparation for the operating in the world upon graduation. Parents should openly discuss the documentation with the student and have the student rehearse a disclosure of his or her disability. While disability programs certainly attempt to mediate issues that arise between students and faculty or staff, students should also become comfortable discussing their academic needs, including what accommodations they receive and why. Finally, students should considering meeting with their faculty members prior to the beginning of the quarter to allow sufficient time to discuss any important matters and to create a more personal connection with the faculty member.

Disability Services in the Higher Education Setting

Having considered the context in which disability services are provided, we now turn our attention to understanding the types of disability services actually available. We emphasize herein only those services that we feel to be germane for students with learning disabilities and ADHD. Higher education disability offices are often divided into service modules (e.g., alternate media, testing accommodations, assistive technology, classroom accommodations, and counseling/advising), each with their own procedures, policies, and staff members. For students who manifest functional impairments in print-based language—whether in the area of reading (e.g., diminished accuracy and/or speed of word decoding, reading comprehension, visual tracking, and retention of reading material) or writing (e.g., dysgraphic weakness in fine motor control, slow writing speed, illegible writing, or dysphonetic writing)—each of these modules may play a role in accommodating them.

Given the frequency of print-based language difficulties among students with LD, it is not surprising that usage of alternate media services, in which reading materials are modified into more accessible formats, is so prevalent among LD students. While conventional alternate media programs center around books on audio tape, the field has seen a revolutionary shift in recent years toward the use of electronic text (etext) programs such as Kurzweil 3000, WYNN, and Open Book. Etext has several characteristics that provide unique benefits for readers with learning disabilities and, in some cases, ADHD. These include a multisensory presentation of reading material (using visual highlighting and high-quality text to speech), complete adaptability of both visual and auditory formats (e.g., speed, pitch, and gender of voice, as well as magnification options and adjustability of font and background color), instant random navigation of book content, the ability to conduct book-wide keyword or content searches, and the ability to extract essential content for study guide generation or conversion to audio format (for listening or rehearsal during times when a visual approach to reading is untenable, such as driving or working out).

Functional impairments intrinsic to learning disabilities may also lead to the prescription of selective testing accommodations. Typical examples include recording exams in audio tape, converting exams into etext, allowing the use of a computer with appropriate spell check and/or grammar check, use of speaking calculators, additional time to process and respond to the exam questions, or the allocation of a distraction-reduced environment in situations where distractibility is a factor in testing performance.

Assistive technology may also play in a role in a student's service plan, whether in the assistive technology center or in the student's own residence. Dysphonetic spelling may be addressed in a number of ways, including the use of (1) computer-based, phoneme-based, spell checking systems such as Read and Write; (2) voice dictation software such as Dragon NaturallySpeaking and IBM ViaVoice, which allows the conversion of spoken content into printed text; or (3) phoneme-based, word-prediction software, such as Aurora or Co:Writer, which completes words and phrases with limited typing from the student and which may be programmed to meet individual spelling patterns and/or inclusion of technical vocabulary.

Deficits in written composition may also be improved with the use of appropriate software. Mind-mapping programs such as Inspiration or Mind Manager, which provides visual representations of writing content, allow students with weaker linguistic or organizational skills the opportunity to organize their materials in a visual manner and automatically generate a hierarchical outline prior to beginning the generative phase of writing. In addition, speaking word processors such as Type and Talk and Write:Outloud afford students the opportunity to proofread their work in an auditory manner; either supplementing or even supplanting the more traditional, visual scanning approach for students who receptive oral skills exceed their receptive print skills. This provides substantially greater independence in editing their written work.

Finally, portable electronic devices such as the Franklin Speaking Language Master can provide greater flexibility in service usage, particularly in locations that preclude conventional computer-based interventions (e.g., laboratories, field excursions, community libraries). These include loaning portable keyboards such as the Alphasmart or Laser PC6 to students for whom handwriting is problematic, and portable electronic devices combining phoneme-based spell checking with speech synthesis and an expanded collegiate thesaurus, as well as active noise-canceling headphones, which can serve to substantially reduce background noise in nonideal study environments such as dorm rooms or study halls.

Classroom accommodations may also be indicated for LD students, particularly in circumstances where functional impairments impact lecture acquisition. Depending on the nature of the student's learning style, peer notetakers, authorization to tape record lecture, or loaned electronic keyboards may be offered. In addition, some interesting preliminary work has begun to explore the efficacy of real-time captioning services (whereby lectures are transcribed into visual format via computers) for students with LD and/or ADHD. Finally, nontechnical suggestions may be made to the students such as seating oneself near the center front of the classroom to focus the student's visual field away from auditory or visual distractions caused by other students.

In summary, successful students with learning disabilities tend to utilize a variety of services and resources within the disability office while at the same time modifying their own habits and choices to optimize their learning efficiency. They also share other positive characteristics, such as maintaining effective and timely communication with the disability office, ensuring the timeliness of service requests, and maintaining an optimistic, focused, and committed approach to their academic tenure.

Alternatives to the 4-Year Higher Education Setting

Our emphasis throughout this chapter has been primarily on 4-year institutions, including some comparisons with 2-year or community colleges. Your client may also want to consider alternatives to this traditional path, such as certificate programs through community colleges or attending a 2-year college before transferring to a 4-year university; vocational schools; or specialized disability schools. While we cannot cover these options comprehensively, you may want to explore them as a possible "best fit" for your client. Following is a brief summary of these alternatives and the key benefits and limitations they entail.

Two-Year Schools or Community Colleges

These schools typically offer 2-year degrees, such as associate arts and associate science, and a variety of certificate programs in specialized areas. Many students attend community collages initially and transfer to 4-year institutions to complete their bachelor of arts or sciences degrees (Table 7).

Vocational or Trade and Technical Schools

These schools provide training in occupations such as automotive repair, cosmetology, drafting, and computer technology (Table 8).

Specialized Disability Schools

These schools are designed for students with disabilities and can therefore cater to specialized needs throughout the curriculum (Table 9).

TABLE 7   Two-Year Schools or Community Colleges

Key benefits

    Will offer testing or reevaluation assessment services

    Better environment if remedial academic work is needed

    Offer greater degree of support to students

    Offer more flexibility in time for completion of requirements

    Curriculum flexibility is greater through nondegree programs of study

    Lower costs help reduce financial pressure

    Greater variety of instructors who often offer more support for nontraditional students

    Can be a good way to adjust to college life before more demanding 4-year environment

Key limitations

    Course equivalency issues for transfer students can be complex

    A 4-year college may not honor disability-related course substitutions

---

TABLE 8   Vocational in Trade and Technical Schools

Key benefits

    Hands-on learning and experience

    Curriculum requirements result in shorter educational track

    Less emphasis on academic skills

    More focused, specialized learning for specific trade area

Key limitations

    Do not offer traditional baccalaureate degrees

    Lack breadth and depth of broad education

    May not offer a good stepping stone to career advancement

---

TABLE 9   Specialyed Disability Schools

Key benefits

    Offer smaller courses

    Provide personalized disability service

    Disability sensitive staff and faculty

    Peers have similar background and experiences with disability

Key limitations

    Such schools are often quite expensive

    Usually geographically far from home (reduced family support)

    May not offer breadth of curriculum options

STUDENT SUCCESS PROFILE

It is hoped that we have raised important factors for you and your clients to consider when making decisions about higher education for your students with learning and attention difficulties. You now have an idea of how to conduct a "fearless assessment" of your client, considering both the specific areas of learning or attention difficulties and important factors necessary for success in postsecondary settings. You also have an increased awareness of higher education settings, the support they provide, and the demand they may place on your client. Based on our own clinical experiences, we have also developed a form that you can use to summarize your client's clinical and academic potential for success in higher education settings (see Appendix 10). This form is intended as a tool to guide your discussions with your client, integrating your assessment of their functioning with an evaluation of the various campus options and features you might consider. It can also assist you in developing action plans that you, your client, or the family may want to take in exploring possibilities in higher education. For those readers seeking additional resources to build upon the information provided within this chapter, we encourage you to examine Appendix 11, where you will find supplemental materials in the form of recommendations for books as well as web-based material.

However, you may still be wondering, as we do from time to time, is there an "ideal" student profile that indicates the best chance of success in such settings? How can you help clients make the path selection of "best fit" for them?

One of the joys of this field is seeing the uniqueness of individuals, which makes it even more difficult to determine an "ideal" profile. We have seen many students succeed when we feared they might not and seen others falter when it seemed they had everything they needed to succeed. It is more often the "intangible" aspects of personality, perseverance, character, and life circumstances that appear to tip the balance in one direction or the other. We have learned never to predict who will succeed and who will not or who will seem to fail this time only to succeed later when their abilities and life circumstances will come together more graciously. Rather, we stand in awe of all that it takes for these students to achieve their goals in the face of obstacles and their continued passion and capacity to make their dreams come true.

While the summary form we provide lends itself to a "formal" assessment process, the most important assessment you can make will be one that considers a truly holistic view of your client, which is far greater than the sum total of factors listed here. This entails an understanding not just of abilities, but also of your client's unique personality, spirit, and heart. As a therapist, you are in a unique position to bring your in-depth insight of your client's true self together with their strengths and weaknesses due to their disabilities. While we encourage you to take a realistic view, this more holistic perspective may at times lead you to support clients in achieving their academic goals, even when others have been less encouraging. Despite obstacles you can clearly see, it may be that your belief in the totality of who they are and who they can become will be the better determinate of how you view their potential for success. This should be the most "fearless" assessment you make.

REFERENCES

Barkley, R. A. (1997). *ADHD and the nature of self-control.* New York: Guilford Press

Barkley, R. A. (1998). *Attention-deficit hyperactivity disorder: A handbook for diagnosis and treatment* (2nd ed.), New York: Guilford Press.

Brinckerhoff, L. C., McGuire, J. M., & Shaw, S. F. (2002). *Postsecondary education and transition for students with learning disabilities* (2nd ed.). Austin, TX: PRO-ED.

Butterfield, E. C., & Albertson, L. R. (1995). On making cognitive theory more general and developmentally pertinent. In F. Weinert & W. Schneider (Eds.), *Research on memory development* (pp. 73 99). Hillsdale, NJ: Lawrence Erlbaum Associates.

Cobb, J. (2002). *Learning how to learn: Getting into and surviving college when you have a learning disability.* Washington, DC: CWLA Press.

Dendy, C. (2000). *Teaching teens with/ADD and ADHD.* Bethesda, MD: Woodbine House.

Erikson, E. H. (1963). *Childhood and society* (2nd ed.). New York: W. W. Norton & Company.

Hallowell, E. M. (1995). Psychotherapy of adult attention deficit disorder. In K. D. Nadeau (Ed.), *A comprehensive guide to attention deficit disorder in adults: Research, diagnosis, and treatment.* New York: Brunner/Mazel Publishers.

Hallowell, E. M., & Ratey, J. J. (1994). *Driven to distraction: Recognizing and coping with attention deficit disorder from childhood through adulthood.* New York: Simon & Schuster.

Henderson, C. (1999). *College freshmen with disabilities statistical year 1998: A biennial statistical profile.* Washington, DC: American Council on Education, HEATH Resource Center.

Hooper, S. R., & Olley, J. G. (1996). Psychological comorbidity in adults with learning disabilities. In N. Gregg, C. Hoy, & A. F. Gay (Eds.), *Adults with learning disabilities: Theoretical and practical perspectives.* New York: Guildford Press.

Katz, M. (2002). Promising practices: The SALT Center. *Attention, 9* (August), 12–13.

Lyon, G. R. (1996). The need for conceptual and theoretical clarity in the study of attention, memory, and executive function. In G. R. Lyon & N. A. Krasnegor (Eds.), *Attention, memory and executive function.* Baltimore, MD: Paul H. Brookes.

Murphy, K. (1995). Empowering the adult with ADD. In K. D. Nadeau (Ed.), *A comprehensive guide to attention deficit disorder in adults: Research, diagnosis, and treatment.* New York: Brunner/Mazel.

Murphy, K. (1997). Interpersonal and social problems in adults with ADD. In *ADD and adults: Strategies for success from CH.A.D.D.* Rosenberg Communications, Inc.

Nadeau, K. G. (1995). Life management skills for the adult with ADD. In K. D. Nadeau (Ed.), *A comprehensive guide to attention deficit disorder in adults: Research, diagnosis, and treatment.* New York: Brunner/Mazel.

Palombo, J. (2001). *Learning disorders and disorders of the self in children and adolescents.* New York: W. W. Norton & Company.

Parker, D., & Byron, J. (1998). Differences between college students with LD and AD/HD: Practical implications for service providers. In P. Quinn & A. McCormick (Eds.), *Rethinking AD/HD: A guide to fostering success in students with AD/HD at the college level* (pp. 14–30). Bethesda, MD: Advantage Books.

Quinn, P. O. (Ed.) (1994). *ADD and the college student: A guide for high school and college students with attention deficit disorder.* New York: Magination Press.

Smith, T. E. C., Dowdy, C. A., Polloway, E. A., & Blalock, G. E. (1997). *Children and adults with learning disabilities.* Needham Heights, MA: Advantage Books.

Sousa, D. A. (2001). *How the special needs brain learns.* Thousand Oaks, CA: Corwin Press.

Torgesen, J. K. (1996). A model of memory from an information processing perspective: The special case of phonological memory. In G. R. Lyon & N. A. Krasnegor (Eds.), *Attention, memory and executive function.* Baltimore, MD: Paul H. Brookes.

Vogel, S. A., & Adelman, P. B. (1990). Intervention effectiveness at the postsecondary level for the learning disabled. In T. E. Scruggs & B. Y. L. Wong (Eds.), *Intervention research in learning disabilities.* New York: Springer-Verlag.

Weiss, G., & Hechtman, L. (1993). *Hyperactive children grown up* (2nd ed). New York: Guilford Press.

Williams, J. P. (1990). The use of schema in research on the problem solving of learning disabled adolescents. In T. E. Scruggs & B. Y. L. Wong (Eds.), *Intervention research in learning disabilities.* New York: Springer-Verlag.

Zigmond & Thornton (1986). Follow-up of post-secondary age learning disabled graduates and drop-outs. *LD Research,* 1(1), 50–55.

## CHAPTER 12

Physician's Contribution to the Treatment of Attention Deficit Hyperactivity Disorder and Learning Disabilities: Implications for Medication Management and Collaborative Treatment

David Coffey

Mental health practitioners are being flooded with requests for the evaluation of children suspected to have attention deficit hyperactivity disorder (ADHD) and learning disabilities (LD) due to the high prevalence and rapidly increasing public awareness of these debilitating conditions. Psychiatrists, pediatricians, psychologists, speech pathologists, educational specialists, therapists, family members, and teachers have formidable opportunities to collaborate to enhance social, occupational, and academic functioning of a large number of children and adults. The LD prevalence is estimated to be about 15% (AACAP, 1998) of the general population and ADHD in the range of 2–18% (Rowland, 2002). Some studies show that roughly one-third of children diagnosed for ADHD meet the criterion for one or more learning disabilities and that half of those diagnosed with LD meet the criterion for at least one DSM IV axis I disorder. Cantwell (1996) was fond of saying, about ADHD, "comorbidity is the rule, not the exception" and that "multimodal management has been promulgated as the treatment of choice." The author believes the same can hold true for LD. With effort and coordination, mental health practitioners can collaborate to help individuals affected by these disorders to realize their full potential.

Often a psychiatrist will cocase manager the treatment team along with a therapist. This chapter focuses on the psychiatrist's contributions to the team, although many pediatricians and neurologists feel comfortable filling the role of medication consultation and treatment coordination as well. In some cases the psychiatrist may choose to limit their role to medication prescription and monitoring when another team member serves as captain, or the extent of psychiatric symptoms are well controlled with medication alone. In other cases, a psychiatrist will serve as a therapist, medication prescriber, and case manager. This chapter is divided into two phases of the psychiatrist's role: evaluation and treatment.

EVALUATION OF ADHD AND LD

The American Academy of Child and Adolescent Psychiatry (AACAP) has set guidelines for the evaluation of ADHD (Dulcan et al., 1997) and for LD (AACAP, 1998). The evaluation process includes initial interviews of the patient and their parents, reviewing reports and previous assessments, and touching base with allied health professionals and educators to clarify and establish roles that each will play on the team.

Referrals come from a variety of sources, but most commonly from a parent, teacher, or therapist. The psychiatrist will ordinarily make initial contact with the parents by phone to clarify the reason for the referral and familiarize the parents with the evaluation process. Psychiatrists allow one to three hours for the evaluation, often splitting the process over 2 days. This allows time for accumulation of school records and surveys, and communication with essential potential team members, before meeting with the patient and parents to give treatment recommendations. Psychiatrists will often tell the parents to bring along copies of all previous evaluations, as well as report cards and achievement tests.

Interviews

The evaluation begins with interviews. It is essential for the psychiatrist to interview parents and their children separately whenever possible, although some younger children may require a parent to be in the room in order to be comfortable. In the case of teenagers, it is a usual practice for the psychiatrist to conduct an interview and mental status exam of a teenager first. This helps establish the agency of the teen as well as foster an environment of confidentiality and trust. An interview of the parents then follows. Some teens may request to be present for the parent interview and this may be accommodated when appropriate. With younger children, the order is reversed and the parent interview is conducted first followed by a meeting with the child.

The parent interview process includes eliciting present concerns about their child's home life, school performance, and peer relationships. The psychiatrist listens for descriptions of concerns that may be consistent with ADHD and LD but also asks questions to distinguish them from concerns more consistent with other psychiatric conditions. Table 1 lists a variety of childhood and teenage psychiatric disorders that look like or are often comorbid with ADHD and LD. In particular, childhood and teenage anxiety and mood disorders can be very difficult to distinguish from ADHD and LD. Children who are anxious can not concentrate and children that are depressed often experience problems with academic performance.

After the parents communicate their concerns, the psychiatrist will ask questions about interactions with parents, siblings, and pets; methods of discipline used in the home; eating habits; sleeping habits; and sleeping arrangements. With regard to peers, the psychiatrist will ask questions about friendships, acceptance by peers, after-school activities, and interests. When interviewing the parents of teens it is wise to query parents about their impressions of their child's exposure to alcohol, drugs, and sexual experiences. On the subject of school, the psychiatrist will ask about current academic performance, studying habits, and tutoring, as well as recent disciplinary actions taken by the school. Teenagers and some younger children may be capable of covering the same ground conversing in an interview, but many younger children and some teenagers do best talking with the psychiatrist over the course of play. Often psychiatrists will have available a variety of toys and games to make children and some younger teens comfortable while being observed for mental status findings as well as being interviewed.

With teenagers, after laying the groundwork of the essential boundaries for confidentiality, it is important to screen for alcohol, drug use, and sexual experiences. The social, cognitive, and impulse control vulnerabilities of teens diagnosed with ADHD and LD make them extraordinarily susceptible to the temptations and consequences of drug and alcohol use and relatively unsafe sexual practices. Comprehensive

TABLE 1   ADHD Comorbid and Look-a-like Diagnoses[a]

Adjustment disorder with symptoms of anxiety and/or depression
Anxiety NOS
Arithmetic disorder
Asperger's disorder
Autism
Bipolar disorder I
Bipolar disorder II
Conduct disorder
Cyclothymia
Depression NOS
Dysgarphia
Dysthymia
Enuresis
Expressive language disorder
Generalized anxiety disorder
Hearing impairment
Hyperthyroidism
Hypothyroidism
Major depressive disorder
Mathematics disorder
Mixed receptive-expressive language disorder
Motor tic disorder
Obsessive-compulsive disorder
Oppositional defiant disorder
Panic disorder
Pervasive developmental disorder NOS
Phonation disorder
Posttraumatic stress disorder
Prodomal borderline personality disorder symptoms
Receptive language disorder
Schizophrenia
Schizophreniform disorder
Separation anxiety disorder
Social anxiety disorder
Substance use and dependence
Tourette's disorder
Vision impairment
Vocal tic disorder
Writing disorder

---

[a] Psychiatric disorders in **boldface** are frequently comorbid or look-a-like disorders. Look-a-like disorders only are in italics. Frequently comorbid disorders only are in regular type.

psychiatric treatment calls for careful screening upon intake and throughout the treatment process for evidence of behaviors putting teens at risk for HIV and other sexually transmitted diseases, sexual trauma, and substance abuse.

Once the present history concerns have been obtained, the focus of the interview will turn to past medical treatment, past psychiatric treatment, academic, and family history. A complete medical history is obtained with, for example, particular attention to medical conditions, which may predispose to ADHD or LD whose treatment or natural history may interfere with the underlying illness or potential treatments for these mental health conditions. For example, often times β-agonists prescribed for asthma can increase hyperactivity and anxiety, which in turn can diminish concentration. Of course, a complete list of current medications and past medications is listed as well as past psychiatric treatment. Screening for allergies to medications that the patient may have is also recommended. If a child or teen has not had a checkup in the last year or is experiencing medical symptoms, a recommendation to follow up with their pediatrician should be made.

The psychiatrist asks for details about previous psychiatric treatments focusing on what psychosocial interventions have been tried, what previous psychotropic medications have been tried, at what dosage, and what responses and side effect were experienced. An extensive family psychiatric history is ascertained with particular focus on screening for the history of family members being diagnosed or suspected of having LD, ADHD, mood disorders, and other mental health conditions. A family history of alcohol and drug use will also be ascertained due to the strong relationship between ADHD and a family history of substance use disorders. In teenagers, screening for suspected drug and alcohol use is also quite important due to the poor prognosis for individuals diagnosed LD and ADHD who get involved in drug or alcohol use.

A sensitive, developmental, and educational history is obtained from parents, including exposures to alcohol, drugs, and prescribed medications during periods of pregnancy. Fetal exposure to medications, cocaine, alcohol, and cigarette smoking has been linked to symptoms seen in LD and ADHD. A further developmental history would not be limited to, but certainly include, a history of any complications of pregnancy, labor, and delivery, some details about the period of infancy through preschool, including screening for difficulties attaining developmental milestones, colic, difficulties sleeping, and feeding and potty training. Finally, it is important to evaluate for difficulties separating from parents in the early weeks of preschool.

A detailed educational history from preschool through high school is important in evaluating for ADHD and LD. For each period of schooling, details about classroom behavior, academic performance, teacher comments, school disciplinary measures, and social acceptance are elicited. Often parents will reveal changes of school or repeating grades as part of this history. We pay particularly close attention to the school history from preschool to second grades given that one of the present DSM-IV criterions for diagnosing ADHD includes evidence of symptoms by the age of 7 years. It is also prudent to get a detailed educational history of the parents to uncover the possibility of suspected but undiagnosed ADHD and LD given that there is evidence that ADHD and LD may have familial inheritance patterns.

During the intake process the psychiatrist endeavors to detect or elicit patient and family attitudes toward various treatment modalities. Some families may be highly resistant to the idea of medication, others to psychotherapeutic interventions or to educational treatments. The psychiatrist may also make note of the family's financial resources, geographic location, family dynamics, and time availability during the intake. The family's attitudes about various treatment modalities, as well as their resources, must be taken into account when formulating an optimal as well as feasible treatment plan.

Mental Status Examination

Varying degrees of formal and informal mental status examination are performed to assess the patient's general appearance, psychomotor coordination and activity level, relatedness, and interaction style. The child's mood, affect, thought process, and thought content are noted. As we play with an elementary school child or converse with a teenager about their interests, the psychiatrist can informally ascertain the patient's self-esteem and screen for psychotic or disorganized thought process, as well as listen for anxious or depressed thought content. Informal cognitive assessment can take place continuously through the course of conversation or playing games to check the patient's degree of distractibility, concentration, and hyperactivity.

Often times, the psychiatrist will ask the patients to draw pictures to assess their fine motor skills and may apply some common cognitive tests for memory and concentration. After completing the initial interviews and mental status examination the psychiatrist will prepare to begin document review and contact with other potential team members by obtaining written informed consent from the parents to exchange information.

Document Review and Contact with Team Members

The psychiatrist must obtain information from potential team members and previous treating therapists and psychiatrists to compete the assessment phase of the evaluation. Sometimes parents may have already recently completed thorough cognitive or educational testing, speech and language evaluation, or a previous psychiatric evaluation. In such cases document review is warranted and often leads to contact with the individuals who compiled these tests for clarification. At other times, initial or updated testing may be called for in order to diagnose the child properly. In these situations, it may be necessary to postpone or modify feedback and treatment planning until referrals are made to the appropriate individuals and their assessments are available. The psychiatrist reviews the schools records, paying careful attention not only to trends in grades and achievement tests, but also descriptions of classroom behavior, study habits, and disciplinary measures. Many psychiatrists distribute surveys to parents and teachers, such as the Achenbach child behavior checklist and Connors scales and review their results. On some occasions the psychiatrist may go on a school visit to observe the patient in the classroom setting.

A review of intelligence and achievement tests is essential to clarify the diagnosis of LD. A careful review of cognitive testing is crucial to determine patient's relative assets and limitations in executive functioning, planning, memory, auditory and visual processing, and visual motor integration. Such an analysis can help construct a road map for teachers, educational specialists, tutors, and parents to utilize available cognitive strengths to compensate for weaknesses.

Likewise, a review of pediatric records is important to establish baseline medical strengths and weaknesses. The psychiatrist also screens for medical conditions that mimic psychiatric symptoms. Particular attention is paid to the patient's height and weight over the years, which is plotted on a growth curve. Healthy children tend to stay in the same percentile of height and weight as they grow. ADHD medications can often

TABLE 2   Potential Treatment Team Members

Classroom shadow	Patient
Educational specialist	Pediatrician
Family practitioner	Psychiatric nurse
Family therapist	Psychiatrist
Homework helper	Psychologist
In-home behaviorist	School principal
Individual therapist	School psychologist
Legal advocate	Social skills facilitator
Marriage and family counselor	Social worker
Neurologist	Special education teacher
Neuropsychologist	Speech pathologist
Occupational therapist	Teacher
Parent trainer	Teacher's aide
Parents	Tutor

interfere with appetite, weight gain, and growth. Later reference to the growth curve can indicate if the patient's height and weight are falling off the trajectory predicted by earlier growth. A review of routine blood and urine tests can determine if medical conditions exist that may contraindicate some medication options.

In addition to document review, it is important for the psychiatrist to contact the other team members to get their perspective on the patient and enlist support in forming a comprehensive treatment plan. The team members vary from patient to patient but it may include an individual psychotherapist, a family therapist, an educational specialist, a tutor, teachers, a speech and language therapist, an occupational therapist, and others. See Table 2 for a list of the wide variety of potential team members.

Once all the groundwork is completed, the psychiatrist is ready to formulate a diagnosis and present a treatment plan to the patient and their family. The diagnostic formulation takes into account the history and mental status exam obtained in the interviews, the review of medical and educational records, as well as cognitive and speech and language testing, and the communication with treatment team members.

TREATMENT

Given that treatment for ADHD and LD is multimodal, a family may have a number of treatment interventions and combinations of treatment interventions to consider in order to achieve the best results. The psychiatrist takes into account the family's psychodynamics, financial resources, resistances to treatment, location, and time availability when formulating a treatment plan. Some situations will require the application of intervention in series rather than all at once. The interventions can be classified as psychopharmacologic and psychosocial. Psychopharmacology for ADHD is managed primarily with stimulants, but antihypertensives and antidepressants may also play a role. Psychosocial interventions target academic, patient education, and psychotherapeutic needs. When it comes to academics, the psychiatrist's role is to monitor academic progress and identify interventions as a case manager. This is often imbedded in the psychiatrist's role as an educator themselves by providing patients and their family information about the natural history of LD and ADHD.

Psychsocial Interventions: Academic and Patient Education

The manner in which symptoms of ADHD and LD present themselves change as child grows, as do the educational challenges they encounter. A psychiatrist can help families set realistic expectations for the unique situations each child may encounter as they develop and their symptoms evolve. Initially the psychiatrist may introduce the importance of obtaining psychoeducational testing from their public school district or from a private neuropsychologist. For children who are on track academically, it is important for the psychiatrist to review quarterly report cards and annual achievement test results provided by the school to detect any trends toward lower than expected performance.

This may trigger the need for medication adjustment, or the introduction of educational interventions by teachers, or perhaps a referral to an educational specialist. The psychiatrist may be able to provide parents with information on how to appeal to their school district or county mental health department for special services such as smaller classrooms, classroom accommodations, tutoring, computer software, and other interventions. In some cases the psychiatrist may advocate for the patient in this process by writing letters or reports or by attending school meetings to plan for school-based academic intervention. When warranted, the psychiatrist may play a crucial role in communicating to parents the need for a classroom staffed by specialists with a small student to teacher ratio in a highly structured setting. When such a setting cannot be found in the public school, a nonpublic school may be required in order for the patient's academic milestones to be met. In some cases the psychiatrist may recommend a professional advocate to assist in the process to obtain classroom accommodations, a shadow/helper, special classes, or funding for a nonpublic school.

For parents who are resistant to treatment for ADHD and LD it is often beneficial for the psychiatrist to educate the family about the higher risks for drug and alcohol use among individuals diagnosed with ADHD, which have been established by Tapert et al. (2002). Lynsky and Hall (2001) established that a higher incidence of substance use disorders occurs in individuals diagnosed with ADHD and conduct disorder. Social skills impairment (Greene et al., 1999) also predicts poor outcomes for ADHD children and teens. For this reason, social skills groups have become a beneficial psychotherapeutic treatment for children diagnosed with ADHD and LD (Frankel et al., 1997). This and other psychotherapies are discussed next.

Psychosocial Interventions: Psychotherapy

The most commonly applied psychotherapeutic interventions for children diagnosed with ADHD and LD are parent training, individual psychotherapy, and group therapy. A cardinal symptom of ADHD is social immaturity. Social skills groups can offer techniques for approaching potential new friends, how to handle difficulties with sharing toys, handling one-on-one play dates, parties, and teasing by peers (Frankel et al., 1997). Teenagers may derive benefits from group therapy facilitated by a therapist who is skilled at utilizing the group process as a means to enhance skillful social communication (Dulcan et al., 1999). The impulsivity, distractibility, and hyperactivity of most children, not only those diagnosed with ADHD, often challenge parents to their limits not only in social settings but at home.

Parent training can offer techniques for dispensing discipline at home without resorting to physical punishment (Webster-Stratton & Hammond, 1990; Pelham et al., 1998)). With ADHD's high comorbidity of oppositional defiant disorder and conduct disorder may be parents stretched to the breaking point of using physical force. Unfortunately, the use of physical force can promote conduct and psychological problems, exacerbating the difficulties ADHD and LD children face. When oppositional and conduct symptoms are part of the presentation of ADHD and LD, there are alternatives to the use of physical force that can restore confidence in parents who are often frustrated and overwhelmed by the severity of impulsivity, disorganization, and hyperactivity experienced with their ADHD and LD children (Weinberg, 1999). Parent training can take the form of a group process with several couples meeting with a facilitator or in a consultation setting where the parents meet with a parent trainer alone. In some severe situations, a behavioral specialist may make house calls to observe first hand how, where, and when difficulties with behavior arise and implement customized strategies for parents. Regardless of the format, parents are given a variety of tools, such as giving commands effectively, use of time out, praise, active ignoring of distracting behaviors, natural consequences, use of a token economy and removal of privileges for undesirable behaviors, and proper use of tone and eye contact. Weinberg (1999) reported parents completing parent training developed "increased knowledge" and "lower stress."

Parents often do not find the behavioral techniques of parent training to be effective with teenagers. Parents and teens can achieve similar results, however, by participating in family psychotherapy (Stubbe & Weiss, 2000). Experienced family therapists can artfully help diminish family tensions and find creative ways for the family to collaborate on consequences for impulsive behaviors. Other therapies common in individuals with LD and ADHD are individual psychotherapy and drug and alcohol-related treatment programs. Individual therapy provided by psychiatrists is most often indicated for the frequent comorbidites associated with ADHD and LD, the most common of these being anxiety and mood disorders. Unfortunately, the comorbidity of drug and alcohol use among teenagers with these disorders is fairly high and treatment of them should not be ignored as in part of the treatment of these individuals. Depending on its severity, drug and alcohol use can be handled in the context of individual and family therapy provided by the psychiatrist or others, but when that it is not sufficient, referral to outpatient or residential substance use treatment centers is warranted.

MEDICATIONS

There has been a substantial growth in the number of psychotropic medications prescribed for children diagnosed with ADHD in recent years. Some of them are very well studied for their safety and efficacy in children, others less so. Some major categories of medications prescribed are stimulants, antidepressants, and antihypertensives.

Stimulant Medications

Stimulant medications are probably the most commonly prescribed medications for children with LD and ADHD. They are the gold standard of treatment for ADHD and have the most robust track record for safety and efficacy. Stimulant medications are purported to derive their benefit by compensating for insufficient dopamine or improper dopamine regulation in the brain, rendering it less capable of screening out noise from the environment. Proper regulation of dopamine can greatly reduce hyperactivity and impulsivity as well. Stimulant medications are useful for all three subtypes of ADHD: inattentive, hyperactive/impulsive, and combined types (Greenhill, 1995).

The most commonly prescribed stimulant medications are Methylphenidate (MPH) and Dexedrine (DEX) and their derivatives. A third type of stimulant, Pemoline(Cylert), has fallen out of favor in recent years because of its association to reports of liver failure secondary to fulminate liver necrosis. Although some physicians continue to use this medication when others fail, close monitoring of liver function with biannual blood tests is required to ensure safety. More commonly, psychiatrists are utilizing MPH- and DEX-based products (Shevell & Screiber, 1997).

Stimulants derive their benefits by recycling dopamine in the synapse of the brain before they are reabsorbed for eventual disposal. See Table 3 for a list of DEX and MPH products and their duration of benefits. In head-to-head studies, MPH and DEX appear to be equal in efficacy (Arnold et al., 1978). Each was shown to be effective in significantly reducing symptoms of ADHD in 70% of cases. If three or more stimulant preparations are tried, the chance of success in a clinically significant reduction of symptoms is an astounding 96% (Elia et al., 1991). There are few medication classes in all of pediatrics as well studied for their efficacy than stimulants (Dulcan, 1997). They have both been shown to be effective, not only for problems with concentration and distractibility, but they also assist in the reduction of hyperactivity and impulsivity. They also share an identical side effects profile. A review of Table 3 reveals a variety of durations of benefit for the different preparations of MPH and DEX.

TABLE 3   Stimulant Medications, Duration of Benefit, and Dosage Range

	Duration (hours)	Dosage (mg)
Dexedrine-based products		
Dexedrine	3	2.5–45/day split 2–4x/day
Dexedrine spansules	5	5–45/day split 1–3x/day
Adderall	5	5–45/day split 1–3x/day
Adderall XR	12	5–50/day
Methylphenidate-based products		
Ritalin	3	5–90/day split 2–4x/day
Methylphenidate (generic)	3	5–90/day split 2–4x/day
Ritalin SR	5	20–40/day split 1–2x/day
Ritalin LA	8	20–60/day split 2–4x/day
Methylyn	8	10–60/day split 1–2x/day
Metadate CD	8	20–60/day split 1–2x/day
Concerta	12	18–54/day

Recent trends in pharmaceutical manufacturer development have been to make longer-acting agents. The rationale behind this is to decrease the need for dosing more than once a day. The shorter-acting agents require children to take multiple doses to get through the school day and after school activities such as homework and extracurricular activities in which the stimulant medication may be helpful. Often, however, the longer-acting agents yield less desirable benefits and require coadministration of shorter-acting agents to target situations when concentration is most needed, such as a tough math class or after-dinner homework.

A psychiatrist may prescribe one or more stimulants to correspond to the patient's schedule and their need to take advantage of the medication's ability to boost their concentration and limit hyperactivity and impulsivity while minimizing side effects.

Table 4 lists the most common side effects seen with stimulant medications. The most common and problematic are difficulties falling asleep and growth retardation (Efron et al., 1997). Growth problems are purported to be due to the appetite suppression and its consequential weight loss associated with stimulants (Zeiner, 1995). Thus comprehensive care of a child treated with stimulants requires monitoring of height and weight through collaboration with the child's pediatrician or by direct height and weight measurements at the psychiatrist's office. When a child appears to be falling off their projected growth curve, the psychiatrist will advise the patient and their parents to strategically time meals and dosing

TABLE 4   Common Side Effects of DEX and MPH Products

Difficulty falling asleep
Appetite suppression/weight loss
Nervousness
Moodiness (usually as the medication wears off)
Headache
Stomachache
Rapid heart beat
Psychomotor and vocal tic exacerbation
Rebound hyperactivity when medication wears off

---

and to alter dosage or type of stimulant preparation. Often, taking holidays from stimulant medication on weekends or school breaks are sufficient for children to catch up in their growth. Similar strategies, such as adjusting timing of dosing and dosage, can be helpful in reducing problems with insomnia. When all else fails, use of a bedtime dose of an antihypertensive (see discussion later) or Benadryl may prove beneficial to enhance sleep.

Psychomotor and vocal tics are often associated with ADHD. Tics are repetitive short bursting movements or utterances. Most commonly they consist of winking, blinking, grimacing, throat clearing, snorting, or utterances of one-syllable words or word fragments. Individuals who experience chronic vocal as well as motor tics are diagnosed with Tourette's disorder. Studies suggest that the coincidence of tics and ADHD is due largely to the comorbidity of ADHD and tic disorders, not due to medication inducing the onset of a tic disorder. A recent case control study followed a group of children diagnosed with ADHD but never medicated with stimulants or had evidence on examination or history of motor or vocal tics. The children were split up into MPH and placebo groups and followed for a year. At the end of 1 year, approximately one in seven children in each group developed psychomotor or vocal tics or both. The conclusion was that the onset of tics is most likely due to the well-known comorbidity of ADHD and tic disorders rather than the effect of medication (Law, 1999). It has been well established that stimulant medications can exacerbate existing tics, although many children diagnosed with both ADHD and tic disorders experience no change or a reduction of tic frequency or intensity when stimulants are administered. Nevertheless, when tics emerge or worsen with the administration of a stimulant, dosage reduction or switching to another stimulant or perhaps an antidepressant is warranted.

Another problematic area that comes up when discussing the use of stimulants with patients and parents is their knowledge that DEX and MPH have the potential to be abused as street drugs, weight loss pills, and agents that promote staying awake for prolonged hours. It is wise that when these questions come up that the psychiatrist points out that abuse of these medications as a street drug occurs only when dosed at 10–20 times that which is beneficial for ADHD. Although psychiatrists acknowledge that these medications interfere with sleep and maintaining normal weight, these are two side effects that must be monitored closely in frequent visits and that when they arise we will intervene to prevent them from persisting. Finally, reminding parents that sparing the use of stimulants may put their child at risk of the very outcome they are trying to avoid—substance abuse (Biederman et al., 1999).

Once a stimulant medication is selected, the psychiatrist will often advise parents to try a few different doses, each for 3 to 7 days starting from a small dose to incrementally larger doses. During that time the psychiatrist will ask the parents and teachers to rate efficacy and side effects. Often this is done using a survey, the most common being the Connors scale. Psychiatrists often review the results of these surveys at different doses to determine which dose works the best. Excessive dosing of stimulants can lead to less than optimal responses, and it is not uncommon to see a regression in benefit if the dose is too high, even if side effects are not present. Some physiatrists utilize computer software tests, such as the continuous performance test or the test of varying attention at each dose to get a objective rating of attention.

Antidepressant Medications

Antidepressants have been a useful intervention for psychiatrists treating ADHD due to their efficacy in treating comorbid disorders. Tricyclic antidepressants (TCAs) in particular are a second line treatment for ADHD when stimulants fail or they cannot be tolerated due to side effects (Spencer et al., 1993). Tables 5 and 6 list the names of commonly prescribed antidepressants. Tricyclic antidepressants and serotonin reputake inhibitors (SRIs) have proven effective for a variety of childhood and teenage psychiatric disorders, including separation anxiety disorder (Masi et al., 2001; Klein et al., 1992), obsessive compulsive disorder (Piacentini and Bergman, 2000, Bernstein et al., 1996), and post traumtic stress disorder (Putnum & Hulsmann, 2002). At the time of this writing, only

TABLE 5   Antidepressants and Common Side Effects[a]

Medication (brand name)	Side effects
Tricyclic antidepressants (T/C) Tofranil Nortyptelline Amytrptilline	Dizziness upon standing, dry mouth, drowsiness, sexual dysfunction
Serotonin reuptake inhibitors (C) Fluoxetine (Prozac) Sertraline (Zoloft) Paroxetine (Paxil) Fluvoxamine (Luvox) Citoprolam (Celexa)	Headache, sleep, appetite, and gastro intestinal disturbances, sexual dysfunction, psychomotor restlessness
Other Buproprion (Wellbutrin, Wellbutrin SR) (T)	Headache, insomnia, dry mouth, decreased appetite
Venlafexine (Effexor, Effexor XR)	Same as Serotonin reuptake inhibitors with added risk of elevating blood pressure

[a] **T**, medications used to treat ADHD; **C**, medications used to treat comorbid conditions.

TABLE 6   Antidepressants and Common Dosages

Medication (brand name)	Dosage (mg)	
Tricyclic antidepressants Desipramine (Elavil) Imipramine (Tofranil)	25–200 25–200	
Serotonin reuptake inhibitors Fluoxetine (Prozac) Sertraline (Zoloft) Fluvoxamine (Luvox) Paroxetine (Paxil) Citoprolam (Celexa)	5–60 12.5–200 50–300 5–50 5–60	
Other Buproprion (Wellbutrin, Wellbutrin SR)	75–450	often split into two to three doses
Venlafexine (Effexor, Effexor XR)	37.5–375	often split into two doses

fluoxetine, fluvoxamine, and sertraline are FDA approved for use in children. Even though the pediatric indication is limited to obsessive-compulsive disorders, studies have established the safety of continuous use over 1 to 2 years. Imipramine is FDA approved for children, but only for the treatment of enuresis. Nevertheless, imipramine, desipramine, and all of the SRIs have been shown to be effective in treating childhood anxiety in preliminary studies. Often times children with comorbid anxiety disorder cannot tolerate the increased anxiety caused by stimulants and require the coadministration of a stimulant and an antidepressant. Benefits of TCAs for depression have been less well established. In fact, many studies have shown a placebo to be equally effective to tricyclic antidepressants for childhood depression. However, early evidence suggests that fluoxetine may be effective for childhood and teenage onset depression (Emslee et al., 2002). Tables 5 and 6 list antidepressants used of ADHD treatment or management of comorbid conditions, their side effects, and dosage ranges.

TCAs are to be used with caution due to cardiovascular side effects. Cardiovascular effects include orthostatic hypotension and alteration of cardiac conduction (Jackson et al., 1987). Orthostatic hypotension is the experience of lightheadedness or dizziness upon standing that can lead to falls and, in the in the worst case, head injury. Parents are warned to look for signs of orthostasis and report them immediately to the psychiatrist so hydration and/or taper of the TCA can be recommended. Children beginning TCAs who have preexisting cardiac conduction blocks have died suddenly from the administration of TCAs. Children who have been on TCAs for a prolonged period of time can experience progression from a normal state toward one of delay in the conduction of signals in the heart that regulate its contractions in the proper sequence. Psychiatrists who utilize TCAs, both for treatment of ADHD or for its comorbid conditions, must warn parents of these risks and obtain baseline and annual electrocardiograms (EKGs). For these reasons, SRIs have rapidly replaced the role of TCAs in managing comorbid conditions, and alternatives to TCAs are needed when first line treatment of ADHD with stimulants fails.

Case series studies of venlafexine and buproprion have shown nearly equal efficacy to MPH and DEX for the treatment of adults diagnosed with ADHD. Results of studies of efficacy of venlafexine and buproprion in children and teenagers are not available at this time (Popper, 1997). Venlafexine may derive its benefit for ADHD because of its norepinephrine-stimulating effects, as does buproprion for its dopamine-stimulating effects. Neither of these medications is currently FDA approved for children and should be used with caution and only in cases where stimulants have not been effective or side effects are not well tolerated.

Antihypertensive Medications

Antihypertensives(AHs) have been useful in the treatment of ADHD to take advantage of their propensity to decrease hyperactivity and impulsivity as well as promote sleep. It is unclear how they convey their benefit psychopharmacologically, and their benefits in reducing hyperactivity and impulsivity may be as a result of their sedating properties (Steingard et al., 1993). The two AHs commonly prescribed for ADHD are guaneficine (Tenex) and clonidine (Catapress). The dosages are much smaller, ordinarily 0.05–0.3 mg, split up into one to three doses in the case of clonidine and 0.5–4 mg split into one to four doses a day for gauneficine. Although both medications have been prescribed in much larger doses, there is the rare risk of rebound hypertension if children skip or miss doses. This problem is more common with clonidine than guaneficine (Leckman et al., 1986; Scahill et al., 2001). For this reason, some psychiatrists prescribe clonidine in a patch form that is distributed slowly throughout the day to avoid the problem of skipped doses in the course of the day.

AHs may also confer a side benefit of reducing vocal and motor tics, as well as some nervous habits, such as excessive scratching and picking of skin for some individuals (Riddle et al., 1995). Thus AHs can fill some important niches in the treatment of ADHD. They may be useful for the child diagnosed with the primarily hyperactive type of ADHD who cannot tolerate stimulants due to their side effects or for when similar patients or their parents are resistant to the idea of stimulants due to their association with street drugs. A very common use for AHs is as adjuncts to MPH and DEX products when rebound hyperactivity, insomnia, or suboptimally treated hyperactivity and impulsivity symptoms arise. Unfortunately, there have been a handful of reported cases of sudden death in children who were taking a combination of MPH and clonidine (Fenichel, 1995).

Since these cases were reported, reviews of autopsies were not able to clearly establish a causative link between the administration of these medications and the sudden death of the children reported. Further monitoring of reports of large numbers of cases of children treated with these

TABLE 7   Multiaxial Diagnosis and Treatment Plan for a 7 Year Old

Axis I	1. Attention deficit hyperactivity disorder—Combined type
	2. Oppositional defiant disorder
	3. Anxiety disorder NOS with skin-scratching habit
	4. Arithmetic disorder
	5. Phonation disorder
Axis II	None
Axis III	Asthma
Axis IV	Parent–child Problem
Axis V	60

Treatment plan:

Problem 1. Behavioral disturbances at home
1. Referral to LCSW for parent training
2. Possible trial of Concerta after anxiety symptoms addressed

Problem 2. Academics
1. Advise parents to request special education classroom for math
2. Concur with math tutor
3. Review report cards quarterly and annual achievement testing annually. Ongoing screening for potential need for tutor or educational specialist

Problem 3. Anxiety
1. One-month weekly extended therapy evaluation with LCSW to identify source of anxiety and offer relaxation techniques and habit reversal techniques with phone conference at conclusion to assess for potential efficacy
2. Consider trial of Zoloft if psychotherapy therapy ineffective
3. Contact pediatrician to discuss alternatives to Allbuterol for asthma to reduce anxiety and picking of skin

Problem 4. Poor concentration
1. Consider trial of 18, 36, and 54 mg of Concerta after anxiety symptoms stabilize
2. Will circulate Conners scales to teachers for each dosage level

Problem 5. Speech
1. Suggest parents request speech therapy two times a week at school
2. Repeat speech and language testing in 12 months to assess efficacy of speech therapy

combinations of medications have not been associated with abnormal EKGs, cardiac irregularities, or cardiac symptoms (Fenichel, 1995). Some psychiatrists are resuming the practice of prescribing these medications in combination with annual monitoring of blood pressure and EKGs. Others are abandoning the practice of coadministration of MPH and clonidine.

CONCLUSION

Monitoring the benefits and risks of stimulants, antidepressants, and anti-hypertensives is often the main focus of psychiatrists in the role of treating children diagnosed with ADHD and LD. However, psychiatrists may also function as case managers, cocase managers, educators, and therapists on a team of clinicians and educators in the mulimodal treatment of these disorders. Table 7 shows an example of a treatment plan.

Psychiatrists are constantly screening for trends in academic, medical, social, family functioning, cognitive, and speech development that can require the adjustment of existing interventions or the application of new interventions that the psychiatrist or other team members will provide. Over the course of treatment, communication between the psychiatrist and other team members is vital. Proactive, responsive, and confidential communication between team members can enhance the likelihood that a treatment plan will be successful. Whether the psychiatrist can execute a comprehensive multimodal treatment plan alone or as part of a team, patients can overcome the limitations imposed by ADHD and LD and reach the academic and interpersonal milestones they are fully capable of achieving.

REFERENCES

AACAP (1998). Practice parameters for the assessment and treatment of children and adolescentswith language and learning disorders. *Journal of the American Academy of Child & Adolescent Psychiatry*, 37(10 Suppl.), 46S–62S.

Arnold, L. E., Christopher, J., Huestis, R., & Smeltzer, D. J. (1978). Methylphenidate vs dextroamphetamine vs caffeine in minimal brain dysfunction: Controlled comparison by placebo washout design with Bayes' analysis. *Archives of General Psychiatry*, 35(4), 463–473.

Bernstein, G. A., Borchardt, C. M., & Perwein, A. R. (1996). Anxiety disorders in children and adolescents: A review of the past 10 years. *Journal of the American Academy of Child and Adolescent Psychiatry*, 35(9), 1110–1119.

Biederman, J., Wilens, T., Mick, E., Spencer, T., & Farone, S. V. (1999). Pharmacotherapy of attention-deficit/hyperactivity disorder reduces risk for substance use disorder. *Pediatrics*, 104(2), e20.

Cantwell, D. P. (1996). Attention deficit disorder: A review of the past 10 years. *Journal of the American Academy of Child and Adolescent Psychiatry*, 35(8), 978–987.

Dulcan, M. (1997). Practice parameters for the assessment and treatment of children, adolescents, and adults with ADHD. *Journal of the American Academy of Child and Adolescent Psychiatry*, 36(10 Suppl.), 85S–121S.

Efron, D., Jarman, F., & Baker, M. (1997). Side effects of methylphenidate and dexamphetamine in children with attention deficit hyperactivity disorder: A double-blind, crossover trial. *Pediatrics*, 100(4), 662–664.

Elia, J., Borcherding, B. G., Rapoport, J. L., & Keysor, C. S. (1991). Methylphenidate and dextroamphetamine treatments of hyperactivity: Are there true nonresponders? *Psychiatry Research*, 36, 141–155.

Emslie, G. J., Heilgenstein, J. H., Wagner, K. D., Hoog, S. l., Ernst, D. E., Brown, E., Nilsson, M., & Jacobson, J. G. (2002). Fluoxetine for acute treatment of depression in children and adolescents: a placebo-controlled, randomized clinical trial. *Journal of the American Academy of Child and Adolescent Psychiatry*, 41(10), 1205–1215.

Fenichel, R. R. (1995). Combining methylphenidate and clonidine: The role of post-marketing surveillance. *Journal of Child and Adolescent Psychopharmacology*, 5, 155–156.

Frankel, F., Myatt, R., Cantwel, D. P., & Feinberg, D. T. (1997). Parent-assisted transfer of children's social skills training: Effects on children with and without attention-deficit hyperactivity disorder. *Journal of the American Academy of Child and Adolescent Psychiatry*, 36(8), 1056–1064.

Greene, R. W., Biederman, J., Faraone, S. W., Wilens, T. E., Mick, E., & Blier, H. K. (1999). Further validation of social impairment as a predictor of substance use disorders: Findings from a sample of siblings of boys with and without ADHD. *Journal of Clinical Child Psychology*, 28(3), 349–354.

Greenhill, L. L. (1995). Attention-deficit hyperactivity disorder: The stimulants. *Child and Adolescent Psychiatric Clinics of North America*, 4, 123–168.

Jackson, W. R., Roose, S. P., & Glassman, A. H. (1987). Cardiovascular toxicity and tricyclic antidepressants. *Biomedicine and Pharmacotherapy*, 41(7), 377–382.

Klein, R. G., Kolcwicz, I I. S., & Kanner, A. (1992). Imipramine treatment of children with separation anxiety disorder. *Journal of the American Academy of Child and Adolescent Psychiatry*, 31(1), 21–28.

Law, S. F., & Schacher, R. J. (1999). Do typical clinical doses of methylphenidate cause tics in children treated for attention-deficit hyperactivity disorder? *Journal of the American Academy of Child and Adolescent Psychiatry*, 38(8), 944–951.

Leckman, J. F., Ort, S., & Caruso, K. A. (1986). Rebound phenomena in Tourette's syndrome after abrupt withdrawal of clonidine. *Archives of General Psychiatry*, 43, 1168–1176.

Lynskey, M. T., Hall, W. (2001). Attention deficit hyperactivity disorder and substance use disorders: Is there a causal link? *Addiction*, 96(6), 815–822.

Masi, H., Mucci, M., & Millipiedi, S. (2001). Separation anxiety disorder in children and adolescents: Epidemiology, diagnosis and management. *CNS Drugs*, 15(2), 93–104.

Pelham, W. E., Jr., Wheeler, T., & Chronia, A. (1998). Empirically supported psychosocial treatments for attention deficit hyperactivity disorder. *Journal of Clinical Child Psychology*, 27(2), 190–205.

Piacentini, J., & Bergman, R. L. (2000). Obsessive-compulsive disorder in children. *Psychiatry Clinics of North America*, 23(3), 519–33.

Popper, C. W. (1997). Antidepressants in the treatment of attention-deficit/hyperactivity disorder. *Journal of Clinical Psychiatry*, 58 (Suppl. 14), 14–29; discussion 30-1.

Putnum, F. W., & Hulsmann, J. E. (2002). Pharmacotherapy for survivors of childhood trauma. *Seminars in Clinical Neuropsychiatry*, 7(2), 129–136.

Riddle, M. A., Lynch, K. A., Scahill, L., de Vries, A., Cohen, D. J., & Leckman, J. F. (1995). Methylphenidate discontinuation and reinitiation during long-term treatment of children with Tourette's disorder and attention-deficit hyperactivity disorder: A pilot study. *Journal of Child and Adolescent Psychopharmacology*, 5, 205–214.

Rowland, A. S., Lesesne, C. A., & Abramowitz, A. J. (2002). The epidemiology of attention-deficit/hyperactivity disorder (ADHD): A public health view. *Mental Retardation and Developmental Disabilities Research Reviews*, 8(3), 162–170.

Scahill, L., Chappell, P. B., Kim, Y. S., Schultz, R. T., Katsovich, L., Shepard, E., Arnsten, A. F., Cohen, D. J., & Leckman, J. F. (2001). A placebo-controlled study of guanfacine in the treatment of children with tic disorders and attention deficit hyperactivity disorder. *American Journal of Psychiatry*, 158(7), 1067–1074.

Shevell, M., & Schreiber, R. (1997). Pemoline-associated hepatic failure: A critical analysis of the literature. *Pediatric Neurology*, 16(1), 14–16.

Spencer, T., Biederman, J., Wilens, T., Steingard, R., & Geist, D. (1993). Nortriptyline treatment of children with attention-deficit hyperactivity disorder and tic disorder or Tourette's syndrome. *Journal of the American Academy of Child and Adolescent Psychiatry*, 32, 205–210.

Steingard, R., Biederman, J., Spencer, T., Wilens, T., & Gonzalez, A. (1993), Comparison of clonidine response in the treatment of attention-deficit hyperactivity disorder with and without comorbid tic disorders. *Journal of the American Academy of Child and Adolescent Psychiatry*, 32, 350–353.

Stubbe, D. E., & Weiss, G. (2000). Psychosocial interventions. Individual psychotherapy with the child, and family interventions. *Child and Adolescent Psychiatry Clinics of North America*, 9(3), 663–670.

Tapert, S. F., Baratta, M. V., Abrantes, A. M., & Brown S. A. (2002). Attention dysfunction predicts substance involvement in community youths. *Journal of the American Academy of Child and Adolescent Psychiatry*. 41(6), 680–684.

Webster-Stratton, C., & Hammond, M. (1990). Predictors of treatment outcome in parent training for families with conduct problem children. *Behavioral Therapy*, 21, 319–337.

Weinberg, H. A. (1999). Parent training for attention-deficit hyperactivity disorder: Parental and child outcome. *Journal of Clinical Psychology*, 55(7), 907–913.

Zeiner, P. (1995). Body growth and cardiovascular function after extended treatment (1.75 years) with methylphenidate in boys with attention-deficit hyperactivity disorder. *Journal of Child and Adolescent Psychopharmacology*, 5, 129–138.

## CHAPTER 13

Complementary Therapeutic Interventions: Neurofeedback, Metacognition, and Nutrition for Long-Term Improvement in Attention Deficit Hyperactivity Disorder[1]

Lynda Thompson

INTRODUCTION

What parents want for their children, and what adults with attentional problems want for themselves, is the ability to manage their symptoms in a positive way for long-term success. This chapter introduces three interventions: neurofeedback, cognitive strategies, and nutritional considerations, which have the potential for making a difference, not just for 4 to 8 hours, but for a lifetime. All three approaches are without negative side effects and are based on learning. With neurofeedback you learn what it

---

[1] With respect to nomenclature, the term attention deficit hyperactivity disorder with the three subtypes inattentive (IN), hyperactive/impulsive(HI), and combined(CB) was adopted in the 1994 revision of the DSM-IV. It is fine for defining research criteria but is, in the author's experience, more cumbersome in everyday practice than the term attention deficit disorder (ADD modified as being with or without hyperactivity), which was used in the DSM-III published in 1980. ADHD tends to leave parents somewhat confused if the child does not have the hyperactive symptoms. This chapter thus uses the older term (ADD), although ADHD is used if citing research that uses that acronym.

feels like to concentrate using computerized feedback about what your brain waves are doing. With metacognition you learn how to learn; i.e., you become aware of how you plan, gain knowledge, and remember things. With nutrition you learn how to eat properly. All three interventions can be used with a range of clients, from those who have a true disorder (remembering that an ADHD diagnosis requires that their daily functioning is impaired to a clinically significant degree due to the symptoms) through to those who want to improve performance to attain optimal functioning.

Neurofeedback is appropriate because those with attention deficit disorder have brain wave patterns that are different. They are not abnormal but they are immature. These patterns can be changed toward more mature patterns with training (Mann et al., 1992; Monastra et al., 1999; Sterman, 2000). Metacognition is particularly helpful in those with ADD because they tend to be impulsive rather than reflective in their thinking. Thus they have to be taught to use cognitive strategies that help them stop and think. Nutritional changes make sense because evidence shows that a change in diet is beneficial to those children with ADHD who have sensitivities to certain foods or additives (Arnold, 1998).

None of these interventions are stand alone and all three can be combined with each other, with medication, and with other approaches that help manage symptoms. There is no cure and, indeed, ADD is not a disease in the usual sense where you are looking for a cure. It is, rather, a constellation of symptoms and a style of interacting with the environment that has both positive and negative aspects. The goal is to manage the negative ones and channel the energy in positive directions. There are many wonderful traits observed in association with being more in your

---

Using ADD underscores attentional weaknesses being the main problem. Hyperactivity, however, is the symptom that improves most noticeably with the administration of a stimulant drug. Perhaps the adoption of ADHD by the American Psychiatric Association was, in part, a recognition that it is those hyperactive and impulsive children who are the focus of research. Russell Barkley, a noted researcher and writer in the field of ADHD, actually states at the beginning of his lectures and in his writing (Barkley, 1998) that he is not talking about the inattentive type. Similarly, in the book, *Stimulant Drugs and ADHD*, the author notes in the first chapter that "this book is largely concerned with the CB type" (Solanto, 2001). In the authors own clinic, where parents and clients can self-refer and where there is thus the luxury of seeing more of the ADD cases without hyperkinesis and without comorbidity with oppositional defiant disorder or conduct disorder, we work with many of the "ADHD, inattentive type." This doubtless reinforces the authors bias toward using ADD as the umbrella term in clinical work, though the authors respects the needs of researchers who must use the latest terminology from the *Diagnostic and Statistical Manual of Mental Disorders*.

own world: more spontaneous, more creative, a good sense of humor, and more persistent when keen on something. If we called these traits the Edison syndrome, after Thomas Edison who clearly had attention deficit disorder, then people would be reminded of the positive instead of the bothersome aspects of this style.

There are other important lifestyle factors, in particular, sleep and exercise, that are also of particular importance for those with ADD but are beyond the scope of this chapter. For an excellent discussion of the former, read *The Promise of Sleep* by William Dement, the physician who set up the first sleep laboratory in the United States. Exercise improves blood flow to the brain, acts as an antidote to depression, and puts the energy of the ADD child to productive use. Obviously needed but not always achieved easily is a positive environment for the child, both at home and at school. These children need to be treated with respect or the damage to self-esteem can compound their difficulties so management techniques (behavior modification) are also very important. A book that covers a multimodal approach to parenting the child with attentional differences, with chapters on managing behavior, setting up for success at home and school, neurofeedback, and diet, is *The A.D.D. Book: New Understandings, New Approaches to Parenting Your Child* by pediatrician William Sears and myself.

Before commencing the more detailed descriptions of these three non-medication interventions for ADHD, here is a brief discussion of why we need to go beyond medications in the first place.

WHY NOT JUST USE MEDICATIONS?

The major limitation of the use of medications is stated succinctly in the American Medical Association's 1998 council report on diagnosis and treatment of ADHD, which states "It is important to emphasize that pharmacotherapy alone, while highly effective for short-term symptomatic improvement, has not yet been shown to improve the long-term outcome for any domain of functioning (classroom behavior, learning, impulsivity, etc.)."

This echoes the findings of a review of articles concerning stimulant medication done by James Swanson and colleagues in 1993. They concluded that what one should expect of stimulants is the short-term management of behavior and noted that research did not support the expectation of academic gains or improvement in social skills when medication is discontinued.

There is abundant literature on medication effects in the treatment of ADHD; indeed, it is the best researched area in all of child psychiatry. This is appropriate, as the introduction in the program and abstracts from the National Institutes of Health Consensus Development Conference held in November 1998 began with the sentence, "Attention deficit hyperactivity disorder, or ADHD, is the most common behavioral disorder of childhood, estimated to affect 3 to 5 per cent of school-age children." When it came to treatment, presentations at that conference were overwhelmingly about medication, although there was one review by Eugene Arnold on treatment alternatives and one by William Pelham on psychosocial interventions. Arnold concluded that both diet and biofeedback had enough evidence that they warranted further research with a sham-controlled trial, which is discussed later.

Drugs are effective in most cases: 70 to 75% of children with the diagnosis and about 50% of preschoolers and adults have a positive response to the acute administration of a stimulant (Barkley, 1998; Goldman et al., 1998; Greenhill, 1998). Methylphenidate (Ritalin) has a rapid onset of action (1.5 hours), although the duration (4 hours) is short (Swanson, 2001). Medications are a necessary component of management for children who require immediate crisis intervention. Examples of those who need a fast-acting form of chemical restraint would be those children with extreme hyperactivity who cannot stay in their seat, are being isolated or sent to the principal's office regularly, or those who are so impulsive and managed by the moment that there is actual danger, such as running out onto the road.

Longer-acting stimulant medications, such as Concerta, which is a paste form of methylphenidate, have been developed and are increasingly popular but there is still a down side: some children do not respond favorably, some actually get worse, some have unacceptable side effects (appetite suppression, stomach and headaches, insomnia), and some have other conditions that may worsen with the administration of stimulants, such as tics or heart problems. The biggest limitation is that the child is back to where he started when the drug wears off, an observation made by Charles Bradley, the first to experiment with stimulants for children. He used benzedrine with 30 children with a variety of behavioral disorders severe enough to require hospitalization. Bradley wrote the following concerning the changes in school performance. "The improvement . . . appeared promptly the first day benzedrine was given and disappeared on the first day it was discontinued." Thus the limitation is the same today as it was in 1937: the child has not learned to manage symptoms by himself. Perhaps he is a little worse off if he is among those who have rebound effects. Finally, although the action of psychostimulants is starting to be understood (Grace, 2001; Arnsten, 2001; Swanson & Volkow, 2001), the long-term effects of chronic stimulant use have not been studied.

NEUROFEEDBACK

Overview

Neurofeedback for ADD (also called neurotherapy, EEG biofeedback, or brain wave biofeedback) involves learning how to shift brain wave patterns in order to produce a mental state associated with being calm and focused. Psychologists call it operant conditioning of brain waves. Basic research done back in the 1960s established that it was possible to train the brain by rewarding the production of certain brain wave patterns (Sterman, 1996). This initial research was done with animals, especially cats. With cats, they used a reward of milk and chicken broth and the animals learned to produce particular rhythms in the electroencephalogram (EEG) in order to get that reward. With humans, one does not use food but just information as the reward. When the person knows they are being successful, as shown by computerized feedback, then they are more likely to produce particular brain wave patterns again. Without being able to articulate how they do it, the individual, using neurofeedback, learns what it feels like to be calm, to concentrate, and to maintain their focus even for boring tasks.

The advantage of neurofeedback over other effective interventions, such as medication or behavior modification, is that neurofeedback does generalize. The effects are seen not just while the person's brain activity is being monitored and they are getting feedback in the form of auditory and visual displays on the computer, but after enough training (usually at least 40 sessions), the differences are evident at home, in school, and on the playing field. Additionally, the benefits appear to last. One study has a 10-year follow-up (Lubar, 1995). A description of neurofeedback and the research behind it will help elucidate how this training fits into the overall management of ADD and explain why it is worth the time and expense to change neuronal firing patterns in the brain as evidenced by EEG changes. It empowers the person, either adult or child, to be in control rather than continue through life with others having to constantly adjust the environment to suit the person with ADD in order that they be successful.

Scientific Basis for Neurofeedback

People with the diagnosis of ADD (or ADHD) pay attention differently and there are also differences in their brain function and structure. The EEG shows more slow wave (theta) activity in central and frontal locations (Mann et al., 1992; Jantzen & Fitzsimmons, 1995). The frontal region of the brain is involved in the executive functions that include planning, inhibiting what is inappropriate, and problem solving.

Other brain imaging techniques show the same lack of activation in the frontal lobes, whether it is using PET (positron emmission tomography) scans for glucose metabolism (Zametkin, 1991) or SPECT (single photo emmission computed tomography) scans that show decreased perfusion (blood flow) to the frontal region (Amen, 2001). The increased theta activity parallels other aspects of immaturity in those with ADD because having these brain waves dominant is the normal pattern for young children. If you see that pattern in older children and adults you know they will have short attention spans, almost like preschoolers or primary grade children, even though they may have very high intelligence and great reasoning skills. You can compare the amount of slow wave activity in non-ADHD as compared to those with ADHD using a ratio that compares the amount of slow wave activity as compared to fast wave activity, a so-called theta beta ratio (Monastra et al., 2000).

Another avenue of research involves using 19 channels of EEG information to produce brain maps and, once again, there are distinct patterns seen in those with ADD. These QEEG techniques are especially helpful in complicated cases, such as those who have learning disabilities as well as ADD, in people who have had head injuries and subsequently developed problems paying attention, or in those who suffer from epilepsy and are also hyperactive. Whenever doing neurofeedback, one should plan which frequencies to train (theta, alpha, sensorimotor rhythm, or beta) according to an initial assessment that will typically include history taking, computerized continuous performance tests (such as the TOVA (test of variables of attention) or IVA (intermediate visual and auditory continuos pertormance test)), questionnaires (preferably parent and teacher), and EEG data. The EEG can be either a single channel or a 19 channel recording depending on the complexity of the presenting symptoms.

Learning Self-regulation

The goal of neurofeedback is to have the person in control of their activity level, their concentration, and their ability to stop and think before taking action. In other words, learning to shift your brain wave patterns leads to self-regulation of behavior, both outward behavior and the inner behavior of thinking and planning. Michael Lyon's personal experience with neurofeedback, as mentioned in his book *Healing the Hyperactive Brain*, recounts his shift from being a marginal student with ADHD to being a top student in science who got early acceptance into medical school. Writing in 2000 he notes, "The skills I learned through neurofeedback in the 1970s are still at my disposal." His book is about functional medicine approaches to helping ADD with a main emphasis on diet and the immune system, and he also sees neurofeedback as playing a role in overcoming limitations associated with ADHD.

ADD is not just about limitations. A positive analogy for understanding how those with ADD pay attention is Thom Hartmann's idea of hunters in a farmer's world. Neurofeedback training allows those with the hunter mind (good at scanning for something to go after and then locking on to go after it) to learn how to pay attention like a farmer and get on with routine chores. There are also some areas where the hunters have the edge; e.g., although most children with ADD will do better in individual sports than in team sports, there are many talented athletes among people with this diagnosis. Boys diagnosed with ADD make great goalies, which the author first noted when assessing hyperactive boys when doing doctoral research in the 1970s. The goalie does not have to pay attention to strategy in the dressing room and he may daydream when the action is at the other end of the ice, but as soon as the puck crosses the blue line he is in hyperfocus and not even screaming fans can ruin his concentration. Parents are proud of their goalie, but they get frustrated when the same hyperfocus occurs in front of the TV or computer and they have to call him 10 times before he finally comes for dinner. When children learn to self-regulate using neurofeedback, they keep the positive aspects of ADD and learn how to manage the bothersome symptoms. They are really learning how to have mental flexibility and switch from one mental state to another as needed. It is like using all the gears when driving a car instead of just the low gears.

Neurofeedback Procedures

Everyone is constantly producing electricity as the neurons in the brain (pyramidal cells) communicate with each other and the EEG provides a method of monitoring that activity. It is no more invasive than putting a temperature-sensitive strip across a child's forehead to see if they have a fever. To put the sensors in place and achieve good impedance readings (indicating a good connection between electrode and skin), the child's hair is parted neatly on the top of the head and a dab of conductive paste is put on the scalp where a small spot has been cleaned gently using a mildly abrasive gel. A sensor smaller than a dime is placed on the conductive paste. Small clip-on electrodes are similarly placed on the ear lobes, one to act as an electrically less active reference point and one as a ground. Wires from the three electrodes are attached by a short cable to a sensitive electronic filter and amplifier, and a sophisticated computer program allows the child to see his own brain waves on the monitor screen.

The trainer helps the child understand the wave patterns and how focused concentration, fidgeting, and opening and closing the eyes all make changes in the various video displays that depend on EEG wave patterns. The game-like displays allow the child to play a computer game just using their concentration: if they stay focused, the game moves. It might involve a fish going through a maze, or a car that morphs, or simple bar graphs depending on the program used. If they tune out, the game stops. The child's attentiveness thus controls what happens on the screen.

Children understand the analogy that exercise for the brain is like exercise for the body. You do not feel immediate changes but things improve with practice over time. A gymnast or martial arts expert trains their body and their mind; indeed, neurofeedback can be used not just to treat deficiencies in attention, but also to help athletes attain a mental edge. With both concentration and sports the skill must in part become automatic (unconscious), although conscious metacognitive strategies (learning skills and "tricks") are also taught. With neurofeedback the student is exercising the nerve pathways that control attention and mental processing. As these neural pathways are exercised, students develop a sense of what concentration feels like and, after practicing these exercises over a period of time, the pathways involved in attention and learning seem to work more efficiently. This enhanced brain activity becomes a natural part of the child's functioning. It makes possible things that were very difficult before training. One young man who did training during the summer before going to university said, "Now I can do the grunt work," meaning pages of math questions or memory work for his pharmacology course. A teenager who had taken Ritalin for 7 years and became able to attend high school off medication reported, "For the first time in my life, I feel in control." The student's attention span improved significantly by training to increase particular brain wave frequencies (beta activity between 16 and 20 Hz) while carrying out assigned tasks. Daydreaming is decreased by training to decrease the production of slow waves (theta activity in the 4- to 8-Hz range). Fidgeting and hyperactivity are decreased by training the child to increase their sensorimotor rhythm activity (12- to 15-Hz range). The particular frequency ranges and placement of electrodes are chosen for each client according to their own initial brain wave patterns and profile of symptoms.

How about Research?

The field of neurofeedback came out of the research laboratories, and there is always a need for more research. The question is what kind of research is appropriate. Research is expensive and drug companies (who have little interest in a nondrug alternative) sponsor much of the research in the field of ADHD. Even the more neutral granting bodies, such as the National Institutes of Health, have on their grant review committees those who have received funds from drug manufacturers and are thus more comfortable with the paradigms for medication studies. Indeed, some of them have stated that neurofeedback is "scientifically unproven," which, translated into practical terms, simply means no double-blind, placebo-controlled studies. That model is not, however, the design that is appropriate for studying neurofeedback because it is very difficult to design a sham control condition in order to have a placebo condition. You cannot just produce a sugar pill version of neurofeedback the way one can for a short-acting drug. Because neurofeedback is based on the person receiving information about their own physiology, there is a large component of self-awareness involved. People readily recognize if the feedback does not reflect their mental state. Niels Bierbaumer at the University of Tuebingen in southern Germany gave up on one placebo-controlled study because everyone in the control group recognized that they were not getting true feedback (personal communication).

A better way to judge the effectiveness of neurofeedback is with outcome studies, including comparing groups who receive neurofeedback with those who receive medication. One such study showed that neuro-feedback had equal efficacy with Ritalin for symptom management (Rossiter & LaVaque, 1995). When pre- and posttestings are done on those that receive neurofeedback, the findings are of decreased ADD symptoms, as shown by computerized continuous performance tests such as the TOVA, improved performance on intelligence measures with gains of at least 10 points on IQ tests, and improvement on academic measures (Lubar, 1995; Linden et al., 1996; Thompson & Thompson, 1998). In the final analysis, it is again like the exercise analogy: one observes healthy outcomes with these procedures and that is what counts with clients. As that clinical evidence mounts it will be hard to continue to be critical. Then research can focus on how to do neurofeedback most efficiently and how to deliver it to more people at less cost.

Organizations Concerned with Neurofeedback

A number of groups hold conferences and provide training in the field, including the Association for Applied Psychophysiology and Biofeedback (www.aapb.org), the Society for Neuronal Regulation (www.snr-jnt.org), and the Winter Brain Meeting organized each year by Futurehealth (www.futurehealth.com). All three promote education in the field. There are some university courses as well, such as an undergraduate course taught by David Kaiser at the Rochester Institute of Technology, pro-grams at North Texas University, or, at the graduate level, courses through the California School of Professional Psychology. The Biofeedback Foundation of Europe (www.bfe.org) was established to provide educational opportunities concerning both regular biofeedback and neurofeedback and they sponsor an annual meeting in Europe as well as supporting workshops and presentations in North America.

Since 1991 there has been accreditation for practitioners of biofeedback through the Biofeedback Certification Institute of America (www.bcia.org), and in 1996 they added specialty certification in EEG biofeedback. They maintain a state-by-state and international listing of people doing neurofeedback (and also those doing general biofeedback) who uphold their standards and have met certification criteria, which include a professional background in a health related field (psychologists, nurses, doctors, occupational therapists, etc.), supervised experience, didactic instruction, and successful completion of a written examination. Awareness and the provision of neurofeedback are growing internationally with branches of the AAPB and the SNR in Australia as well.

Parents looking for service can contact the BCIA through their web site or by mail, sending a stamped envelope with return address, to find a practitioner. The address is 10200 West 44th Avenue, Suite 310, Wheat Ridge, CO 80033-2840. There are also many practitioners who are not yet certified and then it is appropriate to ask what their training has been and what their experience is with children who have ADD.

METACOGNITION

Metacognition refers to executive thinking strategies. The term came into use in the mid-1970s, but the phenomenon is well known to any good instructor or, for that matter, any talented student. It is thinking that goes beyond (*meta* in Greek) regular *cognition* (perceiving, thinking, remembering) and involves being consciously aware of how one learns and remembers things. The techniques can be learned for specific tasks, such as how to approach a particular kind of math problem, and the approach should then generalize to other learning tasks. Good students seem to figure them out and apply them by themselves, but those with ADD benefit from direct instruction in metacognitive strategies.

The part of the brain most involved in metacognition is the prefrontal cortex where our executive functions such as planning and inhibition reside. As noted earlier, ADD is primarily a diagnosis made in those with less activation in the frontal lobes (slower EEG, less glucose metabolism, less blood flow) and so it is not surprising that these strategies are less developed. The frontal lobes are still maturing into the second decade of life so the use of metacognitive strategies parallels maturation. Specific coaching and modeling of this style of thinking are needed in those with ADD.

The basics of metacognition involve three steps: (1) figuring out what the job is, (2) deciding on how to do the job, and (3) monitoring how you are doing as you implement your strategy. The last evaluation step is an important component as it encourages the person to learn from experience, something that seems harder for those with ADD. There is no published catalogue of metacognitive strategies, they simply involve doing a kind of task analysis of the components of a job and then getting on with completing the task and seeing how things work out. It can be applied at any level, from reading readiness skills to writing a thesis in graduate school.

The latter example comes to mind because one of our clients at the ADD center was a bright and vivacious woman who simply had not been able to finish her Master's degree because she could not get her thoughts organized on paper to finish the thesis requirement. The research was all done and analyzed but for months she had been unable to get the writing done. We (1) analyzed the job (write a certain number of chapters with the following headings . . .), (2) decided on a way to break it down into small steps (outline chapter 1, and dozens more steps going through to putting the references in alphabetical order), and (3) monitored the progress through writing the draft, polishing it, and doing the final copy (one-third of the allotted time for each of those writing steps). By monitoring herself she learned which techniques worked best; e.g., dictating the draft as compared to writing it on the computer. When she spoke to me after her training was complete (yes, the thesis got done) she remarked that her head used to be as busy as our international airport with ideas coming and going, but now the ideas were just as many and as creative but it was like an airport with a control tower.

Active reading strategies are among the most important metacognitive strategies. If must be stressed that you have to have a personal reason for reading the passage in the first place or you will drift off in the first paragraph. Before you even open the book you must come up with ideas and questions regarding what you want to learn and what you expect to find in the text. With that prepared mind you are ready to organize information. Once you open the book you skim the contents, paying special attention to headings and illustrations, which helps generate more questions. Only then do you actually begin reading and, while reading, you keep actively involved by making mental summaries, jot notes, underlining, connecting the new information to things already known, making sketches or putting information into a grid, picturing what you read, and coming up with mnemonic devices to remember series of things (like acronyms, such as HOMES for the names of the Great Lakes). After reading you review both what you have read and which of the techniques you used worked best. If someone has never before tried to put all the facts into a funny picture that can be a powerful addition to their strategies repertoire.

Even very basic tasks benefit from a metacognitive approach. Children with ADD are prone to making careless errors, such as adding when the sign says subtract or not answering the question that was asked. If they get in the habit of asking themselves, "What's the job here?" then they are less likely to jump in impulsively and do the wrong thing. Say the question is 6 − 4 = ?. Then the "job" is to subtract. The next step is to decide on the strategy: count on your fingers, add on from 4 up to 6, count backward four numbers from six, make six tally marks and cross off four of them, find six things (fish in your desk for old bits of erasers) and take away four, use a number line that the teacher stuck to your desk, etc. After you finish, hopefully arriving at 2 for an answer, you check how you did and think about (evaluate) what you did. Maybe getting out the bits of eraser got you in trouble with the teacher or took too long and you ended up missing part of recess. Maybe you discovered that adding on was easier and more accurate than counting backward. You decide you will try that method for the next subtraction question. Taking a little time to use a metacognitive approach will save time in the long run. It also reduces procrastination because you know what the first step is as you always start by defining the job.

In addition to metacognition, specific cognitive areas can benefit from a tune-up, and there are specific computer software programs designed to enhance such functions as reaction time, visual discrimination, and spatial reasoning, to name but a few. Similarly, there is abundant software for training specific academic skills, such as the LEXIA program that uses a multisensory approach to teaching phonemic awareness and building reading skills. All these things can be combined with the mix being dictated by the unique needs of each individual child.

NEUROFEEDBACK + METACOGNITION

Combining neurofeedback and metacognition is the approach that holds particular excitement for the author because of first-hand experience in the last decade with the effectiveness of this combination in hundreds of clients from the kindergarten level to age 63 years. When a chart review was done concerning 111 clients seen during the first years of operation of the author's ADD center, significant improvements were documented in behavior measured by a continuous performance test (TOVA), intellectual functioning measured by the Wechsler scales, and academic levels on the wide range achievement test. There were also EEG changes in the direction of more mature patterns (Thompson & Thompson, 1998). This replicated the findings of other researchers (Linden et al., 1996; Lubar,

1995, 1997; Lubar & Lubar, 1999). The greatest contribution to the field of neurofeedback applications for ADD has come from a physiological psychologist, Joel Lubar, who is a professor at the University of Tennessee. He and his wife, Judith, who is a social worker and gifted therapist, have spent over 25 years teaching and training about the use of neurofeedback for ADD. They report a 90% success rate with these methods at their southeastern biofeedback institute.

NUTRITION

Nutrition is part of learning good lifestyle habits. Obviously eating the foods that support optimal functioning for the brain and the body is important for everyone. The optimal diet will differ from person to person due to individual differences. There is evidence that subgroups of people who show ADHD symptoms may have particular dietary challenges. These occur largely in three areas: food sensitivities; deficiencies of important nutrients, such as essential fatty acids; or too much of certain toxins, such as lead or mercury (reviewed by Hill & Castro, 2002). Parents of children with ADD need to have a higher level of awareness of nutritional issues, especially if there is hyperactivity or behavior problems that seem to be triggered by certain foods, the so-called food–mood connection (Sears & Thompson, 1998).

Good nutrition is something that can be regarded as common sense, although as Covey has said in his books about successful habits, common sense is not always common practice. Children with ADD are often the ones who are hard to get up in the morning and then they are rushed and more likely to skip breakfast or eat a suboptimal one. Then they feel hungry and have a sweet snack during their first break, which then produces the sugar-high, sugar-low phenomenon. When the blood sugar levels go down (hypoglycemia), then the body reacts with the release of stress hormones to increase the blood sugar, which can contribute to diminished attention and behavior problems. The effect can be so sudden and dramatic that ski coaches the author knows will not allow their young racers to go on the course if they have eaten a chocolate bar. Such snacks are only for after the race.

Studies indicate that essential fatty acid deficiencies are more common in those with ADD who are hyperactive, have dry skin or hair, excessive thirst, and frequent urination. Trying supplements and foods rich in omega-3 fatty acids from sources such as fish oils, ground flaxseed, and flax oil, cold water fish such as salmon, soybeans, eggs, and evening primrose oil makes more sense as a first intervention than prescribing a stimulant drug in such children (reviewed by Sears & Sears, 1999; Hill & Castro, 2002). Iron deficiency is another thing to watch for as insufficient iron can lead to ADD symptoms. Low iron levels have been linked to poor math performance, and levels do not have to be so low as to indicate anemia for the effects to be measurable. Adolescent females are particularly prone to being iron deficient. Only give iron supplements if serum ferritin levels are low (a more sensitive test than checking hemoglobin), as iron can build up in the body and can even be toxic at high levels. Taking a balanced multivitamin, multimineral supplement makes sense for all children, as research shows that it improves school performance, behavior, and even IQ scores. Megavitamin therapy, however, has not been shown to be helpful (Arnold, 1998). The basic nutritional supplements recommended by Michael Lyons in his book *Healing the Hyperactive Brain* include antioxidants (vitamins C and E and grape seed extract), a multivitamin/multimineral supplement, plus extra calcium and magnesium, and an essential fatty acid supplement.

Supplements have a place but a balanced diet should be at the core of a healthy lifestyle. It should start with breast feeding, which conveys a protective advantage against hyperactive symptoms (Sears & Sears, 1999). Breast milk is rich in essential fatty acids needed to build healthy brains and, in particular, it is used in the production of myelin, which allows for a faster transmission of messages in the nervous system. There are no essential fatty acids in most formulas in the United States, although there are in Japan. At any age, breakfast is important and should include milk or some other source of calcium (since that mineral has calming effects on behavior) and have a balance between complex carbohydrates and protein. Try eggs, toast, yogurt, and orange juice or granola cereal with milk and a piece of fruit. Be aware of the glycemic index of different foods, the rate at which a sugar enters the cells of the body. The gastrointestinal tract determines how much the pancreas is stimulated to release the insulin that causes the sugar to empty from the blood into the cells. Steady blood sugar levels are needed for more even moods and behavior. Eating frequently (grazing rather than gorging) also helps mood and behavior to be more even. Avoiding fast food and the wrong kinds of fat (anything that says "hydrogenated") is just as important as having the right kind of fat. Healthy fats come from sources such as seafood, vegetable oils, nuts, soybeans, avocados, and flaxseed.

Not just food but water is important. Dehydration can impair concentration. It is thus obviously important to drink enough fluids each day. The high activity level of many children with ADD makes this particularly important because they will become dehydrated as they are running around or doing sports and yet they may not want to take the time to have a drink if they are hyperfocused on their chosen activity. Studies with skiers, who are less likely to realize they are perspiring and losing water because they are out in the cold, have shown that they not only perform better but they enjoy themselves more when they drink water (from a small backpack equipped with a plastic tube) as they travel up the chairlift between runs. Sometimes parents resent a child who is cranky at the end of a wonderful excursion, but if they did not take enough liquid refreshment for that day at the beach or the amusement park, they should not be too quick to blame the child, as dehydration is probably contributing to the negative mood. Adults need one-half to three-fourths of an ounce of water per pound per day (eight 8-ounce glasses if you weigh 120 pounds) and more is required if you are exercising or the weather is hot. Thirst is not a good indicator of when you need to drink, so if you rely on the child to drink enough according to thirst, he probably will not be hydrated adequately. Anything that contributes to a more positive mood *and* better brain function *and* muscles that tire less quickly is obviously a bonus, so keep the water bottles handy.

Even if food and water intake is healthy, you may have to watch out for toxins that produce learning and behavior problems. Heavy metals, especially lead and mercury, are common culprits that produce symptoms that mimic ADD. A study done in Ottawa, Canada, in the days before unleaded gasoline was introduced showed that children identified as having LD problems tended to live nearest the main highway. Charts showing the increase in the use of Ritalin since 1985 and the increase in children's exposure to mercury during the same time period can be superimposed on one another and they look almost identical. Some children may be more vulnerable to the buildup of heavy metals in their bodies, particularly mercury, due to differences in absorbtion and excretion so some individuals are more at risk, not only for ADD symptoms but also perhaps for autistic spectrum disorders (Bradstreet, 2002). Certainly the author's own clinical experience has been that there are more children presenting with Asperger's syndrome in the last few years and most of them were initially diagnosed as having ADHD. Heavy metals are the most obvious toxins; if levels are measured and found to be high, then medical treatments such as chelation should be undertaken.

More subtle than toxic exposure is the question of food sensitivities and allergies. There seem to be higher rates of both in children with ADD. If a child always seems stuffy or displays the dark circles under his eyes that pediatricians have nicknamed allergy shiners then you should suspect food or environmental sensitivities. An elimination diet can usually identify the former; e.g., remove dairy products for 2 weeks and see if the child's stuffy nose problem is eliminated. Bill Sears in *The Family Nutrition Book* suggests trying first to eliminate "the nasty nine": dairy products, soy, egg whites, wheat, peanuts, tree nuts, citrus fruits, shellfish, and food additives (monosodium glutamate, artificial color, preservatives). These account for over 90% of food allergies. Allergies certainly affect attention, as anyone with hay fever can tell you in the fall: just when they have to return to school the allergy to ragweed is worst. Allergies can mimic ADD symptoms or a child can have both ADD and allergies so that he has a double challenge.

CONCLUSION

The wave of the future will certainly be brain wave training, as people realize that empowering students through neurofeedback—having them learn the skill of being calm and concentrating—is both cost effective and good for self-esteem. Everyone is happier when the energy that used to get the child in trouble is channeled in positive ways. With neurofeedback training the child finally pays attention to paying attention. Add in metacognition and they learn how to learn. Give them proper nutrition and they have the right fuel on which to run their minds and bodies. The positive traits of ADD are still there—the creativity, sense of humor, spontaneity, the ability to scan for something of interest, and the switch to hyperfocus when pursuing that interest—but now they have the ability to concentrate in the middle zone. They have trained their brains and have more flexible minds so that they can use their potential and, rather than being too much in their own world, they can make a positive contribution to the world around them.

REFERENCES

Amen, D. G. (2001). *Healing ADD.* New York: Putnam.

Amen, D. G., Carmichael, B. D., & Thisted, R. A. (1997). High-resolution brain SPECT imaging in ADHD. *Annals of Clinical Psychiatry*, 9(2), 81–86.

Arnold, E. (1998). Treatment alternatives for attention deficit hyperactivity disorder. In *Program and Abstracts of the NIH Consensus Development Conference on Diagnosis and Treatment of Attention Deficit Hyperactivity Disorder.* Bethesda, MD: National Institutes of Health.

Arnsten, A. F. T. (2001). Dopaminergic and noradrenergic influences on cognitive functions medicated by prefrontal cortex. In M. V. Solanto, A. M. T. Arnsten, & F. X. Castellanos (Eds.), *Stimulant drugs and ADHD basic and clinical neuroscience* (pp. 185–208). New York: Oxford University Press.

Barkley, R. A. (1998). *Attention deficit hyperactivity disorder: A handbook for diagnosis and treatment (2nd ed).* New York: Guilford Press.

Bradstreet, J. (2002). Personal communication regarding submission made to the U.S. Senate on increased rates of autism.

Chabot, R. J., di Michele, F., Prichep, L., & John, E. R. (2001). The clinical role of computerized EEG in the evaluation and treatment of learning and attention disorders in children and adolescents. *Journal of Neuropsychiatry and Clinical Neurosciences*, 13(2), 171–186.

Chabot, R. J., Orgill, A. A., Crawford, G., Harris, M. J., & Serfontein, G. (1999). Behavioural and electrophysiological predictors of treatment response to stimulants in children with attention disorders. *Journal of Child Neurology*, 14(6), 343–351.

Chabot, R. J., & Serfontein, G. (1996). Quantitative electroencephalographic profiles of children with attention deficit disorder. *Biological Psychiatry*, 40, 951–963.

Cheng, Pui-wan (1993). Metacognition and giftedness: The state of the relationship. *Gifted Child Quarterly*, 37(3).

Filipek, P. A., Semrud-Clikeman, M., Steingard, R. J., Rendshaw, P. F., Kennedy, D. N., & Biederman, M. D. (1997). Volumetric MRI analysis comparing attention-deficit hyperactivity disorder and normal controls. *Neurobiology*, 47, 618–628.

Frank, Y., & Pavlakis, S. G. (2001). Brain imagining in neurobehavioural disorders. *Pediatric Neurology*, 25(4), 278–287.

Goldman, L. S., Genel, M., Bezman, R., Slanetz, P. J., for the Council on Scientific Affairs, American Medical Association (1998). Diagnosis and treatment of attention-deficit/hyperactivity disorder in children and adolescents. *Journal of the American Medical Association*, 279(14), 1100–1107.

Grace, A. A. (2001). Psychostimulant actions on dopamine and limbic system function: Relevance to the psthophysiology and treatment of ADHD. In M. V. Solanto, A. M. T. Arnsten, & F. X. Castellanos (Eds.), *Stimulant drugs and ADHD basic and clinical neuroscience* (pp. 134–157). New York: Oxford Univ. Press.

Greenhill, L. L. (1998). Stimulant medications. In *Program and Abstracts of the NIH Consensus Development Conference on Diagnosis and Treatment of Attention Deficit Hyperactivity Disorder.* Bethesda, MD: National Institutes of Health.

Gruzelier, J. (2002). Neurofeedback training to enhance musical performance. *Proceedings of the Annual Meeting of the Association for Applied Psychophysiology and Biofeedback.* Las Vegas, March, 2002.

Guberman, Alan (1994). Hyperkinetic movement disorders. In A. Guberman (Ed.), *An introduction to clinical neurology.* New York: Little, Brown & Co.

Hill, R. W., & Castro, E. (2002). *Getting rid of Ritalin.* Charlottesville, VA: Hampton Roads.

Hynd, G. W., Hern, K. L., Novey, E. S., & Eliopulos, D. (1993). Attention deficit hyperactivity disorder and asymmetry of the caudate nucleus. *Journal of Child Neurology*, 8, 339–347.

Janzen, T., & Fitzsimmons, G. (1995). Differences in baseline EEG measures for ADD and normally achieving preadolescent males. *Biofeedback and Self-Regulation*, 20(1), 65–82.

John, E. R. (1989). The role of quantitative EEG topographic mapping or "neurometrics" in the diagnosis of psychiatric and neurological disorders: The pros. *Electroencephalography and Clinical Neurophysioogy*, 73, 2–4.

LaHoste, G. L., Swanson, J. M., Wigal, S. B., Glabe, C., Wigal, T., King, N., & Kennedy, J. L. (1996). Dopamine D 4 receptor gene polymorphism is associated with attention-deficit hyperactivity disorder. *Molecular Psychiatry*, 1, 121–124.

Landers, D. M., Petruzzello, S. J., Salazar, W., Crews, D. J., Kubitz, K. A., Gannon, T. L., & Han, M. (1991). The influence of electrocortical biofeedback on performance in pre-elite archers. *Medicine and Science in Sports and Exercise*, 23(1), 123–128.

Linden, M., Habib, T., & Radojevic, V. (1996). A controlled study of the effects of EEG biofeedback on cognition and behavior of children with attention deficit disorder and learning disabilities. *Biofeedback and Self Regulation*, 21(1), 106–111.

Love, A. J., & Thompson, M. G. G. (1988). Language disorders and attention deficit disorders in a child psychiatric outpatient population. *The American Journal of Orthopsychiatry*, 58(1).

Lubar, J. F. (1995). Neurofeedback for the management of attention-deficit/hyperactivity disorder. In M. S. Schwartz (Ed.), *Biofeedback: A practitioner's guide* (2nd ed., pp. 493–522). New York: Guilford Press.

Lubar, J. F. (1997). Neocortical dynamics: Implications for understanding the role of neurofeedback and related techniques for the enhancement of attention. *Applied Psychophysiology and Biofeedback*, 22(2), 111–126.

Lubar, J. F., & Lubar, J. (1999). Neurofeedback assessment and treatment for attention deficit/hyperactivity disorders. In J. R. Evans, & A. Abarbanel (Eds.), *Introduction to quantitative EEG and neurofeedback*. New York: Academic Press.

Malone, M., & Swanson, J. (1994). Hemispheric processing and methylphonidate effects in attention-deficit hyperactivity disorder. *Journal of Child Neurology*, 9(2), 181–189.

Mann, C. A., Lubar, J. F., Zimmerman, A. W., Miller, C. A., & Muenchen, R. A. (1992). Quantitative analysis of EEG in boys with attention-deficit-hyperactivity disorder: Controlled study with clinical implications. *Pediatric Neurology*, 8(1), 30–36.

Monastra, V. J., Lubar, J. F., Linden, M., VanDeusen, P., Green, G., Wing, Wm., Phillips, A., & Fenger, T. N. (1999). Assessing attention deficit hyperactivity disorder via quantitative electroencephalography: An initial validation atudy. *Neuropsychology*, 13(3), 424–433.

Munoz, D. P., Hampton, K. A., Moore, K. D., & Armstrong, I. T. (1998). Control of saccadic eye movements and visual fixation in children and adults with ADHD. In *Proceedings of the Annual Meeting of the Society for Neurosciences*. Los Angeles, CA.

Palincsar, A. S., & Brown, D. A. (1987). Enhancing instructional time through attention to metacognition. *Journal of Learning Disabilities*, 20(2).

Pavlakis, F. Y. (2001). Brain imaging in neurobehavioral disorders: Review. *Pediatric Neurology*, 25(4), 278–287.

Pelham, W. E. (1998). Psychosocial interventions. In *Program and Abstracts of the NIH Consensus Development Conference on Diagnosis and Treatment of Attention Deficit Hyperactivity Disorder*. Bethesda, MD: National Institutes of Health.

Peterson, G. (2000). Operant conditioning. In *Proceedings of the Annual Meeting of the Society for Neuronal Regulation*. Minneapolis, MN.

Robbins, J. (2000). *A symphony in the brain*. New York: Atlantic Monthly Press.

Rossiter, T. R., & LaVaque, T. J. (1995). A comparison of EEG biofeedback and psychostimulants in treating attention deficit hyperactivity disorders. *Journal of Neurotherapy*.

Sears, W., & Sears, M. (1999). *The Family Nutrition Book*. New York: Little Brown & Co.

Sears, W., & Thompson, L. (1998). *The A.D.D. Book: New understandings, new approaches to parenting your child*. New York: Little, Brown and Company.

Shouse, M. N., & Lubar, J. F. (1979). Sensorimotor rhythm (SMR) operant conditioning and methylphenidate in the treatment of hyperkinesis. *Biofeedback and Self-Regulation*, 4, 299–311.

Solanto, M. V. (2001). Attention-deficit/hyperactivity disorder: Clinical features. In M. V. Solanto, A. M. T. Arnsten, & F. X. Castellanos (Eds.), *Stimulant drugs and ADHD basic and clinical neuroscience*. New York: Oxford Univ. Press.

Sterman, M. B. (1996). Physiological origins and functional correlates of EEG rhythmic activities: Implications for self-regulation. *Biofeedback and Self-Regulation*, 21, 3–33.

Sterman, M. B. (1999). *Atlas of topometric clinical displays: Functional interpretations and neurofeedback strategies*. Los Angeles: Sterman-Kaiser Imaging Laboratory.

Sterman, M. B. (2000). EEG markers for attention deficit disorder: Pharmacological and neurofeedback applications. *Child Study Journal*, 30(1).

Swanson, J. M., McBurnett, K., Wigal, T., Pfiffner, L. J., Williams, L., Christian, D. L., Tamm, L., Willcutt, E., Crowley, K., Clevenger, W., Khouam, N., Woo, C., Crinella, F. M., & Fisher, T. M. (1993). The effect of stimulant medication on children with attention deficit disorder: A "review of reviews." *Exceptional Children*, 60(2), 154–162.

Swanson, J. M., & Volkow, N. (2001). Pharmacokinetic and pharmacodynamic properties of methylphenidate in humans. In M. V. Solanto, A. M. T. Arnsten, & F. X. Castellanos (Eds.), *Stimulant drugs and ADHD basic and clinical neuroscience* (pp. 259–282). New York: Oxford Univ. Press.

Tansey, M. A. (1993). Ten year stability of EEG biofeedback results for a hyperactive boy who failed fourth grade perpetually impaired class. *Biofeedback and Self-Regulation*, 118, 33–44.

Thatcher, R. W. (1999). EEG data base-guided neurotherapy. In J. R. Evans, & A. Abarbanel (Eds.), *Quantitative EEG and neurofeedback*. New York:Academic Press.

Thompson, L., & Thompson, M. (1998). Neurofeedback combined with training in metacognitive strategies: Effectiveness in students with ADD. *Applied Psychophysiology and Biofeedback*, 23(4), 243–263.

Thompson, L. M. (1979). *The effect of methylphenidate on self-concept and locus of control of hyperactive children*. Thesis submitted in conformity with the requirements for the Degree of Doctor of Philosophy in the University of Toronto.

Weins, W. J. (1983). Metacognition and the adolescent passive learner. *Journal of Learning Disabilities*, 16(3).

Zametkin, A. J., Nordahl, T. E., Gross, M., King, A. C., Semple, W. E., Rumsey, J. H., Hamburger, S., & Cohen, R. M. (1990). Cerebral glucose metabolism in adults with hyperactivity of childhood onset. *New England Journal of Medicine*, 323(20), 1361–1366.

## CHAPTER 14

Cognitive Training and Computers: An Innovative Approach

Joseph A. Sandford

Computer technology has made tremendous advances. Advances in technology have made it possible to develop sophisticated training programs focusing on cognitive development in children with attention deficit hyperactivity disorder (ADHD) and learning disabilities (LD). This chapter discusses the following areas: (1) cognitive training software versus educational programs and video games; (2) the advantages of computers in cognitive training; (3) cognitive training, what to train; and (4) utilizing a cognitive training system with children with ADHD and LD. This chapter combines the author's clinical knowledge and research in cognitive development and computer instruction to offer an insightful discussion on technology and its place in remediating academic and clinical goals for children with ADHD and LD.

COGNITIVE TRAINING SOFTWARE VERSUS EDUCATIONAL PROGRAMS AND VIDEO GAMES

Cognitive training software differs from educational and general computer software or video games in that it was designed for use in a synergistic "drill for skill" and meta-cognitive approach to cognitive training. This model for training cognitive skills is hierarchical, and the programs are designed to specifically target one or more specific cognitive skill. Inherent in this hierarchical system of training cognitive skills is the concept of passing a series of stages, which consist of programs with increasing more complex stimuli and requirements for "passing." Cognitive training software for children with ADHD and LD offers the opportunity to train a variety of important cognitive skills involving selective attention, problem solving, patience, mental processing speed, comprehension and remembrance of rules, frustration tolerance, and sustained attention. These aspects of cognitive training software are an important way in which it differs from educational and video game software that may train some cognitive skills in an incidental way.

Cognitive training software can be programmed to train specific cognitive skills. For example, using computer software, it is possible to train selective attention by adding visual and auditory distractions and continuously playing background sounds *during* a cognitive training exercise. The player must then discriminate relevant stimuli and feedback from irrelevant stimuli, which are also presented simultaneously. The removal of auditory and visual cues along with auditory and visual feedback can also be utilized to train frustration tolerance and the *retention* of the exercise rules. The length *of* time that an exercise task must be performed can also be varied in order to train sustained attention and patience. Higher and more difficult stages are not only more complex, but they require more time. Options can also be built in to specifically train the patience of the player by inhibiting impulsive mouse clicking or movement.

The speed of mental processing is also considered an important part of cognitive training. Individuals with ADHD and LD were found to be slower in their reaction time, more variable in their responses, and make more errors in a video game-like test of attention, particularly with their nondominant hand (Mitchell et al., 1990). The training of mental speed can be adjusted automatically for each individual. A baseline measurement of a player's mental processing speed to the specific cognitive exercise is calculated and is then adjusted faster or slower for each stimulus presented depending on whether a correct or an incorrect response is made, respectively. It will only resemble educational and video game software in that the cognitive exercises are usually somewhat game-like in format.

In contrast to cognitive training software, educational software focuses on specific academic skills that involve the mastery of relevant information pertaining to the topic (e.g., science, social studies, algebra) and the rules or procedures related to this field of study. Cognitive training software is "process oriented" and does not involve learning any new facts or procedures specific to an academic field. From one perspective, cognitive training software can be conceived of as helping an individual develop the basic processing skills necessary for later mastery of the higher level, more complex academic topic areas. For example, the training of the cognitive skills of phonemic awareness and phonics is important in the development of reading skills, and the ability to read well is essential to the successful mastery of almost all academic areas of study. In school, cognitive training software and educational software can both be incorporated in a special education program. A synergy using this integrated approach is likely to result. This successful synergy can be achieved based on the enhancement of self-esteem that often occurs when the student uses the cognitive training software and can perform a task successfully, thus developing a "winning" attitude that can easily generalize to other academic work.

Video games differ significantly from cognitive training software in that their primary purpose is to entertain. In today's video games, the theme and role-playing activities often involve acts of violence, such as shooting at monsters or other humans, brutally fighting with opponents, or blowing up the property of others. Even when a violent theme is not the basis of a video game, players are often rewarded for impulsive responding (e.g., driving a car in a careless and reckless manner) and must make thoughtless, hyperactive responses often involving poking, pushing, hitting, or running into objects in order to earn points. The most popular action video games address a very limited number of cognitive skills, which consist of mainly visual tracking, divided attention, and visual discrimination. Thus, video games are likely to be of minimal value in enhancing cognitive skills and are not designed for this purpose.

Many children with ADHD are often very talented video game players and will play these games for hours on end whenever permitted by their parents. The positive and negative impact of this behavior has been explored in the research literature to a limited degree. A search of the scientific literature did not find any studies in which playing video game skills was associated with reductions in ADHD or LD symptoms. One study did find a brief improvement in mental processing speed. Skosnik and colleagues (2000) observed a significant decrease in reaction time speed on an attention task after healthy, normal (i.e., no identified disorders) college students played 15 minutes of a stressful video game. This finding showed that after achieving a high level of arousal, individuals were quicker to respond. Research has also identified a possible reason why young people with ADHD and LD may enjoy video games so much and can sustain their attention while playing. This ability to pay attention during video games could be explained by the fact that endogenous increases in dopamine levels were observed using a positron emission tomography scan while individuals played a video game (Koepp et al.,1998). Thus, an individual's emotional arousal and motivation to pay close attention during a video game may apparently lead the metabolism of the brain to adjust by producing more dopamine. Young people who play more video games than others in the same age group have been found to be more socially immature, and those adolescents who preferred the more violent games were found to be more aggressive (Salokoski et al., 2002). Thus, frequent playing of video games may increase negative psychosocial behavior and has very limited positive benefits. They function in society as entertainment that is often mindless in nature.

The appeal of video games to children with ADHD may also be enhanced because hyperactive and impulsive responses are often rewarded and game stimuli are novel and constantly changing. Based on these scientific findings, it is recommended that most parents censor the violent video games and significantly limit the time their children spend playing the nonviolent ones.

A new concept of educational video games called edutainment has been created that blends video game-like interaction and the mastery of educational content areas such as math, reading, or science. These software programs can be effective in training problem-solving skills and academic knowledge. They are not typically designed though to target the training of specific cognitive skills, nor do they usually offer the opportunity for repetitive practice, detailed scoring, hierarchical levels of difficulty, immediate feedback, or session summary feedback. Trainers, teachers, or therapists will play few roles in the use of edutainment software, and few options are provided to direct or control what cognitive skills are trained. These edutainment games are likely to be useful in training mostly academic skills and knowledge. They help train general and higher level problem-solving cognitive skills, but are not designed to improve a wide range of cognitive skills.

The unique characteristics of well-designed cognitive training software are related to the various control options, data collected, and feedback given. A cognitive trainer needs to be able to control a number of diverse program control variables. The possible program control options include the length in time of each exercise, the level of difficulty, selection of age-appropriate stimuli, and the criterion for passing an exercise. Useful options to adapt the training protocols to the needs of persons with cognitive difficulties also include the verbal presentation of instructions for those who do not read well, clearly understandable auditory and visual feedback, visual and auditory cues to help reinforce and direct attention, and a cumulative point system for each exercise. In order to train important general cognitive skills that transcend the drill for skill approach, *various options can be programmed*. Options such as visual and auditory distractors to enhance selective attention, feedback to train mental processing speed, problem-solving (i.e., "think for yourself") challenges, and feedback for sequential repeated correct responses can be selected for implementation in cognitive training protocols. Also, feedback and cues can be selectively eliminated to require more effort and focus under purposely "boring" training conditions for the specific training of self-control "when the going gets tough" and to enhance a player's frustration tolerance. The ability to tightly control, start and stop programs, pick exercise options easily, and have numerous opportunities to provide feedback and facilitate reflective thought in the player are all important factors in the cognitive training process. These elements in software are seldom available in either video or educational software.

Cognitive training software also provides useful and detailed data to chart progress that will aid the trainer in understanding what causes a player's errors. Summary data of sessions can help the players see their progress and illustrate mastery of a potential skill. A cumulative percent grade, the current "stage" (i.e., a rating of progress and difficulty of the most recent exercise passed), time played, average reaction time, and score (i.e., typically money earned) are important variables for most players. Detailed scoring for each stage of training completed, along with specific information about relevant errors, is needed to help the cognitive trainer "tailor" and adjust the player's training program. This amount of detail in scoring or a detailed cumulative record of important error data is ever available in a video or educational game, severely limiting the application of this type of software in cognitive training.

ADVANTAGES OF COMPUTERS IN COGNITIVE TRAINING

In some form, cognitive training can go on throughout life. It is a positive, beneficial, and mentally healthy behavior in which all human beings can engage (Kotulak, 1996). Research has found that the effect of a structured cognitive training program is powerful enough to reverse aging-related declines in reasoning, memory, and mental processing speed typically observed in healthy older adults (Ball et al., 2002). Noncomputer alternatives such as crossword puzzles, find-the-hidden object picture books, card games such as concentration, motor skill games such as Operation, anagrams, math word challenges, mazes, charades, search for hidden word books, birthday party games, and TV show games such as Wheel of Fortune, Jeopardy, and Who Wants to Be a Millionaire all train various cognitive abilities in some manner. Learning to write, paint, and play sports also develops many cognitive skills. In this way, these games and exercises do enhance the mental skills of most individuals. However, when there are significant impairments in a number of cognitive skill areas, then a more intense, highly structured and comprehensive computerized approach can be beneficial. Intensive cognitive training is often required because of an accident (e.g., traumatic head injury), developmental delays caused by inherited genetic factors (e.g., LD), neurochemical imbalances in the brain biochemistry (i.e., dopamine deficiencies in ADHD or exposure to cocaine in the womb), or a disease such as a stroke. In these cases you do not need a computer to do cognitive training, but it helps!

Technological advances in computers have just begun to be applied in the field of cognitive training. Most home personal computers now have the ability to talk, sing, and can even make robots dance! Computer screen resolution and the available colors have improved dramatically since the early 1990s. The life-like display of full color photos and video is now the standard. A number of versatile input devices exist that can be adapted for almost any physical disability, including individuals who can only communicate through eye blinks. These devices are used to facilitate cognitive training by providing accommodations for a wide variety of physical limitations and disabilities. Almost all of these input devices emulate the common computer mouse input methodology. These input devices include trackballs, touch screens, mouse joysticks, touchpads, sip'n'puff mouth sticks, modified keyboards, and specialized switches. It is easily possible for a cognitive trainer to have simultaneously connected and an immediately usable optical mouse, keyboard, sip'n'puff mouth stick, PS/2 trackball, and USB touch screen. Just plug them in and play!

A number of advantages were discussed in the previous section in using computers in cognitive training. Score and record keeping, measuring response times, generating new and different cognitive exercises for drill and practice, performing summary calculations needed to measure progress, and providing acceptable immediate feedback are often very challenging using noncomputerized approaches to cognitive training. Trainers can be distracted easily by the demands to keep a score, interact, and participate with the player using noncomputerized game activities. These distractions will often make it difficult to focus on the nonverbal cues of the player and, thus, limit the trainer's ability to understand and help the individual when they may be slightly frustrated or confused. It is possible to have one trainer and an assistant to the trainer whose main purpose is to keep a score, set up the exercise material, and keep records. However, a computer can function in many ways as the more versatile "assistant." Cognitive exercise generation, record keeping, scoring, timing, and data calculations are made quickly and accurately by the computer. The computer can also store results automatically, and these data can later be displayed, printed, or analyzed to evaluate a player's progress.

In most traditional or common games, the trainer will also have to be a player, which puts him in the role of competing with the player who is supposed to be trained. In these circumstances, the trainer will often be faced with the dilemma of "faking bad" or "throwing the game" in order not to win all the time. Giving appropriate and immediate feedback in order to facilitate learning when errors are made is also difficult in social or individual game formats. There is often a negative emotional reaction on the part of most players to social statements of "that is not right," "wrong choice," "you missed," and so on even in a private setting. For most social games to function in cognitive training, other players will need to be involved so that the trainer can function in the role of a "coach" and not as a competitor. This may mean that it will be difficult without a group of individuals to plan and conduct cognitive training when using game and educational exercises provided in such cognitive training systems as REHABIT. The REHABIT program, which is a noncomputerized approach, developed by Reitan and Wolfson (1988), consists primarily of commercially available games and toys. The various training "exercises" in this cognitive rehabilitation system have been identified by the creators of REHABIT in respect to what cognitive skills are trained by each of them. However, competition and social interaction can be added easily to computerized cognitive training by having the players try to "beat the computer" (i.e., pass a stage) and the trainer can socially interact in a supportive role as their coach. While computerized cognitive training generally is implemented on a one-to-one basis, players can take turns competing with each other on the same computer or work separately on the same exercise on computers located side by side. Also, feedback from the computer, even when spoken, is not usually interpreted negatively by players, as being judged by a human. The computer is not perceived as judging them and, thus, the player is more able to use the informational aspect of the feedback provided to help them correct errors and learn how to respond more quickly.

These traditional games and their components must always be stored properly and in the case of the REHABIT system, which consists of hundreds of components, a storage room will be needed. Thus, portability of a cognitive training system that does not use a computer may be somewhat limited. With a laptop computer (which can be as powerful as a large stand-alone desktop computer), a computerized cognitive training system can be taken almost anywhere a trainer wants to go! The flexibility to adapt computerized cognitive systems is also possible. Most effectively designed programs are developed with many options and different stages of difficulty in order to handle individual differences. The stimuli and order of presentation using computerized exercises can be randomly generated very quickly, creating almost endless "new" exercises for training. Creating new training variations usually takes much more time when using noncomputerized cognitive training methods. A structured, easily followed hierarchy of progressively more difficult cognitive training exercises is also constructed much more easily using a computerized training model. The computer system can be programmed to control the presentation of the various stages of difficulty based on how the player performs in comparison to preset criteria.

This management logic for automatically adjusting the difficulty level has been implemented successfully in the SmartDriver, SoundSmart, and new Captain's Log programs in order to specifically facilitate their home use. Through home use, a computerized cognitive training system is more cost effective and can greatly extend the needed training hours required for the beneficial effects of the essential drill for the skill component of a comprehensive cognitive training system. Even with intensive home-based training programs, the trainer is still needed to select specific training exercises, provide guidance in using relevant program options, target and train specific meta-cognitive concepts, and reinforce, supervise, and enhance the generalization and successful implementation of the overall cognitive training program. Thus, using a computer can greatly enhance the power of a cognitive training program in many ways, but it does not do away with the need for a skilled and knowledgeable cognitive trainer.

COGNITIVE TRAINING:
WHAT DO YOU TRAIN?

Research has clearly established that deficits in executive functioning involving self-regulation are a significant casual factor contributing to the maladaptive social behavior and poor academic performance of individuals with ADHD (Clark et al., 2002). The cognitive deficits that contribute to poor executive functioning of individuals with ADHD and LD include (1) spatial short-term memory, (2) working memory, (3) set-shifting mental flexibility, (4) planning ability, (5) abstract verbal reasoning, (6) visual processing speed, (7) complex information processing speed, (8) selective attention, (9) behavioral response inhibition, (10) spatial recognition memory, (11) sustained attention, (12) motor control, (13) verbal learning, (14) strategy generation, and (15) divided attention (Adams & Scowling, 2001; Kempton et al., 1999; Mariani & Barkley, 1997; Roodenrys et al., 2001; Shallice et al., 2002; Woods et al., 2002). While many individuals with ADHD and LD will have deficits in at least some of the aforementioned identified cognitive skills, cognitive training is conceptualized as working best if specific deficits and areas of strength are identified for each individual. This can be accomplished through a comprehensive neuropsychological test battery and/or using rating scales completed by therapists, teachers, and/or parents that rank various cognitive strengths and weaknesses.

Using this approach, training exercises can then be selected from a computerized cognitive training system such as the Captain's Log "mental gym" (Sandford et al., 1985) in which each program is identified in terms of the specific cognitive abilities it targets (Sandford & Sandford, 2000). In addition to the Captain's Log, other popular computerized cognitive training systems include Fast Forward, Earobics, Thinkable, Parrot Software, NeurXercise, and LocuTour. The reader can find out more information about any these software programs by doing a search on the internet (the author recommends the search engine www.google.com) using their names as key words. Using the internet, it is possible to locate many different computerized cognitive training programs, commercial computer games, edutainment software, tape-based structured exercises, cognitive rehabilitation workbook activities, and structured cognitive/educational individual and group training programs that can be adapted or created to train specific cognitive skills. Two articles that readers may find useful that list and review various cognitive training tools and techniques are by Cicerone et al. (2000) and Lynch (1998). The next section demonstrates how a neuropsychologist using advanced computer technology develops a cognitive training program.

UTILIZING A COGNITIVE TRAINING SYSTEM WITH CHILDREN WITH ADHD AND LD: A SNAPSHOT INTO THE DEVELOPMENT OF THE TECHNOLOGY

Cognitive training can be incorporated easily into a cognitive behavioral treatment approach to help individuals with ADHD and LD more fully to develop their mental abilities for sustaining attention and maintaining self-control. The training of specific cognitive skills can be an important part of a multimodal treatment approach when working with individuals with ADHD and LD. Cognitive training does not preclude using any other therapeutic techniques, including psychopharmacological, environmental accommodations, or various therapeutic interventions. Advances in brain research and neuroimaging may, in the near future, document the development of neuronal networks in various centers in the brain of individuals with ADHD and LD as a result of cognitive training exercises. Used interactively, these types of "brain-building" exercises can provide positive feedback for paying attention. Enabling the person to "win" through sustaining attention and demonstrating relevant self-control to a task then enhance self-esteem. Specific cognitive deficits such as poor listening skills can be identified and targeted for training. A treatment plan can be directed by the therapist in weekly 1-hour sessions and then extended using structured cognitive training exercises in the home environment through workbooks, parental/sibling interaction, and in-home computerized cognitive training exercises, thus facilitating a long-lasting cognitive and behavioral change.

As the principal author and developer of the Captain's Log cognitive training system (Sandford et al., 1985), the author has had the opportunity to conceptualize, design, develop, refine, and test cognitive training software with hundreds of clients of all ages and disabilities over many years. In an ongoing effort to develop new software that took advantage of improvements in computer technology, the author first created a standalone program to primarily train visual attention and tracking called SmartDriver (Sandford, 1999). Recognizing a need for more auditory cognitive training exercises, the author created the SoundSmart series, which consists of 11 programs (Sandford & Turner, 2001). Currently, an entirely new version of Captain's Log is being developed with numerous enhancements to take advantage of the advances in computer technology and the author's clinical experience in this field. In developing a general nomenclature for use in describing cognitive training, the author decided to label those who actively participate in the training, "players," and those individuals who direct the training simply, "trainers." In this model, trainers include psychologists, occupational therapists, speech language professionals, special education teachers, and parents. Thus, cognitive training utilizing technology is conceived as a cross-disciplinary tool that can be used by a wide variety of individuals from a variety of domains. This software cannot be used though in a "vacuum" and does require specific knowledge and skill in selecting what to train, how to train, and the use of cognitive behavioral techniques to generalize the training. It is most beneficial when it is part of a comprehensive cognitive training program. Thus, all cognitive training software is viewed as a set of tools that are the means for helping individuals achieve for themselves improvements in mental, educational, and psychosocial functioning in many aspects of their life activities.

Essential to any individual's ability to learn and process general, social, and academic information is the **p**rimary **i**nformation **p**rocessing **s**ystem (**PIPS**). **PIPS** is defined as an individual's general cognitive capability to accurately and efficiently identify, discriminate, and process relevant ongoing information in his/her environment. It is dependent on working memory and central processing speed capabilities. All of the exercises in the Captain's Log system or any other comprehensive cognitive training system will help enhance this critically important information processing system. By working systematically on deficit areas that impair aspects of information processing, individuals can improve their memory and overall ability to learn and retain new information. The **PIPS** model recognizes that each individual has a meta-cognitive system that must be trained using cognitive behavioral techniques while simultaneously training specific cognitive skills using a "drill for skill" approach.

The 20 specific cognitive skills listed in Table 1 can be trained using the Captain's Log system (Sandford & Sandford, 2000). Each of the 33 cognitive training exercises in the Captain's Log system has been identified as training one or more of these cognitive skills. Other cognitive training systems, such as REHABIT, can also be "mapped" to the specific cognitive skills listed below. This list is not all inclusive, but it is comprehensive. Various models of attention and cognition may define these skills somewhat differently or additional cognitive abilities may be defined and added to the scope of cognitive training goals. This list provides a functional definition and model of many important cognitive abilities. The cognitive skills included in it are listed in alphabetical order in Table 1.

It is not possible to train all 20 cognitive skills at once. Generally, not all skills will need to be trained. Each of the cognitive abilities can be rated for an individual on a one-to-five scale with number one representing an area where improvement is needed and five an area of cognitive strength. It is suggested that no more than four target cognitive skills be the focus of training. This rating can be used to identify four important cognitive skills to train. In addition, one area of strength needs to be selected that can be utilized to enhance self-confidence and self-esteem. Clinical judgment based on neuropsychological test scores, clinical observations, the client's needs, rating scales, parental input, and educational information or teachers' input can all be used in selecting the areas where training needs to start.

For individuals with ADHD and LD, it is important to determine the specific emotional and self-control skills that need to be trained. For example, some individuals are very slow in their mental processing speed. In this case, the speed option is available in many of the Captain's Log programs to train an individual to improve his mental processing speed relative to his own baseline speed. Other players are impatient and need to learn to wait until instructions are fully spoken and visual cues indicate that it is time to proceed. Patience training tracks are available in the SoundSmart auditory attention training programs for such individual needs. If individuals are having problems with auditory discrimination, then it may be recommended that they use the listening track in the SoundSmart series. This training track in SoundSmart provides distracting sounds, unusual pauses in instructions, distorted speech, and background sounds in order to systematically train auditory discrimination and attention. Many of the new Captain's Log programs also offer the ability to train patience and listening skills via program options.

It is often important to train individuals with ADHD in the ability to ignore distractions and irrelevant information. The Captain's Log helps train both selective and focused attention by providing the option to add visual and/or auditory distracting stimuli during a training exercise. Problem-solving skills can be specifically trained in many of the Captain's Log programs by selecting the "challenge mode." In this mode, no instructions or hints are given and the player must figure out what the rules are

TABLE 1   A List of Cognitive Skills

1. **Alternating attention:** The ability to shift the focus of attention quickly back and forth between two different sets of stimuli in the same sensory modality and respond appropriately
2. **Auditory processing speed:** The time it takes to perceive relevant auditory stimuli, encode and interpret it, and then make an appropriate response
3. **Central processing speed:** The time it takes to encode, categorize, and understand the meaning of any sensory stimuli that is the focus of attention
4. **Conceptual reasoning:** Cognitive skills that include *concept formation* (the capacity to analyze relationships between objects), *abstraction* (the ability to think symbolically), *deductive logic* (the application of general rules or concepts in making a decision for a specific set of stimuli), and/or *inductive logic* (the analysis of feedback or identification of relevant details in formulating a concept to use in decision making)
5. **Detailed reading:** The ability to read, understand, and implement detailed instructions correctly
6. **Divided attention:** The capability to attend to, process, and respond appropriately to two or more different types of sensory stimuli (typically visual and auditory) that occur simultaneously or in close temporal proximity in the environment
7. **Fine motor control:** The ability to accurately control fine motor movements and avoid making erroneous responses
8. **Fine motor speed:** The time it takes to perform a simple motoric response independent of central processing speed
9. **Focused attention:** The ability to recognize and respond to specific relevant stimuli
10. **General attention:** The ability to focus, sustain, and selectively attend to relevant stimuli and make correct responses (a combination of focused, sustained, and selective attention as defined previously)
11. **Response inhibition:** The capability of understanding and holding in working memory a rule that defines a correct response and using this rule to help avoid automatically reacting to an incorrect stimulus
12. **Selective attention:** The capacity to continue making a correct response during a task when competing or distracting stimuli are present
13. **Sustained attention:** The capability of maintaining consistent and accurate responses during a continuous and repetitive activity
14. **Visuospatial classification:** The ability to accurately discriminate relevant features, count, and group visual objects based on a concept or rule
15. **Visuospatial sequencing:** The ability to discriminate and discern the sequential order of visual objects accurately based on a concept or rule
16. **Visual perception:** The ability to accurately discriminate and respond appropriately to fixed visual objects within the field of vision
17. **Visual processing speed:** The time it takes to perceive relevant visual stimuli, encode, interpret, and make an appropriate response
18. **Visual scanning:** The ability to accurately discriminate and respond appropriately to visual objects that appear without a cue and randomly over time within the field of vision
19. **Visual tracking:** The ability to follow a continuous visual cue, discriminate accurately, and respond appropriately to visual objects that move continuously within the field of vision
20. **Working memory:** The ability to encode and "hold" perceptual information *while processing it* and the capability to recall and apply relevant procedural rules in order to respond accurately

for the specific cognitive training task. The SoundSmart challenge track works differently. It is designed to train frustration tolerance by requiring quick responses (i.e., mental processing speed training track) while distracting sounds are playing (i.e., listening track). The individual must also be patient and not make any response until all instructions are spoken and the visual cue to "go" is given (i.e., the traffic light cue changes to the color green). Thus, when training the cognitive skills of individuals with ADHD and LD the trainer needs to identify if mental processing speed, patience, auditory discrimination, selective and focused attention, problem solving, and frustration tolerance need to be addressed specifically using the various options and training tracks available in the Captain's Log and SoundSmart programs.

Training through technology has the potential for a positive, interactive therapeutic experience for individuals with ADHD and LD. Simply telling individuals that they need to be more patient, not overreact, work harder, do their homework, or use their problem-solving skills does not work very well for young children and adolescents in changing their behavior in the school or home setting. In almost all cases, their parents and teachers have already tried this "instructional/educational" approach repeatedly before seeking therapeutic assistance. In addition, the use of a self-instructional approach in cognitive behavioral psychotherapy has not been found to be effective in improving the functioning of children who have ADHD, except when combined with external contingency reinforcement (Hinshaw, 2000). In contrast, the therapeutic training of cognitive abilities can be presented easily as game-like by using stimulating computer exercises that provide feedback and utilize a point system to reflect progress. Children with ADHD and LD learn best by "doing" and through immediate feedback. Computerized cognitive training provides a system and set of tools that these individuals can enjoy and help them rediscover the meta-concepts that you "win" by paying attention and that learning can be fun.

The positive experience of winning by paying attention, maintaining self-control, completing a task, and experiencing active focused mental activity as fun could help at a meta-cognitive level. A person's motivation and willingness to perform other directed work type activities could be influenced by his emotional state and mental attitude toward the activity. As school progresses and the challenges of learning new material increase, individuals with ADHD can easily develop a learned helplessness toward new learning. While teachers recognize that on "good days" these individuals can learn to do the new schoolwork if they would only try, instead they often give up, get off a task, or shut down emotionally. For these individuals, cognitive training is needed in order to help them develop frustration tolerance and coping skills to reduce overemotional reactivity, the ability to set personal goals, the recognition of the need to delay immediate gratification, and the enhancement of their self-confidence. Changes in motivation, attitude, and one's emotional state can best be achieved therapeutically through an interactive positive learning experience. Trying to "make" a person feel, think, and act differently by criticizing or telling him or her to "get with the program, get the lead out, shape up or ship out, or my way or the highway" will usually result in the opposite desired effect, decreasing motivation and increasing negative, angry thoughts. If an individual is guided in a set of cognitive exercises and experiences for themselves ways to improve their "score" and pass to the next level, then their self-confidence builds and they learn "I can do it." In this therapeutic interaction, learning to pay attention can become fun and is associated with a pleasurable experience. The joy of learning something new (i.e., the "ah-ha" experience) can be remembered. Mastery and insight stemming from the person's new understanding (which may need to be pointed out and emphasized for some) and a renewed confidence in the effort to learn (reinforced positively by the therapist) can lead to a change in one's attitude and motivation to do mental work. Thus, cognitive training exercises can be used to specifically enhance an individual's feeling of self-esteem and self-control.

SUMMARY AND CONCLUSIONS

Cognitive training through the use of computer software offers the potential for a positive, interactive therapeutic experience for individuals with ADHD and LD. Telling someone to pay attention, be more patient, not overreact, do not be negative, or work harder rarely leads to positive, sustainable behavior change. Change can occur though through personal experience and feedback. If cognitive exercises are fun and "game-like," then motivation is increased and "learning by doing" can occur. An individual must improve specific areas of a cognitive deficit and also learn "higher level" meta-concepts of self-regulation and problem solving if cognitive training is to be helpful in changing how individuals with ADHD or LD function in their life.

Research has clearly established that deficits in executive functioning lead to maladaptive social behavior and poor academic performance for individuals with ADHD. It needs to be determined on an individual basis what specific emotional and self-control skills need to be trained. More than 20 specific cognitive abilities can be trained, including mental processing speed, auditory discrimination, and visual tracking. Training works best if based on a hierarchical system with increasing more complex stimuli and requirements for "passing." The primary purpose of cognitive training software is to "train the cognitive skills." Thus, it must be based on neuropsychological and behavioral principles and incorporate clinical training options. You do not have to have a computer to do cognitive training, but it eliminates many of the mundane tasks, such as scoring, so that the trainer can focus on the important meta-cognitive aspects of training.

Cognitive training software resembles educational or video game programs only superficially. Its purpose is not to instruct in academic topics, test knowledge, or entertain. While the exercises are usually somewhat game-like in format, their purpose is very different from other software genre. Cognitive exercises are carefully designed "tools" to help improve the basic mental processes important for higher level learning. Through cognitive training exercises, an individual with ADHD or LD can learn how a meta-cognitive strategy can help them choose a positive, helpful attitude and response instead of an overemotional, negative reaction. Players are not competing with others, but striving toward personally set goals.

With computers you can practice cognitive skills daily at home, let it keep the score, and stay mentally fit. One important advantage of computerized cognitive training lies in the ability for the trainer to assign "homework." Using home versions of this genre of software, players can work on their own and master the "drill of skill" part of cognitive training at a lower cost and with equal effectiveness. The trainer becomes the coach and works on meta-cognitive training in weekly sessions. Thus, the computer has a clearly defined role in cognitive training that makes cognitive training more available to a larger number of people.

Cognitive computer training is a valuable approach, but the training is work. Thus, resistance to cognitive training exercises is to be expected, as cognitive training only works if the player practice consistently. Positive reinforcement such as tangible reinforcers can be utilized to provide concrete rewards when necessary to overcome this resistance. Just as improvements from physical exercise are not visible immediately, the same is true for cognitive training. One of the global goals of cognitive training is to help individuals with ADHD and LD master feelings of boredom and learn how to sustain their attention when necessary to a repetitive task with a high degree of accuracy. Thus, most players need to be "coached" that progress requires mental discipline and that positive changes will not occur overnight, but over time.

The application of technology with this population has great promise. Advances in brain research, neuroimaging, and computer technology offer the potential to enhance cognitive training. Taking a holistic approach to the treatment of ADHD and LD that incorporates advances in computer technology, brain research and neuroimaging may lead to a reduced need for psychopharmacological intervention. It offers the potential of enhancing the effectiveness of current practices in remediating LD and symptoms of ADHD.

REFERENCES

Abikoff, H., & Gittelman, R. (1984). Does behavior therapy normalize the classroom behavior of hyperactive children? *Archives of General Psychiatry*, 41, 449–454.

Adams, J. W., & Snowling, M. J (2001). Executive function and reading impairments in children reported by their teachers as "hyperactive." *British Journal of Developmental Psychology*, 19(2), 293–306.

Agency for Healthcare Research and Quality (1999). Diagnosis of attention-deficit/hyperactivity disorder. Summary, Technical Review: Number 3, Rockville, MD. www.ahrq.gov/clinic/epcsums/adhdsutr.htm.

American Psychiatric Association (1994). *Diagnostic and statistical manual of mental disorders* (4th ed.). Washington, DC: Author.

Ball, K., Berch, D., Helmers, K., Jobe, J., Leveck, M., Marsiske, M., Morris, J., Rebok, G., Smith, D., Tennstedt, S., Unverzagt, F., & Willis, S. (2002). Effects of cognitive training interventions with older adults: A randomized controlled trial. *Journal of the American Medical Association*, 288(18), 2271–2281.

Barkley, R. A. (1997). *ADHD and the nature of self-control*. New York: Guilford Press.

Barkley, R. A. (1998). *Attention deficit hyperactivity disorder: A handbook for diagnosis and treatment* (2nd ed.). New York: Guilford Press.

Barkley, R. A., & Cunningham, C. E. (1978). Do stimulant drugs improve the academic performance of hyperkinetic children? *Clinical Pediatrics*, 17, 85–92.

Baumgaertel, A. (1999). Alternative and controversial treatments for attention-deficit/hyperactivity disorder, *The Pediatric Clinics of North America*, 46(5), 977–993.

Bell, M., Bryson, G., Greig, T., Corcoran, C., & Wexler, B. (2001). Neurocognitive enhancement therapy with work therapy: Effects on neuropsychological test performance. *Archives of General Psychiatry*, 58(8), 763–768.

Brodeur, D. A., & Pond, M. (2001). The development of selective attention in children with attention deficit hyperactivity disorder. *Journal of Abnormal Child Psychology*, 29(3), 229–239.

Brodsky, P. (1988). Follow-up on the youngest REHABIT client: Importance of caution. *Perceptual and Motor Skills*, 66(2), 383–386.

Burda, P. C., Starkey, T. W., Dominguez, F., & Vera, V. (1994). Computer-assisted cognitive rehabilitation of chronic psychiatric inpatients. *Computers in Human Behavior*, 10(3), 359–368.

Cicerone, K., Dahlberg, C., Kalmar, K., Langenbahn, D., Malec, J., Bergquist, T., Felicetti, T., Giacino, J., Harley, J. P., Harrington, D., Herzog, J., Kniepp, S., Laatsch, L., & Morse, P. (2000). Evidence-based cognitive rehabilitation: Recommendations for clinical practice. *Archives of Physical Medicine and Rehabilitation*, 81, 1596–1615.

Clark, C., Prior, M., & Kinsella, G. (2002). The relationship between executive function abilities, adaptive behavior, and academic achievement in children with externalizing behavior problems. *Journal of Child Psychology and Psychiatry and Allied Disciplines*, 43(6), 785–796.

Colin, B., Denney. (2001). Stimulant effects in attention deficit hyperactivity disorder: Theoretical and empirical issues. *Journal of Clinical Child Psychology*, 30(1), 98–109.

Conners, C. K., Epstein, J. N., March, J. S., Angold, A., Wells, K. C., Klaric, J., et al. (2001). Multimodal treatment of ADHD in the MTA: An alternative outcome analysis. *Journal of the American Academy of Child and Adolescent Psychiatry*, 40, 159–167.

DuPaul, G. J., & Eckert, T. L. (1998). Overcoming learning difficulties. *Reading and Writing Quarterly*, 14(1), 59–82.

Faraone, S. V., Biederman, J., Monuteaux, M. C., & Seidman, L. J. (2001). A psychometric measure of learning disability predicts educational failure four years later in boys with attention deficit hyperactivity disorder. *Journal of Attention Disorders*, 4, 220–230.

Fine, A. H., Goldman, L., & Sandford, J. A. (1994). Innovative techniques in the treatment of ADHD: An analysis of the impact of EEG biofeedback training and cognitive computer generated training. Paper presented at the annual convention of the American Psychological Association, Los Angeles, CA.

Fletcher, K. E., Fischer, M., Barkley, R. A., & Smallish, L. (1996). A sequential analysis of the mother-adolescent interactions of ADHD, ADHD/ODD, and normal teenagers during neutral and conflict discussions. *Journal of Abnormal Child Psychology*, 24(3), 271–297.

Flicek, M. (1992). Social status of boys with both academic problems and attention-deficit hyperactivity disorder. *Journal of Abnormal Child Psychology*, 20(4), 353–366.

Frankenberger, W., & Cannon, C. (1999). Effects of Ritalin on academic achievement from first to fifth grade. *International Journal of Disability, Development and Education*, 46(2), 199–221.

Gardner, J. E., & Bates, P. (1991). Attitudes and attributions on use of microcomputers in school by students who are mentally handicapped. *Education and Training in Mental Retardation*, 26(1), 98–107.

Hansen, S., Meissler, K., & Ovens, R. (2000). Kids together: A group play therapy model for children with ADHD symptomalogy. *Journal of Child and Adolescent Group Therapy*, 10(4), 191–211.

Henker, B., & Whalen, C. K. (1999). Hyperactivity and attention deficits. *American Psychologist*, 44(2), 216–223.

Hinshaw, S. P. (1987). On the distinction between attentional deficits/hyperactivity and conduct problems/aggression in child psychopathology. *Psychological Bulletin*, 101, 443–463.

Hinshaw, S. P. (2000). Attention-deficit/hyperactivity disorder: The search for viable treatments. In P. C. Kendall (Ed.), *Child and adolescent therapy: Cognitive–behavioral procedures* (2nd ed., pp. 88–128). New York: Guilford Press.

Hinshaw, S. P., Henker, B., Whalen, C. K. Erhardt, Drew Dunnington, Robert, E. (1989). Aggressive, prosocial, and nonsocial behavior in hyperactive boys dose effects of methylphenidate in naturalistic settings. *Journal of Consulting and Clinical Psychology*, 57(9), 636–643.

Hopkins, M. (1991). The value of information technology for children with emotional and behavioural difficulties. *Maladjustment and Therapeutic Education*, 9(3), 143–151.

Hynd, G. W., Hern, K. L., Voeller, K. K., & Marshall, R. M. (1991). Neurobiological basis of attention-deficit hyperactivity disorder (ADHD). *School Psychology Review*, 20(2), 174–186.

Kempton, S., Vance, A., Maruff, P., Luk, E., Costin, J., & Pantelis, C. (1999). Executive function and attention deficit hyperactivity disorder: Stimulant medication and better executive function performance in children. *Psychological Medicine*, 29(3), 527–538.

Knivsberg, A. M., Reichelt, K. L., & Nødland, M. (1999). Comorbidity, or coexistence, between dyslexia and attention deficit hyperactivity disorder. *British Journal of Special Education*, 26(1), 42–47.

Koepp, M., Gunn, R., Lawrence, A., Cunningham, V., Dagher, A., Jones, T., Brooks, D., Bench, C., & Grasby, P. (1998). Evidence for striatal dopamine release during a video game. *Nature*, 393(6682), 266–268.

Kotulak, R. (1996). *Inside the brain*. Kansas City, MO: Andrews and McMeel.

Kotwal, D., Burns, W. J., & Montgomery, D. (1996). Computer assisted cognitive training for ADHD: A case study. *Behavior Modification*, 20(1), 85–96.

Kramer, A. F. (2001). Methylphenidate effects on task-switching performance in attention-deficit/hyperactivity disorder. *Journal of the American Academy of Child and Adolescent Psychiatry*, 40(11), 1277–1284.

Leuchter, A. F., Cook, I. A., Witte, E. A., Morgan, M., & Abrams, M. (2002). Changes in brain function of depressed subjects during treatment with placebo. *American Journal of Psychiatry*, 159(1), 122–129.

Levine, M. (2002). *A mind at a time*. New York: Simon & Schuster.

Lynch, W. (1998). Software update 1998: Commercial programs useful in cognitive retraining. *Journal of Head Trauma Rehabilitation*, 13(5), 91–94.

Mariani, M., & Barkley, R. (1997). Neuropsychological and academic functioning in preschool boys with attention deficit hyperactivity disorder. *Developmental Neuropsychology*, 13(1), 111–129.

Mitchell, W., Chavez, J., Baker, S., & Guzman, B. (1990). Reaction time, impulsivity, and attention in hyperactive children and controls: A video game technique. *Journal of Child Neurology*, 5(3), 195–204.

NIH Consensus Development Panel (1999). Consensus development conference statement: Rehabilitation of persons with traumatic brain injury. *Journal of the American Medical Association*, 282(10), 974–983.

NIH Consensus Development Panel (2000). Consensus development conference statement: Diagnosis and treatment of attention-deficit/hyperactivity disorder (ADHD). *Journal of American Academy of Child and Adolescent Psychiatry*, 39(2), 182–193.

Rao, S. M., & Bieliauskas, L. A. (1983). Cognitive rehabilitation two and one-half years post right temporal lobectomy. *Journal of Clinical Neuropsychology*, 5(4), 313–320.

Rapport, L. J., Voorhis, A. J., Tzelepis, A., & Friedman, S. R. (2001). Executive functioning in adult attention-deficit hyperactivity disorder. *The Clinical Neuropsychologist*, 15(4), 479–491.

Rapport, M. D., & Kelly, K. (1991). Psychostimulant effects on learning and cognitive functions: Findings and implications for children with attention deficit hyperactivity disorder. *Clinical Psychology Review*, 11, 61–92.

Reitan, R., & Wolfson, D. (1988). The Halstead-Reitan Neuropsychological Test Battery and REHABIT: A model for integrating evaluation and remediation of cognitive impairment. *Cognitive Rehabilitation*, 6(3), 10–17.

Riccio, C. A., Cecil, R. R., & Lowe, P. A. (2001). *Clinical applications of continuous performance tests: Measuring attention and impulsive responding in children and adults*. New York: Wiley.

Roodenrys, S., Koloski, N., & Grainger, J. (2001). Working memory function in attention deficit hyperactivity disordered and reading disabled children. *British Journal of Developmental Psychology*, 19(3), 325–337.

Runnheim, V. A., Frankenberger, W. R., & Hazelkorn, M. N. (1996). Medicating students with emotional and behavioral disorders and ADHD: A state survey. *Behavioral Disorders*, 21, 306–314.

Salokoski, T., Mustonen, A., Sipari, T., & Pulkkinen, L. (2002). Computer games playing in childhood. *Psykologia*, 37(2), 128–137.

Sandford, J. (1999). *SmartDriver*. Richmond, VA: BrainTrain.

Sandford, J. A., Fine, A. H., & Goldman, L. (1995). *Validity study of iva: A visual and auditory CPT*. Paper presented at the annual convention of the American Psychological Association, New York, NY.

Sandford, J., & Sandford, V. (2000). *The captain's log workbook: Protocols for training and testing using the captain's log cognitive training system*. Richmond, VA: BrainTrain.

Sandford, J., & Turner, A. (2001). *SoundSmart*. Richmond, VA: BrainTrain.

Sandford, J., & Turner, A. (1994). *Integrated visual and auditory continuous performance test*. Richmond, VA: BrainTrain.

Sandford, J., Turner, A., & Browne, R. (1985). *Captain's log: Cognitive training system*. Richmond, VA: BrainTrain.

Schreiber, M., Lutz, K., Schweizer, A., Kalveram, K., & Jaencke, L. (1998). Development and evaluation of an interactive computer-based training as a rehabilitation tool for dementia. *Psychologishche Beitrage*, 40(1), 85–102.

Seidman, L. J., Biederman, J., Faraone, S. V., Weber, W., & Ouellette, C. (1997). Toward defining a neuropsychology of attention deficit-hyperactivity disorder: Performance of children and adolescents from a large clinically referred sample. *Journal of Consulting and Clinical Psychology*, 65, 150–160.

Semrud-Clikeman, M. S., Biederman, J., Sprich, S., Krifcher, B., Norman, D., & Faraone, S. (1992). Comorbidity between ADHD and learning disability: A review and report in a clinically referred sample. *Journal of the American Academy of Child and Adolescent Psychiatry*, 31, 439–448.

Shallice, T., Marzocchi, G. M., Coser, S., Savio, M. D., Meuter, R., & Rumiati, R. (2002). Executive function profile of children with attention deficit hyperactivity disorder. *Developmental Neuropsychology*, 21(1), 43–71.

Skosnik, P., Chatterton, R., Swisher, T., & Park, S. (2000). Modulation of attentional inhibition by norepinephrine and cortisol after psychological stress. *International Journal of Psychophysiology*, 36(1), 59–68.

Slate, S. E., Meyer, T. L., Burns, W. J., & Montgomery, D. D. (1998). Computerized cognitive training for severely emotionally disturbed children with ADHD. *Behavior Modification*, 22(3), 415–437.

Tinius, T., & Tinius, K. A. (2000). Changes after EEG biofeedback and cognitive retraining in adults with mild traumatic brain injury and attention deficit hyperactivity disorder. *Journal of Neurotherapy*, 4(2), 27–44.

Turner, A., & Sandford, J. A. (1995). *A normative study of IVA: Integrated visual and auditory continuous performance test.* Paper presented at the annual convention of the American Psychological Association, New York, NY.

Whalen, C. K., & Henker, B. (1985). The social worlds of hyperactive (ADHD) children. *Clinical Psychology Review*, 5, 447–478.

Whalen, C. K., & Henker, B. (1991). Therapies for hyperactive children comparisons, combinations, and compromises. *Journal of Consulting and Clinical Psychology*, 59(1), 126–137.

Woods, S. P., Lovejoy, D. W., & Ball, J. D. (2002). Neuropsychological characteristics of adults with ADHD: A comprehensive review of initial studies. *The Clinical Neuropsychologist*, 16(1), 12–34.

## CHAPTER 15

Future Directions in the Holistic Treatment of Children with Learning and Attention Disorders: Concerns and Guidelines

Aubrey H. Fine and Ronald A. Kotkin with contributions from Mary Fowler, Steve Forness, Peter Jensen, Mark Katz, Mark Lerner, Michael Posner and James Swanson and Bruce McCandliss

Over the course of the last century, numerous developments and changes have taken place in the treatment and diagnosis of learning disabilities (LD) and attention deficit hyperactivity disorder (ADHD). Perhaps some of our advancements are solely due to the scientific discoveries achieved over the past century. Neuroimaging and medical research have unraveled some of the mysteries of both learning and attention problems. We have also witnessed a continued effort in advocacy by parents and society as a whole urging politicians to not ignore the needs of this population. Consequently, through media, popular press, and legislation, there has been great pressure from within to not accept mediocrity. People are continuing to ask more questions and are not accepting "no" for an answer.

Large-scale research studies such as the MTA and efficacy research in the field of LD are providing the clinical community with clearer impressions of what treatments seem to have the most promise. We are now more aware of the genetics and the neurobiology of both these syndromes, and we can only continue to look toward the future for more solid discoveries.

The true test to our futuristic thinking is in our ability to conceptually look at this multifaceted field and determine what steps scientifically, medically, and educationally we will take in the next 20–50 years. Eric Hoffer (1954), in *The Passionate State Of Mind*, once stated "*The only way to predict the future is to have power to shape the future.*" We now possess some of the science and medical tools to make an impact. Ironically, no one will truly be able to evaluate our predictions until the future becomes our present. That being understood, as editors we set forth to try and get some of our questions answered. We generated a series of questions that presented a glimpse into the future for the assessment and treatment of children with ADHD/LD. To broaden our breath to secure information, we invited several respected individuals who are on the cutting edge of parent advocacy, brain research, treatment, medical practice, and education to make a contribution.

What follows are the questions we posed to each expert and their predictions for the future. We conclude the chapter by integrating their impressions with some of our own conclusions.

QUESTION 1. HOW WILL ADHD AND LD BE DIAGNOSED IN THE FUTURE?

Peter S. Jensen, M.D., Director, Center for the Advancement of Children's Mental Health, Columbia University

Most often the medical diagnosis of any illness is *not* an exact science. Yet uncertainty is *particularly common* in the case of mental disorders, especially those conditions with behavioral manifestations that overlap with normal states. ADHD and LD are both excellent examples of such conditions. For ADHD and LD (as well as for most psychiatric disorders generally), there are no clear diagnostic tests, biological indicators, or genetic markers. The current state of practice is that physicians must rely on determining if a specific pattern of behaviors, emotions, and/or thoughts is present, if this pattern is of sufficient duration, severity, consistency, and intensity, and if this pattern is associated with impairment in the child's day-to-day functioning. This diagnostic approach can be even more imprecise with children, whose behavior, emotions, and thoughts change continuously over the course of development. Such uncertainties and varying factors help explain why parents get different opinions from different experts and why we as professionals often arrive at different diagnoses.

While diagnoses are still imprecise, scientific advances and medical practice would be impossible without diagnoses giving names to sets of medical signs and symptoms. Names make it possible for scientists, health care providers, families and consumers, and policy-makers to communicate, but diagnosis is more than simply naming or labeling. When research supports it, a diagnosis can be used by professionals to make important predictions about a child's likely response to a specific intervention, the course the condition will likely take, and its eventual outcome.

Thus, careful diagnosis is the backbone of clinical research and the cornerstone of clinical practice. Historically, medical classification systems were based on externally observable descriptions: some type of medical "sign" plus symptoms, observable by the doctor or other health care professional. However, as research has advanced, diagnoses more often are based on understanding of the inner workings and structures of organs or bodily systems. This means that diagnoses for conditions such as ADHD and LD *can and should* change as our understanding of various syndromes advances, whether by studies of genes, brain processes, pathophysiology, or treatment. Unfortunately, research does not always proceed at an even pace, and as a consequence, various disorders across all of medicine are defined according to different principles, depending on the state of knowledge in that area.

For example, some medical disorders are diagnosed based mostly on the presence of structural pathology, as in ulcerative colitis. At other times, a disorder may be defined and diagnosed principally on the subjective nature of symptom presentation, as in migraine headache, for which we have no biologic tests. At other times, a diagnosis may be simply based on the deviation from a known physiologic norm, such as hypertension. In such an instance, we define a certain level of higher blood pressure as "hypertension" *not* because we can demonstrate that the cardiovascular system is defective per se, but only because we can predict that persons with higher blood pressures have a statistically increased likelihood (but not a certainty) of particular medical outcomes (stroke or heart disease). Better yet, we might be able to do something about it (diet, antihypertensive medication, exercise, etc.). In terms of diagnosis, however, usually the best situation of all is when we know the specific cause, such as streptococcal tonsillitis or sickle cell anemia. Sometimes, though not always, knowledge of a disorder's causes allows us to do a better job to prevent or treat it.

With ADHD and LD, causes are as of yet far from known, as are precise measures of any such putative causes. So to establish a diagnosis of either of these conditions, the doctor or other health care professional must first obtain a careful clinical description and history, get information from all available persons who can describe the child well, consider the child's current age and developmental status, learn about the possible history of similar problems in any relatives, and "rule out" all other known causes of the particular symptoms.

However, all diagnoses and diagnostic systems (including those for ADHD and LD) are shaped by current norms and values, medical "fashions," as well as the limitations of the current science. In the early 1960s, most severe psychiatric disorders in adults were characterized as "schizophrenia," while in fact our understanding today is much more refined, vis-à-vis major depressive disorder, bipolar disorder, and a range of schizophrenia-type disorders. Even conditions such as peptic ulcer, long thought to be due to excess stomach acid and/or stress, have been recently reconceptualized and better understood as principally due to a particular bacterium, *Helicobacter pylori*.

As our understanding of ADHD and LD progresses, we can expect to eventually determine that various manifestations of ADHD are related to specific allelic variations, other ADHD manifestations are related to adverse events such as perinatal trauma, lead exposure, or maternal smoking, and still others related only to combinations of such factors. If we use the example of the behavioral symptom of a "cough," consider that the presence of a cough alone may not convey much information of any clinical significance. However, if that cough is accompanied by spiking fever, long duration, râles, and purulent sputum, the likelihood of the diagnosis of bacterial pneumonia is much higher than with a cough without such accompanying symptoms, and that cough with such symptoms is again quite different than a cough that is associated with bloody sputum, gradual weight loss, and no fever (e.g., perhaps cancer or tuberculosis). In the same way, increasing knowledge and research of ADHD symptoms with or without the presence of specific alleles, neuropsychological test scores, neuroimaging profiles, or family histories will just as surely lead us to different ADHD manifestations that have at their root quite different etiologic processes.

So how will ADHD and LD be diagnosed in the future? It seems unlikely that the requirement of overt clinical symptomatology will ever be dispensable. However, this same constellation of clinical symptomatology, when accompanied or modified by other symptoms (e.g., see Jensen et al., 2001), specific allelic variations (e.g., see Swanson et al., 2001), specific family histories, or specific neuroimaging profiles (see Posner's letter), may convey quite different clinical meanings and future diagnoses, just as coughs of different types are now understood to result in many different diagnoses if accompanied by other positive information and/or diagnostic tests. Thus, while there are currently three major subtypes of ADHD, we might expect research advances to ultimately reveal many different disorders, many different etiologic pathways, and, quite possibly, an array of different treatment and prevention strategies, depending on the particular etiologies of that form of inattention, hyperactivity, and impulsivity. Sophisticated diagnoses of ADHD and LD of the future will become increasingly dependent on tools such as neuroimaging, genetic profiling, neuropsychologic and physiologic testing, and consideration of other accompanying symptoms and clinical characteristics. The irony is that we will not be using these tools to diagnose ADHD and LD per se, but to make diagnoses of future constructs that bear only an approximate relationship to current ADHD/LD concepts, perhaps no more tightly linked than is "cough" with our current concepts of tuberculosis, cancer, and pneumonia.

QUESTION 2. FUTURE DIRECTIONS IN THE ASSESSMENT AND TREATMENT OF ADHD AND LD: A PARENT'S PERSPECTIVE

Mary Fowler, parent, author and former Vice President of Government Affairs of CHADD

The past two decades have brought a plethora of information about ADHD into the public sphere. Thankfully, the availability of scientifically reliable and valid findings regarding ADHD for the professional and lay audiences has created greater awareness and understanding of the disorder and its management. Nonetheless, in most community settings, the best practice has not necessarily become common practice (MTA, 1999). While many competent, caring, and dedicated professionals do exist, far too many children and youth with ADHD still do not receive adequate, much less ideal, diagnosis and treatment.

The American Academy of Pediatrics (AAP, 2002) issued practice guidelines based on the diagnostic assessment protocol and multimodal treatment approach that have long been recommended in the clinical literature (Barkley, 1990) and widely reported in the lay literature (e.g.,

Fowler, 1990; Fowler, 1992). In short, though published recently, these guidelines are nothing new. Still, community practice lags behind recommendations, which is not surprising given the constraints of most private practices and client resources. These guidelines cannot be followed readily, or improved upon, without systemic changes and paradigm shifts.

Furthermore, the multivariate nature of ADHD and its look-alike symptomatology demand a differential diagnosis by well-trained practitioners. Yet, in 2002, many children are "identified" as having ADHD rather than diagnosed as such. The distinction between "identification" and "diagnosis" is no mere semantic issue. Identification is akin to "if it walks and quacks like a duck, then it's a duck" logic. To the unskilled or quickly glancing eye, many conditions walk and talk like ADHD, and ADHD can look like other issues. In addition, many parents report that they have had to "shop around" to find up to date, knowledgeable, competent professional help. Seemingly, value judgment and dismissal of the potentially serious nature of this disorder enter into the clinical picture and into school service delivery systems far more than they should.

How schools deal with students known or suspected to have ADHD is also a significant issue of concern. While schools should not be expected to diagnose, nor should they do so, they can be expected to "identify" possible ADHD. Consider common school practice. When presented with a student who "looks ADHD," school personnel, which may include child study members, either "identify" or "not identify" the student as having ADHD, depending on unwritten district policies or personal opinion. They then proceed with an educational response or nonresponse often without suggesting or initiating an appropriate diagnostic protocol by licensed clinical professionals. Parents who place their trust in a school's misguided response often lose valuable diagnostic information and early intervention time.

Poor school practice stems from fairly common misperceptions. Some school personnel consider ADHD to be a learning disability. Some children with milder symptomatology may be impacted primarily in the learning environment; appropriate school-based interventions may "solve" the problems, but this rosy scenario is generally the exception. In other instances, school personnel may view the problem as solely "medical" and thus up to the parents to solve. More commonly, school staff view a child's difficulties as willful noncompliance, boredom, the product of poor parenting practice, or rooted in dysfunctional "What do you expect?"

families. Such misattribution provides an easy answer and a ready excuse to drop the ball. A school's nonresponse may either lead the parent to look further (many do not) or assume the child or themselves are to blame.

Poor diagnostic practice often leads to "intervention" rather than "treatment"—another distinction that is not merely semantic. Interventions generally invoke situation-specific responses while treatment infers a systemic, multimodal approach that involves patient, parent, and educator education, training in pharmacological and behavior management approaches, advocacy, study skills, social awareness, time management, and so on. More often than should happen, the diagnosis gets treated rather than the individual so that the person's unique clinical picture is overlooked by generalization. Too often the intervention is medication and nothing else. While the efficacy of medication has been well documented (MTA, 1999), pills do not teach skills. As with diagnosis, individual-specific, eclectic treatments are not easily or inexpensively put into practice, which may explain, but not excuse, why multimodal approaches do not occur as common practice.

So what can be done to follow current best practice until the time when scientific advances bring a better understanding of ADHD along with more efficient diagnostic procedures and treatments?

Topping my list would be the cessation of overreliance on any single parent or parent dyad to expertly fill all the roles that effective ADHD management may require: parent, teacher trainer, educational supervisor, advocate, behavioral specialist, medication monitor, coach, mentor, critical friend, home instructor, problem solver, trouble shooter, and quality/assurance control for educational programs and medical regiments. No wonder some parents "quit" when their children become teens and the problems have not been resolved or, in some cases, have become exacerbated. The parents are exasperated—or overwhelmed. Consider those parents newly seeking help who come with denial, guilt, shame, and faulty conclusions. Worn and torn from their struggles, they need support, often lack the resources to get it, and then find that they have to lead the charge!

My wish for the treatment of ADHD and LD would be that of shared responsibility between members of a treatment team. While ultimately parents have the primary responsibility for decisions affecting their children, they would be better able to make nonreactive and informed decisions when the full burden of management is lifted from their already weighted down shoulders. Through collaboration, they could also have better access to services.

While my ideal concept has yet to be brought to its utopian form, models do exist that can be adapted and replicated to assist parents in securing an appropriate diagnosis and better treatments for their children. For example, in Israel, the Joint, a Jewish foundation, funded "Parents Empowering Parents," an outreach program created by Beyahad, the Israeli national association on ADHD. Under the supervision of Beyahad's founder and chairperson, a small group of parents were "super" trained in ADHD management and various trouble-shooting techniques. Each team leader had responsibility for a region of the country. They then went into their respective regions and trained other parents about home management, school problem solving, medication management, etc. The team leaders serve as ready reference and support personnel so that parents in need have a well-informed source to guide them and provide immediate feedback, support, and referral to other experts (personal communication).

Another model that has widespread potential for the United States is the Harvard University RALLY (responsible advocacy for life and learning in youth) program. This program, originally designed for "at risk" youth, was developed in 1994 as a collaborative effort among McLean Hospital, the Harvard Graduate School of Education, the Howard Taft Middle School, and the special education department of the Boston public schools. (RALLY has been expanded to work with students with ADHD. Studies have not yet been conducted to determine efficacy, but anecdotal reports have been quite favorable.)

The primary goal of RALLY is to "expand children's schools into a hub for services, creating partnerships with neighborhood-based after-school programs, universities, health care and mental health providers" (RALLY program literature). To meet their goal, RALLY trains service providers called "prevention practitioners" who then are paired with teachers and preselected students within the classroom. (In the Boston program, the prevention practitioners are Harvard Graduate School of Education students.)

Prevention practitioners provide academic and social assistance, develop supportive relationships, and create the bridges between the child, school, family, and community. They consult with parents, trouble shoot, and do some parent training. (In a sense, the Israeli "joint" follows a modified prevention practitioner model.) Prevention practitioners pull services into the school and also form partnerships with after-school and community programs, e.g., Boys & Girls Clubs, Big Brothers Association, the YMCAs, and the Boston Police. RALLY staff also consult with other school districts throughout the United States interested in replicating their program. The promise of consultation is that it has the potential to bring the cutting edge research and resources a university research project can offer its neighborhood into other communities. The promise also extends to those who cannot afford the high cost or private services.

My hope for the future diagnosis and treatment of ADHD is for the creation of a readily available community-based model that takes the myriad needs of children with ADHD, their families, schools, and communities into account. These children and their caregivers need villages not islands. There should be passenger ferries to cross the gulf from piecemeal, catch as catch can interventions to comprehensive systems of competent service delivery that can be responsive to children and their parents in a timely fashion. Furthermore, those competent, caring, dedicated clinicians within the community settings, as well as educators, also deserve to have the same level of support and access to greater services that those with ADHD, their parents, and caregivers should have.

QUESTION 3. WHAT WILL THE FUTURE HOLD FOR EDUCATION OF CHILDREN WITH ADHD AND LEARNING DISABILITIES?

Steve Forness, Ed.D., Professor, Hospital School, Principal, and Chief, Educational Psychologist, UCLA Neuropsychiatric Hospital

This is a very interesting question and one that could certainly be answered at several levels. For children with ADHD in particular, it may be that success in school will be tied only partially to education itself. This is because there are increasingly impressive findings on the efficacy of stimulant and related medication on a wide variety of academic and other school outcome measures. Meta-analyses now show that medication alone improves performance in academic skills, by almost half a standard deviation, in children with ADHD. MTA findings also demonstrate enhanced performance on both reading and social skills in children with ADHD by combining behavioral and medication treatments, as compared to using behavioral interventions only. How we teach such children may actually prove less important in the future than whether they have effective psychopharmacologic treatment.

The take-home lesson from the MTA study, however, is also that such improvements from medication very much depend on cooperation from teachers, both in helping to assess initial effectiveness of the medication or its dosage and in careful collaboration with families and prescribing physicians over the longer term. Children in the MTA study whose families sought out medication on their own, as part of the community contrast condition, did not improve as significantly. This was arguably because such collaboration was largely absent from community practice, whereas medication treatment in the MTA study was titrated very carefully through systematic feedback from both teachers and parents. Monthly visits to the prescribing physician also helped ensure that adjustments could be made to maintain the most effective dose.

The task for the future, however, is not only to develop collaborative skills in teachers, but to study various ways in which teachers can collaborate effectively. While the usual 10 item teacher rating scales of ADHD symptoms are necessary in the titration of medication, they may not always prove to be sufficient. With a few exceptions, behavioral researchers in education have paid less attention to other medication outcome measures that might improve this process, but I suspect that more attention will be paid in the future. Teachers in the future may also have to be much more aware of issues in child psychopharmacology in general. Because direct marketing of stimulant or related medications is quickly becoming the norm, parents may increasingly seek out teacher opinion on these issues.

Another important direction for the future of ADHD and learning disabilities concerns the nature of comorbidity. We have long thought that some children with ADHD fail to develop reading skills because of their inattentiveness so they later develop learning disabilities. We have also taught that some children who have poor reading skills develop inattentiveness because they cannot process effectively either the verbal or the written demands of the classroom so they are at risk for ADHD. Evidence from studies such as those by Bruce Pennington, Erik Willcutt, and others at the Institute for Behavioral Genetics at Colorado University, however, suggest a third possibility. Comorbidity of ADHD and LD may instead derive from a common source. They suggest that this source is an executive functioning deficit, involving such problems as working memory. This might in turn suggest that the usual emphasis on teaching phonologic awareness and decoding may be necessary but not sufficient as reading instruction for children with ADHD and comorbid LD. It is not altogether clear, however, that remedial approaches based on executive functioning are that well developed or have been that well studied in children with such comorbidity. The future instruction of children with comorbid ADHD and LD may nonetheless turn out to be very different from phonologic remedial approaches that are now predominant for children with learning disabilities.

Other instructional or classroom approaches for children with ADHD are currently extensive and involve basic techniques, such as seating the child in a section of the classroom that will minimize distraction while enhancing access to individual help from the teacher, providing teacher cues and reminders to remain on task or to reflect before acting, judicious use of teacher praise or ignoring, and home–school report cards for feedback and reinforcement. Cooperative learning, social skills training, and self-monitoring approaches are also being used increasingly more for children with ADHD and LD. It is of interest that all those techniques, however, are not markedly different from those used for children with a wide range of learning or behavioral disorders, both in general and in special education settings. A question for the future is therefore likely to be what combination of methods or techniques is most effective for children with ADHD and LD in particular.

One of the admitted limitations of the behavioral treatment package in the MTA study was that a wide variety of components were involved. Thus the relative contribution of each component to its overall success could not necessarily be determined. I suspect the future might suggest a basic "package" of classroom interventions for children with ADHD, although it is too early to predict what that package might look like. It is conceivable that a package could be developed as a fundamental approach necessary to instruction or classroom management, with a list of supplementary techniques that could be added as each child's unique needs dictate.

Although my comments earlier concern primarily ADHD, or ADHD comorbid with LD, it is important to stress that education of children with LD may also change rather dramatically. Such changes are already underway. The general acceptance of early instruction in phonologic awareness, even for children as young as preschoolers, seems to suggest that such instruction will be seen routinely in the future as primary prevention. Failure to develop such skills may then pinpoint children at risk for LD who need more intensive instruction as early as kindergarten. Whether the traditional concept of LD diagnosis requiring discrepancy between IQ and academic performance will still be relevant is open to question, but ruling out low IQ will still be seen as an important factor in diagnosis. Some progress in genetic screening for LD may also occur, but the complexity of the reading process and the pervasiveness of comorbid psychiatric diagnoses in children with LD may hinder this progress for some time to come. Such complexity, as noted for comorbid ADHD and LD described previously, may also lead to the same need for a basic "package" of LD interventions, with add ons depending on the individual needs of each child.

A final concern for the future involves issues of special education eligibility and placement. As most professionals and parents are aware, there is no category of special education for children with ADHD. Children with ADHD are currently eligible for the LD category only if they have comorbid LD. Children with ADHD are eligible for the category of emotional disturbance (ED) if they meet one of the five criteria for that category involving an inability to learn, unsatisfactory social relationships, inappropriate types of behavior or feelings, depressed or unhappy mood, and physical symptoms or fears associated with school or personal problems. Both these categories are problematic for eligibility for children with ADHD for a variety of reasons. The category of other health impaired (OHI) has thus become a category of convenience, especially since ADHD is now listed as one of the medical conditions that could qualify a child in this category under federal law. Estimates are that more than half of children in the OHI category are there because of ADHD. Such will continue to be the case in the future, as OHI is now the fastest growing category of special education.

It is difficult to see that this eligibility picture will change in the future, as the trend in special education is away from specific labels or diagnoses. Not all children with ADHD, of course, need special education and 504 accommodations are sometimes sufficient to bring about teacher awareness of a child's problems, along with enough individual instruction to make a difference. In some ways, it is surprising that ADHD has received as much attention as it has from special education professionals, as they generally do not conduct their research according to specific psychiatric diagnoses. In the future this may change somewhat, given the impressive body of research on ADHD by other professionals. School professionals may also develop increasing sophistication related to the treatment significance of comorbidity of LD or ADHD with other psychiatric disorders, such as conduct disorders, depression, or anxiety.

The trend toward mainstreaming or full inclusion of children with disabilities in general education classrooms will continue to be problematic for some children with ADHD or LD. Special class placement probably needs to remain an option particularly for children with serious comorbid disorders or children who are nonresponsive to, or noncompliant with, medication treatment. I would like to think that the sheer reality of these children's predicament would not be lost on special educators; but, thus far, evidence-based practice seems less apt to carry the day than some of the misguided values of current full inclusionists.

In conclusion, the next few years may see some changes in instruction and classroom management for children with comorbid ADHD and LD, partly because of increasing recognition of a core deficit in executive functioning. Collaboration between teachers and prescribing physicians may continue to be enhanced, not so much because it is a good idea but because direct marketing of psychopharmacologic products to parents may force teachers to become more expert in this area. A basic intervention "package" for children with ADHD and LD may become more of a reality, with add ons selected to address specific needs of individual children. Special education eligibility may not change dramatically, but some recognition of the significance of comorbidity issues in ADHD may lead to more recognition for a continuing need for special classroom placement as opposed to full inclusion. Although it is hazardous to speculate about the future, progress in school recognition for ADHD and in LD prevention gives me some reason to hope that the next few years may bring significant changes in schooling for children with ADHD and LD.

QUESTIONS 4. IN THE NEXT 20 YEARS, WHAT ADVANCES WILL WE SEE IN HOW SCHOOLS RESPOND TO CHILDREN AND YOUTH WITH LEARNING AND ATTENTION PROBLEMS?

Mark Katz, Ph.D. psychologist

Researchers and other professionals who study developmental trajectories over the life span have known for some time now that many adults who struggled during their years in school have gone on to lead meaningful and productive lives (Werner & Smith, 1992, 2001; Masten, 2001; Katz, 1997). Counted among these now successful adults are those who experienced learning and attention problems. We appear, according to these professionals, to be much more resilient than we think we are—a realization that in the future may actually alter how we come to view the lives of many children and youth who struggle with learning and attention problems. The question in the future will not be "if" the lives of these children and youth will reverse course, but rather "when" and, more importantly perhaps, can their schools do anything differently to speed the process along.

There will be very good reasons to believe, in fact, that their schools can. Better yet, some of the same programs and practices that may eventually help reverse the developmental trajectories of struggling children may also prevent their problems from ever emerging in the first place.

Why the hopeful tone? Because there is compelling evidence that it may finally be possible to overcome a major barrier that has prevented many students' lives from changing for the better, no matter how committed their families and schools were. A barrier that up until very recently seemed virtually insurmountable. The barrier? School culture.

Why is school culture—or what researchers, educators, and others sometimes refer to as a school's social climate—such a major barrier to so many struggling students? Because it is a school's culture that sets the tone for how learning differences at school are perceived, whether they are perceived as sources of shame or humiliation or, to the contrary, whether differences are recognized, even celebrated.

If students who learn differently, or who are challenged in other ways, see being different as unsafe—as increasing their sense of danger—it is not likely that they will be very motivated to accept special help when doing so further exposes their differences. Even the best, well-thought out programs may very well fail when vulnerable students perceive the social climate as unsafe.

The future is where our most successful school programs and practices will begin to turn young people's lives around, including the lives of children with learning and attention problems. They will change the social climate of school. Being at school will feel safe, especially so for children and youth who learn differently.

How do you change a social climate? According to some researchers, it starts with modeling (Embry, et al., 1996)—with character education for adults. Researchers have shown that when large numbers of individuals come together to model, promote, teach, and reinforce a set of behaviors designed to increase safe, responsible, and respectful solutions to common problems, the social climate starts to change (Sprague, 2001).

Important behavioral skills—those needed to promote safety, enhance personal relationships, increase understanding, and embrace differences—are modeled, taught, rehearsed, and retaught, much in the same way as reading is. And taught in those situations where danger typically lurks, settings where bullies feel safe, while their victims live in terror. It is in these situations, on the playground, at lunch, on the bus, or during transition times, where students often need a repertoire of new behavioral and emotional problem skills when problems arise.

The buzz word? "Buy in." When it comes to changing a school's culture, everyone has something important to contribute, and everyone has something to be gained: teachers and administrators, secretaries and bus drivers, students and parents. There are no bystanders, and for good reason. Researchers have known for some time now that bystander behavior is a major factor in determining whether aggressive and violent behaviors at school can be expected to increase or decrease (Olweus, 1993).

It has been said that there is nothing so wrong with us that what is right with us cannot fix. One of the first orders of business for programs that set out to change a social climate is to find and nourish strengths. These programs and practices spend time focusing on things that are working well in children's lives and, at every opportunity, highlight children's accomplishments.

While it may be our biological nature, observed even in infancy, to notice differences and to be fascinated by them, those working to change school cultures know that the inferences and the judgments that we make about differences are learned. This being the case, students can actually learn to embrace differences. There are a lot of important skills that schools impart to students before they enter the adult world, but few are more important than this one. The ability to understand and embrace differences.

Is it easy to change a school's culture? Hardly. Is it possible? Yes. Is it important? It is critical. Where do you start? Begin first by learning about some of the successful programs currently being replicated by schools around the United States Resources like the Institute on Violence and Destructive Behavior (IVDB) at the University of Oregon can help (see reference section). Other resources are available as well, and those interested in learning more about them are encouraged to contact me directly.

QUESTION 5. WHAT IS THE ROLE OF PHYSICIANS IN THE FUTURE OF ADHD AND LD?

Marc Lerner, M.D., F.A.A.P. Clinical Professor of Pediatrics, University of California, Irvine

Physicians have a number of roles to play in the care of individuals with ADHD and/or LD. This role begins in the earliest phases of pregnancy. It is well established that handicapping conditions may result from untimely toxic or teratogenic exposures during critical phases of development of the fetus and nervous system. Examples include folic acid deficiency, leading to spina bifida and specific learning problems, the attention and cognitive deficits resulting from substantial alcohol exposure during pregnancy, and the school difficulties that challenge survivors of severely premature births.

Opportunities for the prevention of school problems may grow through public health initiatives (folic acid supplementation of breads and grains) and public education (community service announcements promoting abstinence from alcohol during pregnancy). Physicians can promote the emerging medical findings of improved nutrition during pregnancy and prenatal care, but will need continued advocacy and a broad social consensus to fund critical perinatal interventions to protect children before birth. Beginning with the newborn child, primary care physicians are in a unique position of longitudinal contact with the growing and developing child and their family. This relationship offers the opportunity for early identification and referral of children at risk for attention and learning difficulties. At the same time, most primary care physicians are weakly committed to the careful monitoring of development. The reasons are multiple.

First, physician training begins in hospital and critical care settings, and only partially establishes the skill set needed for outpatient screening of development. This weakness is being addressed through advances in physician education (competency-based curricula). The early professional identification of a cadre of primary care doctors may lead to a separate track in the medical school or postgraduate education to train doctors on the front line of ADHD and LD identification. Ambulatory-based physicians are under a considerable time pressure to provide health maintenance (feeding and care recommendations), complete medical interventions (immunizations, laboratory studies), and provide medical treatment.

Doctors need empirically derived (research-based) support for the techniques of developmental assessment and to establish the value of treatments for learning and attention problems. Specific learning disabilities are often diagnosed when a clinician documents an inadequacy or underperformance of learning, whether in language, social, or academic domains. The earliest signs of these concerns may be a delay in early communication, difficult early temperament or skills of rhyming, phonemic awareness, or sound symbol association. Office-friendly assessment tools are not broadly available to identify problems in these critical areas of child development. One of the great opportunities of the coming decade will be the chance to improve communication to facilitate patient management.

At present, a minority of pediatricians have the benefit of regular school input in monitoring a child's symptoms and response to an ADHD medication or a nonmedical treatment plan. It is quite difficult to join teachers, parents, and doctors into a cohesive team to promote optimal health and learning. The use of web-based technologies should begin to break down communication barriers and improve outcomes in the areas of learning and attention. Pediatricians hope to utilize their ongoing contact with the growing child to apply newly emerging neuroscience techniques to gain accuracy in the diagnosis of school problems. These scientific advances will need to be scrutinized for their reliability and validity. In addition, physicians will need to address the risks of labeling and loss of privacy that already place some individuals with genetically mediated disease at risk of loss of privacy, employment, and/or health insurance. Finally, economic contributions to learning risk must be addressed. These risks range from the heightened risk of school failure of the child born into poor and or single parent homes to the at-risk medical insurance contracts that provide a disincentive when doctors are asked to pay for costly evaluations and treatments from a capitated health insurance fee. While the evaluation of developmental concerns is part of the comprehensive mission of primary care doctors (AAP, 2001), time and reimbursement barriers still exist and must be addressed to truly extend medical care to children and families in need.

Some physicians will maintain a primary care role (pediatricians and family practitioners) whereas others will work as consultants (developmental–behavioral pediatricians, child and adolescent psychiatrists, child neurologists). Primary care physicians will emphasize screening activities and address the myriad of medical concerns that can disrupt learning or imitate learning disorders through their impact on the nervous system. These physicians should be addressing the child who does not hear well, who loses attention through subtle seizures, or who can not pay attention due to obstructive sleep apnea, with daytime fatigue and sleepiness. Consultants often will provide more detailed neurobehavioral and developmental assessment and address the needs of children with complicated problems (e.g., children with multiple simultaneous concerns or uncommon, atypical development). Recent changes in the health care system have sometimes split the health coverage for physical illness from coverage for mental health and developmental disorders. This artificial separation is one of the newest challenges to a thoughtful medical response to learning and attention problems.

Physician specialists in the areas of attention and learning are likely to be assisted by exciting scientific growth in the next 20 years. Some of these advances will emerge from collaboration with colleagues in the fields of bioinformatics, genetics, imaging, pharmacology, and psychology. A child's learning simultaneously expresses the interaction of a child's constitutional (inborn) nature and of their individual experiences. Advances in the mapping of the human genome (DNA sequence) will be followed by a new understanding of gene function and expression. The application of such findings (genomics) will likely allow physicians to predict one's response to medications before they are given in distinction to our current trial-and-error methods. Side effects will be avoided, rather than managed. Advances in the management of biological information may allow the processing and analysis of information (such as brain EEG data obtained while a child is concentrating) in a fashion that can support diagnosis or document treatment effects. Finally, technological advances may transition current interventions that are deemed bypass strategies (computers that can read a scanned page for the dyslexic child or voice recognition programs to deliver typed pages from the spoken word of a dysgraphic child) into broader and more powerful application. The result will be an increase in the speed and efficiency of learning, attention, and communication (such as a system to recognize thought and simultaneously deliver typed copy or scanners that can immediately translate printed words into multiple languages). We can anticipate safer and more efficient interventions for children with learning and attention problems in coming generations.

QUESTION 6. WHAT WILL THE RECENT ADVANCES IN BRAIN RESEARCH CONTRIBUTE TO THE TREATMENT OF ADHD AND LD?

Michael Posner, Sackler Institute, University of Oregon

Two developments of the last decade have transformed the potential for advancing our understanding of the biological basis of ADHD and learning disabilities. They may also have the potential for aiding diagnosis and treatment of ADHD and learning disorders.

For the first time, we can glimpse inside the human brain as people think (Posner & Raichle, 1994). Although some aspects of this technology have been around for a long time, only in the last decade did it become clear that a new era had arrived in our ability to create local images of human brain activity through changes related to the cerebral blood flow. When combined with electrical or magnetic recordings from outside the skull, one can observe in real time the circuits computing aspects of a task such as reading words or attending to a scene (Dale et al., 2000).

Being able to see things has always had a dramatic impact in science. The microscope allowed people to see things too small to be observed by our senses. At the beginning of the 20th century, Santiago Ramon y Cajal (1937) was able for the first time to observe individual nerve cells. Our current ability to see the consequences of human thought depends on the operation of these nerve cells. When neurons are active, they change their own local blood supply. This makes it possible to trace areas of the brain that are active during cognitive processes by measuring local changes in blood flow or changes in the bloods oxygen content.

The second development was sequencing the entire human genome (Ventner et al., 2000). Now it was possible not only to study the functional anatomy of brain networks, but also to examine how genetic differences might influence individual variations in the potential to use these networks in order to acquire and perform skills. The route from genetic endowment to difficulties in attention and learning is not simple nor should it be separated from an understanding of specific brain networks.

How can these methods be combined to improve the diagnosis and treatment of attentional and learning disorders? Two specific examples, of initial efforts to use imaging and genetic data in this way, might help clarify the future potential of brain studies using these methods. Studies of ADHD have suggested that a specific allele (the 7 repeat) of a dopamine receptor gene (DRD4) increases the likelihood of ADHD (Swanson et al., 2001). However, this gene does not appear to do so by reducing the efficiency of attention or other cognitive functions (Swanson et al., 2000). Studies of brain networks of attention have shown that one particular network (executive network) is heavily modulated by dopamine systems expressed in the anterior cingulate and prefrontal cortex (Posner & Petersen, 1990; Posner & Fan, 2003). A recent preliminary finding is that a different allele of the same dopamine gene (DRD4, 4 repeat) may reduce the efficiency of this brain network (Fossella et al., 2002). It seems possible that the 7 repeat allele is related to behaviors associated with ADHD, such as a high need for varied sensory input, but that other alleles may be related to difficulties in attention and other cognitive deficits. If this proves to be true, genotyping the dopamine genes of children given the behavioral diagnosis of ADHD and then using specific tests of attention not influenced by prior learning (Fan et al., 2002) we might be able to determine whether the deficit arises in attention network efficiency or from other behavioral causes. We might want to treat those with the behavioral deficit with behavioral or cognitive intervention, whereas those with an underlying attentional problem might do better with pharmacological interventions. All of this remains very speculative at present, but it is used here merely to suggest how future diagnosis and treatment of ADHD might be related to the functioning of underlying brain systems.

A second example lies in studies of children having difficulty in learning to read (dyslexia). Imaging studies have shown the importance of developing two brain areas in learning fluent reading. The visual word form area of the left temporal–occipital boundary packages visual letters into chunks so that no scanning of the input is needed to see the word as a whole (Posner & McCandliss, 1999). The phonological area in the superior temporal lobe serves to assign sound to the visual chunks (Shaywitz & Shaywitz, 1998). Children with difficulties related to the word form can read slowly but lack fluency, whereas those with phonological difficulties cannot sound out new words and are limited to reading familiar words and guessing at those they do not know. Genetic analysis (Olson et al., 1999) has shown how independent contributions of different genes influence these brain areas.

Although something is known about the general location of some of the genes related to these networks (e.g., chromosome 6), much more needs to be done to understand the specific alleles involved and the role of training. However, what we already know about brain networks underlying skilled reading suggests methods of remediation that have been successful in improving the performance of children (McCandliss et al., 2003). Future studies can be guided by examining the improvements in brain networks that accompany these interventions (McCandliss et al., 2001).

This brief note suggests how studies using brain imaging and molecular genetic methods may become important in the diagnosis and treatment of attentional and learning deficits. No one can predict the exact forms of remediation to which the new knowledge will point, but we can be hopeful that new understanding will be useful in the treatment of disorders.

QUESTION 7. WILL BEHAVIORAL AND MEDICAL ADVANCES LEAD TO A CURE OF ADHD?

James Swanson, Ph.D., Professor of Pediatrics, Director of the Child Development Center, University of California, Irvine

The diagnoses of ADHD by DSM-IV and ICD-10 criteria depends on the manifestation of specific behaviors that result in significant impairment. As defined in these manuals, and in most ratings scales of ADHD symptoms, each item must be judged by this standard of impairment, which defines the presence of psychopathology. One way to "cure" ADHD is to reduce impairment so this essential criterion is no longer met.

In the MTA study, the traditional treatments for ADHD (stimulant medication and behavior modification) effectively reduced impairment over time. As outlined by Swanson et al. (2001), an operational definition of "success" was defined by a cutoff on ratings of the ADHD and ODD symptoms on the SNAP rating scale, which uses rating categories defined by psychopathology. That is, the items on the SNAP are stated categorically as in the DSM-IV manual (i.e., Does this child "often fail to give close attention to detail . . . ," with choices of no ("not at all" = 0) or yes with a graded response ("just a little" = 1, "quite a bit" = 2, "very much" = 3). An average rating greater than 1.0 (i.e., more then "just a little") was defined as the cutoff for psychopathology. Based on this logic, at the end of the 14-month treatment phase of the MTA, each subject was classified as a "success" or not.

If "success" defined by lack of psychopathology is accepted as a cure for ADHD, then the cure rate for the MTA treatments was remarkably high: 68% for the combined treatment, 56% for the medication alone treatment, 34% for the behavior modification alone treatment, and 25% for the community treatment. In addition, the comorbidity rates decreased by about 50% for the high prevalent cooccurring conditions, ODD (from about 40 to 20%) and anxiety (from about 30 to 15%), as well as for the low prevalence disorders.

Current treatments can reduce impairment so that the essential feature for the diagnosis of ADHD is no longer present, so we do not have to wait for the future to bring this type of "cure." However, this is not the full story. The current treatments are symptomatic and are expected to produce this dramatic reduction in impairment only when they are applied. This logic suggests that lifelong treatment with medication and application of behavior modification would be required to maintain this "cure," and if treatment is stopped, then a relapse would be expected.

This in the bane of treatments for ADHD: they do not last. With current medications, there seems to be little change in status of the individual over time, except for acute tolerance (tachyphalaxis), which builds up each day but dissipates overnight when the medication is no longer in the system (Swanson et al., 1999). In the long term, impairment returns when medication is stopped, which occurred in almost all cases in an early long-term follow-up study (Abikoff and Hetchman, 2002), this occurred in the MTA, too (MTA Group, in press).

The long-term outcome of the behavior modification alone group showed a different pattern. When the treatment phase ended, fewer cases were classified as "successes" (34% versus 56% for medication alone), but over time there was little deterioration. Thus, it appears that fewer ADHD children were "cured" by behavioral than by pharmacological intervention, but the "cure" may be longer lasting for the behavioral intervention. This longer duration may be because the behavioral interventions were continued after the MTA staff were withdrawn. The behavioral intervention in the MTA was based on work with parents and teachers, who then implemented token systems (daily report cards) and developed coping skills to deal with problems associated with ADHD symptoms in their children and students. Part of the MTA behavioral treatment was designed to prepare parents and teachers to continue the intervention alone when the MTA staff were withdrawn. Of course, if this naturalistic continuation were the reason for the long-lasting effects, then if the delivery of the psychosocial intervention was eventually stopped, a return of symptoms would be expected.

Initially, MTA proponents of the psychosocial approach were disappointed by the clear superiority of the pharmacological approach. Secondary analysis of the MTA provided some clarification of the relative effectiveness of behavioral treatment, but still the limitations were disappointing (Pelham, 1999). One reason for the limited efficacy of the behavioral treatments may have been poor attendance in the parent training component (MTA Group, 1999b). Cunningham et al. (1993, 1995, 1998, 2000) have proposed a new model for parent training based on group problem solving, which may correct this deficiency. Sonuga-Barke et al. (2001) have used an approach and utilized "home visitors" in the United Kingdom health care system. These visitors provided a behavioral intervention with preschool children with ADHD. The findings suggested a large effect size (.48) in the reduction of ADHD symptoms.

In retrospect, what seemed to be a low "success" or cure rate (34%) now seems clinically and socially significant. If applied to all children with ADHD, the type of psychosocial treatment used in the MTA may result in the cure of over 1 million of the 3 million school-aged children estimated to have ADHD. In the future, we hope to increase the percentage of children who are successfully treated with psychosocial interventions, but we are also concerned about eventual relapse, even if it is partial relapse (see Biederman et al., 2000).

So we and others are working to develop a new type of behavioral treatment (attention training) that may have permanent effects on children with ADHD. The background for this comes from evidence of brain plasticity from the field of cognitive neurosciences (see Posner et al., 2000). According to this approach, the neural networks that have been described for the components of attention (alerting, orienting, and executive control) are inefficient in ADHD children. However, if these components are viewed as skills that can be improved by practice, then very specific attention training may alter brain development and provide a cure of the basic underlying deficit of ADHD. This offers an approach to increase the potency of the behavioral treatment of the MTA (which was directed primarily toward work with parents and teachers) by working directly with ADHD children.

Barkley (2000) suggested that the effects of the BEH intervention were limited because it did not target underlying core deficits of ADHD. The existence of one (Barkley, 1997) or multiple (Sergeant et al., 1999) core deficits is debated, but the empirical information from multiple paradigms (see Swanson et al. 1998b) suggests that the underactivity of key brain regions is a characteristic of the disorder. One of the science-based interventions noted in this letter is based on the controversial but plausible hypothesis that direct intervention may correct the neural underactivity of ADHD children. This emphasis has strong scientific support from a growing literature in the cognitive neurosciences that suggests "training" can alter brain organization in animals (e.g., Merzenich and Jenkins, 1995; Greenough et al., 1999; Posner et al., 2001) and in humans (Tallal et al., 1996; Ungerledier et al., 2001; Posner et al., 2001). This basic science research suggests promising new targets and techniques for psychosocial interventions (e.g., specific training activities for children) to supplement usual psychosocial treatments (e.g., parent training and teacher training for school-based token systems with home-based reward) that were developed in the mid-1960s (Patterson, 1967; O'Leary et al., 1969) and are still applied essentially unchanged.

This new direction challenges the concept of domain specificity of training that was formulated over 100 years in psychology (Thorndike & Woodworth, 1901) and has remained dominant since then (Chase & Simon, 1973). Domain specificity suggests that skills developed in one domain do not transfer to enhance skills in another domain. Both Posner et al. (2001) and Posner (2002) review this history of domain specificity and present a theoretical rationale and extensive empirical support from the cognitive neurosciences of the concept of brain plasticity (that the training can alter neural organization) and of the possibility of generalization (that targeted change at the neural level can have broad effects on cognition and behavior). Brain plasticity is not limited to early childhood (Bruer, 1999).

Over the past several years, the Sackler Institute at Cornell University in New York City has focused on these issues. This preliminary work included a 2-year comprehensive assessment by six panels, each consisting of five to seven experts, of the literature on the developing human brain, supported by a grant from the McDonnell Foundation (see Posner et al., 2001). This status report provided the intellectual and theoretical basis for our proposal and contributed to our decision to focus on attention training (ATT) as a new, science-based psychosocial intervention for ADHD.

ATT is based on the concept that attention is an organ system (i.e., has a specific anatomy defined by neural networks; see Posner and Raichle, 1994) that serves a general central function, despite highly distributed effects across sensory modalities and cognitive domains (Posner, 2002). ATT assumes that processes of neural plasticity allow for improved efficiency of this general process with focused and extended practice, and the first applications in animals (see Washburn and Rumbaugh, 1992) and in humans (see Kerns et al., 1999) support this approach. Over the past decade at the University of Oregon, a multidisciplinary group including cognitive neuroscientists (e.g., M. Posner), electrophysiologists (e.g., B. McCandliss), developmental psychologists (e.g., M. Rothbart), and rehabilitation specialists (e.g., M. Sohlberg) developed specific tasks to selectively activate these neural networks by the use of warning signals (for alerting), visual–spatial cues (for orienting), and cognitive conflict (for executive control). These activation tasks have been used as part of "attention training" in adults to accelerate recovery of function following brain injury (see Sohlberg et al., 1987; 2000) and to train attention in toddlers (see Posner, 2001).

Swanson et al. (1998a) proposed that the deficits of ADHD may be characterized as inefficiencies in these attentional networks. Also, this approach has been used by Washburn and Rumbaugh (1992) in a NASA-sponsored program to develop a program to train monkeys to attend to tasks. They observed an impact on the control of attention in the laboratory setting and in emotional status in the natural setting and, on the basis of this Rumbaugh and Washburn (1996), suggested this as an animal model for ADHD and its treatment with nonpharmacological intervention.

Considerable effort has already been devoted to ATT as an intervention. Posner and Rothbart (personal communication, 2001) have conducted a project funded by the National Science Foundation to train attention in school aged-children (5 to 8 years) and a project funded by the McDonnell Foundation to apply ATT to train attention in toddlers. McCandliss and Posner (personal communication) used support from the IBM Foundation to refine ATT tasks for use with children. Rumbaugh et al. (1989) and Rumbaugh and Washburn (1996) developed computer-based tasks (similar to "computer games") to train monkeys and chimpanzees to perform high-level cognitive tasks that require sustained attention (long bouts of work), selective attention (response to cues), and executive control of attention (resolution of conflicting response tendencies).

At the Sackler Institute, McCandliss (2002) have been developing child-friendly versions of computer-based tasks for attention training. We have generated several categories of attention training tasks. General tasks involve the manipulation of a joystick to follow a target (*side, chase, pursuit, hole,* and *maze*) and matching target stimuli to sample stimuli, deciding whether two stimuli are the same or different, and searching for target stimuli among distracting stimuli (*matching-to-sample, delayed matching-to-sample, same/different*, and *visual search*). The critical tasks are related to the three attentional networks, including *warn* and *wait* (altering); *position* and *meaning* (orienting); and *numbers* (numeral–magnitude conflict), *colors* (color–word conflict), and *compatible* (stimulus–response conflict) (conflict resolution).

The ATT intervention is based on the concept of "skill training," but in a way quite different than in many prior training programs. We view the components of attention (alerting, orienting, and executing) as skills that can be enhanced by training. The concept of "domain specificity" of training suggest that transfer or generalization does not occur. Our approach challenges this dogma, based on the theoretical advances in the cognitive neurosciences (see Posner et al., 2001; Posner, 2002). We propose a distinctly different approach than in "cognitive therapy" (see Abikoff, 1991), which is affected by domain specificity and does not generalize. By focusing on the underlying central attentional skills that are called upon by many tasks and by improving the efficiency of the underlying network that performs the underlying process, we expect to observe improved performance on multiple tasks (i.e., we expect transfer of training).

We hope in the future that attention training may provide a way to cure the underlying deficit of ADHD so the need to continue treatment for a lifetime may not be a requirement for the long-term reduction of impairment of ADHD symptoms.

QUESTION 8. WILL ADVANCES IN PSYCHOLOGICAL AND NEUROBIOLOGICAL UNDERSTANDING OF LEARNING DISABILITIES LEAD TO SOME FORM OF CURE?

Bruce D. McCandliss, Ph.D.—Assistant Professor of Psychology in Psychiatry, Sackler Institute for Developmental Psychobiology, Weill Medical College of Cornell University

Understanding learning disability at the psychological and neurobiological level may play a large and productive role in the study and generation of useful treatments, and provide insights as to *why* some treatments work well, and for whom they work best. However, the general term *learning disability* largely serves as a catchall phrase within the context of educational systems, serving to delineate which children require special services above and beyond the typical classroom setting. Given the non-specific nature of learning disabilities as a syndrome, it is informative to examine the special services typically provided to such children. Data from the '94–95 school year indicates that the U.S. Department of Education provided special services to approximately 2.56 million children (4.4%) designated to have some form of specific learning disability, with an estimated 2.01 million (3.54%) receiving special services for reading disability. This pattern underscores the often cited observation that among all the identified forms of specific learning disabilities, those that impact the process of learning to read pose what is perhaps the most pervasive problem for our school children.

Focusing on a specific form of learning disability, such as reading disability, serves to illustrate one pathway through which investigations at the level of psychological function and neurobiological activity might contribute to the process of understanding, innovating, and refining treatment approaches. Although specific reading disability represents just one form of learning disability, this prevalent and well-studied example provides an illustration of the connection between intervention and basic research at the levels of complex symptoms, core cognitive deficits, and underlying brain circuitry.

A great deal of developmental, cognitive, and neuroscience research has made progress in characterizing commonly recurring patterns of deficits associated with reading disability. Many reading difficulties identified in the classroom can be systematically linked to a more fundamental cognitive deficit, often referred to as "a core phonological deficit" (for review see National Reading Panel, 2000). Strong convergent research demonstrates that the most common form developmental reading disability is specifically linked to an underlying core cognitive deficit in a process that is more basic than reading itself: the ability to focus the mind on the phonemes (basic sound units) within words, break them apart, and put them together. This skill is an important precursor to the specific challenge of learning to read.

By linking the symptoms of reading difficulties with a core cognitive deficit, the field made several important advances in understanding reading disabilities. Objective measures were refined and standardized to specifically assess phonological abilities in early school years. Furthermore, linking reading disability to a core cognitive deficit provided a new theoretical basis for the creation and refinement of interventions designed to strengthen this cognitive ability in identified children, and young children at risk. In over 20 controlled studies of normal and disabled readers, the impact of such interventions led to effect sizes that fell in the "medium" to "strong" range for improving reading skills measured shortly afterward, with many children moving from scores that indicate impairments to scores indicating normal performance. Such positive short-term results provide a promising outlook toward alleviating, if not curing, a major form of learning disability. Furthermore, these results cast a new light on reading disability, not as an inability to learn, but more an inability to learn from commonly used teaching methods.

However, a number of issues remain that demonstrate that there is a still a long way to go. First, there are still formidable barriers between such research-based intervention approaches and the channels of dissemination of materials in educational that could provide such treatment to large numbers of children in need. Perhaps even more crucial, there are still open questions concerning whether children with reading disabilities are best considered as "cured" after an intervention helps them score in the average range on standardized tests (for discussion, see Olson, 2002). Longitudinal research is needed to investigate how such boosts in core cognitive skills translate into later reading success. Additionally, research tools are needed that enables us to tell the difference between an interventions that merely reduces a surface level symptom, such as poor performance on a particular cognitive test, and those that lead to long-lasting remediation of a core cognitive process that might transfer to new situations. Finally, it may be the case that for more severe disabilities, the possibility of detecting and addressing a core cognitive deficit early in development is the best hope for making a substantial impact.

Recent advances in brain imaging may prove to be a valuable tool in overcoming many of challenges we face in understanding the causes of reading disabilities and understanding the successes and limitations in interventions. When skilled readers (both adults and children) actively process the sounds within written or spoken words, neural activity typically increases over resting baseline levels, especially in language-related left posterior brain areas (i.e. peri-sylvian regions, located somewhat behind the left ear). This does not occur, however, in the brains of reading disabled individuals—brain activity in these left posterior language areas demonstrate no difference between a control task and task require actively processing the sounds within words. This research provides a neurobiological marker for a common form of reading disability (i.e. development alphonological reading disability) that helps advance efforts to link psychological learning difficulties to individual differences in brain structure and function. As our ability to measure such phenomena within an individual improves, we will gain greater insight into how individual differences in brain activity translates into difficulties in learning to read under instruction approaches typically found in schools.

Even with the last two years, the field has advanced rapidly to the point where intervention studies are often coordinated with brain imaging studies, and this combination has opened up the possibility of linking specific interventions to changes brain circuitry. Several studies have demonstrated that intervention efforts focused at core phonological deficits and reading skills not only boost cognitive measures of these skills, but lead to systematic changes in activity within specific brain regions implicated in reading disability (see for example, McCandliss, et al., 2001; Simos, et al., 2002; Temple et al., 2003). These early studies serve as demonstrations that brain activity patterns associated with reading disability can be changed via short-term interventions in a way that is measurable at the neurobiological level.

Even in light of these advances, we are clearly far from the day in which an individual's fMRI will bear directly on the planning of a comprehensive and individualized treatment program. However, these studies mark the beginning of a long-term research process that will eventually map out the relationship between critical design principles that drive particular interventions to produce changes within particular cognitive skills and within particular supporting brain systems. Furthermore, as neurobiological measures are applied to younger and younger children and infants, new possibilities are opened up for early intervention for young children at risk. The fruit of such research is likely to prove valuable in understanding how specific interventions interact with specific individual deficits. Such work may provide a basis for understanding why it is that some interventions work remarkably well, and may eventually contribute to the practice of customizing specific interventions to meet needs of individual children.

Reading disabilities provide a clear example of how a specific learning disability can be investigated at the level of complex presenting symptoms, underlying core cognitive deficits, and associated brain regions. Furthermore, this example serves to demonstrate that patterns of brain activity can be modified via learning activities that target core cognitive deficits in processing. Research and discovery concerning other learning disabilities may follow similar pathways of development, from mapping complex symptoms to core cognitive deficits, linking core cognitive deficits to individual differences in the structure and function of brain systems, and developing intervention techniques that target these systems with interventions that are well-adapted to learner's current skills and needs.

CONCLUSIONS: WHERE HAVE WE BEEN AND WHERE ARE WE GOING?

The questions we have posed to a parent, physician, educator, nueropsychologist, psychiatrist, and psychologist were designed to give our readers a look into the future assessment and treatment of ADHD and LD. New and exciting advances in genetic profiling, neuropsychology, psychopharmacology, and brain imaging will serve to change the way we diagnosis and treat ADHD and LD. Practitioners from the field of medicine and education will need to collaborate in their efforts to make more refined assessments and recommendations for treatment. It will be possible to determine who will benefit from which medication and avoid negative side effects. More refined approaches to teaching reading and addressing LD will be possible through the use of computer technology. Advances in neurobiology and behavioral technology hold the promise of a possible cure for ADHD and LD.

The effective use of these advances will require cross training and multidisciplinary teams with knowledge of neuropsychological tests, brain imaging, and advanced technology for bypassing educational limitations. Paraprofessionals may become a cost-effective means for providing a continuity of services and intervention across, families, schools, and communities. Community-based collaborative services may serve to bridge the gap among home, school, and community.

Intervention in the school will center on changing the climate of the school to better accept individual differences. Programs that are replicable and have shown to be effective in providing early intervention and safer environments for children will be implemented on a large scale. School-wide programs will be implemented to "bully proof" schools. This will require better systems of dissemination of information and training in the use of "best practice" approaches that are grounded in research. Universities, state and federal agencies, and schools need to develop a more streamlined method of taking research to practice. Training should be focused on developing competency in the implementation of innovative programs rather than mere exposure to ideas. This will require new models for teacher training and preservice and in-service training of teachers and support staff. The contributors to this chapter have provided us with a road map for advancement of the field. The challenge is in breaking from the past to make the future happen. It is hoped that by providing a glimpse of converging fields of study we have painted an optimistic view of the future.

REFERENCES

Abikoff, H. (1991). Cognitive training in ADHD children. Less to it than meets the eye. *Journal of Learning Disability*, 24: 205–209.

Abikoff H., & Hechtman L. (2002). *Long-term effects of Stimulant Medication*. Unpublished Manuscript.

American Academy of Pediatrics (2000). Committee on psychosocial aspects of child and family health: The new morbidity revisited: *Pediatrics*, 108, 1227–1230.

American Academy of Pediatrics (May, 2002). Committee on quality improvement, sub-committee on attention-deficit/hyperactivity disorder. "Diagnosis and evaluation of children with attention-deficit/hyperactivity disorder." *Pediatrics vol 105*, no. 5, 1158–1170.

Barkley, R. A. (1997). Behavioral inhibition, sustained attention, and executive functions: Constructing a unifying theory of ADHD. *Psychological Bulletin*, 121, 65–94.

Barkley, R. A. (2000). Commentary on the multimodality treatment study of children with ADHD. *Journal of Abnormal Child Psychology*, 28, 595–599.

Barkley, R. A. (1990). *Attention Deficit Hyperactivity Disorder: A Handbook for Diagnosis and Treatment*, New York: Guildford.

Bruer, J. T. (1999). *The Myth of the First Three Years*. New York: Free Press.

Cajal, S. R. Y. (1937). *Recollection of my life*. Philadelphia: American Philosophical Society.

Chase, W., & Simon, H. (1973). The mind's eye in chess. In WG Chase, *Visual Information Processing* (pp 215–281).

Cunningham, C. E. (1998). Large group, community based, parenting courses. In R. A. Barkley (Ed.) *Attention Deficit Hyperactivity: A Handbook for Diagnosis and Treatment*. New York: Guilford Press.

Cunningham, C. E., Boyle, M., Offord, D., Racine, Y., Hundert, J., Secord, M., & McDonald, J. (2000). Tri ministry project: Diagnostic and demographic correlates of school-based parenting course utilization. *Journal of Consulting and Clinical Psychology*, 68, 928–933.

Cunningham, C. E., Bremner, B., & Boyle, M. (1995). Large group school-based courses for parents of preschoolers at risk for disruptive behavior disorders: Utilization, outcome, and cost effectiveness. *Journal of Child Psychology and Psychiatry*, 36, 1141–1159.

Cunningham, C. E., Bremner, R. B., & Secord-Gilbert, M. (1993). Increasing the availability, accessibility, and cost efficacy of services for families of ADHD children: A school-based systems-oriented parenting course. *Canadian Journal of School Psychology*, 9, 1–15.

Dale, A. M., Liu, A. K., Fischi, B. R., Ruckner, R., Beliveau, J. W., Lewine, J. D., & Halgren, E. (2000). Dynamic statistical parameter mapping: Combining fMRI and MEG for high resolution cortical activity. *Neuron*, 26, 55–67.

Embry, D., Flannery, D. J., Vazsonyi, A. T., Powell, K. E., & Atha, H. (1996). PeaceBuilders: A theoretically driven, school-based model for early violence prevention. *American Journal of Preventive Medicine*, 12, 91–100.

Fan, J., McCandliss, B. D., Sommer, T., Raz, M., & Posner, M. I. (2002). Testing the efficiency and independence of attentional networks. *Journal of Cognitive Neuroscience*, 14(3), 340–347.

Fossella, J., Posner, M. I., Fan, J., Swanson, J. M., & Pfaff, D. W. (2002). Attentional phenotypes for the analysis of higher mental function. *Scientific World Journal*, 2, 217–223.

Fowler, M. (1990). *Maybe You Know My Kid (1st Ed.)*. New York: Carol Publishing Group.

Fowler, M. (1992). *CHADD Educators Manual*. CHADD, Landover, MD.

Greenough, W. T., Black, J. E., Klintsova, A., Bates, K. E., & Weiler, J. (1999). Experience and plasticity in brain structure: Possible implications of basic research findings for developmental disorders. In S. H. Broman & J. M. Fletcher, et al. (Eds.), *The Changing Nervous System: Neurobehavioral Consequences of Early Brain Disorders* (pp. 51–70). New York, NY: Oxford University Press.

Jensen, P. S., Hinshaw, S. P., Kraemer, H. C., Lenora, N., Newcorn, J. H., Abikoff, H. B., March, J. S., Arnold, L. E., Cantwell, D. P., Conners, C. K., Elliott, G. R., Greenhill, L. L., Hechtman, L., Hoza, B., Pelham, W. E., Severe, J. B., Swanson, J. M., Wells, K. C., Vitiello, B., & Wigal, T. (2001). ADHD comorbidity findings from the MTA study: Comparing comorbid subgroups. *J. Am. Acad. Child Adolesc. Psychiatry* 40, 147–158.

Katz, M. (1997). *On playing a poor hand well: Insights from the lives of those who have overcome childhood risks and adversities*. New York: Norton.

Kerns, K.A., Eso, K., & Thompson, J. (1999). Investigation of a direct intervention for improving attention in young children with ADHD. *Developmental Neuropsychology*, 16, 273–295.

Masten, A. S. (2001). Ordinary magic: Resilience processes in development. *American Psychologist*, 56(3), 227–238.

McCandliss, B. D. (2002). Attention Training: What Can We Learn from Interventions for Reading Disability? Presentation at the Annual Conference of CHADD, Miami Beach, FL.

McCandliss, B. D., Maritnez, A., Sandak, R., Beck, I., Perfetti, C., & Schnieder, W. S. (2001). A cognitive intervention for reading impaired children produces increased recruitment of left peri-sylvian regions during word reading: An fMRI study. *Neuroscience Abstracts*, 27, 961–964.

McCandliss, B. D., Sandak, R., Beck, I., & Perfetti, C. (2003). Focusing attention on decoding for children with poor reading skills: Design and preliminary tests of the Word Building intervention. *Scientific Studies of Reading*.

Merzenich, M. M., & Jenkins, W. M. (1995). In *Maturational Windows and Adult Cortical Plasticity*, B Julesz and I Kovacs, Eds. (pp 247–272) New York: Addison-Wesley.

MTA Cooperative Group. (1999a). A 14-month randomized clinical trial of treatment strategies for attention deficit hyperactivity disorder. *Archives of General Psychiatry*, 56, 1073–1086.

MTA Cooperative Group. (1999b). Moderators and mediators of treatment response for children with attention-deficit/hyperactivity disorder. *Archives of General Psychiatry, 56,* 1088–1096.

MTA Cooperative Group. (in press). Differential deterioration of effects in the MTA treatment groups: change from the end of treatment to the first follow-up. *Pediatrics.*

O'Leary, K. D., Becker, W. C., Evans, M. B., & Saudargas, R. A. (1969). A token reinforcement program in a public school: a replication and analysis. *Journal of Applied Behavior Analysis, 2,* 3–13.

Olson, R. K., Datta, H., Gayan, J., & DeFries (1999). A behavioral-genetic analysis of reading disabilities and component processes. In R. Klein & P. McMullen (Eds.), *Converging methods for understanding reading and dyslexia* (pp. 133–151). Cambridge: MIT Press.

Olweus, D. (1993). *Bullying at school.* Malden, MA: Blackwell.

Patterson, G. (1967). *Families.* Austin TX: Research Press.

Pelham, W. E. (1999). the NIMH multimodality treatment study for ADHD. Just say yes to medication. *Clinical Child Psych Newsletter. 14,* 1–3.

Posner, M. I. (2001). Developing brains: The work of the sackler institute. *Clinical Neuroscience Research, 1,* 258–266.

Posner, M. I. (2002). Issues in Psychology: Domain Specificity of Skills and Knowledge. Manuscript in preparation.

Posner, M. I., & Fan, J. (in press). Attention as an organ system. In J. Pomerantz (Ed.), *Neurobiology of perception and communication: From synapse to society.* Cambridge, UK: Cambridge University Press.

Posner, M. I., & Gilbert, C. D. (2000). Attention and primary visual cortex. *Proceedings of the National Academy of Sciences, 96,* 2585–2587.

Posner, M. I., & McCandliss, B. D. (1999). Brain circuitry during reading. In R. Klein & P. McMullen (Eds.), *Converging methods for understanding reading and dyslexia* (pp. 305–337). Cambridge: MIT Press.

Posner, M. I., & Petersen, S. E. (1990). The attention system of the human brain. *Annual Review of Neuroscience, 13,* 25–42.

Posner, M. I., & Raichle, M. E. (1994). *Images of mind.* Scientific American Books.

Posner, M. I., & Raichle, M. E. (Eds.) (1998). Overview: The neuroimaging of human brain function. *Proceedings of the National Academy of Sciences of the United States of America, 95,* 763–764.

Rumbaugh, D. M., & Washburn, D. A. (1996). Attention and memory in learning: A comparative adaptational perspective. In GR Lyon and NA Krasnegor (Eds.), *Attention, Memory and Executive Function.* Baltimore: Paul H. Brookes.

Sergeant J. A., Oosterlaan J., van der Meere J. (1999). Information processing and energetic factors in attention-deficit/hyperactivity disorder. In Quay H and Hogan (Eds.). *Handbook of Disruptive Behavior Disorders.* New York: Plenum Press.

Shaywitz, S. E., & Shywitz, B. A. (1998). Functional disruption in the organization of the brain for reading in dyslexia. *Proceedings of the National Academic of Sciences of the United States of America, 95,* 2636.

Sohlberg, M. M., & Mateer, C. A. (1987). Effectiveness of an attention training program. *Journal of Clinical and Experimental Neuropsychology, 19,* 117–130.

Sohlberg, M. M., McLaughlin, K. A., Pavese, A., Heidrich, A., & Posner, M. I. (2000). Evaluation of attention process training and brain injury education in persons with acquired brain injury. *Journal of Clinical and Experimental Neuropsychology, 22,* 656–576.

Sonuga-Barke, E. J. S., Daley, D., Thomson, M., Laver-Bradbury, C., & Weeks, A. (2001). parent-based therapies for preschool ADHD: A randomized, controlled trial with a community sample. *J. Am. Acad. Child Adolesc Psychiatry,* 40, 402–408.

Sprague, J. (2001). *BEST II (building effective schools together) training.* San Diego: San Diego County Department of Education.

Swanson, J., Deutsch, C., Cantwell, D., Posner, M., Kenndy, J., Barr, C., Moyzis, R., Schuck, S., Flodman, P., & Spence, A. (2001). Genes and attention-deficit hyperactivity disorder. *Clinical Neuroscience Research,* 1(3), 207–216.

Swanson, J. M., Gupta, S., Guinta, D., Flynn, D., Agler, D., Lemer, M., Williams, L., Shoulson, I., Wigal, S. (1999). Acute Tolerance to Methylphenidate in the Treatment of Attention Deficit Hyperactivity Disorder in Children. *Clinical Pharmacology and Therapeutics,* 66, 295–305.

Swanson, J., Oosterlaan, J., Murias, M., Moyzis, R., Schuck, S., Mann, M., Feldman, P., Spence, M. A., Sergeant, J., Smith, M., Kennedy J., & Posner, M. I. (2000). ADHD children with 7-repeat allele of the DRD4 gene have extreme behavior but normal performance on critical neuropsychological tests of attention. *Proceedings of the National Academic of Sciences of the United States of America,* 97, 4754–4759.

Swanson, J. M., Sergeant, J. A., Taylor, E., Sonuga-Barke, E. J. S., Jenscn, P. S., Cantwell, D. P. (1998b). Attention-deficit hyperactivity disorder and hyperkinetic disorder. *The Lancet, 351,* 429–433.

Tallal, P., Miller, N. E., Bedi, G., Wang, X., Nagarajan, S. S., Srikantan, S., Schreiner, C., Jenkins, W. M., & Merzenich, M. M. (1996). Language comprehension in language-learning impaired children improved with acoustically modified speech. *Science, 271,* 81–84.

Thorndike, E. L., & Woodworth, R. S. (1901). The influence of one methal function upon the efficiency of other functions. *Psychological Review, 8,* 247–267; 384–395; 553–564.

Ungerledier (2001). Presentation at the Memory and Learning Conference, UC Irvine.

Ventner, et al. (2001). The sequence of the human genome. *Science,* 291, 1304–1350.

Washburn, D. A., & Rumbaugh, D. M. (1992). Testing primates with joystick-based automated apparatus: Lessons from the language research center's computerized test system. *Behavior Research Methods, Instruments, and Computers, 24,* 157–164.

Werner, E. (1995). Resilience in development. *Current Directions in Psychological Science, American Psychological Society,* 81–85.

Werner, E., & Smith, R. (1992). *Overcoming the odds: High risk children from birth to adulthood.* Ithaca, NY: Cornell University.

Werner, E., & Smith, R. (2001). *Journeys from childhood to midlife: Risk, resilience, and recovery.* Ithaca, NY: Cornell University.

Appendices

Baseball Analogy of ADHD: Inattentive Subtype

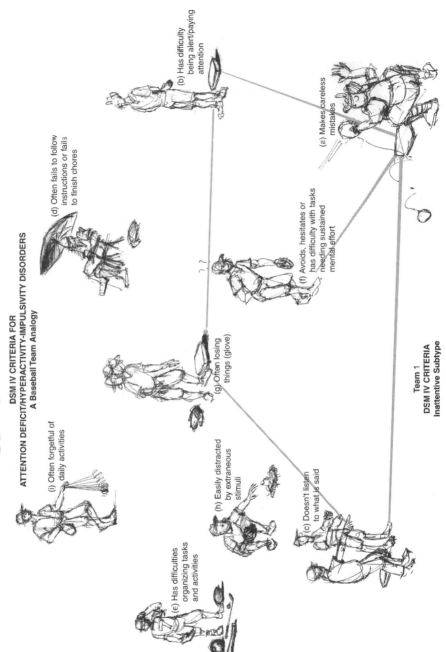

**DSM IV CRITERIA FOR
ATTENTION DEFICIT/HYPERACTIVITY-IMPULSIVITY DISORDERS
A Baseball Team Analogy**

(d) Often fails to follow instructions or fails to finish chores

(b) Has difficulty being alert/paying attention

(a) Makes careless mistakes

(f) Avoids, hesitates or has difficulty with tasks needing sustained mental effort

(i) Often forgetful of daily activities

(g) Often losing things (glove)

(h) Easily distracted by extraneous stimuli

(c) Doesn't listen to what is said

(e) Has difficulties organizing tasks and activities

**Team 1
DSM IV CRITERIA
Inattentive Subtype**

Baseball Analogy of ADHD: Hyperactivity/ Impulsive Subtype

DSM IV CRITERIA FOR
ATTENTION DEFICIT/HYPERACTIVITY-IMPULSIVITY DISORDERS
A Baseball Team Analogy

(f) Often talks excessively

(b) Often leaves seat when expected to remain seated

(c) Runs or climbs about excessively in situations where it is inappropriate

(e) Always "on the go" or acts as if "driven by a motor"

(h) Often has difficulty waiting in lines or awaiting turn

(a) Often fidgets with hands or feet or squirms in seat

(d) Often has difficulty playing quietly

(i) Often interrupts or intrudes on others' conversations

(g) Blurts out answers before questions have been completed

Team 2
DSM IV CRITERIA
Hyperactive-Impusulsive Subtype

481

The Iceberg

THE ADD/ADHD ICEBERG

Only 1/8 of an iceberg is visible!!
Most of it is hidden beneath the surface!!

THE TIP OF THE ICEBERG:
The Obvious ADD/ADHD Behaviors

IMPULSIVITY
Lacks self-control   Difficulty awaiting turn
Blurts out   Interrupts
Tells untruths   Intrudes
Talks back   Loses temper

HYPERACTIVITY
Restless   Talks a lot
Fidgets   Can't sit still
Runs or climbs a lot   Always on the go

INATTENTION
Disorganized   Doesn't follow through
Doesn't pay attention   Is forgetful
Doesn't seem to listen   Distractible
Makes careless mistakes   Loses things
Doesn't do school work

"HIDDEN BENEATH THE SURFACE"
The Not So Obvious Behaviors!!

NEUROTRANSMITTER DEFICITS
IMPACT BEHAVIOR
Inefficient levels of neurotransmitters,
norepinephrine, dopamine, & serotonin,
result in reduced brain activity on thinking tasks.

COEXISTING CONDITIONS
2/3 have at least one other condition
Anxiety (37%)   Depression (28%)
Bipolar (12%)   Substance Abuse (5%)
Tourette Disorder (11%)
Obsessive Compulsive Disorder –
Oppositional Defiant Disorder (59%)
Conduct Disorder (43%)

WEAK EXECUTIVE FUNCTIONING
Working Memory and Recall
Activation, Alertness, and Effort
Internalizing language
Controlling emotions
Complex Problem Solving

SERIOUS LEARNING PROBLEMS (90%)
Specific Learning Disability (25-30%)
Poor working memory   Can't memorize easily
Forgets teacher and parent requests
Slow math calculation   Slow retrieval of information
Poor written expression   Difficulty writing essays
Poor listening and reading comprehension
Difficulty describing the world in words
Difficulty rapidly putting words together
Disorganization   Slow cognitive processing
Poor fine motor coordination   Poor handwriting
Inattention   Impulsive learning style

SLEEP DISTURBANCE (50%)
Doesn't get restful sleep
Can't fall asleep
Can't wake up
Late for school
Sleeps in class
Sleep deprived   Irritable
Morning battles with parents

TWO TO FOUR YEAR
DEVELOPMENTAL DELAY
Less mature
Less responsible
14 yr. old acts like 10

NOT LEARNING EASILY FROM
REWARDS AND PUNISHMENT
Repeats misbehavior
May be difficult to discipline
Less likely to follow rules
Difficulty managing his own behavior
Doesn't study past behavior
Doesn't learn from past behavior
Acts without sense of hindsight
Must have immediate rewards
Long-term rewards don't work
Doesn't examine his own behavior
Difficulty changing his behavior

IMPAIRED SENSE OF TIME
Doesn't judge passage of time accurately
Loses track of time   Often late
Doesn't have skills to plan ahead
Forgets long-term projects or is late
Difficulty estimating time required for tasks
Difficulty planning for future
Impatient   Hates waiting
Time creeps   Homework takes forever
Avoids doing homework

LOW FRUSTRATION TOLERANCE
Difficulty Controlling Emotions
Short fuse   Emotionally reactive
Loses temper easily
May give up more easily
Doesn't stick with things
Speaks or acts before thinking
Concerned with own feelings
Difficulty seeing other's perspective
May be self-centered
May be selfish

****

ADD/ADHD is often more complex than most people realize!
Like icebergs, many problems related to ADD/ADHD are not visible. ADD/ADHD may be mild, moderate, or severe,
is likely to coexist with other conditions, and may be a disability for some students.

Reprinted with permission from Chris A. Zeigler Dendy.

Executive Functioning: The River Rafting Metaphor

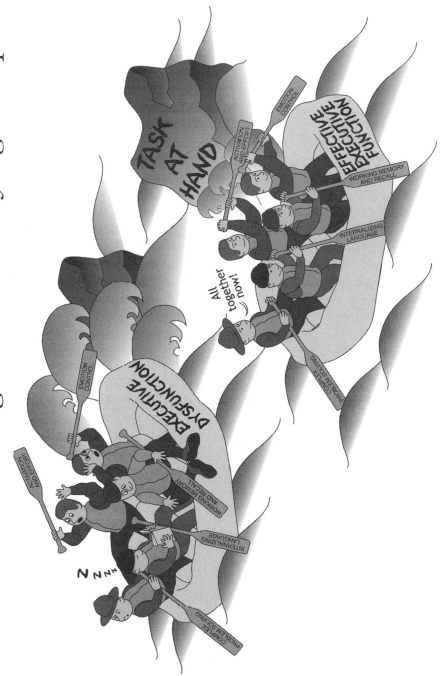

Chapter 2 The SNAP-IV Teacher and Parent Rating Scale

James M. Swanson, Ph.D., University of California, Irvine, CA 92715

Name:_____

Gender:_____ Age:_____ Grade:_____

Ethnicity (circle one which best applies):
African-American   Asian   Caucasian   Hispanic

Other_____

Completed by:_____

Type of Class:_____ Class size:_____

For each item, check the column which best describes this child:	Not At All	Just A Little	Quite A Bit	Very Much
1. Often fails to give close attention to details or makes careless mistakes in schoolwork or tasks	_____	_____	_____	_____
2. Often has difficulty sustaining attention in tasks or play activities	_____	_____	_____	_____
3. Often does not seem to listen when spoken to directly	_____	_____	_____	_____
4. Often does not follow through on instructions and fails to finish schoolwork, chores, or duties	_____	_____	_____	_____
5. Often has difficulty organizing tasks and activities	_____	_____	_____	_____

Reprinted with permission of James M. Swanson

For each item, check the column
which best describes this child:

	Not At All	Just A Little	Quite A Bit	Very Much
6. Often avoids, dislikes, or reluctantly engages in tasks requiring sustained mental effort	_____	_____	_____	_____
7. Often loses things necessary for activities (e.g., toys, school assignments, pencils, or books)	_____	_____	_____	_____
8. Often is distracted by extraneous stimuli	_____	_____	_____	_____
9. Often is forgetful in daily activities	_____	_____	_____	_____
10. Often has difficulty maintaining alertness, orienting to requests, or executing directions	_____	_____	_____	_____
11. Often fidgets with hands or feet or squirms in seat	_____	_____	_____	_____
12. Often leaves seat in classroom or in other situations in which remaining seated is expected	_____	_____	_____	_____
13. Often runs about or climbs excessively in situations in which it is inappropriate	_____	_____	_____	_____
14. Often has difficulty playing or engaging in leisure activities quietly	_____	_____	_____	_____
15. Often is "on the go" or often acts as if "driven by a motor"	_____	_____	_____	_____
16. Often talks excessively	_____	_____	_____	_____
17. Often blurts out answers before questions have been completed	_____	_____	_____	_____
18. Often has difficulty awaiting turn	_____	_____	_____	_____
19. Often interrupts or intrudes on others (e.g., butts into conversations/games)	_____	_____	_____	_____
20. Often has difficulty sitting still, being quiet, or inhibiting impulses in the classroom or at home	_____	_____	_____	_____
21. Often loses temper	_____	_____	_____	_____
22. Often argues with adults	_____	_____	_____	_____
23. Often actively defies or refuses adult requests or rules	_____	_____	_____	_____
24. Often deliberately does things that annoy other people	_____	_____	_____	_____
25. Often blames others for his or her mistakes or misbehavior	_____	_____	_____	_____
26. Often touchy or easily annoyed by others	_____	_____	_____	_____
27 Often is angry and resentful	_____	_____	_____	_____
28. Often is spiteful or vindictive	_____	_____	_____	_____
29. Often is quarrelsome	_____	_____	_____	_____
30. Often is negative, defiant, disobedient, or hostile toward authority figures	_____	_____	_____	_____

For each item, check the column which best describes this child:	Not At All	Just A Little	Quite A Bit	Very Much
31. Often makes noises (e.g., humming or odd sounds)				
32. Often is excitable, impulsive				
33. Often cries easily				
34. Often is uncooperative				
35. Often acts "smart"				
36. Often is restless or overactive				
37. Often disturbs other children				
38. Often changes mood quickly and drastically				
39. Often easily frustrated if demand are not met immediately				
40. Often teases other children and interferes with their activities				
41. Often is aggressive to other children (e.g., picks fights or bullies)				
42. Often is destructive with property of others (e.g., vandalism)				
43. Often is deceitful (e.g., steals, lies, forges, copies the work of others, or "cons" others)				
44. Often and seriously violates rules (e.g., is truant, runs away, or completely ignores class rules)				
45. Has persistent pattern of violating the basic rights of others or major societal norms				
46. Has episodes of failure to resist aggressive impulses (to assault others or to destroy property)				
47. Has motor or verbal tics (sudden, rapid, recurrent, nonrhythmic motor or verbal activity)				
48. Has repetitive motor behavior (e.g., hand waving, body rocking, or picking at skin)				
49. Has obsessions (persistent and intrusive inappropriate ideas, thoughts, or impulses)				
50. Has compulsions (repetitive behaviors or mental acts to reduce anxiety or distress)				
51. Often is restless or seems keyed up or on edge				
52. Often is easily fatigued				
53. Often has difficulty concentrating (mind goes blank)				
54. Often is irritable				
55. Often has muscle tension				

For each item, check the column which best describes this child:	Not At All	Just A Little	Quite A Bit	Very Much
56. Often has excessive anxiety and worry (e.g., apprehensive expectation)	_____	_____	_____	_____
57. Often has daytime sleepiness (unintended sleeping in inappropriate situations)	_____	_____	_____	_____
58. Often has excessive emotionality and attention-seeking behavior	_____	_____	_____	_____
59. Often has need for undue admiration, grandiose behavior, or lack of empathy	_____	_____	_____	_____
60. Often has instability in relationships with others, reactive mood, and impulsivity	_____	_____	_____	_____
61 Sometimes for at least a week has inflated self esteem or grandiosity	_____	_____	_____	_____
62. Sometimes for at least a week is more talkative than usual or seems pressured to keep talking	_____	_____	_____	_____
63. Sometimes for at least a week has flight of ideas or says that thoughts are racing	_____	_____	_____	_____
64. Sometimes for at least a week has elevated, expansive or euphoric mood	_____	_____	_____	_____
65. Sometimes for at least a week is excessively involved in pleasurable but risky activities	_____	_____	_____	_____
66. Sometimes for at least 2 weeks has depressed mood (sad, hopeless, discouraged)	_____	_____	_____	_____
67. Sometimes for at least 2 weeks has irritable or cranky mood (not just when frustrated)	_____	_____	_____	_____
68. Sometimes for at least 2 weeks has markedly diminished interest or pleasure in most activities	_____	_____	_____	_____
69. Sometimes for at least 2 weeks has psychomotor agitation (even more active than usual)	_____	_____	_____	_____
70. Sometimes for at least 2 weeks has psychomotor retardation (slowed down in most activities)	_____	_____	_____	_____
71. Sometimes for at least 2 weeks is fatigued or has loss of energy	_____	_____	_____	_____
72. Sometimes for at least 2 weeks has feelings of worthlessness or excessive, inappropriate guilt	_____	_____	_____	_____
73. Sometimes for at least 2 weeks has diminished ability to think or concentrate	_____	_____	_____	_____
74. Chronic low self-esteem most of the time for at least a year	_____	_____	_____	_____

For each item, check the column which best describes this child:	Not At All	Just A Little	Quite A Bit	Very Much
75. Chronic poor concentration or difficulty making decisions most of the time for at least a year	_____	_____	_____	_____
76. Chronic feelings of hopelessness most of the time for at least a year	_____	_____	_____	_____
77. Currently is hypervigilant (overly watchful or alert) or has exaggerated startle response	_____	_____	_____	_____
78. Currently is irritable, has anger outbursts, or has difficulty concentrating	_____	_____	_____	_____
79. Currently has an emotional (e.g., nervous, worried, hopeless, tearful) response to stress	_____	_____	_____	_____
80. Currently has a behavioral (e.g., fighting, vandalism, truancy) response to stress	_____	_____	_____	_____
81. Has difficulty getting started on classroom assignments	_____	_____	_____	_____
82. Has difficulty staying on task for an entire classroom period	_____	_____	_____	_____
83. Has problems in completion of work on classroom assignments	_____	_____	_____	_____
84. Has problems in accuracy or neatness of written work in the classroom	_____	_____	_____	_____
85. Has difficulty attending to a group classroom activity or discussion	_____	_____	_____	_____
86. Has difficulty making transitions to the next topic or classroom period	_____	_____	_____	_____
87. Has problems in interactions with peers in the classroom	_____	_____	_____	_____
88. Has problems in interactions with staff (teacher or aide)	_____	_____	_____	_____
89. Has difficulty remaining quiet according to classroom rules	_____	_____	_____	_____
90. Has difficulty staying seated according to classroom rules	_____	_____	_____	_____

Scoring Instructions for the SNAP-IV-C Rating Scale

The SNAP-IV Rating Scale is a revision of the Swanson, Nolan and Pelham (SNAP) Questionnaire (Swanson et al, 1983). The items from the DSM-IV (1994) criteria for Attention-Deficit/Hyperactivity Disorder (ADHD) are included for the two subsets of symptoms: inattention (items #1–#9) and hyperactivity/impulsivity (items #11–#19). Also, items are included from the DSM-IV criteria for Oppositional Defiant Disorder (items #21–#28) since it often is present in children with ADHD. Items have been added to summarize the Inattention domain (#10) and the Hyperactivity/Impulsivity domain (#20) of ADHD. Two other items were added: an item from DSM-III-R (#29) that was not included in the DSM-IV list for ODD, and an item to summarize the ODD domain (#30).

In addition to the DSM-IV items for ADHD and ODD, the SNAP-IV contains items from the Conners Index Questionnaire (Conners, 1968) and the IOWA Conners Questionnaire (Loney and Milich, 1985). The IOWA was developed using divergent validity to separate items which measure inattention/overactivity (I/O—items #4, #8, #11, #31, #32) from those items which measure aggression/defiance (A/D—items #21, #23, #29, #34, #35). The Conners Index (items #4, #8, #11, #21, #32, #33, #36, #37, #38, #39) was developed by selecting the items which loaded highest on the multiple factors of the Conners Questionnaire, and thus represents a general index of childhood problems.

The SNAP-IV is based on a 0 to 3 rating scale: Not at All = 0, Just A Little = 1, Quite A Bit = 2, and Very Much = 3. Subscale scores on the SNAP-IV are calculated by summing the scores on the items in the subset and dividing by the number of items in the subset. The score for any subset is expressed as the Average Rating-Per-Item, as shown for ratings on the ADHD-Inattentive (ADHD-I) subset:

	Not At All	Just A Little	Quite A Bit	Very Much	Item Score	
1. Makes careless mistakes			_X_		2	
2. Can't pay attention				_X_	3	
3. Doesn't listen				_X_	3	
4. Fails to finish work			_X_		2	ADHD-In Total = 18,
5. Disorganized		_X_			1	Average = 18/9 = 2.0
6. Can't concentrate				_X_	3	
7. Loses things		_X_			1	
8. Distractible				_X_	3	
9. Forgetful	_X_				0	

A scoring template for the DSM-IV subtypes of ADHD (In and H/Im), for ODD; for the dimensions of the CLAM (I/O and A/D); and for the Conners Index are presented below:

ADHD-In	ADHD-H/Im	ODD	I/O	A/D	Conners Index
# 1 _____	#11 _____	#21 _____	# 4 _____	#21 _____	# 4 _____
# 2 _____	#12 _____	#22 _____	# 8 _____	#23 _____	# 8 _____
# 3 _____	#13 _____	#23 _____	#11 _____	#29 _____	#11 _____
# 4 _____	#14 _____	#24 _____	#31 _____	#34 _____	#21 _____
# 5 _____	#15 _____	#25 _____	#32 _____	#35 _____	#32 _____
# 6 _____	#16 _____	#26 _____			#33 _____
# 7 _____	#17 _____	#27 _____			#36 _____
# 8 _____	#18 _____	#28 _____			#37 _____
# 9 _____	#19 _____				#38 _____
					#39 _____

Total In = _____ H/Im = _____ ODD = _____ I/O = _____ A/D = _____ CI = _____
Average = _____ = _____ = _____ = _____ = _____ = _____

C = _____
= _____

		Teacher	Parent
Tentative 5% Cutoffs:	ADHD-In	2.56	1.78
	ADHD-H/Im	1.78	1.44
	ADHD-C	2.00	1.67
	ODD	1.38	1.88

The items on page 2 of the SNAP-IV Rating Scale are from other DSM-IV disorders which may overlap with or masquerade as symptoms of ADHD. In some cases, these may be comorbid disorders, but in other cases the presence of one or more of these disorders may be sufficient to exclude a diagnosis of ADHD. The SNAP-IV is not designed to be used in the formal process of diagnosing these non-ADHD disorders, but if symptoms on page 2 of the SNAP-IV receive a high ("Quite A Bit" or "Very Much") rating, then an assessment of the implicated non-ADHD disorders may be warranted.

The DSM-IV Manual should be consulted to follow-up with an evaluation of these non-ADHD disorders. The DSM Codes and the page numbers in the DSM Manual are specified below to help in the assessment of possible conditions which may exclude or qualify a diagnosis of ADHD. A referral to a psychiatrist or a clinical psychologist may be required.

#41-#45 Conduct Disorder	(DSM 312.8, p. 85)
#46 Intermittent Explosive Disorder	(DSM 312.34, p. 609)
#47 Tourette's Disorder	(DSM 307.23, p. 103)
#48 Stereotypic Movement Disorder	(DSM 307.3, p. 121)
#49-#50 Obsessive-Compulsive Disorder	(DSM 300.3, p. 417)
#51-#56 Generalized Anxiety Disorder	(DSM 300.02, p. 432)
#57 Narcolepsy	(DSM 347, p. 562)
#58 Histrionic Personality Disorder	(DSM 301.50, p. 655)
#59 Narcissistic Personality Disorder	(DSM 301.81, p. 658)
#60 Borderline Personality Disorder	(DSM 301.83, p. 650)
#61-#65 Manic Episode	(DSM 296.00, p. 328)
#66-#73 Major Depressive Episode	(DSM 296.2, p. 320)
#74-#76 Dysthymic Disorder	(DSM 300.4, p. 345)
#77-#78 Posttraumatic Stress Disorder	(DSM 309.81, p. 424)
#79-#80 Adjustment Disorder	(DSM 309, p. 623)

Finally, the SNAP-IV includes the 10 items of the Swanson, Kotkin, Agler, Mylnn, and Pelham (SKAMP) Rating Scale. These items are classroom manifestations of inattention, hyperactivity, and impulsivity (i.e., getting started, staying on task, interactions with others, completing work, and shifting activities). The SKAMP may be used to estimate severity of impairment in the classroom.

It is important to note that many disorders may produce impairment in the classroom setting, not just ADHD. Therefore, this rating scale is presented last to the possible exclusion conditions (on page 2 of the SNAP-IV) will be considered in addition to the inclusion criteria for ADHD (on page 1 of the SNAP-IV). Both should be considered before interpreting the SKAMP measure of classroom impairment or attributing high ratings on the SKAMP to ADHD.

ACADEMIC

#81	_____
#82	_____
#83	_____
#84	_____
#85	_____
#86	_____

Total = _____
Avg. = _____

Orienting (#81,#86)   = _____
Maintaining (#82,#83)   = _____
Directing (#84,#85)   = _____

DEPORTMENT

#87	_____
#88	_____
#89	_____
#90	_____

= _____
= _____

Attention to Other (#87,#88) = _____
Attention to Rules (#89,#90) = _____

The Classwide SNAP-IV Teacher Rating Scale
James M. Swanson, Ph.D., University of California, Irvine, CA 92715

Teacher's Name _____   Class Size _____

Class Type (Regular, Special Education, Other-Specify) _____

For each item, check the column which best describes <u>each</u> child in your class. Use copies of this page, and assign a code (if necessary) for each student.	Not At All	Just A Little	Quite A Bit	Very Much

Code _____   Gender (M or F) _____

Age _____   Other _____

	Not At All	Just A Little	Quite A Bit	Very Much
1. Often has difficulty maintaining alertness, orienting to requests, or executing directions	_____	_____	_____	_____
2. Often has difficulty sitting still, being quiet, or inhibiting impulses in the classroom or at home	_____	_____	_____	_____
3. Often is negative, defiant, disobedient, or hostile toward authority figures	_____	_____	_____	_____
4. Often has excessive anxiety and worry (e.g., apprehensive expectation)	_____	_____	_____	_____
5. Often seems sad, hopeless, discouraged, or not interested in enjoyable activities	_____	_____	_____	_____

Code _____   Gender (M or F) _____

Age _____   Other _____

	Not At All	Just A Little	Quite A Bit	Very Much
1. Often has difficulty maintaining alertness, orienting to requests, or executing directions	_____	_____	_____	_____
2. Often has difficulty sitting still, being quiet, or inhibiting impulses in the classroom or at home	_____	_____	_____	_____
3. Often is negative, defiant, disobedient, or hostile toward authority figures	_____	_____	_____	_____
4. Often has excessive anxiety and worry (e.g., apprehensive expectation)	_____	_____	_____	_____
5. Often seems sad, hopeless, discouraged, or not interested in enjoyable activities	_____	_____	_____	_____

For each item, check the column which best describes <u>each</u> child in your class.
Use copies of this page, and assign a code (if necessary) for each student.

	Not At All	Just A Little	Quite A Bit	Very Much

Code _____ Gender (M or F) _____

Age _____ Other _____

1. Often has difficulty maintaining alertness, orienting to requests, or executing directions   _____ _____ _____ _____

2. Often has difficulty sitting still, being quiet, or inhibiting impulses in the classroom or at home   _____ _____ _____ _____

3. Often is negative, defiant, disobedient, or hostile toward authority figures   _____ _____ _____ _____

4. Often has excessive anxiety and worry (e.g., apprehensive expectation)   _____ _____ _____ _____

5. Often seems sad, hopeless, discouraged, or not interested in enjoyable activities   _____ _____ _____ _____

Code _____ Gender (M or F) _____

Age _____ Other _____

1. Often has difficulty maintaining alertness, orienting to requests, or executing directions   _____ _____ _____ _____

2. Often has difficulty sitting still, being quiet, or inhibiting impulses in the classroom or at home   _____ _____ _____ _____

3. Often is negative, defiant, disobedient, or hostile toward authority figures   _____ _____ _____ _____

4. Often has excessive anxiety and worry (e.g., apprehensive expectation)   _____ _____ _____ _____

5. Often seems sad, hopeless, discouraged, or not interested in enjoyable activities   _____ _____ _____ _____

Code _____ Gender (M or F) _____

Age _____ Other _____

1. Often has difficulty maintaining alertness, orienting to requests, or executing directions   _____ _____ _____ _____

2. Often has difficulty sitting still, being quiet, or inhibiting impulses in the classroom or at home   _____ _____ _____ _____

3. Often is negative, defiant, disobedient, or hostile toward authority figures   _____ _____ _____ _____

4. Often has excessive anxiety and worry (e.g., apprehensive expectation)   _____ _____ _____ _____

5. Often seems sad, hopeless, discouraged, or not interested in enjoyable activities   _____ _____ _____ _____

For each item, check the column which best describes <u>each</u> child in your class. Use copies of this page, and assign a code (if necessary) for each student.	Not At All	Just A Little	Quite A Bit	Very Much

Code _____ Gender (M or F) _____

Age _____ Other _____

	Not At All	Just A Little	Quite A Bit	Very Much
1. Often has difficulty maintaining alertness, orienting to requests, or executing directions	_____	_____	_____	_____
2. Often has difficulty sitting still, being quiet, or inhibiting impulses in the classroom or at home	_____	_____	_____	_____
3. Often is negative, defiant, disobedient, or hostile toward authority figures	_____	_____	_____	_____
4. Often has excessive anxiety and worry (e.g., apprehensive expectation)	_____	_____	_____	_____
5. Often seems sad, hopeless, discouraged, or not interested in enjoyable activities	_____	_____	_____	_____

Code _____ Gender (M or F) _____

Age _____ Other _____

	Not At All	Just A Little	Quite A Bit	Very Much
1. Often has difficulty maintaining alertness, orienting to requests, or executing directions	_____	_____	_____	_____
2. Often has difficulty sitting still, being quiet, or inhibiting impulses in the classroom or at home	_____	_____	_____	_____
3. Often is negative, defiant, disobedient, or hostile toward authority figures	_____	_____	_____	_____
4. Often has excessive anxiety and worry (e.g., apprehensive expectation)	_____	_____	_____	_____
5. Often seems sad, hopeless, discouraged, or not interested in enjoyable activities	_____	_____	_____	_____

Optional Narrative Comments_____

SNAP-IV (Plus CLAM, COMORBID, and SKAMP)
James M. Swanson, Ph.D., UCI Child Development Center, Irvine, CA 92715

INSTRUCTIONS FOR USING THE SNAP-IV DISK

This instruction sheet provides the scoring instructions for the latest version of the SNAP-IV rating scale. The SNAP-IV includes: (a) the DSM-IV items for ADHD (#1–#20, with summary item #10 for Inattention and summary item #20 for Hyper/Imp added) and ODD (#21–#30, with summary item #30 and DSM-III-R item #29 added), (b) the CLAM items not covered by the ADHD and ODD items (#31–#40), (c) selected items from possible comorbid disorders (#41–#80), and (d) SKAMP items (#81–#90).

The paper version of the SNAP-IV (copy attached) can be administered and scored by hand according to the instructions on the attached sheet. A new version of the SNAP-IV can be administered and scored by computer according to the instructions given below. The new version can also be used to score a completed paper version of the SNAP-IV.

The computerized version of the SNAP-IV is for the DOS 5.0 operating system on an IBM-compatible computer. It is based on a complied FoxPro database program, but you do not need to have the FoxPro database system on your computer. Everything required is provided on two disks. Put Disk 1 in Drive A, select Run from the Program Manager, and type "a:\setup". Put Disk 2 in Drive A when prompted on the screen. This will load the program and put a SNAP icon on your Program Manager display.

The SNAP program keeps a database record on all cases scored by the program. A stored record can be retrieved and printed to avoid the requirement to keep a paper copy. Also, the SNAP disk can be used to print a blank SNAP to provide a paper copy of the rating scale to be completed by pencil or pen.

Here are some instructions for using the SNAP-IV disk:

Getting started:
1. From the Program Manager, double click on the SNAP-IV icon
2. From the SNAP-IV screen, double click on the SNAP-IV icon to get options ("File", "Reports")
3. Click on "File" to to get options on the display ("Rate", "Locate", "Delete", "Exit")

4. Click on "Rate" (to enter data on a new case) or "Locate" to retrieve an old case

Rating a new case (after clicking on "Rate"):
1. Fill in the areas for subject and rater information
2. 10 items will be displayed at a time (on each screen)
2. Use the "pull down" menu to view choices for each item
3. For each item, select "Not at all", Just a Little", "Quite a Bit", or "Very Much"
4. At end of page, click on "Next" to get the next 10 items (on the next screen)
5. At end of scale (item #90), click on "Done"
6. The items will be scored and a Summary Report will be displayed
7. Click "Print" or "Exit"

Locating an old case (after clicking on "Locate"):
1. Names and dates of stored rating forms will appear on the screen
2. Click on the name you want to retrieve
3. After name is highlighted, press the "escape" key or "double click" to close the window
4. The SNAP-IV items will appear, 10 items per screen
5. Click on "Continue" to get each page displayed
6. At end of scale (item #90), click on "Print" to send to printer
7. Click on "Exit" to stop

Stopping:
1. Click on "File" to get options
2. Click on the "Exit" option

The Swan Rating Form
Chapter 2

The SWAN Rating Scale with Items Defined by Dimensions Encompassing Normal Behavior

Compared to other children, how does this child do the following:	far below avg.	below avg.	slightly below avg.	avg.	slightly above avg.	above avg.	far above avg.
1. Give close attention to detail and avoid careless mistakes							
2. Sustain attention on tasks or play activities							
3. Listen when spoken to directly							
4. Follow through on instructions and finish school work or chores							
5. Organize tasks and activities							
6. Engage in tasks that require sustained mental effort							
7. Keep track of things necessary for activities							
8. Ignore extraneous stimuli							
9. Remember daily activities							
10. Sit still (control movement of hands or feet or control squirming)							
11. Stay seated (when required by class rules or social conventions)							
12. Modulate motor activity (inhibit inappropriate running or climbing)							
13. Play quietly (keep noise level reasonable)							

Reprinted with permission of James M. Swanson

Compared to other children, how does this child do the following:	far below avg.	below	slightly below avg.	avg.	slightly above avg.	above	far above avg.
14. Settle down and rest (control constant activity)	___	___	___	___	___	___	___
15. Modulate verbal activity (control excess talking)	___	___	___	___	___	___	___
16. Reflect on questions (control blurting out answers)	___	___	___	___	___	___	___
17. Await turn (stand in line and take turns)	___	___	___	___	___	___	___
18. Enter into conversations & games without interrupting or intruding	___	___	___	___	___	___	___

Assessment of Specific Neurodevelopmental Functions

Craig Pohlman, Ph.D., Senior Psychologist, Student Success Services, All Kinds of Minds (used with permission)

ASSESSMENT OF ATTENTION

Attention is a complex, multifaceted, and elusive construct that interfaces with all other neurodevelopmental functions. Weak attention controls can be easily overlooked in their subtle forms. Consequently, assessment of attention should consider multiple sources of information. Reports may vary from setting to setting, which may reflect varying demands on the student. For example, some parents report few concerns about attention at home (where the student has relatively fewer work demands) while the student's teacher reports significant concerns.

The mental energy controls are best assessed through observation and history (interview data or questionnaires). Observing the student over the course of the evaluation can provide much information about alertness and consistency of mental energy. Observations in the classroom or information provided by the teacher are similarly useful. Parents are in the best position to report on a sleep/arousal balance.

Attention is an area often assessed in neuropsychology, and several tests developed for this field can be useful regarding the processing and production controls. Direct testing of attention can be very revealing, but consideration of the context is always warranted; a testing environment is much different than a classroom.

Within the processing controls, tests exist for *saliency determination* (sometimes referred to as "selective attention") and *focal maintenance* (sometimes referred to as "sustained attention"). For example, continuous performance tests (such as tests of variables of attention, TOVA) and target tag tasks (such as NEPSY visual attention) tap a student's ability to discriminate between important and unimportant information and to maintain attention over a period of time.

The pattern of responses on any task can also reveal difficulties with *focal maintenance*. Students with a weakness in this area often display variability in their accuracy. For example, they might get four items correct in a row, then miss three get three, miss two, etc. Perhaps the clearest indicator of this type of phenomenon is missing easier items and then correctly answering more difficult items; should this occur on a language test, for example, language would likely be intact (because the student answered correctly the harder items), with *focal maintenance* compromising overall performance.

Assessment of *cognitive activation, depth/detail of processing*, and *satisfaction level* needs to rely more on qualitative techniques than direct testing. Students can reveal the strength of their *cognitive activation control* through the extent to which they elaborate on ideas; for example, students with strong *cognitive activation* frequently link information (such as a test item) with their own knowledge and experience and might make seemingly tangential comments.

Depth of processing can sometimes be assessed during language tasks. For example, some students make errors on receptive language tests (such as following complex directions) that they can correct if the item is repeated for them; in contrast, a student with weak receptive language would not benefit as much from repetition of items. Also, learning curve information on multiple learning trial tasks (see Assessment of Memory) can be used to assess *depth of processing*. For example, some students have difficulty recalling words from the first couple of trials, but then show a strong learning curve, suggesting shallow processing of information that benefits from multiple presentation of the material.

Several of the production controls are similar to what are commonly referred to in the literature as *executive functions*. Hence, many of the assessments designed for measuring executive functions can be used to tap the production controls. Examples include the Wisconsin card sorting test and the tower subtest from the NEPSY. Beyond such direct measures, the production controls can be assessed qualitatively through observation and report. For example, a rushed, haphazard approach to tasks (vs planning or using strategies) can suggest weaknesses in *previewing, facilitation/inhibition*, and *pacing* (*tempo control*). Also, the degree to which the student detects and corrects errors in their work can inform *self-monitoring*. Direct tests of *reinforceability* do not seem available, requiring reports from home and school concerning the student's ability to use previous experience to guide current output.

ASSESSMENT OF MEMORY

Memory is commonly divided into three systems: *short term, active working,* and *long term* (both *consolidation* and *retrieval/access*). A useful distinction to make within each of these systems is the type of material committed to memory. The main distinction here is between visual material and verbal material. Memory assessments can be categorized as visual or verbal. In addition, some tasks tap multimodal memory, which usually involves the pairing of a piece of visual information (e.g., a face) with a piece of verbal information (e.g., a name). Multimodal memory is necessary for learning sound–symbol correspondences.

Another consideration in memory testing is the degree of context or meaning of the material. Some students show interesting contrasts in their ability to recall two general types of material. In particular, some students are much more adept at recalling contextualized or meaningful material (e.g., words on a shopping list) than decontextualized information with less meaning (e.g., a string of digits or unrelated words). Some verbal memory tasks contain items that are both contextualized and decontextualized; close analysis of specific items is warranted to determine any pattern in student performance; also, one must determine if the student has been exposed to material (e.g., through instruction or experience) before judging whether they have remembered it. Chunk size (e.g., a small set of words vs sentences vs a passage) is also something to consider, as some students have particular difficulty memorizing larger volumes of material.

Tests of memory include the children's memory scale and subtests from the Wechsler intelligence scale for children—(third edition). Multiple learning trial tasks, such as the California verbal learning test, involve presenting the student with information several times and asking them to recall the material after each presentation. These types of tests allow the clinician to become a teacher and to observe how the student responds to instruction. Performance on the first learning trial is often related to attention. Tasks can involve verbal material (e.g., a list of words), visual information (e.g., an array of figures), or multimodal material (e.g., a series of face–name pairs). Such tasks provide information about learning curves, which can inform *depth/detail of processing* (described earlier in Assessment of Attention). Verbal versions of these tasks typically include words belonging to categories. The degree to which the student can identify categories and use them to help recall is an important observation about strategy use (the California verbal learning test assesses this directly). Many multiple learning trial tasks include an interference task (i.e., introduction of new information, such as a different list of words); weak performance after interference material may relate to weak active working memory, as the student had trouble suspending the original information. Also, many include delayed recall and recognition trials for the assessment of long-term memory.

Comparing the student's performance on recall and recognition tasks can help tease apart *consolidation* difficulty from *retrieval* difficulty. Recall tasks involve free recall (i.e., no cue given to support retrieval), whereas recognition tasks do provide access cues for the student. If a student is unsuccessful with free recall, but performs better on a recognition trial, the implication is that they consolidated the information, but had trouble with retrieval. In contrast, difficulty with recognition tasks suggests that the student did not consolidate the material in the first place. Cued recall tasks are akin to recognition tasks in that they facilitate retrieval, allowing for the assessment of consolidation of material; the California verbal learning test includes cued recall trials (e.g., providing the student with a category of words included in the list, such as animals).

ASSESSMENT OF LANGUAGE

In addition to using tests designed to tap language, observations of this construct can be made throughout an assessment. How readily the student understands instructions is an important observation. Also, quality of language output can be noted throughout testing (e.g., degree of elaboration, word retrieval and usage, articulation). *Pragmatics* and *automatic* language can be assessed through conversation with the student (e.g., while discussing affinities). Many students show dramatic differences between their *automatic* and *literate* (i.e., academic) language function; for example, they might sound fluent during casual conversation but fall apart on more challenging or decontextualized tasks.

As mentioned earlier in Assessment of Attention, some students have difficulty after the first presentation of material (e.g., oral directions) due to shallow processing. When students do not benefit from repetition, however, weak receptive language is the likely culprit (as opposed to weak attention).

ASSESSMENT OF CROSS-CONSTRUCT PHENOMENA

One of the critical features of the neurodevelopmental framework is the inclusion of cross-construct phenomena, which are general aspects of functioning that interface with all eight constructs. For the most part, these phenomena are assessed indirectly during testing of neurodevelopmental functions (e.g., short term visual memory).

Phenomenon	Explanation
Rate of processing/production	Working with sufficient speed
Chunk size, volume of input/output	Processing and producing in sufficiently large amounts or sizes
Junctions between functions	Interfaces between constructs for learning or task completion
Metacognition	Thinking about thinking, reflecting on functions being used for tasks
Strategy use	Having tactics or techniques to facilitate learning or output
Domain-specific function	Functions that work much better in some subject areas than others

The processing/production rate can be observed during any number of tasks. Judgements of rate are usually qualitative, although some instruments provide normative data for work rate (e.g., NEPSY). Some measures involve time limits and bonus points for quick performance; consideration of accuracy beyond time limits is important when testing students who work at a slower rate.

Chunk size often is a factor on memory and language tasks. Memory tasks can be roughly divided by chunk size: small (e.g., word list) vs medium (e.g., sentences) vs large (e.g., passages).

Most assessment tasks tap multiple neurodevelopmental functions. A digit span task involves short-term memory and temporal–sequential ordering, which is an example of a "junction between functions."

Talking with the student about school and their learning is the best method to assess metacognition. One way to start the discussion is to ask what aspects of school are difficult and what are easy. This kind of dialogue can also be woven into a testing session by asking the student if tasks were easy or hard for them, and why. Students who are adept at explaining their own strengths and weaknesses have strong metacognition.

Strategy use is also assessed by interviewing the student about how they solved problems or completed tasks. For example, after a memory task the student could be asked what technique they used to commit the material to memory. Some students, especially younger ones, may need guidance to explain their strategy use, such as providing examples. For instance, when interviewing a student after a digit recall task, the examiner could say, "Some students tell me that they remember the numbers by saying them over and over in their head, and others tell me that they try to see the numbers in their mind. What did you do?" Also, some instruments, such as the cognitive assessment system, provide the examiner with prompts for observing strategy use.

Attention Coding Exercise for children

A coding sheet makes an excellent attention focus exercise. An example of a coding exercise form follows these instructions. To begin, the therapist needs to prepare or decide on the *interrupter signal*. This can be a tape that is recorded with a *beep* or other sound which is a signal to the student to stop working, record a tally at the top of the sheet, and, *immediately,* return to task. If a tape is not used, the therapist may provide a verbal signal, sound a tone, or ring a bell as the interrupter cue.

The student begins the coding exercisetransferring the information to the boxes on the work page. Whenever the *interrupter signal* is heard, the student marks a tally at the top of the page and returns to work. This exercise teaches the student to return to task quickly from an interruption. This is an important skill in a classroom setting because teachers frequently interrupt the class to give additional instruction, correct one student, or respond to a student. All of the students are drawn off-task in these circumstances but the student with attention issues often remains off-task because she is unaccustomed to returning to task immediately. This exercise will retrain this habit and aid the student in becoming focused for sustained periods of work.

A Coding Exercise grid example follows: The student is asked to fill in the numerals which match the symbols at the top of the grid. The box below the name is used for recording tally marks.

EDU-<u>Therapeutics</u> Coding Task

Name _____   Date _____

☐	_	✓	_	→	☒
1	2	3	4	5	6
→	☒	☐	_	✓	☒
_	☐	→	✓	_	☒
☐	_	→	☒	✓	_
→	_	_	✓	☐	→
☐	_	☒	→	_	✓
☒	_	✓	_	☐	_
→	☐	☒	✓	_	→
_	☒	☐	_	→	✓

EDU-<u>Therapeutics,</u> Joan Smith, Ed.D.   1-800-50-LEARN

<u>EDU-Therapeutics</u>   Memory Exercises

Memory exercises always begin with assessment to identify the digit span for symbols. The digit span may be different for pictorial recall, numeral, shape and letter recall. Exercises should start at the level of the child or adult.

Teacher/Parent Report of Behavior

Child: _____ Date: _____

Person completing form: _____

Please list your concerns regarding this child's behavior, academic, and/or social problems in priority order. Please be as specific as possible.

1.

2.

3.

4.

If academic concerns are not listed, how does the child do academically?

If social concerns are not listed, how does the child do in interacting with others?

Other comments:

Data Collection/Report
of Behavior

INSTRUCTIONS

One of the most difficult tasks in assessing the effectiveness of an intervention is collecting objective data. Most teachers feel it is a waste of time. However, it is the only way to know the effect of an intervention. If we do not take a baseline (collect data on the target behavior prior to intervention), we may stop an effective intervention prematurely, continue an intervention that is not working, or rely on faulty subjective impressions. A behavior may actually be improving but we fail to recognize the improvement because we are angry or frustrated. As a member of the intervention team we can only evaluate the effectiveness of our suggested interventions based on data collected by the teacher. In order to increase the likelihood that a teacher will keep data, the procedures for collecting data need to be simple and practical. The procedures outlined here are designed to be simple and practical.

A. Academic

Select an academic subject in which the student produces a written response. Make sure the student has the same amount of time to complete the assignment daily. The problems should be of roughly equivalent difficulty. If you cannot hold the time the same then record the beginning and ending times for the assignment. Collect the student's papers daily and at the end of the week record.

515

1. Daily number of problems attempted.
2. Daily number of problems correct.
3. Daily number of minutes the child was given to work on the problem.

B. Nonacademic Behavior

Pick a time period in which you can observe and record behavior (no more than 10 minutes). Tell students that it is an independent work period and they are to work quietly. Pick one student to observe.

Record a plus each time the student talks out or talks to his neighbor. Record daily for 1 week during the same 10-minute period.

Form:

Student _____ Date _____

Person completing form _____

Behavior(s) being observed _____

_____

_____

Date	Time	Tally or duration

SKAMP

MCSKAMP Rating Scale—Parent Version

Your name: _____Relationship to child: _____ Date: _____

> Circle the number that corresponds to this child's behavior TODAY: <u>do not</u> mark between choices. Note that the rating of "NORMAL, NO IMPAIRMENT" should be given only when the child's behavior is within the range of the child or expected behaviors of typical children who do not have chronic attentional or behavioral problems.

PLEASE BE SURE TO ANSWER EVERY ITEM

GENERAL BEHAVIOR TODAY	Normal No Impairment	Slight Impairment	Mild Impairment	Moderate Impairment	Severe Impairment	Very Severe Impairment	Maximal Impairment
1. Getting up and ready for the day's activities	⓪	①	②	③	④	⑤	⑥
2. Sticking to games or activities after school or during the day	⓪	①	②	③	④	⑤	⑥
3. Completing assigned work							
Homework	⓪	①	②	③	④	⑤	⑥
Chores	⓪	①	②	③	④	⑤	⑥
4. Performing work accurately							
Homework	⓪	①	②	③	④	⑤	⑥
Chores	⓪	①	②	③	④	⑤	⑥
5. Being careful and neat (e.g., when cleaning up toys, rooms)	⓪	①	②	③	④	⑤	⑥
6. Interacting with others:							
children (e.g., friends or siblings)	⓪	①	②	③	④	⑤	⑥
adults (e.g., parents or others)	⓪	①	②	③	④	⑤	⑥
7. Remaining quiet when the situation requires it	⓪	①	②	③	④	⑤	⑥
8. Staying seated and still when the situation requires it	⓪	①	②	③	④	⑤	⑥
9. Complying with usual requests or directions of parents	⓪	①	②	③	④	⑤	⑥
10. Following the rules established for the home	⓪	①	②	③	④	⑤	⑥
SPECIFIC BEHAVIOR TODAY:							
B1	⓪	①	②	③	④	⑤	⑥
B2	⓪	①	②	③	④	⑤	⑥
B3	⓪	①	②	③	④	⑤	⑥
B4	⓪	①	②	③	④	⑤	⑥
B5	⓪	①	②	③	④	⑤	⑥

Permission to reprint given by James M. Swanson

Behavior Plan

Child _____ Date _____

Team Members _____

Desired behavior _____

_____

Description of plan

Who is responsible for implementing the plan

Data collection process

Next meeting or phone conference

Other

Example of DRC Component Definition and Contract Letter

Nick's new behavioral management stickers
Developed by ⟨parents⟩, ⟨teacher⟩, following a parent teacher conference on xx/xx/xx.

Definitions:
Nick will be responsible to write down all assignments in his Daily Agenda and then take the agenda to ⟨Teacher⟩ immediately after school or as soon as ⟨Teacher⟩ is available after school (it is his responsibility to wait until she is ready and available to accurately complete the sticker).

Nick To be signed after school	
HW Accuracy/Compliance	☹ ☺ ☺
Binder Reminder	→ ☺ ☺
Behavior	☹ ☺ ☺
Teacher's Signature (only when done)	_____

Item 1: Homework Accuracy
  HW Accuracy/Compliance   ☹ ☺ ☺
☹Previous night's HW or due assignments were incomplete or not turned in on time
☺Previous night's HW or due assignments were complete but not up to teacher's level of expectations
☺Previous night's HW or due assignments were completed up to expectations

Item 2: Binder Reminder assignment log accurately filled out from posted assignment board

Binder Reminder   ➔ ☺ ☺

☺Nick needed prompting, was inaccurate, or was incomplete in copying down necessary assignments

☺Nick was accurate in writing down all necessary assignments

Item 3: Behavior in the class during the day

Behavior   ☹ ☺ ☺

☹Behavior was not appropriate: Nick required prompting above grade level expectations: Nick required repeated redirections from teacher: Significant improvement necessary

☺Behavior needed improvement: Nick's behavior stood out from the rest of the class

☺Behavior was in line with the rest of his classmates: Nick's behavior did not stand out from the rest of the class

Item 4: Signature

Teacher's Signature (only when done) _____

⟨Teacher⟩ will sign the sticker after circling the daily rating 'faces'

Substitutes will sign the sticker – although they may not choose to rate Nick – Their signature only indicates that Nick was compliant with his obligation to take the binder to the teacher at the end of the day

Intervention Strategies for Success (ISS-BIRP)

Student: _____   DOB: _____   School/Grade: _____

Rater: _____   Date: _____   Teacher: _____

How long rater has known student: _____

Key	intervention rating (intervention activity required)
④	..........Critical (frequent and consistent intervention on a <u>daily</u> basis {consult treatment team})
③	..........Highly recommended (consistent intervention on a <u>daily</u> basis)
②	..........Helpful to student (intermittent <u>daily</u> attention)
①	..........Not critical for this student (intervention may require infrequent attention)
⓪	..........Not recommended for this student

Behavioral Interventions (100)

⓪①②③④ ....use verbal prompts for specific desired behaviors (101)

⓪①②③④ ....use nonverbal prompts for specific desired behavior (102)

⓪①②③④ ....praise specific desired behaviors (103)

⓪①②③④ ....use concrete reinforcers (104)

⓪①②③④ ....send positive notes home (105)

⓪①②③④ ....assist in problem solving to reduce negative outcomes (106)

⓪①②③④ ....use student self-monitoring strategies for desired behaviors (107)

⓪①②③④ ....keep classroom rules simple and clear (108)

⓪①②③④ ....use negative consequences (punishment) consistently for noncompliance (109)

⓪①②③④ ....allow short breaks between assignments (110)

⓪①②③④ ....tolerate minor inappropriate behaviors not drastically outside classroom limits (111)

⓪①②③④ ....allow appropriate out-of-seat movement within classroom (112)

⓪①②③④ ....contract with the student (113)

⓪①②③④ ....send daily progress reports home (114)

⓪①②③④ ....send weekly progress reports home (115)

⓪①②③④ ....provide social skills instruction (116)

⓪①②③④ ....give explicit redirection before applying negative consequences for inattentive/impulsive actions (117)

⓪①②③④ ....assign student to be peer tutor (118)

⓪①②③④ ....increase the immediacy of rewards (119)

⓪①②③④ ....utilize a classroom behavior management system (120)

⓪①②③④ ....utilize a school based reinforcement (121)

⓪①②③④ ....utilize a brief in-class time out procedure when appropriate (122)

⓪①②③④ ....develop a written plan to utilize hands-on behavioral interventions (199)

⓪①②③④ ....other: _____

_____

Physical Arrangement of Room/Environment (200)

⓪①②③④ ....seat near the teacher's primary location (201)

⓪①②③④ ....seat near board/presentation area (202)

⓪①②③④ ....seat near or facing positive peer role model (203)

⓪①②③④ ....stand near when giving directions/presenting lessons (204)

⓪①②③④ ....avoid distracting auditory stimuli (205)

⓪①②③④ ....avoid distracting visual stimuli (206)

⓪①②③④ ....increase distance between students' desks (207)

⓪①②③④ ....provide study carrel (208)

Organization (300)

⓪①②③④ ....provide daily assignment and work schedule for students (301)

⓪①②③④ ....provide daily assignment and work schedule for parents (302)

⓪①②③④ ....monitor desk and notebook organization (303)

⓪①②③④ ....post assignments in consistent location (304)

⓪①②③④ ....leave assignments posted throughout the school day (305)

⓪①②③④ ....provid student with a homework assignment log structure (306)

⓪①②③④ ....monitor student's assignment log and organization (307)

⓪①②③④ ....allow student to have an extra set of books at home (308)

⓪①②③④ ....encourage utilization of any existing telephone homework verification (309)

Lesson Preparation (400)

⓪①②③④ ....write key points on the board (401)

⓪①②③④ ....provide written outline (402)

⓪①②③④ ....utilize visual aids (403)

⓪①②③④ ....pre-teach vocabulary (404)

⓪①②③④ ....pre-read oral reading assignments (405)

⓪①②③④ ....have student review key points orally (406)

⓪①②③④ ....check for understanding regularly (407)

⓪①②③④ ....make sure directions are understood (408)

⓪①②③④ ....include a variety of activities during each lesson (409)

⓪①②③④ ....supplement lessons with computer-assisted instruction (410)

⓪①②③④ ....monitor student when using manipulatives (411)

⓪①②③④ ....deliver lengthy presentations in small segments (412)

⓪①②③④ ....monitor student during cooperative learning groups (413)

⓪①②③④ ....check work carefully for both completion and accuracy (414)

⓪①②③④ ....structure and prompt use of proactive academic activities for lag time (415)

Assignments/worksheets (500)

⓪①②③④ ....allow for additional time to complete tasks (501)

⓪①②③④ ....simplify complex directions (502)

⓪①②③④ ....hand worksheets out one at a time (503)

⓪①②③④ ....hand worksheets out stapled together (504)

⓪①②③④ ....reduce the reading level of the assignments (505)

⓪①②③④ ....modify homework assignments (506)

⓪①②③④ ....decrease quantity of homework (507)

⓪①②③④ ....allow calculator use for computation support when necessary (508)

⓪①②③④ ....mark student's correct answers, not incorrect ones (509)

⓪①②③④ ....utilize computer for additional drill and practice (510)

⓪①②③④ ....provide study skills training/learning strategies (511)

⓪①②③④ ....break large and long-term assignments into small segments (512)

⓪①②③④ ....use self-monitoring devices for assignment progression (513)

⓪①②③④ ....develop school-based reinforcement for homework completion (514)

⓪①②③④ ....front load parents as to assignments (515)

⓪①②③④ ....instruct parents in study skills utilized at school (516)

⓪①②③④ ....deemphasize penmanship in assignment grading (517)

⓪①②③④ ....facilitate tutoring assistance from peers (518)

⓪①②③④ ....use cross grade tutors (519)

⓪①②③④ ....have student rephrase instructions before beginning assignment (520)

Assignments/worksheets (500)

⓪①②③④ ....monitor student when pairing students to check work (521)

⓪①②③④ ....provide instruction/support in self-checking and proofreading (522)

⓪①②③④ ....assist student in setting short-term assignment goals (523)

⓪①②③④ ....allow computer-printed assignments (524)

⓪①②③④ ....give additional supported guided practice (525)

Test Taking (600)

⓪①②③④ ....pretest to identify areas needing study (601)

⓪①②③④ ....prompt relaxation techniques prior to taking tests and exams (602)

⓪①②③④ ....modify exams to allow text access (603)

⓪①②③④ ....modify exams to be given orally (604)

⓪①②③④ ....allow extra time to complete exams (605)

⓪①②③④ ....use objective test items (multiple choice) (606)

⓪①②③④ ....grade individually, giving subjective determination of concept mastery (607)

①①②③④ ....read test items to student when necessary (608)

①①②③④ ....assess frequently over short periods of time (609)

①①②③④ ....consider computation and process in addition to final product when interpreting tests and exams (610)

①①②③④ ....require fewer correct responses to demonstrate concept/skill mastery (611)

①①②③④ ....other: _____

_____

Behavioral Intervention Responsibilty Plan

Teacher: _____

School: _____

Parent(s): _____

_____

Needs Assessment

Please identify interventions (by item #) requiring external support services with responsible team members

Aide: _____

_____

Resource Teacher: _____

_____

Site Psychologist: _____

_____

Principal: _____

_____

District Program Specialist: _____

_____

Behavioral Intervention Case Mgr: _____

D. Flynn/R. Kotkin © 2002. Reprinted with permission.

Suggested Letters Accessing Special Education Services

Sample Letter 1: Request for an Initial Evaluation for Special Education Services

Today's Date (include month, day, and year)
Your Full Return Address

Name of Principal
Full Address

Dear (name of Principal),

I am writing to request that my son/daughter, (full name), be evaluated for special education services. I have been worried lately that he/she is not doing very well in school and that he/she may need some special help in order to learn. He/she is in the (grade level and name of current teacher) at (name of school).
Specifically, I am worried because (name of your child) does/does not (keep this paragraph short, but give one or two reasons for your concern about your child).

I understand that I have to give written permission in order to have (name of child) tested. However, I would first like to know more about the tests, the testing process, and when this can be done. I would be happy to talk with you or another school official about my child. You can send me information or can call me during the day at (daytime telephone number). Thank you.

Sincerely yours,
Your full name

Permission to reprint these letters has been given by the National Information Center for Children and Youth with Disabilities

Sample letter 2: Request for a Meeting to Review the IEP

Today's Date (include month, day, and year)
Your Full Return Address

Name of Principal
Full Address

Dear (name of Principal),

I am writing to request an IEP review meeting. I would like to discuss making some possible changes in (child's name, grade level, and teacher) IEP as I feel that . . .

I would also like to have (name of specialists) attend. I think that his/her/their ideas about the changes we may make will be valuable.

I (or my husband/wife and I) can arrange to meet with you on (days) between (give a range of time, such as between 3:00 and 5:00). Please let me know what time would be best for you.

I look forward from hearing from you soon. My daytime telephone number is (••) ••—••. Thank you for your time.

Sincerely yours,
Your full name

Sample Letter 3: Request for a Change of Placement

Today's Date (include month, day, and year)
Your Full Return Address

Name of Principal
Full Address

Dear (name of Principal),

I am writing to request a meeting to discuss a change in class placement for (full name of your child). He/she is currently in (grade/school/name of teacher). I feel he/she would do better in (name of alternative placement).

I am most concerned about . . . (keep this brief and mention your child's needs, not problems with people).

I would also like to have (name of teacher(s) and/or any specialists you would like) attend.

I (or my husband/wife and I) can arrange to meet with you on (days) between (give a range of time, such as between 3:00 and 5:00). Please let me know what time would be best for you.

I look forward from hearing from you soon. My daytime telephone number is (••) ••–••. Thank you for your time.

Sincerely yours,
Your full name

Sample Letter 4: Request for Records

Today's Date (include month, day, and year)
Your Full Return Address

Name of Principal
Full Address

Dear (name of Principal),

I am writing to schedule a time to come to school and review all of my child's records, both cumulative and confidential. My child's name is . . . , her grade is . . . , and his/her teacher is. . . . I will also need copies of all or some of these records.

Please let me know where and when I can come in to see them. (I need these records by . . .). You can reach me during the day at (your daytime telephone number).

I look forward to hearing form you soon. Thank you for your consideration.

Sincerely yours,
Your full name

Reflective Listening: A Viable Approach to Enhance Communication

An excellent approach to enhancing the dialogue between parent and child is known as responsive listening. This strategy is defined as attending and responding accurately and sensitively to the verbal and nonverbal messages that come from the child. Parents need to learn not only to respond to the content of what a child is saying, but also respond to the message.

When responding to the child's feelings, we must not only be aware of what the child is saying verbally, but also pay attention to what the child is expressing nonverbally (postural and facial expressions). Sometimes there is a tremendous dichotomy between what is being said and nonverbal behaviors. This contradiction may lead to making an inaccurate assumption. Clarification may be needed to really get to the root of the child's issues. Nonverbal expressions tell us a great deal about how the child is handling an experience. The child's tone of voice, as well as facial expressions, is also an invaluable source of communication.

For example, a child may say to his/her parents after coming home from a game, "Things are not going so good for me. Not on the field, not with my teammates, and not with the coach. I don't feel I am holding up my part of the bargain and I feel like a failure. I want to quit." What is the child trying to tell us? The main theme of the conversation suggests that the child feels very down. He is feeling discouraged because he thinks everything on the team is falling apart, especially as it relates to him. As a parent, if you were in his position, wouldn't you also feel very dejected?

To develop a responsive statement, a parent will have to integrate two components. In the first part of our response, we will formulate a statement that accurately integrates what we perceive the child feels. We must try and select a feeling word, which is the most accurate, both in intensity and in actual feeling. We may do this by using a simple "You feel _____" formulation.

To assist in developing a more comprehensive "feeling" vocabulary, parents may want to practice formulating as least 5–10 feeling words for the feeling states of sadness, happiness, anxiety, shame, and anger. For example, other words for sadness could be demoralized, dejected, distressed, lousy, and lonely. However, the word angry could also be expressed as feeling annoyed, furious, mad, and enraged. To be effective, the parent must feel competent and comfortable utilizing feeling words. That is why it is suggested that you should practice responsive listening and develop a vocabulary that best suits your personality. Although practicing may feel awkward, the experience will make you feel more competent while communicating.

The second part of the response, after identifying how the child feels, is putting the feeling together with the content of the child's statements. The content gives meaning to the child's expressions of the experiences. Remember the feelings that you just identified are about the content. The content provides the reason the child feels the way s/he does.

The formula one uses after formulating the feeling component of a sentence (e.g., You feel _____) is to immediately follow the statement "You feel . . ." "because _____). Now you have been able to capture both the feeling and the content of what the child has said. Using responsive listening allows a parent to attempt to read the mind of a child by first clarifying how the child feels as well as clarifying the content that was shared. Returning to our first example, the parent may respond that "You feel demoralized because everything seems to be going wrong for you on the team."

What is exciting about this approach is that when you are correct, children feel understood and are encouraged to clarify and continue talking. When you are incorrect, children often do notice your genuineness in communicating and are willing to modify your statement and continue opening up.

A few more strategies are now added that complement responsive listening. These strategies may be helpful in helping you encourage more optimal discussions with your children.

1. Paraphrasing. This approach is utilized when a parent attempts to rephrase what a child has said. Sometimes this is very helpful, especially when the child may not be clear and a parent wants clarification.

2. Probing. Some people do not realize that it is helpful to ask children questions to get more information. Unfortunately, they asked close-ended questions, which only require a yes or no answer. It is helpful for parents to use open-ended probes such as "Tell me about your day" or "What do you think of. . . ."

3. Redirecting or summarizing. It is impossible to always be reflective when talking to our children. At times we may need to ask questions or redirect the discussion. That is entirely appropriate. Once that occurs, parents can return to applying the strategies already noted. Finally, it is imperative for parents to realize that it is extremely helpful while communicating to summarize what has already been stated and review the highlights. This lets the child know what has been discussed previously and ascertains if any clarification is needed.

Fact sheet for 1-2-3 Magic Effective Discipline for Children 2-12

Thomas W. Phelan, Ph.D.

1. The 1-2-3 is simple, but not always easy! The first step in disciplining kids is to discipline yourself. Get started right away with counting, then add START behavior tactics in 7-10 days.

2. STOP BEHAVIOR: arguing, whining, fighting, teasing, tantrums, yelling, etc. For this minor obnoxious behavior you will use the 1-2-3, or "counting," method.

START BEHAVIOR: eating, going to bed, getting up in the morning, homework, cleaning rooms, practicing, etc. To encourage good behavior you will have 6 tactics. You may use one or more of them.

3. Watch out for the "little adult assumption." Kids are not born reasonable and unselfish, but if you believe this you will talk too much and perhaps fall into the Talk-Persuade-Argue-Yell-Hit syndrome.

4. The Two Biggest Parenting Mistakes: Too Much Talking, Too Much Emotion.

5. The 1-2-3: two brief warnings ("That's 1," "That's 2") followed by a "rest period" or time out if the child hits three. No Talking, No Emotion. No explanations after unless absolutely necessary.

6. FAQs:

How long between counts?

What if they do something real bad, e.g., hit you or swear?

Will they hate their rooms?

What if they won't go to their room?

What if they won't come out?

What if they wreck the room?

Etc.

7. What to do in public. Get 1-2-3 rolling at home first, then use it in the grocery store the same as at home. Beware of the threat of public embarrassment!

8. Variations:

Sibling rivalry: count both mostly and don't ask the world's stupidest question.

Tantrums: once child is in time out, start time out after tantrum is over.

Pouting: ignore 'passive' pouting, but count aggressive pouters.

9. The Kickoff Conversation: let the kids know a change is coming! The kids will look at you like you've just lost your mind.

10. The Six Kinds of Testing and Manipulation:

1. BADGERING
2. INTIMIDATION (TEMPER)
3. THREAT
4. MARTYRDOM
5. BUTTER UP
6. PHYSICAL TACTICS

11. Does your child have a favorite tactic? That's not good, because this means it's probably working for them! By and large, T&M is STOP behavior.

12. General Rules:

A. We parents were built backwards.
B. Train the kids or keep your mouth shut. Training does not mean   nagging, screaming or hitting.

13. The Six START Behavior Tactics:

1. Sloppy Positive Verbal Feedback
2. Kitchen Timers
3. Docking System
4. Natural Consequences
5. Charting
6. 1-2-3 (different version) for things that take less than 2 minutes

14. START Behavior examples: cleaning rooms, up and out, bedtime, nighttime waking, homework.

15. The authoritative parent: active listening and counting. Discuss discussions and count attacks.

16. The Family Meeting: the road from dictatorship to democracy.

17. Slipping: long-term and short-term. It's not hard to get back on the wagon!

18. Cautions: parental loss of control, marital conflict, kids' responses, etc. Train those sitters and grandparents.

19. The Payoff: kids' self-esteem, parents' self-esteem. Children who listen and kids you can enjoy.

20. Get started!

Surviving Your Adolescents: How to Manage And Let Go Of Your 13-18 Year Olds

1. Teenagers may come from a Different Planet, but their parents do not have infinite time, energy, skill and patience.
2. What is a normal adolescent?
   A. Change
   B. Weirdness
   C. Distance
   D. Peer focus
   E. Inexperience
   F. Self-consciousness
   G. Risk taking
   E. Straight arrows, experimenters and emotionally disturbed
3. Sorting Out Problems
   A. Your teens already have their MBAs (Minor-But-Aggravating behaviors), such as phone use, messy rooms, appearance and "musical" preferences.
   B. MBAs vs. Serious problems: anxiety, depression, ADHD, conduct disorder, manic-depression, eating disorders, etc.
   C. How are you (the parent) doing?
   D. Rate yourself on a scale from 1-10

E. Emotional Dumping: take the Anger Addiction Test
  1. Is your anger regular?
  2. Do you enjoy it?
  3. Do you look for things?
F. Perhaps you need assistance before trying to deal with a trouble-some teenager!

4. Communication and Safety
  A. Reasons for getting along
  B. Safety: The "Big Three" risks for teens: driving, drinking and drugs, sex
  C. Chain them to a post?
  D. Research reveals a connection between an open and friendly parent/teen relationship and adolescent safety

5. Getting Along
  A. The 4 Cardinal Sins: what not to do
    1. Nagging
    2. Spontaneous discussions about problems
    3. Insight transplants (lectures)
    4. Arguing
  B. How to avoid the 4 Sins
  C. What to do:
    1. Active listening (attitude test, what do kids your age . . . ?)
    2. Talking about yourself
    3. Shared fun
    4. Positive reinforcement
  D. Rate your relationship: Great, Average, Rotten

6. Managing Problems
  A. Understanding your job: 4 possible roles
  B. Think and clarify your role before talking
  C. Observer
  D. Advisor
  E. Negotiator
  F. Director
    1. Major/Minor
    2. Professional Evaluation
    3. Kick out of house
  G. Managing risk-taking
    1. Driving
    2. Alcohol and drugs
    3. Sex

7. Teen Testing and Manipulation
    A. BADGERING
    B. INTIMIDATION (TEMPER)
    C. THREAT
    D. MARTYRDOM
    E. BUTTER UP
    F. PHYSICAL TACTICS
8. What to expect in the future

Clinical and Academic Assessment for Higher Education Success

Client Information and Relevant History

Client name _____

Initial assessment/ follow-up assessment   Date _____
(circle one)

Type of learning disorder _____

Comorbid diagnoses _____

Medications _____

Relevant history summary _____

_____

_____

_____

_____

_____

_____

_____

_____

_____

Goals _____

_____

_____

Client Functioning

Cognitive abilities (per test results)	weak	Somewhat weak	Adequate	Somewhat strong	Strong
Overall resources					
Information processing—Verbal					
Information processing—Nonverbal					
Perceptual—Visual processing					
Perceptual—Auditory Processing					
Memory—Longterm					
Memory—Shortterm					
Attention					
Visual–Motor					
Executive functioning/Organization					
Overall cognitive assessment					

Academic skills (per test results)	Weak	Somewhat weak	Adequate	Somewhat strong	Strong
Reading—Basic skills					
Reading—Comprehension					
Writing—Basic skills					
Writing—Content					
Writing—Organization					
Math—Calculation skills					
Math—Conceptual					
Overall academic skills assessment					

Cognitive learning style

___ Visual   ___ Auditory   ___ Visual–auditory combination

___ Hands-on (kinesthetic)

Comments/planning and action items

_____
_____
_____
_____
_____
_____
_____
_____

General academic preparation	Weak	Somewhat weak	Adequate	Somewhat strong	Strong
Fundamental academic skills					
Use of accommodation tools/strategies					
College prep coursework completed					
Math					
English					
Other					
Overall academic prep assessment					

Comments/planning and action items

_____
_____
_____
_____
_____
_____
_____

Areas of interest/ motivation	Weak	Somewhat weak	Adequate	Somewhat strong	Strong
Commitment to higher education					
Eventual grad/professional school					
Interest in specific field(s)					
Knowledge of specific fields					
Internship/job/volunteer experience					
Overall interest/motivation assessment					

Comments/planning and action items

_____

_____

_____

_____

_____

_____

_____

_____

Executive functioning areas	Weak	Somewhat weak	Adequate	Somewhat strong	Strong
Planning					
Organization					
Time management					
Attentional modulation					
Behavioral modulation					
Overall executive functioning					

Comments/planning and action items

_____

_____

_____

_____

_____

_____

_____

_____

Social–emotional issues	Weak	Somewhat weak	Adequate	Somewhat strong	Strong
Developmental maturity					
Self-awareness					
Self-acceptance					
Independence					
Problem-solving/ego strength					
Social/interpersonal skills					
Comorbid factors					
Overall social–emotional					

Comments/planning and action items

_____

_____

_____

_____

_____

_____

_____

_____

Source of support	Weak	Somewhat weak	Adequate	Somewhat strong	Strong
Family					
Friends/relationships					
Therapeutic					
Medication intervention					
College services					
Overall support assessment					

Comments/planning and action items

_____

_____

_____

_____

_____

_____

_____

_____

Evaluation of Campus Environment

Types of higher education settings	Inadequate fit	Adequate fit	Good fit	Excellent fit
College—4 year				
College—2 year				
College with specialized disability program				
Vocational Education				
Trade School				

Comments/planning and action items

_____

_____

_____

_____

_____

_____

_____

Documentation requirements	Yes	No	To be done	Completed
Confirms disability				
Verifies need for accommodations				
Includes service history				
Documentation is recent				

Comments/planning and action items

_____

_____

_____

_____

_____

_____

_____

Campus features to explore	Inadequate	Adequate	Good	Excellent
Major options/curriculum requirements				
Support services (e.g., tutoring, learning skills programs, counseling, career center)				
Orientation and advising services				

Comments/planning and action items

_____

_____

_____

_____

_____

_____

_____

_____

DSS services/resources available	Inadequate	Adequate	Good	Excellent
Alternate media				
Testing accommodations				
Assistive technology				
Classroom accommodations				
Counseling/advising				

Comments/planning and action items

_____

_____

_____

_____

_____

_____

_____

_____

Supplemental Materials for Transition into Higher Education

RECOMMENDED BOOKS

Brown, D. S. (2000). *Learning a living: A guide to planning your career and finding a job for people with learning disabilities, attention deficit disorder, and dyslexia.* Bethesda, MD: Woodbine House.

> A career guide that targets the unique needs of high school and college students, as well as young adults with LD and ADHD. Emphasizes self-understanding, understanding occupational search processes, and using both technological and interpersonal resources.

Cobb, J. (2001). *Learning how to learn: Getting into and surviving college when you have a learning disability.* Washington, DC: Child Welfare League of America.

> A useful, easy-to-read manual for high school and college students that provides a host of tips and strategies on all aspects of postsecondary life.

Goldstein, S., Crawford, R., Goldstein, M., & Latham, P. H. (1996). *Managing attention and learning disorders in late adolescence and adulthood: A guide for practitioners.* New York: Wiley.

> A comprehensive volume for clinicians who wish to delve deeply into the latest on assessment, diagnosis, treatment, and outcome research for those with ADHD and LD.

Guyer, B. (1997). *The pretenders: Gifted people who have difficulty learning.* Homewood, IL: High Tide Press.

> Compiles stories from diverse adults who struggle to work with (and around) their learning disabilities. Offers insight into their daily challenges and solutions as they navigate their jobs and lives.

Kravets, M., & Wax, I. F. (2001). *The K&W guide to colleges for students with learning disabilities or attention deficit disorder* (5th ed.). New York: Princeton Review Publishing.

> Collects a great deal of information from a wide variety of colleges on the scope and breadth of disability support systems available. Helps clinicians to better understand and prepare their client for their transition.

McEwan, E. K. (2000). *Managing attention and learning disorders: super survival strategies.* Wheaton, IL: Harold Shaw Publishers.

> A solutions-oriented book geared toward both those with ADHD and/or LD as well as their significant others and caregivers. Covers strategies for managing a wide variety of aspects of living.

Nosek, K. (1995). *The dyslexic scholar: Helping your child succeed in the school system.* Dallas, TX: Taylor Publishers.

> Geared toward helping caregivers and parents understand and successfully navigate the K–12 special education system. Includes step-by-step sections on the special education process, legal mandates, and transition planning.

Quinn, P. Q. (2002). *ADD and the college student: A guide for high school and college students with attention deficit disorder* (Rev. ed.). New York: Magination Press.

> A brief, practical guide recently revised with the latest perspectives and recommendations from this widely published and respected scholar.

Reiff, H. B., Gerber, P. J., & Ginsberg, R. (1997). *Exceeding expectations: Highly successful adults with learning disabilities.* Austin: TX: PRO-ED.

> A book that explores the strategies, mechanisms, and characteristics used by adults with LD that allow for successful navigation of life challenges. Includes educational, emotional, and occupational considerations.

Rodis, P., Garrod, A., & Boscardin, M. L. (2001). *Learning disabilities and life stories.* Boston: Allyn & Bacon.

> A powerful collection of essays by students with LD and ADHD and those who serve them. Offers a phenomenological perspective on disability as it pertains to emotional, educational, occupational, and social adjustment.

RECOMMENDED WEB SITES

General Disability Links

Information Sites

HEATH Resource Center, www.heath.gwu.edu
> Huge site specializing in information on postsecondary education. Offers a summer precollegiate program, resource guides, and many links.

ican, www.icanonline.net
> Online disability community focusing on news, events, discussion boards, and products of interest.

Job Accommodation Network, www.jan.wvu.edu
> Site specializing in workplace accommodations for persons with disabilities. Offers an online database of accommodations, publications, and referrals.

SchwabLearning, www.schwablearning.org
An attractive, nicely organized site with a large numbers of articles on diagnosing, understanding, and effectively managing disabilities.

National Organizations

Association on Higher Education and Disability, www.ahead.org
Organization committed to advancing opportunities for persons with disabilities in the postsecondary environment. Offers an annual conference and professional development materials.
Council for Exceptional Children, www.cec.sped.org
Organization focused on improving educational outcomes for children with disabilities. Provides advocacy, discussion forums, and a variety of publications.

Governmental/Grant-Funded Agencies

ADA Home Page, www.usdoj.gov/crt/ada
A comprehensive resource on all aspects of this critical law. Includes publications, a toll-free telephone number, and a mediation service.
Educational Resources Information Center (ERIC), ericec.gov
A massive collection of articles, fact sheets, and research on education, including a clearinghouse devoted to disabilities and gifted education.
National Center for the Dissemination of Disability Research, www.ncddr.org
Promotes and aggregates research on all aspects of disability living, including technology, education, health activities, and employment.
National Information Center for Children and Youth with Disabilities, www.nichcy.org
Excellent collection of articles, bibliographies, and fact sheets, including a large number targeted at parents.
Office for Civil Rights, U.S. Department of Education, www.ed.gov/offices/OCR
Responsible for ensuring equal access to educational opportunities for persons with disabilities. Includes materials specifically addressing the postsecondary realm.

ADHD Links

About.com info on ADHD, add.about.com
   Specializes in the latest news and products related to ADHD.
   Includes diagnostic and treatment information for patients, parents,
   caregivers, and significant others.
ADDitude Magazine, www.additudemag.com
   Bimonthly magazine devoted to topical issues related to ADHD.
   Includes articles on treatment options, relationships, workplace and
   school issues, and personal growth.
Attention Deficit Disorder Association, www.add.org
   International organization devoted to improving the lives of those
   with ADHD. Offers an annual conference, periodicals, and videos.
   Emphasizes education, inclusion, and acceptance.
Children and Adult with Attention Deficit Disorder, www.chadd.org
   National organization that focuses on information, advocacy, and
   referrals. Also offers a national conference, a magazine, local
   support groups, and national research center.
MentalHealth.net info on ADHD, adhd.mentalhealth.net
   Large collection of documents and links related to ADHD. Clear
   content with easy navigation makes them an especially useful site
   to recommend for patients.
National Institute of Mental Health info on ADHD,
   www.nimh.nih.gov/publicat/adhdmenu.cfm
   Site emphasizes latest research and scholarly literature on ADHD.
   Includes articles and books on the clinical, psychological, medical,
   and educational aspects of the disorder.
One ADD Place, www.oneaddplace.com
   An online community devoted to information, support, and
   referrals. Targets clients, although offers some content useful to
   clinicians.

LD Links

Council for Learning Disabilities, www.cldinternational.org
   International organization focused on advancing the educational
   pursuits of those with LD. Offers scholarly journal articles, fact
   sheets, and both links and information related to conferences and
   other professional development opportunities.

International Dyslexia Association, www.interdys.org
    International organization focused on education, research,
    advocacy, and support. Has sections just for adults, educators, and
    college students. Lots of reading materials, an annual conference,
    professional development opportunities, and more.
LD Online, www.ldonline.org
    A terrific site. Specifically targets professionals (clinical and
    educational). Offers content from respected experts, discussion
    boards, good links, and relevant product reviews.
LD Resources, www.ldresources.com
    A small site with an easy to navigate structure. Includes
    information and links related to LD diagnosis, symptomology,
    technology tools, and educational issues/resources.
Learning Disabilities Association of America, www.ldanatl.org
    National organization devoted to education, advocacy, research, and
    social tolerance. Information on their national conference, state
    chapters, news and research sections, and reading materials is
    available.
National Center for Learning Disabilities, www.ld.org
    A strong site with broad, though comprehensive content. Easy
    navigation links allow you to explore sections on research,
    treatment, legal matters, and news related to LD.
National Institute of Mental Health info on LD,
    www.nimh.nih.gov/publicat/ldmenu.cfm
    Site includes latest research and scholarly work on LD. Includes
    materials on the clinical, psychological, medical, and educational
    aspects of LD.

Assistive Technology Links

AbilityHub, www.abilityhub.com
    A wealth of information on assistive technology, organized by
    disability or product type.
AbilityNet, www.abilitynet.org.uk/content/home.htm
    A nice overview of AT issues plus detailed fact sheets on specific
    products and services.
AbleData, www.abledata.com
    Includes a reading library and a forum for consumers to offer
    opinions on AT products.

AssistiveTech.net, assistivetech.net
  Huge library of information on AT products, large link collection, and discussion groups.
Closing the Gap, www.closingthegap.com
  Organization hosts an annual conference on AT usage in education and offers a newspaper and large resource directory.
Disabilities, Opportunities, Internetworking, and Technology Program, www.washington.edu/doit
  Specializes in AT information for postsecondary environments. Targets the needs of students, staff, and faculty via publications and a host of multimedia materials.
Equal Access to Software and Information, www.rit.edu/~easi
  Offers training and certification in AT and access to the *Information Technology and Disabilities* journal.
Tech Connections, www.techconnections.org
  Excellent collection of articles on AT, browsable descriptions and recommendations by disability or product type, and a user forum.
Trace Resource Center, trace.wisc.edu
  Huge collection of links, product descriptions, and news on AT products. Offers much technical information for those wishing to explore the field in more detail.

Cognitive Training: Suggestions for Generalizing its Effects

In academic and life settings, attitude can play as important a role as ability in achieving success. A negative outlook can make success impossible, and a positive outlook can make the impossible goal into a reality. Learning to keep a positive attitude while maintaining the stamina and effort necessary to meet the challenges of cognitive training exercises can be a critical component in how the training sessions impact and generalize to successful functioning in school, work and interpersonal relationships.

Below is a list of words of encouragement that can be used to motivate performance and incorporate positive self-programming into the cognitive training paradigm. These concepts are designed to help an individual develop and internalize a positive self-concept in the face of challenges. Generally, three of these positive metacognitive concepts per session should be selected and displayed on a sign where the player can see it. Examples of positive self-programming statements are listed below:

Keep your mind on your work, don't be fooled!
Try, try again—Persistence pays off!
Keep trying—never give up.
Do you want to be a winner or a loser?
Are you going to beat the computer or let the computer beat you?
Being a winner takes persistence!
Do it again!
Take your time.
Work a little faster.
Only Perfect Practice makes Perfect.
Set a goal and practice until you achieve it!

Effort counts.
One Step at a Time.
Keep Your Cool!
Attention Counts.
You can do it!
No one knows his/her full potential.
No effort is wasted.
Choose to be a Winner!
Take a Chance! Surprise Yourself!

The trainer can introduce each concept by discussing with players what it means to them, and then ask the players if they can think of any examples of how this specific attitude can help them function more successfully in their school, home and work life. Each of the following concepts can be incorporated at an appropriate time during the training session by restating it and pointing out its relevance to the player concerning what has just happened. For example, when a player clearly pays attention and "wins" then the trainer can cheer them with the statement see, "Attention Counts." When players are not sure that they will succeed in passing a stage, the trainer can use the phrase "Take a Chance! Surprise Yourself!" If a player gets upset and frustrated because they fail to pass a stage then the trainer can remind them, "Keep Your Cool!" and point to the sign. These metacognitive concepts are important in generalizing cognitive training and can be shared with parents or significant others who can remind players of them during incidents, challenges and opportunities that are encountered in daily life where they are relevant.

The trainer can also set specific goals or tasks to motivate performance, challenge a higher level of performance, encourage sustained efforts, train divided attention, or improve a player's ability to ignore real-life distractions. Examples of these types of exercises that can help generalize the effects of cognitive training to real life and enrich the regular training regimen are:

1. **BE A WINNER**—Beat your last score.
2. **TWO MINDS ARE BETTER THAN ONE**—Coach the trainer to beat their last score.
3. **KEEP YOUR COOL**—Stay relaxed, do diaphragmatic, deep breathing while you work.
4. **BE A HIGH ACHIEVER**—Complete three cognitive exercises in a row at 95% or higher.

5. **SLOW BUT SURE**—Take your time and improve your accuracy the second time you do a task
6. **BE NOBODY'S FOOL**—Improve your previous score and don't be fooled or distracted by others.
7. **DIVIDE AND CONQUER**—Correctly answer 10 mental math problems while doing an exercise.
8. **LISTEN AND REMEMBER**—Listen to and remember a sequence of letters and numbers while doing an exercise.
9. **DO THE BIG BRAIN CHALLENGE**—Perform two cognitive exercises at the same time and get 95% or better on both! (Note: requires two computers to be placed next to each other)
10. **DO YOUR BEST**—Accept a challenging task and make a point of not overreacting when you make an error.

Making index cards out of the brief descriptions of the above cognitive exercises can be useful. The player or trainer can then random select an exercise to try. The concepts related to the exercise can be discussed as part of the training in order to generalize these metaconcepts. Also, similar new exercises can be created by either the player or trainer for experimentation.

In cognitive training, the emphasis should be on working smarter, not necessarily harder. The above exercises can lead an individual to develop practical cognitive strategies for success in real-life tasks. For example, the experience of *failure*, "I am bad and will never succeed" can be replaced by continued striving for *success*, "I did not succeed this time, but I will try again and do my best." The positive self-programming statements provided above can serve to remind the player that "they always have a choice" in that they can choose how to respond. However, in order to "see" things differently the player needs to practice and then *learn from their experience* for themselves how a metacognitive strategy can help them choose a more positive, helpful attitude and response instead of an over emotional, negative reaction. For this change to occur options must be practiced, reinforced and introduced in the more controlled, therapeutic environment of the training session. This part of the cognitive training process can then inspire the player to maintain hope and perseverance in coping with the demands and continuing to pursue the goals required in their life. The overall training model needs to emphasize to the player that one is not competing with others, only working from the point where one *is* and moving towards their defined goal of how one wants to be or how one wants to perform.

Index